Acclaim for Jake Tapper's
THE OUTPOST

"*The Outpost* is a mind-boggling, all-too-true story of heroism, hubris, failed strategy, and heartbreaking sacrifice. If you want to understand how the war in Afghanistan went off the rails, you need to read this book."
　　　　　—Jon Krakauer, author of *Into Thin Air* and
　　　　　　　　　　　　　　　　　　Where Men Win Glory

"One of the most important books of the year. Jake Tapper's book is meticulously researched, excellently written, and a must-read for everyone who does more than just mouth the phrase 'I support the troops.'"
　　　　　—Curt Schleier, *Minneapolis Star Tribune*

"The power of *The Outpost* lies in Tapper's development of the main characters.... He juxtaposes dramatic battles, complete with limbs blown off and eyes dangling from sockets, with poignant scenes of wives and parents first learning of the deaths of their loved ones."
　　　　　—Seth Jones, *Washington Post*

"Brilliant, dedicated reporting by a journalist who goes to ground to get the truth. A sad, real tale about this war, America, and the brave warriors who live—and die—at the point of the spear."
　　　　　—Bob Woodward, author of *Plan of Attack,*
　　　　　　　　　　The Commanders, and *Obama's Wars*

"There have been many books written on the subject of America's seemingly endless engagement in Afghanistan, but none better than *The Outpost*." 　　　　　—Jeffrey Goldberg, *The Atlantic*

"Jake Tapper has woven an intricate account about battlefield bravery hamstrung by military bureaucracy....His voice is understated, not polemical—just a good reporter letting the facts speak for themselves."
　　　　　—Tony Perry, *Los Angeles Times*

"Jake Tapper has written perhaps the best book set in Afghanistan to date....He provides a window into the false hopes and visions that enabled this failed experiment, an attempt to create government in spaces that had actively avoided such."   —Douglas Ollivant, *Foreign Policy*

"As Rudyard Kipling did in the nineteenth century, now, in his magnificent book, Jake Tapper takes us to an untamed part of Afghanistan at war. Journey to *The Outpost* to understand what our troops go through — and why they go through it."
> —James Bradley, author of *Flags of Our Fathers,*
> *Flyboys,* and *The Imperial Cruise*

"The seminal work of documentary journalism to emerge out of the post-9/11 war in Afghanistan."   —Anand Sankar, *Business Standard*

"Analyzing the consequences of decisions, large and small, is what makes Tapper's book so important....For those wishing to understand the middle years of the war, they could do no better than to read *The Outpost.*"   —Nate Rawlings, *Time*

"A fascinating history...Tapper delivers a blow-by-blow account of [the soldiers'] actions, their personal stories, and the tortured, often incomprehensible command decisions that kept them fighting despite inadequate support and an ally, Pakistan, that actively encouraged the enemy."
> —*Publishers Weekly*

"Mr. Tapper lays bare the poor decision-making that shattered dozens of American lives in the pursuit of an ill-conceived goal."
> —Sarah Chayes, *Wall Street Journal*

"*The Outpost* is valuable because its faithful account of bravery, stupidity, and inertia makes the objective case for admiration and outrage."
> —Sam Jacobson, *Commentary*

"A heartbreaking chronicle of the rotation of soldiers asked to oversee an underfunded, often thankless mission."   —Sam Stein, *Huffington Post*

"The Army uses the term 'BLUF' — bottom line up front. The BLUF on Jake Tapper's new book on Afghanistan, *The Outpost,* is that you need to read it."   — Kurt Schlichter, Breitbart.com

"A heartbreaking, detailed day-to-day account.... Tapper does what all great narrators do: He brings to life the individual men in a way that allows readers to see each soldier in full, with their unique backgrounds, hopes, dreams, and families."   — Susan Gardner, DailyKos.com

"A chronicle of the commitment and heroism of individual soldiers. As such, it can rarely have been surpassed in the history of military writing."
                                        — John Hinderaker, PowerLineBlog.com

"This is a narrative, not a polemic, and Tapper patiently lays out the history of what happened at Keating in a gripping, forceful style.... This unadorned, powerful account challenges the purposes and wisdom of America's ongoing military presence [in Afghanistan].... A timely indictment of a thoughtless waste of young American lives."
                                        — *Kirkus Reviews*

THE OUTPOST

AN UNTOLD STORY OF AMERICAN VALOR

Jake Tapper

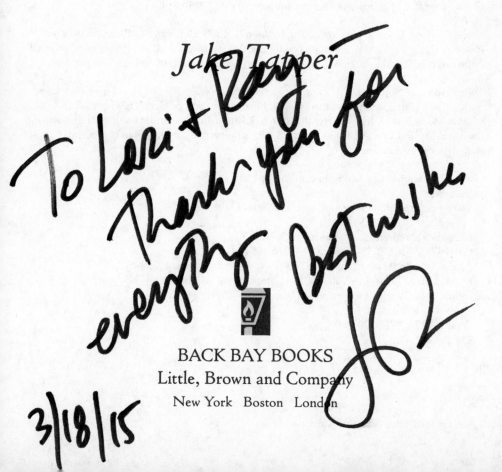

To Lori + Roger
Thank you for
everything
Best wishes

3/18/15

BACK BAY BOOKS

Little, Brown and Company

New York   Boston   London

Back Bay Books / Little, Brown and Company
Hachette Book Group
237 Park Avenue, New York, NY 10017
littlebrown.com

Originally published in hardcover by Little, Brown and Company, November 2012
First Back Bay paperback edition, October 2013

Back Bay Books is an imprint of Little, Brown and Company. The Back Bay Books name and
logo are trademarks of Hachette Book Group, Inc.

The publisher is not responsible for websites (or their content) that are not owned by the
publisher.

The Hachette Speakers Bureau provides a wide range of authors for speaking events. To find
out more, go to hachettespeakersbureau.com or call (866) 376-6591.

"Folsom Prison Blues" words and music by John R. Cash. Copyright © 1956 (renewed 1984)
House of Cash, Inc. (BMI), administered by Bug Music, Inc., a BMG Chrysalis company. All
rights reserved. Used by permission. Reprinted by permission of Hal Leonard Corporation.

"When You Say Nothing at All" words and music by Don Schlitz and Paul Overstreet. Copy-
right © 1988 Universal Music Corp., Don Schlitz Music, Screen Gems–EMI Music, Inc., and
Scarlett Moon Music, Inc. All rights for Don Schlitz Music controlled and administered by
Universal Music Corp. All rights reserved. Used by permission. Reprinted by permission of
Hal Leonard Corporation.

Library of Congress Cataloging-in-Publication Data
Tapper, Jake.
    The outpost : an untold story of American valor / Jake Tapper. — 1st ed.
        p. cm.
    Includes bibliographical references and index.
    ISBN 978-0-316-18539-4 (hc) / 978-0-316-18540-0 (pb)
    1. Kamdesh, Battle of, Afghanistan, 2009. 2. Combat Outpost Keating
(Afghanistan). 3. Afghan War, 2001 — Campaigns — Afghanistan — Nuristan
(Region). 4. Counterinsurgency — Afghanistan — Nuristan (Region).
5. Taliban. I. Title.
    DS371.4123.K36T36 2012
    958.104'742 — dc23   2012023094

10 9 8 7 6 5 4 3 2 1

RRD-C

Printed in the United States of America

Contents

Contents

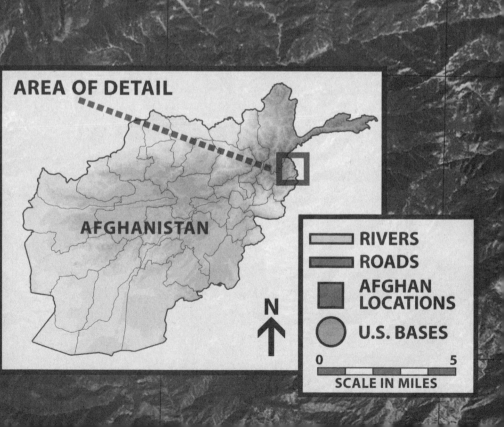

LANDAY-SIN RIVER

MANDIGAL

**COMBAT
OUTPOST
KEATING**

URMUL

AGASI

MIRDESH

AGRO

KAMDESH

**OBSERVATION
POST FRITSCHE**

KAMU

KUSHTOZ

**COMBAT
OUTPOST
LOWELL**

DARREH YE
KUSHTOZ
RIVER

AREA OF DETAIL

AFGHANISTAN

RIVERS
ROADS
AFGHAN
LOCATIONS
U.S. BASES

N

0   5
SCALE IN MILES

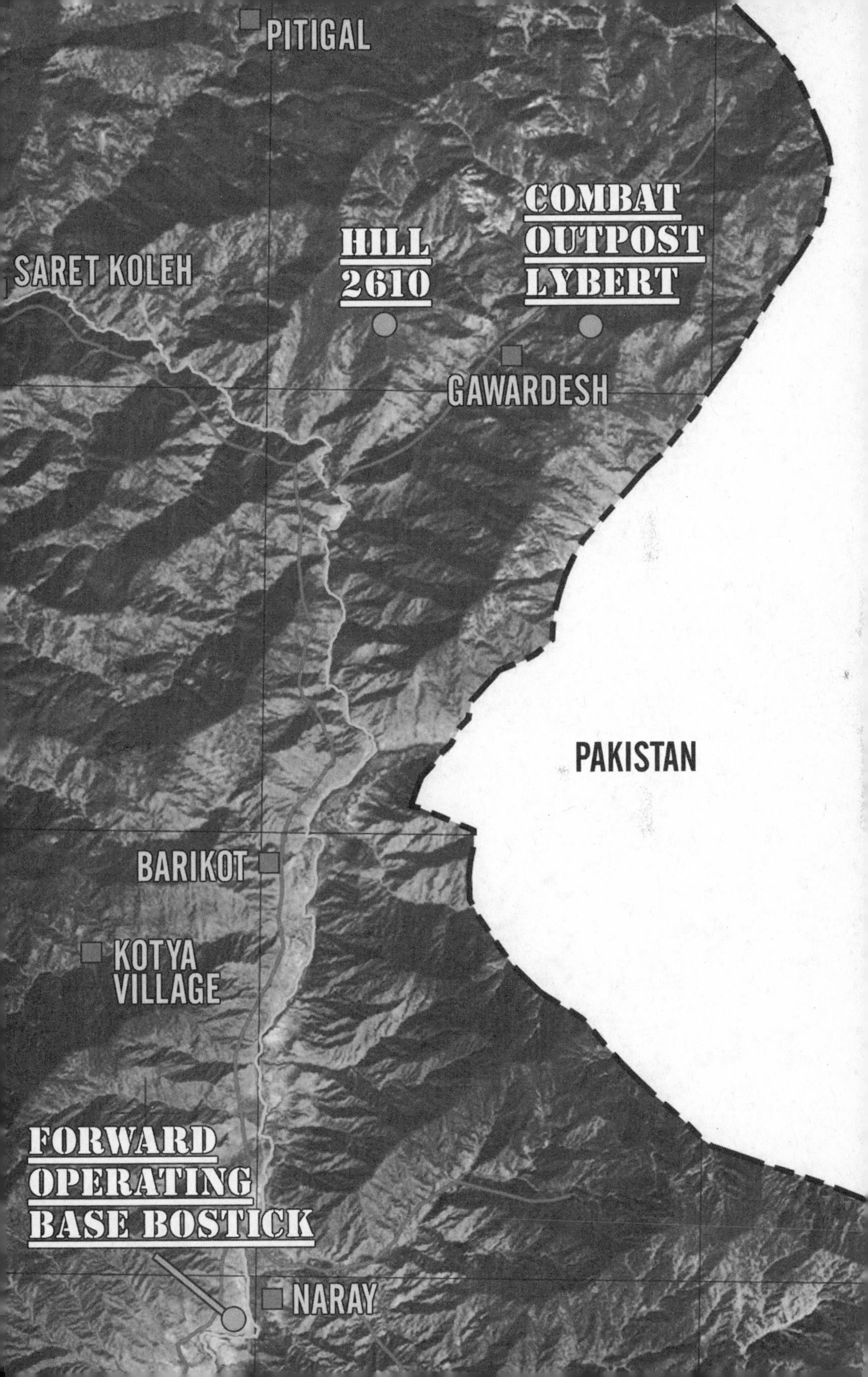

PITIGAL

SARET KOLEH

HILL
2610

COMBAT
OUTPOST
LYBERT

GAWARDESH

PAKISTAN

BARIKOT

KOTYA
VILLAGE

FORWARD
OPERATING
BASE BOSTICK

NARAY

Author's Note

The most difficult choice I faced in writing this book lay in deciding how honest to be about the horrors of war: the injuries, the deaths, all the things that make war so terrifying. The media in the United States — taking their cue from the American public — often shy away from such coverage, and that has not served the nation well, to say nothing of the troops or the people in those countries that the U.S. government says it's trying to help. Certainly, there are good reasons to avoid descriptions that are too graphic, including, primarily, the desire to shield families of troops who have been wounded or killed from details that may be new and upsetting to them. Ultimately, with all of this in mind, I opted to withhold some information — but not a lot.

The Cavalrymen's Poem

Halfway down the trail to Hell,
In a shady meadow green
Are the Souls of all dead troopers camped,
Near a good old-time canteen.
And this eternal resting place
Is known as Fiddlers' Green.

Marching past, straight through to Hell
The Infantry are seen.
Accompanied by the Engineers,
Artillery and Marines,
For none but the shades of Cavalrymen
Dismount at Fiddlers' Green.

Though some go curving down the trail
To seek a warmer scene,
No trooper ever gets to Hell
Ere he's emptied his canteen.
And so rides back to drink again
With friends at Fiddlers' Green.

And so when man and horse go down
Beneath a saber keen,
Or in a roaring charge of fierce melee
You stop a bullet clean,
And the hostiles come to get your scalp,
Just empty your canteen,
And put your pistol to your head
And go to Fiddlers' Green.

—*Anonymous*

THE OUTPOST

Focus

I t was madness.

At Jalalabad Airfield, in eastern Afghanistan in the summer of 2006, a young intelligence analyst named Jacob Whittaker tried with great difficulty to understand exactly what he was hearing.

The 10th Mountain Division of the United States Army wanted to do *what?*

Whittaker had to choose his words carefully. He was just a low-ranking "specialist" with the Idaho National Guard, a very low man on a very tall totem pole. A round-faced twenty-six-year-old, Whittaker had simple tastes — Boise State football, comic books — and a reputation for mulishness belied by his innocent appearance.

Whittaker stared at his superior officer, Second Lieutenant Ryan Lockner, who was running this briefing for him and Sergeant Aaron Ives. Lockner headed intelligence for Task Force Talon, the Army's aviation component at Jalalabad Airfield, in Nangarhar Province, adjacent to the Pakistan border. Military leaders considered this area, officially designated Regional Command East, the most dangerous part of an increasingly dangerous country.

Lockner had an assignment. Soldiers from the 10th Mountain — a light infantry division designed for quick deployment and fighting in harsh conditions — had recently come to this hot corner of Afghanistan and would soon be spreading throughout the region, setting up outposts

3

and bases. More specifically, they would be establishing a camp in Nuristan Province.

The members of the intelligence team led by Lockner didn't know much about Nuristan, as U.S. forces had generally been focusing their efforts on Kunar Province, which had become a haven for Taliban insurgents and foreign fighters sneaking in from Pakistan to oppose the American "infidels." During one operation in Kunar the previous summer, in 2005, nineteen U.S. troops—Special Forces—had been killed by such insurgents, and since then, the United States had increased its presence there. Helicopters flying in and out of Kunar Province were fired upon at least twice a week, every week, with small arms and/or rocket-propelled grenades (RPGs).

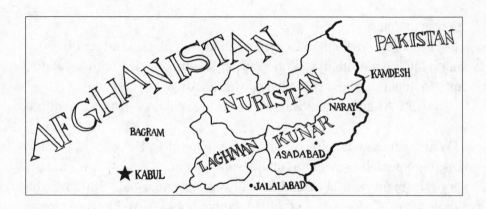

Nuristan was farther north, a province so mythically untamed that one of the greatest writers of the English language, Rudyard Kipling, had chosen it as the setting for his 1888 novella "The Man Who Would Be King." One of Kipling's British adventurers, Daniel Dravot, describes Nuristan as a place where "no one has gone . . . and they fight, and in any place where they fight a man who knows how to drill men can always be a King." "You'll be cut to pieces before you're fifty miles across the Border," warns Kipling's narrator. "The people are utter brutes, and even if you reached them you couldn't do anything."

The region's previous brigade commander, Colonel Pat Donahue, hadn't thought Nuristan had much strategic value, so conventional forces hadn't been posted there, and no one had troubled to find out much about the native people, the Nuristanis, a distinct and outlying ethnic group within Afghanistan. In a departure from his predecessor's policy, Donahue's replacement—Colonel John "Mick" Nicholson, the commander of the 10th Mountain Division's 3rd Brigade, known as the Spartan Brigade—ordered the establishment of small outposts throughout the area in the summer of 2006, in an attempt not only to stop the Taliban fighters who were streaming in from Pakistan, often with bushels of weapons, but also to win over the locals, who were predisposed to a suspicion of outsiders.

Lockner had just returned from Forward Operating Base Naray, in Kunar Province, where he'd met with officers of the 10th Mountain Division's 3rd Squadron, 71st Cavalry Regiment, or "3-71 Cav."[1] They'd told him of their plan to set up an outpost in the Kamdesh District of Nuristan Province, for which he would be in charge of identifying suitable helicopter landing zones. The new base would sit adjacent to the Nuristan hamlet of Urmul.[2] A small settlement missing from most maps, Urmul was home to fewer than forty families of Nuristanis, or roughly two hundred people, who lived in houses made of wood and rock and mud sealant. The residents were primarily subsistence farmers trying to eke out a living through both crops and livestock, but the U.S. Army knew little more than that about them. Coalition forces likewise had next to no intelligence about the enemy in Nuristan—its numbers, its location, its intentions, or, most important, its capabilities—which was one of the reasons the brass was pushing to build a base there. This was the essential difficulty of the task at hand: the higher-ups in the U.S. Army needed to know about the enemy in this unexplored province, so in order to learn as much as they could, they were going to stick a small group of troops in its midst. For all Lockner knew when he flew over Urmul to reconnoiter, the hamlet might have been Osama bin Laden's secret compound.

"They're going to build another outpost," Lockner told Whittaker and Ives back at Jalalabad Airfield. "So I need you to take this terrain analysis I started, finish it, and make it pretty so I can brief it in the morning."

---

[1] A squadron comprises some five hundred to six hundred soldiers.

[2] The noted Nuristan linguist and expert Richard Strand suggests that a more accurate spelling of "Urmul" would be "Ümür." Here as elsewhere, however, for the purposes of narrative ease for the reader, this book will defer to the more popular—if not necessarily the more accurate—Afghan spelling and reference.

Many troops were far more proficient in PowerPoint than they were with firearms, so Whittaker understood just what Lockner meant by "make it pretty": the slides for the presentation needed to look crisp and to make a compelling case.

"Where are they going?" Whittaker asked.

Lockner gestured at the topographical map. "Right over here, north-west of Naray," he said. "Where the Darreh ye Kushtaz and Landay-Sin Rivers meet."

Whittaker looked at the spot, stunned. "Right *there?*" he asked.

"Right there," confirmed Lockner. "Can you do it?"

"I can do it; I have all night," Whittaker said. "But sir . . . that is a really awful place for a base." This new camp in the Kamdesh District would, like the dangerous Korangal outpost that their pilots knew too well, be surrounded by higher ground. But whereas the base in the Korangal was situated about halfway up a mountainside, in a former lumberyard, the one in Kamdesh would sit in a cup within the valley's deepest cleft, ringed by three steep mountains that formed part of the five-hundred-mile-long Hindu Kush mountain range. Blocked off on its northern, western, and southern sides by rivers and mountains, it would moreover be a mere fourteen miles distant from the official Pakistan border — a porous boundary that meant little to the insurgents who regularly crossed it to kill Americans and Afghan government officials before taking refuge in caves or in the mountains or returning to their haven across the border. The camp would be one of the most remote outposts in this most remote part of a country that was itself cut off from much of the rest of the world, and the area all around it would be filled with people who wanted to kill those stationed there.

"So it's located at the base of a mountain peak?" Whittaker asked. It didn't take a Powell or a Schwarzkopf to know that as a matter of basic military strategy, it was better to be at the top of a hill than at the bottom of a valley.

"Yes."

"And it's flanked by a river on the west and another river to the north?" Whittaker continued.

"And there's no good road to get to it — they're still building that," Lockner volunteered.

The Army had been coordinating efforts to build up the vulnerable and narrow path from Naray to Kamdesh, but rain, steep cliffs, insurgent threats, and high turnover rates among local construction workers had led to frequent delays. The road, often running along the edge of a cliff that spilled into the Landay-Sin River, was a mere thirteen feet wide at its widest, and in some spots only half that—narrower than many military vehicles. A soldier could be killed just driving on that road, without ever coming into contact with a single enemy fighter.

"And it's an eternity away by helicopter if something goes wrong," Whittaker said.

"Yup," agreed Lockner.

"Sir, this is a really bad idea," said Whittaker. "*A. Really. Bad. Idea.* Anyone we drop off there is going to die." As he said it, he thought he saw Lockner's eyes glaze over.

Whittaker was known for being inquisitive and sometimes downright melodramatic, but even for him, this was an outsized response to a mission briefing. Those who worked with him understood that he always believed he was the smartest person in the room. He knew it put people off and made them less likely to listen to him when he had something especially important to say, but he was still young and had not yet learned how to check his behavior.

"What's the point of this base?" Whittaker asked. "It's on the low ground. It can't be supported in any meaningful way. The troops there will be *horribly* outnumbered by potential bad guys in the town next door. They can't even really go out and do anything because the rivers, the town, and the mountains will block any patrol routes."

He couldn't stop himself.

"All they can do is die," he added.

Lockner, too, had been surprised to learn where the 3-71 Cav officers wanted to put the camp. He understood their logic, at least in theory: with so few air assets, they'd have to rely on the road as the main way to resupply the outpost. And anyway, the troops couldn't just sit on the mountaintops; they had to go to the towns and make friends with the locals. But Lockner himself wouldn't want even to visit there.

Still: it wasn't their job to question where the 3-71 Cav officers had decided to put their camp and their men.

"Noted, bitch," Lockner told Whittaker with a smile. "But do it anyway. We just need to find a place to land the helicopters."

"But sir—"

The lieutenant stopped smiling.

"Whittaker," he said, now angered. He mocked the other man's staccato: *"Fucking. Focus. I. Need you. To make me. Some. Slides. We need. A place. To land. The helicopters."*

Lockner had already spotted one location atop the mountain that seemed perfect for landing helicopters, a rarity in the jagged topography of Nuristan. The second landing zone would need to be down nearer to where the outpost itself would be constructed, close to the local headquarters of the Afghan National Police.

The specialist from Idaho spent that hot night carrying out Lockner's order. The task per se wasn't particularly difficult; it was just a Power-Point presentation. But Whittaker kept staring at the map, hoping that the logic behind it would suddenly be revealed to him, as if it were one of those Magic Eye posters containing a hidden image. He thought about what he would do if he were a commander of one of the local insurgent groups. The hours passed as Whittaker war-gamed attacks on the new outpost. His mind played a cinematic loop of the fate of the camp, one that always ended in disaster. In scenario after scenario, positing one defensive strategy after another, every single time he completed an exercise, everyone at the outpost died.

Ives arrived in the morning to relieve him. Even without the all-nighter, Whittaker hadn't slept well in months; he was the only day-sleeper in a tent that would hit 120 degrees before noon. He looked a mess: razor blades were scarce, and he didn't entirely trust the on-base Pakistani barber and his jerky technique. With all of that, on top of the stress and the dust that coated everyone and everything in Jalalabad, he figured he must resemble a mentally ill homeless person.

Whittaker's fears about the new base were intensified by the memory of a previous scouting mission, Operation Tall Mountain, which he hadn't protested against as aggressively as he now thought he should have. Tipped off by an intelligence report suggesting that a high-value target was using a small trail east of a combat outpost named Ranch House, a team of scouts had gone to a nearby mountain peak to survey the area and try to spot insurgents. At fourteen thousand feet above sea level, the temperature on the peak was just above freezing. Because the helicopters were already overloaded with men, equipment, and supplies, the cold-weather gear and water were scheduled to follow on a second flight—which in fact never left Jalalabad, having been grounded by thunderstorms. The scouts were now trapped on a remote mountain peak without critical supplies. Everyone survived the three-day ordeal, but it was harrowing. In the end, even though the scouts saw nothing of note, the mission was believed to have accomplished something—for some officer somewhere, at least. Whittaker—who had offered up a halfhearted argument that the plan didn't make sense—suspected that the operation had turned into a positive bullet on someone's officer evaluation report.

Now the whole idea of the Kamdesh outpost seemed to be propelled by the same shallow Army logic: Push forward! Move 'em on! Head 'em up! Achievement was what mattered, even if the achievement itself was worthless, whereas delays or a cancellation could be seen as a failure of leadership, which would look bad on an officer's record during the next round of promotions. Whittaker told Ives that he felt he should have fought harder against Operation Tall Mountain; he would never be able to live with himself, he said, if they couldn't find a way to stop the construction of this new base. But by that point he'd learned that in the military mindset, it was usually preferable just to carry out orders and then investigate later, if necessary, rather than to raise questions beforehand about whether a plan might be flawed.

The aviation group named the helicopter pad at the future location of Camp Kamdesh "Landing Zone Copenhagen," after the crew members' favorite brand of chewing tobacco. The one atop the southern mountain was christened Landing Zone Warheit, for Staff Sergeant Dana Warheit, an Air Force staff weather officer who happened to be sitting in the briefing room at that moment and whose surname sounded kind of cool.

Over the next few days, Whittaker would come to call Camp Kamdesh the Custer Combat Outpost. He figured people would ask him what the nickname meant, giving him an opportunity to carefully explain the problems to anyone who would listen; he intended to keep doing that until someone in command finally came around and canceled the mission. Eventually, Lockner had to tell him to knock it off.

Whittaker's fears would be realized more than three years later. Before dawn on October 3, 2009, hundreds of insurgents scattered throughout the village of Urmul and the mountains surrounding the American outpost. The U.S. base had been there since 2006, and insurgents had attacked it from day one. The newest company of U.S. troops had arrived less than five months before, and during that period, the enemy had increased his attacks threefold over the number launched against previous units. But this would be the big one.

The enemy fighters faced Mecca and conducted their morning prayers. Then they grabbed their guns and got into position to attack the Kamdesh outpost.

At 5:58 a.m., as the sun started to rise over the valley, the assault began. Five U.S. soldiers manned five guard stations, near the entrance of the camp and on four Humvees. Those spots were obvious targets for the enemy, as were the command center and the various barracks. Strategically, the Taliban fighters focused on the mortar pit, the location of the only guns at the outpost that could return fire with any effectiveness against their positions on the mountainside: one 60-millimeter and two 120-millimeter mortars, the big guns.

"*Allahu Akbar!*" the insurgents cried, seemingly with the blast of every rocket and the crash of each mortar fired into the air: "God is great."[3]

After a short and intense assault, Taliban fighters began spilling down from the mountains, through the wire, past the Americans' defensive positions, and into the camp.

"Mujahideen have entered the base!" rejoiced one such "holy warrior."

"The Christianity center is under attack!" another of the Taliban cried.

"Long live the mujahideen!" yelled a third. "No helicopters are here yet! Let's just hit them!"

He was right about the aircraft. The Americans at the outpost had called for air support — they had little hope of surviving otherwise — but the Apache attack helicopters had not yet arrived, and they wouldn't get there for more than another hour.

The Americans fought. Over the past three years, U.S. troops had died

---

[3] These words are commonly translated into English as "God is great," though a more accurate translation might be "God is the greatest" or "God is the most transcendent" — meaning, "God is the most powerful being in the universe." In the context of military operations in Afghanistan, "Allahu Akbar" might best be rendered as "God is greater than our enemy."

on their way to construct the outpost; they had died clearing the path to establish the outpost; they had died patrolling the area that surrounded the outpost; they had died driving from the outpost; they had died commanding the outpost; and they had died pursuing the mission of the outpost. Now, as the enemy burst through into their camp, a small group of just over fifty American soldiers had no alternative but to do whatever they could to stay off that grim list. There was no more time for them to wonder why they were there. It was time to fight — and for some, it would be time to die.

BOOK ONE

"With Your Shield or on It"

ROLL CALL

Main Characters: Book One

International Security Assistance Force (ISAF)[4]

January 2006–June 2007

At Jalalabad Airfield, Nangarhar Province:

Colonel John "Mick" Nicholson, Commander, 3rd Infantry Brigade
Combat Team (BCT), 10th Mountain Division

Lieutenant Colonel Chris Cavoli, Commander, 1-32 Infantry Battalion,
3rd BCT, 10th Mountain Division

At Forward Operating Base Naray, Kunar Province:

Lieutenant Colonel Joe Fenty, Squadron Commander, 3-71 Cavalry
Squadron ("3-71 Cav"), 3rd BCT, 10th Mountain Division

Lieutenant Colonel Mike Howard, Squadron Commander, 3-71 Cav

Command Sergeant Major Del Byers, 3-71 Cav Command Sergeant
Major

Major Richard Timmons, 3-71 Cav Executive Officer

Captain Ross Berkoff, 3-71 Cav Intelligence Officer

Captain Pete Stambersky, Delta Company Commander, assigned from
the 710th Brigade Support Battalion

Captain Dennis Sugrue, 3-71 Cav Headquarters Troop Commander

---

[4] ISAF is the acronym for International Security Assistance Force, the formal name of
the coalition fighting the war in Afghanistan. Formed in October 2001 to establish
security in Kabul, ISAF in 2003 had its charter extended by the United Nations to
cover the entirety of the country. In October 2006, ISAF officially expanded into the
region this book is focused on, eastern Afghanistan. The coalition has consisted of
personnel from more than forty countries, including the United States, the United
Kingdom, Germany, Italy, France, Latvia, Poland, and Australia. This book will generally identify the forces as "U.S.," since that was overwhelmingly their nationality,
except where otherwise noted.

Working throughout Kunar and Nuristan Provinces:
Able Troop, 3-71 Cav, 3rd BCT, 10th Mountain Division
   Captain Matt Gooding, Troop Commander
   First Lieutenant Ben Keating, Troop Executive Officer
   First Sergeant Todd Yerger, First Sergeant
   First Lieutenant Vic Johnson, 1st Platoon Leader
   Sergeant Jeremy Larson, 1st Platoon Section Leader
   Sergeant First Class Milton Yagel, 2nd Platoon Sergeant
   Staff Sergeant Adam Sears, 2nd Platoon Senior Scout
   Specialist Shawn Passman, 2nd Platoon gunner for platoon sergeant
   Private First Class Brian M. Moquin, Jr., 2nd Platoon scout
   Private Second Class Nick Pilozzi, 2nd Platoon scout
   Specialist Moises Cerezo, medic attached to 2nd Platoon
   Staff Sergeant Matthew Netzel, Troop Headquarters Platoon Sergeant
   Sergeant Dennis Cline, M60 mortarman attached to Able Troop
Barbarian Troop, 3-71 Cav, 3rd BCT, 10th Mountain Division
   Captain Frank Brooks, Troop Commander
   First Lieutenant Erik Jorgensen, Troop Fire Support Officer
   First Lieutenant Aaron Pearsall, 2nd Platoon Leader
Cherokee Company, 3-71 Cav, 3rd BCT, 10th Mountain Division
   Captain Aaron Swain, Company Commander
   Captain Michael Schmidt, Company Commander
   Staff Sergeant Chris "Cricket" Cunningham, sniper and kill team leader
   Staff Sergeant Jared Monti, fire-support and targeting NCO attached
     to Cherokee Company
   Sergeant Patrick Lybert, recon team leader
   Private First Class Brian Bradbury, fire-support specialist attached to
     Cherokee Company

**On the Provincial Reconstruction Team in Mehtar Lam, Laghman
Province:**
Lieutenant Colonel Tony Feagin, team head

**Trainers of the Afghan National Army (ANA) Troops at Camp
Kamdesh, Nuristan Province:**
Master Sergeant Terry Best
Sergeant Buddy Hughie

On the Home Front:
Kristen Fenty, wife of Lieutenant Colonel Joe Fenty
Gretchen Timmons, wife of Major Richard Timmons
Ken and Beth Keating, parents of Lieutenant Ben Keating
Heather McDougal, girlfriend of Lieutenant Ben Keating

Note: *These Roll Call lists throughout the book are by no means
intended to be complete lists of those who served or even those
mentioned in the book, but rather as a resource for the reader,
a way to keep straight some of the people in the book within their
heirarchy.*

CHAPTER 1

Every Man an Alexander

The bad dreams began long before the troops of 3rd Squadron, 71st Cavalry Regiment, or "3-71 Cav," pushed north in March 2006. The troops blamed the vivid nightmares on the Mefloquine, the pills they were required to take each "Malaria Monday" to guard against that disease. Some Army doctors argued that the pills should stop being distributed, convinced they could cause far worse side effects than just restless nights, including depression, paranoia, hallucinations, and even mental breakdowns. Of course, such symptoms could be tough to detect in a place where depression and paranoia might just be the most appropriate reactions to the surrounding reality.

On March 12, 2006, hours before the first leg of the convoy pulled out and began its nearly four-hundred-mile trek north from Forward Operating Base Salerno, in southeastern Afghanistan, insurgents had already made their presence known. Enemy fighters detonated an improvised explosive device, or IED, in Kunar Province — where First Lieutenant Ben Keating and his men were heading — as another U.S. convoy drove through. The explosion destroyed a Humvee and killed four Army Reservists from an Engineer Battalion out of Asheville, North Carolina.[5]

But Kunar was hardly the only danger zone. Before Keating and the

---

[5] Sergeant Kevin "Big Ake" Akins of Burnsville, North Carolina; Sergeant Anton Hiett of Mount Airy, North Carolina; Specialist Joshua Hill of Fairmount, Indiana; and Staff Sergeant Joseph Ray of Asheville, North Carolina.

other men from 3-71 Cav could even get there, they would have to stop in Kabul, where, on that very day, two insurgents wearing explosive vests killed four civilians and severely wounded two more, one a young girl. (They missed their target, an Afghan politician who ran a government reconciliation commission.) On the same day, other insurgents attacked a convoy of Afghan National Army (ANA) soldiers on the Kabul–Kandahar Highway. Nobody was killed in that attack, but not for the Taliban's lack of trying.

To help his men deal with these kinds of horror stories and with the fear they all felt about moving to an area widely reputed to be barbaric and deadly, Keating tried to keep the mood light as the medium-sized convoy — eight Humvees and two trailers — headed toward possible danger. He joked that this, the lead Humvee, with a Mark 19 grenade launcher in its turret, was only the second brand-new vehicle he'd ever owned. As Able Troop[6] pushed north, the lieutenant held the microphone of his MICH ranger headset up to the speaker of his CD player and provided his men with a sound track:

> She was a fast machine
> She kept her motor clean
> She was the best damn woman that I ever seen . . .

"You Shook Me All Night Long," from AC/DC's album *Back in Black,* was the sort of head-banging anthem that flicked a switch in the minds of young men and set them on a course toward conquest. Keating, at twenty-seven, may have looked the part of an Army stud, but what few knew about him was that he was deeply devout, disapproving if not sanctimonious on the subject of the hedonistic pursuits of the young. The drinking and carousing he'd witnessed as a student at the University of New Hampshire had disgusted him, and shortly after 9/11 he'd delivered a guest sermon at his parents' church, in a small town in Maine, in which he'd lambasted the vacuous immorality of his college peers. He'd mel-

---

[6] Technically, Able Troop was at this point still "Ares" Troop and would not change its nomenclature to "Able" until a few months later. But for simplicity's sake, this book will call the company Able Troop.

lowed since then, but he had remained chaste and was convinced he walked the path of righteousness.

Neither Keating nor any of the other men of 3-71 Cav had much of an idea of what their mission would entail, or for that matter even where they were going, in anything but the vaguest sense. While prepping for the trip north from Forward Operating Base Salerno, they'd heard the whispers, the military gossip:

"Oh, you're going up *north*," soldiers would say. "It's bad up there."

Now off they went, 3-71 Cav, in four different convoys, with additional supplies to be ferried via helicopter. For Able Troop's journey, Keating — his Humvee in the lead — rode shotgun in the truck commander seat as his driver, Private Second Class Nick Pilozzi, steered the vehicle over both paved highways and gritty gravel roads. Sergeant Darian Decker, their gunner, sat on a strap in the turret, holding his Mark 19 grenade launcher. Sergeant Vernon Tiller, Able Troop's chief mechanic, was in back.

A few Humvees behind them, in the command-and-control truck, sat Captain Matt Gooding, the leader of Able Troop. Gooding had planned every part of this trip, coordinating logistics and making sure the convoy would have enough fuel. En route, he would keep the mortarmen on the ground apprised of the convoy's position at all times and alert the pilots of the choppers and planes above whenever ground fire support was out of range.

Keating — the executive officer, or second in command, of Able Troop — took note as the convoy steered through the pass on the road between Khost and Gardez. As he wrote to his parents, the "weather wasn't great — rain in the foothills turned into snow in the mountains. The soil in most of Afghanistan is a heavy clay, rock-hard when dry, but slick as ice after rain or snow. The road has no guardrails or boulders to clearly define its edge, which falls off several hundred feet to the valley floor." The sight of a truck speeding by would make everyone's heart skip a beat. As they rolled through the pass, the temperature changed from a freezing chill to almost 90 degrees within a half hour. The bizarre weather shift was just one of the road trip's surprises, in a journey full of nothing but — especially considering that before their deployment to Afghanistan two months earlier, in January, many 3-71 Cav troops had never been outside the continental United States.

Keating made sure to take pictures all along the way to show to his beloved parents, his older sister, Jessica, and his new girlfriend, Heather McDougal. Although he had spent three years after high school working at her father's apple orchard, picking McIntoshes and Honey Crisps while trying to figure out what to do with his life, Keating hadn't actually known Heather all that well back then. She was just fourteen when they first met, almost a decade ago now, and they'd lost touch after he left the job at the orchard. But the previous fall, Keating and McDougal—now a college junior—had struck up a conversation online, and at Christmas they'd met up again at his parents' church in Maine. They were both surprised by how strong their feelings were for each other. They exchanged intense emails and instant messages whenever they could. It was an unusual way to fall in love, but it was their only option at the moment.

Ever a creature of the modern Army, Keating would later turn his snapshots into a PowerPoint presentation that he sent to McDougal and his family, titled "ROAD TRIP."

Wrote Keating to his family: "The route traversed two high mountain passes of elevations above 2,000 meters ASL [above sea level] and followed the K[u]nar River on a treacherous road from the city of Jalalabad to the camp at Naray." *(Photo courtesy of the Keating family)*

As they traveled, Keating and his men, wary of insurgents who might be hiding among the locals, stopped to set up temporary defensive perimeters that would allow civilians to pass them. Herds of camels ran alongside the convoy where the road flattened out and the danger of slipping off an edge declined. When they reached a rocky plain, further evidence of civilization emerged.

"If you've ever wondered what a people do when they've lived in a place with nothing but rocks and sand for five thousand years," Keating wrote to his friends and family, "wonder no more. Walls, they build walls. There are rock walls everywhere, without rhyme or reason."

Afghan males, mostly boys and elders, would come to the edge of the road, smiling—even laughing—as if they were all in on some joke that the recent arrivals had yet to get. They wore hats, tunics, and loose-fitting trousers, which the U.S. troops referred to as "man-jams."

The gear worn by Keating and his men was more sophisticated: combat uniforms, pixelated grayish camouflage "go-to-work" suits; bulletproof vests; mesh vests with pouches and compartments for canteens, grenades, and ammunition; military combat helmets; and kneepads. This all amounted to no less than fifty pounds per man, and that was before adding a rifle, a supply of water, or an assault pack, not to mention the things they carried, the letters and photographs, the chewing tobacco, the cigarettes, the talismans.

The drivers slowly steered their Humvees and trucks as the flat, barren landscape gave way to densely forested mountains. With the exceptions of the enemy weapons and the cheap Toyota Hiluxes clanking along the roads, this part of Afghanistan did not look to Ben Keating to have changed much since the war with the USSR in the 1980s, or even since the British were felled there almost a century before. Not that his own passport matched his scholarship: aside from a weekend trip to Montreal for a hockey tournament at around the age of ten and a family trip to the United Kingdom when he was twenty, Ben Keating hadn't been outside the United States until this deployment.

In December 2005, Keating had visited a Portland, Maine, bookstore and bought a Christmas present for his father. Sean Naylor's *Not a Good Day to Die* detailed Operation Anaconda, the bloody campaign undertaken by the United States in March 2002 to flush out an Al Qaeda stronghold in southeastern Afghanistan. In an inscription in the front of the book, Keating wrote that the contents would give his dad, Ken, "a pretty clear picture of what the enemy threat looks like."

He continued:

I want to thank you for all that you've taught me. I have excelled thus far in my short career because of what I learned from you on all those afternoons in the woodlots and fields of southern Maine. Even for me, a "Big-Picture Guy," the idea of dying for one's country is a little too abstract. I have no desire to meet my end in Afghanistan, but it's a commitment to family (that I learned from you) which compelled me to join and serve.

Your dedication as a faithful father and pastor taught me to extend my definition of family to my men. I assure you that my men are the answers to the questions you so often ask. I have felt called to this job and blessed by the challenges. I am continually rewarded when I see eighteen-year-old boys bear up under pressure and carry themselves with the newfound pride of men. They fully understand that they are the face of America in the world.

For the men in my command, I have worked very hard to make that your face. Because it is the one that has always represented respect, integrity and love for me. Thank you for all you have given me. I am confident that it will see me through this next challenge as faithfully as all those in the past.

With love and continued admiration,
Ben

Ben Keating was destined for greatness, of this he was sure. After finishing ROTC at the University of New Hampshire, where he was president of the Young Republicans, he had joined the military because he expected someday to be a U.S. senator from Maine, charged with voting on whether or not to send American troops into harm's way, and he didn't think it would be right to ask those future troops to fight if he had never done so himself.

Assigned to something of a ragtag platoon at the Army post at Fort Drum, New York, home of the 10th Mountain Division, Lieutenant Keating had thrown himself into his job, putting overweight soldiers on diets, counseling service members who were having marital problems, and mediating disputes with landlords for those of his troops who didn't live on base. He loved leading his men, and he wasn't particularly happy about being taken away from them when he was promoted to be the executive officer, or "XO," of Able Troop, responsible for administration, logistics, and millions of dollars' worth of equipment. Platoons consist of anywhere from sixteen to forty soldiers, and Keating missed his joes; he preferred mentoring them to serving in what was often an administrative job, even if the paper-pushing was done on the front lines.

As 3-71 Cav's resident warrior-poet, Ben Keating seized any opportunity he could to lecture, and he spent part of the convoy's northward journey teaching the troops about the history of this land they were in and the foreign forces that had invaded it over the centuries. He'd brought along a number of books to Afghanistan that he'd read for college history classes. He was thrilled to be in the country where Alexander the Great had taken an arrow to the leg and almost died, but he was concerned, too, by the stories of how challenging this place had been for both Alexander and Genghis Khan — to say nothing of the USSR, which had withdrawn ignominiously in 1989 after nearly a decade of bloody battle with fierce Afghan warriors, having suffered an estimated fifteen thousand casualties.

Nomadic, self-contained, and agile, the enemies whom 3-71 Cav would face were similar in many ways to the people Alexander had tried to put down here. Because they didn't have much of an organizational structure for him to exploit — unlike the Persians, whom he had decapitated at a stroke by attacking their king, Darius the Great — Alexander believed that the only way to defeat them was to trap them with overwhelming force and either kill or capture them. There was no jugular in their decentralized society. One academic[7] has noted that in Bactria (part of modern-day Afghanistan), Alexander found to his dismay that "allies and enemies were often indistinguishable until it was too late." The confusion worked both ways: Alexander's troops were asked to juggle "awkwardly the jobs of conquerer, peace-keeper, builder and settler. One

---

[7] Frank L. Holt, *Into the Land of Bones: Alexander the Great in Afghanistan* (Los Angeles: University of California Press, 2005), pp. 20–21.

minute they were asked to kill with ruthless and indiscriminate intensity, the next they were expected to show deference to the survivors." Then as now, moreover, the difficult turf provided the natives with a significant home-field advantage, allowing a rebel force of just 10 percent of the population to pose a serious threat to a better-armed and much larger occupying force.

The nickname that the 3rd Infantry Brigade Combat Team (to which 3-71 Cav belonged) had adopted—the Spartans, after the legendary Greek fighters—was used by the unit's officers to build up their men and themselves, likening them to the fierce warriors of yore. They'd even co-opted as their motto "With your shield or on it," which was said to have been a directive from Spartan mothers to their sons, an order to fight to the death in battle, a reminder that dying was preferable to retreating. Beyond that tenuous historical link, however, the direct relevance of Alexander the Great's experience to Ben Keating's mission was debatable, and the problem was, there weren't many people in the Pentagon or the State Department who were capable of engaging in that debate. The military had been focused on hunting down Osama bin Laden, Al Qaeda, and the Taliban for almost five years now, and yet the enemy was still thriving. Some Pentagon leaders were beginning to worship at the altar of COIN, shorthand for "counterinsurgency," a strategy designed to divide the general population from the insurgents through cooperation with local leaders. Under such a program, U.S. troops would offer economic assistance, implement development projects, and expand local government and security forces. The thinking behind COIN had been around for decades, but as a military theory, this population-based approach had only recently begun to regain momentum. Although the Army's Counterinsurgency Field Manual was still being revamped, by a team headed by Army Lieutenant General David Petraeus and Marine Lieutenant General Jim Mattis, ideas about this new way of looking at war in general and at the Afghanistan war in particular had already started to flow throughout the command structure.

The 3rd Brigade commander, Colonel Nicholson, was a believer. Step one, he would say, was to separate the enemy from the people. Step two: link the people to their government. Step three: transform Afghanistan. Because the 3rd Brigade Combat Team was an entirely new command, formed from scratch back at Fort Drum in 2004, its leaders—Nicholson and Lieutenant Colonel Joe Fenty among them — wanted counterinsurgency to be a part of whatever they, and it, did.

Even as the Americans pushed into Kunar and Nuristan Provinces, though, they knew astonishingly little about the region. The citations for the briefing written by one intelligence officer for 3-71 Cav included Wikipedia, from which he drew heavily. As another officer later put it, while there were smart individuals throughout 3-71 Cav, in eastern Afghanistan, "we might as well have been going to the moon."

Few had any doubt that Mick Nicholson would soon make general. He was intelligent, devoted to his troops, and carrying on the family business. His father, Brigadier General John "Jack" Nicholson, was a 1956 graduate of West Point and had spent two and a half years in Vietnam several decades before serving as an undersecretary of Veterans Affairs for President George W. Bush; Jack's brother Jim, a former chairman of the Republican National Committee, was Bush's secretary of Veterans Affairs. By 2006, there were four from Mick's own generation of Nicholsons on active duty, three in the Army and one in the Air Force. Three of them were deployed to the same region simultaneously, in Iraq, Saudi Arabia, and Afghanistan.

Jack hadn't been too happy when his son left West Point after two years to pursue premed studies at Georgetown University, but after graduation Mick changed his mind and returned to the Academy to finish his degree. Since then he had served in Grenada and Sarajevo, among other hotspots. He was working for the chief of staff of the Army when that hijacked plane hit the Pentagon on September 11, 2001; given the location of his office, he almost certainly would have been killed if he'd been at his desk, but he and his wife were moving into their new house that morning, so he hadn't yet gone in to work.

Nicholson was aware that it took an average of fourteen years for a counterinsurgency program to succeed. After five years of war, the United States had just started to expand its presence in this part of Afghanistan. And though he would never say it out loud, Nicholson knew that the whole country was being shortchanged on troops and resources.

If the concept of counterinsurgency was nothing new, it was nevertheless new to this particular administration. Before being elected president, George W. Bush had expressed disdain for "nation building": "I would be very careful about using our troops as nation builders," the then-governor said in the first presidential debate of 2000. The goal of the military was to fight and win wars, he asserted, and U.S. troops had been spread too thin policing conflicts in the Balkans, Somalia, and Haiti. But then came 9/11, and, as Bush said after leaving office, "I changed my mind."

In a speech he gave in April 2002 at the Virginia Military Institute, Bush laid out the new mission: "Peace will be achieved by helping Afghanistan develop its own stable government." He believed the United States had a moral obligation "to leave behind something better," as he later wrote in his memoir. The U.S. "had a strategic interest in helping the Afghan people build a free society. The terrorists took refuge in places of chaos, despair, and repression. A democratic Afghanistan would be a hopeful alternative to the vision of the extremists."

The president's idealism would not, however, immediately be matched by overwhelming success. In the view of many generals, this was due to the fact that he sent fewer than twenty thousand troops into a country the size of Texas, after which both he and his administration began focusing on a new war, in Iraq. By 2006, the Pentagon was still working on establishing a minimal presence in parts of the mountainous country, trying to expand into areas where even the Afghan government was barely visible—especially those regions in which insurgents were able to thrive or at least travel unhindered, such as Nuristan.

And that was where 3-71 Cav would come in.

"This is going to be tough," Keating told his men as they pushed north in the convoy. "It's going to be a struggle and a long fight. But we're going to do it because it's our job."

Keating reveled in both learning and sharing the history of the land. He enjoyed a brief stop he made at the U.S. base at Jalalabad, located on the former site of a Rest-and-Relaxation "resort" built and used by the Soviets during their invasion—though it didn't escape his notice that the swimming pool he walked past on the way to chow was rumored to have served as an execution ground for Taliban firing squads. Jalalabad had also once been home to Osama bin Laden: the Al Qaeda leader moved into a mud-and-brick structure there in 1996 with his three wives and their children, but he was long gone by the time an American missile destroyed the residence in October 2001.

Accompanied by an interpreter, Keating headed to a bazaar, where he delighted in parrying the aggressive sales pitches of the merchants. The salesmen all but fell over themselves to get their items—whatever they happened to be—into the American officer's hands.

"Mister," one said, "very nice jewelry, very good. Good knives, mister. Great blankets, sir, good price."

"Is that from Afghanistan?" Keating asked, pointing. "Did you make it?"

Reliably, the merchant would offer almost frantic confirmation or, even better, insist with a look of shocked reproach, "Oh, no, sir, this very old—given me by my father, who got it from his grandfather...."

Keating bought his own father an old brass Kelvin & Hughes sextant, used for navigation. In change, he was handed a Russian five-ruble bill from 1908. After purchasing some chalices, he received in change some coins that might have been older than the country for which he was fighting.

"Roman, sir, this one and this one," the seller said. "Greek, this one, and this one, and that one." Such remnants were charming, yet they might also inspire foreboding: many empires had been here before.

CHAPTER 2

"Major Joe Fenty, Hard Worker"

Before their convoy pulled out, intelligence officer Captain Ross Berkoff briefed Lieutenant Colonel Joe Fenty on the incidents that had just taken place along their route: the U.S. troops killed in Kunar, the Afghan politician attacked in Kabul, the convoy of Afghan soldiers hit in Ghazni. It wasn't Fenty's style to show fear or even concern, so to Berkoff, his reaction seemed to be, "Okay, so the country is swarming with enemy fighters who are trying to kill Americans. Well, that's why we're here." That was classic Fenty: not glib, not nonchalant, just all business.

Beyond Fenty, the other senior officers of 3-71 Cav tried to seem likewise unconcerned. Their private emotions, however, were another matter. Berkoff felt as if they were driving through the valleys encased in a big tin train emblazoned with the words "IED Me." Early on in the journey, as Fenty's twelve-truck convoy was pulling out from Forward Operating Base Salerno, the local Afghan intelligence chief was targeted by a remote-controlled bomb fitted on a bicycle. He survived, but two children were wounded in the attack.

As an eight-year-old boy growing up in Ronkonkoma, Long Island, Joseph Fenty had made mock dog tags for himself that read "Major Joe Fenty, hard worker." He was forty-one now, and while he was no longer a major, that second part still held. In 3-71 Cav, he was widely admired and considered a true gentleman, though he was perhaps best known for his fanatical physical discipline—the supermarathons he ran, his 3 percent body fat. Earlier in his career, when he was stationed in Alaska, he had become a cross-country skier, and was eventually approached by one of the coaches of the 1992 Olympic team, who asked if he wanted to try out. In Bosnia, he would get off work at three in the morning and go hit the treadmill; it was how he relaxed.

Fenty was relentlessly focused, even compulsive. As part of his continuing education after college, he had studied exercise physiology and kinesiology, the science of human movement, at Troy State University, where he'd learned that wearing a different pair of shoes every day could help guard against lower-leg injuries. When he was in Bosnia, he had a dozen pairs of size 9½ ASICS running shoes, all lined up and rotated daily. This habit amused his roommate, Chris Cavoli, who routinely shuffled Fenty's shoes out of order to mess with the mind of his anal-retentive friend.

He never stopped running, whether back at the home of the 10th Mountain Division, at Fort Drum, New York, where he and Command Sergeant Major Del Byers had run five to ten miles together daily, or on this deployment in Afghanistan, where the two men took advantage of any opportunity to do the same on U.S. bases.

Fenty always tried to work his brain as much as he did his muscles. He made a great effort to educate himself, reading three newspapers a day when he was at home, taking graduate courses, ordering professional journals, attending lecture series, reading books on military history and critical thinking. He was the kind of self-made man and commander whom a general could trust to assemble a new unit from scratch, as he'd done with 3-71 Cav.

As the convoy slowly traveled the hundreds of miles from Forward Operating Base Salerno, Fenty sat in the front truck commander's seat of his Humvee, with Berkoff behind him.

Fenty made it his job to know about his troops and their lives. As they rolled closer to their final destination, he asked Berkoff about his new girlfriend, Rebekah. How had they met?

Actually, Berkoff replied somewhat sheepishly, they'd met online. She was at Syracuse, and he'd been an hour away at Fort Drum, but they both wanted to marry someone Jewish, so they were introduced through J-Date, a website for Jewish singles.

Fenty smiled. He'd met his wife, Kristen, during a spring break in college, he told Berkoff, at a campfire on the beach in St. Petersburg.

Lieutenant Colonel Joe Fenty in his Humvee, March 2006. *(Photo courtesy of Ross Berkoff)*

Fenty and his friends had lost their car keys in the sand, so Kristen and her friend gave them a ride back to where they were staying. She sat on his lap during the drive. Both were students at Belmont Abbey College, and they officially became an item shortly thereafter, on Saint Patrick's Day. Within two weeks, they knew they would be husband and wife. That'd been twenty years ago.

Fenty talked to his troops to get their minds off the forbidding landscape they were entering. Berkoff described the scene in an email home: "Imagine if you can, driving the road distance equal to driving from Richmond to NYC, but instead of 95 North, you are switch-backing over landscape similar in size to our own Rocky Mountains the entire way, oh yeah, not to mention there are no barriers on the roads keeping your truck from tipping over the cliff."

Fenty's chatter also served another purpose: it got his own mind off what he was seeing. This was his second deployment here; in 2002, he had been stationed in northern Balkh Province, where, among other challenging tasks, he'd helped put down a Taliban riot in a detention facility. He knew that some of his soldiers wouldn't make it home; he accepted that, too. He was all business, yes, but in this place, nobody could be all business all the time.

The Special Forces troops who'd been operating in these provinces since 2002 hadn't found any of the senior leaders of Al Qaeda, though they had killed or rounded up some lower-level facilitators. The enemy fighters here belonged primarily to three different groups: the Haqqani network from Pakistan, Mullah Omar's Taliban, and an entity called HIG.[8] Five years earlier, when the Pentagon was planning to attack the Taliban and Al Qaeda in Afghanistan after 9/11, HIG wasn't on anyone's radar. Even just one year before this deployment, when Fenty heard the term being bandied about, he didn't really know what it signified: "HIG"? he thought. Huh? During a May 2005 meeting with 3-71 staff, Fenty—probing his team for information relating to operations and intelligence—bluntly asked his intelligence officer, "Can you tell me exactly what HIG is?" The man— whom Berkoff would soon replace—stared back at his commander. It wasn't an unreasonable question, especially to ask of an intel officer. But the fact that no one in that room knew what HIG was, almost four years into the war, indicated how poor a job the U.S. Army was doing of preparing its officers for the enemy they would soon have to face.

Berkoff was from Fair Lawn, New Jersey, and had gone through ROTC at Tulane; he was the expert in the room. Indeed, he had learned everything he could about HIG. After all, the Hezb-e-Islami Gulbuddin led insurgent operations in the region 3-71 Cav was headed for—Kunar and Nuristan Provinces—and Berkoff figured he and his fellow officers, at least, should know who was going to try to kill them.

For Berkoff, working in intelligence provided not only an intellectual challenge but also something of a rush. Deciding where to bring the fight to the enemy, setting his brain to the problem—it could feel like a more muscular exercise than doing a bench press or a curl. Yes, sometimes he felt as though he might as well be throwing darts at a map or shaking a Magic 8 Ball. But if the intel was good, it would mean that shortly thereafter, far fewer insurgents would be hunting him and his friends.

Berkoff explained to Fenty that HIG was an extremist group formed

---

[8] Pronounced so it rhymes with "fig."

more than a decade before Al Qaeda, during the chaotic years of internal struggle for control of Afghanistan, beginning in the 1970s. After the Afghan government started arresting and executing Islamists in 1974, Gulbuddin Hekmatyar, a young extremist who had been part of the Muslim Youth organization at Kabul University, fled to Pakistan and founded an Islamist group called Hezb-e-Islami, while also establishing ties with the Pakistani intelligence service ISI. By 1979, Hezb-e-Islami had split into several factions, including Hezb-e-Islami Gulbuddin, or HIG.[9]

HIG was among the many groups of mujahideen, or Islamist holy warriors, that had received aid from the U.S. government for their fight against the USSR. Hekmatyar's faction had in fact evolved into one of the U.S. Central Intelligence Agency's favorite Soviet-killing proxies, receiving more money from the U.S. government than any other single group during that period. The funds were not spent on lollipops; the Soviets considered Hekmatyar to be "the bogeyman behind the most unspeakable torture of their captured soldiers," as George Crile would later write in *Charlie Wilson's War*. "Invariably his name was invoked with new arrivals to keep them from wandering off base unaccompanied, lest they fall into the hands of this depraved fanatic whose specialty, they claimed, was skinning infidels alive."

If the mujahideen groups shared a common Soviet enemy, they often fought one another just as fiercely. After the Taliban seized control of Kabul in 1996, the country became unsafe for Hekmatyar, and he fled to Iran. Although he wasn't invited to join the interim Afghan government after the fall of the Taliban in 2001, the Iranians kicked him out, so he returned to Afghanistan anyway. Hamid Karzai and Hekmatyar were longstanding enemies, but Hekmatyar initially extended an olive branch to the new Afghan leader. Within weeks, however, Afghan officials claimed to have uncovered a plot by HIG to overthrow Karzai's government, and more than three hundred fighters loyal to Hekmatyar were arrested. That

---

[9] Another Hezb-e-Islami faction, Hezb-e-Islami Khalis, also fought in the 1980s. On November 12, 1987, its leader, Mohammed Yunnus Khalis, in his capacity as chairman of the Islamic Alliance of Afghan Mujahideen (which at the time was fighting the USSR), met in the Oval Office with President Ronald Reagan. According to intelligence officers, Khalis later helped bin Laden escape at Tora Bora in 2001. He "died in his sleep" in Pakistan in 2006. A third faction—named simply Hezb-e-Islami—is a political party whose members sit in Afghanistan's Parliament, though they do not act as a cohesive group.

was the end of the rapprochement. Soon Hekmatyar was targeted— unsuccessfully—by one of the first CIA Predator drone attacks, in May 2002. He subsequently issued a statement: "Hezb-e-Islami will fight our jihad until foreign troops are gone from Afghanistan and Afghans have set up an Islamic government." In December 2003, tipped off that Hekmatyar and one of his top aides were in a small hamlet in the Waygal Valley in Nuristan, U.S. warplanes pounded the area. Six civilians were killed, including three children. Hekmatyar had left the village hours before.

Berkoff's briefing was for the benefit of only a select few officers, not the entire squadron; the great majority of the troops had no clue as to what HIG was or how deep ran its fanaticism. They also had no idea that soon enough, members of this group they'd never heard of would be trying to kill them.

As Fenty's team pushed north, the view became lusher and more scenic, with raging rivers and tall mountains. Along the way, the convoy traversed the infamous Khost–Gardez Pass, where Soviet troops had been regularly ambushed two decades before, a tradition now extended to include Americans. Upon reaching Forward Operating Base Gardez, Fenty and his men stopped for the night.

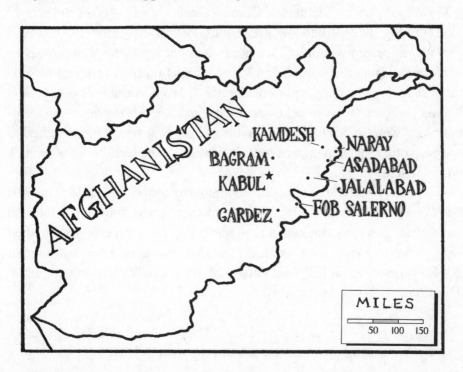

On day two, Fenty's convoy traveled from Gardez to the outskirts of Kabul and then headed toward Jalalabad Airfield, more than 150 miles total. It was not an easy trip. Berkoff was told that a section of the main road was out between Kabul and Jalalabad, near the Surobi Dam. Not damaged, not under repair, just...*out.* No further explanation was forthcoming or even needed. This was Afghanistan; this was how it was. So the next day, the convoy set off on a long alternate route, switchbacking over mountains, back and forth, back and forth. It took eighteen hours, but everyone made it to Jalalabad alive.

Afghanistan was not a nation known for its robust infrastructure. Summer rainstorms could wash roads out, and even under optimal conditions, a road might be so narrow that a convoy would have to take detours via riverbeds just to get through. If staying dry was a priority, the only other option was to brave the steep cliffs, but that involved no small risk. On the same day that Fenty's convoy left Khost, a Marine was killed in one of the provinces they would be stopping in — Nangarhar — when his Humvee accidentally rolled over the edge.[10]

In Nangarhar, at Jalalabad Airfield, Fenty and his men linked up with a battalion from the 10th Mountain that was headquartered there, the 1-32 Infantry, led by Lieutenant Colonel Chris Cavoli — he of the scrambled running shoes. Loud and gregarious, Cavoli was yin to the reserved Fenty's yang. Fenty could go for hours without speaking; Cavoli was as restless as a hyperactive child at Mass. During their assignment in war-torn Yugoslavia, Fenty had considerately played country music at low volume, whereas Cavoli had blasted the Clash and Springsteen. And now both men were in Afghanistan. Cavoli and his best friend were excited to see each other, but Cavoli was most interested in the well-being of Fenty's wife, Kristen.

For years, Kristen Fenty had been unable to conceive a child. That had been okay with her husband: the two of them moved around a lot, and their lifestyle wasn't conducive to parenthood. They were pretty satisfied with things the way they were. All of that changed in the summer of 2005, however, when Kristen Fenty — at the age of forty — got pregnant. Their little girl was due in April.

---

[10] Lance Corporal Nicholas Anderson of Sauk City, Wisconsin.

From: Joe Fenty
Sent: Friday, March 17, 2006
To: Kristen Fenty

Dear, hope all is well. I'm traveling but sure would like to get a note from you. Please let me know how you're feeling. The timing is awful. I'm going to be at the most remote place on the due date....

Miss you and love you,
Joseph

From: Kristen Fenty
Sent: Friday, March 17, 2006
To: Joseph Fenty

Dear, did you get the note I sent you yesterday and in the middle of the night before?...

As part of the book club, [we're] going to hold a "kite run" in May in recognition of the Taliban ban on kite festivals and their resurgence after the U.S. liberation of Kabul. We're going to try to hold a "build a kite for your soldier" craft day and then hold the festival on the parade field....

The house is now spotless and I'm ready to pack for the hospital. I don't want to go through labor, though. I think I'll opt for drugs. Do you have any thoughts?

Do you like Lauren as well as Kelly? I think it will need to be Kelly if she's born today (St. Patrick's Day)—our twentieth anniversary since our hookup....

Love you—
Kristen

On their runs, Fenty would confide to Del Byers that he was worried about how old a dad he would soon be. He was already forty-one.

"Shit, Joe," Byers would say to him, "you can already outrun ninety percent of the U.S. Army—what are you worried about?"

Byers reminded his friend that nothing was easy in the Army, including parenting. Byers's own kids were teenagers, and he was missing most of their high school years.

"You'll get to see her grow up," Byers told Fenty.

In the 1-32 Infantry briefing room, Cavoli introduced Fenty to his staff and commanders. "Give him and his team all the support they need while they're here," he instructed.

Before moving on to their final destination, Fenty and his team took the opportunity afforded by this brief pit stop in Jalalabad—the new headquarters for the brigade in charge of this area of operations—to begin face-to-face planning for a pending operation in Kunar Province, the one that would put Joe Fenty in "the most remote place on the due date." Troops from 3-71 Cav, 1-32 Infantry, and the 2nd Battalion, 3rd Marines, would all participate in what was being called Operation Mountain Lion, after which Fenty and 3-71 Cav would move with full force into Nuristan. On March 19, Fenty's convoy pulled out of Jalalabad.

The road they took followed the Kunar River, which bestowed life on the surrounding country, transforming it from a dusty brown into a lush green. They stopped at Camp Wright—an outpost that was on their way—and hiked eight hundred feet up to a former mujahideen observation post. From there they saw the ancient Nawa Pass leading into Pakistan. It was the same corridor used by Alexander's cavalry twenty-three hundred years before, Berkoff said. Again, the uncomfortable history of empires in this land hung like a noose.

CHAPTER 3

Like Just Another
Day on the Range

The ultimate destination of the 3-71 Cav convoys was a small Special Forces base established in 2004 in Naray District, Kunar Province, near the provincial border with Nuristan. Fenty's men were tasked with building the camp into a fully functioning forward operating base. They would be the first conventional troops to be stationed there.

Soon after their arrival, the 3-71 Cav troops moved into barracks just vacated by what were called ASGs, or Afghan Security Guards—locally hired contractors who were not directly affiliated with either the Afghan National Army or the Afghan National Police. Special Forces Captain Steve Snyder,[11] whose team had been the only U.S. military force at Naray until 3-71 Cav got there, had ordered the Afghans to move into tents, but the locals had left their mark: the barracks reeked of body odor, rotting food, and what smelled like feces. One of the 3-71 Cav officers, Captain Pete Stambersky, smeared Vicks VapoRub under his nose just so he could breathe. Snyder knew it stank in there, but the sting from the enemy rockets in the area was far worse. Better to have a roof over your head, he thought.

Berkoff found the sparse conditions demoralizing. It wasn't just here at

---

[11] Not his real name. In a number of cases in this book, including Snyder's, the real names of Special Forces troops, military intelligence collectors, and Afghans who worked with the Americans have been withheld, either at their own request or out of concern for their safety.

Naray; throughout their tour of U.S. bases in Afghanistan, from Khost to Jalalabad, he and others in 3-71 Cav had been stunned by the enforced austerity whereby soldiers could be simply jammed against one another in rows of green cots. The Iraq veterans among them couldn't believe how grim their Afghanistan quarters were compared to U.S. bases in Iraq— especially since Iraq was the more recent of the two wars, with the United States' having gone into that country more than a year *after* entering Afghanistan. But then again, the officers reminded themselves, Iraq had long been the favored war of their commander in chief, and Afghanistan the one that would be fought on the cheap.

Snyder had been running his twelve-man Special Forces team out of Naray since January. He conducted his operations with a palpable intensity, haunted by the ghosts of nineteen Americans—fellow special-operations troops—who'd been killed before he even arrived.

In June 2005, as part of a mission designated Operation Redwing, a four-man team of Navy SEALs on the trail of an enemy leader named Ahmad Shah was dropped into the mountains of Kunar. There the Americans were attacked by insurgents, who killed three of the four team members and also shot down a Chinook helicopter, killing even more SEALs as well as the special-operations Nightstalker crew and pilots, for a total of nineteen U.S. casualties in all. For the men of Naval Special Warfare, that day marked the largest single loss of life since World War II.[12]

---

[12]The members of the original SEAL team killed were Lieutenant Michael P. Murphy from Patchogue, New York; Petty Officer Second Class Matthew Axelson from Cupertino, California; and Petty Officer Second Class Danny Dietz from Littleton, Colorado. Lost on the Chinook were Chief Petty Officer Jacques J. Fontan of New Orleans, Louisiana; Senior Chief Petty Officer Daniel R. Healy from Exeter, New Hampshire; Lieutenant Commander Erik S. Kristensen from San Diego, California; Petty Officer First Class Jeffrey A. Lucas of Corbett, Oregon; Lieutenant Michael M. McGreevy, Jr., from Portville, New York; Petty Officer Second Class James E. Suh of Deerfield Beach, Florida; Petty Officer First Class Jeffrey S. Taylor from Midway, West Virginia; Petty Officer Second Class Shane Patton of Boulder City, Nevada; Staff Sergeant Shamus O. Goare from Danville, Ohio; Chief Warrant Officer Corey J. Goodnature of Clarks Grove, Minnesota; Sergeant Kip A. Jacoby from Pompano Beach, Florida; Sergeant First Class Marcus V. Muralles from Shelbyville, Indiana; Master Sergeant James W. Ponder III from Franklin, Tennessee; Major Stephen C. Reich from Washington Depot, Connecticut; Sergeant First Class Michael L. Russell from Stafford, Virginia; and Chief Warrant Officer Chris J. Scherkenbach from Jacksonville, Florida. For more on this mission, read Marcus Luttrell with Patrick Robinson, *Lone Survivor: The Eyewitness Account of Operation Redwing and the*

By mid-2005, the commander of special operations in Afghanistan was considering shutting down the base at Naray. Instead, U.S. military leaders went the other way, sending in conventional forces — 3-71 Cav — in part to help Snyder, who welcomed the arrival of Fenty and his squadron.

Snyder's task was to disrupt and/or kill what were then called ACMs, or anticoalition militias — in short, anyone who didn't like the U.S.-led coalition. He knew that the Taliban had been using Pakistan as a safe haven, so his team's first operation was to trek to a length of border reputed to be particularly porous. Dokalam, Afghanistan, was adjacent to Arandu, Pakistan. It was clear that the Afghan Border Police and Pakistani border guards were turning a blind eye on those seeking passage; anyone who wanted to cross could do so anywhere he liked. That changed only when the Afghan Border Police became aware that the Americans were watching. Then the gates suddenly closed, and everyone got to work.

As they made the rounds in their area of operations, Snyder and his men visited hamlets and communities so isolated they could be reached only on foot. The mountain peaks here were more than twelve thousand feet high; even many mountain passes were at ten to eleven thousand feet. When the Americans reached each village, they would ask the elders if they could enter; unfailingly, the locals would welcome the big men with guns, just as they and their forefathers had welcomed so many other men with superior weapons before them. To Snyder, they did not seem of the twenty-first century. Many of them initially mistook the U.S. troops for Soviets, returning after the USSR's withdrawal nearly a generation before. Some were evidently unaware that the USSR had ceased to exist; others hadn't heard about 9/11; still other locals thought 9/11 had been a retaliation for the American invasion of Afghanistan in October 2001. Most of them didn't know how to read; few knew anything of modern medicine. One Afghan came to the base needing medical attention after trying to use wet concrete as a salve for a wound. Snyder noted that the Afghans appeared to have no comprehension of time; they didn't even seem to know how old they were. He would inquire about a certain insurgent, and the Afghans would say they hadn't seen him in two or three days, two or three weeks, two or three years. Everything was in twos or threes.

Lost Heroes of SEAL Team 10 (Boston and New York: Little, Brown, 2009). Luttrell was, as the title of his book indicates, the only member of the original team who survived.

These Special Forces troops had been asked to operate in a world they could not fathom.

Snyder and his intel officer briefed the 3-71 Cav troops on their new home and its bad-guy neighbors. Residing in the village of Kamdesh was a local HIG commander who had gone underground but was believed to shuttle back and forth routinely between Afghanistan and Pakistan. A Taliban leader lived in Pitigal, and another HIG leader in Bazgal; the hamlet of Sedmashal was reportedly home to a bomb-maker known as the Engineer — a nickname often bestowed, in that region, on anyone thought to be educated. In Gawardesh, a local timber smuggler–cum– HIG commander reigned.

And then, in the Kotya Valley,[13] there were the Ayoub brothers. In June 2004, a group of Marines had returned to their small firebase after thirty-six hours on observation patrol. When he checked his gear, one Marine realized he was missing his night-vision goggles. The next day, word came from higher up that he had to go back to the makeshift observation post with the other two members of his fire team to recover the goggles. They didn't find them there, but on their way back, the Marines stumbled across a group of Afghans who were preparing to ambush a U.S. convoy. The Afghans instead attacked the three Marines, killing two of them.[14] The Ayoub brothers — Daoud, Sardar, Mohammed, and others — were presumed to be responsible for the deaths, Snyder said.

---

[13] Some maps located the Kotya Valley just outside of Nuristan Province, in Kunar Province, the result of a dispute over the Ghaziabad District between the two provinces. The borders on the 2002 map drawn up by the interim Afghan government placed Kotya in Kunar, one of many designations that experts considered woefully divorced from reality. Berkoff at one point told the Afghan police chief in Naray, in Kunar Province, that his forces needed to head to Gawardesh — technically in Kunar — only to be informed by the chief that the map was wrong, and Gawardesh was in Nuristan. The Nuristan expert Richard Strand would advise military officers who consulted him on the matter that such errors led to needless jurisdictional disputes and were too often seen by Nuristanis as part of a scheme to steal their land. Joshua Foust, a civilian who worked for the Human Terrain System, would advance a similar argument, maintaining that the bad map-making also caused confusion about which U.S. troops should be in charge where.

[14] On this mission to retrieve his goggles, Private First Class Daniel McClenney of Flat Creek, Tennessee, took with him Lance Corporal Juston Thacker of Princeton, West

As the new commanding officer of the base at Naray, Fenty decided to make getting rid of the Ayoub brothers his first priority. In order to do this, however, he needed to secure the cooperation of the elders of Kotya, so he invited them to Naray to participate in a shura—a consultation with village elders that is an important aspect of governance in many majority Muslim countries. The elders accepted the invitation and came to the base, but they were not receptive to Fenty's overtures; indeed, they asked him to stay away from the valley. They also claimed not to know anything about the Ayoubs.

One U.S. official would later suggest that the Kotya elders had acted cooperatively just in coming to the U.S. base at Fenty's request. "It is not a trivial thing from the perspective of Afghans to respond like a dog when someone whistles," the official explained. "That's especially true for prominent individuals in a community. To look like they're responding as servants to the foreign occupier diminishes their stature in their peers' eyes. So it's not a small thing that they came. That we don't see it and instead get upset when they don't behave in ways that reflect our interests is shortsighted." But to Snyder, it seemed like more of the same "see no evil, hear no evil" bullshit he'd been dealing with for the past three months. They come in, they lie, they want money for projects, he thought. "Get out of here," he told them. He was disgusted.

The sun had yet to rise on the morning of March 29 when roughly one hundred members of 3-71 Cav piled into Humvees and light medium tactical vehicles (LMTVs) and began driving north. Fenty was accompanied on this expedition by Command Sergeant Major Del Byers; Captain Matt Gooding and Able Troop; a kill team—snipers and reconnaissance officers—from Cherokee Company; and a smaller group called a quick reaction force, or QRF, which would stay on the periphery as an emergency reinforcement should more military might be needed.

Before they left, Berkoff handed out photographs of the Ayoubs to the snipers and scouts. He figured the odds were slim that the brothers would show their faces, but you never knew.

Virginia, and Lance Corporal Brian Molby of Troy, Michigan. Molby was the lone survivor.

Cherokee Company[15] commander Captain Aaron Swain was at the head of the twenty-five-truck convoy on its forty-minute trip to the mouth of the valley, a drive that would be followed by a four-hour hike from the road up to the village of Kotya. The floor of the valley itself was only half as wide as a football field; the stream that ran through it was about the width of a two-lane road. On the second leg of the journey, Snyder and his team led the way on foot, ready to fire at any enemy threat at any moment. It was a show of U.S. force such as the valley had never seen before.

Whereas Snyder was there to capture or kill the Ayoub brothers, Fenty also hoped to befriend the people of Kotya and convince them to partner with 3-71 Cav and the Afghan government. If those two missions seemed at odds — helping some Afghans while killing others — that was just a reflection of the complicated nature of the U.S. mission, not to mention the sometimes contradictory relationship between Special Forces and conventional troops.

As Fenty and Byers finished climbing the path and arrived at the edge of the village, atop a steep mountain, they were greeted by elders. Other village leaders were summoned. Fenty and Byers whispered to each other, agreeing that it had all been too easy. Four hours walking through the Kotya Valley, and they hadn't seen a single person. Now, here at the village, they saw only elders and children. The women were obviously indoors, hiding — or more to the point, being hidden — out of religious modesty, but where were the fighting-age men? Were they all out working, tending to their animals? Were they just staying out of sight of the Americans? Or was something more nefarious going on?

The elders sat with Fenty and Byers, who had a translator with them. They briefly chatted. No, the Afghan men said, they didn't know of any insurgent forces in the area. No, there wasn't any intimidation. The

---

[15] Technically, this group of infantrymen, Charlie Company, was nicknamed the Gladiators at this point and would become Cherokee only later in the deployment. But for ease and consistency, this book will refer to the unit as "Cherokee" for the duration. A "troop" and a "company" are the same thing — each comprising three to four platoons of anywhere from one hundred to two hundred soldiers — but the first term is used for Cavalry, and the second for Infantry. While 3-71 Cav was itself a Cavalry unit, Cherokee Company consisted of infantrymen.

Ayoubs? They hadn't been seen in the village for a long time. It was "see no evil, hear no evil" all over again.

For Fenty, there was something discomfiting about the whole situation. Byers had the same feeling. The two thanked the elders for their time and prepared to go. Fenty told the leaders of a Cherokee Company security team, Staff Sergeants Matt Cusson and Nicholas Platt, and a sniper attached to them, Sergeant John Hawes, to mingle with the rest of the 3-71 Cav troops as they left the village and started walking eastward back to the road. Once they all got around the bend and appeared to be on their way out, Fenty said, the security team should split off, stealthily scramble up the mountain on the other side of the valley, take cover, and keep watch on everything.

Fenty picked up his radio and gave his orders: they were leaving. The ruse commenced. Cusson, Platt, Hawes, and the other members of the security team made the turn and then disappeared into the southern mountainside. Once he'd ascended, Hawes hid in a bush. He had grown up shooting in competitions in upstate New York, where his family regularly hunted deer, turkey, and small game. He had won local competitions and coached a junior rifle team, and by his senior year of high school, he was shooting four or five days a week. But he had never actually shot a person, never killed a man. Now he held his sniper rifle with its powerful scope and prepared to do just that.

And then they came.

Just as Fenty had anticipated, about half an hour after the American troops had departed, the fighting-age men of the village started popping up on ridgelines all over the hills and heading back to the settlement. Hawes's radio line was promptly abuzz with the voices of scouts reporting locals jumping out everywhere in front of them—or behind them: the new arrivals were all over both the southern and northern ridgelines. None had weapons. While a local carrying either a weapon or a radio was considered to be a "positive identified threat" and could thereby constitute a legitimate target, the U.S. Rules of Engagement prohibited soldiers from firing upon anyone simply for acting in a suspicious manner. For now, all Hawes and the others could do was stay focused and wait for trouble.

About an hour after the 3-71 Cav troops had left the village, three men started walking along the trail heading east. One carried an AKM—a

Russian Kalashnikov assault rifle, a modernized version of the AK-47 — under his arm. They entered a four-building complex across the valley from where Hawes was hiding.

The security team radioed to the other 3-71 Cav troops to make sure there weren't any Afghan Security Guards who had stayed behind in the valley. There weren't.

Four reconnaissance troops from the security team quietly moved about fifty yards east to check out a vacant building. As they did so, the man who'd been carrying the AKM suddenly appeared on a roof within the housing complex. He was talking on a radio whose antenna was extended. Not spotting the Americans, the man went back inside, only to emerge from another building lower down in the complex. Now he had the AKM *and* the radio.

Cusson placed a call to the squadron's operations center, asking for permission to shoot. "Sounds like PIT to me," Berkoff said — meaning a "positive identified threat." Permission was granted.

The word came back to Cusson: Take him out.

The man with the AKM went over to a rock wall and removed a stone, behind which he had evidently hidden something.

A scout with the security team, Sergeant David Fisher, projected an infrared laser on the man. He was 167 yards away.

Hawes set his scope.

He pulled the trigger. The first shot hit the Afghan in his right pectoral and spun him around. Hawes put two more rounds in his chest, and the man fell down on his back.

There it was: his first kill. To Hawes, it felt like just another day on the range.

Afghans ran from the house. A boy sprinted west, back toward the village, followed by an older man. Other young men now bolted out of the complex and began scrambling over the mountain. Some members of the security team were already on their way to check out the man Hawes had shot when a woman rushed out of the house, snatched the radio and the AKM off the body, and ran back into the complex.

The security team members photographed the dead insurgent and recovered the AKM from inside the house. One of the Americans heard an Afghan man's voice talking over the radio, but because the team didn't have an interpreter along, there was no way of knowing what was being said. Just then, on a different frequency, in English, came word from the scouts in the valley that dozens of men were heading their way from the village. This wasn't good.

While the leaders of the security team had been able to radio their commanders before Hawes took his shot, once the men moved down to the valley floor, communication became intermittent at best. Fenty and Swain both tried to tell the team leaders to find a piece of territory to defend so Swain could lead the quick reaction force into the valley to support them and start a fight; he had mortars and attack helicopters at the ready and was eager to use them. But they could never get that message through to the team leaders, and then it began to get dark and hence too dangerous for two friendly forces to try to link up without good communication. The QRF ran to watch over the valley, while the security team leaders decided on their own that it was time for their troops to leave.

All of the members of the team got out safely, with no exchange of fire. It wasn't clear whether the insurgents just gave up or the security team outran them, but soon enough, the chase had ended. The next day, the local Afghan police would confirm that U.S. troops had killed Daoud Ayoub, the leader of the insurgent cell.

Thus, in a sense, the first-ever operation by conventional U.S. forces in this part of the country had been a success. But the bigger picture was not reassuring. The insurgents hadn't seemed to care that the Americans had them outmanned and outequipped; they'd hidden from them and then brazenly planned an ambush on them. After their leader was shot, his family's first impulse had been to try to grab his weapon and his radio for future use. They didn't seem afraid of the U.S. troops.

And what of the elders of the Kotya Valley? They had demonstrated how their ancestors had survived for centuries in these mountains: by being practical, saying what they needed to say to whoever happened to be in front of them at any given moment.

Berkoff worked with translators to craft a message to be sent to the remaining members of Ayoub's gang: Reconcile or die. The threat was apparently of limited value: a week or so later, intel came in that the

Ayoub brothers' cell had returned. Fenty had Cherokee Company commander Swain fire repeated illumination rounds — basically giant flares – into the valley from the base at Naray. It was his way of letting the Kotya elders know that *he* knew the enemy fighters were back.

At the base itself, meanwhile, Fenty ordered the buildup of showers, laundry facilities, flush toilets, and new picnic benches. A hot meal was served once a day. Resupply air drops began, though not without a glitch: the first ones missed the mark and ended up in the adjacent Kunar River. Locals looking to make a quick dollar jumped into the water, hauled the goods out, and delivered them to the front gate.

A couple of days after Swain began firing the illumination rounds, about a dozen Kotya elders came to Naray and asked to talk to Fenty. He wasn't there, so Swain, the ranking 3-71 Cav officer on the base at the time, met them at the gate.

"Please stop firing the flares," the elders asked. "The rounds are scaring our children and animals."

"I'll stop firing," Swain said. "But I don't want to hear about you guys supporting the Ayoub brothers anymore."

About a week later, the elders returned to Naray. "We've thrown them out of the valley," they told Swain.

When Aaron Swain graduated from West Point, in 1998, the idea that he would one day find himself devoting much of his time and energy to tending to the needs of a band of Afghan elders in an obscure valley would have struck him as being highly improbable. His training had been focused not on dealing with civilians but rather on killing bad guys, and back in the 1990s, the threat of a U.S. war in Afghanistan had seemed slight.

But Swain was now essentially the U.S. ambassador to the Kotya Valley. Deciding he would take an approach different from that adopted by Snyder, whose impatience often manifested itself as hostility, he invited all of the elders to Naray. When they arrived at the base, Swain showed them deference by ordering up a banquet for them.

When they all sat down, he thanked them for throwing the Ayoub brothers out of the valley. "I'm grateful," he said. "I want to get a road built for you, into the valley, to make it easier for you to get in and out."

More than a month later, when reports came in that the bomb-maker known as the Engineer was in the Kotya Valley, Swain lit up the flares again.

*   *   *

The experience of 3-71 Cav in the Kotya Valley would be repeated time and time again across Nuristan as American troops tried to establish a foothold through the policy of counterinsurgency.

Even within a country that could sometimes seem to U.S. troops to be far removed from the twenty-first century, Nuristan's valleys and villages were truly in a class of their own. More than 99 percent of the population of the province was ethnically Nuristani, a profound distinction in Afghanistan, where elsewhere Nuristanis made up only a tiny minority — just 1 percent or so — of the total population. (Some Nuristanis had blue eyes and/or red hair, and a number had physiognomic features that made them look European, feeding the long-discredited myth that as a people, they were descended from the Greeks and Macedonians left behind by Alexander the Great's army.) Even in the hardscrabble context of Afghanistan, those who lived in Nuristan were legendarily tough. All that most Afghans knew about them was that their ancestors had been non-Muslims who were brave and determined warriors, famed for their lethal raids on Muslims in the lowlands. This had inspired the Nuristanis' reputation as mountain-dwelling fighters — tough, effective, and uncivilized. Whether that reputation was still accurate or up to date in 2006 was almost beside the point.

Berkoff had studied Nuristan before he deployed and noted that rebellion seemed to be an important part of its culture. Fenty gave him a copy of an out-of-print book about the region, *The Kafirs of the Hindu Kush,* written by an English army major named George Scott Robertson after he visited there in 1890–91. Because at that point they were the only ethnic group in Afghanistan that had refused to convert to Islam, instead practicing a religion that seemed to have ties to a primitive form of Hinduism, the Nuristanis were known as Kafirs, or "infidels," and Nuristan was called Kafiristan — literally, the "land of the infidels."

In 1896, however — just five years after Robertson's visit — the Kafirs finally accepted Islam, many at knifepoint. Kafiristan then became Nuristan, or the "land of the enlightened." Many Nuristanis became quite devout, even as they maintained their reputation for fanatic rebelliousness. They were said to have been among the first to take up arms against the Communists who brought down the Afghan government in 1978. Some Nuristanis told stories of dramatic and bloody attacks on these intruders, though what was reality and what was myth could be difficult to discern.

During the time of the Soviet occupation of Afghanistan, part of eastern Nuristan became a semiautonomous state referred to as the Dawlat,[16] or the Islamic Revolutionary State of Afghanistan. Adhering to extremist Salafi Islam, and officially recognized by Pakistan and Saudi Arabia, the Dawlat was run by an especially fearsome warlord who chased off or killed his rivals. Among those rivals were fellow Nuristanis.

Northern Kunar and eastern Nuristan were home to at least four major ethnic groups—Mushwani Pashtuns, Salarzai Pashtuns, Nuristanis, and Gujjars—all of whom had argumentative histories with one another and among themselves. Just about the only matter the first three groups could agree upon, in fact, was their disdain for the fourth, the Gujjars, a destitute population of migrant workers whom the others often characterized as thieving squatters.

Each group was further split into subdivisions that carried their own potent political implications. The Nuristanis consisted of Kom, Kata, Kushtoz, and Kalasha communities. These four subgroups were themselves given to feuding, and each subdivision had its separate subpopulations, with accompanying disputes and rivalries. The Kom people, for instance, saw themselves as being organized by different lineages, with each claiming descent from a distant ancestor. They did not count themselves part of the Dawlat. Significant religious differences also divided the populace, as each group practiced a type of Islam that varied in important ways from the next group's. Even within a single group, there might be multiple divisions. The residents of Kamdesh District observed an Islam that differed from others in that its mullahs—the Muslim clergymen—were expected to interpret the holy text and were, therefore, much more apt to introduce their own political bias.

For Nuristanis to take up arms against one another was not uncommon. The Kom had historical tensions with the nearby Kushtozis, and the spark was reignited in the 1990s when the two clans began battling over water rights, among other issues—a clash that inspired such acts of aggression as the planting of landmines on enemies' property. In 1997,

---

[16] Literally, "State."

50

the Kom burned down a Kushtoz village, displacing at least five hundred families.

Considering all of this, it perhaps wasn't surprising that these villagers, while welcoming enough to visitors, didn't immediately cooperate much with the Americans. They were survivors, and they continued to do what had worked for them in the past: withholding information and playing both sides. They had learned long ago from the British, and from the Soviets more recently (though still before many troops from 3-71 Cav were even born), that intruders always, eventually, left. A presentation by the Foreign Military Studies Office at Fort Leavenworth about the decade-long occupation of the area by the USSR noted some "eternal truths" about Afghanistan. One of them was "Switching sides is common." Another was "Loyalty can be rented for a small bag of gold."

CHAPTER 4

War, Fate, and Wind

Private Nick Pilozzi gasped.

Oh my God, I can't breathe, he thought.

It was April 2006, and Pilozzi and others from 3-71 Cav's Able Troop, led by Captain Gooding, had been choppered in and dropped atop a twelve-thousand-foot snow-capped mountain on the southern slope of the Hindu Kush for Operation Mountain Lion. The air was so thin he felt as if he were being slowly, almost subtly, strangled.

Pilozzi, who was eighteen, came from Tonawanda, New York, not far from Buffalo, so he knew from cold. But there was something devastating about the combination of the deep snow, the chill, and the lack of oxygen to be found here on the roof of these mountains. His driving skills were not needed up here; there were no cars or trucks. There wasn't anything except for rocks and snow — anywhere from two to six feet of it. Most of the snow was packed, so the troops were able to walk on it, but they exhausted themselves digging down to rock to position their mortar tube — the cannon from which they would aim and fire explosive rounds — lest the weapon sink into the powder.

The Americans had had no idea it was going to be so cold — just one more indication that they didn't know much about the land they were supposed to be controlling. The troops hadn't packed appropriate cold-weather gear and had just fifteen sleeping bags for thirty men, including the handful of Marines who had joined them. They ended up dividing the bags — some got the Gore-Tex outer layer, others the thick black inner layer — and laying them atop the rock formations that jutted out of the snow. Troops clung to one another for body heat. Everyone survived, but it was the roughest night many of them had ever known. And that was how Private Pilozzi met the Korangal Valley.

(Photo courtesy of Nick Pilozzi)

The Korangal Valley was tough to get into and even tougher to get out of. The region was home to roughly twenty-five thousand Afghans, an insular community with its own particular dialect. Some Korangalis trafficked in illegal timber, selling lumber from the Himalayan cedars that grew in the valley; such traffickers were sufficiently ruthless that their influence far exceeded their numbers. The combination of this criminal culture with its geographic, cultural, and linguistic isolation had made the Korangal an inviting sanctuary for insurgents fighting the USSR in the 1980s, and then later again for those fighting the United States in the 2000s. (The Korangal was close to where those nineteen SEALs and Nightstalker pilots and crewmen had been killed in 2005, during Operation Redwing.)

Now 3-71 Cav had been diverted to the region because Colonel Nicholson wanted to take advantage of the temporary overlap, in Kunar Province, of 3-71 Cav (commanded by Fenty), 1-32 Infantry (led by Cavoli), and the 1st Battalion, 3rd Marines, which was scheduled to leave the country in late May.

Nicholson, who commanded the parent brigade, ordered 3-71 Cav to flank around the valley to the east while 1-32 Infantry blocked the valley from the north. The Marines, along with the brigade tactical command post—Nicholson, the ANA brigade commander, and a small staff—would be dropped by chopper onto mountaintops and were to clear the enemy down into the valley. Their ultimate goal was to set up the Korangal outpost, reach out to the villagers, help establish an Afghan government presence, and kill the enemy: intelligence sources claimed that the insurgent leader Ahmad Shah, thought to be behind the Operation Redwing disaster, plus a known Al Qaeda operative named Abu Ikhlas were in the immediate area.

Fenty had sent Gooding and Able Troop to watch over the southern Korangal Valley while Captain Franklin Brooks and Bravo Troop—who called themselves the Barbarians—moved south into the adjacent Chowkay Valley. Most of Cherokee Company remained back at the base at Naray, with the exception of the kill team, which was also ordered into the Chowkay Valley to patrol for enemy fighters.

The Chowkay Valley was the most popular exit route used by the Korangali Taliban to escape over the border into Pakistan; indeed, Berkoff had briefed Fenty and the 3-71 Cav troop commanders that when confronted by the consistent presence of U.S. troops, the local Taliban leader was likely to "squirt" into Pakistan, after first pushing his team of insurgent fighters into the Chowkay to clear the way for him. The Americans hoped to be waiting there for him.

After they all almost froze to death at twelve thousand feet, Gooding sent Staff Sergeant Matthew Netzel and more than a dozen soldiers from Able Troop's 2nd Platoon down the Korangal to watch over a lumberyard. Among the troops with Netzel was Private First Class Brian Moquin, Jr., a nineteen-year-old from Worcester, Massachusetts, whom Netzel had kept an eye on since the beginning of their deployment.

When Moquin first arrived at 3-71 Cav, it was clear to Netzel that the private had been a problem child growing up—just like half the Army, in Netzel's estimation. Back at Fort Drum, Moquin was late to formation one morning at 0630, so Netzel went to his room and banged on his door.

"What's up, Sergeant?" Moquin said after he finally came to the door, rubbing sleep from his eyes.

"You're fucking not at formation, that's what's up," Netzel said. "Get your uniform on and get in fucking formation."

When the slipups continued, Netzel instituted some "corrective" training, ordering Moquin to do pushups, situps, laps — anything to make his whole body hurt for a few days so he wouldn't ever again forget what a mistake it was to slack. Netzel knew Moquin could potentially be a good soldier; he would always ask questions. After an exercise in which the troops had to disassemble and reassemble their weapons, everyone else in the platoon dispersed, but Moquin remained, repeating the drill.

"Yo, dude," Netzel said. "It's time to wrap shit up."

Moquin smiled at him.

"Out of curiosity," Netzel asked, smiling back, "what are your thoughts about how you're hammering down on your weapon?"

"I don't know about the rest of these guys," Moquin said. "But I plan on coming home. And if it comes down to a weapons system working, I'm going to make sure there are no problems."

Fuckin' A, thought Netzel.

Born and raised in upstate New York, the twenty-five-year-old Netzel understood Moquin in a way that was hard to explain to anyone who hadn't peered into the chasm of drug dependency and mustered the strength to walk away — in both of their cases, into the welcoming arms of the U.S. military. Back home, Netzel had dabbled in a little bit of everything, without much effect. By the age of eighteen, he'd started to sense that if he stayed in his hometown for too long after graduating from high school, he'd end up in jail or in a coffin. This wasn't just a working-class cliché; one day, a friend of his, tripping hard, flying around a room like an airplane, dove out the window of a second-story apartment, landing on the pavement. He survived the fall but was never quite the same. Netzel headed for the military not long after that.

"I have a pretty good idea why you joined the Army," Netzel once said to Moquin at Fort Drum. "But why don't *you* tell me why."

"My life was pretty much going to shit," Moquin replied. "It was either the Army or end up in jail or dead."

Netzel had known he was going to say that.

Moquin was a talented artist, and at Naray, Netzel asked him if he'd design a tattoo for him. "This is what I want," Netzel told him. "A tattered American flag with an Afghan knife. It should also say, 'The price we pay'"—this was the unofficial motto of the 10th Mountain—and should include the designations "OIF 1 and 2" and "OEF 7," referring to Netzel's time with the first two deployments in Iraq for Operation Iraqi Freedom (OIF) and their current stint in Afghanistan, with the seventh rotation for Operation Enduring Freedom (OEF). Moquin drew it all out on a piece of paper and gave it to Netzel a few days later.

"Do you mind if I get it, too?" Moquin asked as he handed over the sketch. "Without 'OIF One and Two,' of course."

Private First Class Brian M. Moquin, Jr.'s tattoo design for Staff Sergeant Matthew Netzel. *(Courtesy Matt Netzel)*

"Hell yeah, do it," Netzel replied. "You drew it up, it's your artwork. We'll go get tatted together when we get back. So hang on to it."

"No, I want you to hang on to it in case anything happens to me," Moquin explained, "because I made it for you."

"Roger," said Netzel. "I'll hang on to it, and we'll get it tatted together." Moquin wrote to his mother:

Hi MOM,

How's everything, I'm doing good. I've done a lot of thinking while I was here. I know I haven't been a great kid and have put you through a lot of things that you didn't deserve. I haven't been a good person to many people and I regret a lot of the things I've done. But I finally found a place for me. I love it here more than anything. I've wanted to get away for so long, I was trapped in my own misery and selfishness. I've grown up a lot here, and I'm going to try my damn hardest to make you proud of me. I'm sorry if you don't hear from me much. I'm very busy and I'm going to be for the next couple years. I love you and I just wanted you to know I haven't forgot about you.

I'm doing the best I can to be the best soldier.

I miss ya,

Love, your son,
Brian.

And now here they were in the Korangal, Netzel and Moquin, in four feet of snow. Almost none of the other soldiers had been in combat before, so Netzel, having been in Iraq, took the lead as they began their trek.

For nearly all of the troops, the steep mountain descent — during which each soldier carried eighty pounds of gear and ammo at a minimum — was one of the toughest physical challenges of their lives. (And these were young men in top physical condition, trained for just such a challenge.) They had to worry constantly — about falling, about the enemy, and about the clumsy morons up above them (someone up top would accidentally kick a rock loose, and then everyone would shout "Rock!" and try to dodge getting hammered by a mini-boulder). It was a painful, full-day hike down. Climbing *up* the mountain would have been easier.

On the fifth night, the members of the platoon reached one of the most difficult points so far in their journey, confronting a cliffside so steep they couldn't descend. They decided to call it a night. In the morning, they'd figure out where to go next.

Sergeant Michael Hendy was on guard duty; he sat behind a rock wall in the pitch black, staring at the path. He heard a hissing.

"I think a battery's leaking," Hendy whispered to Moquin. Batteries for the thermal scope were stacked up for the night; filled with a gas, they would make a *"Ssssss"* sound if they cracked. Hendy turned on a thermal light so he could fix the problem. A four-foot-long pit viper was angrily staring him in the face, raised as if it were coming out of a snake charmer's basket.

Holy shit, Hendy thought.

He jumped back and bellowed for the lowest-ranked private, Taner Edens, to get the snake. Edens snatched up a KA-BAR combat knife.

"Attack!" Hendy yelled from behind Edens, pushing the private toward the snake. The viper turned toward Edens and hissed.

"Abort! Abort!" yelled Hendy, running.

Edens swung. Although the viper was nicked by the KA-BAR knife, it managed to slither off into the brush. The snake's escape didn't make it any easier for the men to get to sleep, but sheer exhaustion soon took over, and they slumbered.

That is, until later that night, when Moquin shook Sergeant Jeremy Larson awake.

"There's contact in the woodline," Moquin whispered. The enemy was out there.

The men got ready. Specialist Shawn Passman crawled over to them in his underwear.

They sat and waited.

No sounds.

Nothing.

Larson peered through Moquin's thermal sight, a camera that picked up infrared radiation, including body heat. He saw the same thing Moquin had seen but caught one detail the other man had missed: the "enemy" was sitting about thirty feet up, in a tree that grew off the cliff.

That can't be the enemy, Larson thought.

He grabbed a blue light and shined it toward the tree.

It was a monkey.

*   *   *

While much of Afghanistan was known for its barrenness, monsoon rains from the subcontinent reached the eastern part of the country, filling the northeastern region with stands of cedar, walnut, fir, oak, pine, and spruce trees. Combined with the clear, untamed streams and rivers of Nuristan and Kunar Provinces, the trees made for gorgeous vistas that reminded some troops of luxury fishing spots in Wyoming or Montana, the kind they'd read about online or in brochures. The one disconnect—other than the insurgents trying to kill them—was the variety of animals they encountered: rhesus monkeys and leopards, horned vipers and wild cats, six-foot-long lizards. More than once, the men stopped to watch as nasty porcupines beat up feral dogs; it became something of a spectator sport. Even more disconcerting were the insects and other critters, including centipedes that were longer than a man's foot, three different types of ants (little red, little black, and crazy-fast tall red), a giant red bee of some sort, scorpions, wolf spiders, and infestations of grasshoppers.

The fauna of their new home often came as a surprise to U.S. troops. Here, Sergeant Paul Rozsa is introduced to a lizard by an Afghan soldier. *(Photo courtesy of Marine Lieutenant Chris Briley)*

Most terrifying of all, though, were the enormous camel spiders, which were technically not spiders[17] and really didn't look as if they were even from this planet. They were typically the size of a soldier's hand, sometimes even bigger, brown in color and with metallic, helmetlike bodies and hairy legs on which they could run as fast as ten miles per hour. Camel spiders were fully capable of eating lizards, scorpions, or birds for dinner. Although not venomous, they could inspire quite a jolt by falling on a soldier in his tent or deciding to seek shade in his sleeping bag. To pass the time during dull stretches, some of the troops would put two of them in a box together and watch them fight.

A few days later, Netzel and his men finally arrived at their destination. Those troops not pulling security were allowed to eat and rest. Netzel and Moquin made small talk about their small-town pasts. Moquin had moved to Worcester, Massachusetts, from nearby Shrewsbury and had to switch high schools, eventually obtaining his GED from a local community college. His parents had split when he was just a year old, he said, and his dad, who wasn't a part of his life, had spent time in prison because of his problems with drugs. Moquin himself had wrestled with drugs; he had been hooked on heroin at one point, before he joined the Army. He had tried it for a simple reason: "I wanted to see why my father loved it more than he loved me," he said.

Originally the plan had been for the 2nd Platoon to watch over the valley from its post for two days and then return, but over the radio, Sergeant First Class Milton Yagel told Netzel that his orders now were to push to the next mountaintop and head down the side to link up with Frank Brooks and the Barbarians, who were planning to meet with the elders at Chalas.

This would end up being a twenty-six-mile haul. During the day, the sun would beat down on the troops oppressively, but after dark, it was bone-chilling cold. One night, Netzel and Moquin shared a hollowed-out tree in which they slept standing up. Before drowsing off, they talked about Moquin's girlfriend; just before arriving at the base at Naray, he'd changed his life insurance policy to make her his beneficiary.

---

[17] Camel spiders, like spiders, are members of the class Arachnida, but they're of a different order, Solifugae.

"Hey, Sarge," Moquin said. "What do you think about this?"

Netzel grunted. He was exhausted.

Moquin went on about how, on R&R, he was going to surprise his girlfriend.

"Surprise her with what?"

"I'm going to ask her to marry me," Moquin explained. The plan was that he would buy an engagement ring, slip it onto a dog collar, put the collar on a puppy, and give her the pet as a sort of double surprise.

Fenty was focused on his men, focused on their missions, but there was something else that occupied his thoughts as well. His wife, Kristen, was one week overdue with their baby. In the green commander's notebook he carried with him everywhere, in the midst of his penciled notations about intel—"New personality in Waygal[18]: Diyan....Has supplies to equip 10X Suicide Bombers"—he had highlighted in black Sharpie "Kristen's Contact Info," with phone numbers for the Samaritan Medical Center near Fort Drum, including Daytime Triage and Evening Maternity, as well as his wife's friends.

"Don't you want to go back for the birth of your child?" Colonel Nicholson had asked him.

"Kristen and I talked about it," Fenty replied. "Right after the baby's born, she'll be tired and off her feet." It'd be better if he waited just a little bit, giving her some time to recuperate. "I'll fly back after Mountain Lion," he said. "My mom's there for her."

As her due date got closer, and then passed, he would call Kristen for news—also speaking to his mother, Charlee Miller, who had driven up to Fort Drum from New York City—but each time the answer was the same: nothing yet. On Friday, April 7, Kristen paid an ambitious visit to a midwife who, hoping to speed things up, expanded her cervix in an attempt to bring on labor.

Early on the morning of April 8, through the unofficial but often far more efficient lines of communication run by military wives, Fenty, in a tiny broom closet of an office at Jalalabad Airfield, heard the news via emails and other messages: Kristen was in labor and about to deliver their baby girl. Her water had broken, and with the aid of her mother-in-law and

---

[18] The Waygal Valley in Nuristan.

Andrea Bushey—the wife of Lieutenant Colonel Dave Bushey, also in Afghanistan—she had gotten into a car, in which the three women had then driven through a blinding upstate New York snowstorm to get to the hospital.

Heart racing, Fenty called her cell phone. Kristen answered.

"They said it's going to be a long time," she informed him. They spoke for a little bit before he told her he'd call again as soon as he could. It was after midnight her time.

At 8:09 a.m. on April 8, the phone rang again in Fort Drum. Fenty was calling back.

"I'm going to take this," Charlee Miller told the nurse.

"Joe," she said as she answered Kristen's phone.

"Mom," he said, obviously desperate for any news.

"Joe, your baby is going to be born right now!" she told him.

At that moment, Kristen let out a bellowing scream, and Lauren was born.

"Stand by," Fenty's mother said. "You're going to hear your baby cry."

Within seconds of the medical team's suctioning baby Lauren's windpipe, she started screaming, and her skin flushed with a beautiful pinkish hue.

"Is she all right?" Fenty asked.

"She's all right," his mother told him.

"Is that the father on the phone?" asked the doctor. "From Afghanistan?"

"Yes, Doctor," Charlee Miller said.

"She's beautiful!" the doctor shouted to Fenty.

"How much does she weigh?" asked Fenty.

"I don't know yet," said his mother.

"I'm going to lose you," Fenty said. "I only have seven seconds left."

The line went dead.

He got through to Kristen herself later in the day. She was weepy. She was worried about him; he was worried about her.

"What's wrong with you?" he asked her, unaware of how difficult childbirth could be and used to his wife's being lucid—not exhausted, hormonal, and recovering from an epidural. Kristen explained her condition.

"What does she look like?" he asked.

"She's beautiful," Kristen said.

*   *   *

On April 19, Staff Sergeant Willie Smith led three other soldiers from Bravo Troop to the Korangal Valley's Abbas Ghar Ridge, where they were put under operational control of the 1-32 Infantry Battalion. Their job was to watch the valleys, the villages, and those sections of the road that were considered particularly vulnerable to insurgent attacks.

They were using a long-range advance scout surveillance system, or LRAS, which allowed thermal-optical surveillance up to fifteen miles, meaning that troops not only could see bodies from a long distance away but also could use the device to confirm enemy deaths, watching bodies lose life as heat from them was slowly — or not so slowly — released into the air. The LRAS in and of itself made obsolete other systems that required scouts to position themselves within the range of enemy fire. This technological advance came with strings attached: it was a terribly expensive and unwieldy machine, weighing about 120 pounds and difficult to haul across inhospitable mountains. The sight — through which scouts would look for the enemy — was as bulky as a medium-sized safe or a 1980s-era living-room television set, at seventeen inches high, twenty-seven inches wide, and thirty-one inches deep. And yet, by 2006, the Raytheon Corporation was closing in on selling its thousandth unit to the Pentagon.

There were just two spots where the LRAS could be set up to cover the first "named area of interest" to which these soldiers from Bravo Troop, 3-71 Cav, had been assigned. One was on a ledge above a steep precipice. The other option would put the LRAS on more stable ground, but trees and other vegetation would interfere with its field of view. Staff Sergeant Smith and his team concluded that the ledge was the only feasible choice.

On April 21, Sergeant Jake McCrae had been scanning the assigned area as instructed for about half an hour when the LRAS's batteries began to die. As he was in the process of replacing them, a gust of wind hit the LRAS, pushing it over the cliff. McCrae tried to hold on to the right-side handle, but there was no stopping the heavy machine once physics became involved. The half-million-dollar piece of equipment crashed at the bottom of the cliff.

In the larger scheme of possible disasters in a war zone, the loss of an LRAS meant very little. But the Pentagon bureaucracy did not see it that way: soldiers were routinely required to account for every tax dollar spent, and the threat of having the cost of any lost equipment docked from their paychecks could loom large. The subsequent investigation into the loss of this LRAS would cause strife among the leadership of 3-71 Cav and, in the end, beget a tragic irony.

It began at 3-71 Cav's new logistical base in Kunar, where Fenty assigned Ben Keating to figure out what had gone wrong and whom to punish for it.

Keating did not want this job. He wasn't eager to punish enlisted men. He identified with them; he felt like he was there to serve them. As a member of the youth leader corps in his parents' church, Keating had taken to heart the notion of leading as a servant, as Jesus had done. He would tell his mother that he'd learned more about how to lead a platoon from youth leader corps than from any of the training he'd gotten at boot camp.

Keating's easygoing veneer masked a complicated mix of self-righteousness and actual righteousness. The intensity of his religious faith was of such an order that even his parents, both of whom were Baptist ministers, sometimes found it jarring. When he was a child, they'd joked that he knew more about the Old Testament than they did. Keating had been something of an odd kid, to be sure, spending hours reading his David C. Cook *Picture Bible,* a 766-page comic-book version of all the texts from Genesis through Revelation. He was particularly taken with the stories of King David and the tale of Jesus washing the feet of his disciples, as rendered in the comic book:

PETER: "No, Lord, I'm not good enough to have you wait on me!"
JESUS: "If you do not let me serve you, Peter, you will have no
   place in my kingdom."
After Jesus has washed all of the disciples' feet, he sits down at the
   table again.
JESUS: "If I, your lord and master, have served you, you should do
   the same for one another. The servant is not greater than his
   master."

And that was Ben Keating. "You don't ever ask your soldiers to do anything you wouldn't do," he would say. "You have to serve them to get the best leadership out of them." Other soldiers might have come to the same conclusion in their own ways, but it was a safe bet that Keating was the only member of the 10th Mountain Division who'd brought with him to Afghanistan a copy of *The Confessions of Saint Augustine* — in Latin.

Keating had a true sense not only of service but of mission as well — and not the small kind, either. During college, after one young woman made it clear that her feelings for him were more like those of a sibling than those of a potential wife, Keating talked it over with his mother. He was very close to both of his parents.

"So how are you with that?" Beth Keating asked him.

They were walking in the woods behind his parents' house.

"I'm okay, Mom," Keating said. "I think I'm supposed to be doing something bigger with my life anyway.

"I need to do this," he went on, referring to his military commitment. "So I guess this isn't the time for me to be thinking of a long-term relationship anyway."

What Keating was now doing in eastern Afghanistan wasn't what he'd had in mind when he talked about serving his troops. All the paperwork made his head hurt, and he'd be in a bad mood all day as he solved problems for people who seemed to him incapable of doing anything for themselves. He would personally sign for some four to five million dollars' worth of equipment daily — money he could never possibly pay back if something got irresponsibly damaged or mislaid. This man whose knowledge and devoutness rivaled those of a cleric was being consumed by work almost entirely clerical.

Now Fenty had ordered him to look into whether Willie Smith and Jake McCrae should have their pay docked for the loss of the LRAS. Keating found the very idea maddening; he saw this as one more instance of the typically myopic Army-brass sensibility that got underneath his skin and irritated him like a rash. He emailed his father, seeking guidance. The maximum pecuniary charge that Smith and McCrae faced was forfeiture of two months' pay. Keating figured that penalty would add up to about one fiftieth of the cost of the LRAS, barely enough to buy one of the system's power cables. He also reasoned that if the Army hit the two men that hard, neither would be likely to reenlist. Taxpayers had every right to seek an accounting for the lost LRAS, but was it really worth losing these two soldiers over? Had there truly been gross negligence? They were at the end of the Earth here, and for the love of God, the mountains of the Hindu Kush were windy. He was inclined to give the soldiers letters of reprimand—still a slap in the face, but one that might keep them in uniform.

Keating discussed his investigation and his thinking with Fenty, who pushed him to make a tougher ruling. Keating suspected that part of what motivated the squadron commander was a desire to impress his bosses, and he resented Fenty for putting him in that position. He resented him even more when he overheard him telling Major Richard Timmons—the squadron XO, and thus the middleman between Fenty and Keating—that he wondered if Keating had the "moral courage" to render such a judgment.

It would be hard to imagine a remark that could have insulted Keating more.

CHAPTER 5

"This Whole Thing Is a Bad Idea"

They set us up, Captain Frank Brooks thought to himself.

On April 29, Brooks had led the Barbarians into Chalas, a village in the Chowkay Valley. They'd been inserted at dawn a few days before, near some colorful poppy fields, their bright flowers all ready for the opium harvest. After surveilling the area for a couple of days, the Barbarians were ready to engage with the elders. Netzel and his men from Able Troop were watching their backs, having trudged half a mile east of the Barbarians' observation post to get a better view of the village.

Brooks and a handful of men from his headquarters element—fire-support officer Lieutenant Erik Jorgensen, his radio man, and two troops who were pulling security—walked down from the observation post to the edge of the hillside village. An Afghan man met them there and took them to the middle level of Chalas, where the buildings were on stilts and looked like oversized steps, to see the seven or so elders. They were all so weatherbeaten and sunburned that it was impossible to guess which of them might be forty years old and which seventy. Sitting on logs and chairs in a spot where a pair of trails converged, the two groups talked for about two hours with the aid of an interpreter. The elders provided some basic history of their village.

"Are you Soviets?" one of the villagers finally asked.

The Barbarians looked at one another.

"No," they explained, "we're Americans, and we're here on behalf of the government of Afghanistan."

"The government of Afghanistan?" the elders remarked. "What is that?"

The Barbarians spent the next fifteen or twenty minutes going over everything from the Soviets' withdrawal from Afghanistan to the 9/11 attacks to the Northern Alliance to the new Kabul government. After that, they moved on to the topic of the cultivation of poppy, used in opium production. The village elders denied growing any poppy, even though the surrounding hillsides were blanketed with it. The Americans noted that there was nothing wrong with their eyesight, and they weren't idiots. The Chalas elders ultimately admitted that they grew the stuff but insisted they didn't sell it to the Taliban—just to "normal" narco-traffickers, they said.

The Americans accepted this.

They next talked about the insurgents in the valley. The elders took the general party line: "Security is good here, we keep the fighters out ourselves, we don't need your help."

Before leaving, Brooks had his interpreter ask one of the elders if he could recommend a better route for them to take up the mountain to return to their camp. The trip down had taken them three hours. The elder told them to follow a drainage ditch up the hill and even offered to guide them. They ended up sucking wind up the trail as they watched the elder, who looked to be about sixty years old, churn along as if he were out on a Sunday stroll. The ditch turned out to lead almost directly back to their observation post. When they arrived there, they thanked the old man, who quickly disappeared.

Home again in their temporary digs, Brooks and his men started to unwind. They put down their weapons, removed their gear, took off their shoes, guzzled water, and lit up their smokes. Erik Jorgensen peeled off the T-shirt he'd been wearing for four days straight. It was pretty ripe.

Jorgensen had been drawn to military service in high school, after reading Stephen Ambrose's *Band of Brothers*. When he signed his ROTC contract in 2000 at Northeastern University in Boston—obligating him to complete four years of active duty following graduation, in exchange for having his tuition paid—he was hoping he'd get lucky and be deployed to Kosovo or Bosnia so he could see some "action." He now chuckled whenever he recalled his gung-ho pre-9/11 naïveté.

As dusk began to settle over the Chowkay Valley, Jorgensen tried to relax, yet he kept thinking that something felt a little off—like that old movie cliché about its being "quiet out there, almost *too* quiet." And then, as if right on cue, there came a series of explosions, followed by yelling. A salvo of rocket-propelled grenades, or RPGs, had been fired at the Barbarians. BOOM. BOOM. BOOM.

Right away, Brooks noticed one thing about these RPGs: they were aimed just south of their position, hitting the path they'd used earlier in the day to walk down to Chalas. The enemy had assumed they were going to take the same route back. Brooks suspected that the elders had known that he and his men would be targeted—except for, perhaps, the one who had escorted them home.

The bangs of the RPGs were immediately succeeded by the rapid DADADADADADA of machine-gun fire. Hollywood has conditioned audiences to think that firepower should sound spectacular, maybe even otherworldly, like the lasers in *Star Wars*. But in truth, the sound of armaments is industrial and mechanical, underlining the factory nature of war and armies: this machine kills that worker, a new worker replaces him; this worker uses his machine to destroy that machine; a new machine needs to take its place.

Shit, thought Brooks. That was no ordinary machine-gun fire; it was from a Russian Dushka,[19] a heavy antiaircraft machine gun, belt-fed with a tripod. This was no small thing, the fact that the enemy had a Dushka: it meant that besides having the territorial advantage, they might be able to outgun the Americans, too. The Barbarians had M240s but no .50-caliber machine guns, the only real match for the Dushka's rate of fire and its 12.7-millimeter round, which could be propelled almost three quarters of a mile and through any type of body armor.

The Dushka raked the entire hillside with bullets, the rounds hitting the building that the Barbarians used for cover with a deadly thud. Jorgensen and the rest scrambled for safety, though they had no idea at first where the fire was coming from.

---

[19] From the acronym DShK, for "Degtyaryova Shpagina Krupnokaliberny"—named after its creators, Vasily Alekseyevich Degtyaryov and Georgi Shpagin. *Krupnokaliberny* translates as "large-caliber." *Dushka* means "sweetie" in Russian.

Before the shooting began, Netzel and four others from Able Troop—Sergeant Michael Hendy, Private First Class Levi Barbee, Private First Class Taner Edens, and Private First Class Brian Bradbury—had been sitting at the tip of a ridgeline overlooking the Barbarians' outpost. They were chatting about how best to prepare for night operations when Netzel looked below them—down to where Brooks and his team had just been breaking down for the night—and saw rocks the size of basketballs exploding.

Everyone dove for cover.

For many of the troops, this was their first experience of having someone actually try to kill them. It wasn't clear who their antagonists were, what group they were affiliated with, what was motivating them. Frankly, none of those things mattered.

The platoon from Able Troop and the Barbarians determined that the position the enemy was firing from was about half a mile away, on a parallel ridgeline to their west. They were slightly higher up than the Americans, maybe a hundred yards or so. Netzel and his men began firing back at the enemy, as did Brooks and his troops, using their M4 carbine assault rifles and M240 machine guns. The M240s were their only major weapon system, and the insurgents were just outside its effective range. The M240 gunners did their best to put fire on the larger Dushka, but it just wasn't working out. Jorgensen was charged with coordinating outside firepower—artillery, mortars, helicopters, or jets—if it was needed. It was. Some two miles away from their position, 3-71 Cav had set up a 120-millimeter mortar team, and Jorgensen now radioed the mortarmen to give them an update, but he was unable to see the target and so couldn't provide a grid coordinate for the enemy's location.

In the middle of the observation post was an abandoned house that Brooks had designated as Barbarian Troop's command post. The lower floor was vile, coated with filth and insects and infested with rats, so the men used only the roof. They called the building Chateau Barbarian.

A rickety ladder led up to Chateau Barbarian's roof, and Jorgensen now scaled up to the top and tried to get into a position from which he could better see the valley. He was followed by Specialist Kraig Hill, whose classification as a "forward observer" meant that he was responsible for serving as the eyes on the ground for gunners, telling pilots, artillery-

A soldier from Barbarian Troop, 3-71 Cav, atop Chateau Barbarian. *(Photo courtesy of Erik Jorgensen)*

men, and mortarmen where to fire. Vulnerable, the two men crawled to a spot where they had a view of the Dushka's location.

It was dusk. Jorgensen and Hill called up to an adjacent ledge where others from Able Troop had camped and were using a laser to pinpoint the enemy position. (Some others from Netzel's patrol, including Brian Moquin, had relocated there as well.) They called back down, giving Jorgensen and Hill a grid coordinate, which they then called in to the mortarmen. Jorgensen looked toward the mortars, saw lights flash as the rounds left the tubes, and watched them crash near the Dushka's position. The troops on the ledge could see more than a dozen figures on the mountain moving back and forth from the Dushka to a nearby shelter of some sort — perhaps a cave? — presumably hauling out ammo. The Dushka fired again.

Netzel was about to call in corrections to the rounds when on the radio he heard his lieutenant calling for a grid correction that would have dropped the rounds right on top of him and his men. Few officers had much confidence in this lieutenant.

"Stay the fuck off the radio!" Netzel barked, then offered the correct adjustments. The mortars fired again. The Dushka went silent, though other enemy fire continued.

Night fell on the Chowkay. Two Apache helicopter pilots checked in with Jorgensen and Kraig Hill, who gave them the relevant grid. Almost simultaneously, a call came in over the radio instructing all friendly positions to turn on their infrared strobe lights so that the Apaches would know which spots to avoid. Netzel and his four troops didn't have a strobe, so he told his men to get behind cover, and he stood, exposed, pointing his rifle at the ground and hitting the button on its laser intermittently, hoping that this would be visible to the pilots. His heart was pounding out of his chest. Ultimately, whether the idea worked or they just got lucky, the Apaches avoided them, opening fire on the Dushka position and the enemy shelter.

Low clouds slid into the area, restricting what the crews of the Apaches could see and where they could safely fly. Fearing that a helicopter might plow into a hillside, the pilots raised the Apaches and left. The troops on the ledge, using an LRAS to track the heat signatures of the insurgents, reported that some of the enemy fighters were still moving in and out of the suspected cave, while others were heading down the back side of the parallel ridgeline.

Now the A-10 Warthogs rolled in. The Warthog is a single-seat straight-wing jet aircraft with superior maneuverability at low speeds and low altitudes. It was designed specifically to provide close air support for troops on the ground. Jorgensen had one crew put a five-hundred-pound bomb right into the enemy's base. Then came another American plane with a two-thousand-pound bomb aimed at the same spot.

The fight was over.

Jorgensen suddenly realized he was freezing. He looked down and saw that under his gear, he was wearing only an undershirt. The enemy had caught him in midchange.

"We were lucky," said Brooks to his men. During that four-hour firefight, the Barbarians had not sustained even a single injury. If the enemy had hit them earlier, when they were on their way down to Chalas, or if they had come back from the village using the same route, things would have gone down quite differently.

The next day, a Barbarian patrol cleared that parallel ridgeline and found blood trails, bits of bone and flesh, and bloody bandages. The insurgents' refuge, whatever it had been—shelter or cave—no longer existed. Intelligence would later report that radio intercepts of the enemy's communications from that day indicated that the fighters were foreign, possibly Chechen, based on a voice analysis.[20]

Brooks and his crew returned to the village days later, wanting to know why the elders hadn't warned them of the attack. The villagers insisted they hadn't known a thing about it. Gooding then went down to meet with the Chalas elders a third time. He wanted to explain to them that the Americans were there to help, but that they could rid the area of the extremists only with the aid of the village. The men served Gooding rice and goat. There were more black flies than grains of rice on the plates. Gooding left the meeting with food poisoning and not much else.

In early May, Colonel Nicholson directed Fenty to begin extracting his troops from the Korangal and Chowkay Valleys. Operation Mountain Lion was complete; now 3-71 Cav's mission to push into Nuristan was to begin. On May 3, Fenty ordered his staff to come up with a plan for Operation Deep Strike, comprising five helicopter extractions of his troops from the Chowkay: eighty-two soldiers waiting with their equipment to be picked up at five different makeshift landing zones by one large helicopter, accompanied by two Apaches, making several trips and dropping off troops and equipment at the temporary base Timmons had set up. The mission would be a go on May 5; the troops were already running out of water and food.

The presence of the Dushka machine gun in the Chowkay Valley had unsettled Fenty, Berkoff, and others at headquarters. Because the Chowkay was so remote, Berkoff had anticipated that the Taliban fighters there would be armed at most with assault rifles, RPG launchers, and a few light machine guns—certainly not with a seventy-five-pound heavy machine gun that could take down a Chinook. In addition to the Dushka attack in the Chowkay Valley, insurgents had shot at three Black Hawk helicopters in the same area just days earlier with small-arms fire and RPGs. Fenty decided that this level of enemy aggression dictated

---

[20] Some intelligence analysts read such "possibly Chechen" labels as meaning, more accurately, "light-skinned persons whose language we can't identify."

that the Americans should fly only after sundown, since U.S. troops and their night-vision goggles still owned the night. But nighttime flight in the mountains, of course, carried its own set of significant risks.

Fenty had other misgivings about this mission. The air-support group Task Force Talon, based at Jalalabad, was the most familiar with Kunar Province, but it had been scheduled for a safety stand-down day — a mandated twenty-four-hour period on the ground, to be spent reviewing policy and procedures and conducting safety training or briefings. Task Force Centaur, headquartered at Bagram Airfield, had been assigned to Operation Deep Strike instead. The fact that its personnel didn't know the area worried Fenty. Some within Task Force Centaur had their own doubts as well. One officer felt that the Army had done Centaur's men "an injustice by sending them to war before they were ready," adding that the "proficiency of crew members is not up to standards." Task Force Centaur, the same officer concluded, was "at best marginally prepared to conduct air operations" in Afghanistan.

The commander of Task Force Centaur, a forty-one-year-old lieutenant colonel named William Metheny, disagreed, though he did suggest that Chief Warrant Officer Third Class Eric Totten and Chief Warrant Officer Second Class Christopher Donaldson, the command pilot and copilot, respectively, take along an extra pilot to sit in the jump seat, to help reduce their workload and enable them to focus their attention outside the aircraft. He also recommended that an additional crew member accompany them to spot through the center cargo door and shout directions. It wasn't as if Chinooks had rearview mirrors, and backing the aircraft onto the improvised landing zones would be tough. The strip for Able Troop, for example — designated PZ (for "pickup zone") Reds — was so small and so perilous that Gooding had nicknamed it Heart-Attack Ridge. Not only would the Chinook likely manage to land only one or two wheels there, the general area was crowded with trees and other obstacles. Plus, they would be flying at night, wearing night-vision goggles.

Totten considered Metheny's advice and opted to bring along another crew member but not a third pilot. With that decision made, he and Donaldson went through the checklist and assessed the mission as posing a moderate risk. Totten was a seasoned pilot, Donaldson was on track to becoming a pilot in command himself, and the two worked well together. The planning, preparation, crew selection, and training for this mission were all good. It was true that the pilots were unfamiliar with the area, and these would be some of the tightest landing zones they'd seen, but they could handle them, Metheny thought.

In the meantime, Fenty flew to Jalalabad Airfield to talk with Colonel Nicholson about where 3-71 Cav would go after all of its troops were back at the base at Naray. The next day, the lieutenant colonel, Timmons, Berkoff, and other officers huddled in a small brigade operations center to brief their commanders on the plans to extract their men from the Chowkay Valley. Online, Brigadier General James Terry, deputy commander of the 10th Mountain Division, participated from Bagram, as did the leadership of the aviation brigade.

It was just a few hours before the Chinook and two accompanying Apaches were scheduled to take off, and Terry said that Operation Deep Strike looked like a high-risk mission to him. "Who's going to be in charge of this?" he asked Fenty.

"We've got Frank Brooks, the troop commander, on the ground out there," Fenty said, the look on his face reading to Berkoff: "That's not the answer Terry wanted to hear; Terry wanted me to say I would command and control this."

"What are your concerns about the risks?" Terry asked.

"Sir," Fenty said, "I believe the real enemy out there will be the terrain."

Staff Sergeant Adam Sears, of Able Troop, had missed most of the action during Operation Mountain Lion, having caught a wicked stomach bug that—combined with the thin air atop the mountain—required him to be evacuated back to a temporary logistical base that Timmons had rented for this mission, an empty compound surrounded by twelve-foot walls, just south of the Chowkay Valley.

On May 5, after recuperating for a few weeks, Sears was transported by a resupply chopper to the landing zone where Brooks and the Barbarians were set up. Moquin and a couple of others met him there and accompanied him back on a goat trail around the mountain ridge to PZ Reds, where Sergeant First Class Yagel directed him to prepare the pickup zone for the helicopter that would be arriving that night.

The twenty-four-year-old Sears had been to air-assault school, so he had some expertise when it came to helicopters. He'd assumed that the bird coming to pick up the troops would be a Black Hawk—a less imposing craft with a smaller rotor-blade span—and was stunned to learn that command was in fact sending a Chinook. Apart from the size differences between the two choppers, Sears's view was that Black Hawk pilots were generally combat pilots, whereas Chinook pilots—while undoubtedly nice enough guys—were more the kind of soldiers who did supply runs from one safe landing zone to another. *This* landing zone, by way of contrast, was covered with dry, sandy soil and sloped 45 degrees downward to the edge of a cliff. And as if that weren't challenging enough, command also wanted to do this at *night?*

"This is crazy," he told Yagel.

The Chinook's larger rotor-blade span—two rotor systems, each with a sixty-foot diameter, compared to the Black Hawk's one big rotor with a diameter of fifty-three feet eight inches—made Sears's task that much more difficult: he would have to get rid of anything the blades might hit if a sudden gust of wind happened to come up. Just five feet from the area where the Chinook would hover stood a tree, a gnarled claw of wood about ten inches in diameter.

"That needs to come down," Sears said. But the only tools they had were two KA-BAR knives. For the next several hours, therefore, they all tried to chop down the tree with the knives—Yagel, Sears, Pilozzi, Moquin, Justin O'Donohoe, Specialist David Timmons, Jr.,[21] Sergeant Dave Young, and a new guy, Staff Sergeant Richard Rodriguez. Without any water to drink, the men had trouble building up the energy to keep going. They would razz one another as each took a turn trying to make a dent in the seemingly indestructible timber. Eventually, under the scorching sun, the group surrendered to the futility of the task.

Sears worked to make the zone as safe as possible in whatever other ways he could, setting up an infrared strobe light to indicate the landing area, close to the tire marks from where a Chinook had landed once before. He and Pilozzi added infrared chemical lights to flag hazards that the pilots should steer clear of. The lights would be visible only to the U.S. troops and pilots, all of whom would need to be wearing night-vision goggles.

The troops readied the cargo, including an LRAS, for rapid loading. They also began cleaning up their mess: it was Army procedure to sanitize the sites of observation posts before troops left them. There were two

---

[21] No relation to Major Richard Timmons.

reasons for this. First, if insurgents were to find evidence of U.S. troops' presence in a certain area, they might booby-trap the location or set up preemptive ambushes around it in the hope that the Americans might return to the same spot (as they in fact often did). And second, leaving this pristine landscape littered with American garbage was apt, understandably, to annoy the locals. Yagel ordered that all the trash be ignited and destroyed in a burn pit on a ledge just under the cliff.

For Sears, doubts remained. He radioed Brooks, who was at the Barbarians' observation post across the valley: "This whole thing is a bad idea," he said. Particularly idiotic, Sears thought, was the choice to send the large Chinook. The landing zone was too small for that bulky aircraft, and flying it at night in these jagged mountains, with their powerful winds, seemed an unnecessary risk. A Black Hawk, sure, but not a Chinook. It seemed like a decision made by someone who wasn't on the ground, someone who hadn't seen where the chopper would be flying.

It was the same argument Brooks had been making to Fenty, especially because the pilots themselves had never flown in the area. But Fenty, after consulting with his commanders, radioed back to tell Brooks that the mission was a go. "Roger," said Brooks. Brooks passed word on to Sears, and he rogered, too.

At Bagram, Metheny once again urged Totten to take a third pilot in the jump seat, to help out.

"No," Totten said. "Lieutenant Colonel Fenty's going to be sitting there."

Fenty had wanted to get closer to the mission, to the temporary base Timmons had set up, as opposed to being stuck in Jalalabad, but Timmons had told him the only way to make that happen was to put him in the jump seat of the Chinook. Fenty could then fly the first leg of the trip, stand by on board as the Chinook picked up as many troops and supplies as it could fit in its hold, and then get off with those men at the temporary base before the Chinook flew off on a second run to pick up more troops and gear at other landing zones. "Do it," Fenty had said.

Totten's handpicked crew included flight engineer Staff Sergeant Christopher Howick, crew chief Sergeant Bryan Brewster, crew member/door gunner Sergeant Jeffery Wiekamp, and observer/door gunner Sergeant John Griffith.

The Chinook itself seemed to be in good shape. Earlier that day, a separate crew had conducted a maintenance inspection on the bird, flown it for more than six hours, and then conducted a second, postflight inspection. Everything had checked out. It had also just gone through its mandatory two-hundred-hour-cycle service inspection. But in the crew's haste to get it back in the air, numerous required forms and records had not been completed correctly, including many items on the maintenance test flight check and the aircraft power check.

Totten was regarded as a strong pilot, though on a previous flight, during an April 11 troop insertion for Operation Mountain Lion, his aircraft had sustained major damage to its undercarriage. No postflight evaluation had been administered on that occasion, however, since Totten's commander believed that it was just a simple matter of a rock's having poked a hole in the chopper floor during a difficult night mission.

Prior to departure, Totten, Donaldson, and the crew attended a go/no-go briefing. The enemy threat, flying conditions, and other matters were assessed. A weather warning was in effect—winds in the area where they would be flying were gusting anywhere from thirty-five to forty-four knots—but that would expire at 6:30 p.m. local time, just when Totten and his team were set to take off.

Joe Fenty tried to call Kristen twice before the mission, which was out of character for him. She had long ago reconciled herself to an important rule that governed the behavior of many military spouses: a husband or wife was far likelier to get back alive and in one piece if he or she focused entirely on the task at hand. When Fenty finally got through to her, the questions he asked were, for him, unusual.

"What does Lauren look like?" he asked.

"She has red hair," Kristen said.

At that point, Lauren let out a wail.

Fenty chuckled. "Is that her?" he asked. "She has some lungs on her." Fenty told his wife that he was going on a mission that would be dangerous. It was quite unlike him to do that. He never wanted to alarm her. But he felt as though he was being pushed by higher-ups to command and control the mission from inside the bird, and to do so at night despite his grave worries.

At 6:38 p.m., the Chinook, accompanied by two Apaches, took off from Bagram, headed for Jalalabad, where Totten and his crew refueled and picked up Fenty. At 7:36 p.m., the three aircraft set out for PZ Reds to extract the men of Able Troop. The Chinook flew slower than planned: Totten was supposed to keep the bird going at 110 knots, but for some reason he flew at 70 to 90 knots instead. Totten did not answer radio calls asking him why that was. On entering the Kunar River Valley, the first Apache hit several pockets of moderate turbulence.

"I'm glad I don't have to land in the LZ"—the landing zone—one of the Apache pilots said. The pilots in the first Apache discussed the wind speed and direction and the turbulence. It might not be a bad idea to call the mission off if conditions got much worse, they agreed. Once the three birds were above PZ Reds, the first Apache flew up and to the southwest to watch over the operation. The other flew low and to the east. "I'm getting my butt kicked up here," said the main pilot at the higher elevation.

Sears, on the ground, made radio contact with Totten, in the Chinook. He told the pilot to land west to east, aiming at the large chemical lights. At 10:02 p.m., the Chinook instead approached PZ Reds from the south. "That part of the LZ's no good for landing," Sears said. Totten didn't respond. The bird landed briefly, but it started to slide, and Totten, clearly aware he couldn't hold it there on the ledge, pulled it up. Sears thought to himself, This is going to be a clusterfuck. The pilot does not seem to be in full control of the Chinook.

At 10:06, Totten managed a two-wheel landing by backing the Chinook in from the east. As Sears had ordered, three of the troops—O'Donohoe, Moquin, and Timmons—sprinted onto the bird with cargo. Others started running the rest of the gear to them: the LRAS system, six or seven duffel bags, ammunition, weapons. They were all wearing their night-vision goggles. It was dark inside the chopper, except for the light coming from the cabin.

One of the Chinook crewmen got off the back ramp of the bird. Sears was surprised to see that he wasn't wearing his night-vision goggles. What the fuck? Sears thought. How could he see the infrared chemical-light markings on the trees and rocks and other hazards on the pickup zone without his goggles on?

Just then, sparks started flying out of the burn pit, perhaps reignited by the air currents from the spinning rotors. The glowing cinders looked a bit like tracer fire. On the radio, Sears tried to explain that it was just ash—nothing to get excited about, he said, though he himself sounded excited. The men in the choppers couldn't understand him and thought he sounded highly agitated.

Seconds later, the Chinook rolled forward off the landing zone.

"I'm having trouble keeping it on the LZ," Totten said.

Sears's voice got higher and even more agitated-sounding. What the fuck was this guy doing? he wondered.

Nick Pilozzi was now inside the bird, having just dropped off a bag filled with a hundred pounds' worth of LRAS batteries. He felt the helicopter lurch forward, and suddenly it was ten feet off the ground. Pilozzi dove out the back of the aircraft, smashing his face when he hit the ground.

Totten yelled excitedly, "Is everyone all right?" He told Sears over the radio, "Just get your rucks and get on."

"We can't do that with our remaining gear," Sears replied, annoyed. It was becoming increasingly difficult for the chopper pilots to understand what he was telling them in his fast-talking Indiana twang. "Do it west to east!" he instructed Totten again. The Chinook took off, with Moquin, O'Donohoe, and Timmons still aboard.

At 10:09, Totten tried to stick a landing for the third time from south to north. As he lowered the aircraft, the Chinook's tail swung to the left, and the rear rotor hit that gnarled tree that the men from 3-71 Cav had worked so hard—but to such little effect—to cut down.

The back blade exploded and came off the chopper. The soldiers at PZ Reds started diving for cover as thousands of pieces of shrapnel sprayed all around them. Sears grabbed Young and dove off the cliff onto a ledge a few feet down. The Chinook's engines started spooling up, building up power, vibrating. Tree-branch parts flew. Totten throttled the engine, and as he did, the exhaust turned from a dull ochre to a hellish crimson. The turbine jet engines on the back of the bird grew red-hot. The Chinook pitched forward and up, its nose rising.

"Fuck, oh fuck, oh fuck," cried Pilozzi. "What the fuck do we do?"

The Chinook started falling down the cliff. It hit the ground about 150 feet down and exploded, and then it kept on rolling, clearing all the trees in its path. It finally stopped 150 feet farther down and ignited into a huge fireball.

"Holy shit," said the pilot of one of the Apaches. "The Chinook is down."

At PZ Reds, the troops started yelling into the valley below:

"If you can hear us, we're coming to get you!"

There were secondary explosions as the fire found ammunition and fuel in the belly of the bird.

Sears, Pilozzi, and others from 3-71 Cav began sliding down into the valley. The fire was throwing off so much light that their night-vision goggles were rendered useless.

They could smell flesh burning.

At the Jalalabad operations center, Berkoff had been monitoring mIRC chat, the military's version of Instant Messenger, transmitted over secured networks. In a special Operation Mountain Lion chat room, the words suddenly popped up: "Chinook Down PZ Reds."

The message came from the logistics base Timmons had set up at the mouth of the Chowkay. At first Berkoff thought it meant that Fenty's chopper had landed safely on PZ Reds. But then he saw a second message: "Chinook Down, Chinook Down. Near PZ Reds." A third one made it clearer still what had happened to the helicopter: "Crashed near PZ Reds."

Berkoff got up and rushed out toward the joint operations center in an adjacent room. Before he even entered, from the hallway, he heard Brooks's familiar, high-pitched southern Virginia drawl, delivering garbled status reports over the radio.

"Give us a BDA"—a battle-damage assessment—"of the crash site," Major Timmons asked Brooks.

"It's bad," came the reply. "There's no way we can even get near the wreckage. It's just too hot down there."

Other staff officers started weighing in: Did Brooks want a pair of rescue jumpers to look for survivors? Could he use a C-130 plane with a giant spotlight to help in the search? There were other offers made, too, to fight the enemy, since back at Jalalabad they thought the chopper might have been shot down, though Brooks and those who'd been there knew that wasn't the case.

Byers grabbed a radio transmitter. "Hey, Barbarian-Six," he said, using Brooks's radio call sign, "I need you to tell me, no shit here, could anybody have survived?"

Everyone paused.

"No," Brooks said. "There's no way anyone could have survived."

81

The whole room, filled with some thirty staff officers, fell silent. Everyone knew that Brooks was probably right. No one made eye contact with anyone else. Many officers looked down at the floor.

A few minutes later, Timmons and Berkoff went out into the hallway to get some air and compose themselves.

The brigade chaplain approached them, extending his arms and offering condolences. Berkoff wasn't ready to believe they were all gone. He ran outside to a dark corner of the airfield, dropped to his knees, and wept.

Berkoff thought about one of his last conversations with Fenty. Two days before, he had seen him at Jalalabad, just returning from the field. Fenty had looked spent; his hair was long, he reeked, and a gray film covered his uniform—the result of four straight weeks' worth of perspiration and Afghan dust. Regardless, upon seeing Berkoff, Fenty had immediately wanted to know about the Jewish chaplain he had arranged to bring to Jalalabad for Passover. "Ross, did you ever see that rabbi that I sent here for seder?" he asked. Even with everything that must have been going on in his head—the mission, his month-old baby girl, the killing of some ANA soldiers a few days earlier in an IED attack on a 3-71 Cav convoy—Fenty never missed a chance to inquire about one of his soldiers.

Now Berkoff got angry. He cursed God.

What the fuck, is this some sort of sick joke? he thought. The man just had his first baby only four weeks ago, and he's never even met her.

Never would.

CHAPTER 6

Maybe That's Just the Wind Blowing the Door

The wreckage of the helicopter, spread all over the side of an eight-thousand-foot-high mountain, was still smoldering the next morning, when Colonel Nicholson and other members of the brigade and squadron leadership arrived.

Thermal imaging had measured the temperature of the crash site at more than 5,400 degrees Fahrenheit.

Nicholson looked at his men, tirelessly combing over the hillside. They were filthy from weeks of combat and hours of rooting around in the residue of a burnt Chinook, covered with dirt and ash and the stink of aviation fuel, their eyes bloodshot, the black grime on their faces carved with streaks of sweat and tears.

It took hours before all ten body bags were laid out on the side of the hill, holding the remains of Joe Fenty, Brian Moquin, Jr., Justin O'Donohoe, and David Timmons, Jr., from 3-71 Cav, and Eric Totten, Christopher Donaldson, Christopher Howick, Bryan Brewster, John Griffith, and Jeffery Wiekamp from Task Force Centaur.

"Which one is Joe?" Nicholson asked.

Someone pointed to his friend. Nicholson put his hand on Fenty's body, prayed, and cried.

From a nearby mountaintop, Timmons phoned his wife, Gretchen, on his Iridium satellite phone. He was choking up. Nicholson had given him permission to violate protocol and tell Gretchen about Joe Fenty's death in order to get her to Kristen Fenty's side as soon as possible. Military spouses were required to fill out "Family Readiness Group" forms on which they listed their closest friends. Gretchen Timmons, Andrea Bushey, and Christina Cavoli—the wife of the 1-32 Infantry commander—were Kristen's contacts.

"We've had a terrible accident," Timmons informed his wife, through tears. "Joe's dead." He told her that he needed her to be strong. He needed her help.

Gretchen was staying with their two small children at Timmons's parents' house in Mechanicsburg, Pennsylvania; they had just returned from Walt Disney World in Orlando, Florida. It was the middle of the night.

Timmons told his wife that she needed to get back home to Fort Drum as soon as possible. She had to be there for Kristen.

Early the next morning, Gretchen jumped into her car with her kids and her mother-in-law and drove the five hours to Fort Drum. After dropping off her family at home, she headed over to the Fentys'. She was shaking as she rang the doorbell.

Kristen answered the door cheerily, holding her month-old baby girl, Lauren. She was surprised to see Gretchen there; she knew she was supposed to be helping her in-laws with a yard sale in Pennsylvania, and then going to a wedding.

"What's up?" Kristen asked, friendly, happy.

Gretchen was stunned: Kristen didn't know.

"Um...I don't know, hey," Gretchen fumbled.

They were close friends, so Gretchen made up an excuse about needing to have some time away from her family after their vacation, and the two women spent the rest of the day together. Kristen was putting together care packages for her husband, placing toiletries, snacks, and some athletic gear—elbow pads and jockstraps—in boxes that would never reach their intended recipient.

Gretchen seemed distracted. She wouldn't look Kristen in the eye. She picked up a pen and doodled on a notepad. At one point, Gretchen herself began to wonder if that conversation with her husband the night before had really happened or if she had just dreamt it.

They took care of the baby, talked about their families, and drank some wine. No one came to the door to tell Kristen what Gretchen couldn't tell her, the information that it would be a violation of military protocol for her to share with her friend.

They watched cable news. A helicopter had gone down in Afghanistan, and all ten soldiers aboard had been killed. A U.S. military spokesman said that the crash had not been the result of an enemy attack. Gretchen kept her mouth shut.

Kristen began to suspect something. She called the rear-detachment commander, Captain Al Goetz, to find out more about the helicopter crash. Goetz's wife answered; she seemed hesitant to talk, but Kristen still wouldn't let herself make the leap.

Around midnight, Gretchen left Kristen's house, drove home, and woke up her mother-in-law. "She still doesn't know," she told her.

Gretchen Timmons got up early the next morning—before seven— and went over to Kristen's again. Kristen was in her pajamas, holding Lauren, when she answered the door. She still didn't know.

"Hey! How're you doing? I got biscotti, but I don't have any coffee," Gretchen explained.

For Kristen, that didn't add up: Gretchen never forgot anything. And while having coffee with a friend before seven wasn't that unusual for military wives, Gretchen always hit the gym first thing in the morning. But again Kristen pushed her suspicions away, figuring her friend was nervous about the news of the crash. She let her in; a pot was already brewing.

Official notification had been delayed because the recovery and identification of the men's bodies had taken some time; Fenty's remains were among the last to be found. He had been strapped into the inner cockpit area, which had burned red-hot for hours after the crash. There wasn't much of him left.

"Gretchen, I know I'm not supposed to ask this, but was it Joe?" Kristen asked.

"Hey, I'm just a wife," Gretchen said.

Kristen heard something at the screen door.

Maybe that's just the heater clicking on, she thought.

Through the top panes of the glass-and-wood door, she saw that the screen door was swinging open.

Maybe that's just the wind blowing the door, thought Kristen.

No, someone was at the door. She opened it.

Two men were standing there: an Army chaplain and Lieutenant Colonel Michael Howard, a neighbor and friend of Joe's.

Everything that she had been trying to push out of her mind was true. Howard grimaced and shook his head.

Kristen began to wail. Gretchen came over, lifted the baby from her arms, and carried her into the kitchen.

For Ben Keating, who had been arguing with Fenty about whether the Army should hold two joes responsible for the wind's having destroyed an expensive piece of reconnaissance equipment, the commander's death was a tragedy cloaked in an ugly irony.

On May 5, Keating had emailed his father, insisting that he was not going to seek the toughest punishment for the soldiers. "Misguided or not, I think it requires some courage to refuse to fry these guys for LTC Fenty, even though he's intimated that that is what he wants," Keating wrote, "simply so that he can show his superiors that we play hardball in 3-71 CAV."

Just after he hit Send, Keating was called to the operations center, where he heard of his commander's fate. The man he was so angry at was now dead.

Three days later, he sent out another email, this one to his friends and family:

From: Ben Keating
8 May 2006

All,

   I want to thank you for the kind words, thoughts and prayers that you offered in the last seventy-two hours. I would have called or written sooner, but there was a mandatory blackout period that is just being lifted for our soldiers now....

   As you probably also know, our Troop suffered the loss of three great young men and the Squadron is struggling with the loss of our Commander, LTC Fenty. It has been a difficult few days; we've been blessed with the exceptional leadership of the Squadron XO, MAJ Timmons, and the Command Sergeant Major, CSM Byers. That these two have held up in the face of losing one of their best friends and mentors is a testament to God's presence here.

This is a surreal environment under typical circumstances; it's an absolutely impossible place to process emotions and feelings in a time like this. Grief will come for most in the days and weeks ahead. The real issue we deal with now is a sort of awakening to the danger here. For three months we've traversed this country's most historied IED routes and patrolled in towns with known enemy threat without incident. The realization that we are mortal and operating in a high-risk area has hit home hard.

We placed our soldiers on a C-17[22] this afternoon; I served as a pallbearer for the Commander's casket. Again, an experience that you've seen played out on the news many times; not an experience you ever expect to find yourself in. Even as we took the flag-draped containers off the trucks and began our slow procession in front of a thousand soldiers, I was emotionally detached. As we climbed the ramp, however, and placed the ten coffins in the cargo hold, the tremendous loss swept over every one of us in the plane's belly. It is certainly a moment I'll never forget, and one I pray never to repeat.

I can tell you that the certain knowledge that I was in your thoughts and prayers was a great feeling. I have [drawn] and continue to draw strength from the relationships I share with you all. I look forward to renewing each of them on my return, and that too will give me the strength I need to lead my Troop through this difficult period. Thank you all so much,

With Love —
Ben

Keating had remained irked by Fenty's "moral courage" comment, even after Timmons reassured him that it had not been made with the degree of seriousness that Keating had projected onto it. The truth was that Fenty had been legitimately concerned that the lieutenant's affection for his men might cloud his judgment. Empathy could be a good thing, but a successful leader did not let emotion get in the way of hard decisions.

---

[22] A Boeing C-17 Globemaster III, a very large transport aircraft used by the military.

In another email to his father, Keating delved into his complicated feelings about the loss of his commander, noting that he had

struggled with where my relationship with LTC Fenty was at the moment he died. There have been a lot of things going on inside this head and I've had to work hard to make sense of it all. I was undeniably angry with him; I was writing an email to you, the first paragraph of which was pretty scathing of the man, at the moment he was losing his life. I was hurt, because I still respected the man a great deal and I honestly believe that at some level he meant what he'd said—to some degree, he questioned my integrity. I was frustrated because in my mind he had become nothing short of some diabolical mastermind who had created a problem set with too many impossible conditions and then beaten up those underneath him for being unable to solve it, all the while refusing to change any of the conditions though it was well within his power to do so.

Ultimately, I never did make sense of it all, and I'm not sure I'm meant to. I do know that my relationship with the man was a rocky one. We very rarely saw eye to eye on anything from personnel to investigations. But I respected the man, and I would think that he appreciated and respected my abilities as well. I learned a great deal from him and perhaps that is all I am supposed to take away from this. I am not going to feel guilt over where we were at when he died—it wouldn't do any good. Nor am I going to harbor any ill will towards him—and expect he would provide me the same if the roles were reversed.

He continued:

I honestly haven't felt any dread as this incident forced us all to inspect our own mortality. I feel as though the Lord fully intends to bring me home safe and put me to work someplace else.

He signed off by telling his father that he would call home soon. In an email to his mother, Keating contemplated the death of Brian Moquin, who had found a home in the Army:

From a discussion I had with him before he went out on that mission, I think he was a long way from having Christ in his heart. But there is no doubt in my mind that the Holy Spirit was at work in a young man with an awful lot of potential during the trials of his final week. What I do know is that he died as a member of a family that loved him very much.

CHAPTER 7

Monuments to an Empire's Hubris

The administrator for Kamdesh District, Gul Mohammed Khan, seemed stoned.

Could that be right? Could he be high?

Captain Aaron Swain, commander of Cherokee Company, stood at the Afghan National Police station near Urmul, in Nuristan, talking to the local leader, whose eyes were glazed like pastries. Swain knew that smoking hashish was a fairly common form of recreation in eastern Afghanistan, but he was still surprised, since it was early in the morning.

It was June 2006, and 3-71 Cav had a new commander: Mike Howard, the man who had broken the news of her husband's death to Kristen Fenty. From Atlanta, Georgia, he'd been commissioned from ROTC at Mercer University in Macon and joined the Army as a poor kid looking for a way to contribute to his country. Ross Berkoff and Staff Sergeant Jared Monti had both served under Howard during their previous 10th Mountain tour and, upon learning who their new leader would be, had joked with each other that the rest of their unit was in for a rude awakening. Howard was a brilliant tactician with a deep understanding of counterinsurgency, they thought, but in terms of "command presence" and "command philosophy," he was the polar opposite of the man he would be replacing. Joe Fenty might have been stringent, but in demeanor he had been laconic, sometimes even Zen. Howard was irascible, with a quick temper that could turn in a blink from cold to downright predatory.

Howard had served in Afghanistan twice before, but this would be an especially trying assignment. The dynamic of taking over for a commander who had been killed was frequently difficult, and for Howard, Joe Fenty had not been just another officer. To nearly all who'd served with him, Fenty had been an inspiring leader, and to Howard he'd also been an across-the-street neighbor and friend. Howard consulted with senior officers and decided to follow through with what Fenty had been working on, having concluded that it wasn't the right time to come barging in with grand new ideas. Joe Fenty's vision, then, would become Howard's own.

What Fenty and his team—Byers, Timmons, Berkoff, and others—had been helping plan was the establishment of a U.S. presence in Nuristan. Howard now ordered Swain to search around the Nuristan village of Kamdesh for a location where a provincial reconstruction team, or PRT, could set up shop. PRTs were a key component of America's counterinsurgency strategy, one singularly focused on economic development. Distributed throughout district centers and in other key locales throughout Afghanistan, the teams were made up of service members, foreign service officers, and construction experts who would work with locals to help their regions grow through jobs, roads, and other projects—thus, the theory went, winning over hearts and minds. Among military officers, PRTs were trendy, a status that had been cemented when one PRT leader, Navy Commander Kimberly Evans, sat in the First Lady's box at President Bush's State of the Union address earlier that year. The new outpost in Nuristan seemed a fitting base for a PRT.

There was a road that ran between Naray and Kamdesh Village, but it was narrow, and Swain doubted it would be strong enough to withstand the weight and width of Humvees. Thus, in order to scout out a site for the regional PRT, he rented a few Toyota Hilux pickup trucks, which were relatively plentiful in the area, and some all-terrain vehicles, or ATVs.

The first time Swain and his team rolled out of Forward Operating Base Naray, they made it only a half-dozen miles up the road, to the village of Barikot, before half of the trucks broke down. They went back to Naray to regroup and try again. This time they used just the ATVs—Polaris Sportsman MV7s, painted Army green. As the sun set, Swain and around a dozen troops put on their night-vision goggles and began motoring north, then west. Snyder and his Special Forces team, who were on a separate mission, also joined them, likewise driving ATVs. Two platoons of Afghan National Army (ANA) troops—some thirty Afghans in total—and about six U.S. mortarmen followed in Ford pickup trucks.

They stopped briefly at Barikot, which was on their way, so Swain could ask the deputy head of the Afghan Border Police, Shamsur Rahman, to come along. Rahman and Swain had developed a strong relationship during a previous operation and had participated together in shuras with the Kotya elders. Rahman was well connected and hailed from Lower Kamdesh Village. He would be an asset on a trip like this.

Rahman wasn't at the station in Barikot—he was on leave—but his boss, Afghan Border Police Commander Ahmed Shah, was there, and Swain considered him a friend as well. Shah cautioned Swain not to go up to Kamdesh Village. "It's a bad place," he said. The road was dangerous; insurgents had tried to blow up his jeep on a recent tour. Swain thanked his friend for the warning, and the team took off again. It was dark by now, so the enemy, presumed not to have night-vision goggles, would be at a disadvantage.

They stopped near the hamlet of Kamu to drop off one of the ANA platoons, under orders to keep watch on a known IED-maker who had a home there. That section of the road was a prime place to hide an IED, and Swain wanted to take precautions to make sure his expedition wouldn't get hit on its way back.

By 2:00 a.m. local time, Swain, Snyder, and their teams had arrived at the hamlet of Urmul, northwest of and down the mountain from Kamdesh Village. They set up security and tried to grab some sleep. After an hour or two, Snyder shook Swain awake. Snyder thought the plan was for both of their teams to hike up the mountain together to Kamdesh Village, and he wanted to get going before it got too hot. A groggy Swain didn't quite understand what Snyder was talking about; he informed him that while his mortarmen would turn the tubes in that direction and offer fire support if needed, Cherokee Company was going to stay at the bottom of the mountain. The 3-71 Cav troops were there, after all, to find a new location close to the road for a U.S. base and a provincial reconstruction team, not to take a three-hour mountain hike. Snyder said that he and his men were going to head out. Swain told his fire-support officer, Sergeant Dennis Cline, where to aim his mortars if the Special Forces troops needed them. He checked the perimeter and then tried to go back to sleep, worrying that the Special Forces troops would mess up his mission to make nice with the locals, as had been known to happen before.

Although referred to as a single village, Kamdesh actually comprised four distinct communities: Upper Kamdesh, Lower Kamdesh, Papristan, and Babarkrom. (Two other, outlying villages, Binorm and Jamjorm, were separate from Kamdesh and had non-Kom Nuristani populations.) On the map, Kamdesh was only a mile distant from Urmul, but the topographic reality meant that the two-thousand-foot climb would take about three hours—for Americans, at least; even geriatric Kamdeshis could make their way up the mountains like spry goats. Of course, it helped that they weren't carrying eighty pounds of gear apiece.

At dawn, Swain awoke, checked his perimeter again, then opened and ate an MRE—short for "meal ready to eat," the basic ration for troops in the field—and headed for the Afghan National Police station down the road. Outside the station sat the hollow shell of a Soviet armored personnel carrier, once used to transport heavy guns, cargo, or half-platoons of Soviet fighters. Nuristani folklore included many tales about how the locals had stood up to the Soviets in the 1980s. They'd attacked the invaders with clubs, stolen their guns, and later ambushed their armored vehicles—or so the stories went. At least five such abandoned vehicles were scattered around the immediate area like trophies, or monuments to an empire's hubris.

One of the many carcasses of Soviet vehicles, this one right outside the outpost. *(Photo courtesy of Matt Meyer)*

93

At Swain's request, an Afghan policeman ran up the mountain to Kamdesh to fetch the district administrator to meet with the Americans. Swain wanted to explain the Army's plan to bring in a provincial reconstruction team—or, in the case of underdeveloped Nuristan, essentially a provincial *con*struction team—to help develop the region. Swain intended to ask the man for his help.

He looked around while he waited. This was a gorgeous part of the world. He gazed up at the steep green mountains and then down into the blue Landay-Sin River. He could see right through the water, all the way to the bottom. Part of him wished he had his kayak and fishing pole.

The Landay-Sin River and its valley. *(Photo by Ross Berkoff)*

Hours later, the policeman returned with the administrator for Kamdesh District, Gul Mohammed Khan—by reputation effective, well connected, and, to some, suspect for his ties to HIG. He, Swain, and a small group of American soldiers and Nuristanis sat in an orchard where small oranges hung from trees. Looking tired and seeming stoned, Moham-med recounted to Swain some of the history of Kamdesh. When asked about insurgents in the area, he insisted that the valley was relatively peaceful, save for the feud between the Kom people and the Kushtozis over water rights and other grievances.

Swain explained what the U.S. military wanted to do in the region. This didn't get much of a reaction from Mohammed. When Swain added that the soldiers would set up camp nearby as the PRT was being built, the district administrator seemed ambivalent.

While preparing to hand over his area of operations to Colonel Nichol-son three months before, Colonel Pat Donahue had made it clear that he didn't think it made much sense to send troops into Nuristan. First, the United States simply didn't have enough soldiers in the country to estab-lish a strong presence there: Regional Command East was a sprawling, mountainous territory roughly the size of Virginia, and the U.S. force there numbered only about five thousand troops.

Second, Nuristan Province was incredibly isolated, and its topography forbidding, with serrated mountains rising as high as eighteen thousand feet. Operations there were grueling; there weren't many functional roads. Third, there wasn't much of a threat involved. Nuristanis were insular, Donahue believed; they didn't like anybody. The men with guns there seemed more like local militias protecting their homes than any-thing else.

His replacement, Mick Nicholson, saw Nuristan quite differently.

In the Pech Valley in Kunar Province, south of Nuristan, Nicholson had witnessed the attacks inflicted on 1-32 Infantry by an enemy well armed with IEDs and rockets, which the Army was convinced were com-ing from Pakistan. Nicholson, Fenty, Byers, Berkoff, and others had talked about the influx of these armaments from across the border. Kamdesh was close to the road where three of the valley systems from the north merged on their way from Pakistan; if 3-71 Cav could secure a loca-tion near this road, the men decided, it might be able to disrupt the threat to 1-32 Infantry in Kunar Province—and to Americans and Afghans in Kabul. Given that American policy forbade troops from entering Paki-stan, where so many enemy forces were safely ensconced, Nicholson also figured that if the brigade could set up outposts in adjacent Nuristan, the

United States might have more success in killing insurgents, possibly even members of Al Qaeda.

The task in Kamdesh District now fell to Nicholson's new commander of 3-71 Cav, Mike Howard. The brigade didn't have enough troops to heavily garrison the entire region, so deployment would have to be strategic and selective. Since his arrival at Forward Operating Base Naray, Howard had spent quite a bit of time talking with Nuristan's governor, Tamim Nuristani. Nuristani's grandfather had been a famous general who fought the British in the Third Anglo-Afghan War, in 1919, and his father had been mayor of Kabul until the Communists took over — at which point Nuristani himself, then in his early twenties, had gone to the United States. He'd driven a cab in New York City, opened a fried chicken joint in Brooklyn, and later owned a chain of pizzerias in Sacramento called Cheeser's. After the Taliban fell, he'd returned to Afghanistan and worked his way into Karzai's good graces until eventually Karzai appointed him governor.

For months, Nuristani had been pushing for the United States to put a PRT in the provincial center of Parun, but American military commanders had visited the area and deemed it too isolated, as it was accessible basically only by air or on foot. Nuristani's second choice was Kamdesh Village. He told Howard that if he could get the Kom people residing in Kamdesh District on the side of the Afghan government, the rest of eastern Nuristan would follow. Nuristani himself was Kata, so he didn't personally have much sway over the elders of Kamdesh — in fact, quite the opposite. But that was all the more reason to locate the PRT near the largest and most influential Kom community, to improve the chances of the combined United States and Afghan government forces being able to win over a population naturally skeptical of its governor. Additionally, from the Americans' perspective, putting a base by the road to Kamdesh not only would stop the insurgents from using that road but also would protect the only means of resupplying the camp itself.

Here in particular, proximity to a road was a crucial feature of the PRT's potential location, because air assets were relatively scarce in Afghanistan. The Pentagon and the Bush White House were focused on Iraq, so that was where the helicopters were. It irked Nicholson. In his area of operations, he was responsible for eleven different provinces, seven million Afghans, and almost three hundred miles of border with

Pakistan—and for all of that, he had only one brigade of troops and one aviation brigade. That was it. By contrast, there were fifteen troop brigades in Iraq, and four aviation brigades. It didn't make sense to him.

"Iraq is smaller and has fewer people than Afghanistan," a frustrated Nicholson would say, trying to explain how nonsensical was the relative dearth of resources in Afghanistan. "And by the way, this is where the war started."

Swain still didn't know where near Kamdesh Village he should put the PRT. He and his troops hopped on their ATVs and drove around a bit, looking for some suitable land, but every possible location either was already being used or was inhospitable to construction.

They went up the road to the west, to Urmul. As they were walking up the mountain from there, on the way to Kamdesh Village, they came upon a school. It looked legitimate. Photographs of Afghan president Hamid Karzai were hung on the wall, a good sign that the locals were supportive of the new government in Kabul. The Americans walked back down the hill and down the road and saw a medical clinic. The sign said it housed an antituberculosis program sponsored by Norwegian Church Aid and the Norwegian Refugee Council. This must be where the bad guys came to get cleaned up before they headed to Pakistan, Swain mused.

The scouting party returned to the Afghan National Police station. Swain looked around the small surrounding compound. This right here might work, he thought. It was by the road, and there was a potential helicopter landing zone right outside the gate, next to the river. Obviously, the site—at the bottom of three steep mountains—wasn't the best place in the world for a base; security would be a concern. But Swain knew that Howard had plans to send at least an entire company—plus mortarmen and snipers—to defend the PRT. It could be properly protected, Swain reasoned, and if they had to put the PRT next to the road, it was going to be at the bottom of the mountains in any case. Moreover, in this location they could be next to the police station, partnering with the government, and Urmul—where the district administrative offices were headquartered—was just down the road to the southwest. Kamdesh Village was right up the mountain to the south. Nothing that the United States did in Afghanistan could be deemed perfect, but this might be good enough, at least for now.

* * *

Snyder and his Special Forces troops were up the mountain, eating lunch with the elders of Upper Kamdesh. Snyder told them about the PRT that Swain was planning on setting up down the mountain, and the elders did not like the idea one bit. Kamdesh was too small, they said. They didn't want U.S. troops nearby.

That's interesting, Snyder thought. It wasn't what the elders had been telling his second in command, or the leaders of 3-71 Cav, over the previous few weeks during shuras at Forward Operating Base Naray, when plans for the PRT were being discussed.

Snyder and his team finished their meal and left their host's house.

"You know, they can't attack us now for three days," Snyder's engineer told him.

"Why not?" Snyder asked.

"We just broke bread with them," the engineer explained, repeating a myth about the region.

As they walked, the children of the village followed them, chanting and yelling, all the way to the edge of Upper Kamdesh. Snyder found this odd. "What are they saying?" he asked his interpreter.

"I can't understand it," the man replied. "They're saying it in Nuristani." The language was incomprehensible to most Afghan interpreters, who were conversant in Pashto and Dari but not in the specific tongue used by these particular hill people. Nuristanis spoke five different languages in all, and within those five, there were a number of discrete dialects.

Adding to Snyder's unease was the behavior of a Kamdesh elder who'd announced that he would join them on their walk down the mountain. The man suddenly turned away from the Americans and proceeded to take a different path. A little farther down the mountain, one of the Kamdesh policemen who were accompanying Snyder and his troops told the interpreter, in Pashto, that he and his men were now out of their jurisdiction, so they, too, were going to break off.

Weird, thought Snyder. And then, a few yards later, tracer rounds started streaming past them: they'd been ambushed.

At first, the bullets did little more than kick up dust. The Special Forces were trained to turn to face their attackers in such situations, orienting their breastplates toward the enemy fire and pushing forward, firing their weapons, to gain dominance.

The insurgents had an answer for this, though: as the Special Forces troops came forward, the enemy fighters sent out small children to stand between them and the Americans.

The Americans held their fire, and the insurgents scrambled away.

One of the Afghan Security Guards with Snyder's group had been shot in the leg. The bullet had hit an artery, and he was bleeding profusely. Snyder and his troops took him into a nearby building and radioed Swain, who in turn called Forward Operating Base Naray and ordered a medevac. One of the Special Forces medics tried to keep the Afghan guard alive, but he soon bled out and died. Sometimes it happened that fast.

Down the mountain from Snyder, Swain unfolded his map and tried to figure out where the insurgents who had ambushed the Special Forces would run. Guessing that they might go southeast of him on the road, past the medical clinic and the school, he ordered Platoon Sergeant Steven Brock to head down there with a mix of American and Afghan troops to head them off. He would meet them there in a few minutes, he said. Meanwhile, a few angry Special Forces troops had returned to Kamdesh Village and detained some elders, demanding answers—an action that embarrassed the Kamdeshis in front of their community.

Special Forces scouts conducting surveillance from surrounding mountains saw a number of Afghan men darting around, and they called this intel in to Snyder, who also began getting similar reports from Apache pilots in the area. Could be innocent, he thought. But likely not.

"We kicked a hornet's nest," Snyder radioed to Cherokee Company. "We're getting out of here." They got on their ATVs and headed back toward Naray, a twenty-five-mile drive. Swain and his men followed suit not long after.

The Americans had been on the road for only a few minutes when Swain saw an RPG coming right at him.

Swain swerved to avoid the incoming rocket and kept driving. It exploded safely behind him. But the battle had commenced.

The glorious Landay-Sin River flowed to their left as they headed downstream, running for their lives. To the north, beyond the river, was a ridge from which insurgents were shooting at them. The 3-71 Cav troops braked their ATVs with a screech, took cover, and began firing back. Sergeant David Fisher—who'd fixed the laser on Daoud Ayoub in the

Kotya Valley—had mounted a machine gun on his ATV, and now he yanked it off, ran up the hill to his right, and started firing at the enemy. Swain crouched behind a rock wall and called Forward Operating Base Naray on his radio: "Tell the Apaches to come back," he said. Cline's mortar team fired their tubes in hand-held mode, aiming for the hillside.

After a few minutes, Swain received bad news about the Apaches: they couldn't come back because they were already engaged in another mission. It was the nature of the beast—there were never enough aircraft in Afghanistan.

"We need to get out of here," Swain told his men. "We can't get air cover." So Fisher provided the only cover available, firing up the mountainside as the rest of the team sped away. He kept shooting even as he jumped on the ATV bringing up the rear, driven by Brock, and zoomed off. Luckily, the insurgents were far away—and they weren't particularly good shots.

Just another day at the Afghanistan office.

After the Marines landed on Guadalcanal and the Solomon Islands during World War II, General Douglas MacArthur and Admiral Chester Nimitz led a charge toward Japan by "island hopping" in the Pacific Ocean, hitting New Guinea, the Gilbert Islands, the Marshalls, the Marianas, Guam, Tinian, the Palaus, and the Philippines. They bypassed some of the enemy's stronger points on their way to Emperor Hirohito, but they built up momentum and eliminated possible threats by taking that path.

Michael Howard now wanted to attempt a version of that strategy— village hopping, Berkoff called it—by clearing out the enemy from communities on the way from Forward Operating Base Naray to the new outpost that 3-71 Cav would be setting up in Kamdesh to support the PRT. In their village hopping, the 3-71 Cav troops would first hit Gawardesh and then proceed westward to chase away and/or kill the enemy, it was hoped, in Bazgal, Kamu, and Mirdesh.

Gawardesh, a border village, was home to Haji Usman, a timber smuggler and HIG commander. His two jobs were not unrelated. In 2006, President Karzai, worried about deforestation—more than 50 percent of the country's forests had disappeared since 1978—banned logging and timber sales within Afghanistan. Instead of ending these practices, however, the ruling merely drove them underground, pushing timber gangsters into the arms of insurgent groups such as HIG and the Taliban. There was only one "official" border crossing point in this region, near Barikot, so insurgents used the mountain pass leading into Gawardesh from the Chitral District in Pakistan to illicitly funnel in supplies and men. Karzai's lumber ban set the conditions for consolidation: trucks and donkeys would transport timber into Pakistan and come back bearing guns and RPGs.

According to standard procedure, before 3-71 Cav pushed into Gawardesh to meet with the elders there, a smaller group from the squadron would go up to make sure no traps had been set for the Americans. Howard ordered Staff Sergeant Chris "Cricket" Cunningham, the twenty-six-year-old leader of Cherokee Company's kill team, to join up with Jared Monti in running a squad of forward observers. Their snipers and scouts would take two days to hike to a ridge overlooking Haji Usman's house near Gawardesh. Only after Cunningham gave the go-ahead would the rest of 3-71 Cav roll in.

After high school, Cunningham had been looking for a way out of Whitingham, Vermont, when one of his older brothers suggested that he join the Army. "Don't sign any papers until they give you one that says 'Ranger' on it," his brother told him—advice that Cunningham followed. Like Byers, Cunningham was a rare member of 3-71 Cav who wore the coveted Ranger scroll on his right shoulder, indicating that he actually had served in combat with the Ranger Regiment rather than merely gone through the course.

For a few months now, Cunningham had been angling to partner with Monti on a mission. He respected the skills of the forward observers on Monti's team, and the two men had become friends. At the end of each day back at Forward Operating Base Naray, they would sit together on a bench in a garden, drinking coffee and shooting the breeze. Missions, commanders, family—they talked about them all. After they got out of the Army, both were thinking about enrolling in the Troops to Teachers program, a joint initiative between the Pentagon and the U.S. Department of Education that helped eligible soldiers start new careers as public school teachers in high-poverty areas.

Monti, a fellow New Englander, came from the working-class town of Raynham, Massachusetts, where he'd been a champion wrestler who always had a smile on his face. That changed after the Army sent him to his first deployment, in Kosovo, where he was given a crash course in what had once been, to him, unimaginable savagery. He would regularly see a townful of Christian adults throwing garbage at Muslim children as they walked to school. To Monti, doing what was morally right was far more important than observing Army rules, so he started driving the kids to school himself, in his Humvee. But there was too much horror there for him to have any real impact on it—too much hatred, too much killing, too many neighbors turned into murderers. He came back from the Balkans a different man, a haunted one.

Jared Monti had always been an innately altruistic person, but it almost seemed as if the more he was exposed to the worst of humanity, the more he lived for his men. One Christmas, he signed over his leave to a soldier who hadn't seen his immigrant wife in two years. That was pure Monti. Returning to his barracks after hitting the mess hall on a separate deployment, in South Korea, Monti had witnessed one private sadistically beating another. He tried to break up the fight verbally, but that didn't work, so he grabbed the aggressor and threw him against a wall. The next day, he got called into the sergeant major's office, where he was chewed out— he was of higher rank than the private, and laying hands on someone of lower rank was a violation of Army rules. He was demoted as a result of the incident. So be it, he'd thought.

Jared Monti during his second deployment to Afghanistan. *(Photo courtesy of the Monti family)*

Monti was just as excited about their teaming up on a mission as his buddy Cricket Cunningham was. Monti would lead the forward observers and artillerymen, while Cunningham would be in charge of the shooters. They met and discussed the operation. The United States had never battled Usman or his fighters before, so they would be operating mostly on hunches. Usman could probably muster up to about fifty fighters, Berkoff told them; he and his men would be able to use their knowledge of the hills to their advantage and would try to outflank the Americans' positions, but Berkoff did not expect they would pose much of a threat in terms of firepower.

Chris Cunningham and Jared Monti planning for their mission to Gawardesh. *(Photo courtesy of Chris Cunningham)*

In his tent at Forward Operating Base Naray, Monti told one of his ranking noncommissioned officers, Sergeant Chris Grzecki, about the mission. "We're going to this area, to overwatch this other area," he said, referring to a map. "This is the mountain we think is best."

He pointed to Hill 2610.

CHAPTER 8

Hill 2610

Before he left on the mission with Cherokee Company's kill team, twenty-eight-year-old Sergeant Patrick Lybert called his younger brother, Noah, back in Ladysmith, Wisconsin, to coordinate a different operation altogether. Lybert was scheduled to return to Fort Drum on leave the following month, July 2006, to visit his fiancée, Carola Hubbard. He had secretly paid for plane tickets for Noah and their mother so they could come to the upstate New York Army base for a surprise wedding.

Because nineteen-year-old Noah was a special-needs kid, Lybert had to make sure he fully comprehended that this was a secret he was supposed to keep not only from Carola but from their mother as well. (Noah understood.) Lybert had always been protective of his younger brother. One classmate in the fourth grade had ended up with a black eye after he suggested that Patrick was something less than a full brother to Noah, who technically had a different father, their mother having divorced and remarried. After graduating from high school, Lybert had told his mother, Cheryl Lee Nussberger, "Don't worry, Ma, I'll take care of Noah." He said he wanted to become Noah's guardian after she passed away.

"Well, Pat, you may have a wife who feels differently," his mother pointed out.

"Nobody will ever be part of my life who doesn't accept Noah," Lybert replied. And Carola fulfilled that prophecy: once Patrick got out of the Army, the two of them intended to move back to Ladysmith. It was all part of the plan and the promise.

When Patrick was home on leave that past January, before being deployed to Afghanistan, his mother had noticed that he seemed to have a new weight on his shoulders. He was due to become a recon team leader, and he took his leadership responsibilities seriously. He couldn't be a pal to his troops, he knew; he had to be tough on them so they would be prepared. "Some of these guys are so green, they're going to get themselves killed," he fretted to Cheryl. "Mom, if any of those guys I'm responsible for get killed, I will never be able to live with myself." So, like any good mother who saw her child worrying, she worried, too.

Lybert joked around a lot—he gave the impression of being a fun-loving, outdoorsy type—but he went into the military with grief in his soul, Cheryl always thought. It predated the Army. Two of his high school friends had died in freak accidents shortly after graduation. Later, when he was working as a "loss-prevention specialist" for the midwest-ern retail chain Shopko, in charge of preventing the theft of merchandise, he'd twice caught young men stealing from the store, and both times they'd ended up killing themselves. One, a seventeen-year-old fellow employee, was videotaped setting goods outside the back door for coconspirators to pick up. Lybert confronted him because that was his job, but then a couple of days later, the boy's aunt called and asked him if he was happy to know that the kid had taken his own life. The other was a foreign exchange student whom Lybert caught shoplifting. The student got on his hands and knees and begged him for mercy, but there was nothing the loss-prevention specialist could do—he was supposed to stop thefts, and this kid, too, was on video. The student was later found floating in a lake. These incidents haunted Lybert.

He'd joined the Army in 2002, done a tour in Iraq, come back, and jumped from 1-32 Infantry to do recon for a new squadron that was being formed at Fort Drum, 3-71 Cav. He loved the Army and had just reupped in March, though he was also eager now to start a family. More immediately, he was looking forward to returning to Fort Drum on leave, to seeing Carola, his mom, and his brother.

"I got the tickets booked," he told his mother, referring to the flight she and Noah would take to upstate New York to meet him.

"I told you not to do that—I'll pay!" she protested.

"I already bought the tickets, Mom," he said. "Hey, I'm going out on this mission. I'll call you when I get back. I love ya, Ma."

The phone went dead.

"I love you, too," Cheryl said into the silence. "Patrick, I love you."

Patrick Lybert didn't normally work with the kill team, but because three soldiers from Cunningham's regular group weren't available—two were on leave, and the third was recuperating from a hernia operation—he and three others went along on this mission. On the night of June 19, Cunningham and Monti led fourteen soldiers in a convoy to a mortar position south of Bazgal, near the Gawardesh Bridge. From there, they began their ascent up the ridge. Because it was crucial that no one see them, they took the most difficult route. Heading up to a ridgeline overlooking the Gremen Valley, they climbed until sunrise. During the day, they rested and conducted surveillance.

The slopes were steep, and their rucksacks were jammed with sixty to a hundred pounds of gear apiece. The men had to tread carefully for fear they might trigger a Soviet-era landmine, fall down the mountain, or, at the very least, sprain an ankle. It was June in Afghanistan, so the temperature shot up to close to 100 degrees Fahrenheit, and the rough climb sapped every bit of their energy. They didn't talk—they had to keep quiet—and Sergeant Chris Grzecki, for one, spent much of his time just praying for the torturous mission to be over.

On the second day of their trek, the troops saw two Toyota Hilux pickup trucks drive into the valley, each loaded with men. After the sun set, the Americans watched headlights flow along the road. It seemed suspicious to them, all of that driving during late hours of the night and through the early morning.

At dawn, they continued their ascent. Specialist John Garner served as point man for the kill team, which meant that he blazed the trails, and he always chose routes that were preposterously far off the beaten path. Sometimes this annoyed those traveling with him, Garner knew, but that was okay with him: he was point, and he would be the first one to get shot or blown up if he made the wrong choice. The others could go where *he* wanted to go.

Garner and Specialist Franklin Woods led the way up the mountain and into a thicket of Afghan pines, the rest of the team following twenty yards behind. Garner was heartened to see the untrammeled pine needles spread across the steep mountainside, covering the ground like a thick carpet, suggesting that the enemy had not been there. And then he noticed a pattern of indentations in the needles, with the ground visible underneath in places.

Footprints.

He called his team leader—John Hawes, the good shot who'd scored his first kill during the Kotya Valley mission—and showed him the evidence of the path, in a steep area where only someone trying to go undetected would walk. The coordinated pattern of broken needles and patches of dirt suggested a group of people walking in single file, Garner thought. Hawes looked and nodded.

"Push forward," he told Garner. "Keep your eyes open."

Garner did so, his sniper rifle pointed out in front of him, his finger on the trigger, the hair on the back of his neck standing at attention. Finally, the team arrived at the top of Hill 2610, where they set up camp in a small clearing on a flat but narrow ridgeline that reminded Hawes of a knife's edge. At an elevation of roughly eighty-five hundred feet, the area measured approximately 160 feet long by 65 feet wide; it sloped downward from north to south and had a tiny goat trail running along its eastern edge. Some of the men set up on the northern side, behind some trees and heavy brush. A few smaller trees, several large boulders, and the remains of a stone wall marked the southern end of their position. Using their scopes, they watched the valley to the east, beyond the steep slope. Normally, the members of the kill team would carry enough food and water to last them for five to seven days, but by the time they all got to the summit, on the third day of their trek, they were almost out of—or "black on"—water. Cunningham called that status in to the base.

About an hour after the team set up camp, Garner saw six men through his spotting scope. They were about two and a half miles away, heading toward them from the Pakistan border. He alerted his chain of command, and soon Cunningham came over to take a look. Were they insurgents? Friendlies? Afghans? No one knew. From the observation point, the Americans could see a suspected HIG safehouse and Haji Usman's home.

Cunningham and Monti were pleased. This, they felt, was a good location.

At Forward Operating Base Naray, Howard called in Brooks and Captain Michael Schmidt, the new commander of Cherokee Company (replacing Swain, who'd been transferred to Peshawar, Pakistan, to work at the U.S. Consulate).

The squadron was supposed to launch into Gawardesh that night or early the next morning, helicoptering in troops from Barbarian Troop and Cherokee Company and entering the village. Were they square? Howard wanted to know. Were they good to go?

Brooks said yes; Schmidt said no. One of his men had just been seriously wounded by an IED, and Cherokee Company needed about twenty-four hours to get things straight.

Years later, the fact that this whole mission was delayed because one man had been wounded would gnaw at Jared Monti's father, Paul. More than once, Jared had complained to his dad that the United States didn't have enough troops in Afghanistan. There weren't enough resources, he said; there weren't enough helicopters.

Paul Monti, a public high school science teacher, was already incensed by what he saw as a near dereliction of duty by President George W. Bush and Defense Secretary Donald Rumsfeld, who for some reason had focused all their attention and the great majority of their available man-power on the war in Iraq. In doing so, Paul Monti believed, they short-changed his son and all the other troops who were fighting in the very country where those responsible for 9/11 had laid out their sinister plans. Why would Bush and Rumsfeld, Paul Monti wondered, send these kids into war without making sure they had enough support and supplies? Why would they create a dynamic that allowed the wounds of one man to jeopardize an entire mission?

On Hill 2610, Cunningham was informed that the mission would be delayed up to forty-eight hours, but he wasn't told why — and it didn't matter why, really. Soldiers did as they were told. But he made it clear to the commanders back at Forward Operating Base Naray that given the change in circumstances, his men would need a resupply of food and water as soon as possible — 420 bottles of water and 160 MREs if they were going to have to last four to five more days on the ridge, as was now the plan. A resupply would unquestionably alert the enemy to their presence, but they had no choice. (They had previously been scheduled for a resupply in conjunction with the pending "air assault," during which troops would be choppered into the area.) All Cunningham could do was request that the chopper drop the supplies as far as it could from their observation post, and in an area not visible to any insurgents in the Gremen Valley.

At about 2:00 p.m. local time, a Black Hawk helicopter dropped the speedball—a container packed with supplies, designed to withstand a fall—around five hundred feet north of Hill 2610, above a ridge on a different mountain.

This is making a bigger signature than I wanted, Cunningham thought. It's too close to us, drawing too much attention. He decided that he would lead eleven soldiers over there to recover the supplies. It might be something of a hike, Cunningham warned them; they should be sure to conserve their water.

Four men stayed behind to keep watch, including Grzecki and Specialist Max Noble, a medic. Through his scope, Noble saw an Afghan with military-style binoculars standing in the valley near a large house, seemingly looking right at them. Although he was carrying a large bag, he didn't have a weapon visible, so the Rules of Engagement prevented Noble from doing much more than noting his location and assigning a target reference point to the building, which he did.

The expeditionary party, led by Cunningham and Monti, now returned with the dropped supplies. Everyone guzzled down water. Noble told Cunningham what he'd seen and then pointed out where the man with the binoculars had been standing.

An hour or so later, on the goat trail adjacent to the team's position, two Afghan women in blue burqas appeared, carrying bags of wheat. They slowly approached the Americans. All that Cunningham, Monti, and the other men could see of them was their eyes, whereas those same eyes could see everything about *them:* the number of U.S. troops; where the heavy guns were positioned; where they'd placed the rectangular Claymore mines that they'd scattered around the camp, set to detonate against any enemy attackers who got too close.

The soldiers looked at one another. What should they do? Should they detain them? For what? For walking in their own country? Garner stood on a boulder above the women, peering down at them. One woman signaled with her hand to ask if she and her companion could pass by. She pointed at a Claymore. The mine was hidden, but when you lived in a country littered with explosives, you learned to watch where you walked.

Garner signaled for her to pass on the trail; she shook her head no and gestured to indicate that she wanted to take another route, circling around their makeshift camp, hugging the cliff, and then heading off into a thick cluster of woods. The soldiers allowed the women to go that way.

As the sun set on the valley, Cunningham, Monti, and Hawes stood behind a big rock and began talking about moving to a different spot. If they did that, they would have to travel on a new path, which was always a risk. That's how the enemy slays U.S. soldiers, Cunningham thought: he waits until we're in a vulnerable place. And there was no guarantee they'd be able to find a better, more defensible post—this area of the ridgeline was wider than others, and there were a few big boulders here that they could use for cover.

They were discussing doubling the number of troops on guard shift for the night when an RPG exploded in the tree above them.

While there are many different types of grenades and RPGs, in general an RPG may be pictured as resembling a rocket about the size of a man's forearm. When fired from a tube, it becomes something like a combination of an immense bullet and an explosive. RPGs can take down helicopters and stop tanks; human bodies—flesh and bone, muscle and tissue—pose little impediment to them.

First comes the force of the explosion, the blast wave that inevitably knocks soldiers down and perhaps knocks them out. The high-pressure shock wave is followed by a "blast wind" that sends an overpressure through the body, causing significant damage to tissue in the ears, lungs, and bowels.

If a soldier survives the initial hit of an RPG and manages to regain his bearings, only then will he notice the effects of the considerable shrapnel produced by the device. The RPG's casing, now in the form of myriad penetrating fragments, will have been hurled in all directions. The irregular shape of these fragments can slow down their trajectory as they fly through tissue, at times making their impact more painful than that of a bullet. A leg or an arm may be turned to mash or even liquefied by shrapnel. If you're a soldier in battle and an RPG hits a tree near you, you get down and hope that another one doesn't land closer.

The first thing Smitty did was look at his watch to see what time he was going to die.

Private First Class Sean "Smitty" Smith was lying down and just putting out a cigarette—a local brand called Pine Light—when the shooting started. He and six other troops were at the northern end of the team's position, near the treeline. The other five were Franklin Woods, Brian Bradbury, Private First Class Derek James, Specialist Matthew Chambers, and Specialist Shawn Heistand.

Woods had heard a shuffling of feet, but before he could say anything, the shooting started, the fire coming so quickly and so ferociously that many of the troops didn't even have time to grab their weapons.

There were approximately fifty Afghans shooting at them from about 150 feet away to the north, and some more immediately to the west—all so close that the troops near the treeline could see their faces as they fired at the Americans with their Russian-made PKM machine guns. Those faces looked calm and collected, wearing the kind of expression that might otherwise be seen at target practice. The insurgents firing the RPGs were to the northwest.

Smitty was scared. This was his first firefight ever. There wasn't much for him to take cover behind, though he didn't think the enemy fighters had noticed him yet. But sooner or later, they surely would.

Smitty and Bradbury were the squad automatic-weapons (SAW) gunners, the designated carriers of portable light machine guns, which produce a heavy volume of fire with something approaching the accuracy of a rifle. Bradbury, lying on his stomach on the front line, used his SAW to suppress enemy fire as best he could. Heistand was firing as well, with his assault rifle.

Smitty didn't have his SAW with him; he'd earlier placed his gun in the spot where he was due to stand guard duty that night. On his belly, he low-crawled backward to a small clearing and snagged a different gun, a sniper rifle. Walking backward, he slowly fired a series of well-aimed shots, then turned around and ran back to the rest of the group behind the boulders.

This attack was distressing not only for newbies such as Smitty but also for the more veteran of the men. The hell they were in represented the most intense enemy fire ever experienced by Cunningham, who was on his fourth tour in Afghanistan. The PKM machine guns the insurgents were firing could deliver up to 650 rounds per minute, and the Afghan RPGs were coming in quickly, one after another after another. Pretty much all the Americans could do was duck behind their cover, hold their weapons above their heads, shoot, and pray.

Using his call sign, "Chaos Three-Five," Monti radioed to squadron headquarters.

"We're under attack by a much larger force," he reported. "We need mortars, heavy artillery, and aircraft to drop bombs."

Monti paused for a minute. Remaining behind the boulder, he fired his M4 carbine rifle toward some approaching enemy fighters to the west of him. Then he threw a grenade at them. It didn't go off, but it caused the insurgents to scatter.

Back on the radio, he called in the two sets of coordinates, for the Americans' position and the insurgents', stressing that they were "danger close"—meaning that the insurgents were in such tight proximity to their prey that there was a significant risk that any mortars fired or bombs dropped might kill Americans, too. But there was no better option, since at this point it looked as though they would soon be overrun.

Shortly thereafter, several mortars landed to the north of the American camp. A mortarman asked Monti by radio if he should adjust his fire, but the enemy bullets and RPGs were flying so furiously that Monti told him he couldn't even raise his head to check where the mortars had hit. He'd just have to keep his fingers crossed and hope they were hitting their mark.

Grzecki and John Garner had been sitting on the eastern part of the hilltop with their spotting scopes, observing the valley, when an RPG exploded in the tree four feet away from them. They promptly dove behind a small boulder for cover, but within moments, the fire was so intense that they couldn't get to their weapons. Grzecki's rifle was sitting next to him, but a flurry of bullets kept him from reaching for it. Garner grabbed his rifle, but when he stood to return fire, an enemy fighter shot it right out of his hand.

Lybert was in front of Garner, crouching behind the small stone wall to the west. Specialist Daniel Linnihan was farther down, also behind the L-shaped wall.

"I need a weapon!" Garner shouted to Lybert.

"Where's yours?" Lybert shouted back.

"It got shot out of my hand!"

"Stay behind cover!" Lybert told him, popping back up just far enough that only the top of his helmet, his eyes, and his rifle were exposed. He continued steadily returning fire at the enemy as the small stone wall he was behind began getting hit with machine-gun fire, chipping the rock and sending up puffs of gray dust. Lybert pulled the trigger of his gun yet again, but then, as Garner looked to him, he stopped, just stopped, and blood started to spill from his right ear. Lybert fell forward.

"Lybert's been hit!" Garner yelled.

Garner fell onto his chest, getting as low to the ground as he could. He wanted to move backward, behind the boulders, but he was afraid he'd get killed if he did.

Behind the cover of the small stone wall, Linnihan crawled over to check on his friend. Lybert was gone.

"Throw me Lybert's weapon!" Garner yelled to Linnihan.

Linnihan reached under the shoulder of the dead soldier, grabbed his M4 rifle, and tossed it to Garner.

"Cover us while we move," Garner and Grzecki screamed to Cunningham and the others behind the boulders.

"Move!" the team yelled back, providing suppressive fire as the two ran to join them behind the larger boulder, followed by a wave of RPGs. Grzecki did a quick check. He could see where every American was, with the exception of Bradbury. The troops at the northern end of the position, near the enemy, had been retreating; Chambers, Smitty, and Woods had made it to cover safely.

Derek James had not. "I got hit in the wrist!" he cried as he low-crawled toward the boulders. "I got shot in the back!" Grzecki reached out and grabbed him and pulled him behind the rocks, where Chambers began treating his wound with gauze, trying to stop the bleeding, unsure whether the bullet had ripped across his back like a skipping stone or drilled in.

The insurgents seemed to be coordinating their movements. While about a dozen of them pushed in directly from the north, others fired RPGs from the northwest, and a third, smaller group started creeping toward the Americans from the goat trail to the east. In their northern position near the woodline, Bradbury and Heistand could hardly have been more exposed: the enemy could see them clearly, and they could see the enemy.

"We need to get to better cover," Heistand told Bradbury. "Let's go!"

Heistand jumped up and retreated toward the boulders. When he arrived at the rocks, Bradbury was no longer with him.

Cunningham had been kneeling behind a tree stump engaging with the enemy; he could feel rounds hitting the wood. Some of the insurgents were close enough that he could hear their low whispers.

Everyone had been calling Bradbury's name for several minutes, with no response. Cunningham loved that kid with the steely gray eyes. He was a soldier's soldier: he did what he was told. He was smart and tough. As they were hiking to the summit of Hill 2610 just a few hours earlier, Bradbury had told Garner and Lybert that he'd had something of an epiphany: after his deployment, he was going to go home, work things out with his wife—with whom he'd been having problems—and raise his three-year-old daughter, Jasmine, the right way. That conversation now seemed as if it had happened a month ago.

Cunningham was convinced they couldn't retreat, primarily because Bradbury was still on their front line, but also for another reason. He believed that if they were to fall back and withdraw down the steep 70-degree slope behind them, they would be repeating a mistake made by the Soviets two decades before. He had studied those battles closely, and he felt certain that if his team gave up the high ground, the insurgents would then be able to pin them down and finish them off. That was why the Russians had never been able to make any progress in the mountains of Afghanistan, Cunningham thought. The best way to fight here was to fight like the enemy, to own the high ground or meet him at the same altitude.

"Bradbury!" Cunningham yelled. "Bradbury!"

Quietly, Bradbury managed to say, "Yeah?" From his voice alone, it was hard to tell where he was—fifty feet away? a hundred?

"You okay, buddy?" Cunningham asked.

"Yeah."

"Okay, buddy, we're going to come get you."

Once the others realized that Bradbury was talking to Cunningham, they started cheering him on — a somewhat incongruous sound amid the heavy volume of rocket and machine-gun fire they were still taking.

"Don't worry, buddy, we're going to get you!" yelled Staff Sergeant Josh Renken.

Cunningham and Smitty were in a decent position to low-crawl to where they thought Bradbury was and drag him back.

"I'm going to get him," Cunningham said.

"No, he's my guy," said Monti. "I'll get him."

Monti tossed Grzecki his radio. "You're Chaos Three-Five now," he said, transferring his call sign, then shouted to Bradbury, "You're going to be all right! We're coming to get you!" Monti stood and ran north, toward Bradbury and the enemy, away from the cover of the boulders, immediately prompting an eruption of machine-gun fire from the insurgents. Diving behind the small stone wall where Lybert's corpse lay, he paused, then stood and began pushing toward Bradbury. The enemy fired upon him again. He dove back behind the wall.

"I need cover!" Monti called to his men.

Hawes grabbed an M203 launcher to fire grenades at the enemy. Others snatched up their rifles.

"I'm going to go again!" Monti yelled, and once again he stood and ran toward Bradbury. Monti's quarry was lying on his back, about sixty feet away, in a small depression in the ground that hid him from both the U.S. troops and the insurgents. Bradbury was in agony; an RPG had ripped apart his arm and shoulder.

Now another RPG found its mark, slamming into Monti's legs, setting off its shock wave and filling the air with shrapnel.

The dust cleared. "My leg's gone!" Monti screamed. "Fuck!" His leg was in fact still there, but it had been deeply cut by the shrapnel, and he was now in shock. When he tried to crawl back, he couldn't. "Help me!" Monti cried. "Cunny, come get me," he pleaded with Cunningham, obviously in excruciating pain. "Come get me."

Cunningham stood and started to move, but the fire was too intense, both from the insurgents, who were frighteningly close, and from the

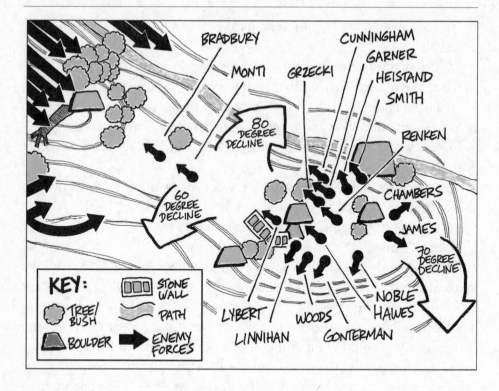

U.S. troops returning their fire. He would have had to run through rounds. Hawes began low-crawling toward Monti, but even on the ground, there was only so far he could go.

For a short while, Monti's fellow troops listened to him scream as he bled out. From a distance, they tried to keep him calm, asking him questions between rounds of returning fire.

"What are you going to do when you get home on leave?" one asked him. "Will you drink a beer with me?"

"Tell my mom and dad I love them," Monti said, his voice fading.

"You'll tell them yourself!" yelled Hawes.

Cunningham could hear an enemy commander shouting out orders to his men.

"Tell them I made my peace with God," Monti said.

He begged for the release of death, and finally it came.

From afar, the fire-support soldiers kept sending mortars that exploded on the ridgeline above the kill team, and as the sun set, Grzecki directed planes that began dropping five-hundred- and two-thousand-pound bombs about five hundred feet away. That was enough to abate the enemy fire.

Cunningham moved up and provided cover, firing his M203 grenade launcher. Hawes reached Lybert and—after confirming that he was dead—gathered up his ammo and threw it back behind the boulders. Insurgents fired at him; Hawes shot back with an M16 rifle that he found near Lybert, then threw a grenade. Next he scurried over to Monti. Also dead. He took and tossed his ammo, too.

Hawes then moved on to Bradbury, where Smitty met him. Bradbury was still alive, though the RPG blast had done serious damage to his arm. Together Hawes and Smitty carried him toward the boulders. Along the way, they passed Monti's body.

"Who's that?" asked Smitty. The fire had been so loud, and the fight so all-consuming, that Smith hadn't been aware of everything that was happening, even just a few yards away.

"Monti," grunted Hawes.

They passed the stone wall.

"Who's that?" asked Smitty.

"Lybert," Hawes answered.

Noble, the medic, immediately started working on Bradbury. His arm was so badly mangled that Noble had to wrap the tourniquet around his shoulder since there wasn't any place left to put it on the limb itself. The medic showed Garner where to hold the special quick-clotting combat gauze on Bradbury's wounds. The gauze burned a bit as its embedded chemical did its work, sealing the skin and flesh.

"You get to go home now," Garner reassured him. "You get to see your baby early."

More rounds came toward them, and Hawes got Garner's attention and pointed to Bradbury's weapon.

"Get to it," Hawes said.

Garner ran back to Bradbury's SAW and started firing. Smitty joined him. Grzecki radioed back to the base: they needed to get a medevac in there, he told them. By now, darkness had fallen upon the mountain.

The enemy retreated, and the kill team assumed a 360-degree posture, ready to fire outward in all directions.

Monti and Lybert lay side by side. Troops pulling guard duty could look through the thermal sights of their rifles and see the remaining heat leave the bodies of their fallen comrades. Viewed through infrared goggles, the two corpses slowly eased from a light shade of gray into the same inky black as everything else around them.

There was nowhere for the medevac helicopter to land, so one of the birds lowered a hoist carrying a combat medic, Staff Sergeant Heathe Craig, of the 159th Medical Company. Just hours before, Craig had been on his computer, using an Internet chat service to play peekaboo with his daughter, Leona, who was just thirteen days shy of her first birthday. His wife, Judy, and their four-year-old son, Jonas, had giggled because Craig's webcam wasn't functioning properly — to his family, in their off-post apartment close to Wiesbaden, Germany, their husband and father appeared upside down and green.

It was in the middle of that happy interlude that Craig had gotten the call, and now here he was, doing one of his least favorite things in the world: sitting on a Jungle Penetrator, the drill-shaped device lowered from a chopper to extract troops, balancing himself as he descended into hostile territory on the side of a mountain. He'd volunteered to be a flight medic after concluding that being a regular scout medic wasn't enough: treating cases of athlete's foot at Fort Leavenworth, Kansas, didn't leave him feeling as if he were really contributing. But *this* — well, this was terrifying.

Craig was lowered into an opening in the trees, just above a boulder on a steep decline to the west of the mountain ridge. Garner lit a strobe light, and Cunningham, standing on the boulder, grabbed the medic, losing his wedding ring in the process. Over the din of the choppers, Craig tried to reassure everyone that the ordeal was over.

"We're going to get you guys out of here!" Craig yelled. "Everyone's going to be okay."

The plan was for the two wounded men both to be choppered to an aid station on the same helicopter. Bradbury was supposed to get in the hoist first, but he had started bleeding again and was slipping in and out of consciousness, so Derek James was first to be strapped into the seat. Craig tied himself to the Jungle Penetrator, so that he was facing James around the upright metal stem, and twirled his finger as a signal for the chopper crewman to pull them up. Upon lifting off, the Jungle Penetrator swung from the boulder over the steep decline and started spinning around. Craig controlled the oscillations as he'd been trained to do, and the two men were quickly yanked into the bird.

Craig went right back down again for Bradbury. They got him onto the seat and strapped in, but he was going to be tougher to hoist up because of his wound. Craig twirled his finger again. The Jungle Penetrator swung out and started spinning again, and as they got closer to the helicopter, the oscillating increased in speed.

Unable to hold himself upright, Bradbury was leaning back, making it more difficult for Craig to manage the rotation. The chopper crewman tried to pull the two men up as fast as he could, but the Jungle Penetrator suddenly began spinning out of control. As the crewman frantically worked, the hoist's cable twisted and turned, rubbing against the sharp edge of the chopper's floor.

Because it was dark, Craig had fastened a small light to his gear. On Hill 2610, Matt Chambers stood and watched the light spin around until it was a blur.

Then the cable snapped. Chambers kept watching as the light stopped spinning into a blur and instead began falling, flying down. Craig and Bradbury plummeted some one hundred feet, onto the western side of the ridge, and landed on rocks.

Oh no, the men thought as they saw it happen. *God,* no.

Cunningham ran down to where they'd fallen, as did Chambers and Noble. Craig and Bradbury were both unconscious and clearly in bad shape, drawing shallow breaths. Cunningham checked Bradbury for spinal injuries, and Chambers did the same for Craig, as the medevac flew away. Cunningham told Chambers to hand him the emergency flight radio attached to Craig's gear. "They're still alive!" he yelled into it. "Get that medevac back here!" There was no response, only static. Because it wasn't his own radio, Cunningham didn't know if it was even working, or if the chopper pilots had heard him.

Chambers could barely see anything, but he could feel that Craig was bleeding profusely. He cradled the medic's head between his legs, trying to hold it and his neck as straight as possible while also making sure that Craig didn't choke on the blood that seemed to be pouring from his nose. Chambers did the best he could, but ultimately he realized that he couldn't do much more than provide the dying man with some small measure of comfort. He cursed his own powerlessness as he heard the last breaths issue from Heathe Craig's mouth.

Hawes came down and tried to help Bradbury, but he was in the same condition as Craig—mortally wounded, being held by a fellow soldier who was unable to do anything to ward off death's inevitable touch.

Cunningham meanwhile ran up the mountain and told Grzecki to call back to command and tell anyone who would listen to send that medevac back. Noble followed him up the hill.

"They're dead," Noble said.

In the operations center at Forward Operating Base Naray, Howard was intensely aware of everything that had gone down on Hill 2610. Four men were dead, and one wounded soldier—Derek James—had been successfully medevacked to the aid station at Naray. Everyone else was accounted for and would likely be okay for the night. Additional food drops were not needed.

Howard went in to his commander's office. Then he came back out to the operations center.

It was time to cut their losses. Howard had decided it wasn't worth it to send a helicopter into an area where an insurgent with an RPG could get lucky and inflict yet another tragedy on 3-71 Cav. There would be no more helicopters that night, he said. He made sure to put plans in place for the spent team to safely walk off the mountain the next day.

"Those guys are just going to have to hold up," he said.

Cunningham, Hawes, and Woods moved the four bodies away from their camp.

As dawn broke, Cunningham saw the look on the faces of his men. He had seen it before: the huge, wide eyes, the result of a lifetime's worth of horror and loss packed into a few hours. The look of men who'd had some part of themselves taken away forever. The look of men who had been hollowed out.

The next medevac brought in hard plastic stretchers, referred to by troops as "Skedcos." The bodies were removed from the mountain, as was the four men's gear. The thirteen surviving members of the kill team walked back down the mountain toward Forward Operating Base Naray.

A few days later, Captain Michael Schmidt and two Cherokee Company platoons air-assaulted into the Gremen Valley. The men of Chero-kee Company watched the building where more than a dozen of the enemy lurked. They took grids and called in bombs. Not much was left by the time it was all over.

Also demolished as a result of this engagement was Howard's village-hopping idea. It was decided that U.S. forces would come back to deal with Bazgal, Kamu, and Mirdesh at a later date. As happened in every military operation, the enemy got a vote.

Still, even with 3-71 Cav reeling now from two major calamities, Nicholson continually reminded Howard of the need to get the Kamdesh PRT established as soon as possible. Winter was guaranteed to be brutal, so they needed to set up the outpost as soon as possible to be prepared for the elements—and to take advantage of when the snows in the passes would keep the enemy away. It had to be done, Nicholson felt, and it had to be done quickly—and so it would be.

CHAPTER 9

"This Will Happen to You"

The establishment of the PRT in Kamdesh District was delayed for several weeks so that 3-71 Cav could concentrate on eliminating the enemy presence operating in and around Gawardesh—that is, the insurgents responsible for the deaths of Monti, Lybert, Bradbury, and Craig. Once that task had been completed, the leaders of the squadron refocused on building the outpost. As a first step, they made plans to begin sending supplies to the Afghan National Police station adjacent to the site. That mission was derailed, however, by a mudslide that blocked a portion of the Landay-Sin River, flooding the road with five feet of water. The overflow washed away large chunks of land, leaving behind a temporary lake about one hundred feet across and five to six feet deep. Local entrepreneurs soon took to lashing together anything inflatable—black inner tubes, animal hides—to ferry people and supplies from one side of the road to the other. For a hefty fee, of course.

Captain Dennis Sugrue, the Headquarters Troop commander, had an engineering background, so he sought to take charge of the situation. Sugrue already had a good idea of the sorts of problems he'd be facing, having joined Howard in the convoy to the future site of PRT Kamdesh the previous month. As was very often the case in Afghanistan, the most dangerous part of the trip was the drive. An uparmored M1114 Humvee had a standard weight of ninety-eight hundred pounds, and steering one on an exceptionally narrow and poorly constructed road was a life-or-death proposition; among other challenges, the edges of the Humvee tires would skirt along the cliffs, causing already suspect retaining walls to crumble further, so that sometimes there was only a few centimeters' margin between continued advance and a fatal plummet.

Since the road was too unstable to support a bulldozer, Sugrue devised a plan utilizing a hydraulic shovel. After troops detonated explosives to blow through the mud, they could use the shovel to dig a channel, through which the water ought then to be able to drain from the road. When that didn't succeed, 3-71 Cav troops began literally floating supplies upriver. In the end, Sugrue cut into the mountain, elevating the road; that solution finally worked. But his chore didn't end there, because huge rocks were constantly tumbling down and blocking the way, obliging Sugrue to hire local men to patrol the future thoroughfare and clear it of debris. There was more: when boulders weren't rolling down onto the road, they were shifting underneath it. On two consecutive days in June, Humvees rolled over off the crumbling side of the road and down the cliff. Thankfully, no one was seriously hurt. To those involved in this civil-engineering nightmare, it became clear that just setting conditions for the birth of the Kamdesh PRT would be close to impossible.

And then one day the order was given: PRT Kamdesh was a go.

Back at Jalalabad Airfield, Jacob Whittaker, the intelligence analyst with the Idaho National Guard, awoke and was told that while he was sleeping, helicopters had landed and dropped off three platoons of soldiers at what would become the new Kamdesh outpost. His jokes about Custer, his alarmist pleas—all of these were now scattered to the wind like so much Afghan dust.

They landed in a cornfield.

At 2:00 a.m. on July 20, 2006, two Chinooks packed with all of Cherokee Company and one platoon from Able Troop dropped down at Landing Zone Warheit. The landing zone sat near the village of Upper Kamdesh, up the mountain to the south of where the Kamdesh outpost would be built. As Apaches hovered nearby to provide additional security, Lieutenant Colonel Howard ran command and control from a Black Hawk in the air; Captain Michael Schmidt led the team on the ground.

The men from Cherokee Company hunkered down for the rest of the night, since there was no need to scare the local Kamdeshis any more than they'd likely already done. (And no need, either, to let them know right away that while landing, the two Chinooks had destroyed an expanse of crops roughly the size of a football field.) They slept on the ground under the stars, though, truth be told, almost no one got much sleep: Landing Zone Warheit was located high up on the mountain and was easily defensible, but nearly everyone was pulling security—all three platoons, some one hundred soldiers—straight through the darkness and on past sunrise.

At daybreak, six gray-bearded elders from Kamdesh appeared. Schmidt introduced himself, and they all squatted, Afghan-style, and chatted. Schmidt told the elders that he and his men were there on a peaceful mission. They were, he explained, headed down the mountain to set up a PRT next to the existing police station, to help the Afghan government provide services and to help the local police force train new recruits. If the elders knew any young men who might be interested in becoming policemen, he added, they should recommend them—it was good work, with steady pay, and recruits' involvement would aid in bringing greater stability to Kamdesh.

Schmidt apologized for the Chinooks' destruction of the cornfield, which he termed unavoidable. The United States would pay for the damages, he said. What he didn't tell them was that he himself had personally picked the location for the landing zone after doing aerial recon of the area: the presence of crops meant there was a low risk of mines.

As a welcoming gesture, the elders offered to have a couple of young men, in their twenties or early thirties, lead the new arrivals down the mountain. Accepting, Schmidt ordered his first sergeant, two platoons, and a medic to remain at Landing Zone Warheit. He also left some mortarmen behind to help protect those descending: if the enemy attacked them, they could call back up the mountain, give the grid coordinates, and have 120-millimeter mortars—the big ones—fired at their attackers from a safe distance. Those coordinates would be an essential piece of information, however, since no one up at LZ Warheit could actually see the future site of the Kamdesh PRT. This lack of a direct sight line was a less than optimal feature, especially considering that Landing Zone Warheit was soon to become the more permanent Observation Post Warheit—but Schmidt had understood that risk from the start and had concluded that having an easily defensible landing zone and firing point for the mortars took priority, in this instance, over having a direct view.

Schmidt took with him a 60-millimeter-mortar team and Cherokee Company's 2nd Platoon, led by Sergeant First Class Steven Brock. As they slowly made their way down the steep path, a number of the men found themselves reflecting on the events of the past several weeks. They'd been in Regional Command East for only four months now, and they'd already lost seven men: Fenty, O'Donohoe, Moquin, David Timmons, Monti, Lybert, and Bradbury. Schmidt knew that war meant loss. He had ancestors who'd served as far back as the Revolutionary War. He had always been drawn to the military, for all the usual reasons—the discipline, the idea of serving a cause greater than himself, the notion of leading a life of purpose. Playing with G.I. Joes had given way to Valley Forge Military Academy, followed by Ranger School. He'd joined the 10th Mountain because it was a force that deployed often. He wanted to lead men in battle.

When Schmidt and his men reached the bottom of the mountain, they were greeted by the chief of the local bureau of the Afghan National Police, Abdul Jalil, who seemed happy to see them.

Taking in the reality of the location of the new PRT, Schmidt himself was not so ebullient. You'd have to be out of your mind to stand here, look around at these mountains, and be okay with this, he thought. Making the same comparison as others before and after him, he felt it was like being at the bottom of a fishbowl. Schmidt knew all too well how thin American military resources were spread in Afghanistan—the United States still had only one brigade in all of Regional Command East—and he understood that because of that, the base needed to be close to the road for resupply and transport. While Observation Post Warheit would be in a great location defensively, it would be far from the road, and its siting wouldn't allow for the monitoring either of insurgents moving into and out of Nuristan or of those returning from Pakistan. But nothing was perfect in this country. If we want to start connecting with the people in Kamdesh, Schmidt thought, we need to be here. If we want to stop fighters and weapons coming from the north, the only way to do it is to be here. He kept reminding himself why this spot made sense.

There were two platoons up at Landing Zone Warheit: Lieutenant Vic Johnson and the 1st Platoon from Able Troop, which had been loaned, or "attached," to Cherokee Company; and First Lieutenant Marc Cleveland and the 1st Platoon from Cherokee Company. Men from both units spent much of the day surveying their new neighborhood, clearing out trees for a more permanent observation post, and shoveling dirt into HESCO barriers—the wire-mesh containers with thick fabric liners that troops use as portable, easily erected obstructions.

At last light going into what would be 3-71 Cav's first full night in Kamdesh District, Vic Johnson was just dozing off near the landing zone when bullets started whizzing overhead, some of them plunking right into those dirt-packed HESCOs. Johnson's radio operator awoke right away and tried calling for support, only to find that the radio's battery had died (not an uncommon occurrence). He then dialed up to ask for help on the single-channel TacSat satellite system, reserved for emergencies. Cleveland and his platoon had the high ground to the south, and they now began returning the enemy's fire. An insurgent RPG landed in a tree without detonating.

Over the TacSat, a soldier at Forward Operating Base Naray asked Johnson if he was taking "effective fire," a term connoting a clear threat to life. "Not really," Johnson said, since the enemy rounds weren't quite hitting their position. But some of his men were feeling pretty rattled by the fire, in particular one first sergeant, huddling in a trench, who prompted a chuckle by contradicting his superior officer's assessment: "It's *really* effective, Lieutenant!" he said.

The attack, more harassment than onslaught, lasted for ten minutes. After that, the men up on Landing Zone Warheit spent another hour or so returning fire without eliciting any enemy response. The Americans didn't stray from their base; they didn't know much about the area and were worried about landmines. But either way, the message couldn't have been clearer: Welcome to Kamdesh.

Lieutenant Vic Johnson at Landing Zone Warheit, July 2006. *(Photo courtesy of Vic Johnson)*

At the bottom of the mountain, Schmidt took a closer look at the plot of land designated for this project. They had a lot of work to do, he thought, to turn this field into an operating PRT.

First off, Cherokee Company had to set up a new landing zone adjacent to the actual site so that birds could start bringing in supplies, including food and water, construction materials for living quarters, and weapons and ammunition, all of which would be too much of a challenge to haul down the mountain from Landing Zone Warheit. The birds would bring in troops, too. Once everything was up and running, Cherokee Company was scheduled to be relieved by the Barbarians.

The landing zone that had originally been sketched out for the site, using aerial recon, had an immense boulder sitting right in the middle of it. The officers doing the planning had known about the boulder, of course, but the engineers thought they could simply blow it up. Now that they were confronted by the reality of this stone monster, however, the

18/07/2006

The site of the future Camp Kamdesh. *(Photo courtesy of Major Thom Sutton)*

troops had second thoughts. Blowing it up might cause collateral damage to the hamlet of Urmul, showering huge chunks of rock on their new neighbors. Instead, Schmidt resolved to find another location for the landing zone.

After considering every possible alternative, he made the decision to locate the landing zone on a small, rocky peninsula to the north of the future PRT. The site wasn't optimal—it was outside the perimeter of the camp, it essentially sat in the middle of the river, and it was accessible only via a narrow bridge that spanned the waterway—but in Schmidt's estimation, there was just no other place on the ground that was large enough to accept a single aircraft.

After a few days of work, they had something approaching a landing zone, though it took a lot of coaxing to get helicopter pilots to even try to land there. The pad was uneven, and a menacing fruit tree clutched the eastern edge. Only the smaller Black Hawks, with just one large rotor, would make the attempt—and even then, most of the pilots would hover a few feet above the pad and instruct the soldiers to jump out. Schmidt

assigned a soldier to destroy the fruit tree using C-4 explosives and detonating cord. Once it was gone, a chopper brought a Bobcat skid steer in
on a sling so the ground could be leveled. After Schmidt's men spent a
few more days getting that huge rock as smooth as they could, Chinook
pilots were willing to land there, and with them came supplies and more
U.S. troops. Lieutenant Colonel Howard arrived and participated in a
shura with elders from villages and settlements throughout the region.
He wanted to describe in detail all the good that the Americans could do
for them.

Dennis Sugrue had been chosen to escort Fenty's body back to Fort
Drum, New York, in May. The experience had wrung him out like a
dishrag. When he returned, he tried to focus on more life-affirming
activities. Mike Howard had told him that the Kamdesh PRT would have
three priorities: bringing electricity to the villages, providing them with
water, and improving the roads. And he said Sugrue, as the commander
of Headquarters Troop, would be the guy to make those things happen.

Only 2 percent[23] of all households in Nuristan had access to safe
drinking water, so raising that statistic would be a major focus. Dividing
the tasks among engineers and locals, 3-71 Cav would repair or build
gravity-fed water-distribution systems in Mandigal, Gawardesh, Urmul,
Kamdesh Village, and other local settlements. Clean water would provide undeniable evidence that the Americans were making life better for
the Nuristanis. Howard's men would also help bring online existing but
nonfunctioning micro-hydroelectric plants in Urmul and Lower Kamdesh and build similar new plants in Mirdesh and Gawardesh.

Improved roads would be further indisputable proof of an American
contribution. Most immediately, the influx of construction wages would
mean a substantial increase in local income. The Americans hired locals
to work on the road that ran up the southern mountain from the Kamdesh
PRT and Urmul, passing through all of the smaller hamlets that made up
Kamdesh proper. Afghan workers, licensed by the government to use
dynamite, were tasked with literally removing the side of the mountain.
They also filled in potholes that at times could seem like small ponds.

---

[23] According to *The National Risk and Vulnerability Assessment 2005,* published by the
Afghan Ministry of Rural Rehabilitation and Development and the Central Statistics Office.

And of course, 3-71 Cav would use local labor to build up the Kamdesh PRT itself.

From the American point of view, roads would link this backward, remote area to the Afghan government, to commerce, to progress. For many Nuristanis, however, roads were a disruption. They would bring government officials to tax them, and modernizers from Kabul to instruct them on how to treat their women.

Within a few months, 3-71 Cav had approved $1.33 million (American) worth of projects in Kamdesh District—a staggering sum in the impoverished context of Nuristan.

Mike Howard had an idea.

Bullets and mortars could get him and his men only so far here. They needed also to fight an information war, to convince the Nuristanis that the Americans and the Afghan government were the good guys, offering them development, education, and a better life, whereas the insurgents were leading Nuristan down a path of nihilism and bloodshed.

"Dennis," Howard said to Sugrue at Forward Operating Base Naray, "I want you to start a radio station."

Oh, shit, Sugrue thought. "All right, sir," he said, though he had absolutely no idea how to go about doing it.

Some AM radio equipment was already sitting unused in a room at Forward Operating Base Naray, left over from a rather modest Special Forces team initiative involving prerecorded messages. Sugrue bought some FM equipment from the local market and approached elders in Naray to ask if they knew of anyone who might be interested in helping with the radio station—maybe someone who had worked on the previous Special Forces project? Soon a man named Gul Rahim showed up at the gate. In his forties, with a strong chin, Rahim was hired to run the station.

Radio Naray started out with a broadcast radius of something like a mile and a half. Some local Afghans had windup radios, and the few who could afford them had small shortwave radios. Locals could listen to programs from the BBC as well as stations in Iran and Pakistan; broadcasts were generally in Dari and Pashto. Sugrue felt there weren't enough radios in the hands of the locals to justify the great effort he was undertaking, so he ordered hundreds more to be distributed throughout the region. Every subsequent patrol would leave the base with windup radios to hand out.

Sugrue's broadcast began at around 10:00 a.m., with fifty minutes of Afghan and Pakistani music from locally purchased CDs. That would be followed by approximately ten minutes of "news"—a script written by Sugrue and his men. A local interpreter would translate it into Pashto (the language spoken by the people of Naray), and a boy from Naray would read it. A typical report would include information about suspected IEDs, bulletins about recent gunfire, and construction updates on various local projects. The recorded broadcast would be repeated hourly, with the last repeat ending at about 3:00 p.m.

They were largely winging it, Sugrue and his team, but slowly they expanded. Sugrue brought in Lieutenant Joseph Lang from Able Troop to head the operation, and by June they were producing around an hour of original programming, including music and readings from the Quran. The boy was replaced by Gul Rahim and another local man. Next, Sugrue bought new equipment, had a tower erected, and fastened an antenna to it to extend the station's reach. Soon Radio Naray was running eight hours of original programming every day, in Pashto and a Nuristani dialect, featuring news, Quran readings (peaceful ones, they made sure!), music, and poetry. If an influential elder stood up and condemned the insurgency at a shura, Lang would see to it that word of it traveled far beyond the room.

They hired a couple of correspondents, including a retired officer from the old Afghan Army who now lived in Pitigal, who became Radio Naray's security reporter. The former colonel would report from the field, then return to the base and write stories for the broadcasters to read; these would eventually also appear in a new, free four-page newspaper that the base began to publish, called *The Light of Naray*. One thousand copies of the paper were distributed each week in the Naray area and Kamdesh District. Given the estimated literacy rates of 17.7 percent in Nuristan Province and 32.6 percent in Kunar Province,[24] the hope was that locals would gather around as one of their fellow villagers read items aloud to them.

Howard would say that he wanted Radio Naray to replicate the "car-bomb effect," but in a positive way. Whenever a car bomb was detonated

---

[24] Ibid.

in Iraq, everyone would learn about it within minutes. Radio Naray's aim was to ensure that *good* news — about the construction of a road, say, or a water pipeline — would spread just as quickly.

The staff at the station never knew how well they were doing at actually reaching the local populace. David Katz, a U.S. State Department official and expert on the region, would later question the timing of the broadcast, observing that Nuristanis tended to listen to the radio only very early in the morning and then again after dark, when they were sitting around with nothing else to do. Radio Naray wasn't on during those hours.

In the distance, from somewhere outside PRT Kamdesh, came the sound of an explosion. Schmidt prepared himself for the worst: a mortar? an IED? an attack?

Within minutes, residents of Kamdesh started running toward the observation post that Cherokee Company was constructing. Schmidt was alarmed. In the short time the Americans had been there, they'd already destroyed some of the locals' crops — not only the original cornfield but also, by now, some valuable walnut and fruit trees felled during the construction of the base. Moreover, they had occupied the locals' land and no doubt had been the subject of an aggressive insurgent propaganda campaign. Schmidt braced himself.

It turned out the villagers were coming to them for help.

It was August 1, 2006, and a young girl from Kamdesh Village had been tending a field when she stepped on a landmine, a remnant of either the conflict between the Kom and the Kushtozis or possibly even — though this was far less likely — the Soviet occupation. Her feet had essentially been blown off. Her family brought her straight to the Americans. A medic applied tourniquets to control the bleeding and stabilized her. Schmidt secured permission to order a medevac to take her and a family member to Jalalabad. She survived.

While the cause of the girl's injury horrified Schmidt, the fact that her family had come to the U.S. troops for assistance reassured him. Had the accident happened at any point before the Americans arrived, the child might very well have died. But she lived, and it was because the locals sought out help from 3-71 Cav; they were pragmatists, and they knew that American medical treatment would give the child her best — if not her only—chance of survival. Lieutenant Colonel Howard made sure that the Radio Naray broadcasters recounted the story over and over.

Nor was this the first such incident. One night less than a week before, an old man had caught his arm in a flour mill. Terrified, wailing in pain, he was brought to the observation post, where he repeatedly begged the interpreter to tell the soldiers to "just kill" him. The Americans wanted him dead anyway, he insisted. The medic on duty, Private First Class Kevin Jonathan "Johnny" Araujo, put on a tourniquet, and he and Vic Johnson stayed by the man's side throughout the night, at one point foiling his attempt to grab the lieutenant's 9-millimeter handgun and kill himself. At first light, the old man was medevacked out and ultimately flown to Bagram, where he had his arm amputated below the elbow. But he, too, lived.

For other Nuristanis, however, associating with the Americans brought less fortunate results.

To Sugrue's mind, the most important development-project priority was the establishment of a system that would distribute potable water in Kamdesh Village. The village was the cultural capital of Nuristan, the elders had told Sugrue. (This claim stretched the truth a tad; in fact, Barg-e-Matal was far more sophisticated.) So if the Americans wanted to reach the Nuristanis, they said, Kamdesh was the place to start. Sugrue's plan was to tap into a spring a little over a mile up the mountain, on an adjacent peak, and use gravity to move the water down to each of the four hamlets that made up Kamdesh. As one of the bigger projects being planned for the area, it was to cost an estimated eighty thousand dollars.

To supervise the initiative, Sugrue hired Haji Akhtar Mohammed, a local man recommended by the powerful district administrator for Kamdesh, Gul Mohammed Khan. Within a few weeks, some other Afghans were trying to get a piece of the water project for themselves, arguing that more than one person should be in charge of the money the Americans were doling out. Sugrue resisted. If they wanted to see their influence increase, he told them, they should get behind this effort and help make it happen, and then they could talk about other projects.

Such was one of the immediate side effects of counterinsurgency: Americans arriving with bags of money for development projects garnered appreciation among those benefiting (though how much loyalty was fostered in the long term was another question) but also, inevitably, prompted jealousy and resentment among those individuals who did not benefit directly, even if their village as a whole stood to gain. In villages that were passed over entirely, the resentment could evolve into uglier emotions such as anger, rage, and fury. When village, tribal, and other rivalries were thrown into the mix, the situation could become downright combustible.

For Haji Akhtar Mohammed and others like him, the association with the United States became a double-edged sword. Keeping a certain distance from these patrons was often critical to avoiding being called a lackey, or worse. The Americans, for their part, had to be mindful that what seemed innocuous to one party might feel profound to another. One afternoon, for example, Sugrue stopped Akhtar Mohammed outside a Kamdesh mosque to check on the progress of the water project. Sugrue saw it as a friendly encounter, but the Nuristani felt emasculated by his public association with the U.S. Army. Seeing him as both a supplicant and a profiteer, some of the villagers concluded that Akhtar Mohammed had been the one responsible for bringing the Americans to Kamdesh in the first place, and thus for provoking the increase in insurgent attacks along the main road from Naray. Many villagers subsequently refused to work for Akhtar Mohammed on the water project.

And that was one of the milder reactions. In August, a group of Afghans working with the United States were attacked by approximately fifteen members of the Taliban during a meeting with the Afghan National Police in the hamlet of Kamu. In a separate incident, insurgents killed three people from the village of Gawardesh, including the police chief, and wounded four other Afghan policemen. The Gawardeshis were on their way to see the district administrator, Gul Mohammed Khan, to get a contract stamped for a new micro-hydroelectric plant and gravity-pipe scheme, when their chief elder, Haji Yunus, was kidnapped and dragged into the hills. This latter act of violence particularly horrified Sugrue: to him, Haji Yunus was the Wyatt Earp of Gawardesh's Wild West. Sugrue would later learn that Yunus had been led into a heavily wooded area of the highlands, roughly seven thousand feet up, known as the Jungle. Intelligence reports over the next few days indicated that he was being moved from village to village, safehouse to safehouse. Three days after Yunus's kidnapping, his mutilated corpse was dumped near the Pakistan border. His throat had been cut. A note was attached to the body: "Don't work with coalition forces. This will happen to you." It was signed by the Taliban leader Mullah Omar.

Yunus's murder further fed into Lieutenant Ben Keating's skepticism. The more time he spent in Afghanistan, the more convinced he became that there was nothing the United States could do to change the dynamics there. Yunus had in fact been kidnapped and killed not by the Taliban but by HIG insurgents, U.S. intelligence reported, but because Mullah Omar was far better known and more feared, HIG allowed him to take "credit" for the murder. It was all in the service of their larger goal: terrorizing anyone who cooperated with the Americans or the Afghan government. Yunus himself had had HIG ties, as had the Gawardesh police chief who'd been shot and killed, but such relationships were worthless, it seemed, under these circumstances. "And guess what?" Keating wrote to his father. "We created, trained and equipped HIG. They were northern Afghanistan's heroes of the Russian War and had heavy ties to the CIA even when we moved in to help kick-start the Northern Alliance at the beginning of this war." This was all true.

Keating wondered: if both the Gawardesh police chief and Haji Yunus had maintained connections to HIG even as they were working with the Americans, what did that suggest about the Afghan National Police commander with whom they were so closely allied, "who is supposedly giving us all of this great intel, but appears to move among these HIG-infested villages with complete immunity"?

The word *futility* kept cropping up in Ben Keating's calls and letters home. "Looking at young men harden under a hail of bullets, and age before my eyes, is heartbreaking," he wrote. He was on edge, more impatient and more prone to anxiety than ever before. Nonetheless, he was thankful that his parents had equipped him to handle such experiences. "I know that when I get home, these stories are from just one chapter in a life that I will continue to use in meaningful ways," he noted.

CHAPTER 10

The Abstract Threat
of Terror

On August 8, insurgents staged their first major, well-coordinated attack on the Kamdesh PRT.

Captain Frank Brooks and the Barbarians had relieved Schmidt and Cherokee Company a week earlier. Brooks was even less impressed with the location of the new PRT than Schmidt had been—it was tactically indefensible, he thought—but he had no choice in the matter: orders were orders. Dropped at Landing Zone Warheit, he felt it would have made much more sense to site the outpost up there, where personnel could defend themselves on the high ground even as they concentrated on building a road up the southern mountain and into Kamdesh Village. Observation Post Warheit was close to Upper Kamdesh, after all.

Enemy fire on the PRT down in the valley had been slowly but steadily increasing, though there had as yet been no injuries. Mostly the enemy was poking the U.S. troops, seeing what they would do, how they would react, but the ominous prodding was bound to end badly in one way or another. Enemy chatter and walk-in reports from villagers about an imminent attack confirmed what the Americans all knew was coming.

On one of his first few days at Observation Post Warheit, Brooks tried to have the squadron fire-support officer (FSO), who was down in the valley at the PRT, orient him to the area via radio. For roughly ten minutes, Brooks struggled to pinpoint the parts of the mountain that the FSO was insisting were right there, to his right and to his left. And then Brooks realized that the FSO had never actually *been* up the mountain and thus didn't understand that what from his view appeared to be the top of the southern mountain was in reality a false summit not even halfway up to OP Warheit.

Oh my God, they don't even know where the top of the mountain is, Brooks thought.

It wasn't that the fire-support officer down at the PRT was unprepared. It was that he was . . . well, *ignorant* wasn't a *fair* word, Brooks knew, but it rang true. The gaps in the FSO's knowledge weren't really his fault; the valley was so disorienting, and the mountains so steep. One peak could obscure everything behind it, and the Army's topographical maps fell short of capturing the domain in any comprehensible way: lines drawn close together on a piece of paper just couldn't capture the myriad elevations, notches, and contours of the area, severe and sharp and unforgiving. Troops would either fly in at night or drive in on the valley road; with minimal time on the ground and little situational awareness, they could hardly help it if their sense of the place was limited to what was visible to them. There was no way any of the troops at PRT Kamdesh could have understood the landscape without spending four or five days just walking around in it—which they didn't have the luxury of being able to do.

So Brooks didn't blame the FSO; probably everyone down there thought the top of that false summit was the top of the mountain. But it was an unsettling revelation for the troop commander, the realization that everything he and his officers had worked out was based on inaccuracies.

"Shit," he said to himself, "we need to start again." All of the predetermined reference points were wrong.

At 9:00 p.m. on August 8, Brooks was just settling in for the night at Observation Post Warheit's headquarters area, a tarp covering a pit walled by HESCOs, when insurgents unleashed a lightning storm of RPGs at his colleagues down at PRT Kamdesh. The attack came from all three surrounding mountains, to the north, the northwest, and the south. The mortarman at Observation Post Warheit jumped to it—"Get up! Get up!" Brooks shouted at everyone, in case the explosions themselves hadn't done the trick—and the rest of the Barbarians prepared to help in whatever way they could. They couldn't see the PRT itself, but they saw the intermittent glow from the RPGs as they detonated in the valley. The troops at the Kamdesh PRT used their machine guns, rifles, and mortars to try to fend off the insurgents surrounding them, then began calling in the grids to Observation Post Warheit so the mortarmen up there could target the enemy positions. The insurgents seemed to have anticipated this move, however, and started attacking OP Warheit's mortar positions from the observation post's south and west. The Americans at both locations pushed back with suppressive fire, and soon enough a team of A-10 Warthog airplanes rolled in and dropped a few five-hundred-pound bombs that devastated the opposition. The Barbarians continued firing even after the enemy retreated; the Warthog pilots targeted insurgents as they attempted to recover the bodies of their fallen comrades, which according to Islamic tradition must be buried within twenty-four hours.

After almost three hours, the engagement was over. Somewhere in the neighborhood of thirty RPGs had landed inside the PRT wire. Remarkably, just as in the Chowkay Valley, none of the Barbarians had been wounded, though there were some minor injuries down at the PRT.

Holy crap, Brooks thought. *I can't believe we just took all of this and walked out without a scratch — again.*

For Brooks and other leaders of 3-71 Cav, the fact that the insurgents had been able to get so close to the PRT further illustrated the major flaw of Observation Post Warheit: there was an entire mountainside below them that the troops at the observation post simply could not see. Clearly PRT Kamdesh would have to expand its perimeter and keep a more aggressive watch.

The larger lesson, Brooks was convinced, lay in the confirmation that this had been an awful place to put a base. He hoped that the attack would make obvious to command the inadequacies of the location, and that the PRT would be moved up the mountain. When Mike Howard visited a couple of days later, Brooks tried to raise the issue with him, but Howard shut him down, indicating that the PRT was going to stay where it was. It needed to be adjacent to the road, period. Able Troop showed up to relieve the Barbarians in late August, and Brooks was happy to pack up and go. It almost didn't matter to him where he was headed next, just so long as he got out of that valley.

PRT Kamdesh was built at the bottom of three mountains. To its immediate southwest was a mountain wall on which "Switchbacks" — paths back and forth — had been blazed. *(Photo courtesy of Kaine Meshkin)*

Constant patrolling was crucial for survival, and daily, one platoon from Able Troop — there were three in all — would hike one of the mountains surrounding the PRT. On August 27, Lieutenant Vic Johnson led 1st Platoon halfway up the southern mountain, on the way to Observation Post Warheit. Lieutenant Colonel Howard and Lieutenant Colonel Tony Feagin — head of the PRT in Laghman Province — had gone up to the observation post earlier that day, as had Able Troop's 2nd Platoon; Johnson and his men were taking a different route.

Out of the blue, some young Nuristani boys ran toward Johnson's troops, yelling something about "bad guys." Johnson, senior scout Staff Sergeant Aaron Jongeneel, and the interpreter tried to figure out what the children were talking about. The boys said they had been leading their donkeys up the trail, loaded with food and water, when some insurgents confronted them, stole their packages, and stabbed the animals. The insurgents had guns, the boys reported, their faces stunned with fear. There were other kids and villagers up the hill, they said.

"Hey, Lieutenant," Jongeneel said, "I'll take a recon team farther up the mountain to see if we can find anything."

Johnson got on the radio as he walked with the recon team. He suspected this might be a trick planned by the enemy, maybe even an ambush, though the kids' fright had looked sincere enough. "We have a report of some bad guys up the hill," he radioed to Howard. "These kids seem pretty scared. We're going to check this out." Johnson relayed the plan to his platoon sergeant, Sergeant First Class Terry Raynor, who said he'd stand by with the rest of the group.

"Red-One," Howard called in to Johnson, "don't go toe to toe with them. Drop mortars."

Vic Johnson thought about this order. He envisioned having his mugshot broadcast around the world on CNN International, suddenly infamous for calling in bombs that slaughtered a group of innocent schoolboys. Moreover, practically speaking, he didn't know where exactly to drop the mortars, since he had no specific intel on the insurgents' location—if there *were* any insurgents, that was.

"Sir, I have civilians in front of me," Johnson said. "We're told other kids are there. I don't think we can drop mortars."

"Fine," Howard said. "Be careful."

At Johnson's direction, one soldier escorted the young Nuristanis down the hill a bit and onto a ledge off to the side, where they would be reasonably safe. Johnson left most of 1st Platoon in place while he and a few others went up the hill to investigate the boys' story. In the brush they found debris and blood, which Johnson assumed must have come from the donkeys. He was starting to think the kids really were telling the truth.

Continuing up the hill, Private First Class Kevin Dwyer spotted an insurgent roughly fifty yards away pointing an RPG at Jongeneel. "Staff Sergeant J!" Dwyer yelled, raising his M-16 rifle and firing, as Jongeneel, so warned, did the same.

Sergeant Jeremy Larson and his immediate crew had discovered the enemy presence in a different manner: by being shot at. Insurgents fired their AK assault rifles[25] at them, and Larson, Private First Class Levi Barbee, and

---

[25] First developed in the USSR, AKs are gas-operated, selective-fire assault rifles, said to be the most widely used weapons in the world.

Specialist Matthew Wilhelm all dropped to a fighting position. Barbee peered up toward the source of the fire through the scope of his M16 rifle.

"They're looking down at us," he said. "I got one in my sight."

"Go ahead and take a shot," Larson said.

Barbee fired, and the insurgents ducked and scattered.

Larson figured the others from 1st Platoon would swing into a flank to help them, so he stayed where he was and told Barbee and Wilhelm to do the same.

About six insurgents had gathered by a tree, offering Larson's squad a rare opportunity to end the conflict almost before it began. Wilhelm had the SAW — the "squad automatic weapon," or M249 light machine gun. He took a bead on the pack of insurgents, aimed his SAW, and . . . nothing happened.

The SAW had jammed.

As the firefight snapped into a greater intensity, Johnson told his interpreter, "Take the kids, the donkeys, whatever, and get them back to the PRT. Get the hell out of here. Tell them you were with Lieutenant Johnson's patrol — they'll know what to do. Make sure everyone gets there. Don't stop for anything."

Johnson grabbed one of his scouts and returned to where Dwyer was firing at the moving group of insurgents. The lieutenant emptied half a magazine of 5.56-millimeter rounds into one insurgent while Jongeneel and his recon team pushed other enemy fighters back with their fire.

At the back of the patrol, Wilhelm took apart the jammed SAW and put it back together. Enemy fire continued to shower down upon the three Americans. The pack of insurgents near the tree dispersed. Larson and Barbee continued to shoot, but they were running out of ammo.

Where the fuck is the rest of the platoon? Larson wondered.

"I need a fucking two-oh-three!" he yelled. "I need a SAW! Can I get some fucking backup?"

Some from 1st Platoon had stayed on the trail; others had headed into the brush. Specialist Clinton Howe now ran up with his M203 grenade launcher. "Hey, man," he said, diving by Larson's side as he fired from behind a bush. "I heard you're looking for a two-oh-three."

They made a plan. The enemy had been trying to work on their right flank, so Howe would launch a grenade from the left side of the bush toward the approaching insurgents, Larson would throw one from the right, and then they would pray to God that Wilhelm's SAW worked.

As Howe stood up to shoot the M203 grenade launcher, Larson rose to his knees to throw his grenade. He hadn't even had a chance to pull the pin when he saw the white puff of smoke from an RPG launcher, its lethal explosive coming right at them. Howe and Wilhelm scooted away. Barbee rolled. Larson dropped down and put his left arm over his face as the RPG landed barely three feet away from him.

Howe woke up in a pool of his own blood, under a tree. "Medic!" he yelled, but a voice told him that the medic was down, so he wiggled out from under the tree, only to promptly fall into a ravine. He took a second to try to clear his head, then got up and made his way over to the voices.

When Larson came to, he couldn't see anything. Both the left side of his face and his left arm had been peppered with shrapnel. Blood was spilling into his eye from a cut on his forehead, and there were holes in his hand and shoulder. He could hear a high-pitched ringing as he crawled toward a tree. Reaching it, he paused to lean against the trunk and then staggered back to the bush where he'd originally been. There he found Howe and Barbee, who had also been hit with shrapnel, as well as Wilhelm.

"Medic!" Larson yelled. Johnny Araujo, the medic, and been following them and was down the mountain a bit, around a bend and behind a crest. But now Larson heard Araujo yelling that he himself was down. Larson quickly descended the hill and found the medic lying on the ground, covered with blood. The RPG had sent a big piece of shrapnel into the right side of his neck; he was now plugging the whole with the fingers of his right hand. Two of the fingers on his left hand had been nearly taken off.

"Dude, are you okay?" Larson asked.

"No, dude," Araujo answered, looking up at Larson. "Are *you* okay?"

Araujo said he was going to pull his fingers out of the hole in his neck for a minute, and then he wanted Larson to describe the blood that started flowing: What color was it? Was it bubbling? Larson agreed to tell him and watched closely as blood started spurting from the hole. It was the same bright crimson that was on Larson's own chest, from where his wounds had bled onto his shirt. Araujo knew that color meant the injury was to an artery, not a vein, indicating that this was a more serious wound. He struggled to apply a special adhesive bandage to seal his neck wound, but there was so much blood it wouldn't stick. He wasn't sure how badly he was hurt or even how long they had been out there. "Hey, man," Araujo said. "I need to get down the mountain."

Johnson, Jongeneel, and the others at the front of the platoon had been granted the rare advantage of getting in the first shot, and the enemy had seemingly retreated. With the fight now almost over, Johnson grudgingly walked toward the spot where someone had been calling his name. Raynor's voice came over the radio: "We need a medevac," he said. With his men spread out all over the mountain, Johnson hadn't known until that moment that the platoon had suffered casualties.

As he hurried down the mountain, he thought about the lessons he'd learned in Ranger School, weighing what he ought to do now. Johnson knew that at all costs, his scouts had to maintain an offensive posture. If they cowered and retreated, the insurgents might further exploit their terrain advantage — they had the high ground — and kill them all.

Larson suddenly appeared in front of him. To Johnson, he seemed a bit disoriented — that was the polite term for it, anyway. "What the fuck are you doing?" Larson asked him. "Where's the medevac? We need to get a medevac, Johnny's bleeding out his neck!"

In fact, Raynor had called for a medevac, but the leadership of 3-71 Cav had nixed it. The hill was too steep and sloping to allow a safe landing, the commanders felt, so the pilots would have had to use a Jungle Penetrator to extract any wounded men. The recent disasters involving tricky helicopter extractions and Jungle Penetrators added an extra layer of hesitation to any decisions to order more such rescue missions.[26]

---

[26] In fact, the Army would learn from Heathe Craig's June 2006 death. In November 2011, when I was briefly embedded with the "All American Dustoff" medevac team next to the Heathe Craig Joint Theater Hospital at Bagram Airfield, the commander, Major Graham Bundy, told me it was his understanding that one of the contributing factors identified in the post-accident investigation was that the rescue hoist cable snapped because the intense oscillations caused it to rub against the lower door track,

"Dude, you need to get the fucking mortars launched!" Larson continued. "Don't let them get away!"

Johnson didn't feel the need to explain himself to Larson, who was known to have a certain attitude, a problem with authority. He'd already made the call not to have mortars fired onto the mountain, given the civilian presence. Moreover, at this point, any mortar fired might hit one of the scattered U.S. troops.

"Just give him the fucking grid and get a goddamn medevac!" Larson yelled. He knew he was approaching insubordination, but he didn't care. He was covered in blood and had been hit by flying shards of metal. Johnson understood that between the adrenaline and his injury, Larson was not in his normal state of mind, so he let it slide.

"I think I'm going to lose my eye. How bad am I hit?" Larson now asked.

Johnson looked at him. "It's not that bad. You're cut above your eye. The blood is streaming in. We're going to have to walk back to the base."

"Let's get out of here," Larson said. "We need to leave now, L.T."

"Jongeneel's team is still out there," Johnson explained. "We don't leave soldiers behind."

A voice came back over Johnson's radio: "Red-One, Titan X-ray, CAS"—close air support—"is coming on station. ETA is five minutes. There are two A-tens coming onto station."

After the A-10 Warthogs flew over their heads, launching flares as a show of force, the troops found one another and consolidated. The fight's over, Johnson thought to himself. By now the insurgents had probably already ditched their weapons and disappeared back into the local populace.

Larson walked back down to where troops were standing in a 360-degree guard station around Araujo as the men of 1st Platoon continued to gather in their last known location. Squadron headquarters ordered the platoon to walk the casualties back to the PRT. Raynor began setting up teams with stretch-

---

which was sharp and pointed. Bundy showed me how all Black Hawks with hoist systems were now required to also have cable deflectors—rounded, not sharp, guards on which the cable could rest—installed along the lower door track. A Pentagon spokesman said the cable deflectors "prevent chafing of the cable should it come in contact with the body of the aircraft" and were required on all Black Hawks with hoist systems as of February 2007.

ers to carry the casualties off the mountain, but he was told it would take at least forty-five minutes for that help to arrive. He was furious, but all he could do was try to figure out how to move the wounded as far down the hill as possible, as quickly as possible, without assistance.

One of the boys' donkeys had survived but managed to tangle its lead rope around a nearby tree. Johnson had an idea: why not put Araujo on the donkey and usher the beast down the hill? Every time they tried to get Araujo on its back, however, the animal bucked him off onto the ground. The medic was in no shape to hold on to the donkey himself, so after a few attempts, they all decided just to head down on foot. The men took turns carrying Araujo.

As he arrived back at the Kamdesh PRT, Johnson saw the rest of the surviving donkeys at the gate. He smiled, reassured that the interpreter had made it back safely with the children.

He sought out First Sergeant Todd Yerger, took a breath, and started going over what had happened. None of his soldiers had been killed, he said, but the enemy had found ways to exploit the Americans' reluctance to risk injuring local villagers, and had taken advantage of the high ground

This image of Araujo (*in the background*), Howe, and Larson after the ambush became a *Time* magazine Photo of the Year. *(Photo copyright 2006 by Robert Nickelsberg of Getty Images)*

and a better knowledge of the mountain. The whole incident might have turned out far worse had the kids not warned them about the insurgents, and had Dwyer not spotted the ambush seconds before it began.

Yerger took out a cigarette.

"Hey, Top," Johnson said, using Army slang for first sergeants, "gimme one of those."

Yerger handed over the pack and a lighter.

It was the first cigarette Johnson had ever had. And the last—it was disgusting, he thought.

Many of the enlisted men did not know about everything that had gone down on the mountain that day, and quite honestly, they didn't care. In their opinion, Vic Johnson had handled things poorly and gotten a bunch of them shot up. They thought he was more interested in ass-kissing the captains than in listening to his men.

That wasn't how Johnson's superiors saw it, however. They saw a lieutenant who'd led a patrol that was ambushed, and who'd responded aggressively while also being cautious about harming the local populace. None of his men had been killed, and no civilians had been, either. "No battle goes down cleanly, like the Xs and Os in a football playbook," one captain would later say.

Larson, Araujo, and Howe were taken from PRT Kamdesh to Forward Operating Base Naray, then to Jalalabad Airfield, then to Bagram. They had their wounds treated and two days later were told they were being sent to the military hospital in Germany. Larson had planned on having a career in the military, but he was eventually discharged early for medical reasons: there was just too much metal in his shoulder.

A few days after their arrival, Ben Keating and Todd Yerger led Matt Netzel and his platoon on a mission to patrol and clear the mountain across the Landay-Sin River from and to the north of the PRT, a task that was supposed to take just a day or two but ended up taking six.

The valley was still new to them, and they hadn't anticipated that the land would be so challenging. Neither Command Sergeant Major Byers nor any of the other head honchos now at the camp had gone up via this route, so no one realized how steep it was. Keating's platoon had to maneuver around and up cliff faces, climbing nearly sheer walls without the benefit of the equipment or the slower pace that might have made such ascents and descents both safer and more tranquil. They didn't see the enemy on this trip, but they did find a rocket pointed at the U.S. camp. (They blew it up with C-4.) They also found the remnants of campfires, which helped them pinpoint some of the locations the insurgents used.

Keating and Netzel talked a lot during this patrol. Keating told Netzel about his new girlfriend back home: he was planning on taking her to Ireland, he said, and thinking seriously about proposing marriage when they got there. Keating also spoke of his doubts about the war effort. He was losing his faith in the cause, he confessed. The shells of the Soviet personnel carriers were constant reminders of the historical determination of the enemy.

"We're here, we have thirty or forty men, and we're expected to hold off this force that destroyed the Soviet Army?" he marveled, shaking his head.

During the period between the end of Operation Mountain Lion and the push to stand up PRT Kamdesh, Keating and Able Troop had been in southern Afghanistan, in Kandahar and Helmand Provinces. Such wide-range roving was the kind of thing made necessary by the fact that the United States had only one full fighting brigade in Afghanistan. Keating's time in the south had been dispiriting. On the first night after his convoy left Kandahar Airfield, the U.S. troops at the front of the line—not from 3-71 Cav—had shot an Afghan man on a motorcycle who they thought was getting too close to them. The man was innocent, and to Keating, it seemed clear that it had been a bad shooting. He'd tried to console the motorcyclist's father while his son writhed in agony on the ground, full of bullet holes, and they waited three hours for a medevac to arrive. The motorcyclist died two days later. That sort of incompetence might kill me, too, Keating thought.

Again and again, Keating felt that some of his peers, his fellow officers, were failing their men. He'd witnessed an instance of friendly fire, from a unit made up of what he judged to be terrible soldiers with no training. During another mess, after U.S. troops were attacked by Taliban forces in a small village, Keating and nine of his men had trapped the insurgents in a copse of trees by a small river; when he called in Apaches to bring Hellfire missiles, one overeager pilot put a Hellfire about 125 feet in front of him and his crew—way, way too close. The explosion reminded Keating of the opening scene of *Saving Private Ryan,* "where everything was ringing and we were all trying to talk with our hands—except for the radio, into which I was very much communicating with my voice," as he later told his father in an email.

His misgivings were complicated. Keating didn't doubt that the insurgents the United States was battling in Afghanistan were evil; in Kandahar, when given a chance to kill the enemy, he was aggressive. He thought of those allied against his country as murderers and rapists, and he believed in the rightness of killing them. It had seemed weird at first to be the leader who had to give the final go to pummel insurgents with mortars, Keating admitted, though it was made a lot easier than he might have expected by the knowledge that the insurgents were trying to kill him and his troops.

He also was coming to recognize the humanity of the Afghan people. He enjoyed his interactions with the local populace, as when he shared tea with an elder who regaled him with stories about being a soldier in the 1960s and confided his hopes for the future for his four-year-old grandson.

But at the end of the day, Keating felt, the American "experiment" in Afghanistan would fail, just as surely as earlier American efforts in Iraq, Haiti, and Somalia had done. The Afghan people just would not stick their necks out far enough to side with the United States and their own government against the insurgency—and he didn't blame them. Their reluctance was part of their DNA, after centuries of occupation by various powers.

Keating had joined the military because he wanted to know what it was like to serve before he—as a future congressman, senator, president—sent others off to fight. What his time in Afghanistan was teaching him was that there needed to be better reasons, stronger threats to national security, before the United States deployed its sons and daughters. The abstract threat of terror was not enough, Keating thought. Having lost his commander, Lieutenant Colonel Fenty, and colleagues such as Monti and Lybert, he couldn't stand the thought of losing one more guy over here. And now here he was, in a place that seemed even more hopeless and futile than Helmand and Kandahar Provinces.

"What the hell are we doing at the base of three mountains?" he asked Netzel.

His friend didn't have an answer.

CHAPTER 11

The Enemy Gets a Vote

The significance of the date—September 11, 2006—didn't cross Sergeant Dennis Cline's mind as he awoke in one of the bunkers that served as the troops' living quarters. He arose and stood in his makeshift house, whose roof was fashioned from timber covered with sandbags and whose walls were made of HESCO barriers packed with dirt. For the twenty-seven-year-old Cline, it was just another day. You get up in the morning, you do your job, and hopefully you go to bed with the stars in the sky above you and your body parts all in one place.

The infantryman from Staunton, Illinois, had done a tour in western Iraq, but he preferred Afghanistan. The war in Iraq was all IEDs and cheap sniper fire, from where you could never be sure. At least here in Afghanistan, the men who considered themselves holy warriors, or mujahideen, would actually engage you in a pitched fight instead of just staging cowardly confrontations, setting roadside bombs and then running away. Yes, IEDs were a problem here, and suicide bombers, too. But usually the insurgents would stay and fight until they were either all dead or out of ammunition, unless they had a very good, very bloody reason for retreating.

Many other troops did contemplate the meaning of 9/11 that morning. Some thought about where they had been five years before. Others debated whether they should leave camp at all that day; maybe it was an anniversary to respect by being extra cautious. Specialist Shawn Passman, a twenty-one-year-old gunner from Hickory, North Carolina, believed the exact opposite.

Today would be a good day to go out and kill a few of 'em for what happened, he thought. Fingers crossed.

On R&R at Fort Drum, Captain Matt Gooding paid a visit to Niagara Falls with his wife, then took in a Bills–Browns game before heading across the ocean and back to business. Stopping at Forward Operating Base Naray en route to PRT Kamdesh, he met with Michael Howard in the lieutenant colonel's office to learn more about the mission Able Troop had already started pursuing in Kamdesh. He was expecting to learn the plan for the squadron's further deployment and get Howard's guidance on Able Troop. Instead, he felt like he was getting quizzed.

"Are you familiar with the term 'COIN'?" Howard inquired. A draft of the Army's counterinsurgency manual had just been updated and pushed out. "What do you know about information operations?"

Gooding thought for a minute about his time in Kosovo, but before he could answer, Howard was talking to him about the weekly newspaper and daily radio programming that 3-71 Cav troops were producing there in Naray.

The test continued. "Do you have any experience overseeing development projects?" Howard asked. "Do you know which funds to use?" Again, Gooding thought about the nation-building projects his unit had worked on years earlier in the war-torn Balkans, but again Howard began describing the myriad efforts undertaken in Kunar and Nuristan by 3-71 Cav. His commander seemed to be enjoying giving him this lecture, so Gooding just listened and let Howard share his knowledge and experiences.

Gooding walked away from the meeting feeling a year behind the squadron and the other leaders in his understanding and execution of the counterinsurgency policy. He didn't know much about the culture of Nuristan, the projects, even which pot of money he was supposed to use. He would have to get his own information operation program up and running. But that was all civil engineering—literally. Howard had never even acknowledged the success of Able Troop's intense combat operations in Helmand Province that summer. While the rest of the squadron was still licking the wounds it had sustained during Operation Mountain Lion, processing the May 5 helicopter crash, and recovering equipment and personnel at Naray, Gooding's troops had spent a grueling summer fighting in some of the most dangerous places in the Taliban's stronghold.

Gooding's briefing with Howard was fairly short, since Howard and the Barbarians were about to head north to a new outpost near Gawardesh. Built high in the mountains, within sight of Hill 2610 and the Pakistan border, it would be called Combat Outpost Lybert.

With Gooding back in Afghanistan, Keating would soon no longer be in charge of Able Troop. Gooding had not yet been to the Kamdesh outpost, so Keating commanded a convoy of Humvees that pulled out from the PRT to link up with him on the morning of September 11, 2006. Keating was driving with two of Berkoff's human-intelligence collectors, Specialist Jessica Saenz and Sergeant Adam Boulio, whom the locals called Adam Khan in a nod to a local song and folktale about a popular bachelor who dies heartbroken. That morning, Saenz and Boulio had met with one of their sources, an Afghan who was plugged in to the local insurgency. He told them that the enemy was setting up on the mountains south of the road and warned them to expect an attack.

Sergeant Dennis Cline was in the fifth of the convoy's five Humvees, sitting in the right rear next to a medic, Specialist Moises Cerezo, from Brooklyn, New York. Shawn Passman sat in the turret with his gun facing backward, aiming behind them. Sergeant First Class Milt Yagel was riding shotgun in front of Cline. Specialist John Barnett drove. It was a gorgeous day in a beautiful land. Passman had joined the Army because he'd never really been anywhere outside of Louisiana and North Carolina, and now here he was, in one of the most breathtakingly scenic corners of the world.

Just a few minutes into their ride, RPGs started sailing toward them. Some of the troops regarded them with nonchalance; for many, the rockets had become part of the everyday ecosystem, like some exotic bird that was native to Afghanistan. Boulio, for his part, was not so relaxed: this was not where they'd anticipated the enemy would be, which made him worry that he and Saenz had either missed some information or been deliberately misled.

Their gunner started firing toward the south as Keating looked back at the other Humvees in the convoy. "Hold on," he said to no one in particular. "Let's see what's going on."

In the back of the convoy, Passman saw an RPG hit a rock wall to the right of the truck, fired from the mountain to the north, on the truck's left, beyond the river. He turned his Mark 19, a 40-millimeter belt-fed automatic grenade launcher, toward the river and fired at the mountain. As he did, he saw two RPGs hit the water. He could hear insurgent AK fire from the mountains to the south, too, on the truck's right.

This is pretty cool, Passman thought. He felt indestructible, as if nothing would or could happen to him. Just try to fuck with me, he thought.

As he drove, Barnett reached his hand back to shake Cerezo's.

"Congrats, Doc, this is your first firefight!" Barnett declared. Just then a bullet pinged off the bulletproof windshield, ricocheting at eye level.

"Oh, shit," Barnett said, turning serious and returning his attention to the task at hand. The convoy stopped. The instructions were to engage with the enemy when fired upon — which was now. As the rest of the convoy seemed to focus on the fire coming from the mountain to the right, Passman fired about a dozen rounds toward the dust cloud on the left. After pummeling the area the RPGs had been fired from, he paused to see if there was any movement there. Cline had a 60-millimeter mortar gun, but one of the insurgents was hitting the truck with small-arms fire, preventing him from opening his door and getting out safely while carrying the bulky weapon. As Yagel leaned forward to look at the southern ridgeline to their right, Cline shifted his body to the right and prepared to open the door. His left hand was on the back of Yagel's seat. Cline turned to the right to look out the window, getting ready to pinpoint the enemy, roll out with his M4 rifle — leaving the 60-millimeter mortar behind — and start firing. At that moment, an RPG hit the right side of the truck, flying through the side wall and exploding on impact.

Everything went black and white and nearly silent. For a moment, each soldier in the Humvee retreated into himself, hearing only his own breathing, the thumping of his heart. That pause was followed by a high-pitched whine that slowly rose as the men revived from the force of the impact and their concussions and became conscious of the world again. The vehicle had an internal Halon fire-protection system that reacted to any spark with an instantaneous emission of chemicals to smother the fire; the resulting fog of retardant added to the soldiers' disorientation. In the haze, all that Cerezo could see at first was Passman's legs in the turret; he thought the gunner had been ripped in half.

Looking again, Cerezo ascertained that the rest of Passman was in fact still there. Cerezo's ears were ringing now. Turning, he saw a big hole in the back of Yagel's seat. He thought Yagel must have been completely obliterated.

As Cline went to reach for his M4, he noticed that his left hand was mangled, shredded, with his pinkie and ring finger hanging off by their tendons. The Humvee was still full of dust and debris.

"Hey, Doc! Doc!" Cline said.

Cerezo looked to his right.

"What, motherfucker?"

"I'm hit," Cline said.

"Where you hit?" asked Cerezo.

"My fucking hand's gone!"

"What?"

"My fucking hand's gone!" He held it up.

"Oh, shit," said Cerezo.

The medic grabbed his aid bag and hopped out of the Humvee. Only then did he realize that the truck was still moving, with no driver behind the wheel: Barnett wasn't there.

The adrenaline rush that nearly every soldier experiences in battle affects each differently. When the hormone adrenaline, or epinephrine, is released, it can constrict air passages and blood vessels, increase the heart rate, cause tunnel vision, relax the bladder, and prompt the nervous system's fight-or-flight response. Adrenaline is such a powerful chemical that people often become quite literally addicted to it, pursuing extreme sports, riding motorcycles, and engaging in other live-on-the-edge activities to feed the addiction. Postdeployment, many soldiers become thrill-seekers for the same reason.

In some individuals, adrenaline excites a self-preservation instinct that can quickly turn into cowardice. In others, it creates clarity and inspires courage. In Keating's Humvee, the gunner's legs were shaking so much that the lieutenant joked, "What the hell are you doing up there, dancing? Keep shooting!"

Barnett had jumped out the driver's door of the last Humvee in the convoy. Cerezo found him behind the vehicle, with his hands on the trunk. "Doc, I'm bailing out," Barnett explained, suffering the effects not only of an adrenaline reaction but also of a head injury: it was apparent that he wasn't quite right. "No, motherfucker!" Cerezo screamed. "Get into the vehicle and stop the truck before it goes off the cliff!"

"Oh, okay," Barnett said, snapping out of it. He climbed into the Humvee and stepped on the brake. Then he grabbed his SAW light machine gun, got out of the truck again, and ran over to a small stone wall on the right side of the road, from whose cover he began firing up at the mountain.

Cerezo meanwhile opened the right rear door of the Humvee, pulled Cline out, and flung him onto the ground, next to the wall. He heard bullets pinging off the Humvee. As the rest of the convoy remained locked in a firefight with the insurgents, Cerezo tied a tourniquet on Cline's forearm and began to assess his other wounds, checking his arteries, ripping off his sleeve.

"Oh, shit," Cerezo exclaimed.

"All right," insisted Cline, "just tell me what the hell's going on! If I'm going to die, I want to know!"

"You're not going to die," Cerezo assured him. But in truth, he wasn't so sure. Shrapnel had taken off Cline's left bicep, and he was bleeding out. Cerezo took the tourniquet off the sergeant's forearm and refastened it around his shoulder area. He put Kerlix gauze in the hole in his arm and wrapped it with Israeli trauma dressing, a multipurpose bandage that applied pressure and sterilized wounds.

Back in the Humvee, Passman saw that Yagel was in the truck and fine, having dodged the RPG by leaning forward toward the windshield. He was on the radio, talking to his first sergeant. Passman now noticed that his own right leg felt wet, and suddenly his back started throbbing.

"Sergeant Yagel, am I bleeding?" he asked.

Yagel himself had chunks of shrapnel in his right shoulder and back. He grabbed Passman's pants, then pulled his hand away. It was covered with blood.

"You're okay," Yagel said. "It's Cline's blood."

From his perch in the turret, Passman began firing at the enemy again. He watched as the senior medic, Sergeant Billy Stalnaker from West Virginia, ran from Humvee to Humvee, taking cover each time and making sure everyone was okay. Todd Yerger followed behind at an unhurried pace, looking as if he were out on a leisurely stroll, with rounds bouncing around him as if they were raindrops.

"Is CAS coming?" Passman asked Yagel, referring to close air support.

"No," Yagel told him. They would have to get out on their own, with no cover.

Next to the stone wall, Cerezo was wondering to himself, What the fuck do I do with Cline's fingers? As he was wrapping them into Cline's hand, Stalnaker ran over to them and hit the wounded man with some morphine. After a minute, Cline got up on his own and stumbled back to the truck.

A sergeant handed Cerezo his M16. "I got one of them," he told the medic. "A kid. Had a gun."

Once all were accounted for and back in the Humvees, the convoy pulled forward a couple of hundred yards, made a U-turn, and headed back toward the Kamdesh PRT. On the way, Cline felt something dripping down his neck. He mentioned it to Cerezo, who checked and saw that some shrapnel had hit the left side of his jugular.

"Don't lose my wedding ring," Cline told him.

After they pulled in to Kamdesh, Cline was put on a stretcher. Netzel ran over to help Passman out of the truck; he was obviously having trouble walking. Netzel touched his leg and came up with a handful of blood. "I think that's Cline's," Passman said. "I think I'm okay." He went to lie down, and Cerezo hurried over. The medic could now see that the gunner had a three-inch gash in his back. Cerezo began to cut off Passman's pants and belt so he could find out what was going on with his leg.

"No, dude, this is a brand-new belt," Passman objected. Cerezo cut it off anyway. The RPG had peppered the gunner's leg with shrapnel from the top of his hip to the bottom of his knee, the fragments ranging from the size of BBs to the size of quarters.

Passman and Cline were medevacked to Forward Operating Base Naray. Amid the haze of his pain, Passman asked a doctor about Cline: "Were you able to save his hand?" "No," the doctor said, in the tone of someone announcing a baseball score. Cline's left hand had been amputated at the elbow.

On their subsequent chopper ride to Bagram, Passman and Cline were placed next to each other. Cline said he wanted to hold Passman's hand with his surviving right hand. He asked Passman about his injuries, about his life. Passman, for his part, couldn't stop looking at Cline's missing arm. They were separated upon landing.

When Gooding was on R&R, Keating had sent him an email: "My puppy is barking," it said.

This was a reference to a statement made by a guest speaker at Fort Drum who had counseled troops on how to prevent posttraumatic stress disorder, or PTSD. The lecturer had likened the typical symptoms of raging emotions, central nervous system reactions, and panicky breathing to "a puppy's barking." Keating's email was his way of signaling that he had hit his limit of combat fatigue and needed to be relieved of command. The timing of Gooding's return would be good, too: Keating was looking forward to his own R&R in October. It would let him clear his head, steady his heart, and come back recharged and ready to lead again.

Howard had told Keating that he wanted him to switch Able Troop's focus from strictly fighting the enemy to counterinsurgency work: more meeting with local leaders and assisting on development projects, less driving around trying to find insurgents. That wasn't so easy: "Nobody told *them*," Keating would quip about the enemy. "The little bastards keep shooting at us every day."

Some of the chatter picked up over the radio indicated that HIG insurgents were not planning on heading to Pakistan for the winter this year. Putting a hopeful spin on it, Army analysts interpreted this as a sign that the enemy was worried that the United States might make progress with its counterinsurgency program during the interim, and that the insurgents might return to a Kamdesh that no longer afforded them refuge; HIG was determined, the analysts believed, to prevent that from happening. Keating felt good about the Americans' chances, but he was also certain that Kamdesh wouldn't be the end of it.

"Ultimately," he wrote to his father, "I think we are going to dismantle this organization"—referring to HIG. "But one thing we're still a little slow on the uptake about is that in this tribal culture, another group will replace them. A group that is just as vulnerable to greed, infighting and murder as the last. We can change the faces and names, [but] we will never change the values and the vision for the future that these people have spent five thousand years developing, perfecting and perpetuating through their common law, religion and teaching."

"I can't wait for you to get here," Keating had emailed Gooding.

The counterinsurgency efforts commenced. Keating, Saenz, and Boulio traveled to the village of Mandigal, to the north of Kamdesh on the way to Barg-e-Matal. Keating planned to join up there with Lieutenant Colonel Tony Feagin to conduct a shura with the village elders, while Saenz and Boulio were hoping to find some locals who might become intelligence sources. Feagin headed the provincial reconstruction team in Mehtar Lam, Laghman Province, and was responsible for all of Nuristan as well. In August, he'd moved into the Kamdesh PRT. While Able Troop was in charge of security at Kamdesh, Feagin was the overall senior mission commander, with a staff of about thirty-five people under him focused on the development of the area, including a civil affairs team, a military engineer officer, and two Army Corps of Engineers civilians.

Saenz and Boulio knew that the best pools of candidates to serve as sources were, first, elders looking to plead their case for a project to be undertaken in their village; and second, twenty- to twenty-five-year-old unemployed, semieducated males, literate and with maybe some high school under their belts but not much more. The likeliest members of this latter group often had something a bit off about them and seemed a touch desperate—perhaps they'd been picked on, or they needed cash to get married or to support a large family. Saenz and Boulio used such weaknesses to persuade these men to work with the United States, offering them a way to feel better about themselves while also helping their nation.

Mandigal was a medium-sized village, typical for the area, with log-and-stone homes stacked one on top of another up the hillside. As the Americans entered the settlement, their eyes were drawn to a wooden overhang resembling a covered bridge, its huge wooden pillars decorated with intricate and ornate carvings, a craft for which the Nuristanis were renowned. Keating and Feagin were met by the elders and escorted to the shura room, in a building next to the main road. Served glasses of scalding tea saturated with sugar and presented with cookies and bowls of raisins, nuts, and jujubes, the U.S. officers and the elders discussed the need for everyone to work together and then went over a prioritized list of projects for the village, the most important of which was a micro-hydroelectric plant.

As Saenz and Boulio, accompanied by First Sergeant Yerger and four of his headquarters soldiers, walked down the main road, villagers gathered on rooftops and in doorways to stare at them. The intelligence collectors made small talk with anyone who seemed even remotely friendly, asking basic questions about the village and the lives of its people, trying to loosen everyone up.

One of the local Afghan policemen told Saenz that he would take her to meet the women of his family if she wanted. Saenz immediately accepted the invitation.

The twenty-five-year-old Saenz had been a student at Texas State University when she watched the second plane hit the tower. Her brother was in an Army Ranger battalion, and her first thought was, What's going to happen to him? In the weeks after 9/11, the two of them often spoke about what she could do next. Saenz wanted to help plan missions, to collect information that would prepare soldiers like her brother for the battlefield. With this in mind, she joined the Army.

Sitting in what appeared to be a biblical-era log-and-stone house in Mandigal, Saenz was a long way from Texas. The villagers gave off the odor of poverty, of dirt and sweat. There was even a faint whiff of urine in the air. The children had distended bellies. They were all very tiny.

"Here," one Afghan woman said to Saenz through her interpreter. "Take my child." She handed her baby to the American.

They were beautiful, the five Afghan women before Saenz—the young mother, her mother and grandmother, her sister and sister-in-law. Their skin tones ranged from fair to deeply tanned, and their eyes were piercing greens and blues. Often when Saenz went out on her intelligence-gathering operations, the locals would tell her that they were descended from Alexander the Great, and these women sure looked it, though experts would have dismissed such claims as folklore.

They were friendly, even warm, these women—hence the young mother's offer to let her hold her baby, Saenz thought. She explained to them what the PRT was all about, how the Americans were there to develop the area and make the Nuristanis' lives better with water-pipe schemes, wells, and schools.

She thought to herself, Sweet! Female sources. Maybe some of them will get upset with their husbands and give me information.

"I work directly for the commander at the camp, on security issues," she told the women. "If you ever see anyone causing problems, let me know."

"Take my child," the young mother said again, though Saenz was already holding her baby.

And then she realized what the woman meant.

" 'Take my child with you,' " the translator elaborated. "Take him with you and raise him in America."

Saenz tried to explain how important it was that the baby be raised by his own parents, how life in the village would improve someday soon, but she wasn't sure even *she* believed that.

Those who write romantically about the military often refer to bands of brothers. But as anyone who has had a sibling knows, brothers fight, and the officers of Able Troop were no exception. Keating had been looking forward to Gooding's arrival. The two were roughly the same age — Keating was twenty-seven, Gooding was thirty — and had attended rival high schools in Maine. Their parents knew many of the same people.

Matt Gooding came from a family steeped in military service. Both of his grandfathers were veterans of World War II, and both of his parents were Vietnam veterans — his dad a Cavalry officer who'd done eighteen months in Da Nang, his mother an Army nurse. In his sophomore year at Ohio University, Gooding, then a criminology major thinking about a career with the DEA, the FBI, or the U.S. Marshals, had looked around and seen a hundred or so other students on the same exact track. So instead he'd taken the road less traveled, at least at Ohio University: he'd joined ROTC, and then he'd just kept on going. On September 11, 2001, Gooding had been in Kosovo with the 3rd Infantry Division. He'd decided to stay in the military beyond his four-year commitment so he could lead a company in combat against those responsible for the attack.

Keating thought Gooding was a good storyteller and a decent guy, fun to talk to one on one, but when it came to combat decisions, his captain drove him crazy. "We fight over every aspect of leadership and the direction of the troop," Keating complained to his father. He was convinced that Gooding was too conservative when it came to using American force.

The truth was, Gooding never really felt comfortable in the mountains. Up here, you never know who you're shooting at, he mused. Even before his immersion in counterinsurgency doctrine, he had been cautious about authorizing his troops to fire or to initiate any "show of force" that might end up killing civilians. He and his men were there, he felt, to win over the local populace.

The problem was, the PRT kept getting attacked: by the fall of 2006, enemy strikes were coming three times a week on average. A rocket missed Command Sergeant Major Byers's helicopter one day by a matter of only seconds—a close call that led command at Forward Operating Base Naray to require more planning before any helicopters were sent in to the Kamdesh PRT, and also to encourage night flights. The PRT was getting lit up, and troops were getting maimed and killed; as far as a lot of the men were concerned, civilians who turned a blind eye toward the insurgency were the enemy as well. Many of the officers felt they had to do something, and Keating was all about doing.

In Gooding's view, Keating personified what troop commanders often referred to as "the Fighting XO"—the second-in-command who was continually exasperated by the "failings" of his immediate superior, a not-uncommon type in any walk of life. Whenever an opportunity arose that would allow him to rally troops and lead them on a convoy or to recon a road, Keating was always the first to volunteer. He didn't seem to be able to get over the fact that he was no longer a platoon leader of men but instead an executive officer in charge of logistics and maintenance, a job that seemed to bore him no end.

Keating's eagerness could, Gooding believed, get the better of him. Within a week of the captain's return, someone with a flashlight was spotted one night on the mountain above the camp. Keating rushed to the command post. "Request permission to engage the enemy," he said to Gooding.

Gooding thought Keating was overreacting because of the large fire-fight the Barbarians had experienced in August—and it wasn't just Keating, either; many of the troops seemed to be on edge, waiting for the next big attack. Gooding himself, however, was decidedly *not* on edge, having just arrived back in country from his R&R, and he told Keating to hold fire until the individual with the flashlight could be definitively identified as a threat. No weapon was ever observed on that occasion, so Gooding never gave permission to engage.

The captain was abiding by the Rules of Engagement, following what he thought of as the steady example of the late Lieutenant Colonel Fenty. He knew he was more conservative in some of his decisions than Keating himself would have been, but he saw his subordinate as still having the young soldier's "I am invincible" attitude, with a dash of the teenage rebel thrown in for good measure.

On another night, a Special Forces team was departing from the camp under the cover of darkness. A guard post witnessed several people moving into a position above the road leading back to Naray. It looked as if they were setting an ambush. Keating organized a patrol and asked Gooding for permission to fire on the Afghans to clear them out. From the road, Keating could not identify any specific weapons or any hostile intent, so Gooding, once again observing the Rules of Engagement, denied him permission to fire. Keating's annoyance was clear in his voice—and Gooding didn't like it. He wasn't fond of making decisions like this, but he also didn't want to kill the members of some family out looking for their lost goat.

A guard at Observation Post Warheit then called in: other enemies, definitively with weapons and a radio, were peering down the mountain.

Gooding now reversed his decision, persuaded that the insurgents above were controlling confederates below. "Permission to engage," he told Keating.

Keating's men fired. Both sides shot back and forth; within forty-five minutes, Apaches were on the scene. The insurgents took cover in the homes of Kamdeshis, and the Apaches took the fight to them. Intelligence would later come in indicating that several of the insurgents had been wounded and were subsequently evacuated to Pakistan. More immediately, however, the troops of 3-71 Cav became aware that innocent Afghans had also been hurt in the action: six civilians, aged three to forty, had been cut up by shrapnel from the Apache's 30-millimeter barrage. Their families took the wounded to Observation Post Warheit, and 3-71 Cav had them medevacked to Bagram.

The next day, nearly three dozen Kamdesh elders came down to the PRT to express their anger over the incident. They met with Feagin and Gooding in a building that was still under construction.

"You told us when you came here that you would not hurt innocent and peaceful people," said one, speaking through a translator.[27] "You have big guns and helicopters with good technology, surely you can tell the difference between those who are innocent and those who are not. You told us if we helped you, the Americans would not harm us. We are prisoners in our villages now!"

---

[27] Journalist Matthew Cole attended this shura and wrote about it in an influential Salon.com story entitled "Watching Afghanistan Fall" (February 2007). The dialogue here is taken from that story.

Feagin—head of the PRT effort—explained that there had been "no intent to target anyone but our enemy. If the enemy continues to fight us, many more will die. I am certain."

At that moment, gunfire sounded in the distance.

"This is part of the problem," Feagin said, motioning in the direction of the fire. "The only thing the enemy can bring is fear, intimidation, and death." He reminded the elders that the six wounded Kamdeshis had been transported to Bagram and were receiving exemplary medical care.

"Mack" took this opportunity to weigh in. Mack was a CIA case officer who had come to the Kamdesh base with some others from his world; they'd built a little cabin there and started their own information-collection business. Most of the time, Mack tried to keep a low profile. This was not one of those times. A muscular former Special Forces soldier, he told the assembled group a story about a neighbor he'd once had at his farm back in the States, whose ill-behaved dog posed a problem. Things got so bad, he said, that he had to ask his neighbor to put the dog down. When the neighbor refused, Mack took matters into his own hands. The implication was, of course, that he and his friends would likewise put down the bad dogs of the valley—the insurgents—if the Kamdesh elders didn't take care of them themselves.

The story did not go over well. Bad dogs? The elders seemed revolted by the metaphor: dogs were reviled in this part of the world. In some cases, insurgents were brothers or sons to these elders, and their actions were motivated by the desire to protect their village. These were not rabid beasts. Don't use analogies, the intelligence collector Adam Boulio reminded himself. They don't translate.

A few days after the shura, Boulio went to the Papristan section of Kamdesh Village to photograph the damage caused by the Apaches and to record the names of those villagers who intended to file claims. He took pictures of bullet-riddled walls and broken windows, but as the hours passed, more and more Kamdeshis began making what seemed to him obviously bogus claims, holding up shoddy mattresses, broken washbasins, and other junk and blaming what was clearly ordinary squalor on the helicopters. Boulio took it all down anyway, noting which losses he thought were real.

Despite Boulio's attempts to smooth things over with the Kamdeshis, Gooding would come to think of the Apache attack and the ill-fated shura as calamitous setbacks in the counterinsurgency effort. In his view, 3-71 Cav never managed to repair the damage these incidents caused.

In a reflective mood, Ben Keating wrote to his father, "I've struggled during quiet times with the question of my mortality. I don't fear death and during my most honest moments I really don't assume its nearness to me. . . . I still believe that God has a plan for my life that extends beyond this deployment; but I'm also very confident that this is a path He has set me on and that I'm treating it in a manner He asks of me. When the bullets start flying all of those thoughts are banished and I just act — further evidence to me that He is with me."

Whether or not the Lord was with Ben Keating, many of the officers of 3-71 Cav increasingly felt that some of the Americans with *them* were leading the mission down an infernal path. No one doubted the motives of Snyder and his Special Forces troops or any of the other special-operations teams that moved in and out of the region. (Mack and his CIA officers were another, and bizarre, matter.) But their actions were sometimes messy, and 3-71 Cav troops had to clean up after them.

There was nothing 3-71 Cav could do about that, however. At Forward Operating Base Naray, a call would come in that "Task Force Blue" — a code name for Navy SEALs — would be arriving in a certain area in two hours, and the 3-71 troops would just have to try to stay out of the way. Questions about the propriety of specific missions were then left to be answered by conventional forces that had had nothing to do with the operations themselves — some of which involved acts committed over the border in Pakistan. CIA teams and Special Forces troops would kill men who they said were insurgent leaders, and who in most cases almost surely were — but when they weren't, it was 3-71 Cav that felt the heat.

For some, collateral damage was a fact of warfare that was as acceptable as the recoil of a gun.

Led by Staff Sergeant Adam Sears, the Hoosier who'd been on the landing zone when Fenty's Chinook crashed, four Humvees containing members of Able Troop's 2nd Platoon left the Kamdesh outpost one October day to investigate a tip that there was an IED under a small bridge about a mile down the road to the east. The squad found nothing at the location in question, so the drivers began turning their vehicles around to return to the base. It was a difficult process, as they had to hit the sweet spot in steering: the road was narrow, but turning the front wheels too sharply could lock up the truck's gearbox.

As fate would have it, one of the sergeants did exactly that, so Sears sent Sergeant Nick Anderson back to the outpost in another vehicle to fetch the particular tool needed to work on the gearbox; he was accompanied by Michael Hendy, whose own Humvee kept stalling. As Anderson made the tight turn in to the gate of the outpost, his Humvee's gearbox seized up as well, and another truck had to come tow it out of the entry control point. Anderson and Hendy grabbed two other Humvees, the proper tool, and a mechanic and went back down the road to where the others were waiting.

It was a gorgeous day, and the men were enjoying the warmth of the sun on their faces. Sometimes it was easy to get lost in those bucolic surroundings and forget the existence of the enemy—and sometimes the men needed to do just that, needed to seek refuge in a momentary lapse in memory, though generally the troops were alert, knowing that otherwise they would make a ripe target.

And make a target they did. Within minutes, an RPG exploded near the Humvees. The troops scurried behind the trucks, taking cover and returning fire. The insurgents were up the mountain next to the road. "Where the fuck is Bozman?" Sears shouted. "Where the fuck is Bozman?" As the fire-support soldier for the platoon, Private First Class Nathan Bozman, then in a different Humvee, was in charge of calling in the grids to the mortar team at the Kamdesh outpost. He calculated the proper grid data to give to the mortarmen, after which they pummeled the hills with 120-millimeter mortar fire, shredding the enemy's general location. The engagement ended, and Sears led the platoon back to the outpost.

The next day, Captain Matt Gooding was told by some of his troops that two local men who worked at the outpost hadn't shown up that morning because their nephew, who was about eleven years old, had been killed by the U.S. mortars fired the day before. The locals said the boy had been innocently walking his cow and had no connection to the insurgents at all—he was just a blameless child, killed by the foreigners who were there purportedly to help them, to protect them.

This was the first anyone from 3-71 Cav had heard about a little boy's having been killed in the firefight, and besides bothering Gooding on a personal, emotional level, it concerned him as a commander. Such a killing could have a huge impact on us, Gooding thought. What if tomorrow *no* workers show up? What if the incident turns all of Kamdesh Village against us?

Sears, Bozman, and the others involved in the firefight felt no remorse. They'd been attacked, and they'd returned fire. It was as simple as that. The bad guys were the ones responsible for the kid's death.

It was different for Gooding. While he hadn't personally fired the mortars, he'd approved the action. It was his first experience, albeit indirect, of killing a civilian, and while he knew that Able Troop had fully abided by the Rules of Engagement, the child's death still upset him. Yes, it was likely that the kid had been helping the insurgents by carrying RPGs and ammo. After all, at least five minutes had passed between the initial ambush and the mortars' being fired, and Gooding couldn't imagine that the boy would have just continued walking with his cow in the same direction from which RPGs were being fired. That, however, was just a hunch, and either way, he felt horrible about the whole thing. Indeed, the grief he felt was as powerful as it might have been if he'd killed one of his own children's classmates, or if he'd run over the boy himself with his car. He emailed his wife, expressing his despair.

"It's not the same," she emailed back. "You're not to blame. You and your men didn't tell the bad guys to ambush you. You had to defend yourselves."

Higher-level officers in the field had some discretionary funds—through the Commanders' Emergency Response Program, or CERP—and for this type of casualty, the Pentagon-approved condolence payment was approximately $3,000 U.S. per lost life. The Kamdesh elders okayed this grant to the uncles, and two days later, with the utmost solemnity, Gooding paid them that sum in the local currency.

As winter approached, Gooding assigned Netzel to supervise the buildup of the camp in preparation for what would assuredly be tough weather, made tougher for those at the PRT by the fact that in the coming months, their post would occasionally be impossible to reach by either air or road. Phones and Internet service were among the camp's few truly modern conveniences, communication lines being a high priority, but otherwise it was a bare-bones affair. In dire need of improvement were the preexisting traditional—and uncomfortable—Nuristan buildings, as well as the dozen or so bunkers topped with lumber that were used as barracks. Netzel hired local Afghans to build new structures made of wood, concrete, cement, and rock. Locals and soldiers installed bunk beds with two-inch-thick mattresses, an outhouse with three toilets, and makeshift urinals—informally called piss-tubes—here and there throughout the site. Some problems Netzel couldn't do much about: the flea infestation was so bad, for example, that many 3-71 Cav troops took to wearing flea collars fastened around their belt loops. There were also a few improvised pleasures, though. The Landay-Sin River was outside the wire—meaning it was off limits except on patrols—but sometimes troops would ask a local laborer to go to the riverbank, fill up a water jug, and bring it back to the post, where they would then hang it from a tree. It would bask in the sun all day, and just before sunset, the men could stand under the jug and enjoy a lukewarm shower. That was what passed for luxury at the outpost.

Subterranean homesick blues: the early flea-laden bunkers for troops at PRT Kamdesh. *(Photo courtesy of Ross Berkoff)*

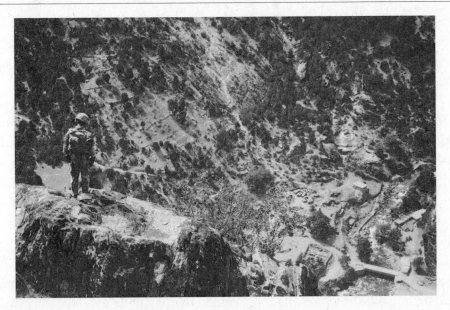

The construction and fortification of the base in Kamdesh had begun in earnest by the fall of 2006, but there was nothing troops could do about its position at the bottom of the Kamdesh Valley. In this photo, Staff Sergeant Lance Blind of 3rd Platoon, Able Troop, looks for enemy bodies after a firefight the night before. *(Photograph by Jeremiah Ridgeway)*

PRT Kamdesh, fall 2006. *(Photo courtesy of Matthew Netzel)*

Even before the weather turned dreadful, helicopter pilots were reluctant to make the journey to the Kamdesh PRT to bring supplies, spooked by the near miss involving Byers's chopper. At Forward Operating Base Naray, therefore, Captain Pete Stambersky made other plans.

Stambersky commanded the forward support unit assigned to the area. Delta Company—attached to 3-71 Cav from the 710th Brigade Support Battalion—comprised about a hundred soldiers who worked as cooks, mechanics, welders, truck drivers, petroleum specialists, and logistics experts. To resupply PRT Kamdesh, Stambersky and his Distribution Platoon leader, First Lieutenant David Heitner, packed five Afghan trucks and two Toyota pickups with needed items. The trucks, driven by locals and nicknamed jingle trucks for the sound made by the colorful decorative chains and pendants hanging from their bodies, were loaded with food, water, building materials, and generators. Because insurgent attacks along the road had been increasing—it seemed that virtually every convoy that passed was being assaulted—Howard told Stambersky to take along a reconnaissance platoon, which brought his total number of gun trucks from six to eleven. To Stambersky, the additional manpower and firepower were welcome, but they also felt ominous.

October 17, 2006, dawned on eastern Afghanistan with a clear sky and temperatures in the sixties. Stambersky instructed the drivers of the jingle trucks to take the rear: he didn't trust them, and he knew that if they weren't in back, it would be easy enough for any one of them to stop his jingle truck and block the Humvees from passing, thus setting the Americans up for an ambush. It was a decision that Michael Howard would later criticize, convinced as he was that their being in the rear made the already vulnerable jingle trucks even more so.

Slowly, steadily, the convoy moved north. Efforts to reconstruct the twenty-five miles of road notwithstanding, the landscape remained perilous. And there was, as always, the enemy. The convoy passed through what was now being called Ambush Alley, where some MPs were already watching over the road. Just past the Gawardesh Bridge, Stambersky and the convoy stopped briefly to pay a local teacher for some work he had done on his school, then resumed their journey to the PRT, approaching the hamlet of Saret Koleh to their right.

Stambersky regularly carried a picture of Jesus in his front pocket; his father had been given the icon in 1948 for his First Communion. On his way to the Kamdesh[28] Valley, the captain patted his chest to assure himself that he had the picture.

It wasn't there.

In the rear seat of Stambersky's Humvee, his forward observer, excited about his impending R&R, couldn't contain himself: "Just nine days till leave and I'll be getting some ass!" he yelled. Stambersky and his driver both told the soldier to shut up—"You're jinxing us," Stambersky said.

RPGs just then began erupting on either side of the convoy, followed by small-arms fire. The vehicles kept pushing ahead. An RPG flew by Stambersky's right window and struck a Humvee driven by some of the Barbarians, detonating the truck's load of ammo. The Humvee burst into flames as the troops—finance guys, carrying a bag of petty cash for Able Troop—spilled out onto the ground and ran behind a rock.

Many vehicles were destroyed in the October 17, 2006, ambush on a convoy on its way to the new outpost. *(Photo courtesy of Pete Stambersky)*

---

[28] The valley in which the outpost was located was actually named Nichingal, but few Americans knew that or referred to it that way. For simplicity's sake, this book will call it the Kamdesh Valley.

Stambersky looked at his gunner, whose .50-caliber machine gun was jamming. An RPG exploded to the left of them, rocking their Humvee and filling it with black plumes even as it continued driving. "Get on the SAW!" Stambersky ordered the gunner, referring to his M249 light machine gun. He then called to each surviving truck to check for casualties and damage. Everyone was okay, but since they couldn't leave the burning truck behind, the convoy stopped, and the battle was joined. Stambersky's forward observer informed the tactical operations center at Forward Operating Base Naray that the convoy was under attack, and the operations center then requested Apaches from Bagram, but the air support would surely take at least forty-five minutes to get there, and likely much longer. Soon, the jingle trucks—all in the back of the convoy, unprotected by and separate from the Americans—began exploding and catching on fire.

From the PRT, Gooding sent out a QRF—quick reaction force—to help Stambersky and his men as they returned fire. Meanwhile, Stambersky's forward observer got on the radio and called for a B-1 bomber. B-1s were regularly dispatched from the U.S. base on the island of Diego Garcia in the Indian Ocean; they would fly around particular regions on shifts, waiting for calls such as this one.

When the QRF approached the ambush location from the Kamdesh PRT twenty minutes later, its members relayed the enemy's coordinates to Stambersky, who shared the ten-digit grid with his forward observer, who gave it to the B-1 pilot.

"We need your initials," the pilot said.

"P.S.," Pete Stambersky said into the transmitter, "drop the bomb!"

A two-thousand-pounder fell.

Then another.

Now, at last, the Apaches got there; they provided cover while Stambersky and his men removed the shell of the burnt-out Humvee from the road so others could pass. In the process, the captain noticed the remains of a Soviet vehicle in the nearby river. For a split second, the metal skeleton reminded him of a couple of different American armored trucks: the V-100 Commando, the M1117 Guardian. Another war—or not.

Passing the QRF on its way, the convoy continued on to the Kamdesh PRT.

It was funny: everyone in Stambersky's convoy had been dreading the trip to the now notoriously hard-to-get-to PRT, but that night it was home sweet home as the troops—many of whom had never had any previous contact with the enemy—shuffled around with expressions of relief and shock on their faces. No smiles, just a muted gratitude at being safe. Better to be here than out there. It was amazing that no one in the convoy had been killed that day.

Stambersky knew that such relief was momentary and illusory. PRT Kamdesh was small and poorly situated. If you looked up, as he did now, all you could see was mountains until your neck was craned back and you could finally see sky. Tomorrow they would assess the damage. Not one of the jingle trucks had made it to Kamdesh; all had been destroyed and would have to be pushed into the river to clear the narrow road. Later, when men from 3-71 Cav went to remove the remnants of the burning trucks—which had been bringing them what were to have become the first hot meals that many of them had had in months—they could smell charred steaks and chicken that had cooked in the conflagration from the attack.

When the base was being set up, any officer who referred to "Camp Kamdesh" or "Combat Outpost Kamdesh" would quickly find himself on the receiving end of Howard's ire.

"Goddang it!" he would snap in the middle of meetings. "For the last time, it's not an outpost! It's a goddang PRT!"

But the September 11, 2006, attack on Keating's convoy, and others like it, made it clear to the commanders that the threat to their convoys and to "PRT Kamdesh" was too great, and too frequent, to enable the base to become a true PRT. Feagin's PRT staff and 3-71 Cav couldn't exactly start building wells, schools, or water-pipe systems if troops and workers were going to keep being attacked with RPGs every time they left the wire. Security was just too frail.

In fact, those up the command chain who were in charge of PRTs would later insist that Kamdesh had never been a definitive location. Yet the 3-71 Cav troops were convinced that it was precisely in order to establish a PRT that they had been working so hard to set up the outpost. In any case, the PRT staff members at the Kamdesh outpost were told in October that when their rotation ended in February, they wouldn't be replaced. Moreover, Lieutenant Colonel Feagin would be leaving in November,

and his replacement would locate at a PRT in Kala Gush, in Nuristan —
roughly sixty miles away from Kamdesh, straight-line distance — which
would be the only PRT for the province. Whatever plans may have
existed for PRT Kamdesh simply were not to be realized. Gooding and
others at the base, which the troops had now started calling Camp Kamdesh instead, would still work on development projects, still focus on
counterinsurgency, but they would soon be doing so on their own, without the help of the official PRT staff.

CHAPTER 12

Matthias the Macedonian and the LMTV

Many of Michael Howard's officers resented him. They thought the lieutenant colonel was all about his own image and his own accomplishments, all about building the northernmost camp in Afghanistan because that demonstrated what a warrior he was. In October, he made a decision that turned that resentment into downright fury, though the men under him never risked charges of insubordination by expressing it directly.

Although more than a quarter million dollars' worth of work had been poured into repairing the road from Naray to Camp Kamdesh, it remained dangerous. A September 2006 analysis had revealed at least sixteen problems limiting, if not in fact precluding, the passage of any vehicle larger than an uparmored Humvee—about 7.5 feet wide, around 4 tons. A more detailed assessment by 3-71 Cav, undertaken little more than a month later, looked at just that part of the road which led from Kamdesh to Mirdesh, not even a tenth of the way to Naray. It identified twelve separate "high-risk" areas that would "greatly hinder trafficability to vehicles larger than a small jingle truck."

And yet that same month, Howard informed his officers that he wanted to send a truck larger than that—8 feet wide, more than 8 tons—from Naray to Kamdesh. He wanted to make sure that 3-71 Cav was 100 percent self-sufficient by ground, he said.

"We're going to drive an LMTV up there, and we're going to get it done," he told Captain Pete Stambersky, referring to a light medium tactical vehicle, a large truck that could carry cargo weighing more than two tons. Because enemy attacks on the road had been increasing, the lieutenant colonel suggested that they go at night. Stambersky laughed. He didn't think his commander was serious.

"Fuck, Pete," Howard said. "Are you with me? Are we going to get this done, or not?"

"Roger, sir," Stambersky replied.

Jesus, Stambersky thought. He really wants to drive an LMTV up that road just to prove it can be done. It doesn't make any sense.

Major Thomas Sutton, who had replaced Timmons as 3-71 Cav's XO in June, shared Stambersky's reservations, knowing that an LMTV weighed around nine tons all by itself, with just fuel and crew. And yet Sutton also understood Howard's intentions. All of the Afghan contractors' jingle trucks were getting shot up; the Army needed to put U.S. trucks, big military might, on the road for resupply. Indeed, it was to make such deliveries easier that Combat Outpost Kamdesh had been put near the road in the first place. Helicopters were getting fired upon, and pilots were increasingly reluctant to fly in the area. Now that repairs had been made to the road, Howard wanted to see if an LMTV could make it up there. Sutton assumed that another part of it was "power projection," as the military called it — flexing muscle to impress the locals.

Captain Frank Brooks of the Barbarians was directed to provide security for the LMTV convoy. Brooks agreed with Stambersky that taking the immense truck to Kamdesh was a bad idea, but he had his orders, and he meant to follow them. Stambersky's troops removed the vehicle's grab rails, bed rails, and rearview mirrors to limit the number of parts that could snag on a rock. They made the eight-foot-wide truck as light and as lean as they could. They worked out a strategy for who would drive and when, as well as how to protect the personnel and equipment. Brooks and Stambersky decided that the trip would take place during the day, so the drivers would have maximum visibility when making their way over the most treacherous and narrow sections of the road. They briefed Sutton about their plan, then Howard.

"I don't want you driving during daylight hours," Howard told them. He was afraid the LMTV would provide the enemy with an irresistible target.

Stambersky later approached Howard near the squadron's operations center.

"Hello, sir," he said. "Can I talk to you?"

"Yeah, Pete," Howard said. "What about?"

"I would be remiss if I didn't talk to you about the dangers involved in driving an LMTV to Kamdesh," Stambersky said. "Especially driving at night. Driving during the day is one thing, but driving that route in the LMTV for the first time at night is going to get somebody killed."

"Pete, we can do it," Howard insisted. "We're going to get it done."

"Sir, I don't think it's the safest thing to do to drive that thing at night," Stambersky said.

"We're going to get it done," Howard repeated. And then he walked away.

Before sunrise on October 29, the convoy pulled out from Forward Operating Base Naray. Stambersky had assigned First Lieutenant David Heitner to command the group, Sergeant Jeffrey Williams to drive the LMTV, and Specialist Tim Martin to serve as its gunner.

Martin sat in the turret clutching an M240B machine gun. This was a smaller and lighter weapon than the options he normally would have gone with—an MK19 grenade launcher or a .50-caliber machine gun—because he didn't want to add any more weight to the LMTV than he had to. He, Heitner, and Williams had limited the gear they packed for the same reason, though they had brought along some nonstandard infrared chemical lights just in case of a rollover—which they agreed was a pretty likely possibility. Still, Martin wasn't nervous—on the contrary, the Kentuckian thought of himself as the most qualified gunner in Stambersky's unit, and he hated to be left out of missions.

The first leg of the convoy was completed in pitch-black darkness, but the sun rose after they stopped at the bridge to Gawardesh. Howard had been upset that the entire mission wouldn't be conducted as he wanted, at night, but ultimately he had given in to Stambersky's insistence—and Brooks's—that that would be an impossible challenge.

At the Gawardesh bridge, the convoy dropped off about a dozen troops to set up mortar tubes as protection for the convoy if the need arose. Williams didn't think he could drive the LMTV any faster than ten miles per hour, not only because of the road's instability but because numerous impediments—tree stumps, stacks of lumber—narrowed it in places. Williams was the most qualified driver in the squadron, with over fifteen years' experience driving vehicles weighing two and a half tons or more, and more than a thousand hours' driving in blackout conditions. If anyone could navigate this route, it was Williams. Even he wasn't sure it was a route that *could* be navigated by anyone. Still, he had no option but to try.

The convoy pashed west, passing Bazgal, when Afghans with weapons were spotted in the mountains across the river. Martin laid down some fire, and the insurgents shot back with small arms and RPGs.

Specialist Jesse Steele, the gunner in the second-to-last Humvee in the convoy, fired his .50-caliber across the river, not realizing that rounds were also coming from directly above them, on the mountain to his left. An RPG hit the left side of Steele's truck, momentarily knocking him unconscious. When he opened his eyes, he was lying on his back, with his left leg twisted behind and under him. The Humvee was still moving. Specialist Javier Valdez tried to help the gunner up, but Steele had no feeling in that leg and couldn't stand. No matter: straining, he hauled himself back into the turret and resumed fire across the river as the convoy continued west.

At a safe point in the road, Brooks stopped the group and took inventory, checking to see who was hurt and who wasn't. The injuries meant that Brooks would have to reorganize his troops for the remainder of the trip. Since Steele couldn't stand up on his own, Brooks took him out of the Humvee turret and had him trade places with Sergeant Justin Pellak, in the rearmost truck.

Forty-five minutes later, the convoy passed Kamu and stopped again. Williams was having difficulty negotiating the LMTV over the narrow road and had had to slow down to a crawl, no faster than three miles per hour. From across the river, two insurgents fired a Dushka at the Americans, their heavy machine gun letting fly piercing metal at the Humvees and the LMTV. Martin responded with his machine gun. From mountains on either side of the convoy, dozens of other insurgents now began firing AKs and other weapons. An RPG hit right in front of the LMTV, and rounds started tweaking off the Humvees' roofs. The lead Humvee took an RPG to its front, knocking the gunner, Specialist Ryan Coulter, around in his turret and spraying his hands and face with shrapnel. Bleeding and in pain, Coulter returned fire across the river to his right with his .50-caliber, then grabbed his M249 SAW with his left arm and fired it up on the mountain to his left.

In the rear truck, Steele thought, Shit, here we go again. Just then the

Humvee's gunner, Specialist Cuong Vo, a slight Vietnamese-American, fell out of the turret and onto Steele's lap, not moving, a bloody bullet hole in his helmet.

"Vo's dead," Steele said, lifting the gunner off his lap by his vest and pushing him over to the side as he pulled himself up into the turret and started shooting Vo's 240.

In the LMTV, Martin heard the whistle of an RPG coming at him from above, from the closer mountain to his left. As he turned to look, the RPG exploded just in front of his gunner's shield, peppering his face, neck, and shoulder with forty-seven pieces of shrapnel. He fell backward into the LMTV, unconscious and covered with blood.

"We got a KIA!" yelled Heitner.

But Martin had not in fact been killed in action, and a few seconds later he awoke, grabbed his helmet, and got back in his turret. He resumed firing at the enemy across the river.

Steele was firing, too, when he heard a terrible scream from inside his Humvee. He looked down and was surprised to see Vo looking right back at him.

"What's going on?" Vo asked.

"Are you okay? You just got shot in the fucking head!"

"Yeah, I know," Vo said. It turned out that the bullet had pierced only the outer layer of his Kevlar helmet and not actually penetrated his head.

The LMTV hit a narrow spot in the road where the route turned to the left. The rear passenger-side tire smashed off a portion of the road, and the LMTV wobbled but pushed forward. About two hundred yards farther on, the rear tire detached another chunk of road, but Williams kept the vehicle from rolling over and continued moving.

Finally, they reached the outpost. In total, six troops were wounded, including Martin, Coulter, Steele, and Vo. It was a bloody mess, an assignment that enraged officers and enlisted men alike—all of whom were convinced that Howard's muscle flexing was not worth the risk to their lives and the lives of their brothers.

At Combat Outpost Kamdesh, Williams inspected the LMTV. The two front tires had been shot and needed to be replaced. Stambersky and Brooks decided to leave the LMTV where it was until the replacements could be delivered.

Williams was relieved; a return trip would be extremely dangerous, he thought. After heading back to Naray by Humvee, he told Command Sergeant Major Byers that there was no way the LMTV could come back until some serious repairs were made to those bad spots on the road.

Over the next few weeks, Williams drove a Humvee in several more convoys to and from Kamdesh, all in blackout conditions. On the second trip, a vehicle manned by maintenance personnel went off a cliff. On the fourth, another Humvee did the same thing in the exact same location. No one was seriously hurt on either occasion. On each successive trip, Williams saw the road get narrower and narrower due to rain. Boulders fell in the roadway; the mud caused vehicles to slide.

By now, his entire chain of command was asking Williams if the LMTV could make it back to Naray. Every time he was asked, he said, "No, the road needs to be fixed first." But no matter how many times he said it, further repairs to that fragile road didn't seem to be on anyone else's agenda.

By November of 2006, there had already been two vehicle rollovers on the narrow road to Combat Outpost Kamdesh. *(Photo courtesy of Ross Berkoff)*

*   *   *

By the end of October, commanders at Forward Operating Base Naray and in Jalalabad were so concerned about enemy attacks in the Kamdesh Valley that the number of supply runs getting through to Combat Outpost Kamdesh had dwindled down to close to none. Pilots didn't want to fly there, and the leaders of convoys didn't want to drive there, either. It got to the point where Gooding and the soldiers from Able Troop had to ration their food and water: they were down to one "meal ready to eat" apiece per day.

On his return from R&R, Keating commanded a convoy from Naray to Kamdesh without getting ambushed. Not only was this great news in itself, but it also meant that a full complement of supplies reached the outpost: ammunition, food and water, and wood and other goods needed to build roofs for barracks. Troops cheered Keating as if he were Audie Murphy and Neil Armstrong rolled into one.

His misgivings about the war's purpose remained, but Keating himself was experiencing something of a rebirth. During his R&R, his romance with Heather McDougal had intensified, and whereas at one point he had talked to Berkoff about joining Military Intelligence, he had now decided on a new career path: he would transfer to a U.S. Army base in South Korea to serve as a specialty platoon leader, an advanced position that would enable him once again to lead a platoon of troops, which he missed doing.

Back at Kamdesh, he led a very one-sided drubbing of some insurgents who were attempting to set up a rocket to fire upon U.S. helicopters. Keating and the platoon killed four enemy fighters and wounded at least ten more. The irony is that *I* was the catalyst for the fight, Keating thought. The same guy who couldn't find a reason for this war anymore rallied a platoon of soldiers, coordinated the attack, and ran around like a wild man with machine guns shooting over his head. Even success was bittersweet. He couldn't wait to leave Afghanistan.

His were not the only blue thoughts. All of Able Troop seemed to be in horrible spirits, as Keating saw it. Every soldier in Able believed he'd be killed the next time he rolled out of the gate — or if not killed, at least wounded in a way that would forever make life a miserable challenge. The men were fired upon nearly every time out, they took casualties regularly — they were like zombies. Leaving the outpost could sure feel like driving into Hell. Toward the end of October, First Lieutenant Candace Mathis and her team of military police were teamed up with Able Troop's 3rd Platoon when they had to push through a complex ambush. In the United States, politicians sometimes speculated that female soldiers might not be strong enough for such duty, or that male soldiers might get too emotional when their female colleagues were attacked, but those notions didn't match the reality of the experience of 3-71 Cav. Actually, with their AT4 rocket launchers, the MPs had stronger firepower than many in the scout platoon; everyone survived this attack relatively unharmed.

The same could not be said for Private First Class Jason Westbrook, who, on November 4, was a gunner in another ambushed convoy. Shrapnel from an RPG clipped off one of his hands, but he didn't even know it until he climbed back into the turret, went to reach for the trigger—it was a butterfly trigger, needing two hands—and saw his right hand dangling from its wrist.

Specialist Steven Dorrell attempts to comfort Private First Class Jason Westbrook after Able Troop's 3rd Platoon was ambushed on November 4, 2006. *(Photo courtesy of Jeremiah Ridgeway)*

When the call came in the next night that another team of insurgents was attempting to dig in a rocket, Ben Keating saw a chance not only to kill the enemy but also to motivate his men. He specifically chose Westbrook's platoon to take with him, hoping that a successful mission might undo some of the damage of the previous day. His strategy seemed to work, though it didn't do Westbrook himself much good: the wound would stay with him forever.

Keating had just finished reading *The Afghan Campaign,* a newly published historical novel by Steven Pressfield that tells the story of Alexander the Great's invasion of Afghanistan, as seen through the eyes of a young Macedonian soldier named Matthias. It had a great impact on the lieutenant from Maine. Alexander the Great "speaks of will—our own and the enemy's," Matthias recalls. "The foe, he declares, has no chance of overcoming us in the field. But if he can sap our resolution by his doggedness, his relentlessness; if he can appall us by his acts of barbarity, he can, if not defeat us, then prevent us from defeating him. Our will must master the enemy's. Our resolve must outlast his."[29]

"We've been up here for less than seven months," Keating told the journalist Matthew Cole when he visited the outpost. "We have a couple of thousand years of history against us," he said, holding up his dog-eared copy of *The Afghan Campaign*. "You do the math."

Still, that was as far as he'd go in public. All day long, Keating spent time with his fellow soldiers, telling them to stop feeling sorry for themselves, urging them to brainstorm more inventive ways of killing the insurgents. He pushed them to figure out how to defeat the enemy even as he thought to himself, You can't! You *can't* defeat this enemy! Yet he was willing to let them continue risking life and limb to try. It was his job, but he felt like a liar.

Upon his return, Keating had been stunned to find the immense LMTV, with two of its tires shot out, parked at the outpost. He was told the story about how Howard had demanded that it be driven up, how the convoy had been attacked twice on the way, how six soldiers had been wounded, including the gunner on the LMTV, Specialist Tim Martin,

---

[29] Steven Pressfield, *The Afghan Campaign* (New York: Broadway Books, 2006). Excerpt copyright 2006 Steven Pressfield, used with permission of the author.

who was awarded a Purple Heart. Gooding was emphatic that the truck needed to go back to Naray; he didn't have room to store it at the outpost, he said.

"Matt, there's no reason for it to come back," Stambersky told him. "Put it at the front gate. Use it as a firing position. Put a gunner in it."

But Gooding needed the space. The whole outpost was only about an acre and a half in area, and the LMTV was taking up valuable territory, not to mention serving as an inviting target—symbolic as well as practical—for the enemy. The camp now housed some 250 soldiers— about a hundred from the Afghan National Army, another hundred American troops, and up to fifty military police, cooks, mechanics, and other support personnel—and there simply wasn't enough room for everyone.

And in any case, Stambersky had been overruled at squadron command, so the message from Naray was clear: the LMTV had to come back for repair and recovery. It had been at Kamdesh too long already, it had to be fixed up, it was an expensive and useful piece of equipment that other troops could use. Squadron XO Sutton conveyed all of this to Able Troop XO Keating.

Ben Keating decided that *he* would take it back. He and Staff Sergeant Vernon Tiller, his most senior mechanic, would drive the LMTV to Naray, say, "Thanks for nothing, assholes," and leave.

"Fuck it," Netzel told Keating. "Don't take it back."

"No, they're insisting, so me and Tiller are gonna do it," Keating said. "I got a bad feeling about it, so no one else is going to take it back but me."

"Want me to come with you?" Netzel asked.

"No, I just want two in the vehicle," Keating said.

Tiller figured they would need extra protection, so he spent an entire day stripping a dead truck of its gunner's protection kit and mounting it on the LMTV. "Who's our gunner gonna be?" Tiller later asked Keating and Netzel. "I put a GPK on the truck, and a weapons mount. All we need is a gunner."

"We can't put a gunner up there," Keating said. "If that vehicle rolls over, the gunner won't make it, you and I both know that. We'll take our chances without. If we get ambushed, we'll ride out the storm."

"This is retarded," Cerezo said when Keating briefed the convoy team on the mission. "This vehicle's not going to make it on this road. Humvees can't even make it."

"It *is* stupid," Keating agreed. "And it's dangerous. So I'm going to drive."

This was no small decision. It was considered a general standing order that officers were not to drive vehicles while on an operation; they were supposed to focus instead on "commanding and controlling" the convoy and were responsible for navigation, security, speed, and maintaining continuous communication with every truck on the move. Keating didn't seem to care.

Dusk had fallen when Lieutenant Vic Johnson from Able Troop's 1st Platoon approached Keating. His hand was wrapped in bandages; just a few days prior, when he and his men were out making sure that no insurgents were hiding in caves, he'd fallen down the side of a steep hill. Needing X-rays, he'd hitched a ride back to the outpost on a D Troop Humvee that had then gotten too close to the edge of the road and flipped, tumbling down the hill and into the Landay-Sin River. He'd nearly drowned but somehow managed to swim to the riverbank while wearing his body armor and holding his weapon. Johnson didn't know much about Keating's mission other than that he was commanding a convoy back to Naray.

"What vehicle are you taking there?" Johnson asked.

"The LMTV," Keating replied.

Johnson told Keating that was a bad idea; the road couldn't even support Humvees, he said.

The two men moved their conversation next to a fire pit, and Johnson tried again.

"Someone is going to have to die before anyone admits these roads are really dangerous," he said.

It had been raining off and on for three days straight when the convoy — five Humvees, four jingle trucks, and the LMTV — left Combat Outpost Kamdesh on the night of November 25.

Earlier that day, Keating had taken out a patrol to inspect his route. Although it had rained or snowed on seven out of the previous ten days, he thought the road was suitable for travel and told Gooding that after the recent construction, the section from Urmul to Kamu was in better shape than it had ever been. Tiller inspected the LMTV and pronounced it to be in good operating condition. He, Keating, and Gooding agreed that hauling an extra Humvee for their return trip would be too cumbersome; they would leave it behind. The truck was prepped, the radios checked. Keating briefed the convoy team on all possible hazards and conditions.

They left at night in order to avoid an enemy attack. The sky was clear, with a quarter slice of moon offering little luminescence. The LMTV and the Humvees had infrared spotlights, and the troops were wearing their night-vision goggles.

Back at Combat Outpost Kamdesh, Gooding assumed that Tiller was driving. That assumption was wrong.

Detailed to provide additional security for Keating's convoy, 3-71 Cav's sniper team, led by Cricket Cunningham, hiked to the high ground along the road to Naray to conduct surveillance. They were there to deal with whatever the night might bring. Wearing their night-vision goggles, they watched as the Humvees slowly made their way down the road to Naray, followed by the LMTV. The road curved slightly to the right, toward the mountain, and then sharply to the left, toward the river ledge. In anticipation of the second curve, Keating steered the LMTV close to the edge of the cliff. The ledge had been reinforced with rocks loosely stacked on top of a stone retaining wall. It was not strong enough for the LMTV, which at its lightest weighed more than eight tons. As their left rear tire passed over the shoulder, Keating and Tiller felt the road give out from under them. The LMTV slid to the left, down toward the river. And then it dropped.

The LMTV landed on its left side, crashing and tumbling, then rolling over and over.

Tiller felt himself roll about four times, and then all of a sudden he just stopped rolling and he wasn't in the LMTV anymore: he was lying spread-eagle on a boulder, about thirty feet from the river. He didn't remember being thrown from the vehicle, but there he was.

Keating, too, fell out of the LMTV before it splashed into the river and became almost entirely submerged.

Tiller was in unbearable pain, mostly from his back. Keating was worse off—much, much worse.

*   *   *

Cerezo was driving the last Humvee in the convoy. He saw a flash of lights from the LMTV.

He looked at Yagel.

"What was that?" Cerezo asked. He braked to a stop.

Specialist Brendan Snell ran up to them. "The LMTV just flipped off the cliff!" he exclaimed. "We got to go get them!"

"Oh, shit," said Cerezo. He hopped out of his truck.

The area where the LMTV had fallen was too steep for them to climb down, Snell told Cerezo, so they tried to descend right there, to the left of Cerezo's Humvee. But the gravel at that spot was too loose and the decline too severe. They quickly went to another location, but that was no good, either.

"Dude, show me where the LMTV went off," Cerezo said.

They ran to the crumbling patch of road. Some of the other troops were now starting to congregate nearby.

"Show me how to get down there, take me," Cerezo ordered an Afghan National Army soldier. The man didn't really respond. Cerezo looked down and saw that the LMTV was underwater, with just one tire poking up from the surface of the river.

"Fuck this," Cerezo said to Snell. "Dude, are you game?"

"I'm game if you're game," Snell said.

"Let's do this," Cerezo replied.

They jumped down onto the steeply descending mountain and started sliding down the gravel-covered slope.

Netzel was listening to it all from the operations center back at Combat Outpost Kamdesh.

Yagel had been leading the convoy. He now came on the radio, his voice loud: "The LMTV just fell down the cliff!"

Yelling from the road, Yagel had been able to speak with Tiller, who was growing more frantic with each passing minute. Tiller had reported to him that Keating was unconscious and out of his reach.

"We're trying to go down and get them," Yagel said. "We need some help!" Keating and Tiller were down a cliff and not easy to get to, and on this dark night, visibility was low. "I need help, please, get us more help," Yagel repeated.

Able Troop responded immediately with two Cavalry sections and an MP platoon, all racing down the road to the site. Cunningham, who heard Yagel's pleas over the radio, called in and requested permission to move down the mountain with his snipers. Permission was granted. He told Gooding and Netzel that he needed to have a Hilux truck, climbing ropes, a Skedco hard plastic stretcher, and a medical kit waiting for him and his team when they came down from their position.

"Okay," said Gooding. "Hurry up, get down there."

Cunningham ran down the hill, on the way selecting a team of troops who he thought could help him:

Matthew Gibson is an SAW gunner; great, take him for security.

John Garner took a course on combat injuries; good, pick him.

Cory Townsend is good with ropes; he went through air-assault training. Let's go.

The four men ran back to Combat Outpost Kamdesh and met up with the ready Toyota, in which sat 3-71 Cav surgeon Major Christopher Martin. Garner hopped behind the wheel, and they sped down the road. The Toyota didn't offer any protection from bullets, but it was the right size and weight for the road.

When Cerezo and Snell reached Tiller, he was leaning against a rock. Hurt, but alive.

"Don't worry about me," he told them. "Go help Keating."

Ejected from the vehicle, Keating had landed between two rocks almost 150 feet down the cliffside, right near the Landay-Sin River. On its way down, the LMTV had rolled over him. He was wedged between the boulders, facing the rocks and the river. His pelvis was pinned down, and water was running over him.

"We have to flip him over," Cerezo said. He, Snell, and Specialist David Mendez, who had joined them, pulled Keating from the rocks and laid him on his back.

Keating suddenly snapped awake and tried to lift himself up. "Get me the fuck out of here!" he cried, and then he blacked out again.

Cerezo identified multiple open fractures to both legs, open wounds on his thighs, open fractures of his left arm, a possible broken back, and head trauma. Keating also had excessive bleeding in his abdomen and groin. His face was banged up, and there was blood by his left eye and his nose.

His left and right feet appeared to be almost completely severed from his legs at the ankles.

The medic cut Keating's clothes off him and began packing his wounds with Kerlix gauze and wrapping him with bandages. The splints he had with him weren't big enough for a guy like Keating, so he took a few of the boxes of MREs that had scattered all over the hillside when the LMTV fell, cut them apart, and fastened the sections together to serve as improvised splints. He got on the radio with Martin, the squadron surgeon, but their conversation kept getting interrupted by others.

"If you are not the fucking doc, or me, get the fuck off the net," Cerezo barked, then went on to describe Keating's condition to the physician.

The troops up the mountain had already ordered a medevac. Keating was still breathing, but it would be a race to get him to the operating room at Forward Operating Base Naray before it was too late.

Cunningham and Garner hooked up two 150-foot ropes to a Humvee and began rappelling down the cliff face. They didn't know how strong the ropes were, but they figured they'd find out soon enough. Less than ten minutes later, the snipers were with Keating, Snell, Cerezo, and Mendez. They put Keating on the Skedco stretcher they'd brought with them. Keating was cold and soaking wet. Every so often he would start to moan a little, and the men would try to talk him up.

"You're gonna make it home to see your girlfriend," Garner said.

The medevac finally arrived, but there was no safe place for it to land, so it began lowering a hoist with a medic. The rotation of the chopper's blades in that tight corridor created a considerable draft, however, and the medic oscillated wildly under the helicopter as he descended. Deciding that the situation was too hazardous, he signaled for the crewman to stop and lift him back into the bird. The medevac extraction was called off, and the bird flew on to Combat Outpost Kamdesh.

Cerezo had been lying on top of Keating to try to warm him up and shield him from the chopper's wind. As soon as the helicopter was called away, he noticed that there was something much more serious going on with Keating than just a loss of consciousness.

"I don't think he's breathing anymore," Cerezo said.

"You've got four minutes to get him breathing again," Cunningham told him. After that, they would need to carry the lieutenant up the steep slope.

Cerezo and Garner, a former emergency medical technician, opened up the Skedco to which Keating had been fastened so they could begin CPR. As they were attempting mouth-to-mouth resuscitation, Keating started vomiting in their mouths: green and black crud burped up from inside him. This caused Garner to vomit in turn, and Cerezo to dry-heave. But they wouldn't give up.

They could feel his life slipping away. They gave Keating as much air as they could from their lungs, trading off over and over. They counted chest compressions—*1, 2, 3, 4, 5, 6, 7, 8, 9, 10, 11, 12, 13, 14*—screaming out the numbers so that the mountains echoed with their desperate cries. Cerezo inserted a King LT tube in Keating's mouth in an effort to help air get into his lungs more easily. It worked: he started breathing again. They snapped him back into the Skedco, and Cunningham wrapped the stretcher around his waist. They all carried Keating the thirty feet up the hill to the bottom of the rope, which Cunningham then secured to both the stretcher and his own belt.

"We're good to go!" Cunningham yelled up the hill. "Start pulling!"

Troops on the road began hauling the rope, and Cunningham started clawing his way up the cliff. Garner and Cerezo continued to breathe for Keating, who wasn't able to do so on his own. The pull rope, rubbing against a rock's sharp edge, snapped. Pushed back suddenly by gravity and Keating's weight, Cunningham dug his feet into the ground while Garner pushed Keating up. Cunningham yelled for Townsend to lower the rope back down so he could fix it, then he hastily refastened it, tying a square knot with two half hitches.

Vehicle parts and MRE boxes were strewn about the slope. Rocks kept falling on the soldiers as they made their way up. When they were half-way up the cliff, Cerezo noted that Keating no longer had a pulse.

They kept pushing.

Cerezo saw that Keating's pupils were fixed and dilated. He was showing no signs of life.

Other troops now began scaling down the cliff toward them, inadvertently knocking loose rocks that hit Garner, Cunningham, and Cerezo. For the most part, Cunningham's helmet protected him, but Garner's head and Cerezo's hand started to bleed from cuts caused by the stones. As the stretcher passed the other troops, the medic and the EMT, both bleeding, continued to push on Keating's chest and offer him their breaths.

Roughly two hours after the accident, Ben Keating at last reached the top of the cliff. Everyone helped the team get him past the ledge. Cory Townsend assisted with the mouth-to-mouth, taking over for Garner. Cerezo told the surgeon that Keating had no pulse, was not breathing on his own, and was cold.

"He's not cold and dead until he's warm and dead," Martin replied.

Martin was quoting an old emergency-room saying, meaning that sometimes when a person's body is cold due to hypothermia, a pulse may be present but not detectable. He was trying to say, in other words, that Keating might still be alive. Cerezo had no idea what the hell he was talking about.

Martin attached a respiratory bag over Keating's nose and mouth and covered him with blankets to combat the hypothermia. Troops put him in the Humvee Ridgeway had been driving and rushed him back to the landing zone at the outpost, where the surgeon gave him a shot of epinephrine before the bird took him to Forward Operating Base Naray, a twenty-minute chopper ride away.

Back on the road, above the wreck of the LMTV, Yagel and Cerezo embraced.

"I don't think he's going to make it," the medic said.

"I know," said Yagel. "I know."

Tiller was still at the bottom of the cliff.

"We gotta go back down there," Cunningham told Cerezo, who seemed preoccupied with Keating's fate. "C'mon, man, do your job, we gotta go down there."

"Get your fucking ass up here, dude!" Cerezo yelled down to the mechanic, mistakenly thinking he wasn't that badly hurt.

Cunningham climbed back down using the same rope. When he got to the bottom, he lay on top of Tiller, offering him his body heat, while waiting for the stretcher to be lowered to them. Once it reached them, Cunningham strapped Tiller into it with the belts of the other troops who had joined them down there, and then they hauled him up the hill. His condition seemed stable.

$*$ $*$ $*$

In the operating room at Forward Operating Base Naray, Keating's body temperature was only 92 degrees. He had no pulse or heart rhythm.

The doctors spent forty minutes aggressively attempting to resuscitate him with an open cardiac massage.

He had bled out.

His heart was empty.

His abdomen became distended with blood.

The open-heart massage didn't work. Keating had suffered too much damage, and it had taken too long to get him from the bottom of that cliff to the operating table.

First Lieutenant Ben Keating was declared dead at 12:20 a.m. ET on Sunday, November 26, 2006.

Ken and Beth Keating had just returned from a trip to Delaware to visit Ken's brother and his family. Their son had called them there and spoken with each relative in turn. It had been a difficult phone call for both Ken and his son, with lots of pauses. Neither wanted to hang up the phone, but eventually there was nothing left for them to say.

On Sunday morning, at church, Beth saw Heather McDougal, whose dad had usher duty that month. McDougal told her that for the first time, she and Ben had used Instant Messenger to talk to each other. Their conversation had taken place before he left on his mission to drive the LMTV from Kamdesh to Naray:

bkeating6: sorry i missed you earlier

applegirl15: hi!

bkeating6: morning gorgeous

applegirl15: hey there...

applegirl15: so how much longer are you in kamdesh for

bkeating6: about 24 hours

bkeating6: [till] tomorrow night...they're pretty much done with operations out here, so the danger isn't too great

applegirl15: ok

bkeating6: just a really boring truck drive

applegirl15: is the weather too bad to fly

bkeating6: don't worry...i'm coming back to you....

The LMTV in the Landay-Sin River. *(Photo from the accident report, U.S. Army)*

That afternoon, Ken Keating watched the Chicago Bears lose to his beloved New England Patriots—a game that his son had said he was hoping to catch at Forward Operating Base Naray. Just in case Ben wasn't able to see it, Ken typed up a synopsis of the Patriots' win and emailed it to his son.

Ken headed to bed at around nine that night. Beth was already under the covers when they heard a car door slam, followed by a knock at the door. Ben Keating's father put his jeans back on, went downstairs, and turned on the porch light. Two soldiers were standing there in their Class A uniforms.

"Beth!" Ken Keating called upstairs. "I think you'd better come down here."

CHAPTER 13

The 7-31

Fittingly, a brutal winter descended over Camp Kamdesh. Gooding had made sure the outpost was prepared, and with firewood burning in potbelly stoves that a local man had purchased in Pakistan and hauled across the border, the troops tried to stay warm. By December, three stone barracks had been constructed at the camp, and two more up at Observation Post Warheit.

The different platoons would rotate onto OP Warheit for two weeks at a time. Not long after Keating died, Able Troop's 2nd Platoon was assigned to the observation post. There, a stray dog made her way into the good graces of Moises Cerezo, the medic who had tried to save Ben Keating and whose hungry soul was grateful for the companionship.

"Dude, we need to give her a bath," Cerezo said to Sergeant Michael Hendy. "She has fleas."

"You're going to freeze her," Hendy cautioned. It was winter, after all, and the only available water was bone-chilling cold. Nonetheless, the two men gave the puppy a bath in a frigid stream that ran nearby. She whimpered and shook. She looked as if she might die at any moment.

Cerezo had his fleece on, and he picked her up and drew her to his body. He held her tightly like that for more than an hour. Her shakes eventually lessened into shivers, which soon calmed to nothing. She began playing with Cerezo. He named her Kelly, but everyone else called her Cali. Cerezo slept the first few nights with her in his bunk, zipped in behind the safety of the mosquito netting that kept out the freaky insects that were always dropping on soldiers at night—immense spiders, glow-in-the-dark centipedes, creatures seemingly from another, horrifying dimension.

Then one night Cerezo saw a flea on his fleece, and that was it for his bunkmate. It was too late, however: fleas had infested the barracks at Observation Post Warheit, leaving some soldiers, including Adam Sears, so badly bitten that they looked as if they had chicken pox. There simply weren't enough flea collars to go around.

Amid subzero temperatures, punishing mountaintop winds, and three feet of snow, Cali's bugs had ruined the only warm and comfortable spot in Cerezo's world: his sleeping bag, which, needless to say, he couldn't wash anywhere. Cali would come into the barracks in the middle of the night, pushing the door open and causing an already cold room to turn into a meat locker.

One morning, Sears awoke to find that the fire in the furnace had gone out. As he grabbed the ax to split some of the chopped firewood, his hand landed in a pile of feces that Cali had deposited on the ax handle. It was the final straw; he snatched up his M16 rifle and chased Cali all over the post. He fired at her, grazing her neck, but she got away, and finally Sears gave up. "I guess it learned its lesson," he said to himself. Sears felt better, at any rate. Cali soon rejoined her new "owners," acting as if nothing had happened, as if Sears hadn't just tried to kill her.

They tried to pass the time constructively. Sergeant Michael Hendy had received some pepperoni in a care package, and he had the bright idea of trying to make pizzas at the observation post, using locally baked flatbread and some tomato sauce the men had bought from the ANA. An interpreter helped the sergeant acquire onions, peppers, and two softball-sized wheels of cheese. Eating dairy up there seemed like a questionable call to some—too many of their fellow troops had sampled the local cheese or milk and ended up suffering a flulike reaction that wrung out their insides—but Hendy was convinced it was worth the risk. Pizza needed cheese, he insisted. Ultimately the question became moot when the wheels were opened and found to be teeming with maggots. Hendy went ahead with the rest of it anyway—the bread, onions, peppers, pepperoni, and tomato sauce. Nick Anderson thought it tasted funny; he looked at the tomato sauce jar and discovered it was two years past its sell-by date. Hendy kept eating.

The winter isolated the men at Combat Outpost Kamdesh and Observation Post Warheit not only from the U.S. Army writ large, but from one another. Anderson bought a goat for a hundred U.S. dollars and asked the ANA cook to prepare it for 2nd Platoon; the result was a crappy stew made of joints and tendons, while the Afghan soldiers kept the good stuff for themselves.

Anderson didn't make that mistake again. He used his own hunting knife to slaughter the next goat, then butchered it himself, dressing it like a deer. Hendy cooked it up after other troops fetched firewood and prepped the meat. This exercise would be enjoyably repeated, both for the sake of dinner and to kill time. In the late afternoon, Anderson would buy a goat from some locals; each one cost between sixty and a hundred U.S. dollars, depending on the seller, which interpreter Anderson had with him, and whether or not the purchase had been arranged ahead of time. They would name each goat—one was Spicoli, after the stoner surfer in *Fast Times at Ridgemont High,* and another was Baba Ganush, the derisive nickname given to a particular insurgent whom Special Forces had targeted—and then take pictures of themselves with their pending dinner. Tied up at the observation post, each goat got one night—and only one—to bleat.

Scene 1: Spicoli and Staff Sergeant Nick Anderson. *(Photo courtesy of Nick Anderson)*

Scene 2: Staff Sergeants Nick Anderson and Adam Sears and, on the makeshift grill made from a HESCO basket, Spicoli. Troops melted the fat in the canteen cup to pour over the meat. *(Photo courtesy of Nick Anderson)*

The enemy had all but disappeared, a seasonal occurrence due to the unforgiving elements. It was assumed that the insurgents had gone to Pakistan, but no one really knew. On December 16, Army Master Sergeant Terry Best, forty-nine, arrived at the Kamdesh outpost by helicopter with the platoon of Afghan National Army soldiers he was in charge of training. The Afghan troops hailed from Kabul, the theory being that sending ANA troops into regions other than their own would discourage the formation of militias with local elders or fighters of a common heritage, ensuring a certain remove that would, it was hoped, allow for a greater sense of objectivity in their military operations. The drawback was that the newcomers would generally be unfamiliar with the local environment and local power brokers, as well as lacking, often, any linguistic and tribal affinity with the local populace.

In this instance, things went sour immediately. The ANA's Afghan commander started regularly smoking hashish. He also availed himself of pharmaceuticals provided by the ANA medic, as evidenced by the used syringes that Best would find during his periodic walkthroughs of the ANA barracks, which were often redolent with the sweet, skunky stench of hash. When Best told Gooding about the problem, the Able Troop leader couldn't have been less surprised. His own experience with ANA soldiers so far was that whenever they joined Americans on missions, at the first sign of danger, they would turn and flee. To Gooding, the idea of Best's foot-patrolling local villages along with eight such Afghan troops—even with the assistance of his staff, Sergeants Buddy Hughie and Chris Henderson of the Oklahoma Army National Guard—seemed downright nuts. Many U.S. soldiers viewed the assignment to serve as an embedded tactical trainer, or ETT, as a sort of punishment, and few wanted to embed with the ANA and become such a naked target for the enemy.

Best contacted the office of the Afghan minister of defense to report the ANA commander's drug use, and officials at the ministry advised him to inventory the unit's medical kit to establish proof. Best did so with the support of First Sergeant Qadar, a competent ANA soldier. His investigation was hardly cheered by some of the ANA troops, two of whom came forward to make a not-so-veiled threat: "Don't fuck with our commander, or you won't be protected," one told Best. Afghanistan was already a haze of switching allegiances and uncertain allies; now two Afghan soldiers whom Best was training were telling him that not only might they not be there in the field for him if he needed them, but they might even willingly allow him to be harmed by others. Qadar had the two yanked out of the company and sent back to ANA headquarters. Confronted with evidence of the ANA commander's drug use, the Afghan Ministry of Defense quickly made the decision to pull both him and the medic who'd been supplying him out of Combat Outpost Kamdesh.

Best had a much more positive impression of the next ANA commander, Shamsullah Khan, who made it clear that he believed his troops needed to be out in the field, protecting their country. Best also liked most of his Afghan trainees; he had cause to be grateful to First Sergeant Qadar yet again after Qadar saved his life by apprehending some insurgents who were planning an attack on him. But his favorite of all was a soldier named Adel, who was an expert at clearing caves and scaling mountains—and a good cook, too.

Among his own men, Best was closest to Buddy Hughie. Hughie had just returned from leave in South Carolina, where his wife, Alexis, had given birth to their first child, a son named Cooper. A smiling and energetic presence, Hughie hailed from Poteau, Oklahoma, where he was active in his local Baptist church. Before he turned two, Buddy, along with his baby sister, Jenny, had been adopted by their grandparents, Mema and Papa, who raised them. With no more than fleeting memories of their on again/off again mother, Buddy Hughie had always protected his sister as if the same unknown evil forces might at any moment snatch her away, too.

Helping people seemed to come naturally to Buddy Hughie, first as an Oklahoma National Guardsman, then as a medic, then as a trainer of Afghan soldiers. He was officially Best's gunner, but for all intents and purposes, he'd assumed the role of his second in command, a de facto opening ever since Best's *actual* second in command had started refusing to participate in combat missions—once even unilaterally calling for a cease-fire in the middle of a firefight. (He attributed his pacifism to his adherence to the teachings of the Church of Jesus Christ of Latter-day Saints; why, in that case, he'd joined the military in the first place remained a bit of a mystery.) The reluctant officer also rebuffed a request from Gooding to join Able Troop on a mission, then later complained to Gooding about the living quarters not being up to snuff. Gooding asked his higher-ups if that officer could be relieved. He was, but when no replacement was offered, Hughie ended up doing the work instead.

On December 15, at Bagram, Governor Nuristani met with the commander of the 10th Mountain Division, Major General Benjamin Freakley, to tell him about the establishment of the Eastern Nuristan Security Shura. Its members, forty-five elders from villages scattered throughout Kamdesh District and Barg-e-Matal District to its north, were to meet regularly and confer on how to keep the region safe. The elders would be paid and considered an official body, in charge of development projects and the like. Nuristani wanted the Security Shura sessions, rather than the Kamdesh outpost, to be the place where locals would take their social, political, and security problems and concerns.

The governor had previously raised some eyebrows among American officers by publicly calling for a U.S. withdrawal from Afghanistan. Nuristani explained to Freakley that he needed to establish credibility so he could initiate direct discussions with some of the more radical elements within Nuristan Province. If the Security Shura was a success, it would demonstrate that the Nuristani people supported Karzai's government, and that the region was capable of providing its own security—and once those conditions were met, then the United States would be able to leave. Wasn't that what they all wanted?

Freakley got it, as did Colonel Nicholson. Some of Nicholson's troops with 1-32 Infantry had just scored a victory in an area of Nuristan that had been harboring insurgents—and they had done it without firing a single shot. The villagers had invited the Americans in for a shura. After conferring with Nicholson, Lieutenant Colonel Cavoli and his men had accepted. The Americans made their case, and the villagers debated among themselves and ultimately voted to expel the insurgents. Ideally, the shura could work as a way of separating the enemy from the people, through social pressure and argument, not bullets.

Governor Nuristani had brought in a controversial local mullah named Fazal Ahad to help guide the Security Shura. When 3-71 Cav first deployed to the region, ten months before, Ahad was on Captain Ross Berkoff's "kill/capture" list. Until recently, he had been the deputy to Mawlawi Afzal, the man who'd once headed the Dawlat, or Islamic Revolutionary State of Afghanistan, which was recognized only by Saudi Arabia and Pakistan. Afzal was thought to have some unsavory connections, and Fazal Ahad was his protégé. Nuristani's idea was that Ahad could work on both sides of the fence. He certainly had sway with the locals.

If the Security Shura was Governor Nuristani's baby, 3-71 Cav helped with child support. The squadron funded gas and supplies so the shura members did not have to pay out of pocket to travel to the meetings, which were held in the community mosques of villages and hamlets throughout the province. The Americans also promoted the Security Shura through Radio Naray and other information operations. Beyond that, however, 3-71 Cav did not get involved. If the locals ever started thinking that the shura was an American creation, its credibility among them would be contaminated.

On Christmas Day, the Kamdesh Valley was judged to be secure enough that senior officers could drop in on Black Hawks with "Christmas chow" to boost the troops' morale. At Combat Outpost Kamdesh, the repast consisted of two military coolers full of cold, holiday-themed foodstuffs: frozen and tasteless canned turkey, pulpy mashed potatoes, coagulated gravy, and the like. The men of 2nd Platoon laughed at the idea of that menu and dug in to hot steaks, onions, and mashed potatoes they'd purchased and prepared on their own. For this special occasion, Anderson had gotten far more ambitious than usual: instead of a goat, 2nd Platoon had bought a cow. He and his fellow happy warriors butchered the beast, packed the meat in bags, and stored their food in a wheelbarrow that they covered with snow.

With the shura process begun, 3-71 Cav turned to overtly pushing an Afghan government program called PTS, which stood for "Programme Tahkim Sulh"[30] in Dari and "Peace Through Strength" in English. President Karzai had established PTS in May 2005, under the auspices of the lofty-sounding Afghanistan National Independent Peace and Reconciliation Commission, in an attempt first to get insurgents to renounce their opposition and then to reintegrate them peacefully by giving them some material benefits — in other words, to co-opt them.[31]

This proved tough going throughout the rest of the country as well as in Nuristan. In December, Governor Nuristani fired Gul Mohammed Khan, the popular district administrator for Kamdesh, and replaced him with a man named Anayatullah. On December 28, Anayatullah met with the Americans and gave them the bad news: village elders throughout Kamdesh were skeptical about the outreach program. Nuristanis found it difficult to believe that anyone whom the Americans believed to be under enemy influence would be either welcomed at an Army base or, more significantly, permitted to leave it again.

Skepticism was far from exclusive to the locals. Many American experts were uncomfortable about the fact that so much of the effort to

---

[30] *Tahkim* means to "reinforce" or "strengthen," and *sulh* means "peace."

[31] PTS originally had nothing to do with the United States, but in some ways, the Americans tried to co-opt this co-opting scheme. They figured if the bad guys were reintegrated through a program in which they played some role, their intel collectors could interview them and obtain useful information. This made perfect sense to the Americans, though from the perspective of the Afghan government, it was not the way PTS was supposed to work.

bring peace to the region now rested on the shoulders of Fazal Ahad, who they believed was motivated only by the desire to get his hands on development dollars. Adam Boulio in particular viewed him as a shady character: Ahad simply isn't our friend, he thought. His speeches in the shura meetings often seemed to contradict and counter American aims, and Boulio believed that Ahad's influence actually turned some neutral elders against the United States and the Afghan government.

The soldiers of Able Troop spent the winter months trying to make inroads among the villagers of Kamdesh, distributing bags of rice, beans, and flour as well as teacher and student kits. Officers at Combat Outpost Kamdesh were even asked to help facilitate a visit by Kushtozi elders to Kamdesh Village, to help broker peace between the warring communities of the Kushtozis and the Kom.

By now, 3-71 Cav had been in Afghanistan for just over a year. The troops were spent and demoralized and still in mourning for their lost comrades. But at least they could console themselves with the knowledge that their deployment was almost over. To prepare for the redeployment back to Fort Drum, several hundred soldiers from across the 3rd Brigade — including a couple of dozen from 3-71 Cav — had already started moving back to the United States via Kuwait and Kyrgyzstan. A few had even spent a couple of nights back home with their families.

Gooding, for his part, had been called to Forward Operating Base Naray for a commanders' huddle to plan for postdeployment training at Fort Drum. It was the first time all of the commanders had been together since they pushed out of Forward Operating Base Salerno in March 2006, and their reunion had a celebratory air.

And why not? They were getting the hell out of Dodge. Berkoff had purchased a plane ticket and booked a week's vacation in Cancún with some college friends. He'd given his counterpart in the 82nd Airborne — which was supposed to replace 3-71 Cav at Naray — his DVDs, his books, and even his bunk. (Berkoff had moved from his little hooch to a tent near the landing zone.)

In the middle of the night on January 22, 2007, the staff and commanders were told to report to Howard's office. As he watched Captain Frank Brooks get up from his cot and head to the lieutenant colonel's office, Erik Jorgensen worried that they must have had a KIA. But no artillery was firing, Jorgensen noticed. And no one was out. Maybe there was an urgent mission of some sort? What was going on?

This was what was going on: the political dominoes had fallen, and as always, the joes in the field were the ones knocked facedown on the floor by the last game tile.

Two and a half months before, back in the United States, the Republicans had taken what President Bush referred to as "a thumpin'" in the November 2006 elections, with the downward trajectory of the war in Iraq being seen as one of the major contributing factors in the Democrats' recapturing of the House and Senate. A head had to roll, and Defense Secretary Rumsfeld offered his up. The brand-new secretary of defense would be Robert Gates, the president of Texas A&M University and former deputy national security adviser and director of the CIA for Bush's father, President George H. W. Bush.

A few days before the leaders of 3-71 Cav were summoned in the middle of the night to meet with Lieutenant Colonel Howard, Gates had visited Afghanistan and met with commanders on the ground. Lieutenant General Karl Eikenberry, the outgoing commander of the U.S. Combined Forces Command Afghanistan,[32] requested that the tours of thirty-two hundred soldiers from the 3rd Brigade—including all four hundred troops from 3-71 Cav—be extended for up to 120 additional days so that the overlap with the incoming brigade would create a mini "surge" of troops. It wasn't easy for Eikenberry to ask for the extension, but it was his only option, as the war in Iraq remained the Bush administration's main effort. Gates agreed.

"Although it is going to be a violent spring and we're going to have violence into the summer, I'm absolutely confident that we will be able to dominate," Eikenberry declared.

So there they all were, in Howard's office: Gooding, Brooks, Schmidt, Stambersky, Berkoff, Sutton, and others. Howard got to it quickly.

"Our deployment has been extended four months," Howard told them. "The new secretary of defense wants and needs more troops here, and

---

[32] U.S. Combined Forces Command Afghanistan had by that point handed over all operational responsibilities to NATO/ISAF and would soon be deactivated.

there are no others—we're the only combat brigade that's ready, and all the other units are committed to Iraq."

Gooding began trembling. It was the same feeling he had when he lost a soldier. He was certain that this decision would mean at least one of his men would die.

Berkoff later wrote to his friends and family:

No words can describe how I felt when I was shaken out of a cold sleep, only to be told that we've been extended another four months. I should have realized something was up when we just received a new shipment of uniforms that were long overdue. I'm sure the Defense Sec. Gates, who's been in his office for all of two weeks and came out here to visit, listened to some NATO general say that we needed more troops in Afghanistan—and that's it. The entire 3rd Brigade, and the 10th Mountain HQ, all ordered to remain. We are now calling back hundreds of soldiers who already went home to return to their posts out here. All our equipment that we sent away, it's coming back, or so we hope. It's just unreal. God help the man who made this decision when we lose another soldier.... All I can say is that I'm sorry for what we're putting you through. I'll be home one day, and if no one else is hiring in the market, I know a few guys here who would make outstanding Bush Administration Protesters for a living.

Captain Brooks returned to his tent with a grim look on his face. He sighed and said, "Someone get all the platoon leaders and platoon sergeants."

Five minutes later, sleep-deprived and dazed, the Barbarians' platoon leaders and sergeants heard the news from their commander.

"Listen, guys, there's no easy way to say this: we've been extended another four months," Brooks told them.

No one spoke; everyone was dumbstruck. Jorgensen was supposed to get married in two months' time, and Brooks himself two months after that. Neither would be able to make his own ceremony.

Gooding called Combat Outpost Kamdesh and asked for First Sergeant Todd Yerger. He broke the news to him, though Yerger had already seen some emails about it. The first sergeant huddled the troops together. He told them he had good news and bad news.

"The bad news is you aren't going home," Yerger said. "The good news is you'll get paid an extra thousand bucks a month."

The men were devastated. Some began to weep.

Back at Naray, Jorgensen sat on his cot and let it all sink in. He pulled on his shoes and walked out toward the phones to call his fiancée, Sheena, and his parents. Turning the corner, he saw a line for the phone that would take hours. So much for that.

He went back to the troop command post and hopped onto the computer to email Sheena and his parents:

I really don't how to say this, so I'm just going to come out and say it.... We've been extended. We're not coming back until June now. I think the most obvious thing is that the wedding will have to be postponed. This info is about three hours old right now, so I don't have a lot of answers. Normally I'd call for something this important, but the phone line has 150 people in it right now and it's only getting longer. I really don't know what to say right now, we're all still in shock. I've got to go now and talk to my soldiers, a lot of them aren't taking it well. I love you guys.

—Erik

Jorgensen's captain, Brooks, was one of those soldiers not taking it so well. Right before Lieutenant Colonel Fenty's helicopter went down, Brooks had been talking to his first sergeant about how he was convinced—had always been convinced—that his girlfriend, Meridith, was "the one." After Fenty and the other nine men died and Brooks got off the mountain, he found the first phone he could use and called her. "I can't tell you what's going on, but we had a pretty bad event happen, and it's made me realize—will you marry me?" he asked her. "Yes," she said. They soon picked a date: June 9, 2007.

Now Brooks was calling her again, this time to tell her that his deployment had been extended and they would have to postpone their wedding. She'd already moved to upstate New York and set up an apartment, believing he'd be there in February. She was distraught, and they both wept. "I don't believe you," she cried. "Why is this happening?"

The move was a surprise and not a surprise. Speculation about an extension had been swirling for weeks, but the anxious troops of 3-71 Cav had been told not to worry. Major General Freakley had visited Forward Operating Base Naray on Christmas Day and given them a short speech: "Gentlemen, I know there are a lot of rumors out there about us getting extended," Freakley said. "Let me be the first to tell you: we will all go home in February!"

He was half right. Freakley himself did go home in February. The men of 3-71 Cav had to stay until June.

The priest had been FOB hopping, flying from base to outpost, tending to the soldiers' spiritual needs as best he could. It was hardly an ideal situation for either the clergyman or his flock, but "ideal" as a concept had been tossed out the window the first day American troops set foot in Afghanistan. Now he was here on a particularly chilly day for the renaming of this outpost in the Kamdesh Valley. It would henceforth be known as Combat Outpost Keating.

"We ask your blessing on the dedication of this camp in the memory of First Lieutenant Benjamin D. Keating, a risen warrior of Able Seven-Three-One," the chaplain prayed during the ceremony. Of course, the squadron wasn't 7-31, it was 3-71, but the chaplain repeated his mistake: "Thank you for the service and sacrifice of Able Seven-Three-One," he said.

What would Ben Keating have made of such an error? He would likely have rolled his eyes and had a laugh at the Army's expense. He had given his life for the Army, and the Army couldn't even get the name of his squadron right.

Gooding had been mired in his own misery after Keating's death; it had taken him a month or so to snap out of it. After he did, having recognized the pit of despair in which he'd been trapped, he was thankful that his depression hadn't come during fighting season. During the ceremony, he tried to keep his tone positive. He unveiled the wooden sign identifying the camp as Combat Outpost Keating — the wood had been cut by Billy Stalnaker, the design was by Specialist Jeremiah "Jeb" Ridgeway — and said that Keating would have been honored.

The Kamdesh outpost was named in honor of First Lieutenant Ben Keating, promoted posthumously. *(Photo courtesy of Matt Netzel)*

It was a rough winter for Captain Matt Gooding. *(Photo courtesy of Matt Netzel)*

Tens of thousands of miles away, in Shapleigh, Maine, Ben Keating's parents, Ken and Beth, were ambivalent about the dedication. They understood the desire of the men of 3-71 Cav to honor their son and, perhaps, to lift their own spirits as they faced the depths of winter at Kamdesh. However, the Keatings had no illusion that the camp would be a permanent fixture in the landscape of Nuristan. (Gooding had mulled over this issue, too.) The monument for their son would be, one way or another, short-lived. The next company would have no idea who Ben Keating had been. New leadership might decide to abandon Combat Outpost Keating altogether. And the site, because of its vulnerability, might be overrun. Indeed, it was the location of the outpost that seemed to trouble Beth Keating the most. She didn't like the notion of her son's memorial standing in such a horribly dangerous part of the world. She was touched that the men Ben had served with had felt so strongly about him, and so affectionate toward him, that they wanted to honor him, and she knew there were limits to what they could do. But it was almost as if someone had decided to rename a sinking ship after her beloved boy just as it slipped below the waves.

CHAPTER 14

Buddy

The insurgents had spent the winter months regrouping. Intelligence reports suggested that they were planning a new offensive in Nuristan with fresh supplies, well-trained snipers, and new commanders. In February 2007, they announced their return with a series of kidnappings, among them that of the son of an elder from Barikot. He was a nice young man, a teenager, who often helped Able Troop at Camp Keating with small tasks—buying the men soda or cigarettes, for example. Howard told Gooding to find out more and to do it quickly. The usual process for collecting intelligence—contacting sources and then arranging for their transport to the outpost—would take too long in this instance. They needed to move *now,* before the kid's corpse was found at the side of the road. Gooding disagreed with the order, but he carried it out, enlisting the help of Adam Boulio, a group of mortarmen, and 1st Platoon, led by Lieutenant Vic Johnson. This would be Able Troop's first mission since the loss of Keating nearly three months before.

Johnson had been watching the calendar, waiting for this day: February 19, the sixty-second anniversary of the beginning of the Battle of Iwo Jima. When he graduated from West Point, his friend and eighth-grade history teacher had given him a Japanese flag that his father had captured in the Philippines during the island-hopping campaign. Johnson wanted to return the honor, so in Bagram he'd bought an American flag for his friend, and that morning at the outpost he'd had some members of Headquarters Troop lower the post flag from the pole and raise his newly purchased Stars and Stripes. It would fly there for a day, and then he could give it to his friend.

Now Johnson rallied his men. Afghan troops would conduct the operation to search for and rescue the boy, with 1st Platoon backing them up. Gooding had been impressed by the ANA soldiers under Master Sergeant Best's tutelage—they were a good company, unlike the many other ANA troops he'd had dealings with before. On this mission, because Best had been called back to Bagram to take care of some bookkeeping responsibilities—turning in receipts and drawing more funds—Buddy Hughie would lead them.

In a recent call to his grandmother, Hughie had admitted that he'd slept only an hour the night before because he and his men had been under fire. He tried to reassure her: the Afghan soldiers had placed sandbags around him for protection, they were a great team, they worked well together as a unit. She was persuaded that Buddy was going to be okay. He was with good people. They were taking care of him.

The convoy left Combat Outpost Keating and headed east toward Naray. Barely a half mile down the road, they encountered Kareem, one of Boulio's sources, walking toward the camp.

Boulio had been informed by a different source that the kidnapped teenager was being held in a particular bandah—a kind of small shack, typically used for livestock and usually consisting of a stone shelter for the herders and pens for animals. This one was owned by a HIG fighter named Abdul. Boulio told Kareem what he'd heard about the kidnapped boy, and Kareem volunteered to lead them to the bandah, which was located amid several others on the northern side of the river. The convoy would need to travel about twenty-five minutes east, pass the hamlet of Kamu, and cross a bridge to get there. One potential problem: they would have to drive by Kareem's village on the way, and if anyone saw him helping the Americans, he might be killed. The insurgents had made that clear.

Some months earlier, when the outpost was first set up, 3-71 Cav had distributed Smith & Wesson 9-millimeter pistols to Afghan policemen in the area. Many of the policemen had proceeded to sell those guns, so the Americans had tried to recall the issued weapons and were on constant lookout to confiscate any found in the field. Boulio now tucked one of these confiscated pistols into Kareem's waistband. "You're going to have to come with me, and we'll make it look like I've caught you with a gun you aren't supposed to have," Boulio told him. A couple of the Afghan troops restrained Kareem and put him in the back of their Ford Ranger.

Gooding thought it would be safer for Kareem to be seen with only ANA soldiers, while Johnson and 1st Platoon hovered nearby as a quick reaction force. Gooding ordered Boulio to stay with him and the mortarmen, just outside Mirdesh; the intel specialist had completed his mission by making contact with his source and then handing that source over to Afghan control.

"I should be going with the group to the bandahs," Boulio argued, furious. "He's my source, and I need to be there to make sure we get to the right place."

But Gooding felt that Boulio and others who worked closely with Afghans often took unnecessary risks to rally their Afghan colleagues. He respected that dedication, but whether by intuition or because he was still mourning the loss of Keating, he was not going to let Adam Boulio out of his sight that day.

With the plan hatched, they now acted, driving to Kareem's hamlet and putting on a show for his neighbors. Elders met Boulio at the bridge. He asked them how Kareem, in the ANA truck, had gotten the pistol. They said they didn't know. Kareem was a good man and not a criminal, they told him through his interpreter. "I believe you," Boulio said. "He will probably be released soon." He then asked for information about the location of the abducted boy, but the elders had nothing to offer.

The ANA troops and Kareem then drove to the bandah, with Johnson and 1st Platoon following a safe distance behind them. Gooding, Boulio, and the mortarmen stayed put. Johnson and his platoon stopped at the "Kamu turnaround," a grassy area adjacent to the road on the southern side of the river, one of the few places on the route from Kamdesh to Barikot wide enough to let Humvees turn around if needed. Hughie, his team of trainers, and the ANA troops continued east toward the bandah.

Kareem led them past the first bridge after Kamu and told them to stop. Hughie and his team stayed in their Humvee; the ANA troops got out of their Ford Rangers, crossed yet another bridge, and then walked quickly toward the bandah. They rounded up three "spotters," HIG insurgents who were obviously on lookout duty, but it was already too late: the insurgents had been tipped off. One band of HIG fighters grabbed the boy and sped off in a Toyota Corolla; another group fled to the south, crossing a third bridge, scaling up a ridgeline, and racing on the high ground toward the Kamu turnaround, where Johnson and 1st Platoon were waiting for the ANA to return.

Tennessee Army National Guard Lieutenant Matt Hall had formerly been part of Best's team, but feeling that he and his colleagues had been utterly neglected by Army brass in their previous post in the Tagab Valley, northeast of Kabul, he'd opted to train ANA troops at Forward Operating Base Naray instead of going to Kamdesh with the master sergeant. At the less remote base at Naray, he figured he could at least try to ensure that for Best, Hughie, and their ANA troops, it wouldn't once again be a matter of "out of sight, out of mind."

Hall's previous job had been as an assistant football coach at Cumberland University, and he loved his ANA troops as he had once loved the kids he coached. He believed in them. Sure, some of the cultural differences took some getting used to — the way the men danced and napped together or held hands, for example, and their hygiene, which, in a land without running water, was certainly, well, *understandable* — but he came to see them as true patriots, a beautiful and friendly people. They wouldn't get paid for months, but they'd stay out there anyway, manning their posts, freezing with no socks or gloves. And they always knew where he was, always had his back.

Hall and his ANA troops now drove from Naray to Kamu to help find this kidnapped teenager. Just after making the turn and getting out of the dead zone where radio contact was impossible, Hall picked a spot in which to set up a checkpoint.

There they met the uncle of the missing young man, on his way toward Forward Operating Base Naray.

"We found him," the uncle told one of the ANA troops. "I'm running to Barikot to go get him."

Hall sent out word over the radio: Good news! The boy had been found.

Hughie stopped his patrol and returned to the Kamu turnaround. He and his fellow trainers got back in their Humvee. Johnson was sitting in his truck, facing east. He could see the ANA troops headed toward him in their Ford Rangers, still half a mile away.

Then Johnson heard a sound — something hitting his roof.

DINK!

It sounded odd. He looked up at his gunner, Sergeant Justin Shelton.

"Shit," Johnson said. "What did you drop?"

That the noise had in fact been made by a bullet became clear within seconds, with an eruption of small-arms fire from AK-47 assault rifles, what sounded like a PK machine gun, and RPGs. The ANA soldiers, in their Ford Rangers, were almost completely exposed. Johnson knew that he and his men had to suppress the enemy fire to protect the Afghans caught out in the open; they were supposed to treat ANA troops exactly as they would have treated American ones.

"Return fire!" Johnson yelled. The members of 1st Platoon fired back toward the enemy while Johnson radioed Gooding and gave him the grid coordinates so the mortar team could pound the ridge. He asked for close air support as well.

Hughie had been sitting shotgun in his Humvee with the other trainers when the attack began. While Henderson, in the gunner turret, fired at the ridgeline with his M240 machine gun, Hughie hopped out to engage the enemy from behind the vehicle. He was joined by an interpreter named Nasir and, a second later, Specialist Cameron Williams, both of whom had been sitting in the back of the truck. Williams fired a single-shot AT4 shoulder-launched rocket toward the ridgeline, then grabbed a second rocket and fired again.

The enemy fighters opened fire on the ANA pickup trucks as the vehicles drove toward Johnson and Hughie. Best and Hughie had been trying for months to teach the ANA troops to do just the opposite in such situations, to ignore their instincts and instead move *toward* the fire — in this case, to hug the ridgeline, which would make it more difficult for the fighters above to aim and fire at them. Heading toward the river made them easy targets.

Because the ANA soldiers and the Americans were on different radio frequencies, Hughie and Nasir ran toward them to point them back toward the mountain. Henderson laid down cover fire, though it was tough to say precisely where the enemy was. He knew about the insurgents on the ridgeline to the east, but now it appeared as if some fire might be coming from the north as well.

One thing that seemed certain was that these insurgents had a new marksman. He fired at Adel—Best's favorite, the wonderful cook—who went down, spilling from his pickup truck onto the ground. Hughie ran toward Adel to administer first aid. He reached him and swung his rifle around so he could access his medic kit. From the ridgeline, the sniper took aim at Hughie and pulled the trigger.

The echo of a single shot reverberated from the mountains.

With adrenaline coursing through his veins, Johnson ran toward Hughie. Bullets rained around him angrily. He thought he was surely going to die, there was no way he wasn't going to get hit, but he kept going. Hughie had just had a baby boy a few months before, and he was a good man who cared about these Afghan troops as few other Americans did.

Johnson hoped that by exposing himself, he might draw the insurgents' fire away from Hughie and his platoon. That might give Hughie a fighting chance of making it out of this one. Johnson's plan seemed to work: an RPG exploded in front of him, slapping shrapnel into his helmet, but on he went, firing into the hills as he ran. When he reached Hughie, he found him lying on his back, his eyes rolled back into his head. The bleeding had almost stopped. There was a hole in his rifle. Johnson screamed at him, but he didn't respond; he tried to find the wound, but it was hidden somewhere under all the body armor Hughie was wearing.

Then Johnson heard a moan from about twenty feet away. He looked and saw a wounded ANA soldier: Adel. He'd been hit in the chest.

Shit, thought Johnson, we have two casualties.

F15 fighter jets zoomed by above, joining in the orchestra of machine-gun fire and drowning out Johnson's voice as he tried to radio for a medic to help Hughie. No one responded, so he quickly decided he'd have to run back to get somebody, through the terrifying downpour of bullets and RPG fire he'd made it through once before. It was Hughie's only chance.

So he did exactly that: he ran back to the American trucks, where he found a 3-71 Cav medic, Specialist Gil Montanez, and then the two of them again raced through the bullet storm to Hughie.

Montanez located the wound; the news was not good. In reaching for his medic bag to treat Adel, Hughie had lifted his arm, and the bullet had found a path to his heart, bypassing his protective breastplate.

"KIA," Johnson said into the radio. Those letters were followed by Hughie's identification code: "Hotel" for Hughie and the last four digits of his Social Security number. As Johnson relayed that information, the medic went over to check out Adel. By this point, the Americans were pounding the ridgeline with 120-millimeter mortars, a 60-millimeter mortar that a 1st Platoon soldier had brought along with him, and bombs dropped from the fighter jets. The enemy had gone relatively silent. Gooding got on the radio and asked Johnson if he wanted him to send in a medevac for Hughie and Adel. Johnson didn't think they could afford to risk it; he wasn't sure if the hills were clear of the enemy. It was the kind of situation no leader ever wanted to be in: he would have to make a decision that could cost the life of a dying soldier—Adel—in order to prevent the possible loss of an aircraft and crew.

"No, sir," he told Gooding.

They packed up the trucks with the wounded and the dead. As they were pulling out, Johnson got a quick look at Adel, who was lying in the back of a pickup, being treated by an Afghan medic. Adel saw him and smiled, flashing him a thumbs-up.

Half an hour later, as Johnson's convoy pulled in to Combat Outpost Keating, a medic pulled up to meet it. He was carrying a pair of body bags. It took Johnson a few seconds to process why there were *two* bags, and then he realized: one was for Hughie, and the other was for Adel, for whom Hughie had given his life. Adel hadn't made it, either.

As Hall had reported, the kidnapped boy had been found—alive—near Barikot. He was sent to Forward Operating Base Naray and from there returned to his father.

That night in Johnson's barracks, no one made a sound.

Gooding was told that an Afghan policeman had been heard on the radio congratulating the enemy for killing Hughie and Adel. Gooding reported this to the Afghan interpreters, who went to the local Afghan police station. The police chief insisted that that particular officer hadn't been there at all that day, that he was away on vacation.

Bullshit, Gooding thought.

Gooding was later informed that the police officer had never returned to work.

*   *   *

"Good job today," Howard said to Gooding, also offering his condolences on the loss of Hughie.

Gooding was spent. Even though Hughie hadn't technically been part of 3-71 Cav, he'd been out there with them because of an order Howard had given—one that Gooding hadn't thought wise but had carried out anyway. Now Hughie was gone.

Howard had another order for Gooding.

"You need to open up an outpost at Kamu tomorrow," he told him. This wasn't entirely a surprise: having read between the lines of previous comments his commander had made, Gooding had been preparing for just this possibility. Near the hamlet of Kamu sat a former hunting lodge that had once belonged to Zahir Shah, the last king of Afghanistan, who'd been deposed in 1973. The lodge itself, or the Palace, as the troops called it, was seamlessly integrated with a large boulder that formed part of its structure, and also incorporated rock features in its landscaping as steps and multitiered terraces. A nearby stream, too, featured in the building's design. The whole thing almost looked as if it had been designed by Frank Lloyd Wright.

Gooding had already hired a contractor to widen the trail from the road to the lodge. His men spent the next day clearing boulders. Soon forty U.S. soldiers were packed into the Palace like cordwood.

On March 17, a crew of Afghan drivers hauled supplies in their jingle trucks from Naray to the new base at Kamu. As they were heading home after dropping off their cargo, around fifty insurgents, dressed as ANA soldiers and Afghan police, stopped them at a fake checkpoint. The insurgents then fired on the three jingle trucks, destroying them, and left them burning in the road. For good measure, they sliced off the drivers' ears.

Best and his forty-two ANA troops were stationed at the Kamu base; they'd been isolated there for weeks, since mudslides had blocked the road to Combat Outpost Keating and floods washed out the road to Naray. When he heard that the truck drivers had been attacked, Best thought of something that had happened the previous summer in the Tagab Valley: he'd bought three sheep to feed to his troops, and the next day, he learned that the merchant who'd sold them to him had been killed for the crime of helping the "infidels." Since then he had always tried to be as discreet as he could about buying bread and meat, and he felt an extra responsibility for any Afghans whose lives were threatened as a result of their helping him and his troops.

Best and his ANA platoon now rushed down the road, through small-arms fire, to help the jingle-truck drivers. Although they had no air support, they were successful in getting through and pulling out the men. The Afghan soldiers even managed to locate the three ears that had been cut off, so after their speedy return to the base at Kamu, the drivers were medevacked out along with their removed appendages, which surgeons were able to reattach.

There were other, similarly motivated attacks, some of them deadlier, including one on an Afghan Security Guard for the outpost, a young man from Mandigal, who was killed on his way to work. Such ambushes belied the progress that Fazal Ahad was making with the Security Shura. Elders and other villagers seemed to be responding to his pleas for Nuristanis to take responsibility for their own security so as to hasten the exit of the Americans. His own background notwithstanding, Ahad was disgusted by what the insurgents were doing in the region.

On April 29, a "night letter" was hammered onto the door of the Upper Kamdesh mosque. Besides listing the names of the Nuristanis who worked as Afghan Security Guards at Combat Outpost Keating, it issued a chilling warning in Pashto:

By the name Allah:

Announcement for the respected Muslims around the world:

The devil is hated by Allah, denied by Allah, denied by the prophet, denied by religion, and denied of the Day of Judgment for Americans.

They change humans from humanity to barbarians. These people are hated by Allah and are trying to turn the world into nonbelievers.

These dirty Americans have killed thousands of children, men, women, religious scholars, true believers, and Arab fighters. They have destroyed Islamic society centers.

At the present time for those who work and obey the American devils by taking contracts for building schools, roads, and power plants; also those who work as police, district administrators, and commanders as well as sold-out mullahs who deny Allah's orders and holy war and deny the holy Quran:

We are telling you that we are continuing our holy war in Allah's will.... Soon we will start our operations.

These infidels are searching street by street and house by house. At the present time these atheists are showing up in the great mujahideen villages. You have every right to kill these atheists if they come back into the village.

Now you know we will not tolerate anyone's complaints.

From,
Mujahideen
Long Live the Islamic Emirate

On the following day, April 30, Fazal Ahad was accompanying two Kushtozi elders to Kamdesh Village to try to help resolve their tribe's long-standing conflict with the Kom. Six insurgents in woodland camouflage uniforms—again disguised as Afghan government security forces—stopped the Kushtozis' cab at a fake checkpoint. They pulled Ahad out of his car. The two elders and their driver were given a choice: Leave now and live, or come with us and die. The three fled east to Mirdesh.

Nicholson, Howard, Berkoff, and other officers were near Barg-e-Matal, in a stone compound that they were thinking of turning into yet another combat outpost, when troops at Forward Operating Base Naray radioed to give them the news that Ahad had been kidnapped. About an hour later, Governor Nuristani called Howard to tell him that Ahad's dead body had been found. His captors had shot him in the face at point-blank range.

Members of the Security Shura were outraged, the governor said, and had already come to confront him. "We have supported you and the coalition; now is the time for you to support us," they'd told him. Nuristani said that he wanted to do something to avenge Ahad's death. The governor—himself from the Kata community—was convinced that at the very least, the Kom elders in Kamdesh Village knew who was behind Ahad's murder. Nuristani intended personally to deliver an ultimatum to the villagers of Kamdesh: Hand over the killers, or ANA commandos will search from house to house until they find them. Implicit in this plan to use ANA commandos was that American troops would be with them. The United States never allowed any ANA unit to conduct uniliteral operations; every mission had to be partnered.

Nuristani also asked Howard if the U.S. Army would be willing to send a Black Hawk helicopter to pick up Ahad's corpse at Combat Outpost Keating and deliver it to Barg-e-Matal, near his home village of Badmuk, for burial. The governor worried that the poor condition of the road from Kamdesh to Barg-e-Matal—which was washed out in many spots from melted snow and spring rains—might prevent Ahad's family from honoring the Islamic tradition that called for burial within one day. Howard asked Nicholson for permission, which Nicholson granted.

The Black Hawk landed in a large, flat field next to the stone compound that Nicholson, Howard, and the others were using. Fazal Ahad's body was cloaked in a white sheet through which his fresh blood had soaked. The corpse was offloaded from the helicopter and placed in a Ford Ranger, which drove down the road running parallel to the river and then up the hill toward the mosque. Hundreds of villagers came out to join the procession, crying and wailing; some men lifted Ahad's body onto a board and carried it part of the way.

John McHugh, an Irish freelance photographer embedded with Best and his ANA troops, was standing at the edge of the village, watching the procession. Almost without warning, McHugh and those around him were caught up in the swarm as it moved toward the mosque. The Irishman felt the piercing glares of the Afghans; he knew from experience that mourning could become violent in a split second. Ahad had been killed for working with the Americans and the Afghan government, and now here were other representatives of those same entities, right in the villagers' midst. McHugh made his way over to Best. "We should get out of here," he said. A local Afghan policeman approached them and anxiously offered the same advice: Get out of here.

They did.

President Bush had mentioned Joe Fenty in a Memorial Day address he delivered at Arlington Cemetery in May 2006, not long after Fenty died. The president noted that only hours before the crash, Fenty "had spoken to his wife, Kristen, about their newborn daughter he was waiting to

meet. Someday she will learn about her dad from the men with whom...
he served. And one of them said this about her father: 'We all wanted to
be more like Joe Fenty. We were all in awe of him.' "

Just under a year later, on May 5, 2007, the first anniversary of his
death, the base at Jalalabad was renamed Forward Operating Base Fenty.

"It was out of this gate and onto that airfield that Joe walked a year ago
today, to board that Chinook to extract his soldiers from a dangerous
spot in the Chowkay Valley," Nicholson said during the renaming ceremony. "It's back to this place that our fallen comrades are brought for
their trip home. So this is an important place, a place of honor and
respect, a place worthy of being named after Lieutenant Colonel Joseph
J. Fenty."

Command Sergeant Major Del Byers said during the ceremony that
Fenty "represented everything that I love about being a soldier. He never
asked another soldier to do anything that he was not prepared to do or
had not done himself. As busy as our commanders are, he always found
time to talk to every soldier regardless of rank or position."

In addition to FOB Fenty at Jalalabad and Camp Keating near Kamdesh, there were two other U.S. bases named after fallen 3-71 Cav troops
who had served in Nuristan: Combat Outpost Lybert, near Gawardesh,
and Combat Outpost Monti, located in an old Afghan Army compound
in Kunar Province. Patrick Lybert and Jared Monti, too, had come to the
region to die. They would not be the last.

CHAPTER 15

"Don't Go Down That Way"

To those around him, Howard seemed torn between, on the one hand, his duty to support Governor Nuristani and the government of Afghanistan and, on the other, his concern over what he knew was Nuristani's ill-advised push for an Afghan commando raid of Kamdesh Village. Howard asked the new senior officer at PRT Kala Gush, Navy Commander Sam Paparo, who'd arrived in March, to try to talk him out of it.

Paparo walked outside his operations center at PRT Kala Gush to get better reception on his Thuraya satellite phone as he dialed the governor. He could never be sure where Nuristani was at any given moment; the Afghan roamed around the country unpredictably, spending a lot of time in Kabul, at his family's ancestral home. Fortunately, he had three different kinds of phones—one satellite and two cell phones—so he was usually reachable.

"What's your overall goal in going to Kamdesh?" Paparo asked the governor. It wasn't likely, the American explained, that Nuristani would be able to find those responsible for Fazal Ahad's assassination through military means. The type of house-to-house search he wanted to undertake yielded virtually no leads 99.99 percent of the time, but it was 100 percent guaranteed to anger the population and turn them against the United States and the Afghan government.

Nuristani, however, was adamant.

Jesus, Paparo thought. This is a huge mistake.

If he insisted on doing it, Paparo said, he ought to instruct the commandos to search only those homes where such intrusion was justified,

219

since indiscriminate searching would be interpreted as mass punishment of a largely neutral population. He further warned Nuristani to make sure every search was conducted with local leaders present as witnesses.

On May 14, ANA soldiers and commandos choppered onto Observation Post Warheit. They were joined there by Tennessee National Guard Lieutenant Matt Hall and some thirty of his ANA troops, Michael Schmidt and Cherokee Company, and Matt Gooding and Able Troop. With the Americans following close behind, the Afghan troops swept through the various sectors of Kamdesh, talking to any Kamdeshis who were out and about, asking them if they knew anything about who had killed Fazal Ahad.

As part of the raid, Best, his trainers, and his forty-two ANA soldiers established a blocking position down the mountain to ensure that anyone who tried to flee the commandos' sweep through Kamdesh would be unable to escape into the ether. It was to be one of their last local tasks: that same day, the Barbarians were to escort a new company of ANA soldiers from Forward Operating Base Naray to relieve Best's team. These fresh Afghan troops had never been to Nuristan before; they were Tajiks and Hazaras, other non-Pashtuns who had served only in the western part of the country.

To avoid an ambush, First Lieutenant Aaron Pearsall, leader of the Barbarians' 2nd Platoon, had originally planned to roll very early in the morning; the Americans had been ambushed often on that road, and he wanted to get the new ANA troops to Kamu before daylight. But the Afghan soldiers weren't ready to leave until an hour after sunup. Pearsall, like his men, had a bad feeling about this mission — a last-minute assignment to escort a new ANA unit they'd never worked with through one of the most dangerous sections of their area of operations — and the late start didn't help. Some of Pearsall's platoon had already left the country to help prepare for the squadron's pending return home, so the lieutenant was down to fourteen soldiers in four Humvees. Rounding out the convoy, in addition to the fifty or so ANA troops in eight Ford Rangers, were three jingle trucks loaded down with supplies like Gypsy caravans.

Pearsall huddled with the trainers and the ANA leaders before they rolled out. His message was simple: This area is one where we've been ambushed many times before. If we get attacked, do not stop. The cliff to the south is too steep, and the dropoff to the river to the north too precipitous—there is nowhere to maneuver. If we get hit, push through. We will do our best to help you, but you must keep driving, no matter what.

And off they went. Pearsall's men had interspersed the ANA vehicles among their own: Humvee, Ford Ranger, Ford Ranger, Humvee, Ford Ranger, and so on, with the jingle trucks near the middle of the pack. The Marine captain and embedded trainers assigned to this ANA company were riding in one of the middle Humvees.

As they passed by Bazgal, an Afghan policeman waved them down.

"Don't go down that way," he warned.

Pearsall stopped the convoy and called command to request an assessment of the road ahead. Could a drone or a plane take a look to make sure no ambush was lying in wait for them? Yes, he was told, and soon a report came in that the only thing up ahead was a sandbag in the road.

Pearsall was skeptical—had the assets looked in the hills? He asked for more planes and/or drones to check it out, but they were all committed to the mission under way at Kamdesh Village, involving the ANA commandos and others from 3-71 Cav. Pearsall made the call to push on.

The "sandbag" in the road turned out to be a dead chicken, and that wasn't the only thing the eyes in the skies got wrong. When the convoy got around the second bend, three shots were fired from across the river, to their right, followed by the best-coordinated ambush 3-71 Cav had ever seen. Dozens of insurgents, up to a hundred of them, opened up on the vehicles with small arms, AK-47s, half a dozen or more PKM machine guns, and RPGs. The fire came from ridgelines on both sides of the road, from up to a dozen different covered fighting positions. The enemy fighters were firing from as little as fifty yards away and with an alarming degree of accuracy.

In the turret of Pearsall's Humvee, Jesse Steele was alternating between guns, firing his .50-caliber across the river and his SAW light machine gun up the near side of the valley. Then all of a sudden he was on his back in the truck.

"Are you okay?" Pearsall asked. He was still focused on the enemy fire.

"What happened?" Steele wondered. His jaw felt funny, as if it had been pushed to the left. He couldn't talk well; his tongue was swelling.

"You got hit," Pearsall said.

"Where?"

"Looks like it nicked you here and here," Pearsall said, pointing to

Steele's lower jaw and neck. He saw that the gunner's wounds were serious, but he didn't want to alarm him.

"Okay," Steele said. He started to prop himself up on his elbows.

"You're not getting back in the turret," Pearsall told him.

Steele turned to Specialist Lorenzo Best.[33] "You gotta get up there," he declared. Best did so. Steele put his hand to his face; when he pulled it away again, it was covered with blood.

Shit, this is more than a nick, Steele thought. He began to administer first aid to himself. It turned out that a round — fired from above, up on the mountain to his left — had gone through his jaw and shattered it before exiting out the left side of his neck. Another round had entered his shoulder, ending up in his chest. Pearsall now pulled out his own first aid bandage and applied pressure to Steele's two wounds.

"Lieutenant, are we going to make it out of this?" Steele asked.

"I don't know, man," Pearsall said. No matter how quickly they sped down the road, and how far they got, it seemed as if the ambush would never end. The enemy was spread out along the road for more than a mile and a half.

"It hurts when I talk," Steele told Pearsall.

"Then stop talking," the lieutenant advised.

Steele put his head down and prayed as RPGs exploded near their truck.

While Pearsall had been clear enough in instructing the Afghans not to stop if the convoy came under attack, that plan was easier to stick to for those in Humvees. For the ANA soldiers, vulnerable in the cabs and beds of open pickup trucks, the first impulse was to pull over and try to take cover — which was exactly what most of them did now. The ANA truck in front of Pearsall's Humvee, and others ahead and behind, stopped dead in the middle of the road as their cargoes of Afghan soldiers jumped out and scrambled for whatever meager shelter they could find — rocks or trees, anything — in the absence of any real cover for them to get behind. That segment of the road was framed by a wall on the uphill side and a cliff drop-off on the downhill; with the enemy shooting from both sides, there was nowhere for the ANA soldiers to hide once they left their vehicles. As the bullets continued to hammer the convoy, Pearsall got out of his Humvee and tried to round up the Afghans,

---

[33] No relation to Master Sergeant Terry Best.

yelling for them to get back in their trucks. He told his own driver to bump the Ford Ranger in front of them to make the point; the ANA driver behind the wheel finally got the message, and the pickup started moving.

While the lead Humvee, the only one in the clear, had continued to speed down the road, the rest of the Barbarians were still stuck behind parked ANA Ford Rangers, as well as a jingle truck that was now in flames from an RPG strike. Pearsall got back in his Humvee and called command, telling the operations center at Forward Operating Base Naray that he needed the 120-millimeter mortars to hit both sides of the road, as close as possible. The incoming fire remained intense: small-arms bullets pinged into and off every truck and Humvee. One ANA driver was shot, and the Ford Ranger he was steering started to roll off the road and into the river to their right. The Marine trainer assigned to the ANA troops got shot in the hand.

Pearsall radioed his acting platoon sergeant, Jason Guthrie, in the rear Humvee. Guthrie reported that he and the other American trucks in the rear were pushing forward, trying to force the ANA through the ambush while they also worked to gather the wounded and dead Afghan soldiers, laying some of the bodies on the hoods and in the beds of trucks. Two specialists with the Barbarians—driver Evan Morales and medic Jonathan Landers—had been struck by RPG shrapnel when Landers braved the enemy fire to rescue a wounded ANA soldier lying by the side of the road. Landers applied a tourniquet to himself, then continued working on the Afghan.

Finally, 120-millimeter mortars fired from near Gawardesh began hitting both sides of the river, dropping disconcertingly close to the convoy but providing a brief moment of respite from enemy fire, during which Pearsall and the others were able to make a break for it. But it was only after the American platoon pulled into the base at Kamu that the lieutenant had his first real chance to survey the damage to his men and equipment. Steele, Landers, Morales, and the Marine embedded trainer were wounded; an unknown number of ANA troops had been wounded or killed. Every one of the Barbarians' trucks had suffered significant damage, with doors blown off, frames cracked, tires spent. It took more than an hour for the Afghans to figure out how many of their own men were missing—first it was three, then eight, then twelve.

*   *   *

Terry Best and ANA Commander Shamsullah Khan were at the bottom of the mountain, awaiting news about the commando raid up the hill, when a Nuristani interpreter approached them. He'd been listening in on the radio used to scan for enemy chatter and had picked up word of an attack down the road to the east, on the way from Naray. Best heard on a different radio that the Barbarians had been hit near Saret Koleh and had pushed through, leaving ANA troops behind.

Best was enraged. This was all too typical of the Americans' attitude toward the ANA troops with whom they were theoretically partnering, he thought. In battle, they were supposed to treat the ANA soldiers just as they would Americans—as Buddy Hughie had done. Instead, the Barbarians had left the Afghans behind. To die.

Best got on the radio and called back to Combat Outpost Keating.

"Request permission to change my mission to go and support the ANA," he said.

"Permission denied," he was told, but he went anyway.

Because he would be passing Kamu on the way, he called two Able Troop NCOs he was close to who were posted there—Staff Sergeant Adam Sears and the recently promoted Staff Sergeant Nick Anderson—and told them where he and his ANA troops were headed.

"I'm going with you, brother," Sears said on the radio. They couldn't just leave the ANA soldiers out there.

When Best reached Kamu, Sears and Anderson were waiting for him in Humvees with some others. They'd heard what had happened; Pearsall and the Barbarians had already arrived at the Kamu outpost with the surviving soldiers from the new ANA company. The Able Troop men followed Best toward the site of the ambush. As they got nearer, they saw that the road was increasingly covered with debris from the attack and objects that had fallen off the trucks: propane tanks, bedding, a Humvee door. Soon they passed the ANA Ford Ranger that had plunged into the Landay-Sin River and was partially submerged. Then they started coming upon the bodies of ANA soldiers, some lying prone on their weapons, others in the middle of the road.

The men got out of their Humvees. Best sent Sergeant Marshall Clark, Hughie's replacement, to join ANA Commander Khan on the high ground. Then Best, Sears, and a squad of ANA troops crossed the footbridge from the road to Saret Koleh, where they would sweep the houses and stables on the north side of the river for insurgents. Two Apaches that had been sent to the area hovered above, ready to provide air support. McHugh, the embedded Irish photographer, accompanied them, snapping away.

When Best and his ANA troops checked out the houses, they found many women and children but almost no fighting-age men. Best looked across the river to the site of the attack and saw six dead Afghan soldiers, obviously laid out by the enemy. He radioed the information to Clark and began walking back over the bridge.

Before he reached the six dead ANA troops, Best skirted the southern mountainside, where he came across the body of the new Afghan company's first sergeant. He'd been shot in the head, execution-style. Best and Sears then happened upon another ANA soldier with multiple wounds at the base of his neck, alive but in deep shock. He muttered a prayer as Sears evaluated him, so the staff sergeant knew he had a decent airway. Several others soon gathered around to try to help him, and they carried him to a truck to get him some medical attention.

Staff Sergeant Adam Sears provides medical assistance to a mortally wounded ANA soldier on May 14, 2007. The Afghan soldier died on his way back to the closest U.S. base. *(Photograph by John D. McHugh, Getty Images)*

Best's Afghan soldiers now began the grim task of stacking corpses in their Ford Rangers. Two of the pickup trucks that the new ANA company had driven from Naray were in the river. Their drivers had been shot and killed where they sat, behind the wheel. Someone would have to go into the river to get them so they could be given a proper Muslim burial.

Whoever did this was efficient, Best thought. These guys were marksmen.

The ANA soldiers looked around for other wounded or slain colleagues. They kept finding corpses.

The Ford Ranger pickup trucks in the river had been packed with enough supplies to last fifty men for four months: ammunition, food, weapons. Best and Sears talked about blowing them up so the enemy couldn't use the goods or, more important, the ammunition. A few minutes later, shots rang out. Sears was northeast of his Humvee, closer to the river. Best and Clark were to the southwest of him, about a hundred yards away, and they scampered to find cover behind the only large rock around. Insurgents fired upon them from both sides of the river. Best's ANA troops started returning fire with their RPK and PK machine guns and their Dushka. Sears and his gunner, Private First Class Dustin Kittle, tried to suppress the enemy fire with the .50-caliber in their Humvee. Behind the boulder, Clark turned to Best and announced, "Dude, we have to go."

"We can't go," Best replied. "When we leave this rock, they'll kill us!" They had to plan their escape, Best said; they couldn't just sprint and hope for the best. He radioed for both the Afghan soldiers and Kittle to target the hills again with suppressive fire. After they finished a burst, Clark fired to the south and Best to the north, and then they both raced toward Sears's position. Clark ducked between the Humvee and a boulder that he thought might shield him from any shots coming from the southern ridgeline. From across the river, a shot drilled directly into his chest plate. The bullet ricocheted off it and hit his arm.

"Shit," said Best. An enemy sniper—a good one. At Sears's location, Nick Anderson applied a tight bandage to Clark's forearm and then called up on the radio to report his injury. Sears couldn't call for artillery because the antenna of his radio had been shot off, so Best did, asking for mortars. The Americans would be "danger close," but there was no other option. They were targets, and there was an expert marksman—likely a foreign fighter, maybe even the same one who'd killed Hughie—training his sights on them.

In the midst of all this commotion, before the Americans could do anything to further protect the photographer embedded with them, McHugh took a bullet to his chest. It went through his intestine and out his lower back. He had never before felt such pain.

Sears jumped up, grabbed McHugh by the back of his belt, and dragged him behind the rock where Clark had been hit. He couldn't identify right away where McHugh's wound was, so Anderson began lifting up the photographer's body armor and at last found the hole in his lower back. They began administering first aid. Best called for the Humvee to move to the rock; he loaded Clark and McHugh into it. Anderson was worried about McHugh: "We need to get out of here," he told Sears. "John's going to bleed out." Kittle just then fell from his turret into the Humvee and let out a bloodcurdling scream. He'd been shot in the collarbone.

The Apaches returned from refueling and began suppressing the enemy while Best and his ANA soldiers, plus Sears and Anderson and their troops, got out of there quickly, rolling back toward Kamu. As they sped away, the Americans saw one of the dead ANA drivers from the first ambush, still stuck behind the wheel of his partially sunken Ford Ranger. They'd have to come back for him.

Once they were safely back at Kamu, and the wounded Clark, Kittle, and McHugh were being treated—they would all survive—Best and Sears hugged each other, their eyes tearing up. They were both shaken and emotionally raw. They'd seen dead bodies everywhere and heard the wounded Kittle screaming out in pain on the way back. It had been hell.

Then, like a storm rolling in, Best's mood shifted.

"I need to find out what the fuck was going through their minds," he said. He went looking for the Barbarian troops who had left the ANA casualties on the road. They were in the hunting lodge. Best approached Pearsall.

"What the fuck is your problem?" he asked. "Why the fuck would you leave those guys behind?"

Pearsall tried to explain that they'd been explicitly told to push through any kill zone: "You don't stop the damn vehicles and jump out," he said. Pearsall was convinced that he and his troops had done everything they could that day to protect both the ANA troops and themselves. If they had acted differently, he said, the day's body count could easily have included fifteen Americans as well.

Best was furious. This is why Afghans and Americans don't get along, he thought. You really think you wouldn't stop to take cover if *you* were in an open pickup truck taking fire? It was pure instinct.

For Best's own well-being, Sears pulled him away and escorted him out.

Fifty ANA soldiers had been sent to Combat Outpost Keating to relieve Best's ANA troops. Sixteen had been killed, and five wounded. In a matter of minutes, the unit had been rendered combat-ineffective.

The insurgents threw a number of the Afghans' bodies into the river, preventing them from being buried within one day. This concerned Berkoff and others in American intelligence because to them, it suggested that some of the killers might have been not local Nuristanis but rather foreign—Chechen, Arab, Pakistani—or "out of area" fighters, perhaps Pashtuns from other parts of Afghanistan who hated the Tajik- and Hazara-filled ANA. Days later, the bodies of dead ANA soldiers would be reported as having washed up on the banks of the Kunar River as far south as Asadabad, more than fifty miles downstream.

Gooding heard about the episode, but he didn't blame Pearsall. Pearsall's patrol had been an afterthought, a mission that wasn't planned and that had gone uncommunicated to those who needed to know about it. No one at either Combat Outpost Keating or the Kamu base had had a clue that Barbarian Troop's 2nd Platoon was on its way with the new ANA troops. More than half of the squadron's combat power was in Upper Kamdesh, with most of the men focused on Governor Nuristani's wild goose chase. Until Pearsall came on the radio asking for the mortars at Kamu to fire on established targets, Gooding hadn't even known he was out there.

While Gooding sympathized with Best's reaction, he also understood that Pearsall had been thrown out the gate with an ANA force that he had never patrolled with or rehearsed contact drills with. It had been a rush to failure, a massacre as predictable as it was tragic. And now more graves were required.

And the commando raid? Nothing had come of it aside from renewed ill will among the residents of Kamdesh toward Governor Nuristani. In the meantime, the Eastern Nuristan Security Shura had essentially died along with Fazal Ahad. Ahad's deputy on the Security Shura, a cleric named Abdul Raouf, told the 3-71 Cav leaders that he had no interest in succeeding his departed friend. "I don't know who killed Ahad," he declared to a reporter. "His number was up. Tomorrow or the next day, my number will come up. They will kill us one by one."

Before Ross Berkoff left Forward Operating Base Naray for good, on May 29, the man who would soon take command of Combat Outpost Keating, Captain Tom Bostick of Bulldog Troop, from 1-91 Cav, 173rd Airborne, approached to ask him a favor: could Berkoff brief him and his team about the insurgency? So Berkoff told them everything he'd learned: who the enemy's key leaders were, where the different cells lurked, which areas to avoid. Berkoff showed Bostick a map and pointed out the specific spots from which the insurgents always attacked.

"Why are you guys driving down the same road every day?" Bostick asked. "You know you're going to get hit."

"We don't have a choice," Berkoff told his fellow captain. "There's only one road."

"You guys gotta get out of your Humvees," Bostick said. "Walk the ridgelines. Talk to villagers."

Berkoff didn't say anything. His brigade had lost forty soldiers and had more than three hundred wounded. Since he first arrived at Forward Operating Base Naray, he'd seen countless others come and go. There had been three different Special Forces detachments, three ANA units, three provincial reconstruction teams. All he wanted to do now was get out of there.

He wished Captain Bostick good luck and left the briefing room.

Gooding had thought he would never leave Combat Outpost Keating, never get out of there alive. But finally, escape was at hand. Able Troop headed to Bagram, but Gooding and First Sergeant Yerger stayed behind for a few days to help mentor Captain Bostick of 1-91 Cav. And that was that.

As he got on the supply helicopter that would take him away from the outpost forever, on June 2, Gooding thought again about how he'd hesitated before naming the camp after Keating. How long would this outpost be here? How ephemeral was this memorial? He had every confidence that 1-91 Cav would keep the camp running, but he knew its success would ultimately depend upon how good the ANA was.

Someday we're going to hand over Combat Outpost Keating, Gooding thought as the bird lifted and he looked down upon the acre and a half of land for which so many men had given their lives. And it's not going to last.

As luck would have it, the chopper was on a supply run, so Gooding got a tour of the area. It stopped at Combat Outpost Lybert, near Gawardesh. It went to the Korangal Valley. It touched down at the observation posts around Naray. The trip was excruciating, like a victory lap but without the victory. At last, hours later, the bird landed at Bagram, which felt so big and safe it might as well have been in Nebraska. Gooding sat there on the tarmac with a bunch of luggage. He was angry about the whole experience—angry about being sent up to the Kamdesh Valley without a campaign plan, angry that what was supposed to be a forty-five-day rotation had ended up being ten horrifying months, angry because no one had had it worse than his team, certainly not any of these soft "POGs"[34]— these rear-echelon folks at Bagram with their air-conditioning, their three hot meals a day and ice cream, their steak-and-lobster Fridays.

He and his troops had done more than most, Gooding thought. They'd kept their heads up the whole time—never said no to a mission, never failed, and executed all with great pride in and support for one another. They'd lost their commander, their XO, many of their friends. They'd been there for longer than anyone, and they'd never gotten the credit they deserved.

That night, Gooding tried to relax. He was going home. To his wife and kids. Everything was going to be okay.

As he walked around the base, he saw a Special Forces unit in full rucksacks on a night run. He thought about how even the guys in Special Forces—badasses, all of them—hadn't liked staying at Combat Outpost Keating. Too dangerous.

Gooding could see the Special Forces troops, but one enlisted man among their ranks apparently didn't see him. He almost ran into Gooding.

"Get the hell out of the way, you POG!" the kid yelled at the weathered captain.

Perfect, Gooding thought.

---

[34] A POG is a "person other than grunt."

Two in the Chest, One in the Head

ROLL CALL

International Security Assistance Force (ISAF)
May 2007–July 2008

At Forward Operating Base Fenty, Jalalabad Airfield, Nangarhar Province:
Colonel Chip Preysler, Commander, 173rd Airborne Brigade Combat
    Team ("173rd Airborne")

At Forward Operating Base Naray, Kunar Province:
Lieutenant Colonel Chris Kolenda, Squadron Commander,
    1st Squadron, 91st Cavalry Regiment ("1-91 Cav"),
    173rd Airborne
Captain Nathan Springer, 1-91 Cav Headquarters Troop Commander
Captain Joey Hutto, 1-91 Cav Assistant Operations Officer

At Combat Outpost Keating and Observation Post Warheit, Nuristan Province:
Bulldog Troop, 1-91 Cav, 173rd Airborne
  Captain Tom Bostick, Commander
  Captain Joey Hutto, Commander
  Second Lieutenant Ken Johnson, Fire Support Officer
    1st Platoon
      First Lieutenant Dave Roller, Platoon Leader
      First Lieutenant Hank Hughes, Platoon Leader
    2nd Platoon
      First Lieutenant John Meyer, Platoon Leader
      First Lieutenant Kyle Marcum, Platoon Leader
      Staff Sergeant Ryan Fritsche
      Sergeant John Wilson
      Private First Class Alberto Barba

3rd Platoon
  First Lieutenant Alex Newsom, Platoon Leader
  Sergeant First Class Rodney O'Dell
  Staff Sergeant John Faulkenberry
  Private First Class Chris Pfeifer
  Private First Class Michael Del Sarto
  Private First Class Jonathan Sultan

On the Provincial Reconstruction Team in Kala Gush, Nuristan Province:
Navy Commander Sam Paparo, team head

Trainer of the Afghan National Army (ANA) Troops at Combat Outpost Keating, Nuristan Province:
Marine Master Sergeant Scott Ingbretsen

On the Home Front:
Sarah Faulkenberry, wife of Staff Sergeant John Faulkenberry
Karen Pfeifer, wife of Private Chris Pfeifer

June 2008–June 2009

At Forward Operating Base Fenty, Jalalabad Airfield, Nangarhar Province:
Colonel John Spiszer, Commander, 3rd Brigade Combat Team,
   1st Infantry Division

At Forward Operating Base Naray, Kunar Province:
Lieutenant Colonel James Markert, Squadron Commander,
   6th Squadron, 4th Cavalry Regiment ("6-4 Cav") of the
   3rd Brigade, 1st Infantry Division

At Combat Outpost Keating and Observation Post Fritsche:
Blackfoot Troop, 6th Squadron, 4th Cavalry Regiment ("6-4 Cav") of
   the 3rd Brigade, 1st Infantry Division
  Captain Robert Yllescas, Troop Commander
  First Lieutenant Joseph Mazzocchi, Executive Officer

Specialist Rick Victorino, Intelligence Officer
First Lieutenant Kyle Tucker, Fire Support Officer
First Lieutenant Kaine Meshkin, Red Platoon Leader
First Lieutenant Chris Safulko, Blue Platoon Leader

Trainer of the ANA Troops at Combat Outpost Keating:
Marine Lieutenant Chris Briley

On the Home Front
Dena Yllescas, wife of Captain Rob Yllescas

CHAPTER 16

"There's Not Going to Be Any Ice Cream"

First Lieutenant Dave Roller couldn't believe his eyes, couldn't help but grin.

Two dozen naked young women?

Are you *kidding* me?

Roller and his platoon were on a ridgeline overlooking the hamlet of Saret Koleh, east of Combat Outpost Keating. They had camped there to watch over the area, to try to discern whether the Nuristanis had any idea that the next day, July 27, 2007, Captain Tom Bostick, the leader of Bulldog Troop, would be coming to the village for a shura. The nearby road was a popular site for insurgent attacks, so there had been occasional sweeps of the hamlet, but until now, no U.S. troops had ever made an official visit. For more than a day, Roller and 1st Platoon had been reporting atmospherics back to Bostick, their commander, at the base: "Trucks are rolling through here," they would say, or, "The weather looks good for tomorrow." Now, through the magnifying scope on his rifle, Roller was finally seeing something really noteworthy.

"Bulldog-Six, this is Red-One," he had murmured over his radio to Bostick a few minutes before, using both of their call signs. "Looks like some women are leaving the village right now."

He'd watched as more than twenty women made their way from Saret Koleh to a stream that fed into the Landay-Sin River. Then kept watching as they started to disrobe.

"Looks like they're about to jump in the creek," Roller whispered.

They ranged in age from about sixteen to thirty. The sun was pounding the mountains on this hot July day, and after jumping into the stream, they splashed one another playfully as they bathed in the cool water.

It was, to say the least, jarring: Roller had seen only about five local women in total during his first two months in Afghanistan, and all of them had been covered from head to toe in burqas. It looks like a goddamn sorority pool party, he thought. He was two thousand feet above the Nuristani women, looking at them from eight hundred yards away, so he couldn't see any real details, just general shapes and colors. Still, there was intelligence to be had here: their romping made him fairly certain that no one in the hamlet of Saret Koleh had any idea that 1st Platoon was watching from just up the hill.

"Red-One, this is Bulldog-Six," Bostick said. "What's going on?"

"Sir, you're not going to believe this," Roller replied. "I got about twenty to twenty-five women here, naked, taking a bath."

It was a comic overture, but a fleeting one, to a day that would end up being the worst of their lives.

First Lieutenant Alex Newsom and his 3rd Platoon were with Bostick at Combat Outpost Kamu that momentous July day, ready to serve as a quick reaction force. Both Roller and Newsom hailed from soft, privileged worlds that they had essentially rejected for lives of blood and muck. Roller had grown up in Coral Gables, Florida, and Newsom in Beverly Hills. Both were handsome: Roller had a tousle-haired all-American look to him, while Newsom was swarthy, with a devilish charm. They were the sort of guys the Army used to great success in recruiting videos, the Army Of One soldiers who were Being All They Can Be.

The two had briefly been classmates at U.S. Army Ranger School, the intense two-month combat leadership course at Fort Benning, Georgia, but they hadn't connected in any meaningful way until they were each assigned a platoon in Bulldog Troop, 1-91 Cavalry Squadron, part of the 173rd Airborne Brigade Combat Team, in Schweinfurt, Germany. After four weeks in Germany, Roller and Newsom had flown back to Fort Benning for a reconnaissance-and-surveillance course focused on conducting operations in small teams and on foot. They'd bonded then, coming to see foot patrols and Vietnam-era tactics as the way to go in

Afghanistan. Their commanders in Germany seemed to want to drive everywhere, while Roller and Newsom pictured themselves as badasses humping through the wooded hills.

It hadn't taken them much time at all to become best friends. They were confident, even cocky, and as mere lieutenants, perhaps a bit too comfortable in their dealings with superior officers. On their way back to Germany after the recon course, having been upgraded to First Class, the two of them drank all the Woodford Reserve bourbon on the plane.

Then Captain Tom Bostick, Jr., came into their lives to kick that silliness out of them.

Bostick, as the cliché went, had been bred to serve. His paternal grandfather, Bill, was an Army sergeant at Pearl Harbor when the Japanese bombs hit. One of Bill's brothers survived the Bataan Death March. The family could trace its military service all the way back to James Bostick of North Carolina, who'd fought the Redcoats during the American Revolution; through him, Captain Bostick was related to the Texas Revolutionary War hero Sion Bostick, who as a seventeen-year-old Texas Army scout had been one of three soldiers responsible for capturing Mexican President Antonio López de Santa Anna. Bostick's father, Tom senior, did an eighteen-month tour in Vietnam with the Marines, after which he came back, married Brenda Keeler in 1968, and got on with his life. A year later, at the naval base in San Diego, Brenda gave birth to Tommy junior.

Tom Bostick, Jr., had joined the Army Reserves while still in high school in Llano, Texas. He went to Panama as a Ranger with Operation Just Cause, the mission against Manuel Noriega; served as an instructor at Fort Benning; and worked in Kuwait at Special Operations Command during Operation Desert Thunder, the international military buildup that responded to Saddam Hussein's threat to violate the international no-fly zone over Iraq. Bostick fell in love with a fellow soldier named Jennifer Dudley, who was in Military Intelligence and had a baby daughter named Jessica from a previous marriage. In September 1991, he got a four-day pass, flew to Fort Meade in Maryland, and married Jennifer. Their daughter Ashlie was born a year later. In 1998, after ten years as an enlisted man, Tom Bostick applied to Officer Candidate School at Fort Benning and got in on his second try. He became an officer and did a tour in Iraq, then another in Afghanistan.

Bostick was one of the company commanders in Vicenza, Italy, with the 173rd Airborne when, in 2006, he first caught the eye of General Frank Helmick, commander of the Southern European Task Force (Airborne). Helmick needed an aide de camp, and Bostick was the obvious choice. It would have been a comfortable job, but Bostick turned it down: he wanted to command troops in the field, even though he had already done that in Iraq and Afghanistan. Helmick admired him for making that decision, and he set it up so that soon Bostick and his girls had moved to Germany, where he was assigned to 1-91 Cav. The squadron had only a handful of experienced Infantry leaders, including Operations Sergeant Major Michael "Ted" Kennedy and Captain Joey Hutto, the squadron's plans officer. Bostick would join that coterie.

The first time the soldiers of Bulldog Troop 1-91 Cav met Bostick, they were standing in formation at the motor pool for the change-of-command ceremony. Bostick explained that they were all a family now. He spoke with compassion and empathy, but what impressed the rank and file most was the knowledge that he had started out as one of them and worked his way up, from enlisted man to officer. He hadn't just joined ROTC in college and then gone right into the military as a lieutenant, without ever putting in any time as a lowly grunt.

It meant a lot to Private First Class Jonathan Sultan of 3rd Platoon that the new commander understood what it was to be a joe. The nineteen-year-old Sultan had enlisted in the Army the year before. He hated his platoon leader, Newsom, who he thought had the energy of a hummingbird—"hated" him, that was, in the way any private would hate a tough lieutenant who rode his men hard and held them to impossible standards. Newsom was constantly pushing the members of his platoon to run and do sit-ups, push-ups, and pull-ups, but the drill they dreaded most was when he'd force them to exercise wearing full body armor and gas masks—the goal being to increase their lung capacity and get them comfortable with the oxygen deprivation they would experience in the mountains of Afghanistan. The more his troops bitched, the harder Newsom pushed—but there was nothing he made them do that he wasn't also doing himself.

As far as Newsom was concerned, Captain Bostick was the hardass: he'd let you fall on your face and learn whatever the lesson was for yourself, and if you still didn't learn it, he'd make damn sure you knew you were failing. Bostick emphasized communications above all. He wanted everyone talking, everyone sharing, not just the radio guy. And he didn't care one bit about rank when cracking down. In the middle of one exercise, he approached Newsom and yanked him out of his truck: "You'd better have the fucking hand mike glued to your fucking helmet, or I'll do it myself," the captain said. Embarrassing though it'd been, Newsom for sure wouldn't make that mistake again: he now knew that the most powerful weapon he had was his radio.

The 173rd Airborne had originally been destined for Iraq, but in February 2007, the Pentagon opted to send the brigade to Afghanistan instead. This change of plans was no small matter, since at the time, the troopers were already training in Germany for urban, not mountain, combat. The brigade quickly revised its mission rehearsal exercises, and the senior officers canceled all Iraq-oriented language and cultural preparation, including advanced courses for Arabic-speaking intelligence officers. Amazingly, six years after 9/11, there were no Pashto speakers on hand to take their place. The time-line for the brigade's departure was also moved up by six weeks.

Lieutenant Dave Roller, for one, was happy about the change. He had trouble justifying the war in Iraq to himself both morally and legally and had been worried about how he would explain the *Why?* to his men. He called his father with the news: he was going to fight the "good" war. Moreover, since there were only two brigades in Afghanistan—compared to what would be almost ten times that many in Iraq during the 2007 surge of troops—Roller was able to suggest to his soldiers that they were headed somewhere "unique" and "special." Bostick had been there before, so that added to his confidence.

The troopers of 1-91 Cav flew from Germany to Kyrgyzstan to Bagram to Jalalabad to Naray, and then Bulldog Troop broke off and moved to Camp Keating. At each stop along the way, conditions became more austere. When they sat down for a meal at Bagram Air Base, Tom Bostick turned to his fire-support officer, Second Lieutenant Kenny Johnson.

"You gonna eat that ice cream?" Bostick asked him.

"No," replied Johnson.

"You should," Bostick said. "Because at Keating there's not going to be any fucking ice cream."

*   *   *

Lieutenant Colonel Mike Howard had handed over command of the area to Lieutenant Colonel Chris Kolenda on May 31, 2007. Kolenda lost his first man two days later.

Kolenda was an unconventional officer with a good heart, a deep belief in the potential of the Afghan people, and often the highest IQ in the room. He was in Jalalabad for a brigade-level meeting, sitting in a commanders' conference, when he was handed a note informing him that there had been a firefight in his area of operations. He excused himself and went to the operations center, where he called back to Forward Operating Base Naray and was told that one of his men was KIA. Kolenda had been in the Army for almost twenty years, and this was the first time — ever — that a soldier under his command had been killed. Private First Class Jacob Lowell, twenty-two, was a big teddy bear of a guy, a football enthusiast who'd been something of a problem child before finding his direction in the Army. That day, a patrol to Gawardesh was ambushed from the high ground; Lowell, the gunner on a Humvee, was shot in the leg. He managed to get back in the turret and kept firing his .50-caliber, but a second bullet — this one to the chest — ended his life.

Although Kolenda hadn't known Lowell personally, a feeling of intense anger, combined with a deep sense of loss, came over him. He told himself he needed to remain calm. He needed to get more troops, more resources, into the fight. He needed to focus on the living, on winning the next battle and then setting conditions that would make it easier to capitalize on future successes. It was not easy. Later, Kolenda and Captain John Page, the 1-503 Infantry Legion Company[35] commander who had led the patrol, analyzed what had happened. This ambush was different from the enemy attacks that 3-71 Cav had experienced during its time in Nuristan. Until the previous month, when all of those ANA troops were slaughtered, nearly every firefight had occurred across a considerable distance, and the insurgents had appeared poorly trained. But in this latest incident, the enemy fighters had been willing to come close to their targets — to venture a "near" ambush, as such an action was known. They hid on the high ground just above the road, behind fea-

---

[35] Legion Company belonged to the 1st Battalion, 503rd Infantry, and had been "attached" to 1-91 Cav. Jacob Lowell had been a member of Legion Company.

tures of the landscape that kept them well concealed. And as had been the case with the ambush of the ANA and Pearsall's platoon, this was a well-planned attack conducted by trained and disciplined fighters.

The Americans seemed to be facing a different enemy in 2007 than they had faced in 2006.

Officers from 3-71 Cav had every good intention when they planned the grand opening of the Naray water-pipe project: they timed it to occur after their own departure, so that their replacements — and most specifically, Captain Nathan Springer of 1-91 Cav's Headquarters Troop — would get a quick success under their belts and earn some goodwill among the locals. Like many of the best-laid plans in Afghanistan, this one made perfect sense on paper.

The project itself wasn't the problem. The contractor had tapped into a spring above and to the east of Naray, which sent clean, potable water flowing down the mountain, through a pipe, to several spots in Naray Village. The problem was this: about halfway down the mountain, between the spring and Naray, sat the hamlet of Shali Kot, which was completely bypassed by the pipe. It was an honest mistake on the part of the United States, if most likely not so on the part of the Naray elders, with whom the contractor had worked in designing the project.

Springer didn't know about any of this before he went to the opening ceremony. There, while inspecting the pipe, he was approached by a Shali Kot elder named Mohammed Ayoub, who made it clear that he thought the omission of his village from the water project was insulting and unfair. He and the other Shali Kot elders claimed that the project not only threatened their own water supply but also violated a previous agreement between them and the elders of Naray regarding water rights. Ayoub let Springer have it — Springer's interpreter could barely keep up with his tirade — and concluded the conversation by calling the American an infidel, an intense pejorative in this part of the world. Hearing this, the head of Naray District, Shamsur Rahman — a six-foot-three behemoth of a man — stepped in and slapped Ayoub several times with the back of his hand for the disrespect he had shown Springer. That ended the ceremony.

There was a lot that the Americans still had to learn about Afghanistan. Maybe they would never learn what they needed to in order to win this war. But Springer knew that to insult (however unintentionally) a village elder who then called you an infidel was not good—not good at all.

Springer told the story to Kolenda, who agreed to budget additional funds to include Shali Kot in the pipe scheme. More important, however, was the larger lesson to be drawn from the episode: money and development projects were a double-edged sword. *Zar, zan, zamin,* Kolenda thought. It was an Afghan saying, the Dari words for "gold, women, land"—the driving forces of conflict in the area, and here *land* also meant "water," and *water* also meant "gold." These were ancient reasons for strife that hadn't gone out of style in Naray and Shali Kot. If the Americans weren't careful, their generosity could create more problems for them than solutions.[36]

Nothing about this country was simple. The population of Kolenda's total area of operations in northern Kunar and eastern Nuristan included at least four of Afghanistan's many ethnic groups, including Pashtuns and Nuristanis. And then there were the political divisions. The villages of Barikot and Naray had ties to the National Islamic Front, a mujahideen party that had been active during the Soviet war, while the Kamdesh elders had long-established links to the rival HIG. The local leader of the National Islamic Front loathed HIG's founder, Gulbuddin Hekmatyar, and the feeling was mutual. Thus, even more than a decade after the Soviets' withdrawal, the Kom Nuristanis living in Naray and the Kom Nuristanis in Kamdesh District were stuck in the clutch of a blood feud. Of course, the religious differences were complicated as well—the several strains of Sunni Islam in the region, for instance, disagreed about the relative importance of certain texts and the role to be played by the mullahs. At the far end of the spectrum was the fanatical Islam being

---

[36] A 2011 study of aid projects in Afghanistan would conclude that though the root causes of unrest and conflict in Afghanistan were often political, international stabilization projects "tended to lay more emphasis on socio-economic rather than political drivers of conflict, and therefore primarily focused on addressing issues such as unemployment, illiteracy, lack of social services, and inadequate infrastructure such as roads. As a result, aid projects were often not addressing the main sources of conflict, and in some cases fueled conflict by distributing resources that rival groups then fought over" (Paul Fishstein and Andrew Wilder, *Winning Hearts and Minds? Examining the Relationship between Aid and Security in Afghanistan,* Tufts University, 2011).

pushed by the Taliban and some of the more extreme seminaries, or madrassas.

Kolenda considered it his duty to understand all of this. He studied the distinctions and the similarities among the various groups and sects, keeping in his head a sort of Venn diagram that looked like a spilled case of Slinkys—which he knew could ultimately make the difference between life and death for his men.

The 3-71 Cav staff officers, immediately impressed with Kolenda during their overlap in May, had referred to him as "The Big Brain." They found his calm demeanor and inquisitive nature a refreshing change from the personal qualities of the man he was replacing, their own squadron commander, whom they called, behind his back, Howard the Tyrant. Kolenda, a Nebraska native, hadn't been satisfied with just an undergraduate degree from the United States Military Academy, so he'd gone on to earn master of arts degrees in modern European history, from the University of Wisconsin, and in national security and strategic studies, from the U.S. Naval War College.

In 2001, the Army War College Foundation Press had published a book he'd edited, *Leadership: The Warrior's Art,* which contained essays by military thinkers, including Kolenda himself, on lessons of leadership gleaned throughout the ages. "The most effective leaders are able to motivate people...not by appealing to fear and interest alone (the 'transactional' approach), but by appealing to ideas more lasting, more meaningful, and ultimately more human," he wrote. In another essay, he examined ideas on the topic from Aristotle, Cicero, Plato, and Xenophon, arguing that the best leaders were those who valued independent thought and individual initiative. In a third piece, he took a critical look at Alexander the Great.

And now here Kolenda was, literally following in Alexander's footsteps, though this was his first time ever commanding on the field of battle. It was a heck of a place for him to make the transition from the world of theory to brutal reality.

Alex Newsom would have been happy to leave the men of departing 3-71 Cav alone, but he and his 3rd Platoon had been posted to Combat Outpost Kamu and needed some guidance on the real estate and the people. The thing was, the 3-71 troops had been at Kamu for only a few weeks themselves and thus didn't have much to offer. What they did know, they shared, but by now they were running on fumes. Indeed, Newsom had never seen American soldiers more burnt out, emotionally and physically, than the guys from 3-71 Cav at Camp Kamu. They'd lost friends and leaders, including Ben Keating, Jared Monti, and Joe Fenty; they'd had their tour extended to almost sixteen months; they were dead-eyed and pale.

After the men of 3rd Platoon were dropped off by chopper on May 18, their seats were occupied by members of 3-71 Cav on their way out. Newsom had with him his platoon sergeant, Sergeant First Class Rodney O'Dell, Staff Sergeant John Faulkenberry, and a couple of dozen others. It was ridiculous: they hadn't even been issued maps for their new area of operations. The day before, Newsom had frantically dashed around the office buildings at Bagram Air Base, eventually prevailing upon a private to hand over his own rather shabby map indicating the location of Combat Outpost Kamu. Such was the level of preparedness they had going in.

The residents of Kamdesh District were still growing accustomed to the idea of having an American presence in their midst. Many locals seemed confused by the new cast of characters, and a number approached Newsom to ask for money that they felt was owed them—for fields ruined by chopper landings, for rental fees for King Zahir's former hunting lodge (now used as part of Combat Outpost Kamu), and on and on. Newsom had no funds to hand over, so he had to do some talking—"Give me some time, and we'll figure this out," he pleaded—but that got him only so far. Soon some of the locals began making veiled threats: if they didn't get paid, bad things would happen. One elder lifted the veil and said straight up to Newsom, "You are going to be ambushed very soon."

Combat Outpost Keating was spartan when Tom Bostick took command in May 2007. The bunkers were bare-bones. There was a junkyard on the grounds, and at the southern edge of the outpost were a burn pit for refuse and a tent that served as the maintenance bay. Nearby, troops urinated in "piss-tubes" and defecated in latrines built over fifty-five-gallon drums cut in half, whose contents would each day be burned using JP-8, the military's kerosene-based fuel. The ignited latrines smelled horrid, fouling the air. Walking in through the front gate, any new arrivals would see, off in the distance to their right, in the southwestern corner of the camp, a small wooden structure; that was the gym. Turning left, or east, as they entered the grounds, they'd pass a bunker on their left, with the mortar pit on their right. The aid station and sleep quarters for 1st Platoon had been constructed adjacent to the former Afghan Department of Forestry building. To their right sat the bunks for 2nd and 3rd Platoons, alongside a site designated for a future morale, welfare, and recreation center, with space for storage on the upper floor and sleeping quarters for transient personnel on the lower.

A view of Combat Outpost Keating from the east, May 2007. *(Photo courtesy of Bulldog Troop)*

Continuing east, next came a newly constructed command post and sleep quarters for Headquarters Platoon, followed by the old Afghan National Police station, and then finally, at the far eastern edge of the outpost, right by the road, some huts for the Afghan National Army company.

Inevitably, new troops would tilt their heads back and take in the peaks looming over them. The southern mountain rose almost right from the border—or "wire"—of Combat Outpost Keating. Somewhere up there were Observation Post Warheit and Kamdesh Village, though neither was visible from the outpost. Those on the base could see, to the west on that southern mountain, the "Switchbacks," as the path running back and forth up the steep slopes was known, from whose track insurgents would sometimes fire.

On the other side of the Landay-Sin River from the camp stood two mountains, one to the northwest, closer to Urmul, and one more directly to the north. The enemy lurked in specific spots there as well, ones so frequently used that the troops of 3-71 Cav had come up with nicknames for them, which they passed on to their successors with 1-91 Cav: the Putting Green was a patch of grass on the mountain to the northwest, and the Northface was straight north. A Marine serving with 1-91 Cav, training ANA troops at the camp, dubbed an area southeast of the outpost the Diving Board. Bostick ordered that construction continue on two additional "hard-stand" buildings, made of concrete and rock and able to withstand a blast. He also directed that a mosque be built on the base.

In early June, Captain Bostick drove the almost six miles from Camp Keating to Combat Outpost Kamu to check the place out. Newsom had briefed him on 3rd Platoon's activities there: patrols that were generally uneventful, a few shura meetings held with elders in Mirdesh and Kamu. The chief elder in Kamu was a retired Afghan Army colonel named Jamil Khan, a man in his late sixties with a huge white cloud of a beard and a significantly disabled arm, who could nonetheless outpace any of the nineteen- or twenty-year-old U.S. troops when they hiked up and down the mountain trails with him. Newsom liked Khan, who seemed to eschew the typical "You're an American, give me money" school of Afghan leadership and had a real sense of military pride and patriotism. He also had a checkered past, according to many: as a colonel in the Afghan Communist Army, Khan had fought against and been defeated by members of the local Kom community, who viewed him as a turncoat. There were various stories floating around about what had happened to his arm: some said he'd been wounded in combat, others that he'd been caught in bed with another man's wife. The one thing the Americans were fairly sure of, in June 2007, was that Jamil Khan was just about the only friend they had in the area.

When he met with his new commander, Newsom had a makeshift cast around his right hand, which he had fractured but not told anyone about. He was supposed to inform Bostick about such things, it was true, but in this instance there was good reason for his reticence: he'd broken his hand on the head of Habibullah, an ANA soldier, with whom he'd gotten into a scuffle one evening when the Afghan was stoned out of his mind and became confrontational. Now, however, Newsom had even worse news to impart: he had heard from the Kamu elders that the school the Americans had built for the kids of Kamu and Mirdesh was a nonstarter, since the parents from each village refused to allow their children to be in class with the children from the other village. The residents of Kamu and Mirdesh had each wanted their own school, and they all felt the Americans hadn't delivered. Moreover, in spite of the poverty of the region, the United States hadn't hired locals to build the new facility. In what might have been the only example of coordinated activity between the two villages in decades, insurgents from Kamu and Mirdesh had been taking turns vandalizing and attacking the building. And this was far from the only evidence of local displeasure with Americans in general. The officers of 3-71 Cav had done their best to make sure their replacements knew what promises they'd made, but the Nuristanis invented many additional ones. These allegedly broken promises fueled a mounting sense of insult and inspired additional threats of revenge.

So Newsom's broken hand was nothing, really — the other breaks were bigger.

The Americans had many names for the insurgents. Officers called them ACMs, short for "anticoalition militias," but that was just the latest acronym circulating on memos from the Pentagon, soon to be replaced by "AAFs," for "anti-Afghan forces." Some officers blandly spoke of them as just "the enemy" or "fighters." Another word sometimes used was *dushman,* a noun of Persian origin meaning, again, "enemy." "Bad guys" was often the shorthand translation; there was almost a comic quality to that term, implying a return to a simpler, childlike black-and-white view of a world that didn't bear much resemblance to the Americans' new home in Nuristan. The Cavalry officers instructed their troops to avoid using religious nicknames, forbidding them from calling the enemy *hajis,* which in Islam is a term of reverence for those who have made the pilgrimage to Mecca. Also prohibited were *muj,* short for *mujahideen,* and *jihadi,* from the same root. In Afghanistan, those words were used to refer to the revered mujahideen who had fought the Soviets (and who at the time had been funded by the United States). Calling the insurgents mujahideen would also imply that they had some religious justification for their attacks. It cannot be said that no one ever used these names, or worse, but such language was officially not permitted.

Many soldiers just called them fuckers.

Bostick had intended to return to Combat Outpost Keating after his visit, taking Newsom's platoon back with him and leaving the platoon from Legion Company (to which the late Jacob Lowell had belonged) at Kamu in its place, but a flurry of new intelligence reports suggesting that the enemy was planning to overrun Combat Outpost Kamu put an end to that plan. The captain needed to stay.

On June 6, the lone local worker at the Kamu outpost failed to show up for work. Bostick radioed Kolenda in Naray, and they discussed the need to prepare for an attack; they planned to send out two patrols. Bostick then briefed his men and listened as Newsom and his platoon sergeant, Rodney O'Dell, both eager to get in the fight, spent half an hour bickering like brothers about which one of them would lead 3rd Platoon troopers into the mountains. Ultimately, O'Dell won out. Newsom would help command from the base with half of the platoon, which would be at the ready as a reserve force.

O'Dell and his half platoon left for the mountain, with orders both to watch over the area and to find a mountain path from Combat Outpost Kamu to Camp Keating so they and the rest of 3rd Platoon could avoid the dangerous road if need be. The platoon from Legion Company moved to take the lower ground. Newsom and Bostick sat on the rooftop of the hunting lodge with their interpreter and other officers, monitoring enemy traffic on the radio. The insurgents were speaking in Nuristani and Pashto and a third language that none of them could discern. For a time, the chatter was fairly vague. Then, in an instant, it got specific.

"We see them in position," an insurgent announced.

Newsom radioed O'Dell and passed on the translation.

"When the Americans get here, we will attack them, and they will fall off this cliff," another insurgent said.

Bostick ordered Sergeant Mark Speight, in charge of the mortars at Combat Outpost Kamu, to have his men fire their 120-millimeter mortars into the hills, targeting the suspected general area where the enemy fighters might be, partly in hopes of learning more about their position: the incoming fire would cause the insurgents to talk, Bostick reasoned, and possibly to reveal some information about their location. (They didn't seem to realize that the Americans could listen in on their radio transmissions.)

The mortarmen fired, and Legion Platoon, on the low ground, assessed where the ordnance had landed. O'Dell and his troops, on the high ground, fired with their M4 carbine rifles in the general direction of where the mortars had hit. Enemy gunfire erupted as a large element of forty or so fighters began conducting a complex maneuver that brought the whole force down the hill toward O'Dell's patrol, with smaller groups providing cover for one another. O'Dell and his troops took cover, returning fire with their M4 carbines. One enemy shot found its mark, hitting a rifleman, Sergeant Wayne Baird; the bullet entered Baird's forearm, traveled through his arm, and blew out his tricep as it exited his body.

O'Dell radioed in the WIA — the soldier "wounded in action." The bullet had hit an artery, and Baird was bleeding out; he would need a medevac. Other troops stabilized the injured sergeant, trying to calm him down and prepare him for the move down the hill. In a valley — a disorienting, vulnerable, echoing space — it can be hard to tell where enemy fire is coming from, but it seemed clear that the enemy was firing upon the patrol from the hillsides to the south and southwest of the base. "We need to reinforce the platoon element up in the hills," Bostick told Newsom.

The enemy fire abated a bit after mortars began raining upon the area where the Americans now knew the insurgents were, allowing some of Baird's fellow troops to help him back toward Combat Outpost Kamu. Newsom and his half of 3rd Platoon grabbed medical supplies and started running up the hill to meet them. Newsom wasn't planning to go far; Bostick and the others back at the hunting lodge would be able to see his and his men's general position.

Up on the hill, Newsom spotted two insurgents some distance away, hiding behind rocks and getting into sniper positions. Just at that moment, two A-10 Warthogs arrived at the outpost.

"I got aircraft here," Bostick radioed up to Newsom. "I'm gonna give 'em to you. Whaddaya got?"

"I got targets," Newsom told Bostick, then provided the relevant coordinates. The A-10s fired and hit their marks. Nothing was left of the insurgents who had been there but a second before.

Bostick also called in an emergency resupply, since 3rd Platoon was getting dangerously low on ammo. Within thirty minutes, a Black Hawk and two Apaches had flown in from Naray. As the Black Hawk passed by him, Newsom saw a mass of muzzle flashes from the *northern* side of the mountain. This was a shock. He and Bostick knew the enemy was to the south, but they'd had no idea a whole mess of insurgents were on the northern side as well. Shit, Newsom thought. Because their guns weren't powerful enough in and of themselves to bring down a bird, the insurgents were trying a tactic that Newsom had read about but never before seen, called volley fire: by amassing the fire of many small arms, the shooters hoped to replicate the effect of a larger weapon. It was another clear sign of discipline and training, if not of the presence of other, more sophisticated enemy fighters.

The Black Hawk landed under fire. The ordnance — mainly a critical supply of 120-millimeter mortars — was quickly offloaded, and the helicopter flew away. But the insurgents didn't stop there; now they started firing at Combat Outpost Kamu, where Bostick was still trying to figure out exactly what was going on.

"Break, break, Bulldog-Six," Newsom said, interrupting the radio chatter, "we see them. What are your recs?"

"I'm going to give you the hundred-and-five-millimeter, and you call it in," Bostick replied.

The 105-millimeter was a long-range howitzer located at Combat Outpost Lybert, more than ten miles to the east of Kamu. Newsom, O'Dell, and forward observer specialist Brett Johnson started working up coordinates to call in, using a hundred-thousand-meter grid square for the area. When they were ready, they radioed the six-digit grid coordinates, but the first rounds ended up being wildly inaccurate, landing about eight hundred yards too far to the left. Newsom called Bostick and relayed the bad news. The men at Combat Outpost Lybert fired again; these rounds hit eight hundred yards too far to the right.

"What the fuck is going on?" Newsom snapped.

Bostick wanted to know the same, and he started hounding Newsom over the radio.

"What the hell are you calling in?" he asked.

"I know what the hell I'm doing," Newsom said. "This is not *me.*"

With the 105-millimeter not functioning properly—it would later be discovered that there was a technical problem with the weapon—the return of the A-10 Warthog jets was a welcome sight. It was getting dark now, and the Warthogs fired white-phosphorous marking rounds at enemy positions.

The chatter picked up on the insurgents' radio frequency; Newsom listened with his interpreter.

"You okay?" one insurgent asked another, presumably one of the targets.

"Yes, I'm all right, they're shooting below me," came the answer.

The A-10 circled around. Newsom told the pilot, "Try fifty yards higher."

The Warthog fired.

A minute later, the enemy chatter started again:

"You all right?"

"Yes, but they're getting closer."

Newsom told the pilot to aim fifty yards higher again.

Fire.

A minute passed.

"You all right?"

"Yes, but they're getting closer. Pray for me."

Newsom advised the pilot, "Aim up just five more yards." He did so.

The first insurgent's voice came again:

"You all right?"

This time the inquiry was met with only static.

By midnight, it seemed to Bostick that the enemy threat had been eliminated. Just in case, though, he ordered 3rd Platoon to stay in the hills until morning. At around 2:00 a.m., O'Dell was on guard duty when, through his night-vision goggles, he saw some insurgents regrouping on the northern mountainside. He radioed Speight, the mortarman, and gave him the grids. Then he gently nudged Newsom awake.

Are you serious? Newsom thought to himself. They're coming *back?* We just hammered that whole area for half the day.

Speight fired the 120-millimeter mortars at the insurgents, pummeling them. That seemed to put an end to that.

Through the morning, 3rd Platoon stayed on the hill. At one point, Afghan Security Guards—local contractors—brought up Pepsis and cookies, but by then two of Newsom's soldiers had already fainted from heat exhaustion. At 11:00 a.m., Bostick finally told Newsom that he and his men could head back to the camp.

Any impulse Newsom may have felt to be celebratory, to slap some backs and pump his fist in the air, was negated by Bostick's clear concern that there would be another attack. He told Newsom to meet him at the operations center so they could make plans for the next two days. It was only later that night, at a barbecue where the men grilled some steaks and took a breath, that Newsom pulled Bostick aside.

"Hey, sir, I had a lot of fun," he told his commander.

"Yeah, I know." Bostick smiled. "It was a good TIC"—meaning "troops in contact," a firefight.

The clash had reminded Newsom of stories he'd read about Special Forces early on in the war—sitting up on an observation post, calling in close air support and mortars. If this is combat, then count me in, Newsom thought to himself, because that shit is fun. "Are they all like that?" he asked.

"Yeah, pretty much," Bostick said. "It's fun stuff."

"I want more!" Newsom exclaimed. Bostick laughed. Newsom vaguely thanked the captain—for trusting him in the field, for staying calm, for being a great commander. Bostick shrugged.

Staff Sergeant Ryan Fritsche[37] was late in getting to Forward Operating Base Naray. His leave back home in Indiana had been extended so he could say good-bye to his father, Bill, who was dying of cancer.

Ryan had scheduled a lot around his father's illness—he and his wife, Brandi, had gotten married the previous September because they weren't certain his dad would make it this long. On May 16, 2007, fifty-two-year-

---

[37] Pronounced "FRITCH-ee."

old Bill Fritsche, surrounded by his family, succumbed to non-Hodgkin's lymphoma.

By June, the younger Fritsche was in Afghanistan. He'd been deployed abroad once before, at a base in Djibouti, between Ethiopia and Somalia, as part of a U.S. effort to hunt terrorists in the Horn of Africa. Fritsche's company had pulled security there for the members of the Army Corps of Engineers as they dug wells and built schools and orphanages. For the whole five years that Fritsche had been in the Army, the United States had been fighting at least one war, if not two, but he'd had yet to see any combat. He'd served as a member of the elite "Old Guard" unit stationed at Arlington National Cemetery. He'd escorted caskets at Dover. He'd marched in President George W. Bush's second inaugural parade. He had never fired a gun at an enemy fighter, nor had one fired at him.

He was a textbook Hoosier, Fritsche — tall, good-looking, a bit meek in bearing, and possessed of a disarming determination. For his first ten days in Afghanistan, he'd been biding time at Forward Operating Base Naray, waiting for a slot to open up out in the field. Then, on June 19, two staff sergeants with 2nd Platoon suffered ankle injuries near Combat Outpost Kamu, and Captain Joey Hutto sent for Fritsche to replace Staff Sergeant Patrick Potts. Potts had been with his men in 2nd Platoon for half a year — working with them, bonding with them, developing close relationships with them.

"I'm nervous about going," Fritsche wrote to his wife. "It's been a long time since I've done any of that stuff. I'm worried I won't remember things I need to. I'm sure I'll be fine, but I'm worried anyway, it's not something that you can get away with being bad at." Since his deployment, he'd also been having dreams that bothered him, mostly about his late father.

Bulldog Troop had only just arrived in Kamdesh District, but the attack on Kamu was something of a last straw for Chris Kolenda. First there'd been the May 14 ambush on Aaron Pearsall of 3-71 Cav and the ANA troops, and then the June 6 attack at Combat Outpost Kamu — and on the latter occasion, according to informants, the fighters had come not just from the immediate area of Kamu but also from the Saret Koleh Valley, down the road to the east, and the Pitigal Valley, northeast toward the Pakistan border.

In the short time that 1-91 Cav had been in Nuristan, none of Kolenda's men had yet ventured into Saret Koleh to reach out to the locals, build rapport, or gather information about the people and the enemy. Kolenda knew that 3-71 Cav hadn't done any of those things, either. He had previously ordered Operation Ghar — *ghar* being Pashto for "mountain" — to develop relationships with the villagers of Gawardesh, a mission led by Captains Page of Legion Company and Springer of 1-91 Cav Headquarters Troop, and now it was time to do the same in Saret Koleh with Operation Ghar Dwa, or "Operation Mountain II." The plan was fairly straightforward: Roller and 1st Platoon would briefly relocate from Combat Outpost Keating to Combat Outpost Kamu, then they'd move again toward Saret Koleh on July 26, splitting up and establishing two observation posts to watch over the area. Lieutenant John Meyer would lead 2nd Platoon and the ANA company as they escorted Bostick and some soldiers from Headquarters Troop to the hamlet. Newsom and 3rd Platoon would serve as the quick reaction force, ready to roll up from Kamu if needed.

After a strategy session at Forward Operating Base Naray, Bostick caught up with one of his closest friends, Joey Hutto. They were both "older captains" in their late thirties, having both worked their way up from the rank of private — a parallel history that had given them an instant rapport when they first met, in Germany. Their families had grown close as well.

Bostick and Hutto sat together for an hour, chugging coffee as if it were beer (since alcohol was prohibited in theater) and talking about their wives and children, and work, too. Hutto was slated to take Bostick's place as commander of Bulldog Troop around New Year's 2008 — welcome news for Bostick, who wanted to be replaced by someone in whom he had confidence, someone he thought would be a competent combat leader in the pitiless mountains of northeastern Afghanistan.

On July 20, less than a week before Operation Ghar Dwa was scheduled to begin, Dave Roller was on the roof of the Kamu hunting lodge when two Black Hawks and an Apache gun team buzzed into the area. As was standard practice, the pilots radioed below to ask the troops if there was anything they could do for their comrades on the ground.

As Roller stood up there talking on the radio with the lead Apache pilot, one of the Black Hawks rolled so low through the valley that its pilot was at just about eye level with him, giving him an alarmingly clear view of what happened next: an RPG was fired out of the hills, missing the Black Hawk but exploding right next to it, propelling shrapnel that clipped the bird's rotor. Flailing and plummeting, the bird landed hard about five hundred yards down the river, around a rocky spur off the mountain. Survivable. Maybe.

"Did you see that?" Roller asked the Apache pilot, who said he wasn't sure. The 1st Platoon leader then alerted everyone else, yelling into the radio, "Guys, you're not going to believe this, but we have a Black Hawk down! We have a Black Hawk down!"

It sounded weird to him even as he said it. Roller had turned eleven on October 3, 1993, the first day of the Battle of Mogadishu. He was sixteen when the definitive account of that battle—Mark Bowden's *Black Hawk Down: A Story of Modern War*—was published, and nineteen when the Ridley Scott film hit theaters. It was the kind of experience that those around him in Coral Gables, Florida, were perfectly content to keep on the page or on the DVD player. But now here he was, saying those same words and meaning them.

Fortunately, the pilots and crew were fine, and they flew off in the other Black Hawk, leaving the men of Bulldog Troop to guard the wounded bird until it could be airlifted to Forward Operating Base Naray. The squadron's assignment to pull security on the helicopter, combined with the impending mission into Saret Koleh, meant that for the first time since the beginning of his deployment, Bostick had all three of his Bulldog Troop platoon lieutenants with him in one place—Roller, John Meyer, and Newsom—along with his fire-support officer, Kenny Johnson. Bostick wasn't one to shower his lieutenants with praise, but he seemed content; his men appeared to be squared away. They all grabbed some MREs and headed to the river.

For his part, when he heard about the attack on the Black Hawk, Kolenda was even more convinced that outreach to Saret Koleh was needed—both the kind of outreach consisting of money and development projects and the kind released by a metal trigger.

Lieutenant Dave Roller, Lieutenant John Meyer, Captain Tom Bostick, and Lieutenant Alex Newsom. *(Photo courtesy of Dave Roller)*

Fritsche did not fit seamlessly into the leadership role in his new platoon. Partly to better acclimate himself to his new troops, he led them on a patrol a couple of days before Operation Ghar Dwa was to begin. On one particularly steep incline, he tripped and stumbled.

"Don't worry, I got you," said Private First Class Alberto Barba, catching him. Barba was a short, likeable kid from South Central Los Angeles who always joked about having been shot at before he even joined the Army.

"You didn't 'get' your last squad leader," Fritsche noted, referring to the fall and ankle injury that had led to his replacing Staff Sergeant Potts. Surely Fritsche meant this as just a joke, a little macho wit, but no one found Potts's mishap amusing.

Sergeant John Wilson didn't care for that crack, that was for sure. In fact, he didn't care much for Fritsche's attitude in general. Wilson had developed a rapport with Potts, and he'd already attempted to do the same with the new guy. Preparing for the mission to Saret Koleh, Fritsche had been tinkering with his radio, taking extra precautions because equipment often broke down in the field. Wilson tried to help him out, but Fritsche didn't seem to want his assistance. Wilson even offered to hook Fritsche up with a "trucker mike," which would allow him to put the radio in his chest rig and hook the speaker — or trucker mike — onto the shoulder of his Kevlar vest, closer to his mouth, thus leaving his hands free to hold his gun. Wilson tracked down three possible trucker mikes and gave them to his new staff sergeant. A warm thank-you was not forthcoming.

Roller and 1st Platoon left on the mission the next day, heading for the observation post from which they would see the naked Afghan women romping in the stream. Back at Combat Outpost Kamu that night, Bostick, Meyer, and Newsom watched several DVD episodes from the first season of the NBC TV show *Heroes* before crashing at around 1:00 a.m.

At 4:00 a.m., Bostick and the top officers and NCOs of Bulldog Troop accompanied Meyer and 2nd Platoon to Saret Koleh. A disappointed Newsom hung back; Bostick had explained to him that his platoon, which had the fewest soldiers, would be needed as a quick reaction force should there be any significant enemy contact — as Bostick was almost certain would be the case. He assured Newsom, in his calm yet focused way, "You *will* be a part of this fight." He would be right.

Third Platoon Private First Class Jonathan Sultan had been on guard duty the night before and expected that as part of the operation, he would be tasked to guard Combat Outpost Kamu. But less than an hour after the assigned troops left the camp, Bostick's radio transmission operator (RTO) said he'd hurt his ankle. Soon Staff Sergeant John Faulkenberry was shaking Sultan awake.

"We've got fifteen minutes to go, we're rolling out, let's go," Faulkenberry told the private. "You're going to be the CO's RTO."

Sultan griped, as was customary. He felt skeptical that the original RTO was really injured; more likely, he thought, he'd heard how dangerous this mission might be and figured out a way to get out of it. But Sultan threw on his gear anyway.

*   *   *

Sultan now caught up with the group at last and was directed to Bostick, Meyer, and Johnson. With them was Air Force Staff Sergeant Patrick Lape, there to coordinate with various combat aircraft should the need arise, including A-10 Warthogs, French Mirage 2000s, and an unmanned Predator drone.

Bostick looked at Sultan warily. "Every single RTO I've ever had has broken on me," he said. "Are you going to break on me?"

"No, sir," Sultan assured him. He didn't know what else to say.

Typically, a "village assessment" would take four to six hours: while Bostick talked to the elders, the medic, Sergeant Rob Fortner, would set up a station directly behind him to care for sick and injured villagers. That morning, however, before they even entered Saret Koleh, Bostick told Fortner that the medic wouldn't be coming along this time; he asked for a rifle team with a light machine gun to accompany him into the village instead.

At roughly 6:30 a.m., Meyer and his 2nd Platoon troops crossed the footbridge over the Landay-Sin River to Saret Koleh. They were followed by other Bulldog Troop soldiers who circled around the village, establishing security. Bostick walked to a spot at the edge of the hamlet by a large grove of trees, where he radioed to Roller. Roller and 1st Platoon were watching everything from above, and Bostick nonchalantly gazed up toward where he thought they were and asked if Roller could see him. Bostick didn't want to wave for fear of giving away 1st Platoon's position.

"Roger," Roller told him.

"Sweet OP," said Bostick, referring to the observation post.

Roller agreed. They had a great position, overlooking the entire valley.

With that piece of business done, Bostick sent the ANA troops into the hamlet to make the initial contact, then went in himself and approached a village elder. At thirty-seven, Bostick was considered aged for a captain in combat, but he had nothing on any of the Nuristani elders he'd met so far, with their decades-old white beards and craggy oaken faces. Bostick was fairly sure that neither this man nor any of the other residents of Saret Koleh had ever before met an American. He and the elder headed into a building for a shura while Fritsche, Wilson, and others from 2nd Platoon pulled security outside. Once again, Wilson made a

Dave Roller's view of Saret Koleh, the Landay-Sin River, and the road. *(Photo courtesy of Dave Roller)*

suggestion to Fritsche, saying that he thought their position might be a tad too exposed, that maybe it would be better if they moved over and stood in the grove of trees instead. Fritsche rejected Wilson's idea.

It wasn't all unpleasantness between the two of them, however: they joked around a bit, then played and exchanged smiles with some village kids, to whom they gave candy. The presence of children was usually a good sign in situations such as this, indicating that the villagers weren't aware of anything bad that was about to happen. A young girl with big, beautiful eyes appeared, reminding Wilson of the iconic Pashtun on the cover of the June 1985 issue of *National Geographic*. She started playing peekaboo with the soldiers from behind a house, granting them a rare moment of innocence and levity.

During the shura, Bostick tried his best, with the aid of his interpreter, to convey that the Americans were there to help. The United States, he explained, wanted to assist the Nuristanis with development, to help

261

them succeed. The old man focused on something else: for months now, he said, mortars had been repeatedly exploding on the mountain next to the village—American mortars, targeting whomever. This needed to stop, he insisted. Bostick expressed concern about the explosions but noted that there were many insurgents in the area. He asked for more information, but the elder offered no additional details.

If Bostick needed further evidence of local insurgent activity, he was about to get it.

CHAPTER 17

"Bulldog-Six, Where Are You?"

Nothing happened, and then everything happened at once.

Per Lieutenant Meyer's orders, Ryan Fritsche led a team out to set up an observation post from which they would watch over the valley. They would cross the bridge, make their way east on the road in the direction of Forward Operating Base Naray, wait for their cue, and then slog up the southern mountain.

"An OP site?" said Wilson, always questioning. "We don't have any cover for it."

"Let's go," Fritsche said. "We're going to push down the road."

Fritsche, Wilson, Private Barba, and their SAW gunner and rifleman, Privates First Class Nic Barnes and James Stevenson, walked over the bridge and then continued on a couple of hundred yards to the east, where, near a large boulder, they came upon two American snipers, Staff Sergeant Bryan Morrow and Specialist Matthew White. The sun was oppressively beating down upon them all, and Fritsche told his men to drop their packs and helmets; the additional weight was too much, he said.

"We saw two guys with AKs run up the hill," Morrow reported. The snipers had been scouting ahead for the rest of the company, and as they were moving up the side of the mountain, they'd glimpsed a young male Nuristani, age eighteen or so, holding a rifle, along with a boy of about twelve, both running away from them.

Why would anyone with a weapon run away? wondered Wilson. He thought of Sun Tzu's *The Art of War* and the concept of a baited ambush. The Chinese military strategist had described the tactic centuries before: "By holding out baits, he keeps him on the march; then with a body of picked men he lies in wait for him."

"We're going to recon the patrol base," Morrow said, meaning they were going to scout out a place for an observation post.

Fritsche turned to his men, Wilson and Barnes, and explained the mission, adding that they would walk in single file because of the steep climb.

"We're not supposed to go until we get word," Wilson reminded him.

But Fritsche shrugged off Wilson's protest. Barba and Stevenson stayed back at the rock while the others started up the hill. White took point, followed by his fellow sniper, Morrow. Fritsche, Wilson, and Barnes came next. After climbing about a hundred yards, they saw the two locals in the distance. All five men broke from their single file and spread out on the hill.

"We're being led into an ambush!" Wilson yelled. "Stop following the kid!"

"Shut up!" Fritsche said through clenched teeth.

"Stick with me," Wilson said to Barnes. "This is bad."

Barnes said he would. Wilson was his team leader as well as his friend. And he shared Wilson's concerns about Fritsche's lack of experience in the field.

Bostick and his team finished up with the shura and left the village, crossing the bridge back to the road to Kamu. On hearing that Fritsche and the snipers were pursuing suspected insurgents up the mountain, Bostick pulled aside the medic, Fortner, and advised him, "Get ready." The ANA troops who'd accompanied them on this operation thought they saw something odd going on at a house back across the bridge, one that had previously been used as a staging ground for an RPG attack. After Bostick gave them the okay to run back and check it out, they recrossed the Landay-Sin River and went into the house. Bostick now turned to his men and said, "Guys, let's get off the road." He, Johnson, Lape, Sultan, and the others headed up into the sloping woods. Bostick was just a few steps up the hill when he stopped.

"Wait," he said.

Pausing, they listened to the radio: lots of enemy chatter. Sultan looked north, back across the river, to the hamlet of Saret Koleh. He saw a villager pick up her child and start running.

Bostick had instructed the ANA troops to rejoin the group once they'd checked out the house on the other side of the bridge, but after exiting the home—where they hadn't found anything—they instead continued walking eastward, away from the bridge and toward a second home across the river.

Up on the southern mountain, Fritsche, Wilson, and Barnes followed the snipers, Morrow and White, as quickly as they could up the steep incline. They came into an open area. It was still and silent—until enemy guns began firing at them from some one hundred yards farther up the mountain. Bullets whizzed by, making a snapping sound. At first the U.S. soldiers weren't sure which way to run, forward or backward, but then they swiftly pulled back and took cover behind some trees down the hill.

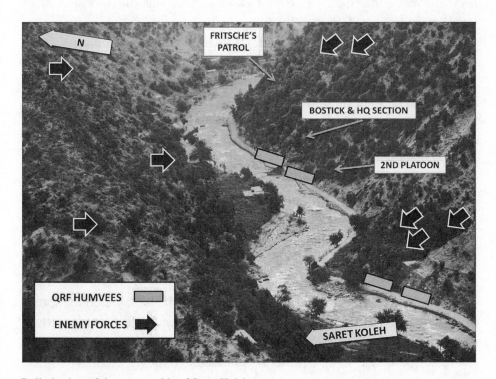

Roller's view of the eastern side of Saret Koleh. *(Photo courtesy of Dave Roller)*

*   *   *

Insurgent fire aimed at Tom Bostick and Headquarters Platoon now also began exploding from the hills above—the same mountain that Fritsche's patrol was on, but farther west. Bullets splashed into the Landay-Sin River.

The ANA troops ran back across the bridge toward the road, returning fire with their AK-47s and RPGs as they went. One ANA soldier fell, shot in the leg: it was Habibullah, on whose head Newsom had broken his hand weeks earlier. Since then, the Afghan had developed trusting relationships with many of the Americans. He'd been hit in the thigh; Rob Fortner met him and hustled him to safety in the trees. Nearby, Bostick, Johnson, Lape, and Sultan took cover in the woods behind some boulders.

Farther to the west on the southern mountain, from his observation post high in the hills, Dave Roller had been watching Bostick and his men and trying to figure out what the ANA troops were looking for. The insurgents now answered that question, as 1st Platoon, too, was hit by a shower of small-arms fire and RPGs.

The enemy had the high ground, attacking from the mountains above the platoon's position and surrounding it from left to right, 270 degrees. Specialist Tommy Alford got his M240B machine gun, ran to the southern edge of 1st Platoon's position, and laid down a streak of bullets. Then he realized that shots were coming from the east as well, so he began returning fire in that direction. A bullet hit him. Blood gushed from his neck. Alford kept firing until he collapsed.

"I'm hit!" he screamed. "Oh my God, I'm hit!"

Private First Class Miles Foltz grabbed his wounded comrade and pulled him behind a large rock, where he began administering first aid. The bullet had torn through the right side of Alford's jaw and exited out his neck. Foltz bandaged up the exit wound; the stream of blood was forceful, as if springing from a bottomless source.

Roller, busy switching among the three radios he had, yelled for someone to pick up Alford's machine gun. Every second spent on something other than coordinating bomb drops would be, for Roller, a second wasted. Specialist Eric Cramer responded to the lieutenant's order, snatching up the M240B, and then he and Foltz took turns trying to save

Alford's life and trying to end the lives of a few insurgents with the machine gun. At one point, when Foltz replaced Alford's saturated bandage, the blood began spilling out again.

"Oh, shit," Foltz said. He plugged the hole in Alford's neck with his hand, then rebandaged the wound and attempted to calm down his injured friend, talking to him as if he were confident that everything was going to be just fine.

Crouched behind a rock, Ryan Fritsche tried to reach the rest of Bulldog Troop to report his patrol's position and give its coordinates, but discovered that his radio wasn't working properly; it kept cutting in and out. Wilson, who had been on guard a short distance away from the group, came back and offered to tinker with it, but once again, Fritsche turned him down.

Not long after that, word came crackling over the radio that Alford had been shot in the neck. All units were ordered to stay where they were until he'd been medevacked out.

Apaches now flew into the valley, and as they swept through, Fritsche, Morrow, White, Barnes, and Wilson could hear the enemy, just a few hundred yards above them, firing at the U.S. helicopters.

Tom Bostick and his patrol were farther down the mountain, to the west, closer to the road. The captain directed Kenny Johnson, his fire-support officer, to get the mortars firing and have them hit the ridge above them to the southwest, where the enemy now had Dave Roller and his men pinned down. They needed to beat back the insurgents so they could get a medevac in there. Johnson called it in, and seconds later, there was a faint boom off in the distance.

"That's it?" asked Bostick. The mortars hadn't landed even remotely close to where they needed to go.

The captain grabbed the radio from Sultan. "Why isn't there fucking mortar fire?" he bellowed. "What the fuck is going on? Why don't I have mortars?!"

He was told that the mortars were being adjusted; apparently the mortarmen were resetting the base plate, which had become unbalanced.

"Fuck this," Bostick said, dropping the radio. He turned to Johnson and gave him an order: "Fix this."

They needed the medevac to drop a Jungle Penetrator up at Roller's observation post so that Alford could be strapped onto it, pulled up into the chopper, and whisked away — *now*.

Roller's voice came over the radio: "Alford's going to die," he announced. "He got shot in the fucking neck — we need a medevac now, or he's gone."

Bostick turned to Johnson and urged him to encourage their friends in the medevac to hurry up and get into the valley. "Tell those pussies to stop being fucking pussies and get out here," he said.

Back at Combat Outpost Kamu, Alex Newsom was still impatient to join the fight, but as the leader of the quick reaction force, he couldn't take any of the men from 3rd Platoon into battle before the first American casualty was reported. Whenever shots were fired, he would radio Bostick to ask if he wanted the QRF to ride in, but he was repeatedly told to hold off. Then word came in of Alford's wound, and the four Humvees in the QRF hit the gas, with Faulkenberry's truck in the lead.

Newsom's team made radio contact with Roller's unit, and just as the QRF pushed east and passed beneath 1st Platoon's position up in the hills, its Humvees took fire from across the river to the north. Faulkenberry's gunner, Private First Class Michael Del Sarto, countered with his M240 machine gun, as did Newsom with both his M240 and his MK19 automatic grenade launcher. At the "casualty collection point" — a just-in-case prearranged spot on the road — 3rd Platoon put on the brakes. Newsom and his men jumped out and began offloading boxes of water and ammo for the troops of 2nd Platoon, who had been moving east on the road when enemy fire began pummeling them from all sides, causing them to scatter into the hills to seek shelter and shoot back. Fortner, the medic from 2nd Platoon, was treating the wounded with little regard for his own safety. He sprinted from the injured ANA soldier to a mortarman who'd been shot, then ran down to help two others who'd been sprayed with shrapnel from an RPG. Calls came in that the mortarman wasn't looking good, so Fortner headed back up the hill to check on him; in the minute or two it took him to get there, he felt as if every enemy fighter in the valley was shooting at him personally. The intimidating cracks of insurgents' bullets terrified him as he scurried up the steep embankment; the ground kept slipping out from under him, and rounds that only barely missed him kicked up debris on all sides. *I'm not going to make it through this day alive*, Fortner thought to himself — and in that moment, he achieved a sort of clarity that caused the hyperactivity around him to slow down and made his task seem easier. He regained his footing and got up the rest of the hill. And then, after he'd done what he could about the mortarman's internal bleeding, something that felt like a baseball bat hit his right elbow, spinning him 180 degrees and dropping him to the ground. His right shoulder had caught a bullet, which he quickly slid out of the wound, patching a piece of gauze into the hole. A bleeding Fortner then helped get the other four wounded men— Habibullah and Privates First Class Scott Craig, Stan Trapyline, and José Rodriguez—to Newsom's Humvees. The medic himself refused to be evacuated. As the QRF pulled out, Fortner stood and yelled at the insurgents in the mountains. "You fucking pussies!" he screamed. "Your bullets feel like bee stings! I'm going to fuck all of you up!" He later wouldn't remember doing it.

Newsom's team drove these first four casualties to a nearby cornfield— maybe twenty-five feet by twenty-five feet—that the lieutenant had decided would serve as a landing zone. From there, a helicopter took them out. Bostick had told Newsom to return to Kamu afterward, but he didn't do it. It was the first time in his career he'd ever disobeyed a direct order. He wanted to stay close to the fight.

Up on the mountain with 1st Platoon, Roller glanced over at Foltz, who was tending to Alford's wounds. Foltz was a touch nerdy, Roller thought, but boy, was he a cool character at that moment. Collected and assured, Foltz gave him a thumbs-up. Roller looked at Alford. He was clearly in a daze, having lost a lot of blood, but he somehow managed to give his lieutenant a thumbs-up as well.

A medevac buzzed into the valley, drawing a cacophony of incoming fire. "Red-One," the pilot radioed to Roller, "we cannot land." Nor would the chopper be able to hover long enough to hoist Alford up on a Jungle Penetrator, he said; it was still too hot in the valley. Roller and the others on the ground would have to get more of the enemy cleared out first. The medevac turned around.

Roller gave the Apache pilots targeting grids so they could bomb and fire upon the insurgents. Twice, the Apaches flew so close that he could see right into their cockpits. It was still not enough. Roller and his Air Force communications officer also tried to get the French and Belgian pilots of some nearby Mirages to offer air support. Although English is the standard language for NATO, it took them all a while — too long — to overcome the considerable language barrier; one of the pilots even read back the instructions for a bomb drop and identified 1st Platoon's position as the target. That mistake was quickly corrected by Roller and, several miles away, by Kolenda's Air Force liaison. Kolenda, infuriated, demanded that Colonel Charles "Chip" Preysler, commander of the 173rd Airborne, see to it that in the future, his men be sent only U.S. aircraft.

On this day, though, the French bombs eventually began to hit their targets, as did the U.S. ordnance, and a credible path was cleared for the medevac. Under heavy fire as tracer rounds reached out from enemy positions throughout the valley, the Black Hawk lowered a medic, Staff Sergeant Peter Rohrs, on a Jungle Penetrator. To the men watching, it seemed nothing short of miraculous that Rohrs made it to the ground. He unhooked his cable and ran to Alford, whom he treated with an IV and more bandages. Rohrs was concerned not only about the specialist's neck wound itself but also about making it worse by hoisting him sitting upright on the Jungle Penetrator — but there wasn't much time to contemplate. He put a neck brace on the injured soldier; that would have to suffice. Amid furious incoming fire, the two men, wrapped around the rescue device, were hoisted into the belly of the Black Hawk. After a perilous rise, Rohrs and Alford entered the medevac, which then turned and sped out of the valley. As the enemy barrage continued, one of the Apache pilots got on the radio: "Hey, guys, I'm hit," he said. "I'm heading back."

Up with Fritsche's patrol, Morrow had seen the shot that hit the Apache; ominously, it had come from right above their position.

Wilson was worried that the pilots might mistake them for insurgents. He expressed his concern to Fritsche, who tried to reassure him that their position had been relayed to the Apaches. Either way, Wilson found it terrifying to see the Apache pilots pointing their 30-millimeter chain guns at — or at least near — them, especially when the patrol's radio wasn't working reliably. It was easy to imagine, he thought, how friendly-fire incidents could happen. Before the radio died once and for all, Fritsche got the call that Bulldog Troop was waiting for him and his team to come down the mountain, and they needed to move now.

*   *   *

As the fight lulled for about ninety minutes, Bostick, Johnson, and Lape walked down toward the road, leaving Sultan behind to cover them. The trio stopped next to two big boulders. Lape climbed up onto a rock to better position his radio. He lit a cigarette. Bostick meanwhile got on the radio to try to find out why the mortars had been so ineffective at helping out Roller and his men; multitasking while doing that, he also directed his platoons into position and cracked a few jokes to relieve the tension. Sultan, who had been providing cover from some yards up the hill, now sucked up an MRE pack. He was facing downhill, toward the north, watching Bostick, Johnson, and Lape. Beyond them was the road, and beyond that the Landay-Sin River, then more mountains.

Without any warning, an RPG exploded between Sultan's position and Bostick's. None of the men was sure which direction it had come from: south, up the hill? north, across the road? Sultan grabbed his rifle and ran downhill. Believing the RPG had been launched from somewhere behind him, uphill to the south, he ducked under a holly oak tree, turned around, and slid into a firing position right near Bostick, Johnson, and Lape, by the two large boulders.

Bullets rained down on the rocks. Shrapnel hit Johnson's chest plate.

"Sir," Johnson said to Bostick, stating the obvious, "they're shooting at us."

"Shoot back," Bostick told him.

An insurgent sniper fired a rifle shot disturbingly close to their position, which was soon followed by an RPG blast near the same spot. The sniper fired again, closer this time. Another RPG followed. Bostick and his team realized that the sniper was showing the enemy RPG team exactly where they were.

"We're taking fire, we don't know where from," Bostick radioed in. "We're going to have to move. We need cover, suppressive fire."

"We should break contact and link up with the rest of Second Platoon," suggested Johnson. Bostick agreed and prepared to lay down suppressive fire to cover their move. Lape got ready to throw a smoke grenade as Bostick stepped out from behind the boulders and fired his rifle. But then suddenly Johnson lost his footing and began sliding down the steep hill.

"We need cover!" Bostick yelled. "I think they're coming from the ea——"

At that moment, an RPG came right at them from up on the mountain to the southeast. It exploded and sent off a shock wave that threw all four men into the air.

West of and up the mountain from Bostick's position, Roller witnessed the RPG explosion and watched as, amid a plume of smoke, Johnson flew downhill some thirty feet, landing near the road.

"Bulldog-Six, Bulldog-Six, where are you?" Roller called on the radio for Bostick. "Bulldog-Six, Bulldog-Six, come in." There was no response.

Alex Newsom's call sign was "Bulldog 3-6," but Roller, worried that something had happened to their captain, didn't think military protocol conveyed what he needed to express at that moment. "Alex, it's Dave," he told Newsom over the radio. "I need you back in the valley."

Newsom knew that Roller's call sign was "Bulldog Red-1," but he followed his friend's lead. "Okay, Dave," he said.

As Newsom and his platoon motored into the danger zone from their spot down the road, not far from the casualty collection point, Faulkenberry turned to the lieutenant.

"Can I look for him?" he asked.

"Let's go," said Newsom.

They roared back into the fight with guns blazing, picking out enemy positions and obliterating them with their big weapons. Newsom yelled to Specialist Andrew Bluhm, the gunner on the MK19 grenade launcher, "Keep shooting! Keep shooting!"

Bluhm didn't need to be told twice.

As Fritsche and his patrol worked to get down the mountain, Newsom and the QRF sped by on the road below, heading west toward Tom Bostick. The battle had started up again.

John Wilson was a native of Littleton, Colorado, so he knew mountains, and he had done a lot of trail running. He led the way as the enemy fired on them from the mountain across the river. While the others—Fritsche, Morrow, and White—returned fire, trying to provide cover, Wilson and Nic Barnes would run from behind a tree, dart diagonally down the steep decline of the mountain, then jump behind another tree. From there, Wilson and Barnes would provide cover as the others ran down to where they were. They did that over and over, trading tasks, with each team covering the other so both could make incremental progress—a strategy known as bounding. Enemy bullets rained down on the covering troops, shredding leaves, bark, and everything else in their vicinity, but the enemy's focus on them meant that the others could crisscross and run down the mountain as well.

The pattern they established had Wilson and Barnes starting their next sprint just before the other three landed safely behind cover. On one relay, Wilson, pausing to hide, looked down and thought he saw tracks on the ground in front of him. He stopped beside a boulder and gingerly walked around it. About twenty feet east of their position, near a dent in the rock wall, three Afghans were looking down the mountain toward the river. Two of them were wearing new ANA battle-dress uniforms and holding AKs. The third looked like an Afghan policeman, complete with police radio and pistol.

Barnes came up on Wilson's right, Morrow on his left.

"What do we do with these guys?" they whispered to one another.

Morrow and Fritsche weren't sure who the men were—they could be ANA, they thought—but Wilson and Barnes were convinced they were insurgents. The Afghans were excited, jubilant—not the sort of behavior to be expected from ANA soldiers in the middle of an ambush. Indeed, to Barnes, the Afghans seemed to be laughing as they watched the Americans below them in the valley being attacked, wounded, and killed.

The debate ended when the Americans noticed that one of the Afghans had a black facemask rolled up on his head that he could pull down to obscure his features. Another held a facemask in his hand.

Wilson turned to Barnes. "Fuck these guys," he said. "Morrow and I will take the two guys on the left," he whispered, referring to the Afghans. "You aim at that one on the right. Let's just mow them down."

Barnes, Morrow, and Wilson fired at their assigned targets. White and Fritsche fired from behind them as well. The three insurgents fell—and for a brief moment, at least, that seemed to be that. The men's relief quickly dissolved, however, when a fourth insurgent with a facemask popped up from behind a nearby group of rocks and sprayed a full magazine at them from his AK, then took cover again. The Americans were already shielded by trees and boulders, so they hunkered down. Bombs now began dropping from a U.S. aircraft, two five-hundred-pounders that whistled angrily on their way down. They landed dangerously close and interrupted the firefight. Wilson ran to check the rear—there had been, after all, dozens of insurgents shooting at them as they moved. Fritsche took cover next to a rock, returned fire, and began trying to work the ailing radio again; he wanted to call Bostick to make sure the pilots dropping the bombs knew where his squad was.

Wilson, higher up on the hill, could see Fritsche's shorn, helmetless head poking up above the boulder. He shouted for Fritsche to crouch down even further, but at the very moment the staff sergeant looked up and their eyes locked, the fourth insurgent fired—and the enemy bullet found its target above Ryan Fritsche's left eyebrow, exploding out the back of his head.

To their west, Jonathan Sultan woke up from the RPG explosion.

He wondered if he was dead. He had seen the explosion, had seen the RPG hit Captain Bostick. He didn't know where his captain was now.

Sultan could see only out of his right eye; his left was hanging out of its socket. His left hand, which had flash-burned when the RPG detonated, was charred black. He could hear nothing but a loud ringing. Then he could just make out someone—Lape?—shouting, "Run! Run! RUN!"

Sultan managed to stand. A piece of shrapnel roughly the size of a baseball had torn through his left shoulder, ripped through his collarbone, and exited out his back. He started running down the hill. He knew that if he stopped, he would die. He wanted to yell out, "Where are you?" to the men of 2nd Platoon, who he believed were down the mountain, but the word *where* kept coming out as "wheer." He stopped for a second. *Wheer. Wheer.* What was wrong with him? Why couldn't he talk? He thought, This is it. A sniper's going to get me. And then he heard, to his left, "Over here, over here, get over here," and Lape pulled him aside and rushed him down to the casualty collection point.

Johnson watched as Lape escorted Sultan down the hill to cover, near a rock by the river. Half of Sultan's face was charred; he reminded Johnson of the Batman villain Two-Face.

Dazed, Sultan thought to himself, If I run into the river, I'll sink. And then he was lying on his back, feeling the cool mist of the Landay-Sin River on his destroyed face.

Morrow checked Fritsche's pulse. "He's dead," the sniper said.

"No shit," replied Wilson. He'd just seen the back of Fritsche's head explode. Blood and gray matter lay on the rock behind him. He wasn't moving. He wasn't breathing. He wasn't bleeding.

They were still pinned down by the fourth insurgent, who by now had been joined by several others. Wilson threw a grenade at them, but it took forever to go off.

One thousand one, one thousand two, one thousand three, one thousand four, one thousand five, BOOM.

No way had it gotten the insurgent, thought Wilson; he'd had too much time to run away, and the explosive had rolled down the mountain. The sergeant grabbed another grenade. He pulled the pin and let it cook off for two seconds.

One thousand one, one thousand two. Throw. *One thousand three*, BOOM.

It went off a second and a half early: Got him, Wilson thought. For once, the Americans' unreliable equipment had worked to their advantage.

"We need to get down the hill," Morrow said. Soldiers are taught never to leave fellow troops behind on the battlefield, including fallen ones, but Morrow was convinced that any attempt on their part to bring Fritsche's corpse down the mountain just then would result in even more casualties. Instead, they'd link up with the rest of their company at the bottom and then return for the staff sergeant. That was the plan, anyway. That was what they told themselves as they ran down the mountain.

When Faulkenberry pulled up in his Humvee at the casualty control point by the river, he saw Rob Fortner working on someone whose face was so mushed up and bloody that he couldn't even tell who it was. It turned out to be Sultan.

"Thank God, it's the Cavalry," the medic managed to crack as he heard the trucks pull up. They sounded as if they were bringing hell with them: the QRF troops were firing their machine guns full-auto nonstop, and a grenade launcher was sending thundering explosions one after another against the enemy across the river. "Where's Captain Bostick at?" Faulkenberry asked Lape and Johnson, who were sitting near Fortner and now looked at him with big doe eyes, shaken up.

They pointed up the hill.

From the road, Faulkenberry could see antennae poking up from the rucksack Johnson and Lape had left behind. He headed up toward the radios and came across a decapitated corpse in a U.S. Army uniform. Flesh was missing from the soldier's right elbow and right knee, and there were marks from several bullet and shrapnel impacts on his body armor. Faulkenberry opened up the armor to check the nametag:

BOSTICK, it said.

All U.S. troops have unique battle-roster IDs — the first letter of their last names followed by the last four digits of their Social Security numbers — but Faulkenberry didn't feel the need to pull the list out of his pocket and consult it. He walked down to his Humvee and got on the radio: "Bulldog-Six KIA," he said. Then he went back up the hill again and began dragging Bostick's body to the road, pulling him by his arms. One of the arms started to come off, so Faulkenberry dragged him by his other arm and his belt. Newsom came over, and the two of them, horrified by their task but determined to see it through, grasped Bostick under his hips and by his clavicle and, with Staff Sergeant Ben Barnes,[38] lifted him into the back of Newsom's truck.

Back at Forward Operating Base Naray, it was all seeming backward.

The commanders had originally thought the real action would be around the other element of the operation, to the east, in Bazgal. Lieutenant Colonel Kolenda had air-assaulted with a Legion Company platoon to a nearby mountain to watch over that area as Command Sergeant Major Vic Pedraza, Nathan Springer, and their men made their way to the Gawardesh Bridge — a mission they accomplished completely unchallenged.

When they heard about the firefight at Saret Koleh, a number of the officers and men at Gawardesh wanted to drive over there to help out Bulldog Troop; Springer and his .50-caliber gunner, Specialist Josh Kirk, were particularly desperate to push west. But part of the road near the Bazgal Bridge had been washed out and was now impassable, so there was nothing any of them could do beyond listening on the radio. Their feeling of impotence tore them up as they followed the unfolding nightmare.

Word that Bulldog-6 was down struck those back at Forward Operating Base Naray like a thunderbolt. With Kolenda in the field, the operations center at Naray was being run by Sergeant Major Ted Kennedy.

---

[38] No relation to Nic Barnes.

Before deployment, Kennedy, Bostick, Joey Hutto, First Sergeant Nuuese Passi, and their wives and children had all gone to Egypt together on vacation. The four men and their families were very close. Major Chris Doneski, who was in the operations center when the tragic news came in, quietly approached Kennedy and asked if he could speak with him. They walked into Kolenda's office. The major shut the door.

"We lost Tom," a stunned Doneski said.

Kennedy doubled over. He made his way to a chair and sat down, speechless. Kennedy and Bostick had been Rangers together, and close friends for years.

After a few minutes, Doneski found operations officer Major Darren Fitz Gerald and told him the same news. The three men huddled and talked about what to do next. Dozens of troops were engaged in battle in a dangerous valley, without a commander.

Joey Hutto was scheduled to relieve Bostick at the end of the year anyway, they noted. "We need to get him up there now," the men agreed.

Hutto happened to be out in the hall just then, looking for Kennedy. The battle had clearly gotten tough, and he wanted to get the big picture, which he knew Kennedy could give him. He was beckoned into Kolenda's office, where a grim-faced Doneski stood, by himself, waiting for him. Doneski looked at Hutto: he obviously had no idea what had happened to his close friend.

"Hey, Joey," Doneski said, "I can't believe I'm telling you this, but Tom's down. We lost Tom."

If Hutto's reaction was less physical than Kennedy's had been, it was still visible: he looked as if he'd been smacked by a wave that had knocked him back, disorienting him.

Soldiers are trained always to finish the task. In the chaos of battle, they're not given time to reflect. There is a job to do, and becoming mired in the quicksand of grief can only result in more deaths, greater anguish.

And yet.

In that moment, Hutto felt the same numbness he'd experienced five years earlier when he lost his oldest brother, Jimmy, his best friend and role model. When his wife told him that his brother was dead—an Alabama game warden, he'd been shot during a drug raid—Joey Hutto had shut down for just a second, and then he'd immediately begun focusing on how the death would affect his thirteen-year-old niece, Hailey, Jimmy's daughter. Now, standing in front of Doneski on this grim afternoon, Hutto went through the exact same process: he became numb, and then all he could think about was Jennifer Bostick and their two girls. Where was Jenn? Did she know yet? Who would be there for her? Were the girls with her?

Doneski gave Hutto twenty seconds to grieve. Then he said, "Joey, I need you to get out there. I need you to take over Bulldog and keep the men together."

Hutto stayed silent.

"Are you okay?" Doneski asked him.

"I'm fine," Hutto said. "When do you want me to go?"

"Get your equipment, I need you to get on an aircraft in about twenty minutes," Doneski told him.

Hutto stepped out of Kolenda's office. He ran into Kennedy, and the two men embraced. "You let me know what you need," Kennedy said.

Hutto jogged to his small bedroom, or hooch, to grab his essentials. He knew he had to focus on Bulldog Troop and help its surviving leaders get control of a devastating situation; they and their men were trapped in hell. But he couldn't stop thinking about Jennifer Bostick and her two daughters. The world seemed a far darker place than it had been just ten minutes before.

Newsom, Faulkenberry, and the other squad leader, Staff Sergeant Ben Barnes, made three trips to the rocks where Bostick had been killed, gathering rucksacks, radios, and GPS equipment. Newsom spotted something shiny in a nearby tree: Bostick's dog tags, hanging from a branch six feet off the ground. He pulled them down and shoved them in his pocket.

Another exclamation of gunfire rang from across the river, and Faulkenberry staggered forward. He'd been shot. He looked down: his left leg was fine—he was standing up straight on it—but his right had been lacerated and had twisted around, so that his foot was facing almost backward. The leg had essentially been cut in half at the thigh. Faulkenberry's pants began to fill up with blood, like a sack being filled with water.

"I'm hit," he announced. He seemed so nonchalant about it that neither

Newsom nor Barnes believed him at first. Then Faulkenberry slumped down onto the ground, twisting his leg with him. He was now facing the river.

Newsom and Barnes came over to him. Barnes pulled out his tourniquet and combat bandages and did what he could while Newsom tried to find a vein for an IV in Faulkenberry's skinny arm. It took him four tries, but finally he got it. RPGs exploded and bullets kicked up all around them, though they didn't even realize it at the time, so focused were they on patching up their wounded colleague, hooking him up to the IV, and feeding him the "pill pack" of three medications that every soldier carries: a Tylenol-strength painkiller, an anti-inflammatory drug, and a general antibiotic. Faulkenberry's sciatic nerve—running from his lower back down his leg—had been severed, so the leg was completely numb except for a throbbing pain. Once they'd gotten him relatively stable, Newsom and Barnes helped him hop down the mountain to the convoy and the other troops.

Down on the road, the insurgents were getting closer and the explosions growing louder, and some of the ANA soldiers started to run away. "Hey, motherfucker!" Newsom yelled at one of the fleeing men, "get back over here!" The Afghan stopped and sheepishly looked back at the American officer.

Newsom's magazines were filled with tracer rounds so he could mark targets for his troops and the low-flying Apaches. "You see what I'm shooting at?" Newsom asked the ANA soldier as he fired into the northern hills. "Shoot there!" He then heard something behind where they were standing, up the mountain to the south and southeast: more insurgents. Time to go, Newsom thought: We have a KIA and WIAs, and those WIAs will soon turn into KIAs if we don't haul ass.

Enemy fire swarmed around them, the bullets as frenzied and chattering as invading locusts. As wounded American and ANA troops fell to the left and right of him, Newsom told all of those still standing to aim their weapons up the mountain, toward the south, and he himself did the same, crouching and walking back toward the vehicles as he pulled the trigger. Fire was also coming from across the river, to the north, the explosions ferocious from that quarter as well.

Morrow, White, Wilson, and Nic Barnes had by now arrived at the Humvees on the road; they were yelling that Fritsche had been killed.

Faulkenberry heard them as he sat, calm and conscious, in the backseat of a Humvee. His gunner, Private First Class Michael Del Sarto, adjusted the bandages that Fortner had applied to the staff sergeant's wound. Faulkenberry's mangled right leg was dangling outside the Humvee, and other soldiers, oblivious to his injury and panicking under fire, kept bumping his knee with the armored door. Finally, fed up, he reached out, grabbed his own leg, pulled it and twisted it inside the Humvee, and slammed the door shut. Let's go, let's go, I'm going to bleed out, he thought. But the trucks weren't budging. They couldn't: bullets and RPGs were peppering the Humvees, seemingly from all sides, and the Americans had little choice but to use the two trucks for cover as they returned fire. (The other two QRF Humvees had earlier pushed down the road to spread out for strategic reasons.) Faulkenberry's head started feeling heavier. His men kept talking to him, trying to keep him awake. He took off his chest rig, packed with ammo and plates of bulletproof Kevlar, to let up some of the pressure on his body.

"We need to go get Fritsche," Newsom announced. He attempted to corral several other guys to come with him.

"Fritsche's dead, sir," Wilson said. "If we go get him, someone else is going to get killed." Wilson knew that what he was proposing they do — or rather, *not* do — was a violation of military protocol, and he hated the notion of leaving anyone behind, but he couldn't stand the thought of losing another soldier in a recovery effort. Maybe if it'd been some other soldier dead up on that hill — Nic Barnes, for instance — then Wilson would have led the charge to get the body and bring it back . . . or maybe not. He had all sorts of complicated feelings about his short relationship with Ryan Fritsche, about their time together on that mountain, and about how Fritsche had died. The bottom line was that Wilson just wanted to get the hell out of there, and he wanted the men who were still living to keep on living. Military funerals had protocols, too.

Fortner, meanwhile, had been worrying about what might happen to Faulkenberry if they didn't get him medevacked out soon; the tourniquet was having only a limited effect. Then the medic heard about Fritsche's being MIA, and he felt torn. Should he volunteer to mount a recovery effort for a fallen brother? It might come at the expense of Faulkenberry's life. "We need to leave now, or John is going to die," Fortner finally told his platoon sergeant.

The Apache attack helicopters continued to work over the enemy positions. The lush forests and rocky landscape made it hard to identify insurgent locations and just as hard to get bombs on top of them, but Roller and his radio man kept feeding coordinates to the pilots of the F-15s and A-10 Warthogs, while the rest of 1st Platoon kept the road clear from their observation post.

The convoy at last began rolling forward.

Newsom ran ahead of the Humvees to keep the momentum going. They were on a road where no cover existed, so there was no sense in their trying to find any: the troops could either shoot and move or stay and die.

Newsom heard a snap and turned to see Private Barba holding his chin, with blood pouring from a hole in his face.

"Sir, I'm shot," Barba said.

"You'll be fine," Newsom said flatly.

As the convoy edged forward—some troops in the trucks, others walking alongside them—a number of soldiers began vomiting, overcome by a combination of dehydration and exhaustion. Along the way, the wounded were dropped off at the landing zone, which offered a modicum of cover from the enemy fire. Private First Class Chris Pfeifer ran up to Faulkenberry's Humvee with a stretcher. "It's going to be okay, Sergeant," he said. "You're going to be all right." The kid had a way of projecting eternal optimism, even in the midst of battle and bloodshed.

Del Sarto, the gunner, stuck by Faulkenberry's side, trying to reassure him. "Here comes the medevac, don't worry!" he fibbed as a helicopter buzzed in. But Faulkenberry was not so out of it that he couldn't see and hear and differentiate among the several kinds of birds.

"Shut up," he told Del Sarto. "I know that's an Apache." Medevacs were Black Hawks.

Soon a Black Hawk did arrive. The landing zone was so small that the pilots would have had every right to refuse to land, but they brought the bird down anyway. Faulkenberry and Sultan, the most seriously wounded of the men, were the last to be loaded on so that they would be the first off when they got to Forward Operating Base Naray. Pfeifer and another private put them in, banged the shell of the Black Hawk to give the all-clear, and watched as it flew them out of Nuristan forever.

The makeshift landing zone. *(Photo courtesy of Alex Newsom)*

The battle was nearly over, but a new commander was finally on his way. Joey Hutto landed at Combat Outpost Kamu and updated Kolenda over the radio: most of the men were now rolling out of the valley, he reported, but Fritsche's body was still on the mountain; they'd have to send a team to go back and get it. Kolenda and Hutto decided that Roller and 1st Platoon should stay where they were, in a good position to call in bombs and cover whatever force went into the valley to recover the corpse. It was not uncommon for this enemy to ransack or even mutilate any bodies left on the battlefield, and the Americans couldn't let that happen to Ryan Fritsche.

Hutto headed to Camp Kamu's operations center, picked up a radio, and prepared formally to assume command.

He froze for a minute.

It was not pleasant, what he had to do: he needed to announce that he was replacing Tom Bostick, his close friend, because he'd been killed. Even though Hutto, as the new commander of Bulldog Troop, had inherited his predecessor's call sign, "Bulldog-6," he decided not to identify himself by that right now; he knew that many of Bostick's troops would be listening, and he was concerned that some of them might not have heard the news yet. It just felt wrong to him—as if by his use of the call sign, he would be not only usurping Bostick's place but also alerting the men to the loss of their leader in the crassest way possible.

Instead he said simply, "Captain Hutto is now on the ground." Kolenda, in his first subsequent transmission, welcomed his new troop commander and called him Joey. It wasn't protocol, but the lieutenant colonel was nothing if not empathetic. He then gave Hutto orders as "Bulldog-6," and that became Hutto's name from then on. And this was how many in the field, among them Nate Springer, learned that their friend and commander Tom Bostick had been killed.

In Martinsville, Indiana, Deputy Sheriff Volitta Fritsche, Ryan's mother, looked out her window and saw several sheriffs' cars in her driveway. She had taken some time off from her job due to her husband's illness and death, but she was scheduled to return to work just two days later, so she couldn't imagine why all her coworkers had shown up at her house.

Then she saw a man she didn't recognize get out of one of the patrol cars. He was dressed in an Army uniform. After he exited the car, he put on a beret. Her heart started pounding.

"This can't be happening," she said aloud.

One of her coworkers knocked on the door. Volitta Fritsche answered it but pointed at the soldier and said, "He can't come in here!"—hoping that somehow, by denying him entry, she might be able to prevent the inevitable.

The soldier, and another, entered anyway. The one she'd seen through the window informed her that her son had been reported missing in action. The news was devastating, but it also gave her a glimmer of hope.

"What does that mean?" she asked. "Does that mean he's still alive?"

"The only information I have, ma'am, is what I told you," said the soldier.

"He could be alive?"

"Yes, ma'am," he said.

"Was he taken prisoner?"

"I don't know, ma'am."

"These people have been beheading prisoners," she said. "Could he have crawled off and be hiding in a cave?"

"Yes, ma'am," the soldier said. "Anything's possible at this point."

After her visitors left, Volitta called her daughter-in-law, Brandi, who had been told the news by a different set of soldiers.

"Where could he be?" asked Brandi, crying.

"He's probably hiding somewhere in the mountains," Volitta suggested. "He's good at that kind of thing. Remember, land navigation is his forte."

"I know," Brandi said. "I'm just so scared."

A few hours later, the soldiers returned to Volitta Fritsche's home to tell her that they had some new information: Ryan was still MIA, but now they also knew that he had been wounded in action.

"Is he okay?" Volitta asked.

"I don't know, ma'am," the soldier replied. "They're reporting he was shot in the head."

"I don't understand," she said. "If they saw him take a hit, and they're back to safety, why don't they know Ryan's condition?"

"They can't find him, ma'am."

" 'Can't find him'? What do you mean, they can't find him? You mean they left him out there?"

"They said the fighting was so intense, they couldn't get him out," the soldier said. "I'm sorry."

"I thought you guys didn't leave anyone behind!" Volitta cried. *"Ryan wouldn't have left one of his guys behind!"*

The Landay-Sin Valley near Saret Koleh was now teeming with U.S. aircraft, bombing every location that the remaining men on the ground—Roller, primarily—called in. Hutto ordered that bombs be dropped in a circle around the spot where Fritsche had last been seen. Newsom wanted to head back into the valley, but he'd been told by Roller that the higher-ups wanted him to hold off for now; they were devising a plan.

Hutto weighted himself down with guilt over Fritsche's death. He was the one who'd sent the staff sergeant to 2nd Platoon; he'd even escorted him to the helicopter that would fly him to Combat Outpost Kamu. On that first night of his new command, Hutto got word to Newsom that he should send a quick reaction force to recover Fritsche's body. A reluctant Morrow went along on the mission, remaining in the Humvee and staying in radio contact with the members of the QRF as they hunted for the corpse.

The searchers couldn't see much by moonlight, and the bombardment had pulverized most of the rocks into loose gravel, which made climbing even more difficult. When they turned on their white lights, they saw further evidence of bombing and strafing runs from earlier in the day. They found several former fighting positions littered with empty water bottles and, in one case, a soft SAW ammo carrier. Morrow guided them over the radio to the location where Fritsche had been killed.

His body wasn't there.

Pfeifer, Newsom's driver that day, sat with the lieutenant in a second Humvee; he was so drained that he kept nodding off behind the wheel. Newsom nudged him every minute or so to wake him up. Each time, Pfeifer would open his eyes and smile: Good to go. The kid was just like that, Newsom thought.

The QRF troops walked down the mountain. Back in their Humvees, they stopped off at the former casualty collection point to pick up some assault packs that were supposed to be there but weren't. The evening, it seemed, had a theme.

The searchers did find some human remains—skull fragments, almost certainly from Bostick—which they collected in an ammunition can that Morrow held in his lap during the drive back to Combat Outpost Kamu. Otherwise, the QRF returned from the mission empty-handed.

As the sun rose on the Landay-Sin Valley, Roller radioed to Hutto that 1st Platoon needed to head back to Combat Outpost Kamu. He and his men were spent, down to thirty seconds' worth of ammunition for the 240 machine gun and almost out of water. Hutto gave them permission, but this, too, added to his guilt over Fritsche: after sending him to the battlefield in the first place, he was now approving Roller's request to leave his body behind there, all alone. And while Hutto believed those who said the kid had been KIA, he hadn't seen it for himself.

In fact, the hunt for Fritsche's body had not been abandoned: Kolenda's boss, Colonel Chip Preysler, committed a different unit from his brigade, the 2nd Battalion, 503rd Infantry Regiment, to conduct another search the next night. Also known as the ROCK Battalion, the unit was led by a contemporary of Kolenda's, Lieutenant Colonel William Ostlund, who gave the impression that he thought his men were tougher than those who'd already tried to find Fritsche—maybe tougher than anyone, period. Ostlund landed his tactical command post on Hill 1696, overlooking the staff sergeant's last known location; the ROCK's Chosen Company landed at Combat Outpost Kamu, where its members were briefed by Hutto and others from 1-91 Cav. Then the seventy or so troops from Chosen Company walked to Saret Koleh. Wilson, eaten up by guilt, joined them. As he hiked the mountain with the Chosen Company troops, the sergeant worried that they wouldn't be able to find Ryan Fritsche—that perhaps he'd never be found at all. He wondered what the insurgents had done to poor Fritsche's corpse. The worst thoughts possible ran through his mind.

But the Chosen Company troops *did* find Fritsche, lying faceup in the very spot where he'd been killed; either he'd been taken away and then returned there by the enemy or the first search party had somehow missed seeing him. He had been stripped of his personal effects and military equipment: his body armor, weapon, and boots were gone. He was wearing just a shirt, pants, and socks. His arms were folded across his chest. His eyelids were closed. An entry wound blemished his left temple, and a matching exit wound showed behind his right ear.

Fritsche was put on a Skedko plastic stretcher and carried down the hill. He was taken to Combat Outpost Kamu, where his remains were officially identified. Three days after Ryan Fritsche was killed, the soldier in his green uniform and Army beret pulled up to Volitta Fritsche's Indiana home for one final visit, this time to tell her that all hope was lost, and her beloved son—the Little Leaguer and high school basketball center with gifts of determination and beauty—was gone.

Dave Roller was distraught at the loss of Bostick; everyone in Bulldog Troop was. But for Roller, the hardest thing of all was his belief that even as he and his fellow soldiers were out there fighting for their lives, no one back home cared. Ninety percent of the American people would rather hear about what Paris Hilton did on a Saturday night than be bothered by reports on that silly war in Afghanistan, Roller thought. Of this he was convinced. That the people they'd been fighting for would never even know their names made the death of soldiers such as Tom Bostick and Ryan Fritsche all the more tragic.

CHAPTER 18

Balloons

The U.S. Army had been moving Joey Hutto around since he was a boy. In the eighth grade, he had relocated from Enterprise, Alabama, when his mom, a single mother, married an Army sergeant who was being moved from Fort Rucker to a base in Missouri. Eventually the sergeant and Hutto's mom split up, and his stepfather faded out of his life, but the Army didn't. He signed up right out of high school, and his fitness and focus were so apparent to one recruiter that Special Forces brought him on board the following year. He spent the next decade running in and out of Central and South America, mostly training host nations' armies in Special Forces tactics—how to clear a building during a hostage situation, how to implement what was then the prevailing theory of counterinsurgency, how to provide security for VIPs, how to combat narcoterrorists. He was commissioned as a second lieutenant at Fort Benning Officer Candidate School in 2002 and ended up in Germany, where he and Bostick became fast friends. At Forward Operating Base Naray, he'd served as the assistant operations officer for 1-91 Cav's Headquarters Troop.

When Hutto touched down at the landing zone at Combat Outpost Keating, he was met by an officer who had just been in Bostick's hooch at the operations center, trying to separate the fallen troop leader's military gear from his civilian items. Hutto thanked him and took over. He entered Bostick's small room and closed the curtain.

Since that split-second embrace with Kennedy back at Forward

Operating Base Naray, Hutto hadn't had a moment to focus on his dear friend: he'd been too involved in coordinating the response to the enemy presence, working to expedite the exit of Bulldog Troop from the battle, and then trying to recover Ryan Fritsche's body. He hadn't even had a chance to talk to his wife yet, because immediately after Bostick's death, the unit had been "blacked out"—meaning that no one could call or write home—for fear that Jennifer Bostick might hear the news through the grapevine and not via official Army channels. This moment behind the curtain of Tom Bostick's hooch was the first time in days that Hutto didn't have soldiers swarming around him, radios going off.

He paused and let himself mourn, allowed himself to cry. For Hutto, being here in Bostick's room was eerily reminiscent of that day five years before when he'd visited his late brother's Alabama home. These were haunted spaces.

After a few minutes, he called the platoon sergeants and platoon leaders in to the operations center so he could start to get a sense of how they did business. He was now in charge of Bulldog Troop, and they all knew the insurgents were going to come at them hard. The enemy would soon see that a new officer was commanding the troops at Camp Keating. They would test him. And they would try to kill him as well.

When she got the news about her husband's potentially lethal wound, John Faulkenberry's wife, Sarah, was back living at home with her parents in Midland, Texas. While her husband was abroad, she was working as an event coordinator at the Petroleum Club. That day, her main task was to make sure everything had been cleaned up after a party held at the club the night before. At around 2:00 p.m., she got in her car and checked the cell phone she'd left there, only to see that she had ten missed calls from Germany, where she and John had been stationed before he deployed.

It's a phone call, it's a phone call, it's a phone call, she told herself. A phone call means he's alive; a knock on the door means he's dead. This is a phone call. That was how Tom Bostick had explained it when he sat down with the Bulldog Troop wives before their husbands deployed. A phone call, a phone call, a phone call, she repeated. Still: her breath was taken away. She couldn't make international calls on her cell, so she zoomed back to her parents' house to place the call from there, running stoplights on the way, passing her father on the road. She was terrified. She saw a note on the front door from afar and felt nauseated; then she got closer and realized that, thank God, it was something about a neighborhood barbecue. She ran inside and ransacked her brain trying to remember how to call Germany. Finally recalling, she dialed the number.

"Have you heard about your husband?" asked the representative for Bulldog Troop, Sergeant Troy Montalvo, over the phone.

"No," she said, panicked. "What the fuck is going on?"

"He's been wounded," Montalvo said. "Stay reachable—we'll know more in the next twelve to twenty-four hours, and we'll get in touch with you."

"Do you know what's wrong with him?" Sarah asked.

"No," he said.

"Was anyone else hurt?" she asked.

"I can't release that information," he said.

Shit, she thought. That means someone was killed.

Sarah called her in-laws to relay what she'd been told about their son, and then at midnight she called Germany again. "Do you know anything else?" she asked Montalvo. He informed her that her husband's wounds were severe enough that he would have to be evacuated from Afghanistan.

At 4:00 a.m., she called a third time. Montalvo now told her that her husband had been severely wounded, was in critical condition, and was currently fully intubated—meaning that a tube had been inserted into his mouth to maintain an open airway. He was on his way to Landstuhl Regional Medical Center in Germany.

Sarah looked up the phone number for Landstuhl and somehow eventually got patched through to the intensive-care-unit doctor in charge of her husband's case. He gave her more details: John had been shot in the leg. Part of his femur had been destroyed, and the bullet had severed his sciatic nerve and lacerated his femoral artery. The wound had triggered pulmonary emboli, or clots in the blood vessels of his lungs, and because he had lost so much blood, his kidneys, pancreas, and other internal organs had started to shut down as his body focused on keeping his heart and lungs going.

"How long do you have to keep him there?" Sarah asked.

"Until Tuesday at the earliest," he said. It was Saturday.

Sarah called American Airlines. A flight to Germany would cost three thousand dollars — money she didn't have.

"Okay," she told the agent, reading off her credit card number.

She arrived in Germany on Sunday. She walked into her husband's room.

"Hey, beautiful," he greeted her.

Heavily medicated, John fluctuated between knowing he was at Landstuhl and thinking he was still on the battlefield.

A few days later, the Army let Sarah fly with him on a larger medevac transport plane to Walter Reed Army Medical Center outside Washington, D.C. John was in so much pain that doctors there decided to put him into a medically induced coma.

Bulldog Troop consolidated itself at Combat Outpost Keating, which the enemy soon began attacking relentlessly. The Americans concluded that the insurgents, apprised of such developments by local informants and collaborators, knew that the American commander was dead and that a replacement, unfamiliar with the area, had been thrown into the valley — meaning that this would be an opportune time to try to kill and chase away these latest occupiers.

Up to that point, there hadn't been much enemy contact at Combat Outpost Keating for Bulldog Troop; the fight had instead been focused almost solely around Combat Outpost Kamu, now overseen by Captain Page and Legion Company. There was a reason for that imbalance, it turned out. Chris Kolenda discovered that in the spring, before Bulldog arrived at Camp Keating, the Kamdesh elders had made a deal with the insurgents in the region: the elders agreed to support them in their attacks on the outpost at Kamu if they, in return, promised not to bring violence to the Kamdesh Village area. But then came the Saret Koleh battle, which took a deadly toll on the Americans but an even deadlier one on the enemy. The insurgents from nearby Combat Outpost Kamu were decimated and exhausted and needed a break to regroup (they would be unable to mount another significant attack for more than a year). That left their comrades up the road, the Kamdesh Village crew, as the only bad guys open for business. Since they knew their own turf far better than they did the environs of Combat Outpost Kamu, they chose the home-field advantage and reneged on their deal with the Kamdesh elders, resuming major attacks on Combat Outpost Keating.

At times, the enemy fighters would synchronize their attacks on the outpost, launching several all at once from different ridges — to the north, south, and southeast. At other times they'd phase them in, first from the north mountain, then from the southern wall, then from the northwest. Sometimes they would pepper the Americans with small-arms fire and nothing else; sometimes rockets rained down, and sometimes RPGs; and occasionally the U.S. outpost would be hit with everything the insurgents had. At one point, the soldiers from Bulldog Troop thought they'd detected a pattern — the attacks would quite often come at 8:30 a.m. — but every time there seemed to be some consistency developing, the enemy would try something new. They seemed to be pros, these insurgents. They were mission-oriented. They weren't just local village kids.

The roads kept on trying to kill the Americans as well. Staff Sergeant Zachary Crawford was commanding a Humvee armed with an MK19 grenade launcher driving northwest on the road to Mandigal. When the truck came to a particularly unsturdy section of the road, Crawford told the driver, Specialist Tabajara DeSouza, to stop the vehicle, then ordered everyone else to hop out. DeSouza tried to drive past the weak patch, but it gave way, sending the Humvee tumbling into the river, where it landed upside down. DeSouza survived the wreck, but the incident gave Kolenda further pause. His troops had already experienced too many close calls in numerous places where the cliffside road was barely wide enough to hold a Humvee, or where it was flat-out untrafficable due to seasonal flooding and erosion. He'd heard how the namesake of Combat Outpost Keating lost his life. The math seemed clear: until the road could be repaired and widened, any benefit to be gleaned from resupplying Kamu and Keating via ground convoy from Naray just wasn't worth the risk involved.

Kolenda's decision was a controversial one, particularly infuriating to the 3-71 Cav vets who had fought so hard trying to secure the road for ground resupply to Keating — or at least trying to show the insurgents that they didn't own it outright. And of course, the location of Combat Outpost Keating had been picked just the previous year mainly *because* of its proximity to that route. But Kolenda stood firm.

With the Americans no longer driving right into their ambushes, the enemy would be forced to come to *them*. And Bulldog Troop would be prepared.

Lieutenant Alex Newsom had always been energetic—he'd worked his platoon hard back in Germany—but in the field, he became a man possessed, and even more so after Bostick and Fritsche were killed. He would hit the gym daily, running on the treadmill with a gas mask over his face to make his workout that much tougher. Determined to keep the enemy off balance, Hutto ordered Bulldog Troop out on constant patrols, varying their times and routes, but the ones Newsom led were so physically challenging that his men started calling him Captain America. Officers who joined Captain America and his platoon on these workouts couldn't believe how strenuous they were. Newsom was nuts, they said, and they joked that "Alex's patrols will shrink your dick." *Relentless,* that was the word for them—maybe with a profane adjective or two in front.

Captain America was ready for action on the morning of August 17, 2007, as the radio buzzed with enemy chatter about an imminent attack. An attack in itself would be nothing unusual; practically every day brought one of those. By now, Newsom's men knew the drill. The Americans' strongest defensive positions and firepower were in the Humvees fitted with .50-caliber and 240 machine guns as well as MK19 grenade launchers, so Newsom, preparing for the enemy action, told his troops to man the trucks. Deciding that an additional defensive position was needed, he took a team up onto the roof of the barracks next to the operations center, where they all took cover behind a wall of sandbags. The men on duty fired into the hills in a short, controlled "recon by fire"— probing for a reaction, shooting at known enemy fighting positions, perhaps even indulging in a bit of chest-thumping.

There were only five of them on the roof—three from 2nd Platoon, plus Ben Barnes and Newsom from 3rd Platoon—so the lieutenant called for more volunteers. "Hey, I need guys up here," Newsom radioed to his men. "We're about to be attacked."

The always willing Chris Pfeifer put himself forward.

Pfeifer's wife was due to deliver their first child, a girl, in a little over a month, and he was—typically—jubilant about it. He didn't complain about missing his daughter's birth; instead he called his wife every single day and showed photos of the very pregnant Karen to anyone who would look at them. The couple had met in Job Corps in Chadron, Nebraska, gotten married in March 2006, and moved to the military base in Germany the following fall.

The troops on the roof fired around the outpost, trying to provoke a response, and they got one: from the Switchbacks up the southern mountain wall, insurgents hit the rooftop with up to forty rounds of automatic small-arms fire. The Americans jumped down behind the sandbags. "Medic!" cried one of the men. "Medic!" Newsom crawled over and saw that Pfeifer had taken a round a couple of centimeters outside his chest plate, between his shoulder and his nipple.

As it turned out, the bullet had carved a path through his spinal cord, lungs, and bowel before entering one of his kidneys and exiting out his back.

Although those in charge of medical care on the front lines are more often than not nicknamed Doc, few of them are actually doctors.

It takes only sixteen weeks to become a medic. The average class size at the Department of Combat Medic Training, at Fort Sam Houston in Texas, is 450. Every two weeks, the Army rotates in a new group of students. The first six or seven weeks offer trainees an introduction to basic medicine, much like that given to those studying to become emergency medical technicians. The lessons are fundamental, covering such topics as how to move patients, how to assess vital signs such as pulse and respiration, how to provide elementary trauma care, and how to control bleeding, as well as reviewing simple anatomy and physiology. In their second phase of training, medics-to-be learn limited primary care: how to perform a basic sick call on a soldier, how to treat headaches and diarrhea, how best to conduct an abdominal or respiratory examination, and how to determine whether a rash is serious. Students are also taught how to distinguish, in the field, between less serious illnesses and those that might require a medevac helicopter.

The third phase of training deals with battlefield medicine. Using historical data from previous wars, student medics learn how soldiers get wounded, the types of wounds they can incur, and what needs to be done to keep a patient alive long enough to get him to a physician assistant or, even better, a doctor. Army studies indicate that if a wounded soldier arrives alive at a combat support hospital where surgeons and nurses can treat him, the chances of his surviving are extremely high—greater than 90 percent. "Surviving," of course, doesn't necessarily entail keeping arms or legs or retaining the ability to function independently back home.

The leading cause of preventable death on the battlefield is bleeding. Having a leg blown off by an IED, for instance, can be fatal if quick steps are not taken to control the blood loss. Even deadlier is internal bleeding, a problem for which medics generally don't have a good answer. A soldier who is bleeding internally needs to be evacuated and delivered to a surgeon immediately if he is to have any hope of survival.

The second-leading cause of preventable death is something called tension pneumothorax. If a bullet punctures a soldier's lung, air can leak from that hole into the "pleural space," or cavity outside the lungs. That air can build up and eventually interfere with the functioning of the heart. This can be a relatively simple problem to correct: a medic can simply stick a big needle in the soldier's chest to relieve the pressure in the pleural space.

Physician assistants (PAs) receive much more training than medics— two years' worth versus the medics' four months' worth—but they are still not doctors. Forced to respond to dire situations with nothing more than a small kit of supplies, including tourniquets, IVs, and combat gauze (a cotton fabric impregnated with a substance that speeds up clotting), they can often work miracles, but there are severe limits to what they can do. The lack of refrigeration facilities at most smaller bases means that no blood can be stored there; instead, PAs have to learn how to do the "buddy transfusion," a risky procedure conducted under emergency conditions, whereby blood withdrawn from a donor—a battlefield volunteer— is pushed directly into the vein of the patient.

Pfeifer's eyes were open; he was conscious but delirious and obviously in great pain. Other members of the team immediately carried him from the roof down to the aid station as Newsom called the operations center to have a medevac ordered. At the aid station, Captain Bert Baker, a former Special Forces medic and the outpost's PA, treated Pfeifer as best he could, but it was clear that the soldier needed to be evacuated at once if he was to stand a chance. There was massive bleeding from the exit wound in his lower back; Baker shoved a combat bandage into the hole. He twice inserted a needle into Pfeifer's chest to let out air that was building up in the cavity, a procedure that succeeded in getting Pfeifer's blood pressure up and his respiration rate down. Luckily, one of his lungs was still working. Baker had held people's lives in his hands before: he'd been a paramedic in St. Louis and a Special Forces medic in Haiti. But in both of those places, a hospital had usually been no more than ten minutes away. At Combat Outpost Keating, it was an hour-and-twenty-minute helicopter flight to the nearest hospital. Baker wasn't sure Chris Pfeifer would make it.

The PA did what he could for the wounded private and then waited for the bird; each passing second was excruciating.

Sarah Faulkenberry left her husband's bedside on August 15 to attend Tom Bostick's funeral at Arlington National Cemetery. She was worried about John, who was still in the intensive care unit. It seemed as though every other day, he had to have some surgery or other to close up his leg wounds. He still had some circulation at the bottom of his right leg, so the doctors were hoping they'd be able to save it.

Then, two days later, Karen Pfeifer, Chris's wife, called her.

Karen was in Germany, on post. She'd just left the mail room after dropping off a huge care package for her husband—containing cashews, baby wipes, sunscreen, short pants, and T-shirts—when she was beckoned into the commander's office and informed that Chris had been shot. He was still alive, she was told, but he'd been critically wounded and had to be evacuated to Forward Operating Base Naray, where he'd undergone surgery. He'd lost a lot of blood, so the command post at Naray had put out a loudspeaker call for O-negative donors, and troops had immediately begun lining up to donate.

Several hours and some forty units of blood later, Pfeifer had been stable enough to be flown to Bagram, where he'd had more surgery and received another forty pints of blood. The commander didn't have much more information to give his wife. The doctors at Bagram, he said, weren't sure when or even *if* Chris would be able to return to Germany.

Army spouses are taught to be there for one another, and Sarah Faulkenberry tried to console Karen Pfeifer. Although the two of them had become friendly while stationed with their husbands in Germany, on one level, Sarah was a bit surprised to get her call. But she knew that Karen had been raised in a foster home and didn't have much of a support network beyond her husband, his family, and her brother, a Marine at Camp Lejeune in North Carolina. Adding to Karen's feelings of isolation and panic was the fact that she was seven and a half months pregnant.

Eventually, just as Sarah herself had been able to accompany John from Germany back to Washington, Karen met her own husband in Germany and flew in a medevac plane with him from Landstuhl to the United States—though instead of landing in the nation's capital, they continued on to San Antonio, Texas, where Chris was to undergo further treatment at Brooke Army Medical Center. The Air Force officers almost didn't let Karen fly because she was thirty-four weeks pregnant and they were worried she'd go into labor during the flight, but ultimately they relented. She told them she was getting on that plane to be by her husband's side, and they weren't going to be able to stop her. If she did go into labor, at least there would be medical staff on board to look after her, thirty thousand feet in the air.

Up the mountain at Observation Post Warheit, Dave Roller and the men of 1st Platoon were getting used to a lifestyle even more spartan than the one down the hill at Combat Outpost Keating. *Hygiene* had become a relative term: six weeks into their stay at Warheit, Roller had yet to use any shampoo and was still on his first bar of soap. The troops bathed in a mountain stream; that part was kind of fun. Roller hadn't worn deodorant in three months, and he rotated his socks, shirts, and uniforms on a monthly basis. The platoon had run out of forks and spoons so many times that it was common to see soldiers sticking any spoons they found into their pockets for later use, or licking forks "clean" so other soldiers could use them.

There were no longer any women permanently stationed at either Observation Post Warheit or Combat Outpost Keating; with plans scotched for a PRT in Kamdesh, First Lieutenant Candace Mathis's MP unit was not replaced. Since Afghan women universally hid from U.S. soldiers, the 1st Platoon troops literally hadn't seen a woman in months—except for Roller, of course, through his scope before the battle at Saret Koleh. It was an odd sensation for the Americans—as if men were the only ones left on the planet. Whenever this one particular female Apache pilot flew in the area, soldiers would crowd around the radio just to hear her voice. They'd never seen her, but they were all convinced she was gorgeous.

The two tribes had been trying to kill each other for years and years now, but Navy Commander Sam Paparo was going to give diplomacy one more shot.

Paparo was head of the area's provincial reconstruction team, which was located about sixty miles distant from Kamdesh, at Kala Gush, in western Nuristan. Insurgents had continued to try to exploit the bitter rivalry between the Kom and the Kushtozis, stoking the dispute that had begun decades before over water rights and persisted ever since. After burning down a Kushtoz village in 1997 and displacing its twelve hundred or so residents, the Kom had placed mines throughout the ruins so the villagers couldn't return. It was in the midst of an attempt to encourage the groups to reconcile that Fazal Ahad, head of the erstwhile Eastern Nuristan Security Shura, had been killed.

Paparo had been working with the United Nations Mining Action Centre for Afghanistan to make Kushtoz hospitable once again. Before that agency could take any action, however, the dispute between the two ethnic groups had to be resolved, and the area made secure enough to allow the U.N. workers to do their jobs in safety. Each of these tasks was considerable. But that was what he and his colleagues were there to do, Paparo told himself. Even if the conflict was generations old and the land insecure, the United States was there to bring peace and stability.

In August, at Parun, the district center of Nuristan, Governor Nuristani, along with some national government officials, hosted a conference to map out a development plan for the province. The governor also invited representatives of the Kom, from Kamdesh Village, and the Kushtozis to come and discuss ways of settling their dispute over water rights. One of the possible solutions being proposed had long been debated by the PRT at Kala Gush: building a canal that would serve both communities. Paparo hoped that a canal might resolve the initial basis for the dispute, though State Department official David Katz had counseled him to refrain from involving the United States in the squabble in any way—the Americans would inevitably become entangled, whether they wanted to or not, Katz said, which would end up making the feud even more difficult to sort out. In any case, at Parun, the matter went unresolved, as the Kom argued that the Kushtozis had no right to the water that would flow through such a canal.

One day at the unfinished compound where the PRT personnel were encamped, Paparo heard a skirmish erupt just outside the gate—thankfully, a fight without armaments. He and other troops from the PRT ran to the entrance of the camp and saw two ancient men beating the life out of each other. Each elder—one Kom, one Kushtozi—was brandishing a large rock, and as the pair rolled around on the ground, each pummeled the other's skull with his stone. Paparo and the U.S. forces balked for a minute; laying hands on these elders might create a whole other host of issues, they knew. But it really looked as if the seniors were prepared to fight each other to the death, so the Americans at last intervened, pulling them apart. Both men had nasty cuts and bruises on their heads.

The physician assistant at the PRT was a Navy lieutenant commander whose previous deployment had been on the White House medical team. Not so long ago, he'd been in Washington, treating the leaders of the United States and their families—the Bushes and Cheneys, the Clintons and Gores—and now here he was in eastern Afghanistan, patching up the lacerations of a couple of old men who were fighting over water rights.

It was a long way indeed from 1600 Pennsylvania Avenue.

The joke about "military intelligence" being an oxymoron was so old as to be beyond a cliché, but Lieutenant Colonel Kolenda and Captain Joey Hutto had in fact begun to seriously doubt the intelligence and conventional wisdom about Kamdesh. They'd been briefed that the insurgents they were fighting against were primarily from Pakistan, which squared with the notion that the fight in the valley related to the larger showdown with Al Qaeda, that all of this had something to do with 9/11. But over time, the 1-91 Cav officers had made a number of observations that called that conclusion into question:

- The fighting stopped during the planting and the harvest and then flared back up again afterward. It didn't seem logical that Pakistanis would defer to the local agricultural calendar.
- On their hand-held radios, the insurgents spoke in the local dialect, Nuristani, which was relatively obscure and difficult to learn.

- The insurgents seemed to know every nook and cranny of the surrounding mountains and valleys.
- The local elders with real influence refused to meet with either the Americans or the district administrator, Anayatullah; those "elders" who did come to the shuras with 1-91 Cav were members of a dwindling group of Anayatullah's cronies.
- Despite both the severely depressed local economy and the relatively high pay offered by the Americans, the number of locals who now worked at Combat Outpost Keating, Combat Outpost Kamu, and Observation Post Warheit could probably be counted on one hand. This could be explained in part by the fact that some young men had begun providing security for the illegal timber-smuggling industry that President Karzai had inadvertently boosted when, concerned about deforestation, he banned the felling and export of trees. But anecdotally, the Americans had also heard that other locals were either working as guards for gem smugglers or joining yet another local growth industry: the insurgency.

Putting the pieces together, Kolenda and Hutto realized that they were facing nothing less than a popular insurrection.

They weren't the only ones. In the Waygal Valley, southwest of Combat Outpost Keating, the 173rd Airborne Task Force ROCK troopers were likewise having difficulty with the natives. Near the village of Aranas, twenty-two U.S. troops, along with some ANA soldiers and Afghan Security Guards, occupied a combat outpost called the Ranch House. Before dawn on August 22, RPGs and small-arms fire hailed down upon them; within minutes, it became frighteningly clear that the enemy planned to overrun the camp. Soon the troops at the Ranch House operations center lost contact with their men at the guard posts. The Afghan Security Guards — locally hired contractors — fled altogether, allowing the insurgents to breach the wire. Then more than three dozen ANA troops ran off toward the western side of the base, and the encroaching insurgents grabbed their ammunition and even some of their RPGs.

Thankfully, A-10 Warthogs arrived on the scene fairly quickly and, under the direction of First Lieutenant Matt Ferrara, began beating back the insurgents with "danger close" runs on enemy positions within the base. The Warthogs provided enough cover for Chosen Company to regain control. By the time the firefight came to its end, an ANA soldier and an Afghan Security Guard had been killed, and half of the U.S. troops had been wounded. The defenders felt certain that their antagonists were not Pakistanis; they were locals.

For Kolenda and Hutto, the attack on the Ranch House reemphasized the need to take every precaution possible to protect such vulnerable outposts in remote areas. Aggressive patrolling and the cultivation of positive relationships with the local population had to be top priorities. But those measures alone wouldn't suffice. Bulldog Troop would also need to conduct regular outpost defense drills specifically to prepare for the worst-case scenario: a breach, or "enemy in the wire." The men would have to be ready.

Having shed his Army uniform and bulletproof Kevlar, wearing just a T-shirt and short pants — as if he were headed out to football practice on the Coral Gables High School field — Dave Roller left Observation Post

Lieutenant Dave Roller meeting with Kamdesh elders. *(Photo courtesy of Dave Roller)*

Warheit with a few of his men to meet with a group of Kamdesh elders. It was mid-September, but the July 27 battle at Saret Koleh remained fresh in his mind, a scar that time would never fully heal.

Desperate, angry, and tired of getting shot at, Roller was ready to give this counterinsurgency business a try. Bostick had been a fantastic commander, but his strength was really more in the kinetic side of things, in fighting, thought Roller. Hutto, in contrast, had spent years working in special operations on unconventional warfare in Latin America, and he regarded counterinsurgency outreach as being common sense. He'd been encouraging his 1st Platoon leader to extend a hand toward the residents of Kamdesh Village. So Roller and his guys took a couple of cases of water with them as a gift, and they all sat down in a circle with the local elders, and Roller, through an interpreter, told the Afghans that he wanted to learn more about them so he could be of better service.

The Kamdeshis didn't understand at first. The Americans wanted to *help* them? Why would conquerors want to help those whose country they were occupying? Why would invaders reach out to them in such a way? It made no sense.

Roller tried to explain that he and his men all had families back in America. He pointed to Sergeant First Class Michael Burns and Staff Sergeant Zachary Crawford. "These men are fathers just like you," he told the elders. "They're husbands and fathers whose wives and children are scared for their lives. They have families that they're responsible for providing for, but they've chosen to be here in Kamdesh to help you." His own parents were terrified he'd be killed, he said, but he and his troops thought it was important to help the people of Nuristan. He was trying to get the Kamdesh elders to see him and his men as real people, with real emotions. Indeed, he was convinced that to the villagers, Americans—with their camouflage helmets, body armor, huge guns, and sunglasses masking their eyes, their bodies festooned with confusing technological devices—appeared robotic, nearly inhuman. That was why Roller had worn his gym clothes to this meeting, so he would look not like an Army officer or any other sort of authority figure but instead like just a young man—a kid, really—who was there to help them, almost as if he were with the Peace Corps.

In August, during his first week at Camp Keating, Hutto had asked Kenny Johnson, in charge of contracting, to call a meeting with local vendors to

Observation Post Warheit. *(Photo courtesy of Rick Victorino)*

discuss various development projects. Some of these projects were funded by the PRT, while others were financed through a special discretionary sum meted out by the commander—in this case, Hutto and Johnson. The distinction meant nothing to the locals who were competing for the money.

The next week, Hutto began making the rounds and holding shuras in local villages, starting with Urmul, followed by Kamdesh. In Urmul, residents made clear their disdain for Kamdesh District's administrator, Anayatullah, who'd taken Gul Mohammed Khan's place. Among the reasons for their antipathy was the fact that Anayatullah's family had been chased out of the area years before; it seemed curious to them that the son of an ostracized family should have been appointed to such a position. The villagers also complained that he was corrupt and didn't look out for their interests. Hutto told the Nuristanis that the United States wanted them to take control of everything—their own governance, development, and security—and suggested that if they did that, the Americans would show more deference to their autonomy and territorial sovereignty. But by the same token, they would also be responsible for any bad guys in their midst who fired upon Camp Keating or attacked the patrols that Hutto was sending out at such a frenetic pace. The villagers seemed receptive to these terms.

Over the next several months, Hutto and Kolenda began establishing close working relationships with elders in the area, and they urged their lieutenants to do the same—whence Roller's excursion from Observation Post Warheit. At Kamdesh, Mawlawi Abdul Rahman had become a prominent elder. Rahman was fairly quiet and not really comfortable speaking in large forums. He wore the only pair of photochromic lenses—glasses that turned dark in the sun—that the Americans ever saw on a Nuristani. He was polite and so indirect that it was sometimes a task to figure out where he stood on an issue. The men of 1-91 Cav knew that Rahman had been a student of Mullah Sadiq's—the HIG leader

Mawlawi Abdul Rahman. *(Photo courtesy of Bulldog Troop)*

who went underground in 2006—but they liked him. Hutto, Kolenda, and their ANA counterparts hoped that Rahman might even persuade Sadiq to encourage HIG fighters' partnering with the Afghan government and the ISAF forces.

The Americans were firm, but they could be deferential, too, when they needed to be.

Marine Master Sergeant Scott Ingbretsen, in charge of training seventy-two ANA soldiers at Combat Outpost Keating and Observation Post War-heit, tried his best to convey the sense that he worked for the Afghans, that it was the ANA commander, Lieutenant Noorullah, who made the decisions for his company. Raised as an Air Force brat, Ingbretsen, now thirty-eight, had joined the Marines because they accepted his application before the Air Force did. He'd done three tours in Iraq, combating IEDs as an explosive-ordnance disposal technician—one of those guys who would be depicted in the 2008 film *The Hurt Locker,* which many in the field would deride for its unrealistic portrayal of such specialists as out-of-control rogues. Ingbretsen approached Nuristani politics and pride with the sensitivity of an expert trying to disable an explosive. When he first met his ANA company, a platoon sergeant was giving a class on hand and arm signals. Afterward, the Afghan sergeant asked him what he'd thought of the class, adding, "I'm sure you're going to change the signals." Ingbretsen reasoned that he'd been preceded as a trainer for that ANA company by any number of other individuals from any number of other countries, most, if not all, of whom had forced the troops to learn their particular motions.

"It probably makes more sense for *me* to learn *your* hand signals," Ingbretsen replied. "There are more of you than there are of me." That went over well. Bomb defused.

Many of the men in Ingbretsen's company had been fighting since they were young teenagers, either as mujahideen or on the other side, as allies of the Soviets. So he figured his job was to professionalize the new Afghan troops—to make sure they understood the importance of representing the Afghan government in ethical and respectful ways. Some of their previous experiences had encouraged habits that were difficult to break. For example, many Afghans had seen that Soviet enlisted men were neither trusted nor respected by their officers, so, following that model, their own enlisted men were considered pretty much personae non gratae. When the usual conflicting tribal, ethnic, and village loyalties were added to the mix, ANA officers and their sergeants hardly stood as paragons of harmony and discipline.

On their first major patrol after their arrival in the area in September 2007, Ingbretsen and his ANA troops visited a couple of small villages, including Upper Kamdesh, where Lieutenant Noorullah sat down with Mohammed Gul, the *malik,* or conduit between the village and the Afghan government. Gul was angry—*very* angry. He told Noorullah how the Americans had, the previous year, bombed a local village; children had died, he said. Noorullah didn't know how to respond. He looked at Ingbretsen, who asked him for permission to speak. It was granted.

Ingbretsen was contrite. "We come from a good country," he said humbly. "The United States wants to do good things for your people. But mistakes happen. All I can do is apologize."

The *malik* looked at the American. "Don't be sad," he said. "It's okay." He invited Ingbretsen and Noorullah to dine with him that night.

Similarly, on another occasion, former district administrator Gul Mohammed Khan invited Hutto to his home in Upper Kamdesh for dinner. It was an impressive spread, as these things went, but Mohammed didn't hold back, laying into Hutto about civilian casualties, night raids, and house-to-house searches. Special Forces teams and other Americans had been coming into Nuristan for years, and it seemed to the Kamdesh elders that all they knew was brute force.

Hutto looked at Mohammed. "I'm sorry that those things happened to you," he said. "I can't change the past. But what we can do is work together on how we interact with one another to support the needs of the people." Such apologies could—and that night, did—completely change a meeting's dynamics. In a culture in which pride and respect were paramount, deference and remorse could go a long way.

On September 6, Hutto and Johnson hosted a shura at Camp Keating. In attendance were district administrator Anayatullah, Afghan National Police commander Abdul Jalil, local ANA commander Lieutenant Noorullah, and a large group of elders from nearby villages and settlements. Anayatullah began the meeting by reading from the Quran and making a passionate plea for cooperation. Security was a big problem, he said. The members of the Eastern Nuristan Security Shura were supposed to have established a security plan, but they hadn't gotten it done. Everyone knew that insurgents lived in the villages; some of the fighters were even related to members of the gathered shura. Indeed, Anayatullah noted, the primary mullah of Kamdesh had a son who was an insurgent.

Anayatullah then asked the elders, "Before the Americans came to Kamdesh, had you ever heard of a development project?" Of course not, he said. The insurgents were making no effort to build a stronger Afghanistan, whereas the United States was trying to help. "So," he announced, "we need to help the Americans." Two days before, insurgents had fired a PKM machine gun into the Camp Keating mosque, which was used primarily by the ANA soldiers and the outpost's Afghan Security Guards. Firing into a mosque? "These are not Muslims," Anayatullah declared, "they are terrorists. If you help the bad guys, we will destroy you. If the local people help the enemy fighters, they are not helping the government; they are considered to be Al Qaeda." Others weighed in, expressing similar sentiments.

Meetings proceeded in this same manner over the next couple of months. Sometimes they took place at Combat Outpost Keating, but it was preferable to hold them in the villages, because "forcing" the Americans to travel to them enhanced the elders' credibility in the eyes of their people. Kolenda and Hutto noticed, in fact, that there seemed to be a direct correlation between their participation in these shuras and a decline in violence. By the end of September, attacks on Camp Keating and OP Warheit, as well as on Bulldog Troop patrols and missions, had ceased.

Shuras generally involved food. A typical meal served by the elders would include goat, rice, and fresh flatbread. Occasionally potatoes or a seasonal cauliflower-like vegetable would be offered. It would be hard to overstate how much Hutto hated eating goat; while chewing the tough, gamey meat, he'd often think to himself that he'd truly rather eat dog—but he'd swallow and take another bite anyway.

Another Nuristani delicacy was ghee, a clarified butter cooked slowly so it would separate, with the residue dropping to the bottom. The Americans found that Nuristan cheese fried in ghee didn't taste bad at all, and the locals liked the stuff so much they sometimes had contests to determine who could chug the most.[39]

---

[39] According to Richard Strand, the Kom have a reputation for being "wild and crazy" and often make bets involving outlandish behavior. One Kamdeshi friend of Strand's

Soon, on their own initiative, elders from the different settlements that made up Kamdesh Village were meeting among themselves and with elders from other villages and hamlets. They reaffirmed that each settlement was responsible for its own security and the security of its portion of the road. They also resolved that the elders of every village would try to persuade the insurgents in their area to lay down their arms and work with them on security and development. Fighters who agreed to do so could expect complete amnesty and acceptance from their communities; fighters who didn't would be banned from their villages. Accomplishing all of that was easier said than done, but it was a lofty goal nonetheless.

The elders also discussed how to distribute humanitarian aid from the United States, how to settle the Kom–Kushtozi dispute, and how to ensure that laborers from each village were hired to work on development projects. There was no resolution of any of these issues, but as far as Kolenda and Hutto were concerned, mere conversation about them could be counted as progress.

As the Chinook bore down at Combat Outpost Keating, Second Lieutenant Kyle Marcum's first reaction was confusion: he thought the pilot was going to land in the river.

Marcum was being brought in to lead 2nd Platoon. (Meyer had transferred to become the XO of Crazyhorse Troop at Combat Outpost Monti, in Kunar Province.) He didn't know any of the guys. He'd found out he was headed to Bulldog Troop on July 27, the day Bostick and Fritsche died. Just that part in itself was tough enough—being told he was joining a company whose commander had been killed only hours before.

And then the bird landed. Marcum got off, looked around, and tilted his head back to gaze up at the mountains, which shot upward on every side.

He was low-key, not an alarmist, a mellow guy from Denver whose path to Kamdesh had begun with ROTC at Montana State University. But now he felt a bit of panic. This is not good, he thought. He stared at the mountains, then looked around again. He simply could not get the topography of it all. An outpost? *Here?*

---

was well known for betting he could climb up a log ladder with a heavy tripod—used to hold large stone pots over a fire—hooked over his erect penis. "He did so and insured his place in local lore forever," Strand says.

A view of Combat Outpost Keating from the northwestern mountain. *(Photo courtesy of Dave Roller)*

The physicians at Brooke Army Medical Center kept Chris Pfeifer heavily drugged to help with the pain. Then, for almost three weeks in that hospital in San Antonio, Chris Pfeifer was sometimes conscious. It wasn't constant—he faded in and out—but when he was awake, he would talk to Karen, ask about their as yet unborn baby girl, and tell her over and over that he loved her.

The bullet had not only damaged many of his internal organs but also, as it exited out his back, paralyzed him. When the doctors at Brooke finally got him stable enough that they could operate on him, they found a huge pocket of infection in his spine that had spread throughout his body. Again and again, Chris's white blood cell count began falling. His heart would slow down, his breathing would stop. The doctors would rush in with the crash cart and bring him back.

Each time he went in for yet another round of surgery—and he had a lot of procedures—he would tell Karen that she needed to be there when he woke up.

On September 22, Sarah Faulkenberry's mother—who had driven

from her home in Midland, Texas, to be with Karen and Chris in San Antonio—called her daughter to report, "It doesn't look good." By then, John Faulkenberry was in much better shape, having been transferred from the ICU at Walter Reed Army Medical Center to ward 57, the orthopedic wing, where combat troops were often sent to recuperate from amputations. John told Sarah to go to Texas to be with Karen Pfeifer, who seemed so very alone except for the baby in her womb. The morning Sarah arrived from Bethesda, Chris Pfeifer crashed again. Doctors shocked his heart repeatedly and brought him back.

Sarah and Karen took shifts, with Sarah sitting at Chris's bedside and holding his hand while Karen, who was mere days away from delivering their baby girl, slept. Sarah would talk to Chris, telling him how John was doing, creating a fantasy world in which she and John moved to San Antonio so they could hang out with Chris and Karen. The men could recover together; their dogs would frolic. Everything would be fine.

The odds of Chris's surviving kept dropping with his white blood cell count. His doctors said they had one last shot: they could try giving him a transfusion of white blood cells from someone who was a match. Chris Pfeifer's blood type was A-positive, and as luck would have it, so was Sarah Faulkenberry's. She, Chris's sister, Nicole Griffiths, and a hospital chaplain were all A-positive, and they all volunteered to donate.

Karen desperately wanted to do something to help. But she was A-negative, and even if she had been a match, her pregnancy would have prevented her from giving blood. So she would wipe Chris's wounds down, assist the nurses, anything.

On September 25, the doctors began the process of transfusion. Chris crashed again. The doctors told Karen and Chris's parents that while they would keep trying everything they could, they seemed to be nearing the point where they might not be able to do anything more for him. They were also worried that even if he did survive, he wouldn't have much quality of life left because of how long it was taking them to revive him after each crash. Every time it happened, his brain was deprived of oxygen for a significant interval.

Karen sat in her husband's room and watched the doctors work. They were trying hard, but it all seemed futile.

Soon the medical team ushered Karen and Chris's parents into a separate room. They had reached that point, the doctors said. There wasn't anything more they could do for Chris short of putting him on life support, which he had specifically noted in his living will he did not want. Karen asked them to put him on life support for fifteen minutes, just long enough to let Sarah, Nicole, and the chaplain—who were at that moment donating their white blood cells for him—get back to his room in the ICU.

Karen was stronger than Sarah had ever seen her. Days before, the first time Chris crashed, his wife had said to him, "If you can't fight no longer, if your body can't take it no longer, it's okay with me if you go. I don't want you to, but if you can't take it no longer, no one will be mad at you." Now, as the medical staff turned off Chris's machines and his life flowed out of him, she told him again that she understood he had to leave. She understood that he would be around to watch over their daughter.

"You've fought long and hard," she told her husband, "but now it's time for you to go. I don't want you to hurt anymore."

Chris was in a medically induced coma, but to his doctors' astonishment, as the life-support machines were being shut down, he reached out for Karen's hand.

They held hands as he slowly stopped breathing.

"He's gone," one doctor finally said.

Karen fled from the room—she didn't want to witness what death would do to Chris's body—and headed to see her obstetrician-gynecologist. She was scheduled for induction the next morning. After almost a full day of labor, she still wasn't delivering, so the ob-gyn performed a C-section. Peyton Pfeifer was born on September 27, two days after her father died. She was silent, almost reverentially so, throughout his funeral on October 10, at Saint Michael's Catholic Church in Spalding, Nebraska. She didn't even cry when the guns were fired at his graveside.

Sarah was there with a wheelchair-bound John Faulkenberry, having been shown how to administer his IV and give him shots. Other members of 1-91 Cav were also in attendance, including a few who were still recuperating from their own injuries, such as Wayne Baird, who served as a pallbearer, and Jonathan Sultan.[40] Although the total population of

---

[40] Baird had suffered nerve damage to, and loss of mobility in, his right arm but was able to remain in the military. Sultan had lost an eye and was subsequently discharged. Faulkenberry ultimately lost his leg and was discharged.

Spalding was only 502, more than 700 people crowded into the church and gathered in the streets to honor the community's first fallen soldier since 1951. Some of Pfeifer's comrades from Bulldog Troop talked about how funny Chris would have found it to see them all there, in his small town.

That afternoon, the schoolchildren of Spalding released dozens of balloons into the air, a colorful bloom that rose to the heaven that was Chris Pfeifer's beloved Nebraska sky.

CHAPTER 19

If You're the Enemy,
Please Stand Up

Dave Roller and Alex Newsom loved the way Joey Hutto would just shoot the breeze with Mawlawi Abdul Rahman, head of the Kamdesh Village shura, as if he were talking to a pal at the local bar. Part of it was Hutto's casual, "Hey, man, let's work out a deal here" style of negotiation and bonding, but it went beyond that, too: the two men would joke around, buddy-buddy, covering a range of topics, often rather bawdy. "You get lucky with your wife last night?" Hutto would ask Rahman, without any fear of giving offense. Sometimes — usually — Hutto's language was even earthier than that, but Rahman's response was always the same: first he'd laugh, then he'd come back at the American captain with the same question.

"I never see her," Hutto would reply. "I'm here!"

In early October, the elders and Anayatullah informed Hutto and Kolenda that they had scheduled a "mega-shura" for the end of the month. The locals were very excited: this council would include representatives from all the major villages in Kamdesh District, from as far east as Gawardesh and as far north as Paprok. The elders selected as the site an old school building five hundred yards or so east of Combat Outpost Keating, and they held planning sessions to map out every last detail: talking points and desired outcomes; seating, food, sound system, pictures, and posters; and — working with Afghan security forces — protection and crowd control.

As Hutto conducted security walkthroughs and rehearsals, he realized that the Kamdesh elders — Mawlawi Abdul Rahman, Gul Mohammed Khan, and others — were completely prepared to handle the meeting on their own. He spoke with Kolenda, and they decided that not only should they let the elders take the lead in this, but they themselves shouldn't even attend unless they were specifically invited. The more evident it was that this process was being driven entirely by Nuristanis, the more successful it would be.

More than eight hundred Nuristanis from all over the district attended the mega-shura. Elders and mullahs from various villages spoke. The basic theme, repeated over and over, was that the elders had to take responsibility for bringing peace and prosperity to their district — and needed, to that end, to form a district shura like the one they'd had in the old days, to govern themselves, to end the violence and foster economic development. Echoing Anayatullah's earlier argument, the elders agreed that those who were trying to kill the Americans were actually harming other Muslims through their false jihad, and therefore were not true Muslims themselves.

The elders referred to the American presence at Combat Outpost Keating as the "PRT," a term that perplexed Kolenda and Hutto when they received reports about the meeting. The force now posted at Camp Keating, 1-91 Cav, was not a provincial reconstruction team; it was a combat unit. But as the two commanders would later learn, "PRT" was the label the elders used to distinguish between those Americans who helped with development and those who caused civilian casualties and searched villagers' homes.

The elders elected one hundred members to serve on the new shura, which was meticulously designed to proportionally represent all of the villages and tribes and clans in Kamdesh District. Thus was born the "Hundred-Man Shura." Rahman was chosen as its head, and an executive committee was appointed to assist him. Anayatullah handed out a list of development projects to the hundreds of assembled Nuristanis. "It's your responsibility to secure your own villages," he reminded them.

The mega-shura continued for a second day and then into a third. While most of the elders returned to their villages after the second day, seventy or so remained behind to try to hammer out a comprehensive security plan, detailing each village's responsibilities and the consequences for violating a pending mega-shura agreement.

Kolenda was delighted. He asked Rahman and Gul Mohammed Khan if the elders might persuade insurgent leaders such as Mohammed Jan— HIG commander for Kamdesh District—to tell their fighters to lay down their arms. Rahman looked at Kolenda and smiled.

"No, that is not how things work here," he said. "Right now the militant leaders are too powerful. They have control of the young men. Our plan is to go from village to village and talk with the people about the future. We will convince the elders and the parents of the fighters, and convince the fighters as well. Once we have enough of them on our side, then we will have the power to persuade the leaders to join us."

From November through the following January, representatives from the Hundred-Man Shura toured Kamdesh District, going from village to village, discussing the way forward, explaining why the Americans were in the area, and talking about how they would all work together. "Jihad is over," the elders said on their journeys. "Stop fighting." To further combat the skepticism of a highly insular people who intensely distrusted outsiders, the Hundred-Man Shura asked the Americans and the Afghan government to draft written agreements regarding peace and cooperation. The shura wanted Karzai and the United States, first, to commit to coordinating with its members on all issues affecting their villages and the district at large, and second, to acknowledge the governance role of the shura itself. (Part of the elders' motivation for both demands, it must be said, was the desire to get more directly involved in the development projects, in order to wield power and disburse money.) Called the Commitment of Mutual Support, the agreement with the Americans stipulated that in exchange for the villagers' assuming greater responsibility for the development contracts and taking the lead in expelling insurgents, U.S. troops would refrain from entering mosques or homes uninvited, unless there was an imminent threat. If a home had to be searched, Bulldog Troop was to confer with local elders and the ANA, and then ANA officers alone would conduct the actual search. If the Americans received intelligence on an insurgent weapons cache, they and the ANA would work with the elders to track it down and seize it. Only if the elders refused to help would the ANA and the Americans be free to take matters into their own hands.

The reaction among some officers and soldiers in the squadron was shock: We're fighting a fucking war, these guys are killing us, and we're supposed to politely ask permission before searching for bad guys? they wondered. But even before this, Chris Kolenda had been diligent about demanding that his officers and NCOs educate all of their troops on the many nuances of counterinsurgency, and after a while, most troops understood why it wasn't always smart to just start kicking down doors, unless the goal was to piss off more people and create more insurgents. As a general rule, the men of Bulldog Troop already knew not to enter a village without first coordinating with its elders, because culturally, it was inappropriate just to show up. American and ANA troops were supposed to wait at the edge of the village while the women withdrew into their homes, and to go in only after the elders told them they could. But such cultural sensitivities hadn't always been a priority. Now they would be, unless there was an "imminent threat."

Roller didn't think that was so much to give up. He was more than willing to trade his infrequent patrols through villages sans permission for the locals' pledge to keep the bad guys out themselves. And most of those he served with understood that this war wasn't like the one in *Saving Private Ryan* or *Band of Brothers:* there would be no surrender by a uniformed enemy army. Second- and third-order effects could metastasize.

Working with the elders, Kolenda and Hutto carved out another exception to the agreement: U.S. troops also had an open invitation to enter a village to inspect a project that the United States was paying for. If the village's shura equivocated on this, or failed to welcome the Americans into the village, the United States would cut off the money or even cancel the project until the elders came into line. Moreover, if insurgents vandalized or destroyed a project, American funding would be stopped until the village elders identified those responsible and worked with Afghan security forces to hold them accountable. If the Nuristanis truly wanted to take ownership of their own affairs, their role couldn't be confined to just managing the cash and handing out the contracts; they would have to do the hard work of self-policing as well.

The new shura also agreed to use its size to enforce a sort of nonviolent resistance against members who broke their word. If any village proved uncooperative and refused to abide by the agreement, the Hundred-Man Shura pledged to drop in en masse and squat there. The village would then have to feed the picketing elders—a very expensive proposition—until the situation was resolved to their satisfaction.

Bulldog Troop signed off on the Commitment of Mutual Support, and Hutto began enforcing it—often with some choice language when he thought a village was slacking or violating the terms.

Hutto and Ingbretsen, the ANA trainer, felt they'd made some headway with elders throughout the district and were eager to expand their range. Hutto requested a shura in Mandigal, and the elders selected a date in November. This exchange was soon followed by radio chatter from insurgents in the area, suggesting that they wouldn't allow the Americans to enter the village—and in any case certainly wouldn't let them leave it alive. As the date neared, Hutto sent his men out on patrols to secure the road leading to Mandigal, and then he devised a plan to fend off an attack: he asked members of the Hundred-Man Shura to swing by Combat Outpost Keating, pick up Ingbretsen and him, and join them at the Mandigal shura. They agreed.

Accompanied by former district administrator Gul Mohammed Khan, Kamdesh Village shura head Abdul Rahman, Afghan National Police commander Jalil, ANA commander Lieutenant Noorullah, and others, the Americans walked breezily into the village. Seats had been set out in a big open space just south of the village mosque, and Hutto and Ingbretsen sat with the elders on a platform in front of a stone wall by the road. The meeting was led by Abdul Hanan, a respected Mandigal elder. Hanan served as a sort of master of ceremonies for the shura, calling upon each man in turn to give his presentation.

Hutto made his usual pitch about the benefits to be had from their all working together: peace, development, prosperity. "I'm not asking you to turn in insurgents," he said. "But I want you to ask the bad guys what future they envision for Kamdesh District."

Lieutenant Noorullah came next, informing the elders that a planned project to build a road north to Barg-e-Matal could be subcontracted so that each village along the way would be responsible for its own section, if it wanted. But, he explained, until the fighting ended, Nuristan would not be able to receive the economic-development funding it desired. And that meant that the elders of Mandigal would need to talk to local insurgents and get them to turn in their weapons and cease hostilities.

Noorullah had connections in the village—his wife was from there—

and he had been working them before this meeting. (His own family sold gems in the Kabul area, and his wife's was involved in the same trade, but on the mining side.) Drawing upon his sources, he had assembled a list of names of insurgents from Mandigal. And right then and there, he called those men out and told them to stand up—right in front of their fathers.

Ingbretsen's interpreter was feeding translations into his earpiece. Ingbretsen and Hutto looked at each other. What was this?

And then the first insurgent stood. He was just a few feet in front of them.

Nervously, Hutto and Ingbretsen whispered to each other, "What are we going to do now?" Since they first entered the village, they'd been hearing enemy chatter on the radio, some of it coming from inside Mandigal. Apart from their interpreters and a couple of Army medics, including Rob Fortner, who were off to one side tending to ailing children, the two Americans were essentially alone, facing a crowd of hundreds of Nuristanis, many of whom were carrying AKs. Sure, there were Afghan police and ANA troops there, as well as the elders who had accompanied them to the shura, but who knew what would happen if bullets started flying?

Hutto looked out into the crowd: some two dozen men were now standing, identifying themselves as enemy fighters. He and Ingbretsen, talking under their breath, quickly came up with a contingency plan. Straight ahead of them was a big wooden arch decorated with intricate patterns. That would be considered twelve o'clock, the two men decided. If the bad guys started shooting, Ingbretsen, on the left, would return fire and clear from ten to twelve o'clock, and Hutto would do the same from twelve to two o'clock. Then they'd turn, drop the fifteen feet down the wall to the gravel road, and run out of town.

The enemy fighters, however, didn't make any moves. Noorullah told the insurgents that they must stop their attacks. "I know who you are," he said. "You need to join the government of the Islamic Republic of Afghanistan. Next time I see you, if you are fighting the government or the Americans, I will kill you."

The insurgents took their seats. It was as strong a message as Hutto and Ingbretsen could have hoped for.

*   *   *

Every officer in the 173rd Airborne was on record as supporting the new counterinsurgency strategy set forth by the Petraeus–Mattis group, but each one had his own take on it, and some thought Kolenda was taking the notion too far. Kolenda felt as if he were being constantly second-guessed by his boss, Colonel Chip Preysler, and by the brigade staff at Forward Operating Base Fenty at Jalalabad. The pushback never came in the form of a denial of development funds; it was more a matter of constant badgering and even condescension: What are you doing? Why aren't you planning another kinetic[41] operation? What's with all of the backslapping and handholding? Despite the fact that 1-91 Cav had obliterated hundreds of insurgents throughout the summer and fall, one brigade staff officer still quipped that Kolenda's men weren't killing enough people.

This frustrated Kolenda to no end. It was true that violence was down in his area of operations, but that wasn't because his men had gone soft. As Kolenda saw it, none of what he was doing had anything to do with being warmhearted. In his opinion, counterinsurgency was a pretty damned cold-blooded strategy, all about being out there with specific goals — establishing stability and defeating the insurgency — and intelligently using the full range of available leverage, from cash, clean water, and education for local children to bullets, when appropriate, to get the desired results. There was an element of manipulation involved. Sure, he wanted the Afghans to have better lives — how could anyone not, after seeing that kind of impoverishment? But there was also something transactional about American promises of clean water, construction jobs, and a brighter future for Afghan kids. This wasn't charity; the bottom line was, these offers were made to save American lives and help destroy anyone who hoped to hurt ISAF troops. Kolenda could never understand why some folks viewed the carrots as being somehow inferior to the sticks.

Preysler, for his part, didn't see himself as pushing back against Kolenda's efforts. As the man in charge of the four provinces in this area of operations, with eleven commands at the lieutenant colonel level under him, each with its own challenges and demands, he had a different per-

---

[41] "Kinetic" operations are combat operations.

spective on matters. His men in the Korangal Valley were getting attacked up to five times a day, every day.[42] Maybe the shuras and promises had helped, but how much? Even if violence was down in 1-91 Cav's zone, all over the rest of its area of operations, the 173rd Airborne was still filling body bags.

This was Preysler's fourth time in combat: he'd been in Afghanistan at the beginning of the war and then again during Operation Anaconda, as well as in Iraq at the beginning of that war. As a battalion commander, Preysler had been featured in Sean Naylor's *Not a Good Day to Die*, the book that Ben Keating gave to his father before he headed overseas. By contrast, this was Kolenda's first time deployed into battle.

Preysler believed that the deaths of Jacob Lowell, Tom Bostick, and Ryan Fritsche, combined with the challenges of the territory, had — understandably — led Kolenda to conclude that conventional tactics wouldn't work in Nuristan, and prompted him to put a great deal of energy into other, nonkinetic courses of action. And while he knew Kolenda might not think he was on board, Preysler felt that in fact, he was — it was just that he was constantly pushing for further analysis.

Kolenda didn't talk with his subordinates about what he viewed as Preysler's skeptical, sometimes even unsupportive attitude, but his troopers readily picked up on wariness from the brigade leaders during their occasional visits to the area. As Kolenda saw it, many of his fellow officers did not understand the situation in Kamdesh, and many seemed to think of counterinsurgency as a simple matter of attrition warfare, with fig leaves of self-governance and development — as if counterinsurgency were just a big show being put on by Kolenda and others, a way of distracting the locals while the "real" Americans tackled the real job of killing bad guys.

At the end of December 2007, Second Lieutenant Hank Hughes, a former Army brat who'd gone to Boston University on an ROTC scholarship, met up with Hutto at Forward Operating Base Naray. The two

---

[42] Sebastian Junger's book *WAR* and documentary film *Restrepo: One Platoon, One Valley, One Year,* which he shot with the late Tim Hetherington, provide captivating looks at fourteen months in the Korangal with one platoon from the 173rd Airborne during this period.

hitched a ride on a chopper to Camp Keating. "You'd better be ready," Hutto warned him in his odd, speedy Southern twang.

Hughes was flying in to replace Dave Roller as leader of 1st Platoon — Roller was being promoted to Bulldog Troop's XO, Hutto's second in command — and the green lieutenant had never before been deployed into a war zone. Hughes looked out the window of the Black Hawk and gulped. He'd been briefed on the physical lay of the land, but actually seeing it was another matter.

Holy shit, he thought.

The bird descended onto the landing zone, at the bottom of the fish-bowl, and Hughes's dreadful astonishment continued. This is really not what a base is supposed to be, he said to himself. This is not what they trained me for. He wondered if the guns on the base could even shoot high enough to reach insurgents at the upper elevations.

Dave Roller greeted Hughes out at the landing zone, noting with approval the Army Ranger tab on the new arrival's left sleeve. The two men were a lot alike in their temperament, confidence, politics (both leaned somewhat left), and stubbornness — which meant, of course, that they didn't particularly get along, at first. Roller was anxious about how the men of his former platoon would fare under the newcomer; perhaps he was even a little jealous of Hughes, who was now their leader, running around on missions with them while Roller himself had to keep inventory. For his part, Hughes found the officers at Combat Outpost Keating a tough crowd: they had come together in battle, in blood, over the loss of their captain and fellow soldiers, and now here he was, this new guy, flying in after Christmas for the remaining seven months of their rotation. Hutto and Marcum, relative newcomers themselves, were reasonably friendly toward him. But Roller — man, he was a very different story.

They clashed about everything. Their more consequential conflicts had to do with tactical decisions. Once, Roller saw Hughes preparing to set up an observation post near Naray while — in Roller's opinion — carrying too much gear with him. With memories of the fateful mission to Saret Koleh still fresh in his mind, he explained to his replacement that redundant equipment would increase his risk of being pinned down. Roller himself, after all, *had* been pinned down before. He advised Hughes that water was more important than extra radios — he could always send a runner or even give hand signals if he ended up needing those. Hughes flat-out told Roller he was wrong, then said he was going to do things his own way. An epic argument commenced. The disagreement was resolved only by the (unrelated) cancellation of the mission.

They fought just as hard about more trivial issues, too. One day, in the gym, the two lieutenants got into a heated argument about the rapper Lil Wayne, who at that point in his career seemed to some to be coasting a bit, maintaining his fan base largely through guest appearances in others' songs and raps and through popular mix tapes. Was Lil Wayne a great rapper? That was open to debate, evidently. Roller asserted that his meteoric record sales meant that the question had been asked and answered. Hughes disagreed: quantity did not indicate quality, he insisted. Referring to Aristotle's *Poetics,* which declared tragic poems superior to epic poems, he dove into the notion of empirical quality. Well, rebutted Roller, getting angrier, Lil Wayne's art had obviously touched a lot of people, so there was clearly something that attracted them to him. How should art be defined? After twenty minutes, the volume increasing with each advance of the minute hand — and Kenny Johnson watching it all, bemused and bewildered — a furious Roller stormed out of the gym, his workout only half done, his heart rate nevertheless well above the fat-burning level.

Later, Hughes talked with Newsom about it: "Why is Dave such a dick to me?" he asked.

Newsom smiled. Hughes had come to Camp Keating full of piss and vinegar, and Roller's immediate reaction had been to hate the new guy, especially because he missed going on missions with his platoon. But even more than that, it was the fact that they were so similar. "Imagine if you were here and then another one of you showed up," Newsom said. "Wouldn't *you* hate you?"

The first real test of the Commitment of Mutual Support between the Hundred-Man Shura and Bulldog Troop came when bullets were fired at Observation Post Warheit.

They were just sporadic rounds coming from somewhere south of Camp Keating — Urmul or, a little farther south, Agro, it wasn't clear which. Either way, they needed to stop. Hutto called for the relevant representatives from the Hundred-Man Shura, Said Amin from Urmul and Hjia Jamo from Agro. He escorted them to the large tent that had been set up for shuras at Camp Keating and invited them to sit down on the carpets. Hutto didn't consider these two to be bad guys, but he didn't treat them as well as he did, say, his buddy Abdul Rahman. They had yet to prove themselves to him. Maybe this would be their chance.

"Where are these rounds coming from?" Hutto asked them through an interpreter. "Who's responsible?"

Amin, from Urmul, said the shots were coming from Agro. Jamo, from Agro, said the insurgents had been firing from Urmul and then running into his settlement.

"Okay," Hutto said. "Until we settle this, you won't get any humanitarian assistance, and funding for your projects will be cut off. You need to figure out who did it, and you need to make it stop."

About a week later, Jamo returned to Combat Outpost Keating and asked to meet with Hutto. "We know who the person is who fired on your camp," he told the American. "But he's not from our village—he's from outside Agro and came in. What do we do?"

"Even if outsiders come in from outside your area, you're responsible," Hutto said. "If you can't control him, tell the ANA or the Afghan National Police."

Not long after that, rounds were fired at Observation Post Warheit from Kamdesh Village. This time, a member of the Hundred-Man Shura knew the identity of the guilty party—but the thing was, the insurgent was the nephew of a *different* member of the Hundred-Man Shura, who was also a contractor. Not only would this second shura member not do anything to stop the shooting, but he wouldn't give the insurgent's precise location to Hutto so that the Americans could take action against him.

Hutto convened several meetings with the leaders of the Kamdesh Village shura—Mawlawi Abdul Rahman and Gul Mohammed Khan—but no information was forthcoming. "You're going to be responsible for our stopping all projects in Kamdesh Village," Hutto told them.

Luckily for the villagers of Kamdesh, the insurgent was arrested near Gawardesh, and the problem went away. The ultimate test of the Commitment of Mutual Support had been avoided—for now. But it all left a bad taste in Hutto's mouth. The Hundred-Man Shura had not yet proven itself.

*   *   *

Winter came to Combat Outpost Keating. General Freakley's replacement, Major General David Rodriguez, the commander of Combined Joint Task Force 82, announced that Observation Post Warheit would be renamed Observation Post Fritsche.

Marcum and 2nd Platoon were assigned to the observation post when a three-day snowstorm hit the mountain in January. At first it was fun — snowball fights, giant snowmen, snow caves — but the weather quickly lost its appeal once the troops realized they were slowly, steadily being buried in up to seven feet of snow.

The local insurgency had been more or less quelled, which Kolenda considered a direct result and reflection of the success of the Hundred-Man Shura. In January, representatives of the shura left for Kabul to meet with President Karzai and tell him that the people of Kamdesh District now supported his government. With the enemy seemingly hibernating for the winter, the troops — when not on guard duty, patrolling, or on missions to visit local villages — spent their time sleeping, watching movies, reading, and trying not to get on one another's nerves.

While most of the region was quiet, some anti-American groups remained active, including the one led by the Gawardesh insurgent/gangster Haji Usman, whom 3-71 Cav had been targeting from Hill 2610 in June 2006 when his militia attacked, killing Patrick Lybert and Jared Monti. Usman and his gang would regularly bypass the legal border crossing into Pakistan, near Barikot, instead using a mountain pass and the Gawardesh Bridge to shuttle lumber and gems east and weapons and insurgents west, into Kunar and Nuristan Provinces. Usman regarded the bridge as the "Gate to Nuristan" and deemed it worth fighting for in order to keep his supply lines open. Camp Lybert had been built almost exclusively to guard this mountain pass and border crossing point.

On January 25, 2008, a team of Green Berets led by Captain Robert Cusick was accompanying an Afghan Border Police and Afghan National Army security patrol near the bridge. Before the patrol passed Checkpoint Delta, a lookout spotted ten armed men crossing the Gawardesh Bridge and then entering a large house nearby. Cusick and the Afghans crossed the bridge themselves to get in position. A platoon from 1-91 Cav Headquarters Troop, now commanded by Captain John Williams, set up nearby. When some two dozen insurgents left the compound and began heading east, toward the Pakistan border, Williams and Cusick and their men opened up on the group. A-10 Warthogs fired their 30-millimeter cannons and sent bombs raining down from above. The insurgent force was cut to pieces in an instant.

Cusick and the ANA platoon were moving forward to gather intelligence from the dead fighters when up to sixty other insurgents who'd been hiding on the hillside began shooting at them. Williams and his troops returned fire, and the Warthogs resumed their bombing and 30-millimeter runs. Cusick was shot through his left lung; the bullet just missed his collarbone. At first he could still give orders, but soon he drifted into shock. Staff Sergeant Robby Miller took command, firing his SAW, throwing grenades, and telling his fellow Special Forces to "Bound back!" as he walked directly toward the enemy fire, giving his brothers in arms a chance to retreat and get Cusick to a medevac.

It was the last time they saw Robby Miller alive. When a quick reaction force arrived on scene an hour later—to assist in extracting Cusick's team and the Afghans and to recover Miller's body—the fight was over.

Despite the tragedy for the Special Forces, the battle produced evidence that the Americans were making progress in the region. Intelligence came in to 1-91 Cav indicating that during the fight, Usman's forces had asked district HIG commander Mohammed Jan to lend them some assistance in combating the Americans. Jan refused; ultimately, he would sign an agreement with the Hundred-Man Shura pledging to stop fighting. Subsequent reports indicated that Haji Usman was no longer welcome in Gawardesh or Bazgal, then later hinted that he was reaching out to Taliban elements in Pakistan. He was going to have to find support from a different group.

A somewhat similar scenario played out with an insurgent leader named Shabbaz, from Lower Kamdesh, who had orchestrated the August attacks on Camp Keating, stolen money from contractors, and destroyed their work, burning buildings, shooting up micro-hydroelectric plants, and blowing up bridges. At times, it was unclear whether Shabbaz was really with HIG or whether he was just an opportunistic local criminal. Hutto instructed the elders to pass along a message to the troublemaker: "What is it you want to accomplish for the people of Nuristan?" But by the fall, it had become clear that any attempt at outreach would be futile, and the shura seemed incapable of getting rid of him on its own.

That changed after the elders returned from their meeting in Kabul with President Karzai, during which they had presented him with a letter stating that the jihad was over and they were on the side of the government, peace, and stability. Karzai had in turn agreed to support the shura with funding and community police. By late February, the newly empowered elders had kicked Shabbaz and other insurgent leaders out of Kamdesh. Shabbaz found refuge in the mountains, where he would, however, be far more vulnerable and less easily able to stage attacks on the Americans.[43]

Special Forces are a rare breed of soldiers. The Army has no troops better trained, and none deadlier, than its Green Berets. They are usually deployed in small, tight-knit groups of a dozen or fewer men. Their strong bonds — which can date back years — often make for exceptional battlefield collaboration and solidarity. They also make the death of a team member an extremely emotional experience for his comrades. All combat losses are tragedies, but for these men, the tragedies are almost always profoundly familial.

Extreme discipline is required of and by Special Forces troops, perhaps even more than is the case for other soldiers. The combination of power, lethality, and, in some ways, a lack of accountability — Special Forces generally don't report to the regular chain of command in the location where they're based — can create a volatile dynamic. It's the captain's job to keep testosterone in check and to mitigate any tension between his Special Forces and other, conventional troops. The men under Robert Cusick's command had no captain to do those things for them during the last two months of their deployment.

In March, the Green Berets at Forward Operating Base Naray concocted a plan that they called Operation Commando Vengeance. They soon thought better of their blunt nomenclature and changed its name to Operation Commando Justice. The mission's purpose was to capture or kill Haji Usman, HIG district commander Mohammed Jan, and HIG leader Mullah Sadiq. The Special Forces were going to set up blocking

---

[43] Specifically, Shabbaz moved east toward Bazgal. One late afternoon a few weeks later, a Predator drone detected a group of enemy fighters near the road west of the Bazgal Bridge, heading toward a cave. Kolenda gave permission to fire, and the Predator launched a missile from eighteen thousand feet. Shabbaz, severely wounded, never bothered anyone again.

positions and then conduct a "deep clear," searching all the homes in Bazgal, Pitigal, and the surrounding area.

Kolenda understood the anger—the impulse toward "commando vengeance"—that the Green Berets felt. Their captain had been wounded, and a brother in arms killed trying to protect him. Their acting on that rage, however, was another matter entirely. HIG fighters were now joining the good guys. Mullah Sadiq was a target for reconciliation, not assassination; his former student Mawlawi Abdul Rahman, the Kamdesh shura and Hundred-Man Shura leader, was fully on board. And Mohammed Jan had refused to help Haji Usman in the fight in which Miller was killed.

Kolenda was convinced that Operation Commando Justice was all about retribution and blood lust. It seemed to be motivated not by a desire to go after real targets, but rather by an angry desire—a hunger, almost—to wreak havoc in two of the largest villages in Kamdesh District just because some of the insurgents involved in the January 21 firefight *might* have come from there. Indeed, the Special Forces didn't appear to have any actionable intelligence indicating that any of the men on their "kill/capture" list were actually *in* Bazgal or Pitigal.

Not surprisingly, the Special Forces troops saw things differently. Commando Justice wasn't rooted in revenge, they insisted. In this particular area of operations, the Special Forces team believed, the United States needed a more kinetic approach. And while Commando Justice would be a higher-risk operation than some, it wasn't as if, one of the Green Berets would later say, they were just going to go in and start dropping bombs, bulldozing houses, and killing people—unless, of course, they found a clear threat. Cusick was monitoring everything from his recovery room back at Fort Bragg, and he was completely supportive of the mission.

Many of the Green Berets thought Kolenda and his men were comparatively soft and insufficiently willing to fight. Moreover, more than half of the dozen members of the Green Beret team had been stationed in the area during a previous rotation, and they felt they knew more about it than anyone from 1-91 Cav. Some resented the fact that Kolenda had never sat down with them to pick their brains or solicit their opinions about operations outside the base.

Kolenda believed this operation would be worse than pointless: it could undo months' worth of work with the Hundred-Man Shura and outreach to local elders. He suggested that the Special Forces instead go after two specific targets: a reported insurgent command-and-control facility between Pitigal and Bazgal and a supply point in the Pitigal Valley. If Haji Usman was still in Kamdesh District, he would likely be in one of those spots. Well, the Special Forces said, we don't answer to you. We're just telling you that we're doing this. Kolenda didn't quite understand what Special Forces did, they decided; he seemed to think all they were about was kicking down doors and killing people. We do plenty of "hearts and minds" work, too, the Green Berets thought.

This is a temper tantrum, Kolenda said to himself. He'd worked seamlessly with a previous Special Forces unit, but there were different dynamics in play with this group. Without Cusick there, these Special Forces troops seemed to Kolenda to be out of control. He called Preysler.

"This is going to be a disaster," he told the colonel. Recalling their darkest days of routine, large-scale fighting in Kamdesh District in July 2007, around the time when Tom Bostick and Ryan Fritsche were killed, Kolenda asked Preysler, "Do you remember how it was last summer? It will be like that times ten." It would undo everything they had accomplished so far, he added.

Other officers from the 173rd Airborne Brigade shared Kolenda's concerns — about the lack of actionable intelligence, the lack of indicators suggesting the presence of an insurgent leader, the lack of sources on the ground to confirm or deny such a presence — and they reached out to the Special Forces as well. They all got the same answer: "We are informing you about what we are doing, not asking for your permission."

At Forward Operating Base Naray, a few days before Operation Commando Justice was scheduled to commence, the leaders of the Hundred-Man Shura arrived for a meeting with an entourage of at least 130 men in tow, some of them questionable characters with known ties to local insurgent groups. The Green Berets on the base were stunned to see these sketchy locals being allowed to cross the wire unharassed. In protest, one Green Beret later tacked up a sign on a barracks walls reading "We don't negotiate with terrorists."

Kolenda had also invited both Preysler and Governor Tamim Nuristani to the shura. A variety of issues were discussed. Kolenda was pushing for the establishment of an Afghan Border Police base at the Gawardesh

Bridge, while the elders were insisting it wasn't the right time—they were close to reaching an agreement with HIG commander Mohammed Jan, and they wanted that wrapped up before they complicated matters by sending the border police into his general area.

Preysler took it all in. During breaks, Governor Nuristani and the ANA commander spoke with various elders. At lunch, the elders joined Hutto, the ANA troops, and the Afghan policemen for a feast of—what else?—goat, rice, and flatbread.

"This is what I'm talking about," Kolenda explained to Preysler. "This is all going to be destroyed. If the Special Forces go forward with their plan, this is all going to be undermined. They'll all go back to the dark side."

Preysler agreed that Kolenda and Bulldog Troop had made significant headway, and that Operation Commando Justice would kick the hornet's nest. But he himself had no authority to cancel the mission, so he picked up the phone and called Bagram, asking for Brigadier General Joseph Votel, deputy commanding general for operations for Combined Joint Task Force 82 and Regional Command East. Preysler briefed Votel about Operation Commando Justice and relayed Kolenda's concerns. "We can't do this mission," the colonel told the general.

Votel likewise had no power to call off a Special Forces operation, but he did control the helicopters that the Green Berets would need to carry it out. Word soon came to Kolenda that the birds had been sent on another mission, forcing Operation Commando Justice to be scrubbed.

A few weeks later, the entire Special Forces team was permanently relocated from Forward Operating Base Naray to Jalalabad. There were no tearful farewells.

Hutto, Roller, and Newsom had taken steps to make Command Outpost Keating less dangerous, including moving the mortar pit from the center of the camp—where it was both too exposed and too easy to suppress—to the southwest corner. In its new spot, the pit hugged a wall, reducing the number of angles from which it could be targeted and requiring enemy fighters to get much closer if they wanted to attack it. But making even this sort of improvement was like adding an airbag to a Ford Pinto—the outpost itself was still located in an extraordinarily dangerous place.

By now, Roller and Newsom had both spent some weeks up at Observation Post Fritsche, which seemed immeasurably less vulnerable than Camp Keating, whether the men were on patrol or in their bunks. Hutto talked with Kolenda about moving all of the U.S. troops at Keating to the observation post. The outpost wouldn't be totally abandoned, he said: the ANA could keep a company there with the Afghan National Police, and maybe it could become a district center, a place for the government, the police, and even some merchants to set up shop.

After several conversations along these lines, Kolenda asked Hutto and his lieutenants to study the matter and present him with some options. As was the wont of every modern Army officer, Roller resolved to turn his and Newsom's thoughts into a PowerPoint presentation—in this case one that showed, in a hundred slides, how the U.S. troops could move up the mountain. The lieutenants' reasoning was solid: Observation Post Fritsche was closer to the district's largest village cluster as well as to the residents who were most supportive of the U.S. efforts. It was inherently safer. And they weren't using the roads much anymore anyway.

Kolenda listened to Roller's presentation. Weighing against a move was the fact that it would limit access to surrounding hamlets such as Mandigal and Agasi. And it wouldn't be easy: it would likely take at least two weeks to relocate everything from Camp Keating up to OP Fritsche using in-demand assets such as helicopters. That last part would be especially difficult—probably even impossible—because the United States didn't have enough birds in the country for the task; they were all in Iraq. Moreover, such an effort would in itself attract enemy attention. During any move, the Americans would be vulnerable.

The lieutenant colonel was also skeptical that the Army could base 120 American troops up at Observation Post Fritsche. Any more than a single U.S. platoon, one ANA platoon, plus headquarters and fire support—sixty troops, maximum—would create significant problems, he believed. One lucky RPG or rocket detonating around too many people in a small area could have catastrophic consequences. Kolenda was looking for ways to reduce the troop presence in Kamdesh and to build up a different outpost in northern Kunar, so he didn't dismiss altogether the *notion* of relocation, but he knew that the true test of 1-91 Cav's counterinsurgency progress would come in March and April, when the fighting season resumed; any changes would be contingent upon the Americans' further success on the ground. Kolenda and Hutto both understood that moving an outpost such as Keating would be best done in winter, when the whole operation would be far less vulnerable to a large-scale attack. So it was a no-go for now; Kolenda would not push to move the camp.

If he *had* advocated for such a move, he would have had to push against two powerful forces deeply entrenched in military thinking and sentiment: perpetual motion and honor.

The Army, like most modern bureaucracies, is hesitant to undo something once it's been done. It's just not how the machinery operates. An outpost has been built, money has been spent, energy has been exerted—why make all that effort for naught? The machinery is built to keep moving forward, not to be dismantled.

Moreover, by this point, many men had fought and died for this terrain. Abandoning the outpost or Kamdesh District would, to some troops, feel like a betrayal. Elsewhere, some in the military had been questioning the wisdom of naming nonpermanent U.S. bases after fallen heroes. Strategic decisions, many officers argued, should not be influenced by mourning. And yet by now, in the region, bases had already been named for Joe Fenty, Jared Monti, Patrick Lybert, Ben Keating, and Ryan Fritsche. Just a few miles away from Forward Operating Base Fenty in Jalalabad, a joint ISAF–ANA base bore Buddy Hughie's surname. At Bagram, patients went to the Heathe Craig Joint Theater Hospital. And soon plans would come to fruition similarly to honor the memory of both Jacob Lowell and Tom Bostick. This practice took the military's reluctance to undo and weighted it down with honor, grief, and sacrifice.

When he began meeting with Abdul Rahman and other Kamdesh elders the previous fall, Kolenda had been intrigued by the way they identified themselves as "good HIG" and insurgents as "bad HIG." At a shura held in mid-May 2008 at Combat Outpost Keating, Kolenda and Hutto set up two white boards, one for Kolenda to write on in English and the other for an interpreter to write on in Pashto for the crowd. They drew three columns—one each for the people of Kamdesh, the Afghan government/U.S. forces, and "bad HIG"—and began discussing the groups' various areas of agreement and disagreement. There was general agreement on almost every item, except that "bad HIG" wanted the United States out of Afghanistan immediately.

By now, in the spring of 2008, it was clear that there were few, if any, bad HIG left. Jan had stopped fighting, and any holdouts from the lower ranks had been kicked out of their villages. When the elders, gathered together once again, were speaking about the progress that had been made, Abdul Rahman noted that the three powers in Kamdesh had changed: they were now the people of Kamdesh, the Afghan government/ U.S. forces, and the Taliban.

The Taliban, thought Kolenda. That's interesting. While the United States and the Afghan government would often use the term "Taliban" as shorthand for any insurgent force, this was the first time he had heard the elders do the same. They knew the difference between "bad HIG" and the Taliban, and Rahman wouldn't have used the word unless the actual Taliban now had a presence in the Landay-Sin Valley.

Kolenda and the interpreter then drew a fourth column, for the Taliban. The elders suggested that the Taliban wanted to promote war and violence, prohibit education and development, and seize power for themselves.

Newsom, Captain America himself, was pleased enough about the success of the Hundred-Man Shura, but he was also a big believer in getting his 3rd Platoon out patrolling the ridgelines. Between December 2007 and July 2008, on his initiative, the number of patrols grew. The ANA would go out during the day so villagers would see Afghan soldiers assuming responsibility for security, but then, once darkness fell, the U.S. troops would head for the mountain in six-man teams, policing with their night-vision goggles, keeping an eye out for any possible threat. The Americans weren't fools.

Roller had ordered up T-shirts emblazoned with Newsom's sardonic take on their difficult mission of helping the good guys and killing the bad guys in this land of gray. "Bravo Troop — Engaging Hearts and Minds," the front of the shirts read. "Two in the chest, one in the head," proclaimed the back.

Captain America wouldn't send his troops out on patrol unless he was willing to go out himself, so some days he went as many as three times. Everyone was spent, and his men cursed him for it.

Occasionally there would be run-ins, but it seemed clear that the insurgents were off their game. Trust led to cooperation; information came in; lives were spared. Counterinsurgency was working. Indeed, Preysler had become such an enthusiastic supporter of his lieutenant colonel's efforts along those lines in Kamdesh that Kolenda often found himself having to manage his boss's expectations. At one point, Colonel Preysler went so far as to suggest that other units could take some lessons from 1-91 Cav — advice that did not go down so well with at least one of the other battalion commanders. At Forward Operating Base Fenty, in Nangarhar Province, Preysler even came up with a "grand vision" that he detailed in "Nangarhar Inc.," a sixty-two-page plan calling for $3.2 billion to be pumped into the region to pay for roughly seven years' worth of infrastructure development projects — though the colonel would be the first to admit that he had no idea where that $3.2 billion might come from.

With his leadership now more encouraging of his efforts, and violence nearly nonexistent in his area, Kolenda figured that things were about as good as they could get. The situation remained fragile, he knew. There wasn't any question that some of those being brought into the confidence of the Hundred-Man Shura were allied or associated with "bad HIG." But Kolenda, ever the optimist, believed this was part of a deliberate effort, by Abdul Rahman and other key shura leaders, to "turn" some of these more nefarious characters and thereby gain greater credibility with the enemy, with the ultimate goal being a laying down of arms. Others in Bulldog Troop were more skeptical, thinking the Hundred-Man Shura members were hedging their bets by supporting both sides.

In May, a number of shura leaders came to Camp Keating to meet with Hutto, Kolenda, and Governor Nuristani. The elders were irate about what they viewed as the empty promises made by President Karzai. He had told them the government would provide funding for the Hundred-Man Shura and local police, but so far, he'd given them nothing. Bulldog Troop covered their food and transportation costs for specific meetings, but the elders also needed money for other trips and internal meetings.

Kolenda doubted that the Afghan president would ever deliver, despite the billions of dollars the United States had supplied to his government. His administration was born vulnerable and then atrophied in its crib. As even Karzai himself had admitted in 2007, "The Taliban are not strong. It is not them that cause the trouble. It is our weakness that is causing trouble."[44]

---

[44] C. J. Chivers, "Karzai Cites Taliban Shift to Terror Attacks," *New York Times,* June 20, 2007.

Kolenda wasn't willing to let all his hard work, all this promise, vanish because of Karzai's incompetence and corruption.

So he didn't let it happen. He pledged to the elders that 1-91 Cav would provide them with funding until the Afghan government ponied up. The leadership of the 173rd Airborne had earlier approved Kolenda's request for a "governance fund" to pay expenses incurred by shura members in connection with their official activities, but he'd been waiting to tell the elders about it until he felt they'd proven themselves to him. The signed documents from Mohammed Jan, the decreasing levels of violence, the absence of illegal checkpoints on the road, the significant decline in the price of local goods due to improved security, and the shura's frequent interaction with people in the villages, with 1-91 Cav, and with Afghan forces — all of these things told Kolenda that the Hundred-Man Shura was showing itself to be a viable partner.

Lieutenant Colonel Chris Kolenda tells the Hundred-Man Shura that 1-91 Cav will enter into an agreement with them. *(Photo courtesy of Bulldog Troop)*

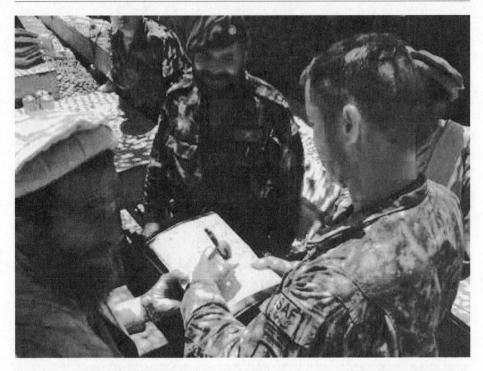

Kolenda signs the Commitment of Mutual Support. *(Photo courtesy of Bulldog Troop)*

After lunch, Kolenda and Hutto changed into Afghan clothing that the elders had given them. When they returned, the elders cheered. A voice in English cried out, "You are a good guest. You are a good guest!"

Kolenda looked up, stunned to hear a Kamdesh elder speaking English. Aktar Mohammed, from Mandigal, now moved closer to Kolenda and, with perfect diction, expressed his appreciation for the respect the Americans showed the Nuristanis, as well as their support of the people. Hutto and Kolenda, he announced, were to be made honorary citizens of Kamdesh. The elders had already given Hutto the name Abdul Wali, meaning "servant of the governor," and now they bestowed upon Kolenda the name Ahmad, "highly praised one."

That evening, in Kamdesh Village, there was a celebration. It was a night that would mark the high point of the Americans' relationship with the people of Kamdesh.

The troops continued to remain vigilant, but the calm meant that they could take some time to enjoy life. They held rib and chili cook-offs. One

Lieutenant Colonel Kolenda makes his entrance in Afghan garb. *(Photo courtesy of Bulldog Troop)*

soldier was put in charge of camp beautification. Flower gardens and a vegetable garden were cultivated. The outpost's roofs were made completely waterproof, and the full-service showers operational. Walls were covered with every color of paint the men could get their hands on. A new gym was constructed, and ground broken for a new, air-conditioned dining hall.

And then the enemy adjusted his tactics.

In May, insurgents in Lower Kamdesh fired a few large-caliber rounds at Combat Outpost Keating — the first attack with a large-caliber weapon in that area since the July 27, 2007, ambush at Saret Koleh, almost a year before. Perhaps the most ominous aspect of the action was the specific weapon used. At first, the men of Bulldog Troop couldn't place it — the explosions were louder than the usual insurgent 7.62-millimeter fire from an AK machine gun, though not as loud as RPG blasts — but then they realized what it was: an immense Dushka machine gun, of the type last seen during the Saret Koleh ambush in the spring of 2007 and, before that, in the Chowkay Valley in 2006. This suggested outside help, likely from Pakistan.

Over the course of a week, there would be one or two Dushka rounds fired, and the shooters seemed to know what they were doing. Bracketing is a process whereby shooters shoot a round over a target, then a round short of it, then keep calibrating back and forth until they have an exact fix on the spot they want to destroy. In this case, the insurgents, over several days, were bracketing the landing zone at Combat Outpost Keating, presumably so they could take out the next chopper that came in.

Shortly after the first Dushka shot, Hutto demanded that the Kamdesh elders come down to Camp Keating. When they arrived a few hours later, he was furious. How could a heavy weapon like a Dushka be in Lower Kamdesh without their knowing about it? It was, he snapped, unacceptable.

Just then, as if to punctuate Hutto's point, a large-caliber round from the Dushka struck a sandbag near the elders.

Abdul Rahman promised he would take care of it.

After the elders returned to the village, the Dushka fire stopped. Rahman later told Hutto that the gun was no longer in Lower Kamdesh. But it soon became clear enough that the Dushka, and the insurgents firing it, were still around and active; they'd just moved out of Kamdesh Village proper. Hutto was not satisfied, and he let Rahman and the other elders know it. A few days later, a soldier at Observation Post Fritsche spotted an insurgent dragging the Dushka up a mountain west of Agasi. After further reconnaissance, Roller radioed it in, and a five-hundred-pound bomb found its way onto the enemy's head. No more Dushka.

But then came the mortars.

CHAPTER 20

"We Will Go to Kamdesh Next"

The mortar round whistled through the air and landed a few hundred yards away from 3rd Platoon. The men had just left Combat Outpost Keating on a patrol. Newsom had been taught in Ranger school that the worst thing to do during a mortar attack was to stay in one place, so they ran and found cover.

"Hey Bulldog-Six, this is Three-Six," he radioed to Hutto. "We're taking mortar fire."

"*What?*" Hutto asked. He couldn't believe it: the insurgents had now gotten their hands on mortars, which were capable of firing immense rounds from a considerable distance, even out of the line of sight. This was no small thing; in fact, it was a potentially lethal development. After some crater analysis, Newsom's men determined that the mortar had come from the north and was a white-phosphorous smoke round, very accurately fired.

Hutto reached out to the Hundred-Man Shura, whose members expressed concern as well. They said they didn't know where the mortars were coming from, and they swore the insurgents were not Nuristanis—a claim backed up by the fact that the enemy chatter the Americans had started picking up was in Urdu.

More mortar attacks followed, professional assaults launched from unknown locations but generally consisting of just a few rounds. New intelligence suggested that several mortars were now in the hands of insurgents throughout Nuristan and Kunar Provinces, and that the enemy had brought in a Pakistani mortarman to train the local talent how to use 82-millimeter Soviet-style weapons. Whenever the rounds came in, Hutto and his men would fire back, but the mortars were coming from too far away to let them pinpoint their target, and the enemy fighters were constantly moving around. Bad—and potentially deadly—news.

One possible location for the enemy mortar tube, intelligence officers believed, was the mountains to the north, on the way toward Mandigal. But where, exactly?

Since joining 1-91 Cav the previous summer, Lieutenant Kyle Marcum had been frustrated by the limited number of paths the troops used on their patrols from Camp Keating. He was sure there were other routes on the mountains that they hadn't yet discovered. Marcum and Newsom now decided to start blazing a new trail north to Mandigal, figuring that sooner or later they would find an existing path that would allow them to sneak into the area and possibly observe the enemy mortar crew at work.

As a first step, Newsom and 3rd Platoon set up an overwatch while about eight guys from 2nd Platoon bushwhacked until they stumbled— as Marcum had suspected they might—upon a substantial trail running all the way north to Mandigal. Encouraged, Marcum, Newsom, and more than a dozen other troops left Camp Keating on the night of June 14, hiked undetected up the newly discovered path, camped out, and waited for the enemy mortar crew to show itself. They'd been in their position for roughly two hours, camped in the dark mountains, when, around midnight, Newsom spotted something through his night-vision goggles. "Am I crazy," he asked Marcum, "or do you see a light moving way up on the mountain over there?"

Marcum looked in the direction in which Newsom was pointing: someone carrying a flashlight appeared to be darting along on the side of the mountain, scurrying from one spot to another, back and forth. They called in the grid to Hutto, back at the operations center at Camp Keating. Hutto checked: it was a location that intelligence officers had already identified as a possible enemy position.

"But why would this guy be running back and forth?" Marcum and Newsom asked each other. Having fired mortars themselves, they figured the most logical explanation was that an insurgent was resupplying the mortar tube from a hidden cache somewhere in the mountain, stockpiling a supply.

Marcum and Newsom called Observation Post Fritsche and asked 1st Platoon to fire the 120-millimeter mortars, giving them the grids. But it was dark, and this wasn't a matter of firing from one end zone to another; the mountain was jagged. The U.S. mortarmen tried, but their mortars ended up missing their target.

Choppers were seldom *where* they were needed *when* they were needed — Combat Outpost Keating was just too remote, and the resources in Afghanistan were spread too thin — but as luck would have it, Marcum was able to pull in an Apache that was on its way to their base for a resupply. He explained the situation to the pilot while Newsom used his infrared laser to point precisely to the insurgent's location. The Apache let loose. Nothing and no one was left standing.

As he settled in for the night — they'd pull out come daybreak — Marcum felt his conscience gnawing at him. He wasn't sure whether they'd sent that Apache to kill an insurgent who was part of a mortar team or just some innocent Afghan out walking with a flashlight. It was an anxious, sickening feeling. The next day he'd know for sure if what he and Newsom had done was right: either the locals would be lined up weeping and complaining, filing financial grievances and perhaps even shredding the Hundred-Man Shura compact, or they would be quiet, and the mortars would stop.

It was a tough night for Kyle Marcum.

The sun rose slowly, and then quickly, and then it began beating down on Marcum, Newsom, and their patrol as they hiked back to Combat Outpost Keating. No villagers ever came to complain about the Americans having killed an innocent man. In this case, no news really was good news.

The mortar attacks stopped. Just a few more weeks and they could all go home.

"Why aren't they here?" Kolenda asked Abdul Rahman.

It was June 21, and Kolenda had come to Combat Outpost Keating to meet with the Hundred-Man Shura, as he'd been doing every three to four weeks since February. As the elders entered Combat Outpost Keating or

Forward Operating Base Naray, Kolenda would check off the villages represented. The absence of a given village's representative would likely have indicated that something was not quite right there, but there had been full attendance—no absences—at all previous meetings. This time, though, the elders from Bazgal and Pitigal were nowhere to be seen, and Kolenda wanted to know why.

"I don't know," Rahman said. He said that he had spoken to both of them just a few days earlier and was expecting them to be there.

Kolenda found that troubling. It might mean that large groups of insurgents from Pakistan or somewhere else had entered those villages and were preventing the elders from attending the shura. Pitigal in particular was easily accessible from Pakistan.

After the meeting, quietly, Lieutenant Colonel Shamsur Rahman, the Afghan Border Police commander from Upper Kamdesh who had very close ties to the villagers, reported that a big Taliban action was scheduled for the next morning. Several hundred insurgents planned to attack the brand-new Afghan Border Police outpost at the Gawardesh Bridge, Camp Kamu, and Combat Outpost Keating—all at once.

At about 2:00 a.m. on June 22, a soldier at a new observation post called Mace,[45] located on a mountaintop overlooking the Gawardesh Bridge, was startled to see more than seventy insurgents moving along a ridgeline. Radio chatter confirmed their intentions. These men were speaking languages other than Nuristani, but even without that clue, the Americans would have known they weren't locals by the way they hiked atop the mountain: Nuristani insurgents would never walk in formation along a ridgeline because it would make them too conspicuous.

Aircraft rolled in—a combination of F-15s, Apaches, A-10 Warthogs, and even the heavily armed AC-130 gunships. Bombs were dropped, and the large force of insurgents was wiped out. The main attack had been annihilated before the Taliban fired even a single shot.

Their being spotted so early on threw off the insurgents' plan to synchronize their various attacks. They next tried Combat Outpost Kamu—now called Combat Outpost Lowell, after Jacob Lowell—but thanks to

---

[45] Named after the weapon called a mace, a kind of bludgeoning club. Two other observation posts in the area were named at the same time: OP Hatchet and OP Brick.

Shamsur Rahman's tip, all of the Americans were on high alert, and a patrol got the jump on the attackers. Close air support eliminated a second enemy force spotted south of Kamu.

Kolenda and Hutto were likewise on alert at the operations center at Camp Keating through the early morning, guzzling coffee, radioing troops, and reading Instant Message–like chat on the mIRC system used for battlefield communications.

Newsom staggered into the operations center at about 5:00 a.m., bleary-eyed and confused as to why Kolenda and Hutto were there. (The lieutenant had been briefed in a general way about the warning, but his platoon was not standing guard that night, so he was less intensely focused on the situation than the others were.) Hutto started to fill him in, but his update was cut short by a call from a guard who'd seen some movement up on the northwest mountain, near the spot nicknamed the Putting Green. Hutto beckoned Marine Lieutenant Chris Briley, the new ANA trainer who'd assumed Ingbretsen's job a couple of months before, into the operations center.

"Chris," Hutto said, "we've got a couple of guys we picked up moving around the Putting Green area."

"Really?" Briley asked. "Because I was going to take an Afghan patrol up there." If he were to do that, his team might be ambushed.

"Why don't you go to the opposite side?" Hutto suggested, referring to the Northface. From the northern mountain, Briley and his troops would be able to see what the enemy was up to on the Putting Green.

The night had yet to fully lift, so Briley and his ANA platoon were still under cover of darkness when they left the wire, walking through and past the landing zone. Just outside the LZ, a loud explosion shook them. At first, Briley thought a U.S. mortar must've accidentally misfired, but then he made out the telltale smoke of an RPG blast: launched from the Putting Green, the grenade had missed them by only about fifty yards. Because it was dark—too dark for the enemy to have seen them from the Putting Green, he thought—Briley became convinced that someone must have alerted the insurgents when the patrol left the outpost, giving them a general area of where to target. Briley and the Afghans ran up to the Northface and began firing their machine guns at the small group of insurgents on the Putting Green. There were fewer than ten enemy fighters there, steadily aiming small arms and RPGs at

Combat Outpost Keating. Briley called in the information to Newsom, who relayed it to Kenny Johnson. Seeing where Briley was firing—he was using the same weapon his Afghan soldiers used, a PKM, and every fifth round he fired was a tracer round—Johnson hit the enemy location with mortars. Close air support soon arrived; A-10 Warthogs strafed the enemy, a bomber dropped a two-thousand-pounder, and that attack, too, was over.

The tip from the Afghan Border Police commander almost certainly saved some lives that early morning; for Kolenda, it was further evidence that having friends among the villagers could be of use. And yet counterweighting that, there was also Chris Briley's haunting suspicion that someone had tipped off the insurgents to his departure.

Later that same day, mortars began raining down again. This team—Urdu-speaking, based on the radio chatter—was clearly well trained, able to make skilled adjustments to its fire. The location of Combat Outpost Keating made it almost impossible for troops there to tell specifically where the explosive volleys were coming from. The men of Bulldog Troop tried different methods—triangulating enemy radio intercepts, translating radio chatter and trying to interpret what the insurgents said they were seeing, crater analysis—but at best, they ended up with educated guesstimates.

Lacking a more specific target, the Americans decided to return fire at what they deemed to be likely enemy locations, using mortars, grenades, unmanned Predator drones, and piloted choppers and planes. Still the enemy mortars continued to fall. The insurgents' skill, their professionalism, unnerved everyone. After Marcum heard translations of some of the insurgents' corrections to previous shots as they bracketed for greater accuracy, he thought to himself, That is literally the exact same correction I would've made. One mortar overshot the outpost by about fifty yards; the next round hit right in the middle of the camp, ripping through the stairs of the morale, welfare, and recreation building; the one after that landed just five yards from the operations center. Newsom was only about five seconds ahead of it and almost got a permanent suntan on his head courtesy of white phosphorous. Indeed, the only reason there were no casualties from the mortars was that the insurgents were firing some kind of smoke round as opposed to a high-explosive round. If it'd been a different kind of mortar, some of the guys from Bulldog

Troop would surely have been killed, just days before they were supposed to go home.

A total of sixteen mortars were fired at Combat Outpost Keating that day and into the evening. One blast after another, one escape after another—the barrage left the men both slap-happy and vacant. At one point, Marcum was running around on the hill at the back of the outpost when another mortar almost got him.

"Hey, Kyle, glad you're not dead," Newsom radioed him.

"Yeah, Alex, same," Marcum casually replied.

Eventually the insurgents stopped firing, presumably because they ran out of munitions. By then, many of the troops at Combat Outpost Keating looked like ghouls. The next day, another sixteen mortar rounds were fired at them by the enemy, until Bulldog Troop located and killed the spotters who were calling in the grids to the insurgent mortar team. Kolenda was very worried, particularly about the havoc the enemy fighters might be able to wreak if they got their hands on high-explosive rounds.

The mortars took their toll at Observation Post Fritsche as well.

The ANA soldiers had a special affection for one of their Marine trainers, Corporal Adam Laman, a stocky, sweet, and smart guy who'd picked up the local language fairly quickly and well. During the intense mortar attacks of June 22, Laman had accompanied an ANA platoon to a position from which they could better observe and suppress the enemy. The insurgents spotted them and began hitting them with small-arms fire and RPGs, one of which exploded right near Laman, showering shrapnel across his body and partially ripping off his left foot. An ANA leader, Nek Mohammed, ran over to try to help him. "Don't worry about me, take care of your own soldiers!" Laman admonished him.

Laman was medevacked to Forward Operating Base Naray, where Roller—who as Bulldog Troop's XO was often up there—went to see him at the aid station.

The room was thick with the ferric scent of blood. Laman was delirious, on painkillers and in shock, when Roller first approached him. Half of his foot was missing, and what was left looked like a mixture of ground beef and spaghetti. Roller grabbed his hand; the Marine seemed relieved to be able to tell someone what had happened. Under the influence of medication, Laman tried to joke around, but after about fifteen minutes, he closed his eyes and stopped talking.

"You're gonna be okay," Roller told him.

When 3-71 Cav handed over Combat Outpost Keating to 1-91 Cav, the soldiers of Able Troop also bequeathed their dog, Cali, to the men of Bulldog Troop, who likewise came to love her. Cali would come out on patrol with them as often as she was allowed to, and even sometimes when she wasn't. She seemed to know instinctively where the men were headed and always ran in front to clear a path. When they slept out on patrol, she was a vigilant guard, helping to put them at ease. If she ran off in a certain direction with an air of purpose, the troops would call the operations center and have someone ask those standing guard to scan that area with thermal sights.

June didn't bring only bad news; Cali delivered yet another litter of puppies. *(Photo courtesy of Bulldog Troop)*

Cali's first litter of puppies had been born around the time Pfeifer was shot. Each platoon was given one, and the rest were divvied out to individual soldiers. Newsom's men called their puppy Franklin, which had been Pfeifer's middle name. The dog soon took on the aggressive personality of 3rd Platoon. He was loyal to the men, fought with other dogs for no discernible reason, stole food, and gorged himself to the point of vomiting.

Just ten seconds of petting a dog, a minute or two of playing with Franklin, would provide soldiers with a brief respite from the tension inherent in this place where danger never stopped lurking. When it got cold at night, the troops would build a fire in the pit and smoke cigars and pet their dogs as if they were on an extended camping trip with the boys. In the winter, they'd let them into the barracks to sleep with them. (By now the dogs were treated for fleas and wore flea collars, so the men didn't have to.)

They were lifesavers in less theoretical ways as well. The puppies began patrolling as their mother did. If the troops tied them up to keep them from accompanying a patrol, they would break free of their restraints and track the men down. On several night patrols, the dogs scurried past the troops and chased away vipers. More often, however, they attacked goats and chickens, and the troops would have to pay the area farmers for their losses — but it was no big deal, really, just an annoyance.

Cali didn't like the locals, and the feeling was mutual — Nuristanis didn't think much of dogs as pets. Whenever the shura convened at Keating, Bulldog Troop would lock up Cali and her puppies, who shared their mother's animus.

The wild dogs in the area did not enjoy the same affection from Bulldog Troop. Hutto, for one, put out a hit on a nasty three-legged mongrel that was a constant menace; the payoff was three packs of Marlboro Lights for a shot and four packs for a knife kill. Tommy Alford had come back to the troop after recuperating from his July 2007 wound, and he collected: three packs of smokes.

That wasn't the only worthwhile kill of the summer. On July 1, an unmanned Predator drone picked up what officers believed to be the foreign insurgents who had been firing mortars at Camp Keating. The drone's pilots consulted with the men of Bulldog Troop and decided to drop a five-hundred-pound bomb and a two-thousand-pound bomb on the insurgent crew. That was the end of that problem. Shortly thereafter,

Abdul Rahman and the Kamdesh shura wrote a letter to a local Taliban leader who was also named Abdul Rahman. (U.S. troops referred to the latter as "Bad" Abdul Rahman to differentiate him from the former.) The letter said that the people of Kamdesh were now "awake," and they wanted him to leave their district for good.

Once the enemy mortarmen had been taken care of, Lieutenant Marcum and 2nd Platoon set out to investigate the attack on Observation Post Fritsche that had ended with Marine Corporal Laman's losing his foot. At first light, Marcum led a patrol to the spot on the hill where Laman had been wounded, about three hundred yards southwest of Fritsche's landing zone. It was a natural fighting position, with a grand view of the valleys and enough cover to get some shots off; it had probably been set up during one of the many Kom–Kushtozi battle periods. Marcum snapped a few pictures.

Lieutenant Kyle Marcum took this photograph right before disaster struck. *(Photo courtesy of Kyle Marcum)*

Nothing really to see here, we might as well keep moving, Marcum thought to himself. He bent over to pick up his M4 rifle, which he'd leaned up against a rock. As he reached for the gun, he pivoted his foot. There was a blast—not a big blast, but an explosion nonetheless. No one was really sure what had caused it. Intelligence reports had been coming in that the Taliban was using different weapons systems, and for some reason, Marcum initially thought that his position had been fired upon with a recoilless rifle. Then he realized that he'd been hit, and that the explosion had come from underneath him: a landmine. Sometimes mines went off not at the first step but at a change in contact. It must have been when he pivoted his now-bleeding foot, he reasoned.

Two of Marcum's troops from 2nd Platoon ran toward him, but the lieutenant held up his hand to stop them. For all any of them knew, they were in the midst of a minefield. Afghanistan is one of the most heavily landmine-laden countries in the world, with cluster munitions, IEDs, and various other lethal remnants of war buried everywhere throughout the land, dating back to the 1970s. It was only common sense to worry that there might be more mines lurking nearby.

Marcum looked down. The landmine had blown off some of his toes, and his foot was throbbing with pain. A medevac was called, and Marcum was flown out of the Kamdesh Valley, never to return. He would end up losing his leg.

In July, 1-91 Cav held a dedication ceremony to change the name of Forward Operating Base Naray. "He died while saving the lives of his paratroopers against a numerically superior foe," Kolenda said of Tom Bostick. "Let all who enter this base, and all who write or speak the name of it, be reminded that freedom is not free."

And then, at the newly christened Forward Operating Base Bostick, the troopers of the 1-91 Cav began transferring command to the 6th Squadron, 4th Cavalry Regiment of the 3rd Brigade, 1st Infantry Division, also known as 6-4 Cav.

It was a distressing time for a handover. That same month, southwest of Kamdesh, in the Waygal Valley in Nuristan, a new American outpost that was being established by Lieutenant Colonel Ostlund's battalion of the 173rd Airborne was attacked by approximately two hundred insurgents. Ostlund's men ultimately repelled the attack, but with nine U.S. troops killed, it would end up being the deadliest day for the United States in Afghanistan since the ill-fated Operation Redwing, in June 2005.

The men of 2nd Platoon, Chosen Company, had less than two weeks left in their fourteen-month rotation, so they were less than thrilled when the order came for them to set up a new combat outpost.

Theirs had been an eventful and difficult deployment. Soon after recovering of Ryan Fritsche's body near Saret Koleh in late July of the previous year, Chosen Company had beaten back the August attack on the Ranch House. Ostlund, the unit's commanding officer, had eventually made the decision to abandon that vulnerable and isolated outpost, which was turned over to local elders on October 2, 2007. Predictably, the enemy seized on the Americans' departure, producing a video that showed insurgents "capturing" and occupying the Ranch House—a propaganda victory.

Then, on November 9, 2007, after a shura in Aranas, near the former Ranch House, Chosen Company's 1st Platoon was ambushed on its way back to Combat Outpost Bella in Kunar Province. Six Americans[46]—including Lieutenant Ferrara, from the Ranch House battle—and two ANA troops were killed, and another eight U.S. and three ANA soldiers were wounded. The significance of the November 9 attack would be disputed, but some experts who have studied what happened to Chosen Company think that day changed everything, with the unit shifting its focus from counterinsurgency to fighting from that point on.

Ostlund was a Nebraskan and former enlisted Ranger who'd earned a master's degree from the Fletcher School at Tufts University with a thesis on the Soviet occupation of Afghanistan. He granted that counterinsurgency certainly had its place, but he thought its success in Nuristan was overstated. The lieutenant colonel believed that much of the local populace was deceptive and dishonest, and he felt that for that reason, a more conventional, fighting mindset was more appropriate to the area. But Ostlund was not entirely dismissive of the Waygal Valley, so he

---

[46] First Lieutenant Matthew Ferrara, of Torrance, California; Sergeant Jeffrey Mersman, of Parker, Kansas; Specialist Sean Langevin, of Walnut Creek, California; Specialist Lester Roque, of Torrance, California; Private First Class Joseph Lancour, of Swartz Creek, Michigan; and Marine Sergeant Phillip Bocks, of Troy, Michigan.

decided to relocate Chosen Company to a new outpost to be built near the hamlet of Wanat.[47] The new site made more sense because it was accessible from a decent road that led from Camp Blessing,[48] in the Pech District of Kunar Province. Wanat, as Waygal's district center, boasted a handful of shops, teahouses, and clinics as well as the district headquarters of the Afghan National Police and a recently completed district administrative building. The area had also benefited from more than a million dollars' worth of United States–funded construction projects that were in the works nearby. It was in the least hostile sector of Ostlund's entire area of operations.

Captain Matthew Myer of Chosen Company was told to prepare a platoon to move to—and build—the new camp. He and Ostlund met with some Wanat elders on May 26, 2008. The meeting didn't go well: the start of the shura was delayed by an hour, the elders took an atypical hourlong break in the middle, and the overall conversation was less than friendly. The elders then insisted that Ostlund and Myer stay for lunch—though they refused to actually eat with the Americans. On its way back to Camp Blessing, just about a mile outside Wanat, Chosen Company was once again ambushed. Two men were seriously wounded. Ostlund and Myer suspected they'd been set up, speculating that the insurgents didn't want the new base to be built and that the villagers had kept quiet about the ambush because they were intimidated.

A little more than a month later, on July 3, insurgents attacked Combat Outpost Bella, launching an assault that carried into the next day. During that second day, the Americans saw two pickup trucks that they thought were fleeing from the spot from which the insurgents had been firing their mortars. Captain Myer radioed to have two Apaches hit the trucks, which they did; the vehicles and most of their seventeen passengers were obliterated. Unbeknownst to Myer or the Apache pilots, among the casualties were a number of civilians, some of them children and staff from Bella's medical clinic. Governor Nuristani was enraged by the killings and told the Al Jazeera television network that the dead had included doctors, women, and children—all of whom had, moreover, been trying

---

[47] Actually "Want," but this book will use the more common version of the name.
[48] Named after Sergeant Jay Blessing, an Army Ranger killed by an IED attack in 2003.

to get away from the fighting, at the behest of the Americans themselves. "The Americans told people around the base to leave, and they left. About seven hundred meters from the district office, they were bombed," Nuristani said, calling the bombing "inexcusable because [the Americans] knew that these civilians were leaving the area." When the U.S. commanders heard of the governor's accusations, they made their displeasure known to President Karzai, who within a matter of hours fired Nuristani. If Karzai truly wanted to persuade the people of Nuristan Province that he was interested in strengthening the government's relationship with them and bettering their lives, then firing the governor probably wasn't the right move for him to make. And if he wanted to demonstrate to the Afghan people that he wasn't a marionette controlled by the Americans, it was definitely the *wrong* move.

Some Afghans would later claim that the deaths of the innocent civilians and aid workers had further hardened the hearts of locals against the Americans.[49] Exacerbating their anger were the initial claims by the United States that those killed had all been insurgents, when that was clearly not the case.

After closing the base at Bella, Myer returned to Camp Blessing, where he had to remain for a few days to provide testimony for an investigation into the July 4 incident that had killed those innocent civilians. The task of command at the new outpost therefore fell to First Lieutenant Jonathan Brostrom, the leader of Chosen Company's 2nd Platoon. The lieutenant would be in charge of securing the camp's location before the heavy engineering equipment was brought in to improve the access road and then construct the outpost itself.

Brostrom was worried. Before leaving for Wanat, back at Camp Blessing, he shared his concerns with his best friend, First Lieutenant Bran-

---

[49] Afghan media reported the casualties as follows: Dr. Nematullah, a doctor at Bella Village's clinic; Kalam Massi, a guard at the clinic; Naeem Massi, a clinic nurse; Sonkra, a landowner near Bella; Rafiullah, Sonkra's son; Sonkra's wife; Noorullah, Rafiullah's son; one of Sonkra's grandchildren, who was eight months old; Sulaiman Klorik, a shopkeeper; Hazrat Ali, a driver; Shoaib Sondi, a shopkeeper; Kafayatullah, a driver; Tabgul, a driver; Dr. Najeebullah, a doctor at Bella's clinic; Sanaullah, a shopkeeper; and two other civilians. Wounded were Wiaullah Muraluddin, a landowner near Bella; Dr. Zainab, a female employee at Bella's clinic; Dr. Nematullah's daughter Asma, eight; Abdullah, a son of Mira Jan, a shopkeeper in Bella; Rohullah, a worker in Waygal; and Ansarullah, a shopkeeper.

don Kennedy. The two men preferred talking about what they were going to do in a few weeks, after they got out of Afghanistan; they thought they might get an apartment together in Italy and take a postdeployment cruise on the Mediterranean. But obstructing their view of this vacation was the unsettling assignment: first Brostrom had to get through this mission.

"What do you think about going up to Wanat?" Kennedy asked him.

"I don't like it," Brostrom admitted. "We're going to get fucked up." The last couple of times that members of Task Force ROCK had driven up there, he said, they'd run into ambushes or IED attacks; he showed Kennedy a smashed window on a Humvee.

But Brostrom never shared these concerns with Ostlund, even though they had several conversations about the assignment. He did tell Myer and others above him that he was worried he had too few men to meet the challenge of setting up an outpost in a hostile area; Ostlund and Myer tried to assuage his fears by providing him with a twenty-four-man ANA platoon, gun trucks, mortars, a Predator drone for the first three days he was there, and more. Brostrum didn't think the ANA platoon would make much of a difference. More generally, he thought Nuristan itself was "almost a lost cause" thanks to the way the war was being fought — on the cheap and undermanned, as he told a military historian at Camp Blessing. "There needs to be a lot more than just a platoon [in Nuristan] if you want to make a big difference," he said.[50]

Brostrum wasn't alone in his misgivings about the mission. "No one in the company wanted to do this Wanat thing," one sergeant, Jesse Queck, later recalled. "We all knew something bad was going to happen." Queck heard that some guys posted on their Facebook pages requests for their friends and families to pray for them. "They felt like this mission was the one they weren't coming back from," he added. One soldier told the sergeant that on his Facebook page, he'd written, "Updated my DD93, ready to go...." The DD93 was the document in which troops provided the

---

[50] As quoted in Greg Jaffe, "The Battle of Wanat," *Washington Post,* October 4, 2009. For details about the battle of Wanat, the author is indebted to Jaffe's reporting, the work of the U.S. Army Combat Studies Institute, and Mark Bowden's "Echoes from a Distant Battlefield," which appeared in the December 2011 issue of *Vanity Fair.*

names of those to be notified should they be wounded or killed, along with a list of their death-gratuity beneficiaries.

From July 8 through 12, 2008, the men of 2nd Platoon, supervised by Brostrom, began building their new camp, which they unofficially named after Sergeant First Class Matthew Ryan Kahler. (Kahler, a fellow member of Chosen Company, had been killed the previous January by an Afghan Security Guard who supposedly shot him by accident.) Area men watched them from the mountains. The local Afghan National Police chief told them that Americans were not welcome in the area.

Thousands of pounds' worth of construction materials were due to be delivered, including wood and concrete that 2nd Platoon would use to build bunkers and defensive positions. But first the contracted Afghan drivers had mechanical problems, and then they were held up because the ROCK Battalion team whose responsibility it was to make sure the roads were clear of IEDs had to deal with a KIA in another area. After that, the IED clearing team had mechanical problems of its own.

The delays meant that the Americans at Camp Kahler had little cover. Water deliveries were also not made because of a scarcity of aircraft. The troops had filters and iodine to purify the local water, but the shortage of bottled water seriously inhibited their ability to work as the hot July sun beat down upon them. With no sense of any imminent threat, and a need to conserve his soldiers' energy, Brostrom did not order any security patrols.

Myer arrived at Combat Outpost Kahler on July 12. At 4:20 a.m. on July 13, hundreds of insurgents began bombarding the camp with what seemed like thousands of RPGs. In addition to rocket-propelled grenades, the enemy had AK rifles and both PKM and RPK light machine guns. The insurgents first targeted the Americans' weapons—their gun trucks, antitank missile system, mortar tubes, and light machine guns. They also attacked the observation post, named Topside, about a hundred yards up a terraced hill.

Myer immediately radioed to Camp Blessing: "Whatever you can give me, I'm going to need," he said. "This is a Ranch House–style attack."

But the camp—like so many others throughout Regional Command East—was remote, and the only support Myer could get, at first, was mortars and field artillery fire from Camp Blessing (roughly five miles away as the crow flew) and artillery fire from Camp Wright at Asadabad (some sixteen miles away), none of which was particularly accurate or effective. In the first two hours of the attack, nine American soldiers were killed,[51] including Lieutenant Brostrom. By the time the smoke finally cleared and the enemy had been beaten back, a total of twenty-seven U.S. troops were wounded, with sixteen of them needing evacuation—the largest number of U.S. casualties in any Afghanistan battle to date.[52]

The night after the Camp Kahler disaster, back at Combat Outpost Keating, Alex Newsom was listening to translations of enemy chatter. It was about 2:00 a.m., and local insurgents were crowing about the victory at Wanat.

"Did you hear about our brothers' victory a couple of valleys over?" one of them asked.

"Yes, it was glorious," said another.

"We will go to Kamdesh next," an enemy fighter pledged.

The attack on Wanat, coming just nine days after his arrival in Afghanistan, had a profound effect on Lieutenant Colonel James Markert, the squadron commander of 6-4 Cav. The forty-year-old Markert was hardly new to battle, having served in Operations Desert Shield and Desert

---

[51] The dead were First Lieutenant Jonathan Brostrom, of Honolulu, Hawaii; Sergeant Israel Garcia, of Long Beach, California; Corporal Jonathan R. Ayers, of Snellville, Georgia; Corporal Jason M. Bogar, of Seattle, Washington; Corporal Jason D. Hovater, of Clinton, Tennessee; Corporal Matthew B. Phillips, of Jasper, Georgia; Corporal Pruitt A. Rainey, of Haw River, North Carolina; Corporal Gunnar W. Zwilling, of Florissant, Missouri; and Specialist Sergio S. Abad, of Morganfield, Kentucky.

[52] The first investigation into what happened at Wanat found no fault with the chain of command. A second investigation, conducted at the behest of First Lieutenant Brostrom's father, a retired Army colonel, concluded with letters of reprimand for Preysler, Ostlund, and Myer for failing to prepare adequate defenses for the outpost. A third investigation by the U.S. Army revoked those letters of reprimand, with General Charles Campbell insisting that the officers had not been negligent. "To criminalize command decisions in a theater of complex combat operations is a grave step indeed," he wrote. "It is also unnecessary, particularly in this case. It is possible for officers to err in judgment—and to thereby incur censure—without violating a criminal statute. This is particularly true where the errors are those of omission, where the standards come from multiple nonpunitive doctrinal publications, where there is less than complete and certain knowledge of enemy capabilities and intent, and where commanders enjoy wide discretion in their exercise of their command prerogatives and responsibilities."

Storm in 1991 and then again in Operation Iraqi Freedom in 2003–2004. But compared with Afghanistan, those tours had been well manned and well supplied. There were, at this point, approximately thirty-three thousand U.S. troops in Afghanistan, only one third of whom were combat troops. Markert's boss—Colonel John Spiszer, commander of the 3rd Brigade Combat Team, 1st Infantry Division—had allowed him to bring more soldiers than he was authorized to have, so his command was technically "over-strength," as Army gobbledygook put it. But no matter how you spun the numbers, the cold, hard fact was that he would have fewer men than the guy he was replacing at Forward Operating Base Bostick, Chris Kolenda.

It was all so different from the other war. There was a saying among the Americans: "If you're in Iraq and you need something, you ask for it. If you're in Afghanistan and you need something, you learn how to do without it."

The new commander of ISAF, General David McKiernan, had visited Afghanistan in April and concluded that there were nowhere near enough troops to deal with the Taliban's burgeoning insurgency. But when the general told President Bush that the United States needed at least thirty thousand more soldiers on the ground—-some of whom would be sent to the south, others to the east—the administration's response was instead to ask its NATO allies to send more troops. Ultimately, that request would go largely unanswered, as leaders of European countries—having already expressed serious misgivings about the U.S. strategy in, and the rising body count from, the war—refrained from increasing their forces. Such reservations were manifest in the rules imposed by these nations on their own soldiers, who were proscribed from serving in combat roles. No, they wouldn't be sending any more of their men and women into Afghanistan.

When the military looked within its own ranks to explain tragedies such as the one at Wanat, colonels, lieutenant colonels, and captains almost always paid the price. But officers at that level, and above, tended to gripe to one another that the real culprits were more often than not the Pentagon generals, defense secretary, vice president, and president who had assigned the U.S. troops a daunting task while irresponsibly undermanning and underequipping the mission. Nine Americans had perished at Camp Kahler, and there were dozens of other little outposts just like it all over Regional Command East. Now Markert was in charge of some of them. At Wanat, the enemy had demonstrated ambition and boldness. The men of 6-4 Cav couldn't let that stand. "We need to have the initiative, not the enemy," Markert told his officers. He instructed Captain Rob Yllescas,[53] who would run Combat Outpost Keating, to make sure that every one of his troops knew to learn from the failure at Wanat, and then he turned to his XO, Major Thomas Nelson, and directed him to order all the wire, sandbags, and HESCO barriers he could get his hands on so that 6-4 Cav could start improving defensive positions across its entire area of operations.

Hutto and Newsom were the last two members of Bulldog Troop to leave the outpost. Newsom spent much of his final two weeks taking Yllescas and the rest of Blackfoot Troop, from 6-4 Cavalry, on patrols, showing them the area. "The enemy's going to attack you in the first four to six weeks to try you out," Hutto cautioned the new guys. "They're going to want to see how good you are. So be ready."

On his farewell visit to Keating, Kolenda went with Hutto and their replacements, Markert and Yllescas, to attend a shura with the Kamdesh elders. The Afghans looked sad, seeming to realize this was the last time they'd ever see the departing officers.

"We want them to go home to their families for a while and then come back," Gul Mohammed Khan said of Hutto and Kolenda. The other elders nodded in agreement, and then, as they bid adieu to the men from 1-91 Cav, they offered the Nuristanis' symbol of affection, extending their right hands to the Americans' hearts.

To: Family and Friends
From: Dave Roller
July 27, 2008

To All,
   I am at an air base in Manas, Kyrgyzstan, waiting for a flight back to Germany. We should be there sometime tomorrow. The deployment is over and there is a lot of reminiscing going on. Today is the one-year anniversary [of the day] my Commander,

---

[53] Pronounced "YES-kess."

MAJ Thomas G. Bostick, and one of our Squad Leaders, SSG William R. Fritsche, were killed in what turned out to be the worst firefight B Troop experienced during our fifteen-month deployment. PFC Christopher F. Pfeifer was shot a few weeks later and died September 25th, 2007. His wife gave birth to their first child two days after he passed away. We're all excited to be coming home, but in many ways it's bittersweet.

The war in Afghanistan seems to be getting a lot of press lately, but it's been our lives for the past fifteen months. It seems like people are just now realizing that we need more soldiers here, but anyone who's lived on a 100m × 100m camp with just twenty other guys with the closest Americans 15km away has known that for some time. Iraq has twenty combat brigades, Afghanistan has two. There's no telling what we could have gotten done if we had more people.

Thank you so much to everyone who has supported us over the last fifteen months. The care packages and the emails and the prayers have made life over here just a little bit easier. But remember, there are still American soldiers in harm's way.

Take care,
David

CHAPTER 21

Chess with No Rules

Dena Yllescas had been holding her twelve-day-old baby girl, Julia, when the phone rang at her home in Nebraska. It was her husband, Rob, who had entered active duty in the U.S. Army the day before, September 10, 2001. "Are you watching TV?" he asked.

"No," she said.

"Turn it on," he said.

She did. Two planes had crashed into the World Trade Center towers.

"I think we're under attack, Dena," Robert Yllescas said.

Robert José Yllescas had been born and raised in Guatemala, his father's native country. His mother had met his father at the University of Nebraska–Lincoln, married him, and moved back to Guatemala with him. Rob was born there and lived there until he relocated to his mother's home state at eighteen to attend college, where he met Dena. Their first date was at the county fair; they were engaged a year later.

Yllescas's goal, for as long as he could remember, had been to be an American soldier: he joined the National Guard as an agronomy major at the University of Nebraska, was commissioned as an officer, and did two tours in Iraq. There he saw things he wished he hadn't seen, among them a close friend getting blown up by an IED. Thankfully, although the friend had lost an arm and leg, he'd lived.

After Yllescas returned from Iraq in 2006, he headed with his growing family to Fort Benning, Georgia, where he enrolled in the Captain's Career Course. Hearing about a new Cavalry unit that was being formed, he reached out to the officer who'd been tasked with creating it; following his completion of the captain's course and U.S. Army Ranger School, Yllescas was assigned to the new unit, 6-4 Cav, and given command of Blackfoot Troop. He had a feeling he'd be sent to Afghanistan—and lo and behold, his orders came in.

A few days before he shipped out, in late June 2008, Yllescas invited some of his friends over to his and Dena's house in Killeen, Texas, near Fort Hood. Dena overheard one of the men saying, "Boy, I'm sure glad I'm not getting put where Rob's going. COP Keating is frickin' dangerous." She brought it up with Rob later, but he said she shouldn't worry: he was going to be careful, he promised.

He was confident, moreover, that the cause was just. Yllescas told his wife, "You know, people can argue over whether or not we should've went to war against Iraq. But no one can argue our war with Afghanistan. Bin Laden is the reason for 9/11. We will hunt him down, and we will find him." Yet beyond that justification, something felt different about this deployment, Dena thought; she sensed a heaviness and dread in her husband. Before he left, she couldn't help but notice how gloomy both he and their daughter Julia—now almost seven—seemed, as if they both knew something she didn't. Rob held Julia's sister, Eva, who was just five months old, as if he were never going to hold her again. "If something happens to me, I know where I'm going," he confided to Dena. "I can live without limbs; I just can't be a vegetable." The declaration stood between them, sensible and honest but with a terrible sense of possibility.

His worries extended to his men. The responsibilities of his pending command in the field weighed greatly on Yllescas. "I know someone's not going to come home alive," he said. "I just hope it's not one of my soldiers. I won't be able to handle it if I lose someone under my command."

Kolenda could always tell who "got it" regarding counterinsurgency and who didn't—who understood that the way to win this war was to show Afghans the better path, and who didn't think the people could be shown anything at all. Yllescas was one of those who got it, Kolenda thought to himself as he handed off his area of operations in northern Kunar and eastern Nuristan to Markert, and Camp Keating to the man from Guatemala. Rob Yllescas at the outpost was like a pig in slop, deeply immersed and excited. He started wearing a headscarf and very much enjoyed his meetings with the villagers, the "shuras." Within days, he believed he'd mastered the entire philosophy of counterinsurgency. He focused more closely on the Kamdesh and Urmul shuras than he did on the Hundred-Man Shura representing the entire area; he wanted to drill down and influence these nearby villages first and then expand outward. "It's like a chess game," Yllescas emailed to his friends and family in July.

You have so many moves and options any one person can move. Now when we think of the game of chess we know the rules, pawns move one space, queen anywhere, etc. Now imagine the game with no rules, you don't get to see the other person's move and he may move several times and you don't know and you play it in the dark. To top it all off the board can be turned around at any given time. That is what it is like out here and I have to crack the code and hope I have the right information to make the best decision.

He sent photos home:

"This is a picture from one of the mountains we have to patrol weekly. It is about a 2,500-foot climb almost straight up." *(Photo courtesy of Dena Yllescas)*

"This is the ONLY way we get re-supplied." *(Photo courtesy of Dena Yllescas)*

"Marine LT Chris Briley (works and trains with the Afghan National Army [ANA]) and myself providing overwatch for a friendly platoon. Marines work a lot with the ANA and having Chris out here is a definite multiplier. He has the ANA in great operational shape." *(Photo courtesy of Dena Yllescas)*

Two ANA troops with "Chris Briley and one of my Platoon Leaders Kaine Meshkin enjoying a fish fry. They caught the fish from the river and fried them up for us. It was actually pretty good." The fish for the fish fry were acquired by Blackfoot Troop soldiers throwing hand grenades into the Landay-Sin River, followed by ANA troops jumping in to collect the dead catch. *(Photo courtesy of Dena Yllescas)*

The ghosts of the troops killed at Wanat on July 13 haunted Yllescas. He conducted regular spot checks on soldiers on guard duty, examining their weapons, making sure they were awake. Intelligence came in from the CIA indicating that the local insurgent leadership was planning a similar strike on Combat Outpost Keating, using the same fighters who had attacked Chosen Company earlier that month. One night, after catching a soldier not paying attention while on guard, Yllescas summoned all of his officers to the operations center and let loose. "You better tighten things up!" he screamed at them. "I will not have the next Wanat on my watch!"

When Marine Lieutenant Chris Briley had arrived at Camp Keating months before, in March 2008, his first impression of Joey Hutto had been that he was somewhat bitter and harsh. But over time, Briley had

361

begun to realize that the captain's prickly demeanor was a result of his taking his job so seriously, and he'd come to look up to the man, to admire him.

Hutto's replacement, Yllescas, couldn't have been more different from him. Whereas Hutto had been rigid and sometimes contemptuous of what he deemed to be nonsense or stupidity, Yllescas was respectful of everything and everyone and always willing to listen to advice and suggestions from others. Briley appreciated that Yllescas knew what he didn't know, and that he wasn't too proud to take lessons from a junior officer. Yllescas let Briley, as the trainer of the ANA company, take the lead in the shuras for those first few weeks, and Briley made flashcards for Yllescas bearing the names and faces of important local figures, supplying politically incorrect mnemonic devices so the new commander of the outpost could learn and remember which Nuristani was which.

While it might very well have been an unfair comparison, since Briley was around the men of Bulldog Troop at the end of their rotation and the Blackfoot Troop soldiers at the beginning of theirs, it nevertheless seemed to him that at their core the companies, too, were night and day. Bulldog was tightly wound, Type A; Briley thought Hutto and Newsom would have to be dragged away from the outpost on their last day. Blackfoot, by contrast, seemed a little green and something of a hodgepodge, having been formed right before deployment. The Blackfoot guys were in nowhere near the physical condition of their predecessors. The first time Briley — happy to help 6-4 Cav raise its game — took Yllescas on a patrol through the mountains, five minutes hadn't passed before the company commander was so winded it looked as if someone had kicked him in the abdomen. Beyond needing to overcome the combination of thin air and a heavy load, Yllescas was a tad chubby, which didn't help.

Hutto had advised Yllescas to push the elders. There were reports of insurgents being as close as Mandigal, and yet the village leaders still claimed not to know where the assailants were. Yllescas threatened to cut off funding for local projects, but that didn't have the immediate effect he'd hoped for. The soldiers of Blackfoot Troop had been at the outpost for only a few weeks when they got their first evidence that the enemy fighters were finding shelter in Kamdesh Village.

The first attack on Blackfoot Troop occurred early in the morning on Saturday, July 27, and was over almost before anyone knew it. Most of the troops were sleeping when an RPG and small-arms fire came in. The U.S. guards and mortarmen returned fire, but it was likely that the attackers had scurried off before their rockets even hit dirt. Hutto, Newsom, and Briley had each told Yllescas to expect something like this — an enemy probing exercise — and here it was. "They wanted to see exactly how you guys would react," Briley reminded Yllescas.

And to Briley, that reaction hadn't been pretty. It was the first time a lot of the guys from 6-4 Cav had ever been under fire, so they were excited, and everyone ran around frantically, Briley felt, not demonstrating the most coherent response. Blackfoot Troop had a long way to go, he thought, and not much time to do it in. And indeed, intelligence soon came in that another attack was scheduled for the following Saturday.

Yllescas tried to put himself in the insurgents' shoes: in that first assault, they'd seen Blackfoot Troop holed up in the outpost, hiding, not pursuing the enemy. So next time, he decided, he'd surprise them by having his troops leave the compound. "We'll have two elements overwatching the outpost," Yllescas told his lieutenants. One patrol would be led by Lieutenant Kaine Meshkin and his men from Red Platoon, including some expert marksmen. The other patrol, made up of ANA soldiers, would be led by Briley, with Red Platoon's Staff Sergeant Juan Santos tagging along. The insurgents would have a rude awakening, Yllescas hoped.

His full name, on his birth certificate, was Kaine Meshkin Ghalam Tehrani, the latter three words being Farsi for "the black pen of Tehran." It was a surname that his grandfather had chosen back in Iran after the shah instituted a census, though no one in the family truly understood what it meant. In America, they went by just the "Meshkin" part.

Born in Arlington, Texas, Meshkin had gone to high school in a small town in South Dakota. His father, who was in the Iranian Air Force before the shah fell, had come to the United States in a military exchange program and fallen in love with the country — and with the American woman whom he would eventually marry, in violation of Iranian military law. That act of love, combined with political statements he made about the brutality of the shah and the Iranian secret police, landed Meshkin senior in an Iranian prison for two years; once he was released, the couple fled back to the States.

Lieutenant Kaine Meshkin hadn't joined the Army because his father was a military man; he'd joined to honor his father's love of America.

Before dusk on Saturday, August 2, 2008, Meshkin led Red Platoon to the Putting Green while Briley and the ANA went to the Northface. Across the valley, one of Meshkin's scouts, Staff Sergeant Ian Boone, spotted a three-man enemy RPG team approaching Camp Keating on the trail from Lower Kamdesh. The insurgents didn't seem to have any idea that the Americans were expecting them. Meshkin called the operations center, and Yllescas gave the order for the squad's designated marksman, Private First Class Marco Maldonado, to shoot.

Maldonado peered through the scope and pulled the trigger. An insurgent fell to the ground. Briley, peering through an infrared sight, saw at least fifteen others walking at the top of the Switchbacks, and he, too, fired.

Immediately after those rounds, the entire mountainside opened up with muzzle flashes. In an eyeblink, the Americans realized that up to a hundred insurgents were in the mountains and the woods, ready to overrun the outpost. The Americans' patrols had indeed surprised the enemy — but that number meant that the surprise went both ways.

The camp was now more heavily fortified than it had been just a few weeks before, thanks to First Lieutenant Joseph Mazzocchi, the XO of Blackfoot Troop. The son of Joseph Mazzocchi, a New York City cement mason who'd worked his way up to be the vice president of his union, NYC Local 780, and Arline Julia Mazzocchi, a high school teaching assistant, Joseph junior had been born in Queens, and for the first couple of decades of his life, his horizons never extended far beyond the Manhattan skyline. Until his senior year of high school, it never occurred to him to join the military. He didn't want to cut his hair or wear a uniform. He didn't want to be told what to do.

He'd been sitting in high school psychology class when he learned about the attacks on September 11, 2001. No one was able to get through to his dad, who was working in Lower Manhattan. His mom was worried sick. Thankfully, Mazzocchi's father made it home that night, accompanied by about six of his fellow masons, all of them covered in dust and ash from the towers.

The grief was international, but for those actually in the areas attacked, it was tangible, a black cloak draped over the lives of residents of those towns and cities. Five of the 343 firefighters killed when the towers fell were from Mazzocchi's small town outside New York City. Mazzocchi didn't understand any of it: the death, the evil, the chasm between Americans and others in the world. His high school graduation was less than a year away, and his parents had offered to take out loans to pay for him to go to college, but Mazzocchi had worked throughout high school and bought himself a car when he was seventeen, so he declined his folks' offer, knowing he could earn his tuition money on his own. He also heard the drumbeat of war, and he found himself marching to it. An ROTC scholarship took him to the University of Scranton, where he majored in history and political science to try to understand the *Why?* of 9/11.

At Fort Knox, Kentucky, in 2006, he met and befriended Meshkin and another young officer named Christopher Safulko. One winter's day, Mazzocchi and Safulko were in the back of a Humvee, shivering and waiting for the "go/no-go" in a training exercise, when they heard some chatter about a new unit that was being formed in Texas: 6-4 Cav. They called the personnel management office on their cell phones, then called Meshkin and told him to do the same. Within thirty-six hours, they all had their orders to report to Fort Hood. They wanted to go to war, and they wanted to fight together.

And then their orders came in. Safulko would be the XO of Apache Troop and was headed to Combat Outpost Lowell at Kamu. Meshkin and Mazzocchi were in Blackfoot Troop, bound for Combat Outpost Keating.

Mazzocchi was one of the first members of 6-4 Cav to arrive in Kamdesh. He landed at Observation Post Fritsche in late June and stayed there for a few days, then hiked down to Camp Keating. He enjoyed the breathtaking vistas but was stunned by how exposed the trail was: descending the mountain, he thought, was like taking a scenic tour of spots from where it would be easy for an insurgent to kill several American soldiers and vanish again before anyone could react. From a distance, it looked as if the trails on the other two mountains were no better.

Few soldiers assigned to a new combat outpost ever seem to feel that their predecessors have sufficiently secured their new home, and

Mazzocchi, at Camp Keating, was no exception. The guard positions were on Humvees, which made sense to him since it allowed increased mobility and kept the insurgents from ever being sure of the guards' exact location. But the mesh HESCO barriers on the outpost's northern and eastern borders appeared to be in disarray. The southern and western borders, meanwhile, were protected by concertina wire — but not enough of it, Mazzocchi thought. When he returned to Forward Operating Base Bostick in early July, he ordered thousands of pounds of lumber, more HESCOs and concertina wire, and pickets for force protection at Camp Keating. He also began working on making Observation Post Fritsche more livable. Camp Keating was the Ritz-Carlton compared to OP Fritsche, which had no kitchen, no hot meals, no showers, and no phones or computers or any other means for soldiers to contact home. The troops of 1-91 Cav had rotated through Fritsche every month because the conditions were so harsh, but Mazzocchi knew that for Yllescas, that practice was unacceptable — OP Fritsche was so close to Upper Kamdesh that it was essential, the new commander believed, for troops to stay up there for longer than just a month at a time, in order to build more enduring relationships with local elders. So Mazzocchi ordered new kitchen supplies, freezers, Internet capability, extra generators, and showers for the observation post. Instead of rotating for one-month stints up at Fritsche, as the members of Bulldog Troop had done, the soldiers of Blackfoot Troop would man the high-ground post in three- to four-month shifts, and no longer would life up there be a short-term hardship to be endured.

Red Platoon, led by Meshkin, was simultaneously improving Camp Keating. Under the supervision of Sergeant First Class William "Wild Bill" Loggins, the men reinforced all the guard positions, relocated some of the heavy weapons, sealed off the entire perimeter of the outpost with the exception of two entry-control points, and encircled the southern and eastern sides of the camp with two layers of triple-strand concertina wire. The added fortification seemed to do its job when the insurgents attacked on August 2, targeting the relatively vulnerable southwestern corner of the outpost, near the Switchbacks. The enemy fighters couldn't get through, and with the help of air support, the Americans massacred them. And yet Mazzochhi was unnerved by the insurgents' sophistication. During the battle, Sergeant First Class Dominic Curry had radioed that the enemy was bounding down the Switchbacks; that the insurgents were aware of this maneuver—the same one used by Ryan Fritsche's team at Saret Koleh—suggested a worrisome level of coordination and complexity.

After the battle, up at Observation Post Fritsche, Sergeant First Class Donald "The Don" Couch led some of his White Platoon troops out to investigate the bodies of the insurgents killed by the Apaches. One of the dead had jammed a pear from a nearby tree into the gaping gunshot wound in his neck. The only explanation the men could come up with was that it had been a feeble attempt to stop the bleeding, an act so desperate that it would later haunt many of the American troops.

The true significance of the August 2 fight was revealed only afterward, when elders from the Kamdesh Village shura asked Yllescas for permission to recover the bodies of some of the fighters who had been killed so they could give them a Muslim burial. The request raised a red flag, especially since several members of Blackfoot Troop were convinced that during the fight, they'd seen a 14.5-millimeter round from a Soviet antitank rifle being fired from a house in Kamdesh Village. That, combined with the fact that Meshkin and his Red Platoon had spotted some insurgents walking on a path from Lower Kamdesh, persuaded the leadership of Blackfoot Troop that it was no longer just a matter of the locals shielding foreign fighters—some of the insurgents were actually their neighbors or even their family members.

So Yllescas canceled all payments to contractors.

Hutto had told his successor to push the elders, and now Yllescas did so—hard. A shura was convened at Combat Outpost Keating on August 20, 2008. The Kamdesh elders seemed eager to resolve matters as they arrived to meet with Yllescas and his fire-support and intel officers, Lieutenant Kyle Tucker and Specialist Rick Victorino,[54] along with new ANA commander Jawed,[55] and the local chief of the Afghan National Police, Ibrahim. Afghan troops prepared food as dozens of elders sauntered into the outpost. After an opening prayer, Mawlawi Abdul Rahman spoke, addressing the issue at hand, the August 2 attack.

---

[54] Not his real name.

[55] Not his real name.

Rahman denied that the guilty parties were from Kamdesh Village; he claimed that the enemy forces in Barg-e-Matal had told insurgents to enter the village in order to target the Americans. "The insurgents come and go as they please," he said. "We cannot stop them. They have good suppliers of weapons and money, and no one stops them."

After an all-too-familiar and all-too-time-consuming back-and-forth between the Americans and the Kamdeshis, the session broke for afternoon prayer. Afterward, Rahman, Ibrahim, Yllescas, and Commander Jawed all went into the ANA commander's office for a private talk. Yes, Rahman finally admitted to Yllescas: the insurgents who'd attacked Camp Keating, some of them *were* from Kamdesh.

Lower Kamdesh, he made sure to specify; Rahman himself was from Upper Kamdesh. *Younger* guys, he further noted, adding that the shura was truly trying to get them to cooperate with the Afghan government and the Afghan security forces — the police and the military.

After Rahman left, Yllescas and other officers remarked on his candor. Yllescas's strategies of withholding contracting funds and then challenging the shura had worked. Even the more radical members of the shura were loath to lose American dollars, and Rahman had realized that he needed to show this new guy, Captain Yllescas, that he understood his responsibilities. In this instance, money had talked — and so had Rahman.

There was nothing funny about the war to Rick Victorino, but sometimes the way it was being fought seemed a bit comical — if darkly so.

Stretched thin and facing a shortage of new soldiers, the U.S. Army had begun lowering its standards for new recruits a few years earlier. Since 2005, the Army had been accepting high school dropouts and people who scored on the lower end of its mental qualification tests. In 2007, the Army brass lowered the bar once again, admitting recruits with criminal records and handing out "moral character" waivers more freely. For Victorino, it wasn't especially difficult to figure out which troops had slipped in under the new rules; there was one guy in 6-4 Cav who everyone was convinced was autistic.

Below par seemed par for the course around here. Eighty Afghan National Police officers were paid for standing their post, but Victorino estimated that there were only really about twenty local policemen who actually showed up for work.

Even more of a problem for Victorino, in his job as an intelligence analyst, was that the Army seemed clueless when it came to institutional knowledge. There was no real information at Combat Outpost Keating about the surrounding area, no historical data about the people or any record of the two previous companies' experiences during their deployments. It took Victorino a few months to realize, for example, that there was more than one "Mandigal," because several towns cloistered nearby had that word as part of their names: Mandigal Bande, Mandigal Sofia, Mandigal Koleh, Mandigal Olya. The intel analyst had to figure this out on his own; there was no way to quickly and reliably reach out to any of his predecessors from 1-91 Cav or 3-71 Cav to seek advice.

And then there were the helicopters.

Pilots were increasingly reluctant to fly into Nuristan or Kunar Provinces, as well as other dangerous parts of Afghanistan, so ISAF had taken to hiring private contractors to carry out resupply runs. The pilots were a motley crew, some of whom—the Eastern Europeans in particular—appeared to be drunk more often than not. These private helicopters, nicknamed Jingle Air, carried no passengers, only cargo, but either way, the sight of the choppers plunking down onto Camp Keating's landing zone, and the pilots, seemingly tanked, rushing out to urinate in the Landay-Sin River, underscored quite a bit that was off about this war—most notably, the thrift, the bizarreness, and the Halfway-Down-the-Trail-to-Hell quality of their location.

At the end of August 2008, one of these contractors' helicopters was hit by enemy fire in the Korangal, causing the aircraft to crash on a landing pad. Two of the crew members were rescued, while a third burned to death inside the bird. It was a complete disaster—and utterly predictable. Victorino didn't laugh about it, but his rotation in Kamdesh certainly gave him a better understanding of why so many dramas about war, such as *Catch-22* and *M*A*S*H,* shared the same warped sense of humor.

Even before he got to Camp Keating, Marine Lieutenant Briley had heard reports of complaints from ANA soldiers that something fishy was going on with their salaries. Once at the outpost, he found that his trainees were at their wits' end because they hadn't been paid in months. Many refused to patrol until the money was in their hands.

ANA commanders had discretion over how funds were allocated, and

Commander Jawed offered nearly every excuse in the book as to why he didn't have enough money to pay his troops. At one point, he insisted that the soldiers had eaten too much food the month before and that their salaries therefore needed to be directed toward the relevant contractors. Another time he swore that he hadn't received enough funds himself. After a couple of incidents like this, Briley brought the problem up with his boss at Forward Operating Base Bostick, Marine Lieutenant Colonel Ty Edwards. On the night the next bag of ANA pay was to be flown to Combat Outpost Keating, Edwards made sure to count the cash personally before it was loaded onto the bird. When the helicopter arrived at Combat Outpost Keating, Briley watched Commander Jawed sprint to the landing zone to grab the bag; he claimed that if he didn't, his troops would pilfer the bills. Surprise, surprise: the next morning, Jawed announced that they'd been shortchanged again.

Briley decided to take action. He called a meeting of the ANA troops and told them that their commander had asked him to teach them all how to do basic accounting, in the name of transparency and education. From now on, he said, their salaries would go through this new system. The first part was a lie, of course; Jawed had asked him to do no such thing, but Briley, while hoping to solve this problem, didn't want the Afghan commander to lose face with his men. The truth was, he was stuck with Jawed, for better or for worse, and he needed to put on a show of solidarity. He also figured the concept of "skimming" was so ingrained in Afghan culture that there was nothing he could do to change it. Suggesting that Jawed had taken the initiative empowered him, in a way, and reassured the ANA troops.

Yllescas squabbled with Commander Jawed fairly regularly about an entrance the ANA commander had created at the eastern side of Combat Outpost Keating to allow people to come and see him more easily. That his visitors were mostly contractors or their representatives only reinforced Yllescas's suspicion that Jawed was stealing, taking money off the top, however adamantly he denied it when confronted about it. In any case, the extra entrance made the outpost less secure; Mazzocchi and Briley often felt compelled to check on it to make sure it was closed.

Despite the challenges he faced, Yllescas was pleased about the impact he and Blackfoot Troop seemed to be making on the locals. And more was in store: there was talk of creating a local radio station to combat the insurgents' propaganda. "When I first took command people told me that there will be a 'burden of command' but I can honestly say I have yet to experience the burden and to the contrary it has been exciting," Yllescas wrote in an email to his family and friends.

By at least one measure, the counterinsurgency program started by Hutto and 1-91 Cav and continued by Yllescas and 6-4 Cav was working. In the surrounding area of operations, between September 2006 and September 2007, more than thirty U.S. troops and Afghan security forces—police and army—had been killed. Between September 2007 and September 2008, the number was down to three.

On guard duty one day at Observation Post Fritsche, Specialist Nathan Nash saw some wild dogs entering and exiting from a nearby bandah, one of the small huts used by mountain herders. Upon closer inspection, he discovered that a bitch had delivered and then abandoned a litter of puppies, which other wild dogs were now coming into the bandah to eat. Nash gave a dollar to a local Afghan boy to bring whatever puppies were left back to the outpost. There was only one, a furry little bag of bones that the men of 3rd Platoon named Doback, after a character in the Will Ferrell comedy *Step Brothers.*

Christopher Safulko had been transferred from Camp Lowell to head Blue Platoon at Camp Keating, and he, for one, spent hours playing with Doback in the mud. The Buffalo, New York, native had been a delinquent youth; his guidance counselor had told his parents that despite his high scores on standardized tests, it was unlikely that young Chris would attend college. But then, on September 11, 2001, Safulko was changing for his high school physical education class when the gym teacher came into the locker room and told the students that planes had hit the World Trade Center. That night, Safulko's mom hugged him tight, weeping and saying over and over, "All of those people, all of those people." The attacks of 9/11 and subsequent photos of the noble 10th Mountain Division troops fighting during Operation Anaconda had called Safulko to duty.

But nothing had turned out to be so black and white in Afghanistan— except perhaps Doback. Safulko became quite attached to the pup. Maybe it was because Doback's intentions were pure, he mused. Or maybe it was because he was so loyal.

Doback and the rest of the dogs, however, were like so many other things the men cared for, things they loved and would have to sacrifice. One day, Meshkin was leading a patrol of Red Platoon soldiers to Observation Post Fritsche. Yllescas had come along to check up on the White Platoon troops, who were at OP Fritsche at the time. The usual contingent of canines from the outpost accompanied them, including the shaggy brown one named Franklin—once the puppy that 1-91 Cav named after Pfeifer—who sometimes seemed just one moon cycle away from wolf. The platoon was halfway to Fritsche when something triggered the dogs to go after an old woman who was working in a small field. The dogs began barking at the woman and then surrounded her; she was clearly terrified. Yllescas fired his gun into the air to scare them off. His plan worked, and the dogs returned to the patrol.

The interpreter, though, had bad news for Yllescas: the old woman had been bitten by the "brown dog," he said.

Franklin.

Yllescas and Meshkin huddled. They agreed to shoot Franklin—right then, right there—so the woman and her family would know that they found what he'd done unacceptable. Meshkin went over to Franklin and pushed him down with one hand. Franklin submitted to him, collapsing and lying on his side as if he knew what was coming. Meshkin put the barrel of his rifle to the dog's head and fired.

"I didn't like doing that," he told Yllescas.

To show the locals that he was trying to set things right, Yllescas then pumped three more rounds into Franklin's body. Meshkin wasn't expecting it and was startled by it.

"Goddammit, he's already dead!" Meshkin exclaimed.

Yllescas's sister-in-law was a veterinarian. "She would kill me if she found out about this," he confided to Meshkin. But she'd want him home in one piece, and if a dog was going to get between him and the locals, then the dog had to go.

CHAPTER 22

After He Finished Washing the Blood Off

T hank you for coming," Rob Yllescas told the members of the Kamdesh shura on October 13. "It makes me happy to come and speak about issues, to resolve them through words and not violence. It is an honor to be with such great men."

They were sitting outside, near the old Afghan National Police station, now used by the ANA company stationed at the outpost. It was a crisp and sunny day.

"Thank you for bringing peace to this area," Yllescas said. "There has not been a large attack against Camp Keating in over two months, and I am very proud of the shura for that. Now we need to expand the peace. We need to go to areas such as Kamu and protect the people."

Anayatullah spoke as well, urging that Kamdeshis obtain voter registration cards so they could have a voice in the presidential and parliamentary elections, scheduled for the following summer. "If we want the right political support, everyone has to participate," the district administrator explained. "Every male eighteen and over has to register." The Nuristanis would get to choose five representatives to Parliament.

There were still many unresolved issues on the agenda—one elder from Paprok, for example, complained that the "security" imposed on his village by the Americans blocked food from getting through to residents—but Yllescas felt good about his progress so far and was looking to extend it. He persuaded the ANA and Afghan National Police commanders to start visiting Kamdesh Village at least once a week, with the goal of establishing a permanent Afghan security presence there, thus denying the enemy any safe haven.

Five days later, on October 18, Yllescas, Anayatullah, Jawed, and about fifty others walked up to Kamdesh. Various platoons were conducting overwatch, but the journey there and back was completed without incident, and the visit itself was a smashing success: Jawed and Anayatullah interacted with the Kamdeshis, more villagers pledged to try to resolve their conflicts through government mediation, and a number of residents expressed interest in acquiring voter ID cards for the upcoming election.

The enemy obviously didn't like any of this. Yllescas, back at Combat Outpost Keating, planned to return to Kamdesh Village the next week, on October 25. But on that day, twenty fighters were spread out in several positions along his path, ready to effect a linear ambush to kill him. In retrospect, it would come to seem that the insurgents might have been focused not just on ambushing Americans in general but on stopping—and killing—Rob Yllescas in particular.

The Americans were ready: Meshkin and a platoon had headed out early to set up an overwatch. They spotted some of the insurgents, fired, and got into a fierce battle. Meshkin called in 120-millimeter mortars, but the rounds were not enough to do the trick, as evidenced by the ongoing fire—from AK-47 assault rifles and a PKM machine gun—that pinned down the lieutenant and two others. Briley and his ANA patrol, on their way to Meshkin's position, were also pinned down, in their case by a large-caliber rifle, likely a powerful PTRD—a single-shot Soviet antitank gun. The Taliban were bringing in their deadliest weapons, ones they could use to fire extremely lethal shots from afar.

The Blackfoot Troop officers wanted to mortar the insurgents, but they couldn't figure out exactly where they were, so back at the operations center, Mazzocchi called in Apaches. The only air support available, however, was some "fixed-wing" aircraft—meaning planes, not choppers—and Yllescas, also at the operations center, didn't want to deal with what could be the long process of getting a bomb drop approved, in order to ensure that no civilians or infrastructure would be harmed. Even if everything happened as quickly as possible, the process would still take as long as fifteen minutes, a lifetime in a firefight.

In the meantime, the Americans had figured out that one of the enemy locations lay to the east, on the other side of a small, rocky spur that jut-ted off the mountain. Briley grabbed an MK19—a belt-fed machine gun that fired 40-millimeter grenade cartridges—and started shooting gre-nades up over the spur. Meshkin called in adjustments from his over-watch position.

"Move the barrel one inch down."...BOOM.

"Now one inch to the left."...BOOM.

The collaboration seemed to work: the screams of insurgents began to echo in the valley. But the PTRD antitank rifle continued to keep Mesh-kin and his troops from Red Platoon pinned down. "Grab some guys from Blue Platoon and push out," Yllescas told Safulko. "Go down the main supply route between Meshkin and the enemy. Draw them out."

Safulko led about a dozen troops down the road to Urmul. Under fire there, and tipped off by a villager that the enemy was hiding behind a pomegranate tree off in the distance, Safulko looked at the map and called the grid in to Meshkin. Believing that the enemy targeting his own patrol was in the same spot, Meshkin called it in to the fire-support offi-cer, Kyle Tucker, and his 120-millimeter mortars.

Yllescas told Mazzocchi to take two gun trucks to the district center: "Destroy that enemy position," he ordered. Mazzocchi led two Humvees outfitted with heavy guns into Urmul to do just that, and Briley and his ANA team followed with a four-foot-long, thirty-pound M240B fully automatic machine gun. Once in place, the gun trucks unleashed more than three hundred .50-caliber rounds and almost four hundred MK19 grenade rounds into the enemy positions. Soon the fight concluded, and the enemy retreated.

"Allahu Akbar, you can kill us," one insurgent taunted on the enemy radio frequency. "We don't care!"

Many of the surviving fighters, it was later reported, returned to their homes in Kamdesh Village. When Yllescas told him about the incident, Markert concluded: the Hundred-Man Shura had lost control. No one in Blackfoot Troop had even been wounded. The Americans had won the battle—killing five or more insurgents and wounding at least three others—but the enemy had won the strategic fight. The fighters had kept Yllescas and his men out of Kamdesh Village; that had been the point of their attack, and in that, they had succeeded. And they had far worse in store.

*   *   *

Up until July, troops had crossed the Landay-Sin River via a solid wooden bridge that linked Combat Outpost Keating to a piece of land in front of a farmer's house on the other side. But right after Hutto and 1-91 Cav left, the farmer suddenly tore it down. "He can no longer guarantee our safety on this bridge," Briley's interpreter told him after chatting with the man. The farmer had said that "people" — he didn't specify who — didn't like his allowing the American soldiers to use it.

A new bridge was then built on the quick, a wooden one made of one-by-four-inch beams laid one after the other, with about an inch of space left between each beam. It was rickety and constructed without nails; pressure and weight kept everything in place. As soldiers crossed it, they could look down and see the river rushing by beneath their feet.

The bridge was a hazard. Troops were forced to cross it one at a time; it was a chokepoint where a soldier could easily be trapped. And even without insurgents trying to pick off those crossing, merely walking on the bridge would cause it to rock and swing violently. A number of troops had seen a little girl drown in the Landay-Sin River after she slipped off the unstable span and was swept away by the rapids. If that could happen to an eighty-pound child, what might befall a two-hundred-pound man lugging another hundred pounds of gear?

The crossing became even more dangerous at the end of October, after someone removed the first six or so boards from the bridge, on the camp side. Meshkin and Red Platoon had to leap across the two-and-a-half-foot gap. This was more than an annoyance.

On October 28, Yllescas and Briley led a joint U.S./ANA patrol north of the outpost. Yllescas was wrapped in his scarf and carrying his own personal knapsack — classic Yllescas, Briley thought, completely confident and reveling in his work. They walked to the bridge. The missing beams had been replaced, surprisingly, with one solid piece of wood, approximately five feet long. No one knew who had done the replacing.

I fucking hate this shit, Briley said to himself. I can't see what's underneath the bridge now.

Kyle Tucker had come along on this patrol for a couple of reasons. First, he wanted to check on the micro-hydroelectric plant that was being set up for Kamdesh and several other nearby settlements; not unexpectedly, even though he had sent an interpreter that morning to alert the contractor that they would be coming to inspect the project, neither the contractor nor his workers were there. The second task the fire-support officer hoped to accomplish was to figure out his mortar targets. Because Blackfoot Troop, unlike Bulldog, hadn't had to deal much with attacks from the north, Tucker carried pages of his predecessor Kenny Johnson's old grids with him so he could conduct target practice. His mortarman, Sergeant Peter Gaitan, was standing by at Camp Keating. Tucker called in the grids, and Gaitan fired up the mortars, but the exercise didn't work all that well: the mortars kept missing their marks.

While Tucker was keeping busy with that, Yllescas and Briley saw a lone man acting suspiciously, walking by the riverbank and looking under rocks. "If we were in Iraq, I would shoot this guy just for cause," Yllescas said. "He's looking for a place to put an IED." But this was a different war, with a different set of rules. Plus, there weren't really many IEDs in this part of Afghanistan.[56] At least not yet.

Separately, before daybreak, Safulko and some of the men from Blue Platoon had moved to the Putting Green, northwest of the outpost, from which they could watch the Afghan National Police checkpoints up the road. There was a lot of foot traffic that day, but only about five pickup trucks for the Afghan police to inspect. Small groups of villagers came down from the mountains to gather firewood, bring livestock to the market, or visit with friends and family nearby. The women of Nuristan did much of the manual labor, and a fair number of them carried large bundles of firewood on their backs. Some men were down by the river gathering rocks that they would use to build modest one- or two-story structures.

The Blackfoot troops watched everything intently; something unusual seemed to be afoot. In their chatter over the enemy radio frequency, the insurgents were being particularly cryptic, and the translations subsequently fed to the Americans were poor. At one point, a man walked in

---

[56] The lack of IEDs was likely due to the fact that the Kamdesh insurgency was ultimately led by local Nuristanis, who did not understand the technical side of IED construction and emplacement. They knew more about, and were more comfortable with, direct-fire ambushes—the same tactic that had been employed to oust the Soviets years earlier. Moreover, IEDs would have destroyed the only road there was, a supply route used more by insurgents—especially after Kolenda stopped ground resupply—than it was by U.S. and Afghan government forces.

front of a woman down the Kamdesh trail, his arms folded. At one of the turning points, he ducked down behind a large rock; after a moment, he resurfaced. He looked suspicious, the soldiers agreed, but he had no weapon. Maybe he had just relieved himself. The couple continued down the trail all the way into Urmul.

A bit later, Safulko spotted two men traveling east on the road, coming toward Keating from the direction of Mandigal. As they approached the checkpoint run by the ANA in front of Camp Keating, they separated and began to walk several hundred feet apart. This struck Safulko as odd—it was as if they were trying to dissociate themselves from each other before they reached the checkpoint. Safulko called the operations center and told Mazzocchi what he'd seen. Mazzocchi radioed the gate and spoke with Staff Sergeant Kris Carroll. ANA troops stopped the two men, who claimed to be on their way to get voter ID cards from the district center down the road. Mazzocchi ran down to the gate to check out the pair himself, but by the time he got there, the ANA soldiers had already released them.

Shortly after noon, the Afghan police up the road called it a day. Around the same time, Yllescas, Briley, Tucker, Staff Sergeant Nicholas Bunch, Sergeant Al Palmieri, and about six ANA troops began walking back to camp. Safulko radioed them and confirmed that he had full observation of them as they prepared to cross the bridge.

Yllescas liked to tease Safulko about his time at Camp Lowell, where the lieutenant and his men had spent much of the summer undersupplied, hanging on by a thread, and getting mortared every day. The mortars had turned life nocturnal for the troops at Kamu: everything they did outside was done at night.

"Hey, Chris," Yllescas radioed back, "I bet you guys never did shit like this at Lowell."

They crossed the bridge one at a time: Briley first, followed by his interpreter, then Bunch, who stood guard when he reached the other side. Then Tucker. As Yllescas crossed, Briley called out to him, "Do you want me to call down the over—"

The Marine didn't get to finish his sentence before a pulverizing explosion knocked him to the ground. When he opened his eyes, he saw Rob Yllescas falling from the sky.

*   *   *

Safulko turned to the bridge and saw a smoke plume billowing upward as the span crumbled into the river. Yllescas — easy to spot even from a distance, with his scarf and his short, stocky frame — was lying faceup on the helicopter landing zone. His legs looked as if they'd been shredded. "Contact!" Tucker yelled into his radio. "Six is down!"[57] rang out over the command net.

Initially, they all thought Yllescas had taken an RPG or a mortar round — the explosion was so large, and his wounds seemingly so severe. But Safulko had never known the insurgents to be quite that accurate. It would be a while before everyone realized that Yllescas must have been hit by a radio-controlled IED. He'd been singled out and targeted.

Two groups of insurgents on the southern side of the outpost — on the Switchbacks — now opened up on Safulko's platoon with small-arms fire, AK-47s, and PKM machine guns. Some of the fire came from the large rock behind which, not long before, Blue Platoon troops had seen that Nuristani man duck.

Briley had a head injury, but he struggled to make his way over to Yllescas. He felt as if he were swimming; everything was blurry and slower than normal. It sounded as if enemy rounds were coming in, but he couldn't be sure. When he finally got to the captain, Briley gasped. No way was Yllescas alive. His hands were mangled. His legs were mutilated. His head had been smashed into his helmet. Briley tried to pull him away from the scene, but pieces of him began falling off, so he stopped. The Marine wondered why he was the only one there. It mystified him.

Disoriented, Briley couldn't physically function the way he wanted to; he found himself on his knees, trying to get to a safer place. He noticed another soldier nearby, behind a rock. "Come help me," Briley pleaded, "come help me." But the soldier wouldn't get out from behind the rock. No one would come out. They all thought the explosion had been an RPG, and their experience with RPGs was that they came in bunches. So everyone on the patrol had immediately taken cover. "Get out of there!" Tucker now yelled at Briley. One casualty was bad enough.

Briley, in emotional shock and experiencing a traumatic brain injury,

---

[57] "Six" is how the commander is commonly referred to over the radio.

was at once furious and confused. He couldn't believe what had happened to Yllescas, what they had done. Yllescas had dedicated himself to improving the lives of these people. The Marine turned to the southern mountains, aimed his two middle fingers as if they were weapons, and screamed at the top of his lungs. "FUCK YOU!" he yelled to Kamdesh, to Nuristan, to Afghanistan. "FUCK YOU!"

There was nowhere for Safulko's platoon to go; while the Putting Green was an excellent observation point, it left troops exposed with few options for escape. All they could really do was hunker down. The Afghan Security Guards who were with the Americans began running up the mountain into a cluster of trees. These local contractors tended to wait and see who they thought was likely to win before they took any action.

"Tell them to take cover and stay put," a nervous Safulko told the interpreter.

Safulko could see the muzzle flashes from the Switchbacks and farther east. Troops at Camp Keating began returning fire, and the enemy shooting ceased. The troops at the outpost held their fire to observe the enemy response, and insurgents to the east of the Switchbacks shot at Safulko's platoon. U.S. mortars shut them right up.

At the operations center, Mazzocchi ordered the mortarmen and troops on guard to suppress any enemy fire while a stretcher was taken out to pick up Yllescas. Meshkin radioed to Forward Operating Base Bostick and asked for a medevac, then told Safulko, "I need you guys to hold your position until the medevac clears out." A call came in to the ops center that a civilian had been spotted near the Switchbacks, a woman out gathering firewood who had unfortunately been caught in the crossfire.

"Continue firing," Meshkin said.

After hearing the explosion, Captain Steven Brewer, a physician assistant who was the senior medical officer at Camp Keating, grabbed his gear and aid bag and headed for the landing zone, where he found soldiers standing, disorganized, around Yllescas. A small group carefully lifted the captain, put him on the stretcher Mazzocchi had sent out, and carried him into the camp. Brewer ran alongside the stretcher. Yllescas was unresponsive but making gurgling sounds. He would need an airway. His left eye was fixed and dilated. The troops laid him on the table in the aid station. "Doc" Brewer realized that his senior medic, Staff Sergeant George Shreffler, wasn't there—he was still out with Safulko's patrol. Brewer thought he heard someone tell him that the medevac was an hour and twenty minutes away. It was one of the many costs of being at a remote outpost.

But it was a cost Meshkin would not tolerate. He sent up an "urgent surgical medevac" request to the 6-4's squadron XO, Major Thomas Nelson, at Forward Operating Base Bostick. They couldn't wait for a Black Hawk from Jalalabad, Meshkin told Nelson, who agreed. But pulling a helicopter out of established protocol was no trivial matter. A Chinook and an Apache were just then refueling and about to leave the base to conduct resupply missions in Kunar. In order to commandeer them to try to save Yllescas's life, Nelson had to get permission from Lieutenant Colonel Markert, who held the birds for a minute while he informed Colonel Spiszer of the plan. "Go to the aid station and grab Doc Cuda," Markert told Nelson, referring to Captain Amanda Cuda, a physician on base at Naray. "You have three minutes to be on that Chinook."

In the meantime, Brewer was trying to get an oral airway down Yllescas's throat to help with his breathing, but Yllescas gagged on it. That was a good sign, that he still had a gag reflex. The PA instead put in a nasal trumpet to make respiration easier. Yllescas's legs had sustained massive injuries. The major bones of both lower legs had been shattered, and blood was spilling out of the wounds, so Brewer ordered the soldiers helping him to tie tourniquets above each knee and then make splints to try to stabilize the captain's legs. His arms were relatively uninjured, except for his left thumb, the skin on which had been pulled back like a banana peel. Brewer inserted the lines for two large IVs containing Hextend—an electrolyte solution that assists in restoring blood volume—into the veins on Yllescas's inner elbows. His airway was obviously still a problem, so Brewer put a mask on the captain's face and started pumping oxygen into his lungs.

Brewer worked for roughly half an hour on Yllescas—stabilizing him, trying to help his breathing and stop his bleeding—before the Chinook carrying Nelson and Doc Cuda arrived. Yllescas was stable by that point, but not by much. At no time did he ever respond to any of Brewer's questions or acknowledge any pain. Landing while the firefight was still sputtering, the Chinook set down so hard that it bounced six feet before stopping on the gravelly landing zone. The waiting stretcher crew rushed forward with Yllescas and placed him in the aircraft, where Cuda and Staff Sergeant Dave Joslin, a medic, began working once again to stabilize him as the Chinook took off and flew back toward Forward Operating Base Bostick.

He was in bad shape. Cuda was trained not to think about patients not surviving—there was no time for anything but effort—but it was clear that at a minimum, Yllescas would certainly lose his legs, which were a mess of muscle, flesh, blood, and bone. Best-case scenario.

Back at Keating, at the LZ, Brewer turned to Briley, who had a head injury and was clearly psychologically traumatized. Brewer escorted him to the aid station and injected him with 10 milligrams of diazepam, better known as Valium. The PA gave the order to evacuate Briley on the next bird.[58]

Villagers came to the entry control point carrying a stretcher on which lay someone completely covered by a blanket. Mazzocchi—now in charge of the outpost—was nervous about letting the stretcher inside the wire. He worried that it might be another IED. It wasn't. The wounded woman who'd been hit while collecting firewood had been brought to the outpost for medical attention. While Brewer worked to get her stabilized, Mazzocchi spoke to her husband, trying to make the quick transition from soldier to diplomat, as he'd learned from Yllescas. He extended his sincere apologies to the man, who was quite upset—largely, it seemed to Mazzocchi, because his wife was a source of revenue for him. Without her, he would have only three people to work his farm. Until he found another wife, he said, his harvest would be delayed. And it was harvest season.

Mazzocchi asked him how much money the woman's wounds might cost him.

Four hundred U.S. dollars, he said.

Mazzocchi gave him five hundred from Blackfoot Troop funds. The man seemed content with that. Brewer worked on his wife for about ninety minutes, after which she was medevacked out for higher-level

---

[58] After a few days' recovery at Bagram, Briley would serve out the rest of his deployment at Forward Operating Base Bostick, replacing his commander, Lieutenant Colonel Ty Edwards. One week before Briley was wounded, Edwards himself had been shot in the head in an ambush—an injury that he, too, survived.

care; when she returned to the area, she was missing one leg below the knee. After that day, whenever Mazzocchi was on patrol and saw him, the woman's husband was always friendly toward him. It disgusted Mazzocchi. He wondered if he could have saved Yllescas if he'd given a thousand dollars to the Kamdesh shura.

On one level, the man had merely been anxious about his subsistence and his family's survival—since in Nuristan, women are responsible for all agricultural work—but Mazzocchi would nonetheless come to see him as representing all men. Not just in Kamdesh, not just in Afghanistan. His concern for the well-being of his wife was entirely about her labor and productivity. He wanted the money because money equaled power and influence.

War, Mazzocchi came to think, was always about money and power and never about anything else. Everyone was out for himself. Mazzocchi would quote from *Leviathan,* the English philosopher Thomas Hobbes's treatise arguing for a strong government to combat man's inherent evil, referring to the "general inclination of all mankind, a perpetual and restless desire of power after power, that ceaseth only in death." Without the constraints of government, human beings would do whatever they wanted, Mazzocchi believed; they were anarchical at their core and concerned only with their own benefit. That was what had motivated Al Qaeda, that was what motivated this Nuristani, and that was what motivated the United States to send thousands of soldiers like himself to this isolated place. He'd joined the Army to find out why 9/11 had happened. He would come to feel that he'd learned why on that October day, when he handed over taxpayers' money to prevent yet another man from becoming an enemy who would try to kill Americans, while his friend and commander Rob Yllescas lay dying on a medevac.

Specialist Rick Victorino was posted at Camp Lowell that day, so another soldier from the intelligence element, Sergeant "Red" Walker,[59] took the lead in trying to figure out who'd been responsible for the remote-controlled IED attack on Captain Yllescas.

Walker went to talk to an Afghan Security Guard commander stationed by the front gate of the outpost, which was now locked down. "This

---

[59] Not his real name.

happened within four hundred feet of the front gate of our camp," Walker said to him. "That's not good. You need to find out what's going on." The commander showed Walker a voter ID card that one of his guards had found by the rocks near the bridge. The photo on the card was of a man in his mid-twenties who had some facial hair. Walker had never seen him before. He asked some of the Afghan Security Guards, but they didn't recognize him, either.

Around that time, three Nuristani men walked by on the road. Walker stopped them and showed them the ID. "You seen this guy?" Walker asked. "No," they all said, and they walked away. But then one of them came back. "Can I see that picture again?" he asked. Walker showed him the card. "That guy is in the hotel right now," the Nuristani said.

The "hotel" was a local inn/restaurant in Urmul, and Walker, along with the Afghan Security Guard commander, headed right for it. As soon as they walked in, they spotted the young man whose picture was on the ID. Walker's eyes locked onto his for a moment, and then the young Afghan ran out a door. Before he could make it very far, though, the Afghan Security Guards caught him and then brought him back to the front gate at the base.

Staff Sergeant Carroll thought he recognized the man from earlier that day — maybe this was the guy who had been walking with another guy and then suddenly wasn't anymore, the one the ANA had cleared before Mazzocchi could talk to him? They sat him on a bench, and Walker, through an interpreter, began asking him questions.

"What's your name?"

"Amin Shir."

"Where are you from?"

"Paprok."

"What are you doing here?"

"I came to Kamdesh to get my voter ID card."

"Who do you know here?"

"Nobody."

"How long have you been here?"

"Three days."

Walker knew that the insurgent group in the Paprok area, which attacked Camp Keating every now and then, was headed by the local Taliban leader named Abdul Rahman — the other, "bad" Abdul Rahman.

"Do you know Abdul Rahman?" Walker asked.

"No," the Afghan said, which Walker knew had to be a lie since everyone in Paprok knew him.

Walker now decided to try out the Expray explosive-detection spray — a three-part, aerosol-based field test kit. He sprayed the contents of the first can onto Shir's hand, wiped it with a collection paper, and waited to see if the paper turned pink, which would indicate the presence of a specific class of explosives that included TNT. Negative. The intel collector then sprayed the second can on the suspect's hand and wiped it with a new collection paper. If this one turned orange, it would mean that Shir had recently come in contact with dynamite or another, similar type of explosive.

Walker was in the middle of spraying the third can when the second paper lit up orange.

"Have you handled a weapon or any explosive within the last forty-eight hours?" Walker asked Shir.

"No," he said. "I've never touched a gun, I've never touched explosives. I don't know what you're talking about. I'm just a farmer."

The U.S. Rules of Engagement prevented the Americans at Combat Outpost Keating from detaining Amin Shir for longer than seventy-two hours. But the ANA had no such restrictions; its soldiers could hold him for as long as they needed to, and then, if and when they ascertained his guilt, they could give him back to Blackfoot Troop to transfer to the detention facility at Bagram. The ANA troops flex-cuffed Shir, searched and took pictures of him, and placed him in custody.

Walker ordered that Shir first be taken to the aid station, so that Doc Brewer could examine him and attest that he hadn't been physically abused or mistreated in any way. Brewer wasn't happy about that; he'd just finished washing Yllescas's blood off, and he didn't want to examine the insurgent responsible for mutilating him. But he did it anyway, verifying that Shir had no broken bones or even any bruises.

Walker next took Shir to the outdoor space between the aid station and the operations center, where he questioned him again. Shir's story had changed: now he said he'd come to Urmul to buy more goats to take back home, because he was a farmer. A little later, he said he'd come to borrow some money to take back home to buy more goats.

Shir also added that he actually did know someone in the area by the name of Hamid,[60] a laborer who worked at Camp Keating. Walker asked Sergeant First Class Shawn Worrell, who was in charge of the day laborers, if he knew a Hamid. Worrell said yes, and he went off to find him. Walker then had Shir blindfolded and brought Hamid in to see him. "Do you know this man?" he asked him.

"I've never seen him before in my life," Hamid said.

Walker handed Amin Shir over to the ANA soldiers, who put him in a cell while the intel specialist contacted his chain of command to commence the process of taking an Afghan detainee into an American holding facility. Then he went back to ask Worrell if he could talk to Hamid again. "Of course," Worrell said. But it turned out that Hamid was no longer at the outpost: he had vanished and was gone forever.

Walker eventually theorized that Shir had come to Urmul and linked up with Hamid three days before he set the explosive. At some point, Hamid described Yllescas to him. The day before the attack, Shir was seen loitering on the concrete bridge near the entrance to Camp Keating (not an uncommon practice for locals), where he confirmed Yllescas's identity by his headscarf, body size, stature, and gait. That night, with the moon at low illumination, Shir crouched by the northern side of the landing zone and then walked around to the wooden bridge.

Based on the size of the area destroyed, and judging from the firsthand accounts of the soldiers who had witnessed the blast, the IED might have contained ten pounds of explosive material. Walker speculated that Shir might have been able to store an IED that small in his pocket, and that when he took it out by the northern side of the landing zone, his voter ID also fell out. It was dark enough that he didn't notice it.

This was all theory, circumstantially buttressed by some eyewitness accounts, but Walker became entirely convinced that Amin Shir had targeted for assassination the man who'd become the greatest threat to the insurgents' influence in Kamdesh.

It was noon in Killeen, Texas, when Dena Yllescas's cell phone rang. She had just finished nursing their baby girl, Eva.

---

[60] Not his real name.

It was the rear detachment notification captain calling. "Your husband has been injured," he said.

For some reason, Dena didn't believe him. She thought he was joking. "Are you serious?" she asked.

"Yes, I'm serious."

He began giving Dena some phone numbers. She was numb, and her hand was shaking. "Rob was hit by an IED," he told her. He was in critical condition at Bagram Air Force Base. She was stunned. She hadn't even known there *were* IEDs in that part of Afghanistan. The captain began listing her husband's injuries, a litany that seemed never-ending and that caused Dena to deeply desire that he shut up: she didn't want to know.

Within hours, Dena's home was overflowing with friends who had heard the news. Another friend had picked up Rob and Dena's daughter Julia from school and taken her to play with her own kids. Dena's sister-in-law Angie had meanwhile volunteered to fly to Texas from Nebraska to get Julia and Eva and bring them back to her home, where she would take care of them while Dena went to be with Rob, wherever that ended up being.

When Julia finally got home, Dena pulled her into her bedroom. "Daddy's been hurt," she told her. "But doctors are taking very good care of him. We need to say lots of prayers for him."

Lieutenant Colonel Markert called Dena a couple of times that day to give her updates and answer any questions she might have. At about 11:30 p.m. in Texas, he called again, and she asked him if she could speak with the doctor who was caring for her husband. "I'll have him call you as soon as he can," Markert said.

On the first night that Amin Shir was being held at Camp Keating, Mazzocchi went to talk to an angry Commander Jawed, who felt responsible for what had happened.

"I'm going to avenge Yllescas," Jawed bitterly declared, "by drowning Shir in the river."

Mazzocchi told him to calm down. "Shedding more blood won't accomplish anything," he said. "We should honor Yllescas by trying to pursue our goals in the valley just as he did."

Jawed remained upset, however, and he insisted on talking to Shir. Mazzocchi accompanied him to make sure he didn't do anything stupid. He was also curious to see what Jawed might get out of the man. Most

U.S. Army soldiers—Mazzocchi included—were prohibited from directly questioning enemy prisoners of war.

After Jawed had finished yelling at the prisoner, Mazzocchi fed him questions to ask Shir: "Why did you do it? Was it because you wanted to defend the valley? Was it because you wanted to defend your family? Why?"

"I don't have any money," Amin Shir said. "They paid me a lot of money for one day's work. I just wanted to make some money."

"Who paid you?" Jawed asked him.

Shir paused.

"Bad people from the Mandigal shura," he said.

So Shir wasn't an insurgent mastermind—he was just a dumb kid trying to make a little cash in a land of scant opportunity. Hobbes had been proven right yet again.

Shortly after midnight, the surgeon called Dena Yllescas. "How much detail do you want?" he asked.

Everything, she told him. Her imagination had been getting the best of her.

Rob Yllescas had arrived at Bagram approximately four hours after the explosion, he said. He had already had his third surgery. His right leg had been amputated just below the knee, and his left leg had been taken off at the knee. He also had a fracture in his left femur, at the hip. More information came in the next day: Rob was in stable condition and would be flown that day to Landstuhl Regional Medical Center in Germany, and from there to Walter Reed Army Medical Center. Markert called and told Dena that some of his colleagues had seen him and said he looked 100 percent better. When Dena explained to Julia that they'd be staying at Walter Reed for a while, the seven-year-old said, "That means daddy has an injury." Julia seemed to connect Walter Reed with Yllescas's friend Ryan, who had been injured in Iraq, spent time at Walter Reed, and had an arm and a leg amputated.

"Yes, Daddy has had an injury," Dena said.

"Did Daddy's legs get chopped off?" Julia asked.

"Yes, baby," Dena told her. "Daddy lost his legs, but he is still Daddy, and he loves you very, very much."

Tears welled up in Julia's eyes. "Is Daddy still going to be able to wrestle with me?" she asked.

"Yes, baby," Dena said, "he will be able to do all of the things he used to do with you. But it will take a while before he can do them again."

Julia thought for a second.

"But Mommy, Eva won't know Daddy," she said.

"You mean, she won't know him without his legs?" Dena asked.

"Yes, Mommy."

"Baby, Eva won't know any different, and Daddy will love you both just like he did before," Dena said. "You know how Ryan has a metal leg? Well, Daddy will have two metal legs."

Julia scrunched up her face. "Well, I'll be painting those legs peach," she declared.

The mood at the outpost was bleak. Feelings of rage, sorrow, loathing, xenophobia, inadequacy, depression—every possible emotion came over the men of Blackfoot Troop. Everyone knew that at best, Yllescas would lose both legs, and that the worst-case scenario was far more probable. Members of Task Force Paladin, newly formed to combat the growing threat of IEDs, flew in from Bagram. The newcomers transferred Amin Shir to Forward Operating Base Bostick and then to the detainee holding center at Bagram.[61]

The day after the attack on Yllescas, Mazzocchi and Meshkin demanded to meet with the Kamdesh shura; there were a lot of questions that the elders needed to answer, they thought. The elders said they were too scared to come to Camp Keating, but eventually a large group of locals met with the Americans at the Afghan National Police station in Urmul.

Meshkin and Mazzocchi took the lead: What was going on in Kamdesh? Who had organized the attack? Why hadn't the Americans been warned?

The elders said they were sorry the attack had occurred, but they insisted they had no information to share, and the more they were pressed, the quieter they got. To Mazzocchi, their response was telling—an admission of guilt. They clearly *had* known that something was going to happen and hadn't done anything to stop it, but they also wanted to make sure they would keep receiving development funds.

---

[61] Shir would ultimately be remanded to Afghan custody. Three years after Yllescas was targeted, according to intelligence sources, Amin Shir was still being held by the Afghan government and awaiting trial.

"Captain Yllescas had been calling for you to meet with us for weeks," Tucker said. "It's comical to me that you have agreed to come down here only now that something bad has happened. As of now, all projects are on hold. We give you all this money and get nothing in return. We know you have the ability to stop the violence, the madness, the chaos. But you don't care! And if *you* don't care, it makes it hard for *us* to care."

One of the elders from the Mandigal shura, an ancient man with a thick white beard, had been staring right into Tucker's eyes as he spoke. Tucker could feel his simmering glare; the old man was looking at him with an expression that seemed to him to be saying, Look at this stupid fucking kid yelling at us. The twenty-four-year-old lieutenant could only imagine the war and poverty that had marked this man's life, only guess how little he must care about being barked at by some young pup in yet another occupier's foreign tongue.

"We're here for only a short time," Tucker said. "Then we're going to return to America, where we have happy lives—where our roads are paved, our children go to school, and our police protect us. You, however, will continue to struggle with violence, as will your children and their children. If you want to make a difference, let us know. We're here to help."

The Americans left Urmul and returned to the outpost.

At 7:30 in the morning at Camp Blessing, in Kunar Province, Captain Dan Pecha was summoned to the operations center to answer a call from Major Keith Rautter, the brigade chief of operations back in Jalalabad.

"You've got two hours to pack up all your gear," Rautter told him. "The chopper's on the way."

The thirty-three-year-old Pecha, an assistant operations officer with the 1st Battalion, 26th Infantry, had been waiting for his opportunity to command a company, likely somewhere in Kunar Province. His wait was over, but he wouldn't be in Kunar. Before lunchtime, Pecha was at Forward Operating Base Bostick, meeting with Markert to talk about his new job: he was moving to 6-4 Cav to command Blackfoot Troop at Combat Outpost Keating.

Pecha would come to think of himself as the polar opposite of the charismatic Yllescas—more low-key and unemotional than his predecessor, more calculated and deliberate. The men of Blackfoot seemed timid around him at first; the troops had been together for almost two years by that point, and they had become close. Pecha had never met Yllescas, but he immediately gathered that he'd been a dynamic leader, and instrumental in bonding together the tight-knit Blackfoot Troop lieutenants. It wouldn't be easy to replace this beloved wounded warrior, but Pecha was confident that his own relationships with Meshkin, Mazzocchi, Safulko, Tucker, and the rest of Blackfoot Troop would develop.

Bonding between the Americans and the locals would be another matter entirely, Pecha knew. Developing such ties required patience and prolonged exchange; when the leader of the effort kept departing, whether through transfer or casualty, the clock was inevitably wound backward. In just two years, the locals in the Kamdesh Valley had gone through seven designated American leaders: Swain, Brooks, and Gooding with 3-71 Cav; Bostick and Hutto with 1-91 Cav; Yllescas and now Pecha himself with 6-4 Cav. And this most recent departure was unprecedented: an attempted assassination of the commander of the outpost. His lieutenants found it incredible that none of the elders knew anything about the plot to kill Yllescas. Someone had housed the culprit, they pointed out; someone had fed him; he must have prayed at a local mosque. Even to Pecha, new on the scene, the apologies that the local powerbrokers were offering sounded insincere.

As surely as the enemy fighters had targeted Yllescas, they now tried to take advantage of his absence. There was an uptick in direct- and indirect-fire attacks, with much larger assaults often coming on Saturdays. (Friday was the Muslim Sabbath, and because the "holy warriors," as they thought of themselves, believed that their cause was in accordance with their faith, they would frequently launch attacks the following morning.) To counteract any insurgent momentum, the Americans significantly stepped up their patrolling. Mazzocchi had ordered that the bridge be rebuilt—troops needed to be able to get to the Northface somehow—but the process further darkened the mood at the outpost. Most of the soldiers were now convinced that at least some of their "allies" in the construction project were gathering information and passing it on to the enemy. Whatever mistrust the U.S. soldiers already had of the Afghan National Army and the Afghan National Police was magnified. Reports came in of ANA troops selling the bullets out of their own guns to the enemy. Day laborers were observed standing behind U.S. fighting positions within Camp Keating and looking up at the mountains, as if they were doing a "reverse sector sketch"—memorizing what the Americans could see from such locations. American troops began following the day laborers around the outpost. One man was caught with a soldier's notebook; it was confiscated, and he was sent away.

At Forward Operating Base Bostick, Markert began wondering if any American in Nuristan or Kunar could ever truly have the support of the locals. And whether it was promised to Hutto, Kolenda, or Yllescas, how much did pledged "support" from elders matter anyway if they were unable to prevent their young men from attacking U.S. troops and bases? To Markert, it seemed that Kolenda's much-touted Hundred-Man Shura was worthless. But at this point, did the shura even have any meaning? Was its backing important? He asked himself, Can it get us *enough* peace? Even if we have people who are behind us in any of the areas north of Naray, they don't have the mass to be — and the United States can't generate the security needed to *make* them — the voice of authority. Markert knew there were some good people in this part of the world, people who would love for it to be a peaceful place. He also knew they weren't the ones with the machine guns and the RPGs.

With the insurgency seemingly gaining strength, the members of the Hundred-Man Shura appeared to be losing interest in talking to the Americans. To some ISAF troops, such a disengagement seemed inevitable. Camp Keating had been attacked a few times with the evident complicity of the local villagers, and Camp Lowell at Kamu had been under fire since 6-4 Cav first arrived in the country. Not only Markert but also Mazzocchi believed that Kolenda and Hutto might have been pushing for too much, too soon.[62] They suspected that however loudly the 1-91 Cav officers may have tooted their own bugle about their counterinsurgency accomplishments, their fifteen months' worth of effort wasn't about to undo decades', if not centuries', worth of habits and traditions of self-preservation.

Robert Yllescas's face was so swollen that when his wife, Dena, walked through the door of his hospital room at Landstuhl on November 1, she

---

[62] Following events from afar, Kolenda wondered how much of 6-4's skepticism about the Hundred-Man Shura became self-fulfilling. Many of the unit's leaders had never seemed willing to listen and learn, he thought, and being a new unit, they had a lot of basics to sort out. "Sadly, the insurgents achieved their intended goal of driving a wedge between the people and the Americans and Afghan forces when they [targeted] Rob," he later wrote.

barely recognized him. He was wearing a neck brace, was hooked up to a ventilator, and had a tracheostomy tube inserted in his neck. She lifted his sheet: his abdomen was so bruised that it was almost black, and so swollen that he looked nine months pregnant. Since the explosion, he had not regained consciousness.

Dena clutched his hand, intertwining their fingers while she, her mother, and her mother-in-law all talked to him and told him stories— about Julia and Eva, about all the friends and family members who were thinking of him and praying for him. Soon the grandmothers left to buy him some clothes. Dena read her husband the letters Julia had written to him. She kissed his hand and told him how much she loved him. She wished she could have a snapshot of the future; she wanted to know where they would be a year from that moment, because right then, everything seemed so hopeless.

And Dena wept.

Nine days later, President George W. Bush gave her a big hug.

"I'm so sorry," the president said. He had tears in his eyes.

They were standing in Rob Yllescas's hospital room at Bethesda Naval Hospital, wearing hospital gowns and surgical masks. Yllescas remained in bad shape, unconscious, with his jaw wired shut and his legs amputated.

It was November 10, 2008. Yllescas was one of 2,561 U.S. service members who'd been wounded in action in Afghanistan since the war started in October 2001; 621 more had been killed there. In Iraq, 30,764 U.S. troops had been wounded in action, and 4,180 killed.

Less than a week before the president paid this bedside visit, Rob and Dena Yllescas had flown to the United States from Germany on the very day that the nation was electing as its next commander in chief a young, inexperienced freshman senator from Illinois, a liberal Democrat named Barack Obama. Public weariness with President Bush's two wars was one of the reasons for Obama's victory over the decorated Vietnam veteran John McCain, a conservative Republican senator from Arizona. Obama seemed less bellicose than McCain. He'd talked about ending the war in Iraq and focusing instead on winning the one in Afghanistan.

President Bush awarded Yllescas the Purple Heart, the medal given to troops wounded in action. Dena tried desperately to wake her husband up. She felt sick, she wanted so badly for him to be awake.

President Bush kept hugging her. "Rob will wake up, and when he does, I will meet him in person again," he said as he held her.

She and the president left the room and removed their gowns and masks. The president signed a 1st Infantry baseball cap of Yllescas's and told Dena about Staff Sergeant Christian Bagge, whose convoy had been hit by IEDs in Iraq. Bush had met Bagge at Brooke Army Medical Center in San Antonio, Texas. From the hospital bed where he lay with no legs, Bagge had told the president, a famous jogger, "I want to run with you." In June 2006, Bagge and Bush had done just that together, on the South Lawn of the White House.

"When Rob's ready and able, maybe you can go wakeboarding with us," Dena said, referring to the water sport that's a combination of snowboarding, waterskiing, and surfing.

The president laughed. "I'm too old to wakeboard," he said.

Dena Yllescas and President George W. Bush. *(Photo courtesy of Dena Yllescas)*

CHAPTER 23

What Was Wrong with Kaine Meshkin

By November 2008, the enemy fighters had evidently decided it was no longer enough merely to attack Camp Keating; now they were going to try to overrun it.

The information came in to Blackfoot Troop piece by piece, through intercepted radio transmissions, tips that locals shared with Rick Victorino, and simple observation: tripwires outside the outpost were cut, insurgent chatter suddenly went silent. Blackfoot Troop's leaders assumed, based on recent history, that the attack would come on a Saturday.

On Friday, November 21, Captain Pecha huddled with Safulko, Victorino, Tucker, and Mazzocchi. Meshkin was on leave. There were two easy ways for insurgents to enter the outpost: through the main entrance and through the ANA's side entrance, adjacent to the road on the east-southeast corner. They had to think like the enemy: which route would the insurgents prefer, and why? After running through a series of scenarios, the men concocted a plan.

Well before dawn on Saturday, Mazzocchi and a patrol snuck up the slope of the northern mountain. Once they were on the Northface, the lieutenant divided his team into two parts, each containing six U.S. troops and two ANA soldiers. He led one group while First Sergeant Howard Johnson took charge of the other. Meanwhile, Pecha, Safulko, and Blue Platoon prepared to patrol the southern wall. That had been Pecha's idea; he'd been at Camp Keating for only a few weeks, but from his conversations with the lieutenants, he'd gathered that the unit had historically stayed away from the southern wall on Saturdays due to the increased likelihood of an attack there. His intent was to have Mazzocchi's troops provide overwatch while he and his team took the fight to the enemy on the other side.

Mazzocchi and Safulko both thought Pecha's plan was a particularly bad one. He and his platoon would be walking uphill and directly into a potentially intense firefight with a larger force. They respected Dan Pecha as a leader, and they knew he wasn't afraid of much, but he was also, now, a symbol in that valley. They had to protect that symbol. The last thing Blackfoot Troop needed was another commander carried off the field of battle, never to return.

First light came. Up at Observation Post Fritsche, White Platoon's Don Couch called in to the operations center to alert command that he'd heard automatic-weapons fire in the distance. That didn't necessarily mean anything; it could be a domestic dispute, a new salvo in the Kom–Kushtozi war, or even just an accidental discharge—such was the Afghanistan sound track. Then one of the guards near the southern wall at Camp Keating reported that he'd seen movement up in the Switchbacks. He wasn't sure, but he thought he'd spotted someone peeking out from behind a rock.

Mazzocchi, on the northern mountain, saw a trip flare go off across the way. Tripwires had been set up on the southern mountain, and someone— almost certainly an insurgent, Mazzocchi felt in his gut, and not one of the monkeys or other wild animals that roamed the area—had disturbed the wire, igniting a smoking flare. Mazzocchi had Tucker tell the mortarmen at Camp Keating and Observation Post Fritsche to prepare to fire.

Then a second trip flare went off. The enemy was coming down the southern mountain from the direction of Kamdesh Village.

Safulko ran to the dining hall to grab some water, after which he intended to make a beeline for the barracks to pick up his patrol. He quickly snatched a couple of bottles out of the refrigerator, stashed them in his backpack, and was just opening the door when—at precisely 6:30 a.m.—the enemy opened up on the outpost with small arms, PKM machine guns, and a volley of RPGs. When the fire hit, the ANA soldiers who'd been milling about on the U.S. side of the base scattered, firing back sporadically in multiple directions before stumbling into the waist- and knee-deep trench systems that wound around the buildings. One RPG went through the wall above the dining-hall door, through the refrigerator, and out the other wall, its shrapnel spraying both cooks, Sergeant Jason Judice and Specialist Jason Pace. Another RPG then exploded through the roof of the operations center, knocking out the generator and landing in Mazzocchi's workspace, polluting the air with its acrid copper smell. All forms of communication were temporarily lost.

The enemy clearly knew the outpost.

Insurgents began peppering a Humvee on which sat a .50-caliber machine gun and an LRAS surveillance device. One round went through the lens of the LRAS and out the other side of the scope, disabling the machine. A soldier carrying both ammunition and an M203 grenade launcher ran to the Humvee; an enemy round knocked the M203 right off his rifle. It was a direct hit from an expert marksman.

Mazzocchi's men returned fire from the northern mountain while he and Staff Sergeant Matthew Crane called in for close air support as well as for 120-millimeter mortars from both Camp Keating and Observation Post Fritsche. Pecha used a backup radio to call Mazzocchi. "You and Crane will be in charge of all indirect fire and air support," he told him. "Our generator's out."

Bullets showered down on Mazzocchi and his men, forcing them to take cover, while Johnson and his troops were pummeled by RPGs. The enemy knew the precise locations of both Mazzocchi's and First Sergeant Johnson's patrols. Mazzocchi saw a group of insurgents, around half a dozen men, on the road. They looked as if they were on their way to the eastern side of the outpost, probably to try to breach the wire near the ANA compound; crossing would be much easier there than elsewhere because in places the wire was jammed down into the dirt, from ANA soldiers regularly hopping over it to take a shortcut into and out of camp. Mazzocchi and his troops fired on the insurgents while Crane redirected the mortar fire, shifting the target from the southern mountain to the enemy on the road. The insurgents heading for the wire retreated.

By then, close air support had arrived, and now the Apaches began hitting the enemy in the mountains with Hellfire missiles, ending the assault. They next provided cover for the U.S. troops as they moved down the northern mountain. On one of their passes, the pilots were at about eye level with the men from 6-4 Cav, and Victorino held up his hands in a University of Texas Hook-'em-Horns gesture as thanks.

The cooks insisted that they were okay and, after some quick treatment for their shrapnel wounds, could stay at Combat Outpost Keating. They even made dinner for the troops that night.

After Mazzocchi returned to the outpost, he surveyed the camp and was surprised to see how hard it had been hit, though he knew the damage could have been much worse if the enemy had managed to breach the wire. "They had us suppressed pretty heavily," Safulko explained to him. "They were spot on." Mazzocchi's seeing the team of insurgents on the road at the eastern side of the outpost had been key to the successful defense. "There's no way we would have been able to detect them if you hadn't been there," Safulko acknowledged. The troops of 6-4 Cav had for the most part made it through in good shape, but that belied how close they had come to catastrophe during this attack.

Two days later, the enemy tried again, firing at the outpost from five surrounding positions. That the insurgents were attacking on a Monday and not a Saturday, and two or three hours into the day instead of at dawn, indicated that they understood the importance of switching up their tactics. Caught off guard, the officers of Blackfoot Troop did not have anyone outside the outpost on patrol. A 107-millimeter rocket crashed into the camp, followed by small-arms fire as a platoon of enemy fighters came from the high ground to the southeast, pinning down the ANA soldiers at their guard posts and in their barracks. Insurgents fired at a U.S. Humvee equipped with an MK19 grenade launcher, but they kept overshooting, spraying the tree behind the truck and causing its leaves to flutter to the ground.

Mazzocchi and Safulko had left the operations center and were standing around the corner from the Humvee. At this point, they expected the insurgents to breach the wire. Safulko called in to Sergeant First Class Curry: "The ANA are pinned down," he told him. Curry led a ready-to-go 240 machine-gun team to a corridor near the ANA's end of the outpost, to prepare for an enemy takeover of the eastern side. If the wire got breached, they would contain the insurgents there.

That turned out not to be necessary. Sergeant Nathan Wagner — a normally quiet kid from the Midwest — ran out of the operations center seeming possessed, armed with an AT4 shoulder-launched rocket. He fired it right at the enemy fighters in the southeast corner of the camp, and they retreated. But in the end, what allowed Blackfoot Troop to keep all of the insurgents at bay — and probably saved the day — was the sheer volume of rounds fired by air support, including two five-hundred-pound bombs dropped by an A-10 Warthog on an enemy position on the North-face, as well as two 30-millimeter gun runs on the same spot.

It was obvious to all, however, that the insurgents had made it their priority to overrun the outpost, and twice now they had come close to succeeding. Once they were inside the wire, there was no telling what damage they could do.

Dena Yllescas put the laptop computer by her husband's hospital bed. She'd downloaded songs from their wedding and others that had meaning for them both: "The Keeper of the Stars" by Tracy Byrd, the Rascal Flatts version of "Bless the Broken Road," "You Save Me" by Kenny Chesney. A slide show of photographs of their two little girls appeared on the screen, each image fading in and then fading out again to make way for the next.

"It's amazing how you can speak right to my heart," sang Keith Whitley.
Without saying a word, you can light up the dark.
Try as I may I could never explain
What I hear when you don't say a thing.

Dena saw tears in Rob's eyes. She wasn't sure if they were because of the music, the pictures, or the pain — or all three. He wasn't able to speak. She cried, too, mourning the loss of the past, terrified of the future.

It had been a good day, as good days went in her new world. The nurse had told her that if she asked Rob to grip her hand, it might just provoke a reflex action. Or, the nurse suggested, she could try to get him to make a thumbs-up sign. Dena asked him to do that, and she could see him try-ing, stiffening his arm in an effort to lift it. At another point, when the doctor was there, she told Rob to blink once if he was in pain and twice if he wasn't. He blinked once. The doctor said he was positive that Rob was responding directly to her command.

It had been surgery after surgery over the previous two weeks, each good sign counterbalanced by a setback. His leg wounds kept bleeding, his fever required a cooling blanket, his blood pressure kept spiking, he had acute kidney failure, he was jaundiced, his blood wasn't clotting well. Rob was in such pain, and his body had suffered such severe trauma, that the doctors often kept him sedated. Dena took pleasure in any indication that he was there with her. She hooked up a radio and turned on conservative talk-radio giant Rush Limbaugh's show, Rob's favorite, and he squeezed her hand tightly as they listened—she hoped he was listening, at any rate. "You'll be fine," she would tell him. "You have to keep working on responding to commands. You're a fighter; you're a Ranger. You finished Ranger school when you didn't think you could go on anymore, and you can use that fight in you to get through this." He had two little girls who were waiting to welcome their daddy back, she said. They could still go ahead with all their plans, including the one to buy an RV and follow Eva and Julia to college so their daughters would never be out of their sight.

Dena, her mother, and her mother-in-law did a lot of praying. At one point, the doctor told them that for some "unknown reason," Rob's bilirubin count had come down, which meant that his jaundice was improving—the doctor wasn't sure why. All three women said at the same time, "*We* know why!" It was the power of prayer, they knew—indeed, they'd been praying specifically for his liver to start working properly.

Yllescas was supposed to receive skin grafts on his leg wounds on November 24, but the plastic surgeon was concerned that given the condition he was in, the grafts wouldn't take—so instead the doctors did a "purse cinch" on his wounds, threading the tissue and cinching it up to make the wound smaller. The next day, Julia and Eva came to visit. Eva, still a baby, was too physically vulnerable to risk exposure to her dad—who was now suffering from a fungal infection, among other things—but Julia, after hesitating for a second in the hallway, put on her gown and bravely went into his room. She seemed scared of him at first but then gradually warmed to him. It was Daddy, she could see that now. And Rob could see Julia, of this Dena was sure.

After Julia's visit, Rob Yllescas started going downhill fast, as if he'd been waiting to see her before saying good-bye. A CAT scan showed fluid in his left lung and his right leg. His breathing became labored. His temperature rose, and his respiration and heart rate increased.

"Last year, Thanksgiving wasn't good for me because I couldn't eat anything," Dena reminded her husband, referring to the gestational diabetes she'd been diagnosed with in 2007, while carrying Eva. "And this year *you* can't eat anything, but next year we will have the best Thanksgiving together with our girls, pigging out!"

On Friday, November 28, Yllescas's pulse was low, and his blood pressure high. Another CAT scan revealed the presence of a large blood clot in the main part of his brain. His doctors gave Dena a choice: either she could let her husband die a peaceful death, or they could attempt an emergency craniotomy. The odds of his dying on the operating table were high, they said. And even if he did survive, he wasn't likely to have much quality of life.

It was the toughest decision of her life. Rob had told her that he didn't want to be a vegetable. But she couldn't believe that a loving God would get him this far and then allow him to die or, worse, live out the rest of his life oblivious to the world around him. Dena talked it over with her mother and her in-laws and decided to ask the doctors to perform the craniotomy. She figured the odds had been against Rob's surviving the IED blast, and yet he'd done that, so he would survive this, too, and somehow emerge cognitively sound. God was working through the doctors, she thought. God knew that Rob had two little daughters who needed him very much.

In a craniotomy, a neurosurgeon removes a section of the patient's skull in order to access his or her brain. The patient's head is locked into position with a three-pin Mayfield skull clamp that will keep it completely immobile while the delicate procedure is performed. First the surgeon cuts into the patient's scalp, folds back the skin and muscles, and removes a flap of bone to reveal the brain's protective covering. That covering, named the dura mater, is itself then folded back, exposing the brain. The surgeon can then get to work on trying to correct whatever the problem is—a blood clot, an aneurysm, a tumor, a bullet, or whatever. When that's done, the bone flap is usually put back in place with small titanium plates and screws, though if the brain swells, that step may be omitted.

During Yllescas's surgery, his wife prayed with a fierce intensity. If he's not going to have any quality of life, God, please just take him home, she asked.

He survived. When the neurosurgeon cut out the bone flap on the right side of Yllescas's skull, however, his brain bulged out. It shrank somewhat after the blood clot was removed, but the trauma of the surgery caused it to start swelling again, and a small section of it had to be excised so that Yllescas could be closed back up. The surgeon didn't know what repercussions this might have. He wasn't able to restore the bone flap; he said that could be replaced down the line with a titanium plate.

Dena was informed that there was a 90 percent chance her husband wouldn't make it to the next morning. A crash cart sat in his room all night. But as the first rays of sun crept through the hospital window shades, Rob was still alive. His vital signs and brain-pressure measurements held steady. Dena saw his eyes moving underneath his eyelids. "I hope you understand why I made the decision I did," she told him.

She saw good signs. When the medical team cleaned out his mouth, he clenched his jaw. When his tracheostomy breathing tube was suctioned, he coughed and moved his shoulders. His brain stem is working, she thought. She held on to that. God got him through the surgery, she said to herself. Why would He do that if He didn't have a plan for Rob?

She heard Julia praying that night. "God, please heal my daddy so he can wrestle with me," said the little girl.

O Lord, please hear my daughter's prayers, Dena asked. They come from this most innocent of children, whose passion and love for her father are unwavering. Lord, please heal my husband. Make him your miracle man. You are the Master Healer.

Two days after his craniectomy, on December 1, Rob Yllescas had a massive stroke. Another clot had interrupted the blood flow to his brain. A CAT scan afforded no hope. There was nothing more for Dena Yllescas to hold on to. She decided to let him go. She promised him that she and the girls would be okay.

Captain Robert Yllescas, age thirty-one, was removed from life support and died quickly.

Mazzocchi sat at a picnic table in the dining hall with Chris Safulko, snacking on Pop-Tarts and talking for hours. He offered Safulko some water from the refrigerator that had been completely blown out by the RPG. (Tongue in cheek, they called it Freedom Water.) Meshkin was still on leave, and Pecha was about to take some R&R, which would leave Mazzocchi in charge of the outpost.

Winter was coming, likely meaning a respite from attacks. No longer did the U.S. forces think this was because the enemy was returning to Pakistan; no, they now realized that most of the insurgents were local, even if they did have Taliban leaders from outside Kamdesh District. The reason for the seasonal break in hostilities, they suspected, was that excessive amounts of snow and ice made it dangerous for the enemy to traverse the mountains to stage serious assaults. They hoped that would be the case this winter, at any rate.

In early November, snow fell on the highest peaks of the surrounding mountains, prompting sighs of relief. Finally, a break, the Americans thought.

A break from attacks, at least—there was still plenty of work to do. The construction quality of the buildings at the outpost was shoddy, and by now every structure leaked. Through the whole winter, soldiers had to set out buckets to catch the drips in nearly every room, then empty them once a day or more—yet another fight just to keep day-to-day operations going. Then, more seriously, the leaders of Blackfoot Troop had to fortify the outpost even further, taking advantage of the bad weather to strengthen fighting positions. This could be accomplished by a few different means, including chopping down surrounding trees and destroying rock outcroppings that the enemy used for cover. Along these same lines, Pecha and his lieutenants decided that they ought to send the insurgents some emphatic messages.

First, if the enemy wanted the outpost, he would have to suffer for it. American troops cleared the entire area around Combat Outpost Keating; if the insurgents tried to breach the wire again, they would have to cross the last fifty to one hundred yards in the open, under U.S. fire. Every yard the enemy fighters gained, they would have to bleed for. Second, the American officers would make it understood that the enemy could no longer move freely in the area. Resuming their aggressive patrols, they would show the insurgents that Blackfoot Troop was always watching.

There was also another, more perplexing challenge facing the Americans: they had to reengage with the locals and reunite with the shura. The IED had destroyed both the trust between the two sides and the troops' sense of security. The officers of Blackfoot Troop figured that the locals had decided the Americans weren't so strong after all: if they couldn't secure their own camp, couldn't protect their own commander, how could they make the valley safe for the Kamdeshis?

Although more skeptical about counterinsurgency than those before him, Pecha nevertheless realized that he had to do whatever he could to restore the trust between his men and the local elders. The insurgents had calculated that by killing Yllescas, they could put an end to the progress that 1-91 Cav, and then 6-4, had made in Kamdesh. One of Yllescas's early dreams had been to turn the shura tent at Keating into a heated building so that Blackfoot Troop could host gatherings there during the winter; by the time he was wounded, however, the building was only 80 percent completed. Now, as part of Pecha's version of a counterinsurgency program, Blackfoot Troop would finish it. The Americans bought the inn where Amin Shir had been found and tore it down; the materials were salvaged to finish the heated shura building. Doc Brewer opened the doors of the aid station, welcoming locals in need of medical care. Mazzocchi, as Pecha's XO, placed orders with headquarters for as many humanitarian-assistance supplies as could be spared. In some ways, the men could never match their earlier efforts, haunted as they were by what had happened to their former commander—yet they were determined to keep trying.

On the night of December 1, First Sergeant Johnson came into the plans room, where all of the officers were assembled.

"Captain Yllescas passed," he said. Everyone fell silent. Within a few minutes, they all went their separate ways, to their bunks or out into the dark.

Kaine Meshkin was home on leave in Fort Hood, Texas, when he got the news.

Dena Yllescas requested that he escort her late husband's body from Bethesda Naval Hospital in Maryland to the funeral in Nebraska. Meshkin immediately agreed, and the Pentagon arranged for him to serve as an escort officer, which required official training in the position's duties and obligations.

The night after he attended the training, Meshkin was sitting at his kitchen table with his wife, Ali, as they went over the details of how each of them would get to Nebraska. He was aware that he had become emotionally numb in Afghanistan. Over there, there wasn't any point in giving in to sorrow or depression, or at least it had seemed that way at the time. Those emotions—as opposed to, say, anger—just weren't practical in an environment in which you had to worry constantly about your own and your comrades' survival. Self-pity could get you killed.

But being back in Texas with Ali and their friends had brought all those pent-up emotions to the fore. Right there at the kitchen table, looking at the handbook detailing his duties as an escort officer for Yllescas's corpse, Meshkin broke down sobbing. He wept uncontrollably, in a way he hadn't done since college, when his mother died of cancer. That had been different, though: that time, he'd felt not only grief but also relief that his mother would no longer be in pain. This was something else. In this moment, all of his pain, frustration, sorrow, anger, and desire for vengeance had finally boiled to the surface.

"I don't know what's wrong with me," he told Ali as his body heaved.

The next day, he flew to Washington, D.C., and was taken to the funeral home where Yllescas's corpse lay. Meshkin was supposed to verify that his former commander's uniform had been put on properly and that he was wearing the right medals and ribbons. He wasn't prepared for what he saw. The morticians were doing everything they could to make Yllescas presentable, but there were clear limits to what they could accomplish. It was the darkest and most solemn moment of the war for Kaine Meshkin. It didn't make any sense, but, enraged and heartbroken, he was seized by a sudden desire to hurt the morticians who were messing with Yllescas's body. I want to beat the shit out of these guys, he thought—though again, he didn't understand why.

Meshkin made sure the captain's uniform, ribbons, and awards were correct. Afterward, he was driven to a hotel and instructed not to drink any alcohol. He'd be picked up in the morning.

Stay cooped up by myself in a hotel, sober, after seeing Rob that way? Meshkin thought. Are you fucking *kidding* me?

He went to an Irish pub and drank—a lot—then stumbled back to his hotel and passed out. He woke up the next morning and went to the funeral home to stay with Yllescas until they boarded the small plane designed especially for escort flights. Meshkin sat up near the cockpit, right next to his friend's casket. Upon landing in Nebraska, he tried to prepare Dena Yllescas for what she was about to see at the funeral home. Her husband's body had deteriorated badly, he told her. Dena insisted on seeing Rob anyway. Afterward, she agreed with Meshkin that an open casket wouldn't be a good idea.

Rob Yllescas was laid to rest at the back end of the Osceola Cemetery, in a peaceful spot near a cornfield. He'd come home.

Soon after Yllescas's funeral, Meshkin returned to the Kamdesh Valley, where it turned out that this winter, in contrast to the previous two, the enemy had decided to *not* take a vacation. The insurgents didn't stage any major attacks on Camp Keating but instead mainly lobbed harassment rounds from a distance: small-arms fire, RPGs, an occasional blast from an antitank PTRD (most likely the same one from October 25). Still, this was a change for the worse.

In accordance with a not-unusual custom whereby officers rotate their

Eva Yllescas, Memorial Day 2009. *(Photo courtesy of Dena Yllescas)*

responsibilities, Lieutenants Meshkin and Mazzocchi switched jobs, Meshkin becoming the XO while Mazzocchi took control of Red Platoon.

In his new role, Mazzocchi led a patrol to the Northface to try to locate and kill the enemy RPG team that had been firing on the camp from the north. No dice—they didn't find it. Meshkin greeted the platoon upon its return, wanting to talk to his colleague about where the enemy team might be shooting from. As the two lieutenants were speaking, Meshkin saw a puff of smoke from the mountain and heard the launch of an RPG. He cringed. The rocket flew about a foot over their heads and detonated on a HESCO barrier right behind them. The blast was deafening. Mazzocchi was knocked unconscious. Meshkin had taken cover—instinctively, he supposed—and now began firing toward the area where he'd seen the smoke. His head felt as if it'd been walloped by a baseball bat; all he could hear was a high-pitched ringing in his right ear. In a state of mental disarray, he emptied a magazine to the north, but the enemy had already escaped behind a ridge. He would have headaches and a ringing in his ear for more than a year afterward.

In December 2008, at Fort Carson, Colorado, Colonel Randy George and Lieutenant Colonel Brad Brown were preparing for the following summer, when they were scheduled to assume control of an area of operations in eastern Afghanistan that included Combat Outpost Keating. More precisely, they were planning to close the outpost.

In six months, George would replace Spiszer, and Brown would take over for Markert. George commanded the 4th Brigade Combat Team, 4th Infantry Division; Brown was in charge of the 3rd Squadron, 61st Cavalry Regiment — or "3-61 Cav" — which was part of George's brigade.

For months, Brown had been reaching out via email to Markert and Kolenda, asking for guidance. Markert recommended that the 3-61 Cav troops practice shooting moving targets on a hill up to seven hundred yards above them; shooting uphill and downhill; and adjusting their aim points — all skills that were critical to surviving at Camp Keating. Make those targets move quickly, Markert wrote. You wouldn't believe how fast the enemy here is.

Kolenda offered similar advice. The mountains are brutal, he added, and you're in Colorado, so take advantage. Everyone should be able to run twelve miles in full gear in less than four hours. And five miles without gear in forty minutes. This was the minimum level of fitness needed, but Kolenda had seen units come to Afghanistan not up to that standard, which would give the men a foundation, at least, for what awaited them in Nuristan.

But beyond the practical preparation, there were bigger issues that Brown just couldn't wrap his head around, the same ones that had flummoxed nearly everyone who'd had anything at all to do with Combat Outpost Keating. The outpost had been put near the road because the troops would need it for travel and resupply, but by 2007, road collapses and frequent ambushes had altered that plan, rendering Camp Keating completely dependent on helicopters for transportation and supply runs. Indeed, the outpost was named after an officer whose very death had highlighted just how unusable the roads were.

It was a familiar chorus, and for George, it was merely a different verse from the same dreadful songbook. The energy invested in counterinsurgency had been extensive, but George didn't think the results had been proportional. The United States had gotten itself in the middle of a variety of blood, land, and tribal feuds, Brown believed, and the government of Afghanistan itself had very little, if any, interest in making serious efforts in that region. The insurgency was actually *gaining* strength, especially in the remote rural areas of eastern Afghanistan. According to one U.S. Army tabulation, the yearly number of attacks against the combat outposts in Kamdesh District had risen dramatically since their establishment, from a few dozen in 2006 (though the United States was there for only part of that year), to 109 in 2007, to 136 by the end of 2008.

As George and Brown came to see it, the Army was committing an inordinate number of troops to try to secure a relatively small percentage of the Afghan population. Moreover, the particular ethos of Kamdesh District in Nuristan Province and the Korangal Valley in Kunar Province — with their geographical isolation, traditional local hostilities, and lack of any real Afghan government presence — meant that the Americans were more irritant than balm to the locals, and more incitement than deterrent to the enemy. Finally, providing air support and making resupply runs for those outposts and observation posts took up time that choppers and their pilots might otherwise be spending on missions in parts of the country more vital to the overall U.S. aims.

Colonel George sent a number of his noncommissioned officers to the outposts so they could see for themselves why they needed to push their soldiers to be fit and able to shoot, move, and communicate in difficult mountainous terrain. This fight would be quite different from what the brigade had gone through during its fifteen-month deployment to Baghdad during the surge. George and Brown, for their part, paid their first visit to Combat Outpost Keating on Saturday, December 6, 2008 — the same day the brigade held a memorial service for Yllescas. The leadership of Blackfoot Troop objected to the memorial being held on the day of the week when the enemy was likeliest to attack, but headquarters insisted.

Once on the ground, George and Brown got out of the bird and looked up and around at the steep mountains — just as Kyle Marcum and virtually everyone else who had been at the outpost over the past two and a half years had done on first arriving.

"What the *hell* are they doing here?" George asked.

"I don't know," Brown replied.

CHAPTER 24

The Puppies

Pecha returned from leave in mid-January. He, Meshkin, and Mazzocchi were sitting on the small enclosed deck right off the aid station, smoking cigars, when a sniper's bullet passed right between them and knocked out a light above Mazzocchi's head. That they had been targeted there suggested to them that locals were telling insurgents that the deck was a good place at which to randomly fire, that American soldiers often hung out there. Or maybe the enemy had just seen the cigar smoke.

Either way, for Pecha, the bullet was yet another reminder that he had to try to improve relations with the locals—a challenge, since the elders from the Kamdesh shura had begun offering excuse after excuse for not visiting Camp Keating: "So-and-so is too old to make the walk," they would say, or "That one doesn't have any shoes," or "The weather is bad." Meanwhile, the outpost continued to provide a significant amount of humanitarian assistance to local villages—blankets, jackets, shoes, and food—and the "Radio Kamdesh" idea was finally starting to come together. Taliban propagandists had been airing clandestine radio broadcasts warning locals that the Americans were planning to kill innocent people, steal their land, and kidnap their children. The enemy radio hosts would stay up all night singing the poetry of jihad; Safulko called these recitations Taliban death jams. Victorino suspected that the broadcasts originated in Kamdesh Village itself, from hand-held radios, the transmissions carrying throughout the area because the village was at such a high elevation. The Americans wanted to mount a counterinformation campaign in Kamdesh District, and to that end, Master Sergeant Ryan Bodmer, a U.S. Army Reserves civil-affairs NCO, was posted to Combat Outpost Keating from the PRT in Kala Gush to oversee the project.

With Markert's support, Bodmer had $130,000 worth of equipment, including a thirty-foot radio tower, shipped to Camp Keating. The goal was to broadcast news and miscellaneous music. Just as Dennis Sugrue of 3-71 Cav had done to promote Radio Naray, Bodmer made sure to distribute hundreds of small, Chinese-made hand-cranked transistor radios to the local populace. The locals, as they did with the humanitarian aid, bickered over the gifts.

At the White House, on January 23, a newly inaugurated President Barack Obama made his way to the Situation Room to talk about Afghanistan.

The commander of international forces in Afghanistan, General Mc-Kiernan, had an outstanding request for thirty thousand additional U.S. troops. While the new president had campaigned on the promise to withdraw American soldiers from Iraq, he had pledged to send *more* men — at least ten thousand, or two brigades' worth — to Afghanistan. But Obama was reluctant to send more troops there without taking a harder look at the overall plan for that war, which he regarded as a mess lacking a clear strategy. During his presidential transition, one of President Bush's top advisers on the wars in Iraq and Afghanistan, Army Lieutenant General Douglas Lute, had briefed the president-elect with a Power-Point presentation that frankly spelled out for him that there was no strategy in Afghanistan that anyone could either articulate or achieve.[63] There were some thirty-six thousand U.S. troops in Afghanistan already, and the president wasn't about to grant McKiernan's request and nearly double that number without undertaking a more comprehensive review of what the United States was doing there — and why this war was in its eighth year, with no end in sight.

Having impressively advanced through the ranks, General David Petraeus, leader of the group that had rewritten the Army's counterinsurgency manual, published in 2006, now headed U.S. Central Command, covering the twenty countries that comprised the European, Pacific, and

---

[63] As first recalled by National Security Adviser Tom Donilon to David Sanger, "Charting Obama's Journey to a Shift on Afghanistan," *New York Times,* May 19, 2012.

African commands, including Afghanistan. Petraeus wanted the president to send in more troops and put even more emphasis on counterinsurgency in the Afghanistan war. He was backed in this call by Admiral Mike Mullen, chairman of the Joint Chiefs of Staff.[64]

Almost a month later, President Obama announced that he would commit an additional seventeen thousand U.S. troops to Afghanistan. "The Taliban is resurgent in Afghanistan, and Al Qaeda supports the insurgency and threatens America from its safe haven along the Pakistani border," he explained. The president said he would be sending a brigade of Marines and a brigade of Army troops "to meet urgent security needs." He meanwhile asked a former CIA official and National Security Council staffer named Bruce Riedel to conduct a sixty-day review of the war and its strategy. The previous year, Riedel had published a book entitled *The Search for Al Qaeda,* in which he suggested that the real threat lay in Pakistan.

Another issue was percolating beyond McKiernan's troop request, and that was McKiernan himself. Mullen and Robert Gates, Obama's (and Bush's) secretary of defense, both had doubts about his leadership and wondered if he was really the right man for the job. To them he seemed too cautious and conventional.

Radio Kamdesh, once it was up and running, featured clerics who preached messages of peace and decried the other voices on the airwaves that were rallying locals to attack Americans. Similar monologues were delivered by the local Afghan National Police chief and ANA commander. After President Obama announced the surge of troops to Afghanistan, the Americans co-opted the information and began broadcasting the falsehood that all of the nearly twenty thousand new troops were headed straight for Kamdesh District. (The other broadcasts reaching the valley, from BBC and Voice of America, never specified where, precisely, the U.S. soldiers were to be posted.) The insurgents pulled back from the area around Combat Outpost Keating for a few weeks,

---

[64] Although as a candidate, Obama had run against his predecessor's foreign policy, he not only embraced Bush's military command structure, in Mullen and Petraeus, but also took the unusual step of asking Bush's secretary of defense, Robert Gates, and White House adviser General Lute to stay on board.

until it became obvious that two new brigades weren't being squeezed into the modest camp.

Forty-four elders came to Camp Keating on February 15 to learn more about Radio Kamdesh and to discuss other topics. They represented all four settlements in Kamdesh Village, plus Mirdesh, Urmul, and Agro. The elders from Paprok couldn't make it due to poor road conditions. The Mandigal elders weren't there, either; the consensus seemed to be that they were protesting the shura because Afghan security forces had killed two insurgents from their village, one of whom had been detained the previous summer for distributing pamphlets near Urmul on how to make bombs. (Yllescas had released him after the Mandigal elders promised to monitor him and keep him out of trouble. They hadn't done either of those things, apparently: according to several Nuristanis, the man had constantly peppered the main entrance to Combat Outpost Keating with small-arms fire.)

During the shura itself, ANA Commander Jawed compared the elders from Mandigal to the thugs from Tora Bora. Anayatullah, the district administrator for Kamdesh, talked up the Americans' new radio station and its benefits for the area. Anyone who wanted to be a journalist, he said, would be welcome to travel around and collect information for broadcasts, with the shura assuming responsibility for correspondents' safety. No matter what issue was brought up during this meeting, the discussion always got snagged in the thicket of security and its insufficiency— as, for example, when Gul Mohammed Khan asked why the Afghan government had promised to bring wheat to their district but then stopped in Barikot.

"The driver would not drive all the way into Kamdesh District due to the security issues," Anayatullah replied.

"There were supposed to be forty-five hundred blankets for Kamdesh District," another elder noted. "Where have they gone?"

"You have to trust us," Anayatullah said. "There were three hundred and thirty blankets, but they were unable to bring them because there were illegal checkpoints past Barikot. The shura needs to do more to provide security."

"Security is the government's responsibility," Abdul Rahman protested. "Providing it is the job of the Afghan National Police and the Afghan National Army."

Anayatullah insisted that he had brought up the matter of security within Kamdesh District several times with the new governor of Nuristan,[65] Jamaluddin Badr, and promised that he would send Governor Badr yet another letter requesting assistance.

"All the other districts have electricity, hospitals, and roads," noted Afghan National Police commander Jalil. "We need to come together for construction in Kamdesh District."

The next day, at a meeting that Camp Keating hosted for all the contractors, Anayatullah spoke bluntly. "Security has been bad in Kamdesh for many years now," he said. "As contractors, you were aware of that when you took on these projects, so you need to stop using it as an excuse for why the projects are not getting done. From now on, you should factor in the cost of hiring security guards before you submit bids. And stop lying about how close the projects are to completion." Kyle Tucker, in charge of development funds for Combat Outpost Keating, informed the seventeen contractors present that they would need to finish the projects they were currently working on before they could be awarded any new contracts.

"You are the most important part of the development of Afghanistan," Pecha told them. "You need to take pride in what you're doing. Even the smallest projects are very important."

Important, maybe, but also endangered. Tucker had looked into the nearly three million dollars that had been committed to projects in Kamdesh District, and the report that he and Pecha wrote up worked its way up the chain of command. Spiszer and Markert decided the money had to stop flying out the door. As Spiszer saw it, 1-91 Cav had initiated these projects without having any means of performing proper oversight or inspections — or any power at all, really, to hold a contractor accountable after the first payment was made. (Then, too, the undermanned 6-4 Cav was at a disadvantage in having less combat strength than 1-91 Cav, hence less ability to get out to the villages to check up on projects.) In any case, the new civil-affairs team at Forward Operating Base Bostick believed that Tucker should cancel every project outright until the violence stopped.

---

[65] Governor Nuristani's immediate replacement was Hazrat Din Noor, who died in a car crash in September 2008. Badr followed Noor in the post.

Tucker pushed back against that notion; he remained convinced that the projects could be used as important bargaining chips. He and Pecha did, however, cancel some projects, and for good reason. The contractors on the Bar Mandigal secondary-road project, for example, were reportedly working for the Taliban; they also rubbed Tucker the wrong way, and besides that, they hadn't done any work. Their total fee would have been $407,197, of which $50,000 had already been paid out. Project canceled. Another contractor had been hired to build a pipe system in Chapo — north of Urmul and up the road toward Barg-e-Matal — to help irrigate the fields there. He had collected $17,000 out of $27,552, but Tucker never saw or heard from him. Canceled. Same problem with the contractor in charge of the pipe project in Sudgul: $11,000 already paid out of $27,552, but no contact with Tucker. Canceled. A micro-hydroelectric plant in Sudgul: $35,000 paid out on a $67,560 contract. Canceled.

Many projects were far enough away, and in areas where security was sufficiently sketchy, that Tucker simply had no direct knowledge of whether or not they were real. He hired a local man with a video camera to drive out to the Marwai secondary road — $118,692.24 paid, in full, for its construction — and document its existence. The man did that and was paid for his time, though Tucker never felt 100 percent sure that the video wasn't of some other, already existing road.

The Americans had spent $19,000 on refurbishing the Kamdesh boys' school, that money having been used to build chairs and desks for the students and to repair the building itself. But then one day Tucker heard that the Taliban had taken over the school and raised their signature white flag over it. So he canceled payment on the remaining $6,000 owed to Mohammed, the contractor.

"We're paying for this school, and you're letting the bad guys live there," he scolded Mohammed.

"We can't control them," the contractor protested. "They have guns! What can we do?"

"Okay," Tucker said. "We'll come in with *our* guns."

"Oh, no," a shocked Mohammed replied, "we don't want you coming into our village with all your guns."

The next time Tucker checked, the flag had been removed. The shura tried to make a big deal out of this, but Tucker wasn't buying it; it wasn't as if the Taliban had abandoned Kamdesh, after all. He imagined the head of the shura telling the Taliban, "The Americans are mad that your flag is up, and they want to cancel the project. Take it down so we can continue to get paid, and we'll give you a slice of the pie."

The Kamdesh girls' school was a whole other box of frustrations. Out of a $25,200 commitment by the United States, $9,200 had already been paid, but Tucker wasn't sure that any girls in the region even *went* to school, given how dedicated the entire female population of Nuristan was to manual labor. The lieutenant sent his quality-control engineer, a local Afghan, to visit the project after receiving reports that the Taliban had blown up the building. The Afghan confirmed that there was a large hole in the roof. "Why are we repairing this if they're never going to use it?" Tucker asked. Project canceled.

Besides canceling nine projects, Tucker also saw five completed while he was in charge. Thirteen others could charitably be considered, well, continual works-in-progress. A total of $1,233,159.66 had been paid out to contractors by the end of Tucker's tour, but there was also a big sum— $1,093,835.40—left unpaid, cash allocated but not disbursed for terminated projects. This annoyed a lot of contractors and villagers. Tucker knew that with American money no longer coming in, some of them would have little incentive to care whether or not the American soldiers were safe. Even worse, some would find work with the insurgency. Tucker tried to leave on good terms with everyone, but he walked away from some of these Nuristanis thinking that things in the valley would almost surely get worse before they got better.

The litter of puppies Cali had birthed in the summer of 2008 had matured into a pack of aggressive beasts, and the antipathy between them and the Nuristanis had grown apace. The dogs provided the U.S. troops with companionship and boosted their morale, as well as offering an added measure of security, but they regularly terrified the locals, barked at Nuristani contractors and security guards, and clamped their jaws around the necks of goats and sheep. Blackfoot Troop's "pets" also attracted other feral curs from the area.

Gulzaman, the head Afghan Security Guard at Observation Post Fritsche, had a house in Kamdesh, but he would often bring his oldest son, Hasanyullah, with him to stay at the observation post. Sometimes he would even entrust Hasanyullah, who was around eight, to the care of Lieutenant Chris Safulko and his troops while he went off on some errand or other. The kid would come to Safulko's hooch, sit on his cot, and browse through American magazines. His presence in itself showed that Gulzaman had a level of trust in the Americans that was not insignificant at this precarious time in the valley.

And then, for some reason, Cali started snarling at the boy.

It started off modestly: a growl here and there, a baring of teeth. But then it quickly devolved into outright hostility toward the boy, who began cowering in Cali's presence. Sergeant First Class Dominic Curry talked it over with Staff Sergeant Ian Boone, and the two of them shared their conclusions with Safulko: they couldn't have this anymore. Cali was causing a huge disruption in an important relationship. And the problem wasn't only with Hasanyullah; every day required the Americans to do some sort of damage control after Cali and another snarling pooch named Willie Pete growled and barked at one or another of the day laborers on the observation post. The Nuristanis were not of the "man's best friend" school, throwing rocks at and even kicking the dogs, and the dynamic was becoming increasingly tense.

Safulko agreed that they couldn't allow Cali to attack and bite Hasanyullah before they acted. So soon after their discussion, Boone approached Willie Pete, who was gnawing on a goat bone he had found in the trash, and shot him in the head. Then another soldier walked over to Cali, who was at the landing zone. *Bang,* she was killed, too.

Many of the troops were upset, but as far as Safulko was concerned, he hadn't had any choice in the matter. It would be great if we could all spend our days hanging out, cooking steaks, and playing with dogs, he thought, but we're soldiers in Afghanistan, we're not on a fucking camping trip.

In March, the enemy mortars returned. Tucker, working out the math based on time of flight and analyses of craters freshly formed at Combat Outpost Keating, developed a general idea of where the enemy was likely firing from: Lower Kamdesh. Several days were spent hunting for the tube, with troops sitting on the Northface and waiting for the mortars to fly so they could try to pinpoint the exact location for counterfire. But the mortars never came.

After Mazzocchi returned from leave in March, he and Red Platoon moved up to Observation Post Fritsche, where he sent word to the Kamdesh elders: Talk to us. But they wouldn't accept the invitation, so Mazzocchi asked Pecha if he could threaten the shura with a warning along the lines of, If you don't come here and talk to us, we're eventually going to find the enemy mortar tube and blast it away, and if anyone from Kamdesh gets hurt, the blood will be on your hands. Do it, Pecha said. So Mazzocchi conveyed that message to a Kamdeshi whom the troops referred to as "Skinny" Gul Mohammed, one of whose sons was suspected of being an insurgent. The Kamdesh elders never turned over the mortar tube, but neither did Blackfoot Troop ever receive fire from it again.

Mazzocchi deemed this a great victory—and one accomplished, moreover, by means of words, not weapons. Then, a week later, enemy mortars started hitting Camp Lowell. The insurgents had just moved the tube down the road.

By this point, Pecha had become convinced that the Hundred-Man Shura was impotent and perhaps even a bit corrupt. Adding to the Americans' general unease was the fact that the new ANA troops who'd arrived in February were green and weak; indeed, the whole Afghan battalion, spread out across Nuristan and Kunar Provinces, seemed incompetent. Intensely frustrated by their limited manpower, Pecha and his lieutenants brainstormed ways to secure the area: Mazzocchi increased the number of joint patrols with the ANA from Observation Post Fritsche, while Pecha worked more closely with the Afghan National Police, in whom he had more faith than he did in the ANA. Neither effort sufficed, however, and attacks on the camp continued. Pecha had been hoping that there might be an influx of U.S. soldiers to Kamdesh as part of President Obama's new troop surge, but no additional forces were forthcoming.

Pecha then gathered his platoon leaders and sergeants and proposed that they set up a new, permanent observation post on the Northface, to be named after Captain Rob Yllescas. They would put eight to ten U.S. troops there, along with four or five ANA soldiers. It would make life safer for all of them, Pecha was convinced. His commanders were not so sure. Lieutenant Colonel Markert had concerns about, first, the addition of yet another target for the enemy, and second, the squadron's ability to haul up enough supplies to create a new OP Yllescas. The idea was officially shot down when Colonel Spiszer visited Camp Keating: Pecha just didn't have enough troop strength to man another observation post, he said. Spiszer also knew that back in Colorado, their replacements were already making plans to close down the base in any event.

From the moment the officers of Blackfoot Troop first heard about the attack at Wanat, in which a huge group of insurgents had surprised and overwhelmed a much smaller American force, they'd sworn they would do everything they could to avoid suffering the same fate — a vow that was repeated at most of the more modest outposts scattered throughout the region. But then, on May 1, Markert called Pecha with some bad news: it had happened again.

Early that morning, a force of up to one hundred insurgents had surrounded, attacked, and overrun nearby Combat Outpost Bari Alai,[66] a recently established Afghan National Army camp in Markert's area of operations, Kunar Province. Three American troops, two coalition troops, four ANA soldiers, and an Afghan interpreter had been killed. Markert, worried that the enemy might try to capitalize on this event by launching another overwhelming attack on a different remote outpost, recommended that Pecha limit not only the number of patrols outside the wire at both Keating and Fritsche but also the distance those patrols were allowed to range from their home base. In response, Pecha staggered his patrols so that there would never be one from Camp Keating out at the same time as one from Observation Post Fritsche. He immediately ordered more troops to stand guard, relying on a pattern-analysis wheel that Victorino had created to provide some predictive guidance about when attacks were most likely to occur. (Thursday, it seemed, was the next-most-volatile day after Saturday.)

What happened at Bari Alai was alarming enough in and of itself, but soon the Americans also began to wonder if there might not be something more sinister to the story — specifically, complicity on the part of Afghan soldiers. The account of the actual attack was all too familiar, beginning with dozens of insurgents staging a well-coordinated assault on the outpost. An RPG killed Staff Sergeant William Vile, an ANA

---

[66] The name was taken from the Pashto word *baryalay,* meaning "successful."

trainer. (The ANA trainers at Bari Alai were members of the U.S. Army, the Michigan National Guard, and the Latvian Army.) The other two Americans killed at the camp[67] were hit by another well-placed RPG that breached the wall and caused a secondary explosion, destroying a bunker; one of the two men was also shot at close range. Two soldiers from Latvia were killed as well, and a third Latvian was severely wounded, while a fourth experienced severe psychological trauma.

But what was different and confusing about this particular incident was that the Taliban, in an unusual move, took prisoner eleven ANA soldiers and a second interpreter. A dozen Afghans—that was a lot of POWs for this war. It seemed suspicious to the Americans. And there were other puzzling aspects, too, starting with the fact that Combat Outpost Bari Alai sat on the top of a mountain and therefore wasn't easy to overrun. Some U.S. officers speculated that there might have been some collusion—that perhaps the "captured" Afghan troops had aided the insurgents. This was a new ANA platoon, and one of the three U.S. soldiers killed that day, James Pirtle, had expressed concern about the Afghan soldiers to his parents. They were insubordinate, he said; they sneaked off the base at night and didn't stay at their guard posts. Other reports indicated that when their superior officers tried to push them to do their jobs, the ANA troops pushed back.

In the wake of the attack, Markert was eager to learn the truth. He didn't expect the same professionalism from Afghan troops that he demanded from his own men and women, but this latest ANA battalion was without question inferior to its predecessors. Days later, a complex rescue mission dubbed Operation King's Ransom, involving more than two thousand troops, was launched into and around the Hel Gal Valley. Coalition forces broadcast a radio message demanding the release of the ANA hostages, who were ultimately freed. At first, the soldiers appeared to be in suspiciously good condition, but then closer examination by physician assistants and medics revealed some light wounds. Only after six

---

[67] Sergeant James Pirtle of Colorado Springs, Colorado, and Specialist Ryan King of Dallas, Georgia, both of whom had spent some time at Observation Post Fritsche earlier in their deployment. William Vile was from Philadelphia; he had served in the Korangal with 1-32 Infantry a couple of years before. The Latvians killed were Sergeant Voldemārs Anševics and Private First Class Andrejs Merkuševs. They were the second and third Latvian troops to die in Afghanistan during this war.

days of interrogation were the ANA troops finally returned to their brigade. Spiszer and Markert never found sufficient evidence that the POWs had been part of a conspiracy. The insurgents had merely gotten some breaks, the investigation indicated, and taken a lucky shot that blew up a bunker and ignited a fire.

A couple more breaks had been given to them by Afghan security forces. An eight-man Afghan National Police post protecting one of the approaches to Bari Alai was abandoned just a few days prior to the attack. There was also supposed to be a full platoon of twenty-eight ANA troops at the Bari Alai outpost, but the company commander had repositioned a dozen of his soldiers at the bottom of the mountain the night before the raid, in preparation for a troop swap. He'd done it because it would make things easier for him and his men.

As Markert often said, "If you're doing something in war because it's easier, you're probably doing the wrong thing."

Had the eleven Afghan troops who were captured surrendered too quickly? In all likelihood, Markert felt, the answer was yes—these were not good soldiers. Indeed, the members of this new battalion of ANA troops in Nuristan and Kunar were quickly becoming notorious. But their actions in this case were evidence of incompetence, not of treachery.

This was of little comfort.

In late May 2009, Colonel George and Lieutenant Colonel Brown of 3-61 Cav were preparing to ship out to Forward Operating Base Fenty at Jalalabad and Forward Operating Base Bostick at Naray, respectively. From those locations, they hoped to shut down Combat Outpost Keating, Observation Post Fritsche, and Camp Lowell in Nuristan Province, as well as Observation Posts Mace and Hatchet in Kunar Province. The troops from these outposts would be sent to other areas of the country that, in George's view, would better support the overall campaign. Forward Operating Base Bostick would thereby become the northernmost U.S. base in northeastern Afghanistan.

Their visit to Nuristan and Kunar the previous December had reinforced the commanders' resolve to pull out of the region. George and Brown believed that Blackfoot Troop had, for the most part, lost its connection to the local population. The officers of 6-4 Cav seemed to them to have little direct knowledge of most of the projects they'd been funding, nor did they have the freedom of maneuver to assess those projects. "In short," Brown wrote to Kolenda after his visit, "6-4 did not appear to be conducting COIN at all."[68] (This was not, of course, how Pecha and his lieutenants saw things.)

The colonel whom Randy George would be replacing, Spiszer, had described Blackfoot Troop as the "cork in the bottle," the roadblock that prevented HIG or the Taliban from traveling from Pakistan through Nuristan to the Waygal and Pech Valleys and possibly beyond. But Brown just didn't see the enemy that way. The insurgents weren't lined up on some Maginot Line, he felt certain; warfare in Afghanistan was much more complex than that. The phrase "cork in the bottle" assumed that the enemy had only one route in or out, whereas evidence suggested that many insurgents were simply walking *around* the few isolated American outposts in the area. When George arrived at Forward Operating Base Fenty, he was pleasantly surprised to find Spiszer amenable to his plan to close the bases. Getting supplies up to Nuristan was difficult, Spiszer confided, and imposed an increasing burden on helicopter and other assets — resources that could be better used elsewhere. The troops up there didn't seem to be getting anywhere with the locals anyway, and critically, there had been no progress made on securing and building up the road. It was all too deadly to resupply troops on foot, and too wasteful by air. Spiszer was on board. Lieutenant Colonel Markert's staff had in fact already twice proposed closing Combat Outpost Keating, but both times the determination had been made — with input from the brigade level — that Blackfoot Troop wouldn't be able to commandeer the eighty Chinook trips it would take to remove all the soldiers and gear. On their second try, the 6-4 Cav planners were told that their troops could either go home on time or close Combat Outpost Keating, but not both: there weren't enough aircraft in the area.

Spiszer's brigade had already learned some hard lessons about how to close down a base. Combat Outpost Lybert had been built only in 2006, near the Pakistan border, but it didn't have a particularly good view of the mountain pass that it had been set up to watch over. The troops were needed elsewhere, and the local Afghan Border Police battalion had no interest in assuming control of COP Lybert, so Spiszer ordered that it be

---

[68] COIN was Army shorthand for "counterinsurgency."

shut down. Before the troops could move out, however, word of their pending exit spread throughout the nearby villages. Half of the Afghan Security Guards who worked at the camp up and quit. The locals were suddenly far more eager to accommodate the enemy fighters—letting them use their homes, for example—to launch attacks on the camp. After all, in a few weeks, the Americans wouldn't be there any longer, but the insurgents surely would. Combat Outpost Lybert went from being tranquil to being a target. One of the enemy bullets killed Private Second Class Michael Murdock, twenty-two years old and from Chocowinity, North Carolina. When the U.S. troops at last pulled out of Camp Lybert, the insurgents claimed to have driven them out. It wasn't true, but propaganda needn't be. Pat Lybert's mom saw YouTube videos of insurgents victoriously parading through the camp named after her late son, and it ripped her apart inside.

Spiszer told the incoming commander of Regional Command East, Major General Curtis Scaparrotti, as well as the ISAF commander, that he believed George's proposal to shut down Keating and Lowell was a good one. He thought the generals seemed receptive to the idea.

CHAPTER 25

Pericles in Kamdesh

Under cover of complete darkness, the men of 3-61 Black Knight Troop's 1st Platoon — led by Lieutenant Andrew "Bundy" Bundermann — arrived at Camp Keating. Black Knight Troop would be the last one stationed at the outpost.

By May 2009, choppers were refusing to venture out to Combat Outpost Keating in anything but the blackest night. It was a surreal experience for these soldiers who were new to the region to be flown from Forward Operating Base Bostick over the mountains and deep into the valleys. The pilots could just see the faint outlines of peaks, but everything else was merely ink. And then suddenly they were landing, and Bundermann could hear the rushing rapids of the Landay-Sin.

Soldiers from Blackfoot Troop were excited to greet the new arrivals. The handoff meant they could go home.

Bundermann and the others were ushered across the bridge and into the outpost. Massive, jagged silhouettes stretching up to the sky surrounded them. This is bizarre, the lieutenant thought. At daybreak, Safulko briefed him and showed him around the place. Bundermann wasn't happy about the location, about its complete and utter vulnerability. The others came in here to set up this PRT and then left, he thought, and now we're stuck holding this bag of shit.

In the barracks that morning, Safulko kept looking at one of the new guys, 3-61 Cav Sergeant Josh Kirk. He knew him from somewhere. Safulko racked his brain trying to figure out where their paths might have crossed.

"Have I met you before?" Kirk asked him.

"I was thinking the exact same thing," Safulko said, somewhat relieved. "Were you in a different unit before this one?"

It turned out that Kirk had been Captain Nathan Springer's gunner in 1-91 Cav. In 2007, after Tom Bostick was killed, when 1-91 Cav was still beating back that ambush, he and Springer were stuck on a road near Bazgal and couldn't make it to Saret Koleh; they could only listen to it all unfold on the radio. Now, Safulko and Kirk realized that at the end of Kirk's last deployment, as 6-4 was transferring into Afghanistan, he had helped guide Safulko and his men around Checkpoint Delta at the Pakistan border. Kirk was back in Afghanistan pretty quickly, Safulko noted: he'd been entitled under Army "stabilization" rules to have twelve months at home. He had returned to Afghanistan before he was required to. "I wasn't going to let my soldiers come here without me," Kirk, a team leader, explained.

Kirk's return to Nuristan made Safulko think, later, of something said by the ancient Athenian general Pericles, in his funeral oration for the war dead:

> Usually decision is the fruit of ignorance, hesitation of reflection. But the palm of courage will surely be adjudged most justly to those, who best know the difference between hardship and pleasure and yet are never tempted to shrink from danger.[69]

Sometimes courage is rooted in ignorance, as when men who don't know what they're about to face rise to the occasion. Joshua Kirk had ample knowledge about how dangerous it was in Nuristan, and yet he had hurried back. The palm of courage.

The arrival of their replacements made the soldiers of Blackfoot Troop even more eager to get home. Sergeant Shane Scherer was chief among them; he was scheduled to get married in about a month.

Dusk came earlier in the valley than in places outside the mountains' muscular shadows. Scherer and some others were milling about outside

---

[69] *The History of the Peloponnesian War,* by Thucydides, written in 431 B.C.E., translated by Richard Crawley. The quote is from book 2, chapter 40.

the communications shack, waiting for Specialist James Witherington to finish his phone call home so they, too, could alert their loved ones to their pending return. Scherer had just finished working out at the camp gym and was in a T-shirt and shorts, casually holding his rifle. He was a big, athletic guy who'd joined the Army two years before, sick of his suit-and-tie job as a parking supervisor for the San Diego convention center.

Specialist Andrew Miller hopped in the Humvee right near them for guard duty. Miller was one of the shorter men at the outpost; the other guys called him Combat Wombat. Dinner had just concluded, and Safulko walked by. He spotted Scherer on a bench, patiently awaiting his turn to use the phone so he could call his fiancée, who was in Texas setting up their apartment.

"Those of you leaving soon, I'd lay low," Safulko said to the group waiting for the phone.

"I'm only going to be out here a minute," Scherer replied. "I'm just calling home."

Scherer understood Safulko's concern. His first reaction upon his arrival at Camp Keating had been disbelief. He, too, had been incredulous that the Army could have established a base at the bottom of a ravine. He'd also felt a nagging worry that there weren't nearly enough troops there, that if a serious enough assault was ever mounted against Camp Keating, the troops wouldn't be able to fend off the enemy before air support arrived. Scherer had asked about it and was told that the guys from the 10th Mountain Division had been there before them, and nothing bad had happened to *them*. The way the military was set up, Scherer figured, once you got an answer, you weren't supposed to keep pushing. And after a while, he got used to being in the fishbowl.

Safulko turned to head back to the barracks. He'd taken three steps when he heard an explosion and the harsh, shredding sound of a B10 recoilless rifle round tearing through Miller's Humvee.

The B10 is an immense piece of machinery, an obsolete Soviet-era weapon usually carried on the back of a truck. The ordnance from a B10 was designed to destroy tanks; in this case, it sliced through Miller's Humvee like a cold knife through warm butter, just missing his legs, exploding on the ground near the men who were waiting for the phone, spraying molten copper everywhere. Everyone nearby was knocked down, and a number of troops were hit by the shrapnel—from Miller in the turret of the Humvee to Safulko on the ground to Witherington in the comms shed — but no one was hurt more seriously than Scherer, in the back of whose head a hunk of that hot copper landed and stuck, penetrating into his brain right behind his right ear. His right arm was nearly severed.

The physician assistant for the incoming 3-61 Cav, Captain Chris Cordova, was in the aid station, chatting with one of his medics, Staff Sergeant Shane Courville, and the outgoing docs, Lieutenant Colonel Mark Burnett (who had replaced Brewer some months before) and George Shreffler. Cordova and Courville had been at the outpost for scarcely half a day. The explosion was followed by PKM machine-gun fire. Don Couch and First Sergeant Howard Johnson carried Scherer into the aid station; Couch was gripping tightly above Scherer's arm to try to stanch the bleeding. Scherer was conscious and kept trying to curl up into the fetal position.

Cordova examined the sergeant's head wound first. He had an inch-deep hole in the back of his skull.

"What happened to me?" Scherer said. "My head fucking hurts."

After examining all of Scherer's other injuries, Cordova decided he needed to focus on stopping the bleeding from his head. Wounds in other parts of the body can be treated with pressure and tourniquets, but — as Cordova knew — that can't be done with vessels right outside the brain. The physician assistant grabbed some combat gauze, put it over the hole, and prayed to God the clotting agent would make the bleeding stop. Thankfully, it did.

Cordova now needed to check Scherer's neurological status. The pupil in his right eye was dilated; pressure from inside his skull was building up and preventing the eye from functioning properly. His breathing was fast and shallow. He had significant brain trauma and, to judge from the fact that the muscles in his arms were locking up, significant neurological damage as well.

Cordova was told that the medevac was going to take at least forty-five minutes to get to them.

This is going to be a long year, he thought.

BOOK THREE

Enemy in the Wire: The End of Combat Outpost Keating

ROLL CALL

International Security Assistance Force (ISAF)
May–October 2009

At International Security Assistance Force (ISAF) Headquarters, Kabul:
General Stanley McChrystal, Commander, ISAF
General David McKiernan, Commander, ISAF

At Forward Operating Base Fenty, Jalalabad Airfield, Nangarhar Province:
Colonel Randy George, Task Force Mountain Warrior/4th Brigade
    Combat Team (BCT), 4th Infantry Division

At Forward Operating Base Bostick, Kunar Province:
Lieutenant Colonel Brad Brown, Squadron Commander, 3-61 Cavalry
    Squadron ("3-61 Cav"), 4th BCT, 4th Infantry Division

At Combat Outpost Keating and Observation Post Fritsche, Nuristan Province:
Black Knight Troop, 3-61 Cav, 4th BCT, 4th Infantry Division
    Captain Melvin Porter, outgoing Commander
    Captain Stoney Portis, incoming Commander
    Lieutenant Robert Hull, Executive Officer
    First Sergeant Ronald Burton
    Captain Chris Cordova, outpost medical officer
    Sergeant Vernon Martin, chief mechanic

Red Platoon
Lieutenant Andrew Bundermann, Platoon Leader
    Sergeant Justin Gallegos, Team Leader

Sergeant Josh Hardt, Team Leader
Sergeant Josh Kirk, Team Leader
Sergeant Brad Larson, Team Leader
Staff Sergeant Clint Romesha, Senior Scout
Specialist Stephan Mace, scout
Specialist Zach Koppes, scout
Specialist Tom Rasmussen, scout
Private First Class Chris Jones, scout

White Platoon
Lieutenant Jordan Bellamy, Platoon Leader
Specialist Keith Stickney, mortarman

Blue Platoon, "The Bastards"
Lieutenant Ben Salentine, Platoon Leader
Sergeant First Class Jonathan Hill
Staff Sergeant Kirk Birchfield
Sergeant John Francis, Team Leader
Sergeant Eric Harder, Team Leader
Specialist Ty Carter, scout
Specialist Ed Faulkner, Jr., scout
Specialist Chris Griffin, scout
Specialist Michael Scusa, scout

Mortar Section
Sergeant First Class John Stephen Breeding, Jr.
Specialist Dan Rodriguez, mortarman
Private First Class Kevin Thomson, mortarman

Latvian Trainers
First Sergeant Janis Lakis
Corporal Martins Dabolins

CHAPTER 26

The General's Competing Considerations

The Greek philosopher Heraclitus once wrote, "No man ever steps in the same river twice, for it is not the same river, and he is not the same man."

Sergeant Joshua Kirk was stepping again into Nuristan, and it was clear that neither the U.S. Army nor the local populace was the same. Kirk—strapping and strong, with a booming voice and an intimidating self-confidence—had been in Nuristan from 2007 through 2008, when 1-91 Cav was making progress with the locals, particularly in Kamdesh District. Stationed in the area of operations once again in 2009, he wrote to friends from his earlier deployment that this was a different world. The security situation had deteriorated significantly since 2007, and the leaders of Bravo Troop from 3-61 Cav—also called Black Knight Troop—did almost no counterinsurgency work, he said. They held only a few shuras, and except for local security patrols, the troops seldom strayed outside the wire. Maybe once or twice a week, the entire troop would stay awake all night to manage the resupply flights from Forward Operating Base Bostick, with one platoon securing the Camp Keating landing zone and the other standing guard and grabbing the supplies. (The third platoon, Blue Platoon—nicknamed the Bastards—was initially up at Observation Post Fritsche.) Occasionally, a platoon would head into the local hamlet of Urmul or go out on a short patrol around OP Fritsche, but the commander of Combat Outpost Keating, Captain Melvin Porter, told his men that there weren't enough of them to safely explore the surrounding area, so patrols generally inspected only histori-cal ambush points. The thirty-seven-year-old Porter struck many of the departing leaders of 6-4 Cav's Blackfoot Troop as being burnt out. He'd already done two tours in Iraq and had seen a fair share of action and death while there. Even back in the States, Porter had seemed spent, at least to his immediate chain of command and those who served under him. Before the unit deployed to Afghanistan, as his lieutenants were running field exercises to prepare for missions, Porter had appeared irri-tated when they expressed a desire for him to lead them, to give them orders. The three platoon leaders—Lieutenant Andrew Bundermann, twenty-four, of Red Platoon, Lieutenant Jordan Bellamy, twenty-five, of White Platoon, and Lieutenant Ben Salentine, twenty-seven, of Blue Platoon—were so concerned about Porter's ability to command that they resolved to stick together and confide any worries they might have to one another. If Porter wouldn't lead the men of 3-61 Cav, then, if push came to shove, one—or all—of them would.

Lieutenant Colonel Brad Brown was also concerned. That Porter didn't seem to get along with his lieutenants—not an uncommon complaint—didn't bother him; the issue was that the captain just didn't appear to be up for another tour as a commander in a war zone. Porter had been consid-ered a good commander in Iraq, but to Brown he now seemed tired. But when Brown brought up the subject with his boss, Colonel Randy George, they realized they didn't have a lot of options: they were already short-staffed when it came to troop commanders, and replacing an even weaker captain in their battalion was a higher priority. There were two captains who could have replaced Porter, but one had a foot injury and was physi-cally limited, while the other was not confident in his tactical ability to take over the position. Brown and George decided that they would send Porter to Afghanistan to command Combat Outpost Keating, and then replace him after ninety days with an up-and-comer named Stoney Portis. Porter had had a good track record in Iraq; Brown knew he was exhausted—they were all exhausted—but he had faith that the captain could keep it together for three months.

Brown had a number of discussions with Porter himself about this plan. This wasn't unusual; company-level commands were routinely changed during deployments, particularly once they passed the two-year mark in that demanding job. Porter had mixed feelings—he was reluctant to give up command, even though he was worn out and ready to move on to another challenge. But orders were orders—though these were ones that Brown would ultimately regret having given.

There was no question that the enemy had been growing more effective: 2008 was the most dangerous year in Afghanistan since the war began, with the frequency of attacks up by as much as 60 percent in some areas. Confronted by this threat, ISAF commander General David McKiernan hadn't demonstrated either the nimbleness or the creativity they needed, in the view of Defense Secretary Robert Gates, chairman of the Joint Chiefs of Staff Admiral Mike Mullen, and Central Command's General David Petraeus.

As Gates saw it, if the U.S. government was going to surge forces in Afghanistan and ask more young men and women to put their lives on the line, the least he could do was put the very best leadership in charge. And with McKiernan continuing as ISAF commander, Gates didn't feel he could look a soldier's anxious mother in the eye and tell her he'd done just that. The best men he had, Gates thought, were Lieutenant General Stanley McChrystal and Major General David Rodriguez, who were both now at the Pentagon after having served abroad.

While McKiernan, Gates thought, was old-school Army, a throwback to the first Gulf War, McChrystal was a more innovative, progressive "New Army" type. Like Petraeus, he was regarded as a "thinking man's soldier," someone who had the flexibility to use all the tools at his disposal, including development and diplomacy. The need for such efforts went well beyond the borders of Afghanistan: media and political dynamics were critical in a long war, as were strong relationships with policy makers in Washington, D.C.

On May 6, 2009, Gates arrived in Afghanistan. He had many public tasks to accomplish, among them visiting surgical facilities on the front lines in Helmand Province and hearing firsthand from troops about the impact of the mine-resistant, ambush-protected vehicles he'd sent there to help curtail American deaths and injuries caused by IEDs.

Gates also had one private mission: to ask General McKiernan to retire early. But McKiernan wouldn't do it. "You're going to have to fire me," he said. So Gates did.

On May 11, back at the Pentagon, Gates spoke at a hurriedly unorganized press conference, talking about President Obama's decision to draw down the war in Iraq and instead focus on Afghanistan, where, the defense secretary declared, "we must do better." Gates insisted that McKiernan had done nothing wrong; it was just that "a fresh approach, a fresh look in the context of the new strategy, probably was in our best interest." Added Mullen, "I just didn't think that we could wait until 2010"— when McKiernan's rotation was scheduled to end—to make the change. Gates said he would recommend to President Obama that McKiernan be replaced by McChrystal, the former commander of Joint Special Operations Command and currently serving as director of the Joint Staff—the three-star general who assists the chairman of the Joint Chiefs of Staff.

In addition to having supervised some highly successful commando special operations in Iraq—including the capture of Saddam Hussein and the killing of Abu Musab al-Zarqawi, the leader of Al Qaeda in Iraq— McChrystal was considered by some of his colleagues to be a shrewd and canny political operator. Some of his contemporaries thought he was manipulative, and some officers from conventional forces viewed him as being typical of the "unaccountable" Special Forces ilk, not used to playing nice with other branches of the military, accustomed solely to getting his own way. Others saw him as brilliant. The president deferred to Gates.

President Obama had already ordered twenty-one thousand more troops to Afghanistan, fulfilling a campaign promise and bringing the total number of U.S. troops in that country to sixty-eight thousand. On June 2, during his Senate confirmation hearings, McChrystal suggested in his prepared remarks that President Obama might need to send even more. He was then asked by Republican senator Lindsey Graham of South Carolina if he would feel "constrained at all" about asking for even more troops if he thought them necessary.

"Sir, I'm not on the job yet, so I—you know, I'm speculating on that," McChrystal said. "Yesterday, in a meeting, Admiral Mullen said that if I was confirmed to ask for what I need—almost quote, unquote. He looked me in the eye said that. So, I believe that if I have a requirement, I can look Mullen in the eye and tell him that's what I need."

"Do you think that's true of the administration also?" Graham inquired.

"Sir, I don't know," McChrystal replied. At the White House, the general's comments were perceived as an announcement to the world that he didn't know whether the president would support him if he needed more troops—and even a suggestion that the commander in chief might not want him to speak candidly about what he thought was necessary to succeed in Afghanistan. Senior White House officials believed that McChrystal—and, they assumed, the Pentagon—was trying to roll them, putting the president in an untenable situation wherein he would have no defensible way to refuse the military when it publicly requested more troops.

McChrystal would later say that his remarks were not aimed at the White House in any way, that he had intended merely to convey that he was trying to stay in his own lane and answer only to his chain of command—in this case, Gates and Mullen.

The broader view from the Pentagon was more complex. From the beginning, the generals thought, President Bush had not provided sufficient troops to do the job effectively in Afghanistan. As a result, Americans were dying, and the mission wasn't succeeding. As to the new president, the generals had been infuriated by a series of leaks, seemingly coming from Vice President Biden's office since March 2009, suggesting that the United States should actually start *withdrawing* troops from Afghanistan, abandoning the counterinsurgency program and pursuing a strategy that was being called CT-plus—consisting of a smaller counterterrorism force focused primarily on taking out bad guys, with some training of Afghan security forces but otherwise not much of an emphasis on nation building. Right or wrong, the generals considered the proposals that were being fed to reporters ill informed and counterproductive. In particular, this notion that their troops could conduct counterterrorist strikes against the enemy without enough troops on the ground to win the support of the Afghan people, and thus help gather intelligence, stirred deep ire. So, yes, the generals were willing to put a little pressure on the suits in D.C.

Such behavior was predictable to senior officials inside the White House—it was common to the Pentagon/White House dynamic—but that didn't mean they were happy about it. President Obama's national security adviser, James Jones, called Gates to make it clear that the generals ought to back off. Jones, a retired Marine Corps general, had been brought in to the administration in part to serve as a liaison between the White House and the Pentagon. Gates assured him that the generals weren't trying to jam the president in any way; they were just being candid, he said.

On June 8, Pentagon spokesman Geoff Morrell announced that Secretary Gates had asked McChrystal, should he be confirmed (as he indeed would be, on June 10), to "go over to Afghanistan to undertake a sixty-day review of the situation on the ground there," and to report on "what changes in the strategy should be made, and particularly from a personnel standpoint, from a manpower standpoint."

This review, too, became something of a controversy. McChrystal saw himself as approaching the task modestly. He would later insist that he hadn't gone into Afghanistan thinking that more troops were needed; he said he was in fact initially inclined to believe that what was necessary was a new strategy and more talented officers, not more bodies. He attempted deference: to try to understand his brief, he scrutinized the president's campaign pledges and the remarks he had made upon sending in the new surge of troops. He knew there was concern in the White House over the direction of U.S. policy in Afghanistan, but he didn't think there was absolute clarity as to the president's concerns versus his goals.

In Kabul, on June 15, McChrystal was interviewed by the *Washington Post*'s Greg Jaffe, and he described in detail the broad assessment of the war that he was about to begin, suggesting that he wanted to focus troops on Afghan population centers and pull them from more remote areas such as the Korangal Valley. The general's informal sixty-day survey was rapidly morphing into something more significant — and more public. Besides doing boots-on-the-ground research, McChrystal invited a number of think-tank folks, such as the conservative Fred Kagan, one of Petraeus's advisers on the Iraq surge, to offer him advice; Kagan began publicly pushing for additional troops to be sent to Afghanistan.

The McChrystal report was much anticipated and, when it was completed, made a momentous impression — which came as something of a surprise to the general himself, he would later say. A number of other assessments had already been done — by Central Command, by the Joint Chiefs of Staff, and by the White House — and McChrystal's had started out as an informal evaluation of the situation. McChrystal didn't think it was the *Washington Post* story or even the Pentagon versus White House angle that created the hype so much as it was the way events just happened to play out: as he arrived in Kabul, the United States' position in the war was deteriorating rapidly, so his report came to be seen as something of an emergency prescription for the illness.

Storm clouds began forming when Jaffe's colleague Bob Woodward, traveling with Jones in Afghanistan, reported on the front page of their newspaper that a conflict was brewing over troop levels, with the Pentagon pushing for more and the White House pushing back. An issue that President Obama thought he had temporarily put to rest with twenty-one thousand new troops and a completed assessment—finished weeks earlier by a team that included one of America's foremost experts on Al Qaeda—now seemed anything but settled. From the White House's point of view, McChrystal had managed to place himself in a position where he would be telling the president what he needed, and the world would see how this new, untested president would respond. While the sniping and suspicions and rhetorical missives fired within the newsprint of the *Washington Post* might have seemed, to the men of 3-61 Cav, to be taking place in another dimension altogether, all of these machinations would have a tremendous impact on them.

In early 2009, as Colonel George and Lieutenant Colonel Brown prepared to deploy to Afghanistan, they refined their plan to close Camp Keating and the other small outposts. Brown was committed to counterinsurgency, which he viewed as a process of creating a series of security bubbles at the local level—connecting Afghans in hamlets and villages to their government through security and economic opportunity—and then expanding those individual bubbles until they merged with others. But the security bubbles at Combat Outposts Keating and Lowell were isolated, and they were not expanding. George and Brown were convinced, in fact, that the various security bubbles in Nuristan were never going to "spread" and link up—there just weren't enough forces to make that happen, and the mountainous land in between was too easy for the enemy to control. Most of the communities in Nuristan Province were separated from one another and from the provincial and national governments by chasms of instability and Taliban violence.

Brown believed there were areas in the region where counterinsurgency was working—from Naray north to Barikot, for example. With more troops—the ones from the remote outposts they wanted to close—they could link the Naray–Barikot security bubble to other security bubbles in the south of Kunar Province. His and George's realignment plan was all about this kind of focus: the idea was to stop spending scarce resources on things that weren't working and start reinforcing success.

Brown and George worried in particular about Combat Outpost Lowell, which they thought most vulnerable. Observation Post Mace, located near Gawardesh and manned by only twenty-four U.S. troops who shared space with a dubious crew of ANA soldiers, was next on their list of concerns. Combat Outpost Keating ranked third.

So they would pull out. But how? And when? George pushed his staff to think hard about what the enemy would do if the United States did pull out. What groundwork would the Americans have to lay beforehand? What would be the most appropriate time line for leaving? The team concluded that the withdrawal wouldn't greatly increase the overall flow of men and materials over the Pakistan border into Afghanistan, since the U.S. presence wasn't affecting that very much anyway. A withdrawal would have a moderate impact on the estimated two thousand residents of Kamdesh Village, some of whom—most likely those who had been working with the Americans—would relocate farther south to be closer to the remaining U.S. troops, at great expense to themselves. They anticipated there might be a slight increase in the number of attacks against Forward Operating Base Bostick and a nearby CIA camp.

The whole team was aware that from the highest general to the lowliest private, members of the military were extremely reluctant to see any base that troops had fought for, that men had died for, shut down. Indeed, to some it was tantamount to surrender, and all the more so when the base bore the name of one of their brothers: Ben Keating, Jacob Lowell, Ryan Fritsche. But the doctrine of counterinsurgency made it fairly clear to George, Brown, and their team that there was no longer any good reason for Americans to be at those bases. No need for more fallen heroes, more names to honor.

The team presented a preliminary proposal to their commanders in February 2009, at division headquarters at Fort Bragg. George, along with other aides, met with Major General Curtis Scaparrotti and Brigadier General William Mayville, Jr., and laid down the framework for their realignment plans. To many attendees, Scaparrotti seemed lukewarm, but Mayville—the deputy commanding general for operations—was wholly in favor.

They agreed that they would try to close Camp Keating by July 6 or 7, 2009. The exit—or exfil, in military lingo, short for "exfiltration"—would by necessity be by air: forty full helicopter loads over several weeks, rotated in and out, one after another, until everyone and everything was gone. Weapons, ammunition, batteries, fuel—these would go in the last six to ten loads.

Yet while Mayville continued to send George and his team positive feedback, as did others, the official go-ahead was never given. George could do nothing without the sign-off of the commanding general of ISAF. The firing of McKiernan and subsequent appointment of McChrystal would make getting that approval more complicated.

Sergeant First Class John Breeding, thirty-eight, from Amarillo, Texas, had been in the Army for twenty-one years and had witnessed terrible things in that time—all of them in the previous five years. In September 2004, he'd been in Ramadi, Iraq, for only three days when the Humvee he was in was blown up by an IED. Three pieces of shrapnel went through his calf, though luckily none of them hit bone. He was laid up for eight weeks, at the end of which, with his wounds bandaged up and gauze in the holes, he took his antibiotics and painkillers and went back to work. Then, in March 2005, during a clearance operation outside Ramadi, one of his company's scout trucks got hit by an IED that had been planted underground. All four troops on the truck were killed.[70] A soldier in Breeding's unit later found one of the victim's heads in a nearby pond.

You couldn't train for that kind of thing, and you couldn't know how you'd handle it until you lived it, Breeding believed. The more carnage he witnessed, the more he felt himself becoming numb to it all.

Breeding was the platoon sergeant for Black Knight Troop's mortar team, and like everyone else in the company, he had been flown to Combat Outpost Keating in darkest night. At first light the next morning, he opened the barracks door and couldn't believe what he was seeing: there was nothing but high ground surrounding the base. Being at the bottom of a fishbowl meant the guns would be less effective—instead of being able to reach a distance of 7,800 yards, they'd fire only up to about 5,500 yards. Whoever was in charge of putting the base here is the dumbest officer in the world, Breeding thought. And lo and behold, within ten minutes of his walking up to the mortar pit, the men of Black Knight Troop were engaged in their first enemy contact.

That was May 27. Throughout that summer, some weeks they'd been attacked once or twice, other weeks every day, and sometimes even twice

---

[70] Captain Sean Grimes, of Southfield, Michigan; Sergeant First Class Donald W. Eacho, of Black Creek, Wisconsin; Corporal Stephen M. McGowan, of Newark, Delaware; and Specialist Wade Michael Twyman, of Vista, California.

daily. To be sure, the attacks were all fairly minor ones: Breeding suspected that the enemy was probing, seeing how the Americans would react.

His team had a concrete bunker in the mortar pit with two bunk beds, and that was where they lived, a tight group that included Breeding, Private First Class Kevin Thomson, and Specialist Daniel Rodriguez. Breeding also had four more men and 120- and 60-millimeter mortars up the mountain at Observation Post Fritsche.

Breeding had served with Rodriguez in Iraq and considered him to be an outstanding soldier. He didn't know much about Thomson, just that he seemed like a nice kid from Nevada, a hard worker who hadn't had an easy life. A substantial six foot four, Thomson had been overweight when he first tried to enlist; the recruiter told him he had to lose a hundred pounds before the Army would take him. So that was what Thomson did, running and panting until he weighed just under two hundred pounds—determined to make something of himself, to prove himself to the ne'er-do-well father who had abandoned him when he was a child, a local policeman who'd impregnated three women in town virtually simultaneously.

Private First Class Kevin Thomson and Sergeant First Class John Breeding at the mortar pit. *(Photo courtesy of Debbie Routson)*

At fourteen, Kevin had tried to commit suicide by drinking carpet cleaner, which he thankfully vomited out in the kitchen sink. His suicidal tendencies were subsequently replaced by self-mutilation; he would cut himself, then lie to his mother about it, saying the carvings were scratches he'd gotten from some bushes. One night, he finally told her that he needed help. She took him to the hospital, where doctors diagnosed him with manic depression. He was prescribed Paxil, but he took himself off it when he turned eighteen and decided the Army offered him a better, disciplined path out of his misery.

He was calm, Thomson. Rodriguez always joked with him that he was too dumb to be scared.

The mortar pit—or "Mortaritaville," as they called it, in homage to Jimmy Buffett's "wastin' away" locale—was not a fun place to be. Its occupants were often fired upon from the relatively close high ground of the Switchbacks and from the looming boulder they dubbed RPG Rock. In a constant state of agitation, the mortarmen would hit golf balls or shag baseballs into Urmul, just to screw with the locals. Their boss, Lieutenant Stephen Cady, was sent a water-balloon launcher by his father, which he then gave to his men for fun; they'd use it to bombard the Afghan National Police station, the villagers, and U.S. soldiers standing guard. Captain Porter didn't seem to know about all of this; as far as the men could remember, he'd been to the mortar pit only once.

The resentment toward Captain Porter that had begun during predeployment were exacerbated at the outpost. Some of the animus was unfair. Porter, for instance, ordered the men of 3-61 Cav to wear full gear every time they stepped outside. The troops found this inconvenient and cumbersome—a helmet weighed roughly three pounds, the full armored vest about ten times that—but given the constant threat of indirect fire, it was a wise measure to take. Porter wasn't alone in enforcing this rule; First Sergeant Ronald Burton, who'd been hit by some of the same shrapnel that had so seriously wounded Shane Scherer[71] in May, was perhaps its most ardent enforcer.

---

[71] Scherer underwent twenty-six separate operations and had to relearn how to walk, talk, and even swallow. "Whatever hit my brain scrambled it," he told me in a 2011 interview, after his remarkable recovery.

Some of the hostile feelings toward Porter were based on strategic differences. The captain was not a strong proponent of the "show of force," whereby mortars, for example, were fired into the hillside to remind everyone in the neighborhood that the United States had superior weaponry. Porter believed there were at least two issues with such displays. First, they were antithetical to the aims of counterinsurgency. If Black Knight Troop were to constantly drop mortars around local homes, killing goats and possibly even residents, it would only reinforce the Kamdeshis' perception of the Americans as hostile occupiers and turn the valley against them even more. Second, whenever the United States used deadly force, there ought to be a reason behind it. The unit was in a location that was very hard to resupply with anything, let alone a pallet of 120-millimeter mortar rounds weighing thirty pounds apiece, and Porter didn't want to expend ordnance for show when it might well be needed for real at a later date.

Many of his men disagreed with this. One time, Private First Class Christopher Jones, armed with an M240 machine gun, was standing guard in the turret atop the shura building while Specialist Thomas Rasmussen manned the .50-caliber at the LRAS-2 guard post (one of two Humvees outfitted with LRAS devices, both of which were used as guard stations). When the camp began taking fire from the Putting Green, Jones and Rasmussen both returned fire, but it didn't seem to accomplish much. At LRAS-2 with Rasmussen, Staff Sergeant Clint Romesha, the sergeant of the guard that day, decided that they needed John Breeding at the mortar pit to fire the 120-millimeter mortars. He called Breeding to make the request, but suddenly the voice of their commander came on the radio.

"Negative," said Porter.

"We have sniper fire, we have movement up on the Putting Green," Romesha protested.

"Do you see weapons?" Porter asked.

"Negative," Romesha admitted.

"Do you have a PID?" Porter asked, meaning a "positive identification"— that is, an enemy with a weapon.

"I see dudes where we're getting sniped at from," Romesha replied. Meaning: No.

"Negative," Porter said.

In a case study in a class at West Point, that would have been the right call. But to troops being fired upon in a remote valley in northeastern Afghanistan, it felt overly cautious. When the enemy sniper stopped shooting, Romesha ran to the mortar pit to speak with Breeding in person so Porter couldn't hear them. Get the 120s ready, he told Breeding. The guns were already laid on, Breeding replied—adding, "Just tell me when you want me to shoot."

Clint Romesha was an intense guy, short and wiry, the son of a leader of the Church of Jesus Christ of Latter-day Saints in Cedarville, California. His parents had hoped he would follow his father into the church leadership, and Romesha had in fact gone to seminary for four years during high school—from five till seven every morning—but ultimately, it just wasn't for him. He didn't even go on a mission, a regular rite for young Mormon men.

Romesha was better suited to this kind of mission, with guns and joes under his command. Leaving the mortar pit at Combat Outpost Keating, he ran back to LRAS-2, and soon enough, the enemy started firing again. Romesha and Rasmussen looked up at the spot. Did they have a "positive identified threat"? Did they see weapons? Well, *maybe* they saw some muzzle flashes....

"We have a PIT," Romesha said on the radio, once more requesting that Breeding fire the 120s. Told that his men had positive identification, Porter now okayed the mortars. Breeding fired. About twenty minutes later, Rasmussen saw movement again in the same spot. "Fire 'em up again," Romesha told Breeding. "We have movement."

"You have a PIT?" Porter asked.

"No," Romesha confessed.

"That's probably just the enemy picking up their dead," Porter said. "Hold your fire. Let them recover their dead."

Behind his back, the soldiers of Black Knight Troop began calling their commander No Mortar Porter. Colonel George and Lieutenant Colonel Brown would later judge Captain Porter's actual decision-making in this instance—and others like it—to have been solid, though they would see a leadership failure in his refusal to explain *why* he wasn't granting permission to fire. Part of Porter's charge, of course, came straight from the top: the U.S. Rules of Engagement dictated that troops needed to see a weapon or, at the very least, a radio in the enemy's hand in order to shoot. On July 6, McChrystal issued a directive underlining this point, urging troops to be even more cautious. "We must avoid the trap of winning tactical victories — but suffering strategic defeats — by causing civilian casualties or excessive damage and thus alienating the people," he wrote. "I recognize that the carefully controlled and disciplined employment of force entails risks to our troops...[b]ut excessive use of force resulting in an alienated population will produce far greater risks." McChrystal also instructed U.S. forces to limit their use of close air support. He added, moreover, that the use of "indirect fires against residential compounds is only authorized under very limited and prescribed conditions." Porter took these commands to heart.

From Forward Operating Base Bostick, Brown kept tabs on Porter, and he remained concerned about his troop leader. True, McChrystal had spoken, but Porter seemed even more reluctant than other commanders to use force when he could. Brown also believed that during the troop overlap, some of the guys from the 6-4 Cav had filled the captain's head with horror stories about how every commander at Camp Keating was a marked man. While it was almost certainly the case that Captain Ylles-cas had been targeted for assassination, Captain Bostick's death in Saret Koleh appeared more random, and Ben Keating — not a commander but an XO — had died in the rollover of an LMTV. Nonetheless, Porter seemed spooked. Brown surmised that the knowledge that he would likely change command and be transferred to a safer post within ninety days had made Porter go to ground; he spent most of his time in the tactical operations center at Keating — the place, the captain himself argued, from which he could best command and control any fight. Porter's radio call sign was "Black Knight–6," but because of his proclivity for holing up in the operations center, his troops also referred to him as "Bunker-6." Porter maintained that he walked around and talked with his troops on a regular basis. But some of them argued that they seldom saw their commander at all.

On the morning of June 28, Sergeant First Class Jeff Jacops was serving as sergeant of the guard, supervising the other troops from White Platoon who were pulling overnight guard duty. As his shift ended, Jacops headed to the barracks to wake up Staff Sergeant Bradley Lee. Suddenly, he heard the unmistakable crack of a recoilless rifle round. Jacops had begun running toward the camp's entry control point when a second round landed ten feet in front of him, hitting a wall, blowing him backward, and knocking him momentarily unconscious. Shrapnel splattered the right side of his face and neck, ripping them open, and exacted a chunk out of his left forearm. When he came to, dazed, he wiggled the fingers on his left hand. Then he realized he was spitting out teeth.

Jacops ran to Doc Cordova at the aid station. His face was bloody and messy; one of his eyes was no longer in the right place, its orbital floor having been shredded. Cordova could see, even through the gore, how terrified the sergeant was as he hit Jacops with morphine, put pressure on his face, and bandaged up his arm. There wasn't much more that could be done for him at Camp Keating beyond waiting for the medevac. The good news was Jacops's fears outpaced the reality of his injuries: he would have some lasting damage to his face—scarring, mainly—but he would be okay.[72] Cordova mopped up Jacops's blood from the floor using the wounded sergeant's T-shirt.

"You're very lucky," Cordova told him. He knew how important reassurance could be to a patient in this situation, especially one who seemed so scared.

"I don't feel so lucky," Jacops replied.

"No, man, you really were lucky," Cordova said. It was remarkable what qualified as good fortune at a place like Camp Keating.

With other troops securing the landing zone, a medevac soon landed, and Jacops was quickly deposited onto it; he jokingly flipped his middle finger to First Sergeant Burton as the chopper took off.

At Forward Operating Base Bostick, the surgeon told Jacops he was going to put him under so he could take a good look at his wounds. Prepping for the anesthesia, he asked his patient, "What did you have for breakfast?"

"A fucking rocket," Jacops replied.

On July 5, at Forward Operating Base Bostick, Brown made his "realignment" presentation to Brigadier General William Fuller, deputy

---

[72] Jacops ultimately lost seven teeth from the right side of his mouth—six on top and one on the bottom—plus part of his jawbone. He kept his eye and would eventually return to 3-61 Cav.

commanding general for operations at Regional Command East. Soon afterward, he made the same pitch to General Mayville. Both men seemed to be on board. Getting the ball rolling, Brown started pulling nonessential gear from Combat Outpost Lowell: spare parts for old vehicles, excess generators, extra air conditioners, and gym equipment.

As part of his battlefield circulation, McChrystal visited Kunar Province around this time. At Forward Operating Base Bostick, Brown personally made the case to him for shutting down Camp Keating, Camp Lowell, Observation Post Fritsche, and other posts in Kunar Province by August at the latest. The bases were defensive in nature, he pointed out, and not mutually supporting; they had minimal value for counterinsurgency efforts and were remote from the population; they could be resupplied and reinforced only by air; and they lacked sufficient troop strength to do anything but defend themselves. They were vulnerable, ineffective, and a poor use of manpower and aviation resources. Moreover, Brown said, the presence of the camps had actually worsened the security situation in Nuristan.

McChrystal seemed attentive and thoughtful, though perhaps a bit taken aback by Brown's presentation—he had come here to get a lay of the land, not to be pressed for a major decision. The general politely told Brown and George that he agreed with their logic and, in principle, their tactical assessment. But there were larger strategic issues involved, McChrystal explained. First, the Afghan presidential election, scheduled for August 20, was fast approaching, and President Karzai and the provincial governors were opposed to any withdrawal of American forces before that; Karzai feared that such a pullout might be taken as a sign of a lack of support for the Afghan government, which could deter turnout, especially among his supporters. And regardless of Karzai's feelings, McChrystal had orders to make sure that ISAF forces maximized voter access in as many areas of the country as possible; pulling U.S. soldiers out of Nuristan and parts of Kunar would undermine that aim.

Karzai also believed that if the United States pulled its troops out of certain discrete districts in Afghanistan, the Taliban would claim a great propaganda victory and make him look weak in front of his people. McChrystal shared his concern about potential Taliban claims and felt it was important for the United States to show that it stood behind the government of Afghanistan—or, more specifically, behind Karzai and his government.

The political situation back home was also sticky. In August, McChrystal was supposed to present his recommendations regarding Afghanistan, after which President Obama would make a decision about what to do next there. McChrystal's swooping down into the country and shutting down a bunch of bases in Nuristan and Kunar Provinces could be interpreted as presumptuous or, at the very least, premature. "I don't want to get ahead of the president," McChrystal said to George. Anytime generals started pulling out troops, it created at least the perception that a big decision had been made, McChrystal thought.

Other considerations would further impede the plan to close the outposts. On June 30, Private First Class Bowe Bergdahl angrily left his base in Paktika Province and was captured by insurgents, prompting a substantial push of planes, helicopters, and surveillance drones to the area in an effort to find him—which proved futile.[73] Shortly thereafter came a major U.S. initiative up in northern Nuristan, at Barg-e-Matal. These two developments would effectively tie up the air assets that would be needed to shut down Combat Outpost Keating and the other remote camps.

Resigned, Brown sent the gym equipment back to Kamu.

Master Sergeant Ryan Bodmer had come to Combat Outpost Keating to run the radio station when Captain Pecha and 6-4 Cav were in charge, and he was shocked by how different things were under Captain Porter and 3-61 Cav. The whole mentality had changed, Bodmer thought. He tried to explain to the leaders of 3-61 Cav how important assertive counterinsurgency was, how the development projects were the only thing keeping the U.S. troops alive—or at the very least, keeping fighting-age Afghan men gainfully occupied—but he didn't get anywhere with them.

---

[73] In a June 7, 2012, *Rolling Stone* story by Michael Hastings, Bergdahl was revealed to have been completely disillusioned by the war, having sent his parents an email shortly before his disappearance that said, "Life is way too short to care for the damnation of others, as well as to spend it helping fools with their ideas that are wrong. I have seen their ideas and I am ashamed to even be American. . . . I am sorry for everything here. These people need help, yet what they get is the most conceited country in the world telling them that they are nothing and they are stupid, that they have no idea how to live." He then walked off his base and was ultimately captured by Taliban insurgents. As of the summer of 2012, he was still missing in action, though there were reports of negotiations between ISAF and the Taliban to free him.

Some of the projects then in progress were funded by Bodmer and the PRT at Kala Gush, and others by 3-61 Cav through special commanders' funds. The PRT projects included a micro-hydroelectric plant, two roads (one of which connected Kamdesh to Agro), a bridge across the Landay-Sin River (as much for the U.S. troops as it was for the locals), and Radio Kamdesh—now called Amman Radio, *amman* being the Nuristani word for "peace." Based on how frequently the Taliban threatened to destroy the radio station and kill its programmers, Bodmer believed he had succeeded in making the station a thorn in their side. Porter wasn't interested; he was on a different page, talking instead about how the United States had no intention of sticking around, saying that any project he couldn't see with his own eyes was going to be canceled—and maybe some of those that he could see, too. Ultimately, with Brown's blessing, Porter decided to cancel almost all of the remaining projects funded by 3-61 Cav.

For his part, Brown believed that apart from the few Afghan contractors who were making money from the projects, the locals didn't have much of a connection at all to the Americans, and vice versa. He respected Bodmer and thought he was working hard, but he felt he was running a one-man show, disconnected from any broader purpose. That wasn't his fault, but it was the reality.

In Bodmer's view, this change of direction was a disaster; as the few remaining projects were canceled, he saw the locals grow despondent and angry over their lost wages.

"This is a huge mistake," Bodmer told Lieutenant Cason Shrode, the 3-61 Cav officer in charge of the development projects; the squadron needed to keep at least four or five projects going through the commanders' funds, he insisted. Shrode's bosses disagreed, saying they weren't in the payoff business. Over the past couple of years, the United States had unwisely, they believed, spent boatloads of cash in Afghanistan. If all of those projects were doing any good, then why had the situation deteriorated? Frankly, Brown thought, if you have to bribe people to convince them not to shoot at you, you're losing.

On July 7, the Taliban violently seized Barg-e-Matal, the remote village in northern Nuristan, up the road from Combat Outpost Keating, with a population of roughly fifteen hundred people. The village sat in a politically important location and was a tempting sanctuary for insurgent groups that were being driven out of Pakistan. President Karzai demanded that General McChrystal send U.S. troops there. The Afghan Border Police who had jurisdiction wouldn't be enough, he said; American forces would be required to retake the town. Karzai and his advisers feared that the loss of Barg-e-Matal, a significant thoroughfare, would suggest to the rest of the world that they were losing control of their country.

Barg-e-Matal was located in the area of operations commanded by Colonel Randy George, and he was afraid of stepping into this tar pit. Once he sent U.S. troops, how would he get them out again? Would dispatching these guys into yet another remote, sparsely populated district—even for just a few days—be worth it? Barg-e-Matal was even more isolated than Camp Keating and other, similar outposts that the brigade was already struggling to maintain. How would sending U.S. soldiers there affect brigade operations elsewhere? To what extent would it deprive other companies of medevacs, Apaches, fixed-wing aircraft, drones, and other needed resources? There were no satisfying answers to these questions.

George's skepticism was met by a direct order from McChrystal to get moving. The message was clear: Karzai wants to do this, it's important to him, and we're going to support him.

On the morning of July 12, coalition forces—specifically, the 1-32 Infantry—and Afghan troops launched Operation Mountain Fire in Barg-e-Matal. The fighting was intense. Army Staff Sergeant Eric Lindstrom, twenty-seven, was killed. A police officer from Flagstaff, Arizona, Lindstrom left behind a wife and seven-month-old twins named Olivia and Riley. That night, when the shooting was done, the American and Afghan forces had regained control of the Barg-e-Matal district center and the surrounding area. Karzai was happy. But the 1-32 Infantry troops, scheduled to leave Barg-e-Matal within four days of the initial assault, would not actually be able to depart until over two months later.

With so many assets—helicopters, drones—pushed north and counterinsurgency efforts in the region down to few or none, life at Camp Keating and up at Observation Post Fritsche involved a decent amount of hanging out. In between patrols and basic maintenance operations—the burning of the contents of the latrines, for instance—uncountable games of Hearts and Spades were played and stacks of DVDs repeatedly viewed.

Specialist Stephan Mace had returned from leave with an Xbox, enabling hours of video gaming. Daily workouts were nothing new for soldiers at the outpost, but the men of Black Knight Troop had so much time on their hands that some began lifting weights twice a day, drinking protein shakes, and taking supplements to jack themselves up.

A few troops experimented with less traditional pursuits. The Bush administration had authorized the use of the interrogation technique known as waterboarding, which was classified throughout the world as torture; upon taking office in 2009, President Obama had banned its use. Some Red Platoon troops, trying to burn time, decided to see what all the fuss was about. In their barracks, Lieutenant Andrew Bundermann, Specialist Tom Rasmussen, Sergeant Justin Gallegos, and Specialist Zach Koppes were all voluntarily waterboarded. Sergeant Brad Larson held a shirt over their faces while Staff Sergeant Clint Romesha poured the water. No one could get past four seconds until Koppes tried; he made it to eight. As far as Koppes was concerned, there was no debate about it: this was torture.

Much less sobering were the inevitable practical jokes. Goats roamed freely across the outpost, so one day Larson lassoed one and with the help of some fellow pranksters shoved it into Bundermann's hooch while he was napping. Another time, Red Platoon super-glued the lieutenant's items to the floor, a feat one-upped by Tom Rasmussen's low-crawling into his hooch and spreading flypaper underfoot.

Christopher Jones had a guitar with him, so when he wasn't pulling guard duty at the entry control point—scanning the mountains and watching people on the road—he'd write and sing songs about the platoon. Among these was the mocking ditty known as "The Davidson Song," about Private First Class Nicholas Davidson of Humboldt County, California:

> *Stutters when he talks*
> *Stumbles when he walks*
> *Trying to find the phone*
> *So he could call back home....*

Another Jones number, about his immediate supervisor, team leader Joshua Kirk, included Specialist Zachary Koppes's free-style rapping:

Whatchoo hearing
Whatchoo heard
Motherfucker got killed by Combat Kirk...
Only man who could turn a kitchen
Into a fighting position....

The lyrics had some truth to them: Kirk's men saw him as being unafraid, unthreatened, and, at times, unrestrained. During firefights, he would tell them, "If you think you need to shoot something, shoot it. It doesn't matter how much ammo you might waste. If you need to kill it, kill it."

Kirk had been born at home in Thomaston, Maine, the son of a Vietnam veteran who transformed himself from the dope-smoking head of a motorcycle gang into a born-again Christian carpenter. When Josh was five, the family moved to fifteen acres of land not far from Bonners Ferry, Idaho, a small town best known for U.S. law enforcement's siege of a compound at nearby Ruby Ridge in 1992. The Kirks had running water but no electricity; their closest neighbors were five miles away. The kids' entertainment was entirely self-created: building forts, sleeping in tents, playing flashlight tag, and, when they were teenagers, engaging in elaborate games of war. One such game, invented by Josh, came to be called Test of Courage; it basically consisted of devising terrifying tasks and daring the other players to attempt them. The challenges started out harmless enough but then quickly escalated to dangerous acts such as exploring an abandoned silver mine, walking on top of the old Eileen Dam, and body-surfing fierce river rapids. In retrospect, it seemed astonishing that no one had ever died.

After high school, Kirk returned to Maine with his father and brother to do some construction work and ended up taking classes at Southern Maine Community College, where, in September 2004, he met Megan Gavin. Holding down a construction job and going to school at the same time soon proved impossible, so the following spring, Kirk enlisted in the Army, attracted by the promise of the G.I. Bill. He was a persistent guy, and he asked Megan to marry him three times before she finally said yes; they were married a few days after he got out of basic training in 2005. Three months before he deployed with 1-91 Cav in 2007, their little girl was born. And now here he was, back in Nuristan.

From: Joshua Kirk
To: Megan Kirk
Sent: Sunday, July 12, 2009

Hey sweetie, just wanted to say that I love you tons! Little pricks have been hitting us all day with B-10 and rpg fire. Lovely and then some!!!! Of course they wont let us patrol more so we can secure this place. instead lets just sit here and take it in the ass. Working on the patroling way more so we can secure it. I would rather hit these dudes out in the brush then wait here, its really driving us nuts, oh well . . . TTYL Love you XOXOOXOXOXOXOXOXOX JK

Sergeant Joshua Kirk. *(Photo courtesy of Megan Gavin Kirk)*

The frequency of firefights at Camp Keating increased significantly, from 136 in 2008 to 212 throughout 2009. When the men of 3-61 Cav took incoming fire, Kirk was a *machine:* he'd hop on the AT4 rocket launcher, then switch to the .50-caliber, then the M203 grenade launcher, then he'd get back on the .50-caliber and shoot that again. Most of the guys at the outpost were pretty tough, but Kirk, he was crazy brave — fearless, thought Jones. Absolutely.

Growing up in Winesburg, Ohio, home of the world's largest Amish community, Specialist Zach Koppes — who'd attended a private Mennonite school — had never pictured himself landing in a place like Combat Outpost Keating.

His path from Winesburg to Kamdesh District had been blazed by his troublemaking ways. He was kicked out of high school for breaking into a file cabinet and stealing (then selling) answers to a test, and then, for far worse infractions, he was kicked out of his family's house. He moved to Colorado to work in landscaping with his uncle Mike but wasn't particularly good at it. Burnt out, he found himself twisting dough behind the counter of an Auntie Anne's Pretzels at a Walmart, embarrassed by what he'd become.

At first, Koppes was just trying to impress a cute girl with talk of joining the military: a commercial came on the TV for the U.S. Navy SEALs, depicting the fierce warriors jumping out of choppers and parachuting into the jungle, and Koppes made an off-the-cuff remark about signing up. But the comment had a weird sort of cling. Joining up would, he figured, solve all his problems. His mother would respect him again, as would his friends. His life's demerits would be erased; he would no longer be twisting pretzels at Walmart. So one day he smoked a bushel of pot and then headed to an Army recruiter's office.

From there, he and five others were driven in a van to a classroom where they took a four-hour test. Afterward, a staff sergeant told him that he'd scored in the top tenth percentile. After basic training, Koppes went back to Ohio before shipping out to Korea. Instead of spending any time with his family — including his thirteen-year-old sister, Eva, who had cystic fibrosis — all Koppes did was smoke pot, hang out with his friends, and hit on girls. He fought with his mom. He fought with his dad. He hadn't changed at all. The problems remained because the real problem was him.

Three months later, Koppes was drinking with his Army buddies at his new home, a base in South Korea, when his commanding officer knocked on the door and took him to the chaplain. "We got a call from the Red Cross about Eva," the chaplain told him. "They don't think she has much time left. We're going to put you on the next plane."

The two of them had been close, though of course Koppes hadn't been around much in the previous few years. He flew to her and ran to her hospital bed. "I'm sorry I wasn't here more," he said to her. "I'm sorry I didn't spend more time with you." He told her how much he loved her. "I love you, too," she replied. She died two days later. Koppes was convinced she'd been hanging on just to say good-bye to him.

Back in South Korea, Koppes straightened up. He worked harder. He earned awards. He took classes. His guilt and grief over Eva melted his rebellious, juvenile shell, revealing a humanity he'd all but forgotten was there. After his rotation on the Korean Peninsula, he transferred to 3-61 Cav—then training at Fort Carson, Colorado—so he could spend more time with his girlfriend, Kaila, who attended the University of Colorado at Colorado Springs. She ended up dumping him three months later, and that was when Zach Koppes became best friends with Specialist Stephan[74] Mace.

He was Koppes's first friend in the squadron. Mace was good-looking, with boundless energy and a wicked sense of humor. He and his brothers had grown up in a small community named Purcellville, in Virginia, where they learned patriotism from their maternal grandfather, an Air Force veteran. Mace loved guns growing up, not just to hunt with but also for the craft of their manufacture. He became an apprentice to a gunsmith and built a rifle for his father for Christmas. After 9/11— Stephan was thirteen at the time—the Army just seemed to make sense.

Everyone in 3-61 Cav seemed to know everyone else from the previous deployment in Iraq; Mace and Koppes were the new guys, and they started hanging out together. They were walking through a Colorado mall together one afternoon when Kaila texted Koppes her official end-of-relationship message. He started to cry.

"I'm not here to hear you cry," Mace said. "Let's go get some booze and party."

After that, they became inseparable; their bond was wild and fierce. When Koppes decided to try to win Kaila back, it was Mace who— intoxicated—drove him to her house. They had purchased mullet wigs and wore them everywhere, and Mace had his on that night. As Koppes

---

[74] Pronounced as "STEFF-in."

and Kaila sat down on a stoop to talk, a wigged Mace humped the campus's giant statue of a mountain lion. Each man's effort proved fruitless.

Koppes got back in the car. "Don't worry about it," Mace said as he revved the motor and drove off with his friend to another adventure. Koppes knew that as long as Mace was around, he would be okay.

Specialist Stephan Mace. *(Photo courtesy of Vanessa Adelson)*

During one of their first firefights at Combat Outpost Keating, Koppes took shrapnel to his head.

He was in the Humvee that was parked on the ANA side of the camp—the eastern side, facing the Diving Board to the northeast. After tearing through his rounds, Koppes had begun reloading his M240 machine gun when a round from the old belt—one that had been dented but not fired—cooked off and fired into the ground. Called a hang-fire, this delay between the trigger being pulled and the bullet being discharged can be deadly. In this case, the bullet, hot from the gun, fired into the ground, and a piece of the metal ricocheted and went right for Koppes, slipping under his helmet and grazing his head. Bleeding and in pain, he was convinced he had been shot by the enemy and started freaking out. Romesha, who'd seen the whole thing happen, grabbed him and took him to the aid station.

Before 3-61 Cav left Colorado, Koppes had promised that any man who saved his life could have anything he wanted to tattooed on Koppes's back. So later that day, his head bandaged from the grazing wound, Koppes came into the Red Platoon barracks and said to Romesha, "Ro, you saved my life, what do you want on my back?"

Romesha thought it was hilarious. Saved his life? Not only was Koppes going to be fine, but clearly he still didn't realize that his had technically been a self-inflicted wound. Trying hard not to laugh, his "savior" suggested that he make plans to have "ROMESHA" indelibly recorded across his shoulder blades.

Command Sergeant Major Rob Wilson, visiting from Forward Operating Base Bostick, had visited Koppes at the aid station and seen for himself that his injuries were minor. In the operations center later that day, Wilson noticed Romesha and Bundermann talking with a suspicious degree of discretion — so he pressed them until Romesha admitted that Koppes's injury had been caused by a hang-fire. There wouldn't be any Purple Heart for a self-inflicted wound, Wilson said.

Eventually, Romesha let the cat out of the bag and told Koppes about the hang-fire. It was a good news/bad news situation: there would be no Purple Heart — but to his own relief and Romesha's perpetual regret, the young ex-Mennonite had been stopped before self-inflicting yet another wound, this one in ink.

CHAPTER 27

The Deer Hunters

Even to close members of his family, Ed Faulkner, Jr., had never seemed comfortable in his own skin, so it might not have been so surprising that he smoked pot in high school and was twice cited for underage possession of alcohol. He was living at home in Burlington, North Carolina, and working at a driving range when he joined the Army in 2005 to get away from the bad influences in his world. His father and both of his grandfathers had served.

In Iraq on January 20, 2007, Faulkner was shot in his left arm by a sniper. He got sent home, had some surgeries, and quickly became addicted to painkillers. One of his best friends from Iraq, Specialist Thomas Blakely "Blake" Nelson, was also addicted—he'd had lower back pain after his deployment—and at some point, heroin entered the picture.

The Black Knight Troop soldiers had a relatively high rate of positive urinalysis for drugs at Fort Carson after they returned from Iraq—an issue that Captain Porter had tried to address. Faulkner and Nelson were at the center of it. Faulkner was disciplined for using meth, and Lieutenant colonel Brown gave him a shot at rehab. Nelson completed his own six-week resident program, but on January 8, 2008, he was found dead in his room at Fort Carson, having overdosed on a combination of prescription drugs and heroin. Out of rehab for less than a week, he left behind a son named Karson. His death was tough enough on Faulkner in the safe and secure environment of Colorado; it didn't get any easier once he deployed to Kamdesh. A few months later, up on Observation Post Fritsche with Blue Platoon—they called themselves the

Bastards—Faulkner tried to deal with the pain of his life and the pain of losing Blake the only way he knew how: he scored some hashish, which was, to say the least, not that difficult to do in Afghanistan.

John Francis—an older, no-nonsense sergeant at thirty-five, from Lindenhurst on Long Island, New York—tried to look out for Faulkner. The kid didn't always make that easy. Francis, a team leader for the Bastards, was sergeant of the guard one night, in charge of calling all the troops at the guard posts, and Faulkner's tower didn't answer when he radioed. The operations center at OP Fritsche had a small camera that could provide a 360-degree view of the entire observation post, so Francis focused the camera on Faulkner's tower and clicked on the night vision. It was pitch black, with no moonlight. Francis pushed the view toward the tower even more and saw some tiny flashes of light. Both wary and curious, Francis grabbed his portable radio and night-vision goggles and walked up to Faulkner's tower post. He quietly proceeded up the stairwell made out of ammo cans, strode onto the dirt platform in the darkness, and paused to watch Faulkner and another private use a cigarette lighter for illumination as they tried to break up a small brick of hash. There was no mistaking what it was; its aroma alone filled the guard tower. For four minutes or so, Francis stood just mere inches from the two and watched them prepare to smoke hash while on guard duty.

"What's up, guys?" Francis finally said, surprising the two enlisted men, who panicked and dropped everything onto the ground.

"Nothing, Sergeant," Faulkner said.

"I called you on the radio," Francis said. "You guys never answered me."

"Oh, check the radio," said Faulkner, "maybe something's wrong with the radio."

Francis went back to the operations center and spent ten minutes deciding what to do. He felt he had no choice. He knew that Faulkner had demons and addiction issues, so he'd made it his mission to try to keep him out of trouble. He watched over the kid as much as he could. But smoking hash on guard duty in the middle of a war zone was unforgivable.

Sergeant First Class Jonathan "Dad" Hill was in the operations center with Lieutenant Ben Salentine monitoring enemy radio chatter, when Francis walked in. He told them what he'd seen, and they discussed what to do. It was tough: Faulkner would be severely punished, they knew, and maybe even removed from duty. But they felt they had to report it because the platoon's integrity was on the line.

Francis and Hill confronted Faulkner and the other private, who both admitted what they'd almost done. Specialist Faulkner was busted down to private but not discharged.

Private Ed Faulkner, Jr. *(Photo courtesy of Jon Hill)*

And then they got back to work.

Ever since their arrival at OP Fritsche in May, Lieutenant Ben Salentine had been pushing the Bastards to turn the observation post into a fortress. Sure, they'd all heard that Colonel George and Lieutenant Colonel Brown wanted to shut the place down, along with Camp Keating, but until that happened, it would make sense to harden their positions by filling sandbags, improving machine-gun locations, whatever. Salentine gave the order, Hill assigned the men to get it done, and Staff Sergeant Kirk Birchfield, the senior scout, and team leaders and Sergeants Francis and Eric Harder organized the creation of the new positions and fortifications. Daily they labored to make Fritsche as impenetrable as possible.

The men of Black Knight Troop tried to enjoy themselves as best they could, but it wasn't always easy. Helicopters would now fly into the area only rarely for resupply, in the blackest night during "Red Illume,"[75] so

---

[75] In the Army's classification system for lunar illumination, Red Illume refers to those times when the moon is not visible at all; Amber Illume to when it's partly showing; and

there were periods when the men had to go without hot meals or mail. It was horrible for morale, but mail was not a priority compared with ammunition, MREs, and water. That's what happens when you're living on the Pakistan border, Salentine thought. All he cared about getting was sustenance and bullets and home to his wife.

Salentine understood that morale was important, and he knew it was tough for troops to blow off steam when they were penned up like livestock. At OP Fritsche, as at Camp Keating, there were plenty of practical jokes. On Salentine's twenty-eighth birthday, for example, his troops packed his room with balloons filled with baby powder. (Only one exploded, hitting Birchfield.) On other occasions, they replaced his shampoo with "fancy sauce," the ketchup-and-mayonnaise mixture referenced in the Will Ferrell comedy *Step Brothers,* and substituted coffee creamer for his talcum powder. John Francis sliced off the bristles of Salentine's toothbrush bit by bit each day until it was bare. Then there were the group activities. On July 4, 2009, the Bastards invited all of the ANA troops and some of the locals to a barbecue. The Afghans cooked up goat, rice, and flatbread while the Americans grilled chicken, hamburgers, and steak. Another project: with his small digital video camera, Sergeant Jory Brown filmed the Bastards dancing, one by one or in small groups, sound tracked it to "Just Dance" by Lady Gaga (the girliest song he could find), and uploaded the clip to YouTube. The footage was a big hit among the men themselves as well as with their families back home, who could find reassurance in the goofiness. After the video-sharing website removed the clip's audio because of copyright infringement, Brown's wife ended up posting the uncensored version on her Facebook page.

Not everyone got into the act. Private First Class Dan Rogers came from a religious family—his father, a former Marine, was a full-time pastor—and he didn't mesh well socially with the rest of the platoon. Rogers looked askance at the cursing and practical jokes and spent his free time playing video games or reading the Book of Romans or Christian fiction. Rogers thought that the only other one in the unit who seemed active in his faith was Specialist Cody Floyd, a medic, and in hope of further salvation, Rogers tried to minister to the other men. He spoke with Specialist Michael

---

Green Illume to when it's full. By May 2009, helicopters wouldn't fly to COP Keating during Green or Amber Illume, only during Red.

Scusa and urged him to get right with Jesus Christ. Scusa was polite about it, noting that his wife went to church, but not all that interested. When Rogers was on guard duty with ANA troops or Afghan Security Guards, he would take advantage of the captive audience and try to save them, too, though usually as soon as he uttered the word *Jesus,* they'd shut down pretty quickly. He never gave up; Bible in hand, he'd ask the Afghans about Islam, and then they'd open up a bit, after which he'd ask them if they'd mind if he shared something about his own beliefs. He'd describe miracles—how Jesus fed the multitudes with five loaves and two fish, for instance. He'd share the Parable of the Sower of Seeds, discuss the Crucifixion. Rogers never worried about getting in trouble for trying to promote his beliefs; he was pretty sure his commanding officers knew he was doing it. They didn't.

Sergeant First Class Hill for sure hadn't heard about Rogers's proselytizing, but he was concerned enough about what he *did* know: Rogers kept falling asleep on guard duty, which was unacceptable—or in Hill's vernacular, "garbage." Called Dad by his men because of his age—thirty-seven—and gruff manner, Hill had been born on an Air Force base in Oklahoma. After high school in Virginia, he'd wasted a year drinking and working at Hardee's; the Army was a ticket out. Hill had the weary manner of a man who'd seen it all, and after two tours through the mass graves and skeleton-riddled roads of booby-trapped Bosnia, maybe he had.

Sergeant First Class Jon Hill. *(Photo courtesy of Jon Hill)*

In early August, the Bastards rotated down to Camp Keating. As soon as Salentine and Hill laid eyes on the outpost, they looked at each other.

"This place is a fucking dump," Hill said. "We need to fortify it like we did at Fritsche."

"You're right, we need to," Salentine concurred.

In their first two days at the outpost, Salentine and Hill brainstormed ways to improve the security at their new home, just as they'd done at Observation Post Fritsche. They wanted to add HESCO barriers, string more wire around the whole camp, place more Claymore mines in more areas, and add two more towers, one facing the Northface and the other by that southern wall. Needing an official okay, they poked their heads into the operations center, and Salentine made his pitch. Porter didn't think the reinforcement was necessary. And anyway, they would all be leaving soon enough. He wouldn't budge.

"It's a no-go," Salentine reported back to Hill as they left the operations center. Salentine was a bit stunned by his captain's obstinance. Being at Combat Outpost Keating is like deer hunting, he thought, but we aren't the ones in the tree stand.

"Why are you here?" asked the journalist.

Captain Porter chuckled and said, "My boss told me to come here."

Porter was sitting in the operations center as Nick Paton Walsh, the Asia correspondent for the United Kingdom's Channel 4 News, threw questions at him, all of it being recorded by cameraman Stuart Webb. The two Brits had come to the outpost to report on the security preparations being taken before the August 20 elections. Webb noticed that sitting prominently on Porter's desk were two books: *The Complete Idiot's Guide to Understanding Islam* and *Bear Went Over the Mountain: Soviet Combat Tactics in Afghanistan.*

Walsh and Webb both knew this would be a trip with some risks. Before leaving Forward Operating Base Bostick, they'd spoken with one pilot who'd flown to Camp Keating and turned right around after a near miss by an RPG. When the journalists flew to the camp, they did so in the dead of night in a bird accompanied by two Apaches, one of which fired a Hellfire missile at the mountain to scare off any would-be attackers. The mountain itself was so close to the landing zone that it looked as if an insurgent could casually stand somewhere nearby and hit any helicopter with a rock. The pilots were concerned that their blades might hit the hillsides as they began their descent. It was the most dangerous flight Webb had ever been on, and insurgents weren't even firing. And that was about the least of it, they realized, when the morning revealed to them just how vulnerable the entire camp was: it was under constant threat of fire from the surrounding hills. A few days before, they were told, an Afghan soldier had been shot in the back as he used the piss-tubes. It was that easy. Webb and Walsh had been to their share of war zones around the world, but in terms of location, Combat Outpost Keating was a new low.

The Americans were reluctant to let the Brits join them outside the wire — it was too risky, they said — so the journalists arranged to meet the camp's Latvian ANA trainers and the Afghan troops by the river, to the northeast of Camp Keating, as they returned to the outpost after a patrol. As Webb began filming, shots rang out. No one was sure which mountain the bullets were coming from, so nobody knew where to take cover. Walsh dove to the ground and jammed his knee so badly he couldn't walk on it. A stray bullet ricocheted into the thigh of one of the Latvians, who let out a shout and fell on top of Webb.

This is fucking serious, Webb said to himself. He started to run toward the Afghan National Police posting, just outside the camp to the northwest, expecting to be shot in the back at any moment. He wasn't. Still, no one knew where to return fire. Then someone saw a muzzle flash, and for the next thirty minutes, the troops at Camp Keating fired into that spot in the hills.

It was roughly the thirty-fifth attack on the camp in just under three months, since the arrival of 3-61 Cav.

"Do you ever think to yourself, Why am I here?" Walsh later asked Lieutenant Bundermann.

"Not really," Bundermann replied. Tall and thin, with a sardonic sense of humor, the lieutenant had graduated from the University of Minnesota two years before and been commissioned as a second lieutenant shortly thereafter. From Michigan, the son of a maintenance mechanic and a nurse, Bundermann had pursued an ROTC scholarship to pay for college, which was about half the reason he was in the Army and standing there right now talking to a journalist at Godforsaken Combat Outpost Keating. The other half of the reason was that he'd needed to do *something* after graduation, and his older brother was already in the Navy.

"That's not my job to ask that question," Bundermann said. He turned to a fellow soldier on guard, Sergeant Joshua Hardt, a team leader from Red Platoon. "Right, Hardt?"

"What?" asked Hardt.

"Ask the question 'Why I'm here' — we don't ask that question, right?"

"Fuck, no," said Hardt. "We don't ask any questions. We get in trouble for asking questions."

Lieutenant Andrew Bundermann. *(Photo courtesy of Jon Hill)*

The mess hall at Combat Outpost Keating used purified river water for cooking and heating bulk meals, but the water purifier was in a constant state of dysfunction, and getting it fixed entailed making a special request for a mechanic from the Support Battalion to fly to Combat Outpost Keating. That was difficult to do, given the dearth of birds available. Before the mechanic could even make the journey, he would have to put in an order for whatever new parts might be needed, and then once the parts had arrived, he'd have to risk getting shot down on the way to or from Keating for the service call. Dying for a water purifier, that would be quite a thing — and yet some troops gave their lives for less.

Porter, mindful of the supply problems, didn't want the cook to use bottled water for making or heating bulk meals. The troops thus lived for periods on cold cuts and sandwiches instead of hot meals. The restricted diet was more of a morale issue than anything else, especially for troops' wives, girlfriends, parents, and siblings, who saw them wasting away, becoming skinnier and skinnier, in each successive photograph sent home or Skype appearance. Many of the families of 3-61 Cav soldiers became convinced that the Army was neglecting their loved ones. In fact, many of the troops *did* feel neglected and abandoned, and they griped about the conditions in emails and calls home. "We barely have food," Sergeant Joshua Hardt told his wife on the phone. "We're lucky to get one hot meal every other day. We have to go out and fight on an empty stomach, while the higher-ups are kicking back and milking it." This was a way for troops to complain without going into detail about what was really on their minds.

Sergeant Joshua Hardt and Olivia Hardt. *(Photo courtesy of Olivia Hardt)*

Joshua Hardt and Olivia Guevara had met in the back row of high school English class and gotten married one week before he deployed to Iraq in 2007. While he was there, they'd talked three times a day, emailed, and chatted via Yahoo! Messenger. Some couples limited their conversations to maybe once a week, perhaps even just once a month, but the Hardts found that too difficult. They needed daily contact—indeed, more than that. Then Hardt came home, but it felt like no more than a blink of an eye before he was off to get in harm's way again, this time in Afghanistan.

Before he left for Kamdesh, back in May, Olivia had been slouched in the passenger's seat as they drove home from a friend's house after a night of card games and long good-byes. They were both quiet, the fact of his imminent departure an unwelcome presence in the car with them.

"Liv, we need to talk," he said, and she swallowed, and that horrible fear in the pit of her stomach grew stronger. "And this time you have to hear me out, because it's important for us to talk about this before I leave."

"That's fine, Joshua, but you have ten minutes," she said. "The thought of you dying makes me sick to my stomach."

He sighed and rubbed his temples with one hand, the other hand on the steering wheel. "Liv, if I don't come home—which won't happen, but if I don't make it—all I want is for you to be happy," he said, speaking slowly. "That's all I want. I don't want you to be sad without me. And you are going to have to be strong, honey.

"And one day I want you to have kids, live in a nice home," he told her. "Don't wait too long to have kids. Because I know you, honey, you will wait till you're in your thirties, and then you'll be too old. More importantly, I want you to find someone who will treat you better than I do and better than I ever have, because you deserve that, Liv," he said. "You deserve someone who is going to treat you like a queen, baby, and if he doesn't, then he doesn't deserve you. But most of all, Liv, I just want you to be happy, baby. As long as you're happy, then I'll be happy."

Olivia was stunned. He'd obviously given this speech a great deal of thought. Hardt had been just an infant when his own parents got divorced, and he'd always wanted to have the family—a mom, a dad, a kitchenful of kids—that he personally had never experienced. But even more than that, he wanted Olivia to have all of that. The only response she could think of was to correct him. "First of all, I don't want kids right away," she said, "and I definitely won't want a husband or a boyfriend for a long time!" She paused. Was she really contemplating a world without her husband? She was only twenty-two; he was twenty-three. She found it utterly impossible to imagine herself simply moving on, starting over. "I really hate talking about this," Olivia declared. But he wouldn't let it go: he kept repeating how much he wanted her to be happy, how he wanted her to have the family he'd never gotten to have.

Hardt had joined the military only because he couldn't figure out what else to do with his life, and Olivia's mother was encouraging him to find a way to support her daughter—not a particularly surprising suggestion for a mother-in-law to make. As it turned out, though, he liked the action and the thrills, and he was an excellent soldier. Whenever the action started, he and Josh Kirk were always the first ones suited up and out the door. But Hardt didn't like Afghanistan, and it was a tougher deployment for him than Iraq. He and Kirk might be quick to action, but the truth was that Joshua Hardt was scared on this tour, and fundamentally less gung-ho than he had been in the past. He didn't like Captain Porter; he didn't like Lieutenant Colonel Brad Brown. He was a Red Platoon team leader, and he felt that his troops were being neglected. It made life difficult for him, and it made him long for his wife in a desperate way. Right now, he just wanted to go home and be a normal husband and have a nine-to-five job.

To: Olivia
Fr: Joshua

hi baby i miss you so much, im so bored and going insane here i just want to be home with you. i think about you all the time and cant wait to see you. we just filled out our leave time and im still on for feb. it might change but for now thats when i will be able to see your beautiful face. i love you so much, i was trying to sleep but i couldnt stop thinking of you. i want to do something when i come home something with just me and you and mean it we always talk about doing something but we never do so this time we will. god i had so much to say but now im drawing a blank. i just miss you so much baby your my world honey and all i want to do is wake up to your beautiful body and that unbelievable smile of yours. that smile has gotten me since the day i met you and will never go away.

anyways i miss you so much and hope your doing alright and dont worry we will be together soon

Afghanistan had consumed Joshua Hardt's selflessness, the best part of him. He didn't have as much access to phones and computers. His insecurities feasted on his psyche. Once, he called Olivia and she didn't answer— she'd left on vacation to spend some time with her parents. He had trouble understanding how her world could go on without him there. Intellectually, Hardt knew that she needed a break from working full time as a preschool teacher while also attending school at Colorado State University at Pueblo. But even so, he felt resentful that she could even think of relaxing without him. "You have it easy," he told her in a surly voicemail in which he chastised her for not answering his call when she knew he was in a war zone, knew that he could die at any moment. "You don't give a shit about me," he said in another of the many nasty messages he left her while she was away with her parents. "I'm busting my ass, and you're having fun."

"Baby we just got [off] the phone tonight after patching up another argument, which of course was my fault," he wrote her by hand on July 24, 2009.

> I love you so much and I always worry about you. It's hard to explain, baby. I had guard tonight and it felt like time stood still for me.... Please don't get any ideas about leaving because I need you so much.... I truly want you to have fun. I just get nervous and really weird and become this jerk. I'm trying to control it but it's hard it's something that will work in time.... I love you so much honey. Your my angel. An angel that keeps me safe and watches over me and protects me.

Joshua and Olivia Hardt were far from alone in their struggle to keep a marriage alive with one spouse in a war zone. But sometimes it sure felt that way.

By the time Brown and 3-61 Cav arrived in the country, the Taliban didn't just control the road near Combat Outpost Keating; they also owned the one around Forward Operating Base Bostick at Naray. The jingle trucks that had once made their way north every two weeks in a relatively casual convoy, unarmed, now had to run a much more sinister gauntlet, laid down by an unholy alliance of insurgents and local gangsters who stopped the convoys at random checkpoints to exact "tolls." Often the drivers would simply flee, leaving their vehicles to be picked apart like carrion. Fuel trucks were a particularly coveted target. Contractors began paying the Taliban not to attack them as they delivered their goods, but locals ultimately refused to drive to Forward Operating Base Bostick without a U.S. escort both ways.

Brown felt besieged. His home base, FOB Bostick, was itself rarely attacked—it was an island of security—but his squadron was fighting for its life whenever its men went beyond the wire. In Naray, he had only one platoon of eighteen guys and a single company commander—and that area was the only one in his larger area of operations with any prospect of success, any likelihood of being worth the fight. Trying to determine how best to manage the situation, Brown reached out via email to previous commanders. Officers from 1-91 Cav insisted that everything had been great until 6-4 Cav replaced them and screwed it all up; the officers of 6-4 Cav said that things had been going to hell anyway, and that 1-91 Cav had just gotten out when the getting was good.

It didn't really matter to Brown whose fault it was, and anyway, he imagined that the truth lay somewhere in the middle. An influx of American development funds intended to help locals pave the main road had ended up in the hands of Taliban fighters who "taxed" local contractors through extortion. With that source of income, combined with the proceeds from a partnership with timber gangsters, the Taliban was offering young local men a fairly lucrative way of life. Brown certainly admired the work Kolenda had done with the Hundred-Man Shura, but ultimately that coalition had been a fragile one and didn't survive Kolenda's departure. The Afghan authorities had made no meaningful effort to take over his role or to empower a capable government official to try.

To Brown, Kolenda's success seemed evidence that a gifted American commander could make himself a "viceroy" in Afghanistan, at least for a while. But that history was almost irrelevant to the immediate needs of 3-61 Cav: Brown, with an insufficient number of troops, was now confronted by a major Taliban surge in Kunar Province. In late June, some of his soldiers with C Troop were out on a mission with ANA soldiers when they were ambushed. The ANA commander—without question the best officer in the 6th Kandak, or Afghan National Army battalion—was sprayed by shrapnel from an RPG. Evacuated from Forward Operating Base Bostick, he never came back. A couple of weeks after that, a platoon from C Troop was ambushed in the same spot; the twenty-nine-year-old platoon sergeant, Sergeant First Class Jay Fabrizi of Seffner, Florida, was killed,[76] and several others wounded. In August, Brown sent troops to meet up with a convoy of twenty-three fuel tankers headed to Naray from Forward Operating Base Fenty, but by the time the convoy reached the linkup point where 3-61 Cav would assume security, only one tanker was left; the rest either had refused to leave Combat Outpost Monti, which lay in between Forward Operating Bases Fenty and Bostick, or had been attacked and burned on the way. During the next convoy security mission, Fabrizi's replacement, Sergeant First Class Johnny Weaver, was wounded by RPG shrapnel, as were two other men, one of whom ended up losing a leg.

By the middle of August, Forward Operating Base Bostick was running terrifyingly low on fuel for its helicopters. Colonel George authorized the closure of Observation Post Hatchet, in Kunar Province, to free up a platoon, and he and the Support Battalion commander, Lieutenant Colonel Bob Law, agreed to start running convoys at night, with air support, surveillance drones, and U.S. military accompaniment.

All of this — the ambushes, the casualties, the extraordinary risk — meant that Brown was even more anxious to shut down the smaller outposts, including Combat Outpost Keating, whose closure would allow Black Knight Troop to come to Kunar to join his fight. It also meant that throughout the summer, he focused on the areas where his men were dying, and not on Combat Outpost Keating.

There had been little preparation made at Camp Keating for the August 20 elections beyond receiving the ballots by air a few days beforehand and planning patrols to keep the enemy from attacking the voting location at the Afghan National Police station. The Bastards left early in the morning and set up at the Northface, high and low, to watch over the camp and the police station. Red Platoon guarded the perimeter. The patrols didn't see a single person visit the voting booths. Not one.

---

[76] Two years before, Fabrizi's sons Jason Allen, nine, and Tyler, six, had lost their stepfather, Specialist Ryan Bell, of Colville, Washington, after he and five other soldiers were killed by an IED in Samarra, Iraq.

Truth was, they didn't really care. Troops from 3-61 Cav were more interested in the enemy's B-10 recoilless rifle than they were in this anemic version of the free and fair exercise of democracy. As the sun began to set, the polling station closed. The troops figured that about four people had voted, yet somehow, as they were later told, all of the ballots had been filled out. Even fishier were the numbers in Barg-e-Matal, where U.S. forces counted only 128 voters, though around twelve thousand votes were said to have been "cast."

The initial results had Karzai winning with 54 percent of the vote, though the election was immediately assailed as riddled with fraud. In what was now familiar Afghan fashion, the organization charged with keeping the process clean and fair—the Independent Elections Commission—was itself accused of corruption. An American diplomat working for the United Nations in Kabul, Peter Galbraith, would be fired by U.N. secretary-general Ban Ki Moon after he later accused his boss, U.N. special envoy Kai Elde, of covering up Karzai's rampant fraud; Galbraith estimated that almost a third of the votes for Karzai were phony. Karzai was hardly alone: Brown heard that allies of Karzai's opponent Abdullah Abdullah had stuffed ballot boxes as well, and paid off elders in Naray to deliver thousands of votes for him. (As was their wont, the Naray elders were said to have taken the cash from Karzai's opponents but then actually voted for Karzai, who subsequently began an expensive construction project to build a three-story mosque in Naray.)

The election fraud meant less to the men of Combat Outpost Keating than did the further evidence provided by the ANA soldiers, around this time, that they were worthless—or, as per Jonathan Hill, "garbage." They refused to follow orders during an election-day mission to take care of that recoilless rifle, though this was merely the latest angry note in the cacophonous earful Brown would get every time he talked to most of his captains: the Afghan troops wouldn't patrol, they wouldn't share information, and when pushed by the Americans, they would say "You're not my commander!" and walk off in a huff. The Afghans' weaknesses were exacerbated during the Muslim holy month of Ramadan, which in 2009 began on Friday, August 21, and would end on the evening of Monday, September 21. During Ramadan, Muslims attempt to achieve spiritual rejuvenation by reading the Quran and abstaining from food and drink during daylight hours. Hungry and thirsty, hot in the late-summer sun, the ANA troops were exhausted and irritable. They would refuse to patrol, making an already inferior platoon completely combat-ineffective. Their attrition and AWOL rates were disastrously high through the summer and got even worse during Ramadan. However much the ANA troops endeared themselves to God, or Allah, during that period, they did not win any friends among the Americans at the outpost.

"So what are you doing there?" Amanda Gallegos asked Sergeant Justin Gallegos over the phone. "Are you building schools?"

Gallegos laughed. His ex-wife was so naive sometimes.

They were from two different worlds. When they met, she was a student at the University of Arizona, an Alaskan transplant–turned–sorority girl with a Honda. He was a big, brash local employed by a water vending-machine company, who had lost two older brothers, both killed—he said—while engaged in gang-related activity. He did not care a lick what others thought of him, his decisions, or his behavior. Justin showed Amanda a side of Tucson that excited her, took her to parties full of drugs and violence. They clicked. However tough he acted toward the rest of the world, he was soft and sweet with her. Yet as soon as it became clear that they were going to stay together, Amanda tried to whip him into shape. She told him he had a choice, boots or books—the Army or college. He chose the former. And right around then, Amanda got pregnant. Their son, Macaidan, was almost five now.

Sergeant Armando Avalos and Sergeant Justin Gallegos. *(Photo courtesy of Amanda Marr)*

Sergeant Gallegos returned from his second deployment to Iraq with posttraumatic stress disorder. He had always been aggressive, sometimes a jerk, but this was something else. If anyone looked at Amanda "wrong," he'd become irate. He promised her he'd take a mood stabilizer, told her a physician assistant had prescribed him Zoloft, but that was a lie; instead he drank too much, became destructive, went to jail for fighting. Every night ended in violence of some sort. Amanda barely recognized him anymore; he was like a pit bull locked in a basement, and all anyone had to do was open the door to unleash the fury.

Gallegos was a loyal friend, but he was a nasty drunk and enjoyed causing trouble, and his Army buddies—fellow Red Platoon soldiers Tom Rasmussen and Stephan Mace, sometimes Sergeant Eric Harder from the Bastards—weren't the kind of friends who helped a guy stay on the straight and narrow. One night, while drinking at a bar before the unit's deployment to Afghanistan, Gallegos clumsily spilled his beer. The waitress came over, bent down to wipe up the mess, and got the rest of Gallegos's beer poured on her head for her trouble. The bouncers escorted him to the parking lot, but he made his way through the kitchen, sat back down at the same table, and had another beer. It took probably twenty minutes for the bouncers to figure out that he had made it back in; they threw him out again.

Harder had his own crooked story. Growing up in the Twin Cities, Minnesota, he never knew who his father was. He was raised by his mother, with his grandpa Jerry Carlson—his mother's stepdad, a Korean War veteran—teaching him how to be a man. When Eric was thirteen, Grandpa Carlson died of throat cancer. That was the teenager's first encounter with death before he joined the Army.

When he was eighteen, Harder talked about joining the military with his close friend Matt Logan. One summer's day, the two of them decided to jump into the St. Croix River, separating Minnesota and Wisconsin. It was illegal to jump in on the Minnesota side, but driving the ten minutes to get to the Wisconsin side was a hassle, and once there, you had to pay for parking—so the Minnesota side it was. Harder jumped first—it was about a forty-foot cliff—and began swimming. Logan followed him. The undertow was strong, and it pulled on both of them, but Harder managed to escape it and swim to the Wisconsin side. When he clambered out and looked back, he saw that Logan was only halfway across the river.

"I'm fucking drowning," Logan called. Harder thought he was joking at first, but then he realized his friend was legitimately having difficulty keeping his head above water. Harder jumped back in and swam to him, but it was too late: Logan had been sucked under. His body was found three days later. Harder had a motorcycle—a blue-and-white Ninja 500—and on the way back from Logan's funeral, distracted, he hit the back corner of a car and messed up his knee. He did stucco work for the next five years. Then he snapped out of his stupor and joined the Army in 2005.

Physically, Gallegos and Harder were men, but emotionally, they seemed something else. Was it because of the PTSD, the camaraderie, their youth? Amanda didn't know, but after a while she didn't care. She divorced Justin, though she sometimes hoped it might be just a temporary thing, until he got his act together.

Then his orders came in to go to Afghanistan.

"You know that I'm not coming home from this one, right?" Gallegos said to her.

Amanda would laugh; it was ridiculous. But Gallegos would say things to Macaidan, preparing him to be the man of the house, and not just for the year of his deployment. "When I'm not here, you take care of your mother," he'd say to his four-year-old son.

"This is not going to go well," Gallegos told his ex-wife. "We're going to be in a fucking valley."

They tried to have a sense of humor about things; it was the only way they'd gotten through his two previous deployments. "It sounds like a horrible idea," she said.

"Yeah, it's awesome," he replied.

And then he went there. He'd email her photos of the fishbowl he now called home. "Doesn't this look like the perfect situation?" he'd write. But it wasn't funny. When he used to call from Iraq, there were times when he'd seemed perfectly relaxed. This was different. At Combat Outpost Keating, he was always on edge. Gallegos told Amanda that he'd had a lot of bad days in Iraq, "but here," he added, "it's *all* bad days."

Sergeant Vernon Martin was stressed out, and Specialist Damien Grissette didn't really understand why. They were on guard duty together, and Martin was trying to explain to him about something deep and powerful, something incredibly important that was going on in his life, but at the same time, he wouldn't say precisely what it was.

"I need to get right with the man upstairs," Martin kept saying to Grissette, over and over.

The two men had first bonded at Bagram Air Base; they were on their way to Combat Outpost Keating and saw a number of caskets on their way out. Inside were the remains of the Americans killed at Bari Alai on May 1. Martin, Grissette, Specialist Ian MacFarlane, and Specialist Andrew Stone were all support staff—mechanics, water, and maintenance. The sight of those caskets badly rattled them. "We're all going to get out of here together," they pledged to one another.

Sergeant Vernon Martin. *(Photo courtesy of Brittany Martin)*

Grissette was unaware of Martin's secret—two secrets, really. The chief mechanic at Camp Keating had a wife, Brittany, and three children, ages six, four, and two. He also had a mistress, Specialist Cashet Burks, a logistics expert with 3-61 Cav who lived at Fort Carson, Colorado. The relationship had started out as a friendship, then turned into a fling, and then grown into something deeper still. Martin and Burks had discussed his leaving his wife, but he'd never actually said he would do it. Burks told him that she'd stick with him either way. The day before Thanksgiving in 2008, Burks informed Martin that she was pregnant. He told her he didn't believe in abortion, and he'd support her in whatever decision she made. That August, she had given birth to a baby girl, Haniyah. Martin was worried about how he was going to break the news to his wife and his other children. He wasn't a particular fan of the Army; he'd joined only because he had a family to support. Now he had two.

Martin was a kindhearted jokester who loved to make people laugh. At Camp Keating, he tried to call Cashet every day. He frequently emailed her as well.

From: Vernon Martin
To: Cashet Burks
Subject: wut up

hey wut up? im a call in a lil bit but yea da civilian came out here to fix our shit so its in the process. i been busy so havent been able to call u. im tired as fuk i do alot of shit out here. me and my two soldiers. shits tiring but oh well. i cant wait to leave dis cop hopefully they move us or close dis mofo. Wut i told u bout that before is starting to come tru. im hearing it on dis end so its inevitable. Thnx for sending me sum stuff. I appreciate u doing things for me and im approaching the position financially to be able to do stuff for u lol so i will. I appreciate ur kindness and luv it. neva take it for granted so jus know that. anyway im a hit u up n a lil bit before i take a nap cuz i got a long nite ahead well luv u chat with u soon.

Among the few in whom Martin confided was Specialist Albert "Cookie" Thomas, Camp Keating's new cook. They knew each other from a deployment in South Korea two years before. The men of Camp Keating hadn't much liked their previous cook or his meager offerings, so soon after the more industrious Thomas arrived for a four-week rotation, they'd essentially kidnapped him. By making the bland foodstuffs edible, even tasty, Cookie single-handedly boosted every soldier's morale.

For Martin, Cookie was a sounding board, and they discussed his predicament over and over. Martin would never leave his wife, he said, though he was afraid she might leave *him* when he told her about Burks. Like Martin, Thomas had grown up without a father, so he understood his friend's vow that there was no way he would ever abandon any of his children.

A couple of months into the deployment, a worried Lieutenant Colonel Brown tried to figure out what to do about Captain Porter. By now, Porter had strained relationships with nearly all of his subordinate leaders— Lieutenants Bundermann, Salentine, Bellamy, and Cady; First Sergeant Burton; and his XO, Lieutenant Robert Hull. To a man, they all felt they had an obligation to help out in those areas where they saw Porter as failing, but upon hearing their recommendations, the captain consistently told them, point blank, that he was the commander, not them.

In one incident, Hull wanted to fire mortars on locations from which the enemy had been repeatedly attacking the camp. Porter said no. "We're getting hit from there," Hull said to him. "It's a pattern we're seeing."

"People live near there," Porter replied. "They don't want to hear explosions in the middle of the night." Thought Hull, Fuck that—these people are trying to kill us. Get off your ass and help us figure out who these people are. But he didn't say it out loud.

As the nation headed into Labor Day weekend, McChrystal's report about the way forward in Afghanistan landed on President Obama's *Resolute* desk with a thud on Wednesday, September 2. The sixty-six-page document warned of "serious and deteriorating" conditions in the country and starkly declared that the war was "underresourced"—meaning, in other words, that McChrystal needed more troops, more funding, more intelligence support, and a vast array of other items. "Failure to gain the initiative and reverse insurgent momentum in the near term (next twelve months)—while Afghan security capacity matures—risks an outcome where defeating the insurgency is no longer possible," the report suggested. McChrystal did not specify how many troops he needed; he would separately present the president with a number of options (and associated risks), one of which would be to send an additional forty-five thousand U.S. troops to join the sixty-two thousand already in the country. A hundred and seven thousand troops would be more than triple the number in Afghanistan when President Obama put his hand on the Bible and swore to protect the nation.

The report's arrival punctuated the failure of national security adviser James Jones to help manage the president's relationship with the generals across the river in Virginia. The mistrust between the White House and the Pentagon that summer was palpable. For their part, White House officials believed that McChrystal had surrounded himself with advisers who'd decided to play the Washington game, by leaking information, chatting up reporters, and trying to curry favor with various insiders.[77] To the White House, it seemed that McChrystal's men, so admiring of the modern "celebrity-general" model that Petraeus embodied (the "surge" of troops in Iraq, undertaken on his recommendation, was now widely credited with having helped rescue that war from disaster), were seeking to anoint another celebrity savior for this war. Indeed, sometimes it looked as though McChrystal and his team were engaged in two wars: one on the ground in Afghanistan, and the other, a separate war of public relations and politics, in Washington, D.C.

Chris Kolenda, now a colonel, was not among this group of press whisperers, but he had become a strategic adviser to McChrystal in June. The new undersecretary of defense for policy, Michele Flournoy, had brought Kolenda into the Pentagon in February, as her adviser on counterinsurgency and her uniformed lead for the Reidel Report. When McChrystal (who had met the former 1-91 Cav squadron leader at the Pentagon) became commander in Afghanistan, he brought Kolenda with him to lead the strategic assessment and implementation strategy (the main parts of the initial assessment requested by Gates), as well as to develop counterinsurgency guidance for all of ISAF.

Kolenda was too focused on his work to pay attention to the very public signals being sent to the president by other McChrystal advisers, but they were unmistakable. On September 18, 2009, reporter Nancy Youssef of McClatchy Newspapers published a story under the headline "Mili-

---

[77] This attitude and these advisers would ultimately bring about the end of McChrystal's military career. He resigned in the summer of 2010, after *Rolling Stone* published "The Runaway General" by Michael Hastings, in which the general and his advisers were quoted making a number of disparaging comments about officials in the Obama administration, from President Obama himself to Vice President Biden to Jones and on and on. McChrystal was replaced as commander of ISAF by Petraeus.

tary Growing Impatient with Obama on Afghanistan." Wrote Youssef: "In Kabul, some members of McChrystal's staff said they don't understand why Obama called Afghanistan a 'war of necessity' but still hasn't given them the resources they need to turn things around quickly. Three officers at the Pentagon and in Kabul told McClatchy that the McChrystal they know would resign before he'd stand behind a faltering policy that he thought would endanger his forces or the strategy. 'Yes, he'll be a good soldier, but he will only go so far,' a senior official in Kabul said. 'He'll hold his ground. He's not going to bend to political pressure.'" That official added, "Dithering is just as destructive as ten car bombs."

Dithering: this one word summed up so much of the ill will between the president and his top general in Afghanistan. But beyond those two men, it also expressed what many other military leaders thought of this president and his decision-making process. Its utterance by a McChrystal aide (presumably) to a reporter, however, was the kind of insubordination that made the president's top advisers seethe.

In September, someone leaked the general's report to Bob Woodward, and on September 20, 2009, the *Washington Post* published a redacted version of it. Woodward's story was entitled "McChrystal: More Forces or 'Mission Failure.'" The leak was seen at the White House as the ultimate attempt to force the president's hand. How could this very green chief executive refuse his top general's request for more troops to fight a war that Obama himself had pledged to win?

In Kabul, McChrystal expressed frustration to Kolenda and other aides about the leaks, as well as about public characterizations of him as being ready to resign if he didn't get what he wanted. The general would subsequently dismiss the latter claim as a complete fabrication; resignation was something he had never even discussed with any of his top aides, he said. As to how Woodward had gotten his hands on a copy of the strategic assessment, McChrystal would maintain that he knew nothing about it: it hadn't come from his team, he insisted, and it was only after the report had been transmitted to Washington, D.C., that the leak had occurred—and very quickly so.

McChrystal's protests notwithstanding, senior White House officials had little doubt that the Pentagon was pushing the president. On one point, however, everyone could agree: all of this was significantly damaging to the United States' strategic interests.

Now that the Afghan presidential elections were over and the White House could assess where to go next, President Obama began holding a series of meetings with his national security team—Gates, Jones, Secretary of State Hillary Clinton, and many others—to review, again, the entire Afghanistan strategy. His top aides were convinced that the president had to regain control of the decision-making process. This was just a mess.

By September, attacks had become so frequent at Camp Keating that many pilots refused to land their helicopters there at all—not at night, not during Red Illume, just...never. Some excuse was always found not to go. Moreover, though the mission at Barg-e-Matal was supposed to end just days after the July 12 air assault, U.S. troops were still there in September, and air assets continued to be diverted to assist them. The overall problem of resupplying missions got worse, with the result that the troops at Combat Outpost Keating and OP Fritsche started running even shorter on supplies. They refrained from using electricity during daylight hours and showered just once a week. They were not alone in their scarcity: the paucity of resupply missions throughout Brown's area of operations had reached a crisis point.

Eric Harder didn't like it, but he understood the pilots' reluctance to land at Keating. Helicopters were *loud*—about ten minutes before the Chinooks arrived, you could hear them coming in. Even waiting until the moon was hiding didn't make it safe enough to fly in the valley, thought Harder. The Taliban could down a bunch of choppers if they planned it right.

ISAF intended to withdraw from Barg-e-Matal at the end of September, so Brown started preparing, once again, for the opportunity to shut down Camps Keating and Lowell. Major General Scaparrotti had made it clear that when the U.S. troops departed from Nuristan, they couldn't leave a vacuum in their wake; there would need to be some kind of security presence, an Afghan one, to prevent the area from becoming a Taliban haven.

Brown had tried to host a district-wide shura meeting upon his arrival that spring, but the key leader of the Kamdesh Village shura, Abdul Rahman (the good one), was away in Pakistan. When Rahman returned that summer, Brown tried again. In July, invitations were sent out to the elders, but the RSVPs came back with regrets—the roads weren't secured, the Nuristani elders said, so they didn't feel they could risk the trip to Forward Operating Base Bostick. In August, immediately after the elections, at the start of Ramadan, Brown tried again. This time, the shura would be held at Combat Outpost Keating. The elders were receptive to the idea.

It was Brown's first shura in the Kamdesh area. "We're not going to stay here forever," he told the elders. "So we've been talking about what will be here in terms of security for you and your people after we leave." He described a plan to create a new Afghan Border Police battalion staffed by Kamdesh locals to protect the area. Brown also made a pitch for Abdul Rahman to become the district administrator for Kamdesh, but Rahman himself rejected the offer: he didn't think the police-force idea would work, he said, and he didn't want to be responsible for it. No one in Kamdesh had enough power to organize and maintain a standing force to keep them safe, he said, and the Afghan government wasn't providing them with the security they needed.

Brown left the shura dejected. He had hoped something good could come out of what seemed to be a Sisyphean process; it might mean that his men would return home safely and not in caskets. He talked about the disappointing meeting with Colonel Shamsur Rahman of the Afghan Border Police, who had good sources of intelligence in the area. How could they fill the power vacuum in preparation for the Americans' leaving? Colonel Rahman suggested that it might make sense to reach out to the long-exiled HIG leader Mullah Sadiq. Sadiq was living in Pakistan, where he'd fled after U.S. Special Forces began pursuing him, likely in 2006;[78] he was considered at the time to be a high-value target to be captured or killed. But HIG's leadership had since reconsidered the group's participation in the insurgency, and Colonel Kolenda and 1-91 Cav had worked on Sadiq as a possible candidate for reconciliation.

---

[78] Others believe Sadiq fled to Pakistan in fear of U.S. forces in 2002. It's possible that both theories are true, given the porous border and the frequent trips made back and forth between Afghanistan and Pakistan by declared enemies of the United States and the Afghan government.

Mullah Sadiq in Kamdesh in the fall of 2009, a photograph given to the members of 3-61 Cav as a "confidence-building measure" to show that he was back from Pakistan. *(Photo courtesy of Brad Brown)*

Sadiq, Colonel Rahman insisted, was not a bad guy. Born into a poor family, he had nevertheless gone to school and was relatively well educated; more important, he was extremely well respected in Kamdesh. After doing some research, Brown learned that Sadiq had actually shared information with U.S. Special Forces when they first arrived in Naray, until the U.S. troops got caught up in a historical grudge dating back to the 1986 murder of mujahideen leader Mohammed Anvar Amin—a feud layered atop an age-old land dispute. Amin's son, a well-connected contractor, blamed his father's death on Sadiq, and he was the informant who told a U.S. Special Forces team that the HIG leader was working with the Taliban and Al Qaeda, thereby causing him to be placed on the "kill/capture" list.[79]

After checking with his chain of command, on September 6, Brown

---

[79] Some U.S. intelligence sources insist that there is no evidence for Amin's son's belief; others maintain that throughout the war with the USSR, HIG repeatedly tried to scuttle Mohammed Anvar Amin, and that Anvar's killer was indeed backed by Sadiq.

sent a letter to Sadiq. "In previous years, the Government of the Islamic Republic of Afghanistan and International Security Forces have worked in close partnership with the shuras and elders throughout Kamdesh District," he wrote. "We would like to rebuild this friendship and return peace to Nuristan, and ask your assistance and wisdom in this effort."

He felt he needed to put the last few years in context, and to apologize for anything that Sadiq might object to, particularly as it related to Afghan casualties. He continued:

> Many civilians have been injured and killed during the fighting, and I offer apologies to the Nuristani people for the bombings that hurt the innocent. We would like to provide support to the people who have suffered in the fighting, and resume development projects to improve the lives of people throughout Kamdesh. But this can only begin when leaders from all the villages work together to provide security.
>
> The Taliban, funded and resourced by criminals in Pakistan, has been able to influence and recruit the young men of Kamdesh to fight the Afghan National Army, Police, and Coalition Forces. We need assistance from leaders like you that are able to reach out and encourage the people of Kamdesh to cease the violence and oust the Taliban. We ask for your guidance in developing a plan that will improve security and development in Kamdesh. The sooner the people of Kamdesh are able to secure themselves from outside influences, the sooner Coalition Forces will be able to return to their homes and families.
>
> In order to better resolve the security problem in Kamdesh, we invite you, or a trusted associate, to attend a shura to discuss security and cooperation. I offer you my personal protection during this meeting. We are willing to meet at the coalition base in Naray or Urmul, at the Afghan Border Police Headquarters in Barikot, the Naray District Center, or any place that is convenient for you.

He ended the letter by saying that he looked forward to working with Sadiq "to help bring peace and development to the people of Kamdesh."

Brown gave copies of the letter to Colonel Rahman and the Afghan

Border Patrol commander Brigadier General Zaman, who had been a member of HIG when the mujahideen were fighting the Soviets. They said they would get it to Sadiq.

Brown hoped he hadn't just made a big mistake.

Colonel Shamsur Rahman reading Lieutenant Colonel Brad Brown's letter to Sadiq. *(Photo courtesy of Greg Jaffe)*

CHAPTER 28

Send Me

Captain Stoney Portis could have been a character straight out of one of the books written by his dad's cousin Charles Portis, author of *True Grit*. Lean and handsome, polite and determined, Stoney Portis was the quintessential soldier. He'd grown up in Niederwald, Texas — "Population: twenty-three," he would later quip. He had to go to the next town, Lockhart, for high school — not that Lockhart was exactly a booming metropolis.

Portis had thought he was going to take command of Black Knight Troop, and relieve Porter at the outpost, immediately after arriving in Afghanistan. But instead he was sent to Jalalabad; Colonel George felt he was needed more immediately in charge of planning missions for the 4th Special Troops Battalion, which contained an intelligence company, a signal communications company, a reconnaissance troop, and two military police companies. That was Portis's charge until August, when George drove from Forward Operating Base Fenty in Jalalabad to Forward Operating Base Finley-Shields,[80] just down the road. It was only then that he told Portis it was time for him to replace Melvin Porter.

Portis's father worked for Texas Parks and Wildlife and was a farmer, cattle rancher, and welder. His mother, an elementary school teacher, had

---

[80] Named after Specialist James Finley, of Lebanon, Missouri, and Private First Class Andrew Shields, of Battleground, Washington, both of whom were killed by an IED on May 31, 2008, in Jalalabad.

died of leukemia when he was sixteen. She had taught Portis and his siblings about the importance of serving, whether through the military, teaching, or the church. Portis's brother and sister both taught high school; his brother was also a youth minister, and his sister for a time had been a missionary in Mexico. Portis's father, an Army veteran, pushed him to go to West Point first if he was going to join the Army; his experience was that officers by and large got to make the decisions, and if his son ever got put in a bad position as a soldier, he wanted him to be the one calling the shots.

Portis graduated from West Point in 2004. Inside his West Point ring, which he wore on his ring finger next to his wedding band, was inscribed "Isaiah 6:8" — the biblical verse, "Then I heard the voice of the Lord saying, 'Who will go for us, whom shall I send?' And I said, 'Here I am. Send me!'"

On August 27, 2009, Portis flew into Forward Operating Base Bostick, where he met with various officers who briefed him on Camp Keating; Lieutenant Colonel Brown was not among them, since he was actually *at* Keating at the time. Air travel in and around Kamdesh was difficult, as Portis would soon learn. On the night of September 2, 2009, he flew to Observation Post Fritsche, where he met with Lieutenant Jordan Bellamy and White Platoon. The place felt to him like an old Western outpost on the edge of Indian country, like Fort Apache — a solitary compound in the middle of nowhere. Two days later, accompanied by a patrol from White Platoon, Portis walked down from the observation post, heading for Camp Keating.

In his more than ten years in the Army, this was the first time Portis ever got blisters. His whole walk down the Switchbacks, he kept thinking, If I were Taliban, I'd shoot at 'em from here and hide behind this tree and escape that way. Over and over, so many places from which to fire. It was only when they were coming down that last stretch of mountain that he first appreciated where Combat Outpost Keating was. Shocked, he could say only, "Holy shit."

Portis didn't know about Rob Yllescas, or Tom Bostick, or Ben Keating. He'd heard their names, but he didn't know their stories. Soon he met Porter, who told him — inaccurately — that Captain Pecha, his predecessor, had stopped patrolling and never left the operations center because he believed he was going to die at Camp Keating. Awesome,

Portis thought. I'm the enemy's new number-one high-value target, and I didn't even know it. Add to that the good news that the U.S. Army had placed the outpost in what he considered to be the most tactically disadvantageous terrain possible, and there weren't many reasons for Portis to be happy about his new assignment.

He was, however, impressed with the soldiers and his new subordinate leaders. When they needed to relieve themselves, the men of 3-61 Cav would put on full body armor just to head to the piss-tubes, even in 100-degree heat. It was a tremendous nuisance, but they did it anyway. That said something positive about their willingness to follow orders, no matter the discomfort and inconvenience. It was a good sign, Portis thought, because Black Knight Troop was living under the most austere and harsh conditions he'd ever seen.

Portis walked around the camp and got his lay of the land. When he entered the shower trailer, Kirk and Rasmussen happened to be in there, on the cusp of disrobing. With his captain's bars, in this remote locale, Portis could have been no one other than the new commander. Kirk turned to Rasmussen and said, "All right, let's get naked." He dropped his shorts and, as God made him, walked over to Portis and stuck out his hand to greet him. "You must be the new commander," he said. "I'm Sergeant Kirk."

Classic Kirk.

Melvin Porter briefed Stoney Portis for three days, and it became clear to the new commander that the men at Camp Keating desperately needed to build up its defenses. He'd heard the whispers, of course, that the camp could be shut down at any moment, but until that happened, he would proceed as if he and his newly assigned troops were going to be there until July 2010, when they would hand the outpost over to the next company. From eye level, the camp looked fortified. The HESCOs were in place, and there was double- and triple-strand concertina wire enveloping the camp. There certainly were some defensive positions that Portis wanted to improve—first off, he thought, there was too much dead space near the entry control point. He understood, however, that there were limits to how much could be done to make the men safe. "COP Keating is practically worthless," he wrote in his journal. "It's in a bowl with high mountains all around us." There were roughly fifty troops here just trying to exist; their only mission was survival.

* * *

Almost immediately, it was evident that Portis was going to be different from Porter. For example, he had a different reaction to the incoming AK-47 and RPG fire from the Putting Green. Hearing it come in, he stepped outside the operations center and looked up with his binoculars at the northwestern mountain.

"Sir, you might want to get behind some cover," suggested "Doc" Courville.

"Yeah," Portis replied absentmindedly. He went back inside the operations center to get his radio. Lieutenant Cason Shrode was in there, on the radio with John Breeding in the mortar pit. "Hey," Portis told Shrode, "you need to put five rounds of 'Willie Pete' " — white phosphorous —"up there now."

Portis walked down the hall, and Shrode ran after him. "Did you just say you want Willie Pete at this grid?" Shrode asked.

"Yeah," Portis said. "And I want it fucking now."

"You sure?" Shrode asked. Portis was. There were no civilians at the location from which the enemy was firing, so there was no reason to hesitate.

Shrode got back on his radio and told a still-skeptical Breeding, "No, he's serious." Portis glared at Shrode, pissed that his instructions had been questioned, let alone debated, in front of other soldiers. "If Willie Pete works," he said bluntly, "use it."

There was a new sheriff in town.

Portis's aunt and uncle had heard the troops lacked even basic equipment, so they sent him a care package that included some Leatherman Multi-Tools, a device containing a knife, pliers, wire cutters, a saw, a hammer, and on and on. Portis told his three platoon leaders each to select a soldier to receive one of the Multi-Tools — someone deserving of special, if informal, recognition.

Salentine picked Specialist Chris Griffin, a member of the Sault Ste. Marie Tribe of Chippewa Indians, from Kincheloe, in the upper peninsula of Michigan. Griffin was a warrior, Salentine thought, who fought and lived with a passion that was second to none. That passion sometimes pushed boundaries—he and Jon Hill almost came to blows once, for instance—but if Salentine could have had ten Griffins, he'd have counted himself lucky.

Specialist Christopher Griffin. *(Photo courtesy of Kerri Griffin Causley)*

Griffin was quiet and kept to himself. He smoked a lot and spent hours reading; before deploying to Iraq, he'd read the entire Quran from cover to cover. He seemed overwhelmed by the Leatherman, as if it were much more than just a hundred-dollar multi-tool, as if he'd never received a gift before. The new commander was surprised to hear, later on, that the twenty-four-year-old had taken the time in the middle of this war zone to write his captain's aunt and uncle a thank-you note for the present.

Colonel George briefed Major General Scaparrotti and the Afghan minister of the interior on the latest developments in his area of operations, and then he renewed his push to close down Combat Outposts Keating and Lowell. Most of the reasons McChrystal had given him for delaying these moves were no longer operative, save for his stated desire not to "get ahead of the president," which also seemed moot. Scaparrotti approved the plan: the troops at Combat Outpost Keating could start packing up on October 4.

On his first official day in charge, September 20, Portis had three tubs of ice cream flown in for his new troops to enjoy after the change-of-command ceremony: cookies-and-cream, mint chocolate chip, and

pralines-and-cream. Later that day, he joined Colonel George and Lieutenant Colonel Brown at a banquet held at the base for the Muslim holiday of
Eid al-Fitr; also in attendance were members of the Afghan National
Police, the leaders of the ANA company stationed at Keating, and some
village elders. There was a lot of friendly chatter as the men sat around a
picnic table together.

"How effective is Combat Outpost Keating?" George asked the ANA
commander.

"We're very effective," he said.

To Portis, this was an example of what U.S. forces referred to as
"Afghan math"—a certain disconnection from reality that Afghans
tended to exhibit when asked to provide honest assessments.

"How effective will Combat Outpost Keating be after we leave?"
George asked.

This time, there was no disconnect: the leader of the ANA laughed.
"When you leave, we'll leave," he said.

George explained that the United States wasn't going to be in Kamdesh in perpetuity, which was why it was important, he said, that the
locals be able to govern themselves and provide their own security. He
didn't intend to signal an imminent departure, but the locals had been
watching the troops ship out sling-loads of nonessential equipment from
the outpost. The conversation suggested to many of the men at the
table—Americans and Afghans alike—that there was a timetable, one
that was obviously already under way.

At least one U.S. officer later recalled that he was stunned to hear
George share this information; he felt sure it would be passed on to the
enemy. "Anger, contempt, shock, disbelief—all emotions that ran though
my mind in the following days," the officer remembered. In his view, and
the view of other members of Black Knight Troop, Colonel George had
just told an untrustworthy group that the Americans were leaving soon.

In his room at Fort Hood in Texas, Rick Victorino—the intel analyst
from 6-4 Cav—frowned. He had left COP Keating four months before,
but he couldn't stop thinking about his time there, and he'd programmed
a Google news alert to let him know whenever the word *Nuristan*
appeared in a media story.

On September 22, journalists at Bagram were informed that General

McChrystal had given commanders the order to begin pulling their troops from remote bases—which would reportedly include Combat Outposts Keating and Lowell. The news immediately made its way to Victorino.

Shit, they're going to be attacked, Victorino thought to himself; they're going to be overrun. He was sure that the information would be quickly rebroadcast by the Taliban to insurgents in the Kamdesh area.

The next day at work, he talked about this development with Mazzocchi and Meshkin. They all agreed: things were about to get rough for the men of Black Knight Troop, 3-61 Cav.

Portis received orders to prepare for a closure of Camp Keating; their last flight out would be on October 10. Just like that. They would have two weeks to tear the camp down. Portis called his team: "Here's the mission," he told them. "We're leaving Combat Outpost Keating."

They all rolled their eyes as if to say, The new guy doesn't understand how it works. They'd been told again and again that Camp Keating was going to be closed down, and nothing ever happened. But Portis impressed upon them that this time, it was real, and so they stayed up all night, planning the move down to the last detail. They decided they would need forty-five sorties, or trips, on Chinooks.

Portis was excited but nervous. His nerves began to fray on Monday, September 28, when he received intelligence that fighters from the Taliban and HIG had held a shura in Upper Kamdesh to try "to resolve the conflict between the two groups in order to attack the COP." A Taliban leader from the Waygal Valley had come to the shura to meet with HIG leaders. Two local officers with the Afghan National Police had also been present.

Portis sought out the recently hired Afghan National Police chief, Shamsullah (whose predecessor had quit), and told him what he had heard. Shamsullah said that the officers had gone without his knowledge, and he promised to talk to them about it. He wouldn't give Portis any details about the meeting, but he did confide that he'd heard from the locals that the outpost was closing. The level of detail the police chief had at his fingertips was stunning: at one point, he said he knew that Black Knight Troop was packing up nonessential gear "and that...we would run non-stop birds all night to backhaul and close Keating and Fritsche starting in ten days (09OCT) for a duration of several days," Portis emailed Brown later that day.

The captain was incredulous. How could Shamsullah know such specifics? Portis had not been particularly pleased when the brigade leadership suggested to the shura elders and the leaders of the ANA and Afghan police that Black Knight troops were headed for the exits, but at least that information had been vague. This was something else, and it worried him. Locally, the only ones officially informed of the plans were Portis's lieutenants and the officers at Forward Operating Base Bostick; the operations centers at both posts were under lock and key. But planning about the closure of Camp Keating had gone all the way up the U.S. chain of command to Kabul; somewhere along the line, someone had said too much to the wrong person.

"Do you think the Taliban and HIG have the same information?" Portis asked Shamsullah.

"Everyone knows this," said the chief.

"Do you think we're going to be attacked?" Portis asked.

"Yes," said Shamsullah. "Tomorrow."

Portis wasn't quite sure how to process this; false warnings of an imminent attack, he knew, were common. He told the police chief that there wasn't an approved plan yet for closing the camp. "We could be told to leave soon, or we could be told to leave after the winter," he fibbed. "I'll keep you informed as best I can, but currently our intentions are to winterize and fly out equipment that needs repairs."

The captain walked away from this discussion filled with anger and unease. Obviously, the Americans couldn't leave a base that they were sharing with the ANA without letting the Afghan commander know they were leaving. But Shamsullah knew an unnerving amount of information about the Americans' plans. Portis wondered if the police chief—who hailed from Mandigal, a center of the local insurgency—might not be playing both sides, having his own survival foremost in his mind. Portis was planning on heading up to Observation Post Fritsche on Thursday, October 1, to check on some equipment—everything would need to be accounted for—and while there, he would meet with the Kamdesh shura to find out whatever he could about this report of a Taliban–HIG détente.

In his email to Brown, Portis wrote that he was "concerned" that local Afghans and members of the Afghan National Police were sharing information about the evacuation of the local outposts, now being called

Operation Mountain Descent. Portis's advisory came at the same time as a report that "Bad" Abdul Rahman was preparing to take Barg-e-Matal back now that 1-32 Infantry troops had withdrawn. It was not uncommon to hear that local Taliban and HIG leaders were meeting, so Portis's news didn't cause anyone to hit the panic button. Since June, the squadron had also gotten numerous tips that more than a hundred fighters were about to attack one base or another, including COP Keating and FOB Bostick. Brown didn't know how seriously to take what Portis had heard. He needed more proof that this threat was real before he could do anything; without more concrete information, he couldn't credibly call in choppers to bring reinforcements. There was also the issue of the moon, which right now was at too bright a point in its illumination cycle to afford the helicopters the darkness they needed to be safe. And anyway, 3-61 Cav would be leaving the Kamdesh Village area within a couple of weeks.

Portis briefed all of his officers and senior noncommissioned officers on what he'd learned, emphasizing the importance of operational security — meaning, keeping their mouths shut. "I don't know how the fuck Shamsullah knows this, but he knows this," he said.

The troops who were primarily tasked with gathering information about potential threats to the outpost were intelligence collector Sergeant Robert Gilberto,[81] intelligence analyst Sergeant Ryan Schulz, and, to a lesser extent, fire-support officer Lieutenant Cason Shrode.

As an intelligence collector, Gilberto could speak with informants and pay sources, whereas Schulz, as an intelligence *analyst,* was forbidden to do either of those things. But for much of September, Gilberto was still at Barg-e-Matal, where he'd been assigned several months before, so COP Keating was without a clique of patiently assembled local informants. Fire-support officer Shrode had stepped in to try to fill the breach; since he was also involved in paying contractors for the few development projects that were still in progress, he had the authority to deal with locals and pay them.

Earlier in the month, after hearing that the Taliban had held a meeting in a nearby village to discuss a potential future attack on the outpost, Schulz and Shrode had requested an unmanned Predator drone to help

---

[81] Not his real name.

them keep an eye on events in their area. That request, however, was rejected by commanders at Regional Command East in Bagram, who prioritized demands on surveillance assets for other missions, particularly at Barg-e-Matal. Shrode and others discussed using the Raven UAV (short for "unmanned aerial vehicle") they had on base. Weighing less than five pounds and flown by remote control, the Raven looked almost like a toy airplane, though the whole system cost about a quarter of a million dollars, and the craft had a range of more than six miles. The Raven, though, was not especially effective in the powerful winds common to Nuristan's mountain ranges; in this situation, the odds were that it would be blown off course and would have to be recovered by 3-61 Cav troops. Without a Predator, they were stuck.

Toward the end of September, Gilberto returned to Combat Outpost Keating. Rumors of future enemy attacks were always coming in to the outpost, but now the intel collector noticed a definite uptick in such warnings. The nearby Afghan National Police station, for instance, received a letter from the local Taliban advising policemen to stay away from the station because an attack on Camp Keating was imminent.

Gilberto shared the intelligence with Schulz and Portis, and they discussed the best next steps to take. One warning referred to an assault planned for dawn the next day, so Portis ordered Black Knight Troop to increase security; dawn broke, but nothing happened. It was terrifically difficult to know which tips to take seriously. Per protocol, Gilberto sent each draft intelligence report up to his team leader at Forward Operating Base Bostick, but for some reason, he didn't see most of these reports included in the squadron's daily intelligence summary.

Likewise, information accumulated at the squadron and brigade levels never made its way down to Combat Outpost Keating. In retrospect, there were plenty of clues that the enemy had something serious in the works. On September 23, one source informed the Americans, insurgents from Kamdesh, Mirdesh, and other communities met in Mandigal. A different source said that half of the insurgents were from Nuristan and the other half from Pakistan, where they were associated with Lashkar-e-Taiba, one of the largest Islamist terrorist groups in South Asia. Yet another source told the Americans that "there are still issues between HIG and TB [Taliban] but for the purposes of attacking Keating they will work together." One local testified that insurgents in Mandigal had 107-millimeter rockets and ten suicide bombers. Another said there were more than two hundred fighters planning on attacking Camp Keating. On Tuesday, September 29, "a large number of people" were reported to be gathering in Lower Kamdesh for an attack on Combat Outpost Keating and Observation Post Fritsche. A report from October 2 stated that thirty to thirty-five men then in Barg-e-Matal were "planning to attack COP Keating…and COP Lowell within the week." The assault force would be made up of locals with RPGs as well as "suicide attackers."

None of this information reached Gilberto and the others at the outpost because at the time, all of these truths were scattered among bushels of lies, gossip, nonsense, misunderstandings, and plans that were never carried out. At the higher levels, largely due to concerns about information oversaturation, such intelligence reports were not widely disseminated: since nobody had the time or the expertise to sift through the bycatch, blanket decisions had to be made that kept intelligence from reaching the field. Too much information can be as worthless as none — that was a lesson of 9/11, and it would soon be a lesson of Combat Outpost Keating as well.

Faruq left the community of Lowluk when he was eight, after his father, a sheep and goat herder, had died. The boy's maternal uncle took him under his wing and sent him to a local madrassa, where clerics who subscribed to fundamentalist Salafi Islam instructed him in the Quran and how to be a good Muslim. Many of these clerics had been trained in special camps that were funded with money from Saudi Arabia and at the very least tolerated by Pakistan's Inter-Services Intelligence agency and its military. Part of the camps' purpose was to create holy warriors who would wage war against the Indians in Kashmir. But after the United States attacked Afghanistan in October 2001, mullahs at Faruq's mosque began preaching that the infidels had now arrived in their homeland to impose their beliefs on and divide the Afghan people. They were not to be trusted, Faruq was told: when they invaded your country, you were obligated to defend yourself and Islam, to help your Muslim brothers.

In 2007, when he was eighteen, Faruq had traveled to the Waygal Valley, where he met Mullah Abdul Rahman Mustaghni, the local Taliban commander whom the 6-4 Cav had referred to as "Bad" Abdul Rahman. Rahman told Faruq that a Taliban fighter's only job was to attack Americans, then to sleep, then to wake and attack Americans again. He operated under the command of the "shadow governor" of Nuristan, the Taliban leader Mullah Dost Mohammad.

Faruq had been following Rahman for two years. Barg-e-Matal was their home base, but they traveled throughout the area. Every week, sometimes every day, they would fire at Americans, with rockets, with guns, with RPGs. Eventually, they were given more powerful weapons by their friends across the border in Pakistan, including heavy machine guns and mortars.

Among Faruq's fellow fighters was one from the local village of Pitigal. Ishranullah's father had been killed years before, in a tribal dispute. At the age of ten, Ishranullah, like Faruq, was sent to a madrassa, this one across the border in Peshawar, a major transit zone between Afghanistan and Pakistan. There he became devout and learned about the "injustices" committed by foreigners. As a Taliban fighter, he also came to hate the Afghan National Army, believing its soldiers to be just as treacherous as the infidels, guilty of spilling the blood of other Muslims while claiming to believe in Allah.

Faruq and Ishranullah were just two out of hundreds of local fighters in an insurgency that was gaining strength in Nuristan. They fought the Americans in Barg-e-Matal and fired upon them at Camp Keating and Observation Post Fritsche. Many came from Kamdesh Village and nearby settlements such as Mandigal, Agasi, and Agro. They did what they were told. And in September 2009, their commanders and Nuristan's Taliban "shadow governor," Dost Mohammed, began planning something truly catastrophic for the Americans, something that would put the Taliban in Nuristan on the map.

By this point, President Obama and White House officials thought they had successfully wrested control of the Afghanistan debate from the men with the bars and stars—McChrystal, Mullen, and Petraeus. Come the end of September, the public and the media would focus on a series of meetings the president had with his "war council"—a large deliberative body made up of top national security advisers, military and civilian, who were to help guide Obama's decision-making about what to do next in Afghanistan and Pakistan. McChrystal was a member of the team, beamed in from Kabul on secure video teleconference, but he was just one of many.

On October 1, McChrystal spoke at the International Institute for Strategic Studies, in London, about the options in Afghanistan. His written speech had been approved through all the proper channels. During the question-and-answer period, he made it clear that he favored sending more troops to that country and maintaining a long-term presence there. The general was asked if he would be happy if within two years, Afghanistan could be handled through a counterterrorist approach, with drone missile strikes and smaller Special Forces teams — which, everyone knew, was the approach favored by Vice President Biden and other top presidential advisers. "The short, glib answer is 'No,'" McChrystal replied. "A strategy that does not leave Afghanistan in a stable position is probably a shortsighted strategy."

McChrystal's remark was immediately seized upon by reporters as yet another shot fired in the Obama-versus-McChrystal troop showdown. White House officials were divided on the question of whether McChrystal was somewhat naive or downright manipulative. This wasn't some offhand comment made to a reporter who happened to catch him in a mess hall at Bagram; McChrystal had flown to London, delivered a speech, and taken questions. And all the while, he was enjoying a spate of positive media: a profile on *60 Minutes* had just aired, and a major story for the *New York Times Magazine* was in the works. The truth was that media coverage of the speech unfairly inflamed the matter, portraying McChrystal as having personally gone after Vice President Biden, and incorrectly reporting that he had referred to Biden's plan as a proposal for "Chaos-istan," when in fact the general had used that term specifically in reference to another study altogether.

McChrystal had gone to London to help bolster Britain's support for the war. When later asked about his comments at the International Institute for Strategic Studies, he said that he'd intended to fully endorse President Obama's stated policy as well as the deliberative process the president had commenced, and after the event, he'd felt he had succeeded in doing that. He was shocked when his remarks were interpreted as criticism of the vice president — in some reports, falsely so. But at this stage in the story, the truth was almost an afterthought.

During his predecessor's term, President Obama had heard members of the Bush administration say, again and again, that they were listening to the commanders in the field. He didn't much care for that. First, it wasn't true: the Bush administration had constantly overruled generals' requests for more troops in Iraq and Afghanistan. Second, President Obama firmly believed that the commander in chief had to be the one who set the mission. Now he was getting fed up with what was coming his way from the generals across the Potomac River and in Kabul. Their campaign was impeding a deliberative process, and the president would not be rolled.

On October 2, President Obama flew to Denmark to try to help his adopted hometown of Chicago win its bid for the 2016 Summer Olympic Games. (His effort failed; the nod went to Rio de Janeiro instead.) He summoned McChrystal to meet with him on Air Force One as it sat on the tarmac at Copenhagen Airport. For twenty-five minutes, one on one, the President made it clear to the general: We're going to do this through our process, not via speeches or public relations. He told McChrystal that it looked untoward for him to be running an active media campaign while his commander in chief was attempting to make a resource decision. He also described the process that he wanted to pursue, in which he — the commander in chief — would review the situation in Afghanistan and Pakistan, the nation's objectives in those two hot spots, and overall U.S. strategy. The general responded that he was entirely dedicated to the mission at hand. It wouldn't be accurate to describe McChrystal as contrite, but the president believed McChrystal left their meeting more on the same page with him — and determined to keep a lower profile.[82]

The degree to which the prickliness between the two men over the previous six months had affected the American evacuation of Camp Keating can't be precisely determined. McChrystal's remark to Colonel George, about not wanting to close the bases in Nuristan prematurely for fear of getting ahead of the president, indicated that he was sensitive to the uncomfortable perceptions that had arisen. By the time of McChrystal's London speech, plans were finally under way to close the camp, but the withdrawal date had already been postponed by some months. The damage had been done.

---

[82] This seemed to last until April 15, 2010, in Paris, when McChrystal and his aides made disparaging comments about the president and his top advisers to *Rolling Stone* reporter Michael Hastings, resulting in the June publication of "The Runaway General," which cost McChrystal his job. (See footnote on page 478.)

CHAPTER 29

Elevator Ride

It was a dilemma: Radio Kamdesh's transmission tower and broadcasting devices were expensive pieces of equipment, but shipping them out would require even more helicopter sorties, draining even more resources. Portis was in favor of either abandoning or destroying it all. Brown and George wanted to reuse the apparatus, concerned that if it was left behind, the Taliban would commandeer it and utilize it for their own propaganda.

On September 29, the argument was resolved by God: lightning struck the radio tower and blew it apart.

On October 1, Portis and the leaders of the Bastards — Lieutenant Salentine and Staff Sergeant Kirk Birchfield — hopped on a helicopter headed for Observation Post Fritsche. The men at Camp Keating called such quick journeys to the top of the southern mountain elevator rides. The attack that Afghan National Police chief Shamsullah had warned of had not happened, but Portis still wanted to find out whatever he could, and he thought some of the folks in Kamdesh Village might be able to help him. He was also hoping to meet with some Kamdesh elders so he could learn more about the HIG–Taliban agreement to cooperate. But his main reason for this elevator ride was inventory: he was looking for equipment, knowing what sticklers Army bureaucrats were.

The men had originally planned to walk up the mountain, but then Salentine noted that the chopper was going up to Fritsche anyway, so

499

what the hell, why *shouldn't* they just take an elevator ride? It was hard to argue with that logic. Portis walked into the operations center and told Bundermann and Shrode where he was going; while he was gone, Bundermann would be in charge of ground forces, and Shrode would supervise the implementation of close air support and mortars.

The trip from Keating to Fritsche normally took just a matter of seconds, but on this occasion, an insurgent fired on the bird. He scored a direct hit.

"The fuel line's been shot out," said the pilot, who immediately took evasive action and left the valley in the rearview mirror, taking with him Portis, Salentine, and Birchfield. They soon enough landed at Forward Operating Base Bostick, safe but disconcertingly far from their troops. Whether or not he meant to do so, the enemy had succeeded in once again depriving the men at Camp Keating of their commander.

"Bad" Abdul Rahman had wanted to attack Combat Outpost Keating on September 30, but he knew that spies had tipped off the Americans. So he waited.

Hundreds of Taliban warriors had been living in the mountains, watching and waiting to pounce. They saw that despite having been tipped off, the Americans did not bring in more troops or equipment to fortify the base.

Rahman noticed, too, and decided that no more patience was required. They would attack before dawn on Saturday, October 3.

On the night of October 2, Jonathan Hill and Eric Harder zoned out in the barracks, watching a Time-Life documentary about World War II. The Bastards complained a lot, but God, it would have been awful to be in World War II, they agreed. Down in the dirt, with no shoes, the Americans got shredded by German artillery as they stormed the beaches of Normandy. "Those guys basically walked into the valley of hell," Hill said.

They made similar observations about Vietnam after they popped in a bootleg DVD of *Apocalypse Now*. It was a little trippier than the actual footage from World War II, of course, especially the part where the deranged Lieutenant Colonel Bill Kilgore told his men it was safe to surf in the Nung River, even as they were taking artillery rounds from the Vietcong.

After watching both DVDs from start to finish, Hill and Harder called it a night.

Specialist Michael Scusa and Specialist Mark Dulaney were up until about 2:00 a.m., shooting the breeze and talking about their plans. Per usual, Scusa wouldn't stop gabbing about his son, Connor, and how big he was getting. Sometimes the guys would tell Scusa to shut up about his wife and son already, but he wouldn't.

Specialist Michael Scusa. *(Photo courtesy of Jon Hill)*

When Scusa entered the Army, he looked so young — with his glasses and boyish face — that the first thing his sergeant told him was that he seemed like he was wearing his big brother's uniform. One of his fellow joes in the Bastards, Specialist Jonathan Adams, thought of Scusa as having walked right out of a remake of *Revenge of the Nerds,* he was so awkward and dorky. But they all came to respect his calm, measured approach to combat, his kindness, and his work ethic. And his devotion to his family: Scusa was going on leave in a few days and couldn't wait to see his wife, Alyssa, his mother, and his little boy.

He and Dulaney were planning on applying for the Warrant Officer Flight Training program, and while on leave, Scusa intended to get some books that the two of them could use to study for the admissions test. They would be Army pilots together, remaining in a combat arms environment but no longer based in hellholes like Camp Keating.

Noor Din was a truck driver when the Taliban fell in 2001. After that, he signed up to become a police officer to help his country. Din saw Nuristanis rejoice at the arrival of the development dollars that the United States spread around for roads and schools. He also saw Nuristan and the local Kamdesh District become a battlefield as the American presence was challenged by insurgent groups. He saw the grief, the anger, when U.S. troops killed innocent Nuristanis. Their apologies—whether in the form of words or cash—were never enough.

As a police officer, Din tried to help the Americans. For years, he told the U.S. soldiers every time he heard about an imminent attack. The information would come to him from locals, and sometimes he would pick it up while listening to walkie-talkie chatter. Whatever intelligence he could muster, he would share: which village the insurgents were coming from, which spot on which mountain they were planning to fire from.

This attack had been coming for days, he knew—ever since word spread that Camp Keating would soon be closing. At that moment, the clock had started ticking down.

And now here it was, zero hour.

The Taliban fighters came to Urmul in the dead of night. The women and children of Urmul fled, as did many of the men, after being cautioned not to alert the American soldiers in the camp just a few hundred yards away. "We don't have any problems with you," the insurgents told the villagers. "We have a problem with the Americans."

At 4:00 a.m. on October 3, 2009, close to three hundred mujahideen—led by their leader, Abdul Rahman, and scattered over the three mountains and throughout the village of Urmul—turned to Mecca and conducted morning prayers. Then they grabbed their guns and got into position.

Faruq and some others went to the Afghan National Police station about a hundred yards to the northwest, outside Combat Outpost Keating. The insurgents shot and killed two policemen; the third policeman on duty fled. The enemy fighters set up a base there. Other mujahideen went to the Urmul mosque. Many more were still in the mountains, where pine, cedar, fir, and oak trees stood like sentries, providing the Taliban plenty of cover. Fifty-three Americans were in the camp. Most would be sleeping. Maybe ten or fifteen would be on guard.

Ishranullah lurked in the hills, excited. On a number of occasions in the past, he'd been disappointed when the Taliban ran out of ammunition and couldn't do anything for weeks. This was not one of those times. The Taliban had truckloads of ammunition. This attack had been planned and coordinated for weeks.

"There were a lot of foot soldiers from all the surrounding villages," a man from Nuristan would later remember. "Each village volunteered a bunch of soldiers. They thought they were doing jihad, that COP Keating was occupying their land, occupying their area. They thought they were doing a service to their area. They were very, very proud.

"They thought, Let's send a message. The message was: Tell the United States you don't mess with us. It was a suicide mission; a lot of the fighters knew they weren't coming back."

Those who weren't involved knew they'd better make themselves scarce if they wanted to live to see another day. As the sun started to rise on the valley and the mujahideen prepared to attack, Noor Din, the police officer, left Urmul and fled north to Mandigal. He did not warn the Americans.

Din's boss did. Afghan National Police chief Shamsullah approached the camp and spoke with an interpreter whom the U.S. troops referred to as "Ron Jeremy" because of his resemblance to that mustachioed adult-film star.

Red Platoon was responsible for guard duty that night. Shortly before 6:00 a.m., the new shift relieved the guys who had been on watch since midnight. Private First Class Nicholas Davidson came a few minutes early to replace Corporal Justin Gregory near the camp's entry control point, in the gun turret of the tower of the shura building. Gregory was giving Davidson the lowdown—"There are fresh batteries in the radios, the ammunition is over here"—when Ron Jeremy ran over to them.

"The Taliban are here!" he said, urgency in his voice. "They're coming!"

Gregory grabbed the radio and called the tactical operations center. "Hey, TOC, this is ECP," he said—short for "entry control point."

"Yeah?" responded Private First Class Jordan Wong, the radio operator for the camp's headquarters.

"Ron Jeremy just ran in and said Taliban are here," Gregory announced. "You got anything on cameras?" There were PTZ ("pan, tilt, and zoom") security cameras all around the borders of the camp, sending feeds to the operations center.

"I'll check it out," said Wong.

Ron Jeremy then ran to the operations center, where he approached Sergeant Jayson Souter, the Headquarters Platoon NCO in charge of fire support.

"The police chief just came to the gate and told me there are four hundred Taliban hiding around the camp, and they're getting ready to attack!" the interpreter exclaimed.

Souter passed the word to Staff Sergeant James Stanley, who was relieving Sergeant Gallegos as sergeant of the guard. Stanley then radioed the news to everyone on guard.

Ron Jeremy next ran over to Staff Sergeant Kevin Daise, who was sitting by the burning barrels near the latrines. "Hey, Sergeant Daise," he said. "The locals said the Taliban kicked them out of town."

"Okay," Daise replied. But how seriously was he supposed to take this warning? There had been so many false alarms over the past few months.

After telling Daise that the enemy was in Urmul, Ron Jeremy proceeded into the latrines to hide.

"Allahu Akbar," the holy warriors said as they prepared their mortars, their B-10 recoilless rifles, their RPGs, their Dushkas.

God is great.

Declared one insurgent in the hills, in his own tongue, "The prophet Mohammed, peace be upon him, says if you throw an arrow toward the enemy, it is as good as freeing a slave for the sake of Allah."

They recorded these and other exclamations on video, for later posting on YouTube, as part of their propaganda campaign.

"We are ready with the help of Allah," said another. "Bring me the ammunition."

Five fifty-eight a.m.

It began.

CHAPTER 30

"Wish Me Luck"

The mortar pit didn't have a computer, so in these early-morning hours Daniel Rodriguez had to go elsewhere to work on the online correspondence course he was taking to earn points for a promotion. Since he was friends with Docs Cordova and Courville, he used the computer at the aid station. Cordova was studying calculus and physics online through Pikes Peak Community College, but this morning, he was slacking: he was in his bunk, having dozed off while reading Malcolm Gladwell's *Outliers*. Rodriguez spent a while on his correspondence course, then surfed the 'net looking for possible vacation options in Australia; he had some leave time coming.

The first RPG hit the aid station, and Rodriguez didn't need any help identifying what the explosion was. He stopped what he was doing and put on his helmet and a non-Army-issued protective vest—one that actually didn't contain any body armor but was much more comfortable than those that did—just in time for the next blast. Cordova and Courville were now awake; they came from the back of the aid station, where their bunks were.

Rodriguez usually carried an M4 carbine, but this morning he had opted instead for his lighter 9-millimeter semiautomatic pistol. Now he cursed himself for that decision, which had been rooted entirely in sloth. Wearing a T-shirt, shorts, and sneakers, he headed for the door, stopping on the way to look back at Courville and Cordova. "Wish me luck," Rodriguez said. He then went to the door, prepared his 9-millimeter to fire, and sprinted out into the open.

The bullets were coming in sporadically, punctuated by occasional RPG bursts, and Rodriguez zigzagged across the grounds to the laundry, then to the showers and the piss-tubes. His first, human instinct had been, of course, to stay in the aid station, but his sense of duty propelled him to the southwestern corner of the camp, to Mortaritaville, to his team: Breeding, Kevin Thomson, and a new guy just a few days into his tour at Camp Keating, Sergeant Janpatrick Barroga.

As Rodriguez ran to the right, he caught a glimpse of the incoming small-arms fire from the Switchbacks in front of him, sparks in the dawn's dim gray. The bullets, shrapnel, and rocks on the ground sounded to him like popcorn kernels bursting. The gravel hit his legs as he ran at full speed; it felt like hail going in the wrong direction, from the ground toward the sky. He dreamed of being a college football player, but this was an altogether different kind of running for the end zone.

Rodriguez was near the Humvee/guard post known as LRAS-2 when he started firing back toward the Switchbacks with his pistol. He had only fifteen rounds, but he used every last one of them as he sprinted breathlessly toward his team and up the stairs to the mortar pit.

The first blast woke them up, but they remained in bed.

"Was that incoming or outgoing?" asked Hill.

"Outgoing," said Harder. Neither of them opened his eyes. They were both exhausted from staying up late watching those DVDs, and one big explosion wasn't all that odd a sound to hear as dawn broke at Camp Keating. They figured Breeding was just firing a mortar.

Then the second explosion came into the camp, and this one shook the Bastards' barracks.

"Nope, that's incoming," said Harder as he got up and threw on his gear. He was wearing only underwear and shorts, but he was sure he'd be up and down in twenty minutes. His sneakers were outside the barracks — they smelled pretty ripe — and he couldn't find a clean pair of socks.

From the mountains came the staccato of heavy machine-gun fire. Harder knew he had to get outside and take care of whoever this was — and then, he thought, he could go back to bed. He pulled on a tan T-shirt and laced up his hiking boots.

"Hurry up and get your shit on!" Harder yelled to his men — Michael

Scusa, Christopher Griffin, Specialist Jeremy Frunk, and Specialist Mark Dulaney. They grabbed their ammunition and weapons. Harder opened the door and saw what was going on outside. He turned to Hill.

"This is a big one," he said, though he had yet to realize just how bad it was.

The first thing John Breeding heard from his position in the mortar pit was a cacophony of RPG explosions, one after another after another. Everyone promptly got suited up. Thomson, his gear already on, was standing by the door, near the radios, and he ran out to remove the tarp from the M240 machine gun so he could fire it into the hills.

Thomson was ripping the poncho liner off the gun, about to run around and fire it, when Rodriguez arrived on the scene.

"Switchbacks!" Rodriguez yelled. "Switchbacks! Target sixty! Hit the Switchbacks!"[83]

But just as Thomson stepped in front of him, Rodriguez saw the private's face explode in a burst of red. A bullet fired from the high ground had found its mark in the Thomson's right cheek, going through his mouth and out his left upper back. He fell onto the ground.

Rodriguez went to him; Kevin Thomson was gurgling, but he couldn't speak. His eyes were filigreed with burst vessels. A pool of blood and parts of his head were spilling into his helmet, into his body armor, onto the ground. The gore had the texture of soup. Rodriguez was at once horrified and nauseated by the sight. Thomson's eyes glazed over and turned black and red.

"Thomson!" Rodriguez yelled. "THOMSON!"

The private was gone. That calm kid from Nevada didn't make a sound; he didn't move. Two minutes into their attack on Combat Outpost Keating, the Taliban had scored their first casualty.

The new guy, Barroga, poked his head out of the mortar pit to see what was going on.

"Get on the sixty!" Rodriguez told him, pointing him to the 60-millimeter mortar tube. But he saw Barroga hesitate. The kid was weighed

---

[83] "Target sixty" was an instruction to get on the 60-millimeter mortar tube and start firing.

down with fear, inexperience, and instant regret. There lay Thomson's body.

Barroga thought he probably could have prevented Thomson's death, could have said to him, "Hey, we're getting shot at, wait two minutes before you run out to throw off the tarp," but this was his first firefight, and he'd been at Camp Keating for only a few days, while Thomson had been there for months. And now ...

"Get inside and take cover!" Rodriguez yelled. "Watch my back."

Rodriguez ran to the M240 machine gun and opened fire at RPG Rock. He saw about half a dozen insurgents there, and he angrily banged rounds at them until the belt was empty. Then, firing with his 9-millimeter, he stepped away and with his free hand tried to pull Thomson's body into the mortar pit's ops center, but the dead soldier's foot was stuck in the steel pickets on which the machine gun was mounted. Rodriguez, significantly smaller than Thomson, couldn't budge him.

Rodriguez ran inside. "Thomson's dead!" he told the other two. "Thomson's dead!"

"Are you sure?" asked Breeding. "Check his pulse!" But through the doorway, Breeding had seen Thomson get shot, and he knew from the limp way he'd fallen that he was dead; he had seen it too many times before.

Rodriguez acknowledged that yes, he had checked Thomson's pulse — and there hadn't been one. Barroga was meanwhile covering the other entrance and radioing to Bundermann in the operations center. With Captain Portis still stuck at Forward Operating Base Bostick, Bundermann was COP Keating's acting commander.

"Tell them we're receiving heavy fire directly into the pit from the Switchbacks and the Putting Green," Breeding told Barroga.

An RPG landed on the plateau outside the door, blowing Rodriguez down; he landed on Breeding.

"You okay?" Rodriguez asked. Breeding was. They picked themselves back up. Rodriguez had taken some shrapnel in his neck. Any time either of them even poked his hand out the door, the mortar pit came under immediate machine-gun fire. The enemy had clearly been told to keep the mortarmen away from their big guns.

Breeding got on the radio. "I got one KIA," he told Bundermann. "We're receiving heavy fire."

"Can you get out to the guns and put rounds down on the Switch-backs?" Bundermann asked.

"No way I can get out to the guns without killing everybody up here," Breeding told him.

"Okay," Bundermann said. "Hold tight." Then the radio went dead.

Breeding looked at Barroga. It felt like the kid had arrived just hours before.

"Are all the TICs this bad?" Barroga asked, using the acronym for "troops in contact"—signifying any instance of enemy fire.

"No, dude," Breeding said. "Not at all. Not at all."

He looked into Barroga's eyes. "I don't know if we're going to get out of this one," he told him. "But we're going to take some of these mother-fuckers with us."

Platoon Sergeant First Class Frank Guerrero was on leave, so Romesha had assumed his duties, sending Specialist Josh Dannelley and Private Chris Jones to the LRAS-1 Humvee/guard post to support Koppes.

Not even ten minutes earlier, Private Davidson had relieved Corporal Justin Gregory at his guard post in the turret of the tower of the shura building. Gregory had heard Ron Jeremy's warning, but not believing it, he had headed to the Red Platoon barracks to go to bed—and now he was throwing his gear back on and grabbing his squad automatic weapon. As he pushed open the front door of the barracks, he heard a din of bullets like he'd never heard before. He stepped back inside and bumped into Ser-geant Kirk and Private First Class Kyle Knight, also on their way out.

"You can't go out that door," Gregory warned them. "You can't go out that door—no way!"

Kirk stopped in his tracks. "Okay, we gotta find another way out," he said.

The three of them headed toward the back door of the barracks. "Knight," Kirk said, "grab that AT-Four." Knight got the single-shot antitank weapon, and the trio went out the back, crept around the build-ing, and started returning fire into the hills as they ran to the area of the shura building and entry control point to help back up Davidson. Kirk had an M203 grenade launcher, and he fired more than ten of the 40-millimeter projectiles while also discharging his M4 carbine. Kyle and Gregory fired their guns, too, and ran like hell.

*   *   *

At the first sound of the attack, Lieutenant Bundermann had run to the operations center, where he was told the base had contact from the Switchbacks. *Contact?* It seemed like much more than that. Bundermann called for a sitrep—a "situation report"—from all the guard posts and was informed that the outpost was taking RPG, sniper fire, and automatic-weapons fire from the Diving Board, the Northface, the Switchbacks, and the ANP Checkpoint some 125 yards to the west, in the direction of Urmul.

Yeah, that'd be contact, he thought.

"Get me air assets from Bostick," Bundermann told Sergeant Ryan Schulz, the intelligence analyst. Air support was at least thirty-five minutes away.

The commander of the outpost, Stoney Portis, wasn't there. The leader of the Bastards, Ben Salentine, wasn't there. It was all on Bundermann.

Observation Post Fritsche was also under attack, the assault having begun at 6:00 a.m. on the dot with a mortar round that landed about fifteen feet behind the guard tower. Specialist Keith Stickney, the senior mortarman present at the observation post, saw the muzzle flash, and then enemy mortars came pounding in. Quickly getting on his .50-caliber, Stickney went through three hundred rounds in his first minute of returning fire, after which he was relieved so he could run to Fritsche's mortar pit.

At first, this one didn't seem that different from all the other attacks. But within fifteen minutes, Stickney realized they were in for a long day. Walls of bullets were hitting the surrounding sandbags. Fire was coming in from every direction. At least a hundred insurgents had surrounded the observation post, as near as Stickney could tell.

White Platoon had only twenty-one U.S. troops up there.

Stickney ran down to the operations center to get the proper grid coordinates. White Platoon leader Lieutenant Jordan Bellamy was talking on the radio to Bundermann; it sounded as if things were even worse down at Combat Outpost Keating. Stickney ran back toward the mortar pit, but before he could reach it, the two other mortarmen—Private First Class Jassey Holmes and Private Second Class Jonathan Santana—screamed for him to get down. Stickney did, ducking behind a wall and narrowly escaping a barrage of RPGs and bullets.

Together, the three mortarmen headed back for the operations center. Spotting them, Bellamy yelled, "Get the fuck back in the mortar pit!"

"No, it's getting torn up!" Stickney screamed back.

The enemy fighters were occupying the Afghan Security Guards' observation post, which was located 150 yards away, between Observation Post Fritsche and the town of Kamdesh, at a fifty-foot elevation above the post. It was the perfect place from which to attack the mortar pit. The night before, Bellamy had noticed that the cameras the Americans had set up at the Security Guards' post were no longer working. He'd sent Staff Sergeant Bradley Lee to find out what the problem was, but in the dark, Lee hadn't been able to tell.

And now it didn't really matter. The men at Observation Post Fritsche were stuck, with a report having come in from one of the guard towers that enemy fighters were within hand-grenade distance of the camp. And with the suspected cooperation of the Afghan Security Guards, the enemy also had the mortar pit pinned down.

The observation post had been set up to help protect Combat Outpost Keating, but for now, the troops down in the valley were on their own.

This is not a normal attack, Bundermann thought. We've got contact from Urmul, the Northface, the Switchbacks, the Diving Board, and everywhere in between. We've got contact from every direction. This is no joke. We need everything we can get, as fast as we can get it.

On the radio, he called Lieutenant Jordan Bellamy with White Platoon, up at Observation Post Fritsche. "I need your mortars," he said, providing the relevant coordinates.

"I can't give them to you," Bellamy said. "We're in some shit up here, too."

While Bundermann and First Sergeant Ronald Burton barked out orders and information to relay to Forward Operating Base Bostick, Schulz and Private First Class Jordan Wong typed updates into the mIRC system.

Wong was "Black Knight_TOC" and Schulz was "Keating2OPS."

6:03 am <Black Knight_TOC> FRITSCHE AND KEATING IN HEAVY CONTACT[84]

---

[84] Some of the shorthand in these mIRC messages has been spelled out—"FRI AND KEA" becoming "FRITSCHE AND KEATING," for instance.

6:03 am <Black Knight_TOC> Requesting Air Tic Be opened

<Keating2OPS> we need it now we have mortars pinned down and fire coming from everywhere

<Keating2OPS> fritsche is taking heavy machine gun fire as well

<Black Knight_TOC> wee need something

<Black Knight_TOC> fritche and keating still taking heavy contact

The men did their jobs, focused on their work, but a tangible sense of dread and panic filled the operations center. This must be what it felt like before a massacre, they thought, a combination of impotence and terror—a doomed sense of being about to be overwhelmed, like sitting in a sand castle as a tidal wave suddenly drew to strength just yards away.

CHAPTER 31

GET SOMETHING UP!

The guard post at the LRAS-2 Humvee was parked on the southern side of the outpost, its gun aimed toward the Switchbacks. Specialist Stephan Mace had been relieved there by Sergeant Brad Larson, but when the firing started, Mace returned, along with Sergeant Justin Gallegos. Things had heated up even more since then. They were being hit with RPGs from three directions, and sniper fire was coming in, bouncing off both the turret and Larson's .50-caliber itself. Larson had a thousand rounds linked and was firing furiously, but within fifteen minutes, the number of insurgent positions focused upon him seemed to have multiplied exponentially.

"Holy fuck," he said.

Out of ammo, Larson got up, leaned over, and was reaching for more rounds when an RPG exploded, scattering pebbles of searing metal into his right arm and armpit. In tremendous pain, he kept shooting. He fired at snipers in the Urmul mosque to the west. He aimed at smoke plumes coming from the Switchbacks. He unloaded on every insurgent he could see. But he couldn't see them all.

There were twenty Afghan National Army troops on the eastern side of the outpost, and they began spilling out of their barracks — most of them without gear on — to assume their battle positions. Within ten minutes, they were out of ammunition. The ineffective ANA commander lost control of the situation as the Afghan soldiers determined that they couldn't withstand the assault, seeming to accept defeat. Cowardice feeds on itself, ravenously, and once the ANA commander gave up trying to convince his troops to fight, the ANA troops themselves simply gave up.

Some sprinted to the far eastern edge of the camp to hop the wire and flee. "This is your country!" yelled one of their Latvian trainers, Janis Lakis. "Hold your position! Hold your position!" They didn't listen. Once outside the wire, some even handed their weapons to insurgents as they passed them.

Within fifteen minutes of the attack, the remainder of the ANA soldiers had completely retreated from their side of the camp. Some sought the protection of the Americans, while others hid in various buildings and barracks. The ANA platoon leader ran into the operations center and screamed, "We need to get the choppers in here so we can get out of here!" He said his men were dying and couldn't fight anymore. (There had also been approximately a dozen private contractors, Afghan Security Guards, employed at the camp; with one exception, they all fled as well.)

That the ANA commander would insist that choppers were needed for his men—who were cowering in corners around the camp—when the Americans couldn't even account for all of their own infuriated those in the operations center.

"Sit the fuck down and shut up!" shouted Burton. But the Afghan commander was in a frenzy and wouldn't listen.

"Choppers are on the way, but they're not going to be able to land unless all of your ANA boys start helping us drive back the attackers!" Cady yelled.

Temperatures continued to rise until Cady finally threatened to kill the ANA commander if he didn't either get his shit together or get the fuck out of the operations center. Cady wasn't the only one whose hand had started inching toward his pistol.

Jonathan Hill had just returned from the operations center and was focused on making sure the battle stations were occupied and the ammo was free-flowing. The soldiers from Red Platoon were in charge of protecting the camp in the guard posts that day, so Hill and the Bastards needed to see to it that they had their gear and radios and a constant supply of ammunition. Their lieutenant, Salentine, was still stuck at Forward Operating Base Bostick.

Machine-gun fire was now coming from the ANA side of the camp, and the ANA barracks itself was on fire. Hill was still trying to get an assessment of where the main attack effort was coming from; no one at the operations center seemed to know. From what he could deduce, the enemy had surrounded them.

Hill opened the north-facing door of the barracks to take a look. Just then, an RPG hit the generator ten feet away, blowing him back into the barracks and onto his back.

"You okay?" Harder asked.

"That thing was close," answered Hill.

"Let me check for shrapnel," Harder said. He patted Hill down, checking for wounds. There weren't any.

"Okay," Hill told him, "go to the ASP"—the ammo supply point—"and get that ammo out to the battle stations."

While troops had ammunition stashed all over the camp, most of the official supply was kept in the ASP, near the camp entrance. It was stored behind two doors, both of which had been locked in an effort to keep Afghans from stealing it. The locks had, in fact, just been reinforced.

Specialist Ty Carter took out his M4 rifle and put five rounds into the ASP lock. But when he opened the door, he realized he'd picked the wrong one—this door led to the mortars and Claymore mines. He needed the door for rounds and bullets. As he exited into the open space, John Francis arrived at the entrance.

"What are you doing?" Francis asked Carter. "Get cover!"

Carter ducked down. "I need to get two-forty ammo for LRAS-two," he said.

"It's in there," Francis replied, referring to the other ammo supply point door.

"It's locked," Carter said. "Can I shoot the other locks off?"

Francis seemed hesitant, but then he said yes; Carter put a round into the second lock and blasted it open. He ran inside, followed by Francis, and they started throwing ammo out to the other soldiers—including Sergeant Matthew Miller and Eric Harder—who now began running over to transport rounds and bullets to the guard posts: *"Take this to LRAS-One. Now!" "Take this to LRAS-Two. Now! Go! Go! Go!"*

An RPG hit the HESCO barrier across from the door of the ammo supply point. It knocked Carter and Francis down and blew Miller into the ammo building. Carter picked Miller up and pushed him out of the building, yelling at him to go back to the barracks.

When Eric Harder and Francis followed Miller a little while later, Hill noticed they'd both been peppered pretty well by shrapnel from the RPG. The fact that Harder was still wearing gym shorts didn't help matters.

Sergeant Justin Gallegos's panicked voice came on the radio, from LRAS-2. "We need ammo right now!" Gallegos said. "This is no bullshit!"

The messages from Wong and Schulz quickly turned from descriptive to desperate:

> 6:10 am <Keating2OPS> we are taking contact from diving board, switchbacks, putting green and b-10 position
> <Keating2OPS> we are taking heavy small arms fire and rpgs
> <Keating2OPS> rpgs from the north face
> <Black Knight_TOC> still taking indirect fire
> 6:15 am <Black Knight_TOC> need something our mortors cant get upo
> <Black Knight_TOC> we are taking casiltys
> <Black Knight_TOC> GET SOMETHING UP!

Sitting in the tower of the shura building, Nicholas Davidson aimed his M240 machine gun at the plume of smoke rising from the Putting Green. After quickly running through his ammo, he was just ducking to reload the gun when a sniper round ricocheted across the turret. Then another whizzed right by his head. "Oh, fuck," Davidson said. He tried to climb down, but an Afghan Security Guard had found a safe harbor in that spot below the turret and was blocking his path.

When Kirk, Knight, and Gregory entered the shura building, it was thick with clouds of dirt and dust. They made their way to the ladder that led to the guard's ledge. "Get the fuck out of there, you goddamn pussy!" Kirk yelled at the Afghan guard. He grabbed him and threw him out of the way. Davidson started to climb down. "Davidson, get back on that two-forty," Kirk ordered.

"I have no ammo," Davidson said.

"We gotta get more ammo," Kirk announced. He turned to Knight, who was on the radio, trying to tell the operations center where to target the mortars. "Give me that AT-Four," Kirk said, grabbing the antitank gun. "Cover me while I fire this," he told Gregory.

Bullets, rockets, and mortars volleyed toward them as if part of a demonic storm. The men had never seen anything like it. Kirk stood by the door and prepped the AT4 rocket launcher, pulling out the safety pin, pulling up the firing pin, opening up the sights. He took a step outside the shura building while Gregory raised his M249 light machine gun and took a knee at the door, half inside and half outside the door frame, aiming at the Putting Green, to the west of the camp. Resting the rocket launcher on his shoulder, Kirk looked into the sights to fire, but before he could press the red firing button, an RPG struck the side of the shura building. The explosion slapped Kirk onto the ground and flattened Gregory onto the building's floor. Gregory took a second to get his bearings and then ran out to try to help Kirk, who was on his back with his feet facing the door, not moving. The RPG had been only part of it: there was also a gunshot wound to Kirk's head. The bullet had gone through his right cheek and out the back of his skull. Blood was pouring from his face. As bullets crackled around his feet, Gregory grabbed Kirk by the shoulder straps of his vest and started pulling him. But Gregory was small, and the man whose limp body he was trying to move was not.

Seeing what was going on, Davidson came out to help. When the two had Kirk in the safety of the shura building, Gregory tried to wipe the blood from the sergeant's face while Davidson called the operations center on the radio, pleading for help.

It was just instinct: when Cordova, Courville, and the other two medics — Sergeant Jeffrey Hobbs and Specialist Cody Floyd — heard the first blast, they immediately headed to the aid station, where they put on surgical gloves and began preparing for casualties.

They did this every three days or so — that is, every time there was an incoming attack — but it didn't take them long to figure out that this one was much worse than anything they'd gone through before. For starters, there were more explosions than they'd ever heard at Camp Keating, and all of them were from enemy fire — the Americans weren't firing back with mortars.

The first casualty call came over the radio: someone was severely wounded over by the shura building.

"Hey, Doc," Courville said to Cordova, "I'm going out there."

While Cordova spoke on the radio to the staff at the aid station at Forward Operating Base Bostick, he threw Courville his M9 aid bag, a slim backpack containing combat gauze, tourniquets, emergency airway devices, IV kits, and more. Out Courville ran, precisely at the moment when an enemy RPG landed in the aid station, spraying shrapnel. Floyd and Hobbs went down, as did Specialist Andrew Stone, a mechanic who had come to alert them about the casualty at the shura building.

Up on their feet again, Floyd and Hobbs took Stone into the back room. Shrapnel had taken out a piece of his calf and hit his chest plate. They treated his wounds, and as they did so, Floyd noticed that Hobbs was bleeding from his chest, and Hobbs noticed that Floyd was bleeding from *his* chest. They looked at each other, and then they briefly looked at themselves. There wasn't much blood, so they kept working.

Over at the shura building, Courville ran to Kirk. He was as limp as a rag doll, but he was alive. Courville shook his shoulders and yelled his name. There was no response.

Courville checked Kirk's body for wounds, doing a "blood sweep." A massive amount of blood was still flooding out of his head and neck. Apart from the bullet wound, Kirk had also, it was clear, taken significant shrapnel to the back of his head. Courville wrapped his head with bandages, cut off his gear, and yelled for a stretcher team.

Davidson brought a stretcher he'd found in the Red Platoon barracks, and Rasmussen provided cover fire so that he, Courville, Stanley, and Vernon Martin could carry Kirk to the aid station. His blood left a crimson trail behind them. During their bumpy scramble, Kirk seemed to look up at Stanley, who couldn't believe this indestructible ass-kicker was down. Kirk? He was a crazily courageous bastard, and now here he was, down — maybe for the count. Stanley had a hard time processing it.

In the aid station, Cordova and Courville got to work on the sergeant while Hobbs and Floyd treated five wounded ANA soldiers. Cordova examined Kirk, who was by now extremely pale. His first priority was to stop the bleeding, always tricky with a head wound. To expand Kirk's blood volume and keep oxygen going to his brain, Cordova used a FAST1 — a device that looked like a flashlight with a needle attached to one end — to introduce a small tube called a cannula into his sternum, or breastbone. He then hooked up an IV to pump fluid through the cannula into his bone marrow. The physician assistant tried to find a pulse in the sergeant's wrists. None. He searched for a pulse in his groin area — none. Finally, he felt a very faint pulse in his neck.

Kirk was alive.

Suddenly, he began gasping for air. Cordova grabbed a tube to insert into his airway and gave Kirk oxygen with a bag valve mask. Courville ventilated oxygen into him. They both knew that even in a best-case scenario, given the distance and danger involved, the medevacs were hours away from landing at Camp Keating.

Cordova tried, but he couldn't completely detach himself from the patient on his table. He and Kirk, Courville, Stanley, Gallegos, Thomson, and Rodriguez were all gym buddies, meeting every night to work out together. Kirk and Gallegos were two of the toughest SOBs he'd ever met, in the gym and outside it. They were strong, obnoxious loudmouths, and he loved them. Kirk, in particular, was fearless.

Cordova tried to resuscitate his friend, performing a series of chest compressions while Courville administered breaths through the airway tube. Kirk had stopped bleeding, but Cordova couldn't tell if that was because he'd been bandaged well or because he had no more blood to give.

The Latvian trainers, Janis Lakis and Martins Dabolins, were furious when they found some of the ANA troops outside the operations center, huddled together and squatting, holding their knees and shaking uncontrollably. Among them was their commander, who had fled his post. Lakis — a big guy with a beard whom the Americans called Bluto — picked the man up.

"Where the fuck are your men? Are any of them manning their battle positions?" Lakis asked.

"The Taliban have taken that side," he said.

"Get your men and go and retake your side of the camp!" Lakis told him.

"You are not my commander!" the Afghan exclaimed, and he ran off.

Specialist Zach Koppes was alone at LRAS-1, the guard post where he'd had some bad luck back in June, resulting in his self-inflicted head wound. It turned out that had been a good day, comparatively speaking.

The rockets and RPGs just kept coming and coming into the camp. Koppes recalled hearing about two pickup trucks full of ordnance that had been stolen recently, and he wondered whether this hell being unleashed upon Keating might be connected to that. A sniper had begun targeting Koppes, his bullets hitting the Kevlar tarp covering the back of the truck with deadly accuracy; if the American had stood up, they would have gone through his head. The tarp was tough, but the bullets were shredding it. Fuck, Koppes thought to himself. This thing's not going to last.

Joshua Dannelley ran over with his Mk 48 machine gun, as did Christopher Jones with MK19 grenades to give to Koppes and several belts of M240 machine-gun ammo for the fighting position right next to the Humvee.

"Keep down! Keep down!" Koppes yelled. "There's a sniper!" But soon it wasn't just a sniper anymore; RPGs began showering down near them, one hitting fifteen feet away.

"My knee! My knee!" yelled Jones, falling to the ground. Dannelley inspected him but couldn't find any external injuries.

Sergeant John Francis had been running ammo back and forth to guard posts for a while when he decided to check in back at the Bastards' barracks. An RPG exploded behind him, lifting him up off the ground and throwing him against a pole. Next thing he knew, he was on his back on the ground, and Specialist Mark Dulaney was on top of him, shaking him.

"You good? You good? You all right?"

Francis opened his eyes.

"Sergeant, you good?"

"I don't know, motherfucker," Francis said. "You're the one looking at me. You tell me if I'm good!"

"Can you get up?" Dulaney asked.

Francis tried, but his left side throbbed with pain.

"You all right?" Dulaney asked again.

"I think I'm all right," Francis said. "I think I got some busted ribs." He would later find out that five of his ribs had been fractured.

"Should we go to the aid station?" Dulaney wondered.

"Fuck, no," Francis said. "We gotta keep fighting till this shit's over."

* * *

Sergeant Breeding and his men did everything they could to get the radio back up, but it wouldn't work. They had no idea what was going on elsewhere in the camp; they were completely disconnected from the rest of the world.

"As long as we're in the bunker, we'll be okay," Breeding told Rodriguez and Barroga.

But the bunker was precisely where the insurgents continued to shoot machine-gun and sniper fire—for good measure adding multiple RPGs to their onslaught, too. Breeding and Rodriguez returned fire with their M4 carbines. They didn't think they had much of a chance of hitting their targets; they just wanted to throw down some lead to keep the bad guys from shooting at them.

Meanwhile, the men on the guard posts at Camp Keating were starting to run low on ammunition. The sheer volume of rounds they were putting out astounded Bundermann. And though some of the American bullets were finding their mark, the counterattack clearly wasn't having much of an effect.

The RPG that had blown Hill onto his back also blew out their generator, and the satellite phone line went dead; the enemy seemed to know exactly what to target. The mIRC system, thankfully, was still online. Forward Operating Base Bostick's ops center alerted Keating's that a pair of F-15 Strike Eagles, the two of them together code-named Dude 25, were on their way, courtesy of Task Force Palehorse.

> 6:12 am <TF_DESTROYER_BTL_CPT> BK DUDE 25 enroute No eta yet
> <TF_PALEHORSE_BTL_CPT> NEGATIVE, AH[85] ARE BEING ALERTED TIME NOW
> <TF_PALEHORSE_BTL_CPT> ITS A 40 MINUTE FLIGHT
> 6:13 am <Keating2OPS> whats the status of air
> 6:14 am <TF_DESTROYER_BTL_CPT> CLOSE AIR SUPPORT 5 minutes

Justin Gallegos, Brad Larson, and Stephan Mace were stuck at LRAS-2. "We're getting attacked from the village," Gallegos told Bundermann, referring to Urmul. "Do I have permission to fire back?"

---

[85] An "AH" is an Apache helicopter.

"Absolutely," Bundermann said. "Light it up." At that point, everything was fair game.

> 6:14 am <Keating2OPS> we are taking fire from inside urmul village
> 6:18 am <Keating2OPS> our mortars are still pinned down unable to fire
> 6:20 am <Keating2OPS> we need cas[86]
> <Keating2OPS> still taking heavy rpgs and machine gun fire
> 6:21 am <Keating2OPS> at both locations fritsche and keating taking heavy contact

All of twenty-three minutes had passed since the attack began.

Ty Carter ran into the Bastards' barracks and was greeted by a scene of chaos and shouting.

"Shut the fuck up!" Hill yelled. Everyone quieted down. "We need to find out who needs what."

"Everyone needs everything," Carter said, gasping for breath.

From Spokane, Washington, Carter had joined the Marines out of high school, but he'd been busted down to a lower rank for fighting. He'd then quit and spent five years as a civilian working aimlessly at a series of odd jobs. He hated that, felt like one in a herd of cattle. He wanted to fight for his fellow soldiers, not earn a paycheck without a sense of honor or direction. He reenlisted in the military in January 2008, opting this time for the Army, figuring the Marines probably wouldn't take him back.

In civilian life, Carter had felt like something of an oddball and an outcast, but in the Army, he felt alive, with purpose. And on this day, he relished his role as a soldier trying to help his fellow troops.

Hill loaded up Specialists Michael Scusa and Jeremy Frunk with more ammunition to take to Gallegos at LRAS-2. "Okay, get the fuck out of here," he told them. Harder stood by the door; he would join them. He opened the door as Scusa, Frunk, and Private First Class Daniel Rogers lined up to run.

---

[86] CAS stands for "close air support."

"Are you ready?" Scusa asked Frunk. Echoes of incoming gunfire filled the barracks.

"Let's go!" Frunk said.

They exited the barracks in earnest.

Hill watched them proudly. Men of valor. No questioning, no protest. He'd given them the order, and they'd run out into the fire.

In the hills of the Northface, a sniper was waiting. One of his bullets hit Scusa in the right side of his neck, lacerating two major blood vessels and the right jugular vein. It also penetrated a larger artery and cut across his spinal cord before exiting out his lower back.

Scusa's head rocked back, and he went limp, falling on the ground.

Frunk tried to grab the loop on the back of Scusa's armored vest in order to drag him to the aid station. As he bent down, the sniper opened up with a dozen more rounds. A bullet went through the side of Frunk's vest, slamming into his back; panicked, the soldier hit the ground and low-crawled back to the barracks, where the next troops were getting ready to run out and resupply those on guard.

"Don't go out! Don't go out! Scusa's hit!" Frunk yelled. The other men lifted Frunk up and brought him back to Hill. He was shaking and scared.

"You okay?" Hill asked.

"Sergeant Hill, I think I've been shot," Frunk said. He'd never been shot before, so he thought his wound was worse than it was. He took off his vest and shirt.

"It's just a graze," Hill told him. "You're okay. Is Scusa wounded?"

Frunk hung his head, shaking it no.

"Where was he hit?" Hill asked.

"I think he got shot in the face," Frunk said.

Sergeant Francis tried to slowly open the door to the barracks to see where Scusa was, but the sniper fired rounds right at him. He shut the door, paused, then opened it again and ran out to Scusa.

Blood was pouring from the specialist's neck. Francis attempted to find the exit wound with his hand, wiping the blood away and feeling for holes. Soon figuring out that the round had gone into Scusa's neck, he probed the area, trying to stop the bleeding, trying to find the jugular. He finally found it and was working to pinch it closed when the sniper shot at him and hit the M203 grenade launcher attached to the M4 carbine that was slung around his arm. The weapon snapped, and the clip fell off.

Good Christ, that was close, Francis thought. "Harder!" he yelled. "I need cover! Harder! I need cover!"

Inside, Hill quickly assigned troops to cover the doors. The other men ransacked their barracks looking for smoke grenades. Hill found some and threw them to Eric Harder, near one of the doors. Harder poked his head outside; he had two grenades in the pouch of his vest. He lobbed one to Francis and held on to one for himself. After waiting but a moment, both men pulled the pins and threw their grenades, building enough billowing smoke to form a wall. Harder rushed out of the barracks, ran through the haze, and helped Francis drag Scusa to the aid station. The smoke did not deter the sniper, who simply fired through it, hitting a nearby Humvee. The bullet fragmented, hitting Francis's arms and legs, but he and Harder kept going.

This is not good, this is not good, this is not good, the men thought. And it was about to get worse, because insurgents were now bounding down the southern wall toward the outpost.

Doc Cordova looked around the aid station and saw mayhem and devastation and blood everywhere. He and Courville were still working on Kirk, and yet another wounded ANA troop had staggered in, bringing the total number of Afghan WIAs to six. One had an eye hanging out of its socket, and another a serious abdominal wound—his guts were literally spilling out of him. The other four had gunshot and shrapnel wounds. Specialist Chris Chappell, peppered with shrapnel, had also briefly stopped in at the aid station; after Cordova treated him with oral antibiotics and pain relievers, he'd headed right back out to the fight.

Into this hell now came Harder and Francis, carrying Scusa. He was completely pale; he had no heartbeat, no pulse. Cordova checked his eyes and wasn't able to provoke any neurological response. Cordova had known the specialist for two years, having first met him in Iraq, and he knew what a sweetheart he was. He also knew that Scusa and Floyd were close, and he wondered how the new medic, today dealing with his first serious casualties, would handle his friend's death.

At 6:30 a.m., Scusa became the first person Cordova had ever pronounced dead. The young man was put in a body bag and carried back to Courville's room.

*   *   *

Back at Forward Operating Base Bostick, Stoney Portis, Ben Salentine, and Kirk Birchfield were crawling out of their skin. They desperately wanted to be of some help, any help, to their brothers back at Camp Keating. But there wasn't anything they could do except sit in the operations center at Naray. The surveillance aircraft hadn't yet made it to the Kamdesh Valley, so they couldn't see anything; they could only read Wong's and Schulz's messages and listen to Bundermann on the radio.

Salentine and Birchfield were conscience-stricken about not being alongside the men they had trained with for just such an event. Portis was new to Black Knight Troop, but as its absent commander, he, too, condemned himself. What leader in his right mind leaves his soldiers? he thought. Logic, at this point, had no case to make.

It felt as if they had to wait forever until they were able to catch a ride, yet the attack wasn't yet an hour old when Portis, Salentine, and Birchfield grabbed backpacks full of ammunition and grenades and got on the first medevac along with Specialist Tim Kugler, a scout from Red Platoon, and two Air Force radio operators. The bird went up, circled over Forward Operating Base Bostick, and then flew up and down the Landay-Sin Valley, killing time, not heading directly for the outpost. Portis finally grew impatient and—because the helicopter's rotors were so loud—began writing notes to the pilot, asking what was keeping them from leaving the area. The pilot wrote back that he was waiting to be told there was somewhere for him to land safely near the besieged outpost; right then, the landing zone was still too hot.

Inside the bird, a cold calm came over the men. They knew what their purpose was. Portis thought, I'm not going to come back from this mission. This is it. This is how I'm going to die. He had written his wife, Alison, a farewell letter and given it to his brother to present to her should he not return. She would be taken care of. Portis got choked up for a second, and then he made his peace with what awaited him in the valley. This was what he had signed up for. He turned his attention to what they would do when they landed. Putting pen to paper, he drew a diagram and began planning with his men how they would exit the helicopter, run for cover, and then join the fight to save Combat Outpost Keating.

*   *   *

Outside the Red Platoon barracks, Clint Romesha yanked Corporal Justin Gregory's Mk 48 machine gun out of his hands. "Grab more ammo and follow me," he told him.

"I'm moving a machine gun into position to cover you," Romesha radioed Gallegos, who was still stuck at LRAS-2. "As soon as I can cover you, if you can, I need you to displace back to Red Platoon barracks."

"I don't know if you can lay down enough fire," Gallegos said. "But if you can, roger." Inside the Humvee, it seemed as if they were being submerged in an ocean of bullets and grenades: Gallegos, Mace, and Larson could only hope the trunk's plating would hold up against the relentless battering. And however determined and skilled and ruthless a soldier Romesha might be, that he alone could provide enough cover fire with one lightweight machine gun seemed unlikely.

Romesha and Gregory scurried over to the generator by the mosque. There, Romesha set the machine gun atop the generator, and Gregory began linking up its ammunition. "I'm setting the machine-gun fire whenever you're ready to move," Romesha radioed to Gallegos.

"Roger," Gallegos responded.

Romesha looked around at the myriad targets up at the Putting Green and throughout the Switchbacks. There were so many to choose from. He picked one enemy position and sent a twenty-to-thirty-round burst toward it. Then he moved to another. Then another. He quickly ran through the two-hundred-round belt.

While Gregory was loading another belt into the gun, Gallegos radioed. "We're not able to move," he said. "We're not able to move." The incoming fire was just too intense, coming from too many different locations.

Romesha had started firing the second belt when, from the blind side to his right, to the north of the camp, an insurgent burst through the entry control point and fired an RPG toward him and Gregory, hitting the generator instead. Romesha, sprayed with shrapnel, momentarily lost his bearings and fell on Gregory. The moment over, he got up and looked at him. "You all right?" he asked.

"Yes," Gregory said.

"Go back to the barracks, I'll cover you," Romesha instructed. He covered the other's mad dash and then began firing into the hills again.

Gallegos came on the radio again. "You're not being effective, it's not working," he told Romesha. "We'll just hang tight here."

Romesha exhaled, fired his last burst of ammo, and ran back down the hill. He found Gregory in a trench near a HESCO barrier, on the southern side of the camp near the Switchbacks. "Wait here, I'm going to get more guys," Romesha told him, handing him back his machine gun. He ran back to the Red Platoon barracks, where he told Christopher Jones and Specialist Josh Dannelley to go help Gregory. Rasmussen looked at Romesha.

"Ro, dude," he said. "You're fucking hit. You're fucking hit."

Romesha looked down. His right forearm was a bloody mess.

"Let me dress that," Rasmussen said, pulling Romesha's pressure dressing from his pocket and then wrapping his friend's forearm tightly with the specialized bandage.

"Where are they?" Jones asked Gregory when he reached him.

"Everywhere!" Gregory said. "Get the fuck down here in the ditch with me!"

As the private jumped in, an RPG blew up the COP Keating mosque. Snipers' bullets, machine-gun fire, hand grenades, RPGs — the insurgents were unloading everything they had. "You need to stay down," Gregory told Jones. "Snipers are targeting us."

"We need to cover people running ammo," said Jones.

As rounds hit right next to their heads, Gregory became convinced that he was going to die, but instead of panic, he felt a sort of peace fall over him like a blanket. He noticed how green the grass was, how blue the sky. He could no longer hear the gunfire and explosions, he no longer noticed the people shooting. He was comfortable with the idea of dying.

At the guard post at LRAS-2, Brad Larson had kept firing his .50-caliber until a well-aimed RPG detonated nearby and hit the gun off the stovepipe so he couldn't shoot it anymore. The weapon now lay half in the turret and half out. Larson tried to get it to work, but it just wouldn't function. Helpless to shoot back, he crawled down into the Humvee, where Gallegos and Mace were sitting and trying to fire their rifles out the windows. The snipers were moving closer to the camp, and anytime either of the men opened one of the Humvee's bulletproof windows, he'd get shot at. The incoming was so ferocious, in fact, that when they stuck their guns out to fire, bullets hit and bounced off the barrels. Since it wasn't particularly easy to aim out the Humvee's windows anyway, they finally just rolled them up.

The snipers' bullets kept pinging off the windshield; if it and the windows hadn't been bulletproof, the Americans surely would have been dead by now. Still, every so often, someone had to stick his neck out, literally, to see what was going on. Larson ducked down from his turret and hopped into the driver's seat. Gallegos was next to him. Mace sat in the back. "Holy shit, there's a lot of them," Gallegos said.

Seemingly out of nowhere, Carter arrived. He was surprised to see that they were all inside the Humvee, with no one in the turret manning the .50-caliber. The COP was under heavy attack, and this was a primary defensive position, but this post wasn't returning fire.

"I got your two-forty ammo," Carter said.

"Either get in or get the hell out of here," Gallegos barked.

Carter climbed in behind him, next to Mace, who was doubled over in pain. He was wounded—he'd taken some shrapnel somewhere along the line—but when Gallegos asked him what was wrong and whether he was okay, Mace said only that he was fine.

"Do you have any M-four rounds?" Larson asked the new arrival. Carter did; he had one magazine left inside his M4 carbine rifle.

Abruptly, the door next to him swung open; it was Vernon Martin. "I heard you guys need ammo?" he asked.

"Get in or get the hell out of here," Gallegos barked again.

Martin paused, so Carter seized him and pulled him into the Humvee. "Get the fuck in here," he said. They found a place for Martin to sit on the gunner's platform.

The bullets and RPGs now increased even more in intensity. An RPG exploded three feet from the turret, causing panic and confusion among the Humvee's occupants. Carter was knocked unconscious; when he came to, a second later, his head ached, and his eyes were out of focus. *Holy shit,* he thought as he regained consciousness. *Where am I?* He began checking himself for holes and found some—as did Larson, who was engaged in a similar investigation. Martin was the worst off of them, having taken a great deal of shrapnel all over his legs and hips, where soldiers typically have no protection from body armor. And now that he had returned to the moment, he felt it: "Motherfucker!" Martin yelled. "It burns! Holy shit, that fucking hurts!"

The men got their bearings, shook off their wounds as best they could, and started talking about what to do next; they knew there would be much worse in store for them if they didn't put their heads together and figure out a way out. It was now clear that the insurgents had armor-piercing capabilities. The RPG had knocked the .50-caliber off its mount entirely, jamming the gun and exploding the primers for the rounds, rendering them useless. It was only a matter of time before the enemy onslaught got through and killed all five of them. They needed to get out of the Humvee. But the rounds were coming in so furiously now that a step outside meant certain death. What could they do?

They didn't have much time. The troops and translators at Observation Post Mace who monitored enemy radio frequencies shared some alarming news over the mIRC system: the attackers were now actively talking about breaching the wire.

Staff Sergeant Kenny Daise ran into the shura building and slipped on Kirk's blood.

Daise picked himself up. He didn't have time to be revolted or saddened. He looked through all of the gear that had been left behind, then grabbed Kirk's M203 grenade launcher and his M4 rounds. The enemy had kept on pounding the shura building with RPGs, and it was so dusty now that none of the soldiers with Daise could see much of anything. He told them to fall back.

"Come with me," Daise said to Private First Class Kyle Knight. The two of them ran from the shura building to a position between the outpost mosque and the nearby generator. As Daise was reloading his M4 rifle, preparing to fire into the hills, he saw the barrel of an AK-47 coming around the corner, which he assumed must belong to either an Afghan Security Guard or one of the remaining ANA soldiers. As the man holding it rounded the corner, their eyes met. He was maybe seventy-five feet away, in his thirties, with a beard, wearing a dirty red overshirt and a white turban. Daise was stunned. This wasn't an Afghan Security Guard; it was an insurgent.

It's the fucking Taliban, thought Daise. Inside our camp.

The Taliban fighter was likewise surprised to see the American. They both raised their weapons, but the insurgent's gun jammed. Daise fired as his target ran back around the corner.

Shit, Daise thought. Oh no. Oh God no.

He had a radio attached to his belt and a hand-mike hooked up to his collar. "Charlie in the wire!" he said, for some reason at first using old Army slang for the Vietcong. He immediately corrected himself: "Enemy in the wire! Enemy in the wire!" On a different radio frequency, Wong repeated what Daise had called in: "We got enemy in the wire! We got enemy in the wire!"

Daise could hear the news repeated and echoed through the camp.

Enemy in the wire.

CHAPTER 32

"They've Got an RPG Pointed Right at Me"

6:49 am <Keating2OPS> enemy in the wire at keating

6:50 am <Black Knight_TOC> ENEMUY IN THE WIRE ENEMY IN THE WIRE!!!

6:51 am <Keating2OPS> how long until cca?[87]

<Keating2OPS> we need support

6:52 am <Keating2OPS> we have enemy on the cop

Less than an hour into their assault on Combat Outpost Keating, insurgents had breached the camp's perimeter. They were coming from the southern wall, near the maintenance shed; they were coming from the ANA side of the outpost; they were even walking through the front entrance.

And as the enemy slithered into the outpost, the operations center took more incoming, and the mIRC system went down. Fortunately, Burton had set up a redundant satellite radio that allowed the ops center to provide news to troops at Forward Operating Base Bostick, one of whom recorded what he was being told so he could pass it on to others:

Bostick: Enemy in the wire at COP keating they breached from the ANA side of the COP to the West

---

[87] CCA stands for "close combat attack," or helicopters.

The F-15s had arrived and dropped two GBUs, or "guided bomb units," on the Switchbacks, but no one was sure if they'd hit anyone.

Hill was bandaging up Francis, whose ribs were cracked.

"Is it getting any better out there?" Hill asked.

"It's crazy," Francis replied. "The gates of hell just opened up on us. We're running around, no shit, in the backyard of hell."

"We've got to pull together," Hill said.

The barracks became quiet for two minutes as the troops regrouped, gathering magazines and supplies. Francis was in his little area at the far end of the barracks, and the next thing he knew, an RPG had come through the door to his room, blowing up his entire hooch.

"Son of a bitch! Motherfucker!" he yelled. Thankfully, no one was hurt, but the RPG explosion started a fire that soon threatened to engulf the north side of the Bastards' barracks. Troops snatched up fire extinguishers to try to stop the conflagration, or at least contain it, but that proved to be a difficult task; the buildings on the outpost, mostly made of stone and wood and topped with plywood roofs secured with sandbags, had been built in close proximity to one another. The fire quickly spread, as did a separate conflagration at the Headquarters Platoon barracks. Leaving the blaze to his men for a moment, Hill headed for the aid station, seeking information about Scusa.

"What's the condition of my soldier?" he asked.

Courville looked down and shook his head.

Soon Romesha, too, stopped in at the aid station. He looked at Courville and did a "Thumbs-up or thumbs-down?" motion. Which was it?

Courville silently responded: thumbs-down.

There were many ANA soldiers there, and Romesha noticed that one of them had leaned his Soviet sniper rifle—a Dragunov—up against the wall. Preferring that to his own M4, Romesha took it and left.

Cordova and the other medics were tag-teaming Kirk; Floyd had been treating him, but now Cordova was looking him over again. Kirk was now taking what medicine calls agonal breaths, labored gasps every ten or fifteen seconds (the colloquial term is "dying breaths"). Cordova gave him two shots of epinephrine and started chest compressions, then breathed for him using a squeeze bag that pushed air into his lungs every six seconds.

After many minutes of trying to keep the sergeant alive by breathing for him with the squeeze bag, Cordova looked down at the floor. They would have to perform CPR on him all day to keep him alive, taking two of the four medical staff out of commission. Any other day, they would have done it without question, but not today. The wounded were already stacked up, and more would be coming in. They would have to stop treating Kirk.

Floyd was torn up. He knew they could keep him alive. He also knew they didn't have the manpower to do so. He understood intellectually that Cordova was making the right call, but he was still filled with fury.

At 6:45 a.m., Cordova pronounced Kirk dead.

Including Thomson, three members of Black Knight Troop had been killed this morning, and the attack was only three quarters of an hour old.

After their sniper picked off Scusa, the insurgents had turned their weapons on Zach Koppes at LRAS-1, relentlessly firing rockets at the Humvee. His radio had gone out, so at one point, Romesha braved the enemy fire and ran up to him.

"This doesn't look good," Romesha said. "We're all going to die." He laughed—he had a pretty dark sense of humor, Romesha. "You okay?"

Koppes looked at him. Bullets were ricocheting off the truck right next to him, but the staff sergeant just stood there looking back at Koppes, smiling the whole time. Holy shit, he's lost his mind, the specialist thought.

"Yeah, I'm good," Koppes finally replied. "I still got this sniper behind me."

"Okay, stay low and hang tight," Romesha told him.

At that moment, the sniper shot at Romesha, who then ducked behind the Humvee and began playing peekaboo with the enemy, trying to draw him out so he could see exactly where he was firing from. He decided that the Taliban fighter was midway up on the Northface, so he fired the Dragunov at the spot.

Then he turned and airily announced to Koppes, "All right, I'm going to head out."

The smoke from the burning ANA building was becoming a problem for Koppes; it stung his eyes and made it tough for him to breathe. And that fire was spreading.

A little later, Koppes saw four enemy fighters moving over the crest of the Diving Board, walking on a path to the Switchbacks. He fired his MK19 grenade launcher at them and watched all four go down. He was about to pull the trigger again when all of a sudden, Sergeant John Francis was running full steam toward him, screaming all the while in his thick Long Island, New York, accent.

Koppes was sure Francis was yelling, "Friendlies on the Diving Board! Friendlies on the Diving Board!" Holy shit, he thought, I killed four Americans who were trying to help us! In a flash, he figured they'd been Special Forces troops, dressed like locals and carrying AK-47s—and then he looked up and saw seven *more* men on the Diving Board, coming down the hill to the ANA side of the camp. Really alarmed now, he thought, Holy shit, I just shot their friends!

But then, as Francis got nearer, Koppes heard him yelling again. This time it was clearer—he wasn't yelling "Friendlies," he was yelling, "*Enemy* on the Diving Board! Enemy on the Diving Board!" So Koppes erased all his misgivings and guilt, pointed his grenade launcher at the insurgents headed down the hill—the one in front looked about fifteen years old—and went up through the line, taking them out one after another.

Bundermann was focused on the men stuck in the Humvee at LRAS-2. There were now five of them: Ty Carter, Justin Gallegos, Brad Larson, Stephan Mace, and Vernon Martin. They might not be able to wait until the Apaches and fixed-wing aircraft got there. The vehicle used as Stand-To Truck 1[88] had a .50-caliber mounted on it; Faulkner was in it and had been firing as much as he could. If someone joined him in that truck, they might be able to drive it closer to LRAS-2 and rescue the trapped soldiers.

Joshua Hardt and Clint Romesha began arguing about the best course of action. Hardt endorsed Bundermann's plan to have someone run out to Stand-To Truck 1 and drive it over to LRAS-2 to provide cover fire—shooting at the enemy snipers and RPG teams in the hills—so the five men could get out of the Humvee and run for safety.

---

[88] "Stand-to" is the period during dawn and dusk when extra guards are added. At this time, Stand-To Truck 1 was parked at the southern edge of the camp, with its gun facing north.

"That's a bad idea," Romesha said. "The fifty-cal is close to black on ammo. The fire up there is too intense — they're telling everyone to keep away. They need to just hunker down and pray for the best."

Hardt looked at Romesha. "I want to take the truck to them," he said.

Romesha studied Hardt's face. Hardt and Kirk — always the first ones out the door whenever there was enemy contact. You couldn't stop them.

"Hardt, you can do this, but you need to be in an effective place to put fire at Urmul," Romesha said. "Don't put yourself in a position where you're out there with your dick slapping in the wind."

Hardt ran off. Romesha knew he wasn't coming back.

Hardt and Specialist Chris Griffin sprinted to Private Ed Faulkner's truck with as much .50-caliber ammunition as they could carry. Griffin got on the gun, Hardt fed it ammo, and Faulkner started driving the truck toward Gallegos and the other men trapped in the Humvee. Hardt radioed Romesha and told him that he'd reached the stand-to truck safely and they were on their way to LRAS-2.

"Call up Gallegos," Romesha said. "You need to coordinate with him."

Hardt did, letting Gallegos know they were coming for them, that they would provide them with cover so all of them could finally get out of there.

"Don't!" Gallegos told Hardt. "Don't bring the fucking Humvee over! You're just going to die!"

But Hardt was determined to get there. Faulkner put his foot on the gas, and the Humvee lurched forward through small-arms fire, accelerating as rounds bounced off the windshield, then the turret. Griffin ducked down to avoid being hit, then sprang up to fire a couple of bursts. An RPG exploded, spraying shrapnel in his face. Faulkner tried to back up the truck to maneuver to LRAS-2, but the tires got stuck on a berm. He tried to go forward, but the Humvee wouldn't move. He tried to go backward again, but it wouldn't move in that direction, either. Insurgents were now targeting them with RPGs, several of which exploded near and then on the Humvee.

"Get out of here!" Gallegos yelled at Hardt over the radio, convinced that his would-be rescuers were on a suicide mission.

"Roger," Hardt said.

"Hardt!" Gallegos screamed. "Will you get the fuck out of here?"

"Sorry we couldn't help," Hardt replied. "We're leaving."

Hardt told Faulkner and Griffin to get out of the Humvee. Griffin hopped out the rear passenger-side door and ran. He was dead within seconds. A bullet hit his left cheek, lacerating his brain before exiting through his left scalp. Another bullet entered his left lower jaw and passed through the base of his skull and the right side of his brain. A third entered his left thigh, traveled upward, and exited out the right side of his chest. A fourth entered his right buttock and exited from his lower back. Bullet after bullet hit Christopher Todd Griffin: his left forearm; his right thigh; the left side of his neck. . . . Griffin hit the ground, his ribs fractured, his brain and liver lacerated, his skull shattered.

Before Hardt could even close the door after Griffin, rounds flew in. Faulkner looked out to the COP and saw three Afghan Security Guards who didn't look right. He alerted Hardt, who peered out the window, then suddenly pulled back into the truck.

"They're shooting an RPG at us!" Hardt exclaimed. The RPG detonated on the driver's-side windshield, spitting shrapnel into the truck, which sprayed the left side of Faulkner's body — up and down his arm, his shoulder blade, and the inside of his thigh. He screamed in pain.

"You're good, you're good," Hardt said, trying to reassure him.

Faulkner had no idea where his rifle was, but he and Hardt both knew they had to get out of the truck. They decided that Faulkner would get out the driver's side, crouch down, and open Hardt's door behind him. He did all of that and then ran toward the dining hall, where he took a left and made for the aid station. By the time he reached the barracks, his face was torn up and his left arm mangled.

"Where's Hardt?" he was asked. "Where's Griffin?!"

"I don't know," Faulkner said. "Hardt told us to abandon the Humvee. I don't know where they are."

Suddenly, Hardt's voice came on the radio.

"Holy fuck," he said. "They've got an RPG pointed right at me."

Then his radio went dead.

Fifty yards in front of him, Gallegos saw an insurgent carrying an American weapon, an M249 light machine gun. The enemy fighter had come up through the trash pit and was making his way toward the main area of the camp. The troops in the Humvee knew they couldn't stay there any longer.

Gallegos was the highest-ranking among them, so Larson asked him, "What the fuck should we do?"

Carter was always eager to talk. "We should use the rocks in front of the Humvee, and then the latrines, and then the laundry trailer for cover and run to the ECP," he said, meaning the entry control point.

Gallegos paused for a second, then threw it to everyone else. "What do you think?" he asked.

"It's not up to us," Carter said. "You're senior."

"Okay," Gallegos said. "That's what we'll do."

Carter and Larson got out of the Humvee and began providing cover with their M4 carbine rifles. Gallegos helped Mace out of the Humvee and then, along with Martin, they tried to run for cover.

Carter crouched down by the sandbags to the front right of the truck. Sparks were exploding off the downed M240 a foot or so in front of him as the enemy targeted the weapons. Larson was to the back right of the vehicle, and he yelled and started shooting; Carter looked to his right and saw another insurgent inside the wire. He was maybe thirty yards away, and he dove behind a bush to avoid Larson's fire. Carter, too, fired, five or six rounds, until he was rocked by another close explosion, from an RPG that detonated a few feet in front of Mace and knocked him down. The shock wave from the RPG had obviously caused Mace some serious internal injuries, but he was still alive. Carter looked back and saw him leaning against the Humvee. Vernon Martin, blood showing on his neck, ran down the hill toward the latrines. Carter continued to provide cover fire.

Gallegos went over to Mace and helped him up, and then he put his arm around him, and they scurried down the hill and around the corner toward the latrines. The area afforded the two soldiers no shelter as insurgents unloaded their weapons on them.

Carter was waiting for Larson to cue him, to tell him he could move, when he saw Gallegos come back around the corner, returning to the Humvee. Bullets were splashing all around his feet, and then one hit him. Gallegos turned around and fired; another round hit him. He kept firing. Mace, on the ground, on his elbows, was also struggling to get back toward the truck. He'd been hit with small-arms fire and RPG shrapnel. Both of his legs had been shredded with enemy metal, and thanks to two bullets in his back that had exited out his front torso, he was bleeding out of his abdomen.

Larson aimed his fire to try to provide cover for Mace, but almost instantly, a sniper round hit his helmet. Larson felt his head snap back, but the Kevlar worked: the bullet stuck in the helmet. He kept firing, yelling to Mace to follow Gallegos back to the Humvee. Mace turned and started crawling in the direction he'd indicated, but Gallegos was hit a third time now, in the head, by machine-gun fire. The bullets spun him around as if he—a man so enormous he was nicknamed Taco Truck—were practically weightless.

As Gallegos landed on the ground, Larson turned around and saw two insurgents walking in the general direction of the Humvee, one with an RPG, the other with a PKM machine gun. Larson snuck around the truck—apparently they hadn't seen him—and waited until they were ten feet away, and then he stood and shot each one in the head. It was the first time he'd ever killed anyone.

"Gallegos is hit!" Carter yelled. "He's down!"

"Get the fuck back in the truck!" Larson yelled back. "I just smoked two dudes back here! They're in the wire! Get the fuck back here!" Carter scrambled back into the Humvee. The gunfire continued steadily showering down upon the camp; more RPGs fell on the truck.

"Gallegos was hit," Carter told Larson. "I don't know what happened to Mace or Martin."

Then Carter saw Mace, ten to fifteen yards in front of the truck, crawling on his elbows, trying to reach them.

"Mace is there," Specialist Carter said. "I'm going to get him."

"No," replied Sergeant Larson.

"I can see him; he's right there," Carter insisted.

"You're no good to him dead," Larson said.

They argued. Larson said it was senseless to try to get Mace. He made a crack about Carter's wanting to earn a medal.

"Fuck the medals, he needs my help," Carter said.

"No," Larson repeated. The indestructible Gallegos had been killed, Mace was gravely wounded, and neither of them knew what had happened to Martin. Larson wasn't about to let Carter be a fourth man down. It was just too hot out there.

Trapped once again inside the Humvee, the two men tried to secure what they knew could very well end up being their coffin. The turret was jammed, and they couldn't close it. The radio wasn't working. They wondered if any of the other Americans at the outpost were still alive.

Specialist Albert "Cookie" Thomas had just delivered ammunition to the troops near the generator when he saw a man in an Afghan Security Guard's uniform pick up an RPG. Thomas didn't think anything of it — he figured those guys were on the Americans' side — so he kept running. Then he looked again and saw the man standing on top of the hill near the dining hall, aiming the RPG at him. It landed right in front of him, but he kept running as the blast went off. Feeling a distinct tingling sensation in his left leg, he looked down and saw that it was in bloody disarray, having been hit by a scattershot of shrapnel.

Realizing that the wire had been breached, Thomas didn't know what to do, so he ran to his hooch in the Headquarters Platoon barracks. He hid in his little area, behind the curtains and shelves constructed to afford some semblance of privacy. Soon he heard noise and then words in a foreign language: Taliban fighters were in the barracks.

Terrified, Thomas looked down at his leg and the oozing blood. As quietly as he could, he reached into his vest and pulled out the tourniquet stored in his cargo pocket. He attached it to his thigh and tried to stem the bleeding. He then eased himself into another small room where computers had been set up. He slid the chair from that room into Private First Class Jordan Wong's hooch. It was pitch black. He aimed his rifle at the curtain; if insurgents pulled it back, he would shoot.

Not a soul in the world knew he was there. Cookie Thomas was positive he wasn't going to get any help. He would be killed by Taliban as he sat in the computer-room chair; he would die in Jordan Wong's hooch. This was how it would end.

CHAPTER 33

Taking This Bitch Back

Forty-five minutes after taking off, shortly after 8:00 a.m., the mede-vac was still hovering over Forward Operating Base Bostick.

"It's still too hot!" the pilot shouted about the area surrounding Camp Keating. "We're going down to refuel!" They landed, and Stoney Portis returned to the Bostick operations center, where the intelligence officer had just finished making a map of Camp Keating. The whole eastern side of the outpost had been colored red, as had much of the western side. The red indicated Taliban control.

"Can you swim?" Carter asked Larson.

Larson thought about the question. He was a really bad swimmer.

"Enough to survive," he finally said.

"Good enough for me," responded Carter. "If this is as bad as we think it is, we should wait until dark, low-crawl to the river, and float down to Lowell."

Larson was quiet; he'd been shot in the shoulder. They were sur-rounded and cut off, with no communications and little ammunition. Everyone friendly in sight was either wounded or dead, and they still had no idea how many Taliban fighters there were. Sure, he could swim.

Clint Romesha stood on the deck off the aid station, in a semiprotected space known as the Café.

He'd had enough. He'd been trying to find out what was going on at

LRAS-2 when he spotted three Afghans by the shura building. Two had AK-47s, the third an RPG. One was wearing camouflage, as the ANA troops often did. He turned to the Latvians, Lakis and Dabolins, who were standing just outside the operations center.

"You don't have ANA on that side of the camp," Romesha confirmed.

"No," said Lakis.

So that was the enemy.

This is a gimme shot, Romesha thought. I couldn't ask for a better shot. The insurgents walked by Stand-To Truck 2, where they casually put down their weapons. They had entered Camp Keating without being met by an ounce of resistance. One began adjusting his bandanna. They seemed to think the camp had been conquered.

They were wrong. Romesha fired and popped the fighter with the bandanna through his neck; he fell like a sack of potatoes. The other two insurgents ran behind the Humvee. Lakis and Dabolins joined Romesha in his position and began firing, Lakis aiming his grenade launcher past the Humvee and dropping two grenades directly on the fighters.

Other invaders showed a similar confidence in their exploration of the outpost. When Gregory and Jones poked their heads up from their ditch, they saw two insurgents roughly twenty feet from them, just walking along nonchalantly as if the battle were over, as if they'd already won. One was wearing a gray overshirt, the other a golden-yellow one with a tan vest over it and a belt of RPK light machine-gun ammunition slung over his shoulder. He carried the RPK itself casually, as if it were a briefcase.

"They're fucking up there," Gregory said. "They're in the wire, they're near the showers."

"We need to kill 'em, kill 'em, kill 'em!" exclaimed Jones.

Gregory and Jones fired, and both insurgents promptly fell to the ground dead. But other enemy fighters in the camp had seen it happen, and with grenades and sniper fire, they started targeting the two Americans. Gregory and Jones ducked back down again. Soon Daise and Dannelley came running over to them.

"It's not looking good, man," Dannelley told them, standing outside the ditch.

"We're kinda pinned down here," Jones said. "There are snipers everywhere."

"Kirk and Scusa have already gotten killed," reported Dannelley. "They're not letting up, and air support's not here." Bullets were flying by to the left and right of his face, but he seemed blissfully unaware of them.

"Get the fuck down," Jones said. "You're getting shot at! You're going to get shot in the fucking face!"

An RPG hit yet another generator, creating a forebodingly dark plume of smoke. The four men took the opportunity to use the cloud as cover, and they ran back to the Red Platoon barracks.

Back inside the LRAS-2 Humvee, Carter looked out the window to see, across the river, about a hundred yards away, a three-man enemy RPG team standing next to the Afghan National Police building. He opened his window and fired six rounds at them with his M4 rifle. Then he fired at another insurgent. And another one, a fighter dressed in dark brown with a ponytail.

Mace crawled out from behind Stand-To Truck 1. Carter opened the window to talk to him. Shots were still coming at them. "Mace, are you all right?" Carter asked.

Too dehydrated to cry, Mace wore his pain on his face. He didn't seem to have the energy to yell. "Help me," Mace said plaintively. "Help me."

"I can get to him, he's right there," Carter told Larson.

"Tell him to stay where he is," Larson said. "He's got cover there."

"Help me, please," Mace pleaded.

"I will get to you as soon as I can," Carter said. He was irate. When the horn on a nearby truck blared, he for some reason became convinced it was a distress call from a fellow soldier. "Can I go to the truck?" he asked Larson. "There's someone calling for help in there. What if I get out and get underneath the Humvee just to see the truck?"

"Fine," Larson agreed.

There were still bursts of intense machine-gun rounds every fifteen seconds or so, but the enemy, having apparently shifted his attention to other targets, seemed no longer to be specifically focused on them. Carter jumped out of the Humvee on his recon mission, only to see that its tires were flat from bullet rounds and there was no way for him, with all his gear on, to fit underneath. He hopped back in with Larson.

"The truck is ten feet away, can I go check for survivors?" he asked.

"Yeah," Larson said. Rounds were still being fired at them, but the enemy was now concentrating more closely on other parts of the camp. Carter jumped out again and ran to the truck. There was no soldier inside, so he recovered some ammunition that was in there and brought it back to the Humvee. He wasn't sure where the sound of the horn had come from.

"Can I go to Mace?" asked Carter, back inside. He'd given Mace his word.

"What do you plan on doing when you get to him?" Larson asked.

"Give him first aid."

"Where are you going to take him?" Larson asked.

They discussed the options and decided that the nearby concrete bridge—outside the camp—would provide the most cover.

"You plan on dragging him that far?" Larson wondered.

"Fuck, no," said Carter. "I plan on carrying him."

Larson rolled down his window so he could fire and cover Carter, who got out and ran to Mace. He was facedown. Carter gently shook him.

"Hey, Mace, you all right?"

Mace mumbled something, and Carter turned him over. He couldn't distinguish between Mace's uniform and his legs; they were all a dark-red mess, with just a stretch of skin and bone keeping his left foot attached to his leg.

"Where does it hurt?" Carter asked. "What should I do? Are you okay?" He applied a tourniquet to Mace's shredded left leg, then used a tree branch he found to splint his ankle. He took out his special "Israeli" bandage—elasticized and fitted with a pressure bar, the invention of an Israeli medic—to stanch bleeding from the largest hole in Mace's abdomen, which was roughly the size of a tangerine. Other cavities were smaller but still gruesome and troubling. One was in the shape of a teardrop, Carter noted. Turning to Mace's bloody right leg, he took out the dagger that'd been a gift from a karaoke buddy back home and cut open Mace's pants. Using tape and gauze, he then tried to plug the holes in that leg.

Mace was in shock and did not seem particularly aware of what was going on. He was pale, and his lips were turning blue.

"Don't worry about your ankle," Carter said. "It will be fine as soon as we can find it." He thought he could discern the faintest chuckle from Mace.

Carter looked at Gallegos, who was lying facedown next to them.

"Sergeant Gallegos is dead," Mace said.

"I believe you, but I need to check his pulse anyway," Carter replied. He reached over and felt the carotid artery in the sergeant's neck. There was no pulse.

"Okay," Carter told Mace, "you play dead. I'm going to check with Larson about what we should do now."

He ran back to the Humvee.

"I don't think it's safe to take him to the bridge, it's too exposed," Carter explained to Larson. "The truck's the only safe place."

Larson agreed and got out of the truck to provide cover for Carter. Carter scurried back to Mace and reached down to hoist him up. He thought about his lifeguard training and how he would've picked Mace up if instead of being shot up he were drowning in a swimming pool. Carter told Mace to wrap his hands around his neck, and then he slid his left arm around Mace's back and under his arms, and his right arm under his legs. Cradling him that way, he carried the wounded soldier while bullets flew by them, tripping over ammo cans and pieces of generator wreckage as they went, until at last they reached the Humvee, where Carter carefully placed Mace in the front seat.

At the operations center, Bundermann was staring at Cason Shrode. Both of them wore grim expressions that said, This is actually happening. And yet Bundermann still looked as if he were headed for the beach, dressed in flip-flops, shorts, and a T-shirt.

"Go get your kit," he told Shrode. His own body armor was back at the barracks; he would need to borrow Shrode's extra set. "Get your rifles," Bundermann added. There was a very real chance that the insurgents would try to take the operations center, and they could not let that happen.

Shrode came back with the body armor. The former high school and West Point football star was much larger than Bundermann, so it was an awkward fit, but it was a hell of a lot better than shorts.

Then, some good news: the Apache pilots radioed, announcing that they would be there in a couple of minutes. Bundermann, fed information by others throughout the outpost, had already given Shrode targets for bomb drops to pass on to the pilots of the fixed-wing aircraft. Now he told Shrode to tell the helicopter pilots that anyone outside the wire should be considered the enemy.

Bundermann stepped outside to the Café and looked out. The whole camp was being lit up; insurgents were firing from everywhere. Shit, Bundermann said to himself. There was absolutely no way the Americans could defend themselves without air support. Since they no longer controlled the entire camp, the men would need to collapse and defend only the core—the operations center, the barracks buildings, and the aid station. Bundermann decided that Black Knight Troop needed to contract, to pull in. That left a dozen troops outside the new perimeter.

I'm not going to be able to keep that part of that camp right now, he thought, so I'm going to focus on keeping and securing this part instead, and then I'm going to kick some Taliban ass.

But it was a gut-wrenching decision.

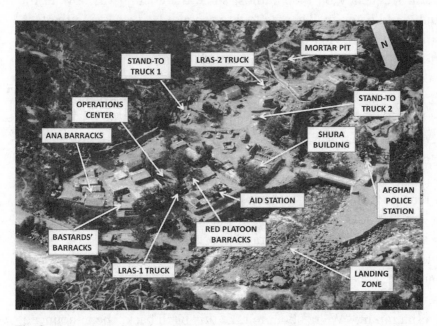

The Outpost. *(Taken from U.S. Army investigation)*

After talking to Brown on the satellite radio that Burton had managed to rig, Bundermann turned to Romesha and Hill, who were at the entrance to the operations center. "We need to fight this out; we need to hold our ground," Bundermann said.

"Fuck that," replied Romesha. "We need to retake this fucking camp and drive the fucking Taliban out!"

"Let's do it," Hill added.

"All right," said Bundermann.

The three men made a plan. Romesha would focus on the western portion of the camp, where the ammo supply point and the entry control point were. Hill would focus on the eastern side, the ANA side.

"I need a machine gun covering me from the south," Romesha said.

Bundermann turned to Hill. "Whoever you've got, put a machine gun by the DFAC"—the dining hall—"looking to the west and north for Romesha."

Hill nodded.

Romesha also suggested that the members of Black Knight Troop use a different frequency on their radios, since the enemy was now in the wire and could listen in. Then he took a second. He was losing the feeling in his right hand. He lifted it to his face and looked at it.

Burton came over to him. "You all right?" he asked.

"I can't feel my hand anymore," Romesha said.

Burton began unwrapping the dressing bandage that Rasmussen had put on him earlier, and almost immediately, the feeling in his hand returned: that big oaf Rasmussen had just wrapped it too tightly, cutting off the circulation.

"Thanks for dressing me for school today, Dad," Romesha said to Burton. "I'll be good."

Bundermann told them to wait to push out until the Apaches were nearby and could provide the distraction of air cover.

Inside the Red Platoon barracks, Knight was pointing an M240 machine gun at the door. Jones had been instructed to grab an Mk 48 lightweight machine gun and stand point inside the barracks as well.

Romesha ran in. "We're about to take this bitch back," he announced. "I need a fucking group of volunteers." He told them he'd need a SAW gunner to handle the squad automatic weapon, a 5.56 machine gun.

Gregory was the only SAW gunner there. "I don't think I can do it," he admitted. He'd hit a wall. A wall of terror, a wall of fatigue—whatever it was, his fellow troops understood. Some had been there themselves.

"I'll do it," Chris Jones offered.

So Romesha had his group: Thomas Rasmussen, Mark Dulaney, Josh Dannelley, Chris Jones, and Sergeant Matthew Miller. Jones took the SAW, and everyone else had an M4 rifle. They knew they were going to be utterly and completely outgunned, but they had no other option.

As they left the barracks, Romesha and Dannelley ran to the hut next door. They kicked the door open and threw a grenade to clear the room. Earlier, Romesha had asked Bundermann to "confirm that there are no friendlies on the other side of the HESCOs here." Bundermann had replied that that was the case, other than the men holed up in the LRAS-2 Humvee and the mortarmen at the mortar pit. As they made their way into the western side of the camp, Romesha told his men that anybody in front of them not in a coalition uniform would be considered an enemy combatant whom they could shoot on sight.

CHAPTER 34

The Apaches

At Forward Operating Base Fenty in Jalalabad, Chief Warrant Officer Third Class Ross Lewallen had just sat down to breakfast with his co-pilot, Chief Warrant Officer Second Class Chad Bardwell, when the portable radio he carried with him sounded a familiar alarm: a medevac was needed.

Lewallen and Bardwell were not themselves medevac pilots, but they often flew along as an armed escort for the unarmed Army medevac helicopters. On this particular morning, as the two men rose from the table in the mess hall and headed to their Apache, they presumed they would be accompanying a bird with a big red cross on its side on a standard wartime medical mission. But during their walk out to the airfield, the radio offered additional information about the situation: Combat Outpost Keating was under intense attack, with small-arms fire and RPGs. The news was delivered matter-of-factly, like a traffic update or a stock-market ticker.

Within twelve minutes, they were in the air, as was another Apache flown by Chief Warrant Officer Third Class Randy Huff and Chief Warrant Officer Second Class Christopher Wright. They were about thirty minutes from Forward Operating Base Bostick, which normally would be their first stop, to refuel, but based on what they were hearing on the radio, Lewallen and Huff decided to go directly to Camp Keating instead. The valley was too dangerous for the medevac but not for the armed Apaches. This would mean they wouldn't have as much fuel when they got there and therefore wouldn't be able to stay as long, but it sounded like there wasn't a minute to spare. They climbed to an altitude of ninety-five hundred feet along the mountain range, keeping an eye out for the enemy the whole time. One lucky shot, a single bullet that cost no more than a gumball, and it could all be over.

As the Apaches neared Forward Operating Base Bostick, the operations center at Jalalabad reported that Camp Keating was being overrun. Everyone not only outside the perimeter but also inside it could be considered hostile. "If this is as bad as you're telling us, we're going to need more Apache support," Wright replied, knowing the message would be conveyed to his commanders.

The pilots knew that the insurgents were used to seeing the U.S. helicopters travel east to west through the valley to the camp, so they decided instead to fly directly over the top of the northern mountain. As they crossed the peak and came around, they could see nothing of Combat Outpost Keating beyond an orange fire and a billowing column of smoke. It looked as if every building at the camp were aflame. They radioed in to Keating's operations center: "Black Knight seven-oh, Black Knight seven-oh, do you read?" The pilots had no idea that the men of Black Knight Troop had lost their generator and were having difficulty responding.

Lewallen felt a sinking feeling in his chest. The entire camp must have been overrun, he thought. Everyone was dead.

But then, all of a sudden, Camp Keating made contact on a different radio frequency.

"We've been compromised," Bundermann announced. "We've got guys inside the wire."

Out his window, Bardwell saw a long finger of roughly thirty Afghans walking down the southern mountain on a trail that ran along the river, heading toward the eastern side of the camp.

"Hey, Ross," he told Lewallen, "I got a whole bunch of guys here."

"Do they have weapons?" Lewallen asked.

"Yeah," said Bardwell.

Lewallen looked. There were so many bad guys that he couldn't believe they were all bad guys.

"We see guys on the road," Lewallen relayed over the radio. "Do you have friendlies on the road?"

"No!" said Bundermann. "Ice 'em!"

"That's not an ANA patrol?" Lewallen said.

"No!" Bundermann reaffirmed.

Apaches can be outfitted with three weapons systems at the same time: up to sixteen Hellfire missiles, each a one-hundred-pound explosive with precision accuracy that follows an aimed laser to its target; unguided Hydra 2.75-inch rockets, propelled from the front of the aircraft; and a chain gun of 30-millimeter high-explosive detonating rounds that can fire at a speed of up to 640 rounds a minute, targeted at whatever the pilot is looking at, provided that the system is linked to his helmet.

At 7:10 a.m., both Apaches let loose with their 30-millimeter chain guns, and the insurgents on the road, who were by then trying to breach the wire, were all killed.

A medevac hovering over the camp was waved away; it was still way too hot for it to land. The two Apaches began trying to solve that problem, firing at insurgents on the Putting Green and the Switchbacks. But now, of course, the helicopters had become enemy targets as well.

Romesha led his team of five into the ammo supply point, where they grabbed grenades, three each. They'd need them to throw around blind corners. By now, the Latvians, Lakis and Dabolins, had joined them.

The arrival of the Apaches provided a welcome distraction as Romesha's team made its way to the shura building. Bullets rebounded off the building, with RPGs and B-10 rounds shaking the walls. Bombs screeched as they were dropped from F-15s, a high-pitched whistle that ended with the deep rumble of explosion. Romesha and Rasmussen looked at each other. "I wonder if this is what it was like during World War Two," Rasmussen said. They were always talking about how bad previous soldiers had had it—in the trenches of Europe, on the beaches of Normandy, in the jungles of Vietnam. Romesha grinned and said, "I'm sure this is just a small taste of what it was like, brother."

Dulaney noticed five insurgents near the maintenance shed, to their south, and he sprayed them with his machine gun; Lakis and Dabolins followed his lead, dropping grenades on them with their M203 grenade launcher.

Romesha realized that the machine gun in the south of the camp that he'd requested from Bundermann and Hill was still not in place. If it had been, they'd have had a great crossfire to kill those five insurgents, but as it was, they were just eight men trying to fight dozens, if not hundreds, of enemy fighters in three different positions—to the north, the west, and the south. Romesha called Bundermann, ready to let loose: no machine gun, no cover, what was the problem? Even more infuriating to Romesha was the attitude he felt he had picked up listening to his fellow soldiers on the radio: some of the guys from Black Knight Troop sounded as if they were giving up.

Fuck no, Romesha thought. We're not going to sit here and roll over and fucking get killed. He could feel his adrenaline flowing. You fucking muj are not going to keep us down, we are going to take this fight to you!

But first he needed everyone to get on the same page. He got on the radio again. "Where the fuck is my machine gun?" he asked Bundermann. "I can't fucking continue without it! You're going to get me and fucking everybody with me trying to take this COP back fucking killed!"

While it didn't feel that way to Romesha, Bundermann had in fact made it a priority to get a machine gun in place to provide him with cover. Problem was, the machine guns were all in use. Hill finally found one in the possession of an Afghan soldier who had taken cover in a drainage ditch outside the operations center. But no matter how hard Hill tried to get the machine gun from him — through argument and brute force — he couldn't do it; here, in the wrong place and at the wrong time, an ANA soldier was finally showing that he had some fight in him.

Hill ran to the Café outside the aid station and found an M240 machine gun. He grabbed it and ran. Better than nothing. His larger goal was to push north and then west from the operations center, to extend the perimeter of controlled territory. He assembled a team of men, and they all ran to the dining hall, where they found Private First Class Daniel Rogers looking fairly hunkered down. "What the fuck?" Hill asked. "How long you been here, Rogers?"

"I don't know," Rogers said. He was now part of Hill's team.

They couldn't push past the dining hall because every time they tried to make a move, bullets hailed down on them from the hills. Figuring it couldn't hurt, Hill set up the M240 machine gun and, streaming a Z-pattern with the gun, unleashed several hundred rounds. He set up Gregory, Rogers, and Davidson in positions to help Romesha and his team, and then he ran back to the Café.

After forty-five minutes of sitting scared in Wong's hooch, Cookie Thomas heard someone come into the barracks. Then he heard a most welcome language: Latvian. Dabolins and Lakis had come in to get more ammunition.

Thank God, Thomas thought. He cried out, and they came to him. The Latvians helped the cook get to the aid station, where Floyd, Hobbs, and Cordova started fixing up his leg.

"If the pain gets any worse, I'll give you morphine," Cordova told him.

"I don't want any until I get out of here," Thomas said. Until he was on a medevac and in the air, he wanted to be as alert as he could be.

At the Café, John Francis looked at Jonathan Hill. "It's been nice fighting with you," he said. "It's been nice serving with you. In case we don't make it out of here."

"Same here," Hill replied.

Chris Jones stood at the corner of the ammo supply point, from which vantage he could see the river and the road toward Urmul.

"We got dudes running outside the wire across the bridge," Romesha said. Jones stood and aimed his rifle. He fired it and took down one of the insurgents. Rasmussen did the same. Jones fired at a third insurgent and killed him as well. Rasmussen looked at Jones. The kid had a huge grin on his face, like it was the coolest thing he'd ever done.

"Stay here at this position," Romesha said. "Anyone who comes up, kill 'em." Jones was handed the Mk 48 light machine gun, and Dannelley was posted nearby to make sure no enemy snuck up on him.

Sure enough, Dannelley soon saw someone through the wall, on the road. "Hey, stop," he yelled. "Fucking stop! *Stop!*" When the man turned around, Dannelley saw that he was holding an AK-47. "What are you doing?" Dannelley said, then shouted, "He's got a gun!" He aimed his M4 rifle at the insurgent, but he had placed it on "safe," so it didn't work for a second; he ducked behind the wall.

"Fucking shoot him!" yelled Romesha.

"Shoot him!" echoed Rasmussen.

Dannelley clicked off the safety on his rifle and stood to fire, but he'd waited too long—the enemy fighter shot him twice in the arm, and he fell to the ground.

Jones fired his Mk 48 machine gun at the insurgent while Romesha, Rasmussen, and Miller threw grenades over the wall. As the grenades exploded, they looked up and saw the spray of a bloody mist and some scraps of the insurgent's clothing rise into the air, then fall. In the craziness of it all, they laughed.

Romesha went over to Dannelley and inspected his injury; it was a sizable flesh wound to his left shoulder and left upper arm, but ultimately he'd be okay. The laughing over, Romesha was now mad. He'd put Dannelley in charge of just one thing: making sure no one snuck up on Jones in the middle of an intense firefight. The kid had seen the insurgent and told him to stop, as if he were on guard duty at the PX back in Colorado. Romesha figured the Rules of Engagement were mostly to blame; these kids were taught they would go to jail if they overreacted even slightly. It was ridiculous, and it created situations like this one, he thought. Such, he mused bitterly, was the "politically correct" Army. But while the Rules of Engagement were whatever McChrystal said they were, Romesha always told his men that at the end of the day, "it's better to be judged by twelve than carried by six." He sent Dannelley to the aid station, and while the rest of them hunkered down, he told Lakis and Dabolins to go back and help out Sergeant Hill.

Bundermann directed Ryan Schulz to replace Dannelley. They still had no cover from the south, so Romesha once again radioed Bundermann, who checked with Hill to see what the holdup was. Hill explained that they were still trying to get a machine gun down there, but he said his own men were busy with other tasks — namely, securing the eastern side of the camp and trying to put out several (literal) fires.

"Let the barracks burn," Romesha said. "They're just barracks."

But it was more urgent than that; the ANA commander had told them their ammo storage building was on fire, cooking off rounds that could have killed men in the base. The staff sergeant decided that his request for cover fire from the south was just never going to be met; that fight was lost. He told Rasmussen, Dulaney, and Miller that the wait was over: it was time to take back the shura building. Jones and Schulz would cover them with grenades as best they could, paying special attention to their southern flank, where they would be completely exposed. It was a rash decision, but it needed to be done, and they couldn't wait any longer. They were going to reclaim the entrance to the camp.

Romesha turned to the three men. "You guys trust me, right?" he said. "This could get bad."

"We'll follow you anywhere," Rasmussen replied.

"You're going to be the point man," Romesha told Rasmussen.

"Roger," Rasmussen said.

A wall made of rocks and sandbags led up to the entry control point building. They didn't know who, if anyone, was in there.

"Let me put a two-oh-three in the building so we don't get whacked," Rasmussen proposed, referring to his M203 single-shot 40-millimeter grenade launcher.

"Cool," said Romesha. "Do it."

Rasmussen stepped around the corner and fired. The grenade shot right through the door and into the building, filling the room with a ball of fire. "Hell, yeah," Rasmussen said.

They ran to the building, and Dulaney opened a whole drum of ammo into it before entering. Inside, they couldn't breathe: the grenade had hit the fire extinguisher, filling the air with fire retardant. Rasmussen started vomiting and ran outside to get some air. At any rate, there weren't any Taliban in there, though some of their weapons had been left behind, including a machine gun and a few AK-47s.

"We've secured the shura building," Romesha called in to Bundermann. He still couldn't see Gallegos or the other men pinned down at LRAS-2. "I can't do anything until I get additional personnel out here."

Romesha looked at one of his men; the battle seemed to be getting to him. He had started shaking and, in Romesha's opinion, was acting a bit checked out and timid, precisely when the utmost courage and focus were demanded. This wasn't so unexpected: endurance folds. But the timing was miserable. Romesha told the soldier to dodge the bullets and run back to the aid station to take a breather, adding that he needed an IV for treatment of dehydration.

Moving to the open doorway, Romesha suggested targets for the Apaches. The camp was receiving a tremendous amount of fire from a spot just above the Urmul mosque. "I need you to put as much firepower as you can in that area," Romesha said. And Bundermann heard him. An F-16 dropped an immense bomb, the shock wave from which nearly lifted the roof off the shura building.

"I'm no structural engineer," Romesha radioed in, "but I don't know how much longer this building can last."

"Do you want me to stop?" asked Bundermann.

"No," Romesha said. "Keep going."

Jordan Bellamy had called from Observation Post Fritsche with good news. Using their Claymores, hand grenades, and machine guns, he and his men had beaten back the enemy enough to get their mortars back up, and the 120-millimeter was ready for use in helping their fellow troops in the valley. Bundermann gave Bellamy a six-digit grid for his 120s to fire at the center of Urmul. "Use Willie Pete," he specified. He wanted smoke blocking the village's view of the outpost.

Bundermann instructed the Apache pilots to lay Hellfires into the Urmul mosque and to take out the Afghan National Police checkpoint. Ordering the destruction of a local mosque was extreme, but to the Americans, using one as a firing base from which to attack them was clearly the greater evil.

In the LRAS-2 truck, Mace's wounds were so serious that Carter knew he would die if he didn't receive medical attention soon.

"That settles it," he told Larson. "I'm going on a recon. If I'm not back in ten minutes, either I made it or don't worry about me."

So much had happened, but in fact it had been only minutes earlier that the other three men in the truck had jumped into the maelstrom. Gallegos had been killed, Mace gravely wounded, and Martin unaccounted for. Carter hopped out of the Humvee and sprinted to the corner of the latrines, where he took a knee. He'd made it. He gasped for air. Carter glimpsed Mace's gun at the corner of the laundry room. That was as far as he'd gotten, Carter figured. He saw Gallegos's radio and snagged it. "This is Blue Four Golf — is anyone still alive?" he asked. He heard some sort of response in English; he wasn't sure exactly what was being said, but it was enough to send him on a sprint back to the Humvee to give the radio to Larson, who dialed up the operations center.

At the operations center, Bundermann got on the radio. "Red Dragon, what's going on?" he asked Larson.

"I'm with Carter," Larson said. "We got Mace. Mace is pretty jacked up. We need to get him to the aid station." And then, with gratitude in his voice, he added, "We didn't know if anyone else was still alive!"

There was a stretcher near their position — someone had brought it out earlier and leaned it up near the truck. Now Bundermann wanted to know if Larson and Carter could get Mace onto it. "We need some cover fire," Larson replied.

Excited that the three of them, at least, were still breathing, Bundermann called Romesha, on the western side of the camp, and Hill, who was in charge of the men on the eastern side. "I'm going to launch mortar rounds from Fritsche," he told them. "When that happens, Ro, anything you and your team can shoot, do it, at the Putting Green, Urmul, and the Northface. Hill, you shoot anything you can at the Diving Board and the Switchbacks. I want every weapons system on the site firing in one minute."

Bundermann radioed Bellamy. "Give me fifteen rounds from the one-twenty and fifteen from the sixty into Urmul." He picked up another radio and asked Larson, "If I lay down a fuck-ton of cover fire, can you guys get back on your own?"

"Fuck yeah," said Larson.

The plan was this: a B-1 bomber would drop its explosives while OP Fritsche, Romesha and his men, and Hill and his men unleashed everything they had at every enemy position they could target—at which point Larson and Carter would grab Mace and sprint to the aid station. Everyone got ready.

Carter scurried out to prepare the stretcher and clear the area, but within seconds, a mortar from OP Fritsche had hit Urmul, and Larson was yelling, "Go! Go! Go!" Prep work now short-circuited, Carter kicked the ammo cans out of the way and snatched up the stretcher. He opened the back door of the Humvee, where Mace was trying ease himself out.

"Mace, you need to shift your legs," Larson said.

"You need to hold the fuck on, because we're going to haul ass," added Carter.

The aggressive fire echoed the morning's earlier sound track, but this time, the bullets and mortars were outgoing, as the men of 3-61 Cav, together and all at once, began giving the enemy everything they had. Mace threw himself onto the stretcher, and Carter and Larson started moving, trying to achieve a balance of speed and smoothness. As they chugged toward the aid station, they passed by the bodies of the two dead insurgents Larson had killed. Not far from them lay a dead U.S. soldier: Chris Griffin. Carter had never been so exhausted; he was in so much pain, and so spent, that tears started streaking from his eyes. He was dehydrated and in agony. As soon as they reached the aid station, the docs grabbed Mace and got to work on him. Carter fell on the ground and started crawling. He had just enough breath to say "Help"—for himself and for all of them.

CHAPTER 35

The Fundamentals

Pushing from the operations center toward the eastern side of the camp, Harder and his team braved the blaze in the Bastards' barracks as a means to escape detection. Lieutenant Stephen Cady was with them; normally Cady worked out of Forward Operating Base Bostick, but he'd flown in a couple of days before—the same day Portis's chopper was hit—to bring the Afghan Security Guards and others their pay. Bad timing.

Exiting via the back door, the group headed toward the ANA barracks, inside of which they could see insurgents, though no one had a clear shot or a particularly good spot with any cover to shoot from.

"Fuck it," Francis said. "Let's start shooting."

They did that, with their M4 rifles, and Francis fired, too, with his M203 grenade launcher, and Harder threw a couple of hand grenades. Some Taliban fell to the ground, direct hits, dead. Other insurgents started screaming. Francis didn't know what they were saying, and he didn't care. He kept shooting and reloading, shooting and reloading.

The seemingly endless supply of insurgents that Harder and his men were seeing was confirmed in commentary from above: "We're picking these guys off here, but they keep coming," an Apache pilot radioed. "They're fucking *everywhere*."

No cover, no weapon—Rodriguez knew this might be his last run. But what choice did he have?

"Can you get out and shoot?" Bundermann had asked the guys at the mortar pit over the radio, now operative again.

Good question. For more than an hour, Breeding, Rodriguez, and Barroga had remained cut off from the rest of the camp, unable to make their radio function, unable to escape their corner. Rodriguez had fired his M240 machine gun at the enemy when he could—sticking the gun out the door and just firing without aiming it—but after sixty rounds, he'd run out of ammunition. From his position, he'd watched the drama unfold at LRAS-2—he'd seen Gallegos help Mace away from the Humvee after the RPG went off so close to him, then witnessed another RPG go off near both of them, knocking Mace to the ground near a gully where an insurgent stood. As he watched, the insurgent had begun firing at Mace.

Breeding had gotten the radio fixed in time for them all to hear Daise shout, "Enemy in the wire!" Hearing enemy fighters coming down the Switchbacks, right near him, Rodriguez had started throwing hand grenades at them over the wall of the mortar pit. He'd then tried to detonate the Claymore mines outside the camp. They didn't work.

"We can't shoot the big gun," Breeding had reported, referring to the 120-millimeter. "We can't get to it." But Rodriguez was itching to lay hands on the 60-millimeter, so Breeding provided cover fire, spraying the hills with the M240 machine gun while his mortarman dashed out the door. Rodriguez got to the mortar pit, grabbed a can of ammo and tucked it under his arm, and with both hands grasped the 60-millimeter and prepared to shoot it at the Northface.

As he turned the weapon, he looked up at the Switchbacks and saw an insurgent retreating. An RPG exploded nearby, hitting ammo cans and sandbags and sending shrapnel into Rodriguez's neck. He kept going. He squeezed the trigger. The 60-millimeter was set at the "Charge 1" level, which made firing it feel like operating a jackhammer; you could break your foot firing at that intensity. Rodriguez sent the explosives into the Northface and then toward the Afghan National Police compound across the bridge. Then he turned, calibrated his mortar tube, and fired at the eastern side of the camp, where he'd been told the enemy had entered and taken over the ANA barracks. There were no friendlies there, he'd been advised.

That last part was no longer true, however. Eric Harder and his team were there.

*   *   *

Harder and John Francis were just seconds away from heading into the ANA side of the camp when Rodriguez's mortars began destroying the buildings in front of them.

"Fuck it," Harder concluded. "Let's fall back. If those dudes aren't dead already, they're not going to survive this."

"Good," said Francis. They retreated. By now, the camp was littered with the tiny metal fins that fell off RPGs before they hit their targets. The fire had leapt into the overflow barracks and the gym and was quickly spreading throughout the area around Harder and Francis. Rounds that had been left inside the barracks would cook and pop and zip by their heads, while abandoned mortars exploded in the ANA barracks. Physically drained and overcome by thirst, Harder ran into the Bastards' barracks, snatched up the mop bucket, and gulped water from it.

By noon, other aircraft had joined the Apaches in the valley. F-15 Eagle fighter jets were screeching far above and had begun dropping two-thousand-pound bombs, causing the entire valley to shake.

Lewallen had done two tours in Iraq—one of them during the invasion—and on this Afghanistan tour had completed some tough missions in the Korangal Valley, but the firefight at Camp Keating was without question the worst he'd ever seen. He was grateful that the man on the other end of the radio—Bundermann—was so cool and collected, able calmly and dispassionately to single out for the pilots those areas from which the outpost was taking the heaviest incoming fire.

The Apaches had repeatedly been coming down, firing, clearing an area, and then floating back to safety. The pilots tried to stay high up when they weren't engaged with the enemy, to avoid all of the small-arms fire that was showering down from the southeastern and southwestern hills. Acting on Bundermann's request, he and Huff, in the other Apache, swooped down to launch a Hellfire missile at the Urmul mosque. Two enemy Dushkas had originally been placed higher up in the hills not far from the landing zone, positioned to shoot down any medevac choppers that tried to land. When the Apaches showed up, the insurgents brought the heavy machine guns downhill, which turned out to be a smart move. One of the Dushkas got Ross Lewallen's Apache, and then again when, within ninety seconds, Randy Huff's bird was hit, too. The helicopters appeared to be okay, but they were both running low on fuel and ammo anyway, so it seemed an opportune — even necessary — time to head back to Forward Operating Base Bostick for a pit stop. Lewallen and Huff would go as quickly as they could, but the reality was that they would be out of pocket for at least an hour, leaving Camp Keating at a disadvantage at a fragile moment in the fight.

Harder wanted to report to Jon Hill that the eastern side of the outpost was secure and then get an update on what else he could do. But the radios were going a bit berserk, so it seemed easier just to run over to his position and have the conversation in person. On his way, Harder ran into Ed Faulkner at the aid station. He was a bloody mess.

"What happened to you?" Harder asked him.

"Man, I don't want to talk about it," Faulkner replied. He showed Harder where he'd gotten hit, in the same arm he'd wounded in Iraq. "I'm going to have two fucking Purple Hearts and just one scar!" he said.

"You all right?" Harder asked.

"I'd be better if I had a cigarette," Faulkner said. Harder threw him a couple.

Cordova and Courville were too focused on Mace to care that Faulkner was violating their no-smoking policy. Mace had been brought in awake and responsive, though pale, and in excruciating pain. As time passed, his level of consciousness ebbed. Cordova asked him if he knew where he was. Mace looked back at him with big wide eyes and mouthed something unintelligible.

The specialist had lost an extraordinary amount of blood. Shrapnel had ripped up his lower left abdomen and lower left back, leaving more than twenty entrance and exit wounds on both sides of his torso and causing internal injuries to his bowel and right adrenal gland, which in turn resulted in extensive bleeding into his abdominal cavity. His right arm had suffered four serious ballistic wounds and seven grazing and superficial wounds. He had nine bullet and shrapnel wounds to his right thigh and six in his left leg, from the thigh to the calf.

Carter had put a tourniquet on Mace's left thigh, and Cordova left it there; it had been on for hours now, and he didn't want to mess with it, though he added a second tourniquet for reinforcement. Cody Floyd held

Mace's left leg together—the foot was nearly coming off—while Jeff Hobbs wrapped it up and splinted it.

Once they'd controlled as much of Mace's external bleeding as they felt they could, Cordova and Courville attempted to insert an IV to begin replenishing his lost blood. They had trouble finding a vein, however, because his vascular system was delivering blood to his most important organs and ignoring his arms and legs. At one point, the medics congratulated themselves on successfully planting an IV in their patient's arm, only to watch him—or his reflexes—immediately yank it out.

Increasingly desperate, they opted to try a FAST1 intraosseous infusion, injecting fluids directly into the marrow of his sternum, just as they'd done with Josh Kirk. They jammed in the FAST1, which dripped with Hextend, a plasma substitute believed to be superior even to the real thing in the treatment of certain kinds of trauma. The solution was pushed into Mace's blood vessels, delivering oxygen to his brain. The IV dripped slowly, but it dripped.

Courville and Cordova then searched again to find a vein, this time for another IV bag of Hextend. They tried Mace's leg, but no luck. In the aid bag was an EZ-IO needle, which Cordova manually forced in just below the soldier's right kneecap. Mindful of the injuries to his abdomen, and the propensity of wounds to the intestines and colon to cause easy infection, Cordova added yet another IV containing antibiotics.

Cordova placed a device on Mace's fingertip to measure the oxygen saturation in his blood. A normal level would be somewhere between 95 and 97 percent; in Mace's case, there was no reading at all. Cordova checked his wrist: no pulse. Then his neck: there was a faint beat there, from his carotid artery. This confirmed that his body was now sending all of his blood exclusively to his vital organs. His blood pressure was weak. He would need to get out of the valley soon if he was to have any hope of surviving.

Courville went to Bundermann to tell him about Mace. "He's got maybe an hour, hour and a half to live if we don't get a bird," the medic reported.

"Doc," Bundermann said. "I'm going to be honest. We're not going to get a bird in here till nightfall."

Courville's heart sank. Before he could even reflect on the situation with Mace, however, there was another, even more pressing problem to address: the fire that was devouring the camp had jumped from the Bastards' barracks to the operations center. At 2:14 p.m., Bundermann, Burton, and everyone else in Headquarters Platoon had to evacuate the building and set up a makeshift ops center in the Red Platoon barracks. Courville hastily helped cut the camouflage net that was attached to both the operations center and the aid station, to minimize the chances that the fire would pursue that route. Then he returned to the aid station and passed on Bundermann's grim assessment.

Cordova, Courville, Hobbs, and Floyd huddled. They needed to try something radical to keep Mace alive for as long as they could. But what?

After getting checked out at the aid station, Larson joined Romesha's team at the shura building.

"Man, I'd really like a Dr. Pepper right now," he told Romesha. "I'm thirsty as hell." That was their drink of choice, the two friends.

"I don't have any on me at the moment," Romesha said with a smile, "but I'll get you some when we get back."

They debriefed.

"Kirk got smoked in the face," Romesha said. "So he's dead." Scusa, too. And Thomson up at the mortar pit. No one knew where Hardt was.

Romesha asked Larson what had happened to the other guys he'd been stuck with in the Humvee. Larson told him that Mace and Gallegos had been messed up pretty good by an RPG and a machine gun. Gallegos was dead, though he didn't know where his body was, and Mace was in the aid station. He wasn't sure where Martin was.

"When I ran Mace to the aid station, we passed by Griffin," Larson added. "He was lying right in front of the shura building." *This* building.

Romesha said they needed to go get Griffin. With all of the bomb drops, the rocks in the walls of the shura building were coming loose, and some of the troops poked holes through the wall so they could cover Rasmussen and Larson as they recovered the specialist's body. They waited until the U.S aircraft were gunning down the insurgents on the Switchbacks, then Romesha, Dulaney, and Specialist Chris Chappell opened up with their guns into the hills. Dulaney almost shot Rasmussen in the head when Ras and Larson sprinted out with a stretcher, but the two men managed to get Griffin onto it and brought him back to the

562

shura building. He was dead, with bullet wounds to his head. One of his legs flopped over the side of the stretcher, looking completely shattered.

"Hardt and Martin still aren't accounted for," Romesha reminded the others. The radios weren't working, and the fire had let up a bit, so he decided to take his chances. Romesha stepped out and began to run to Bundermann, in the operations center.

When the Apaches landed, they were refueled, rearmed, and repaired. While all of that was being seen to, the pilots went into Forward Operating Base Bostick's operations center, where Brown began peppering them with questions.

"Can we get a medevac in there to get these guys out?" Brown asked.

"You can't," said Lewallen.

John Francis was in the middle of telling Jon Hill that he was going to grab two dudes to secure another part of the camp when he heard that gunshot again, the same one echoing in his brain from when Scusa was killed, Frunk was grazed, and the sniper hit his grenade launcher. Francis heard the crack of the gun and stopped talking in midsentence.

"What?" Hill asked.

"That shot," said Francis. "Listen."

"Where's it coming from?" asked Hill.

"Somewhere on the north side," said Francis.

Dabolins had left his sniper rifle on the deck, so Hill grabbed it, and then he and Francis found a spot behind the Café wall where they could look up toward the Northface. The Afghan sniper kept firing at the camp, and every time he did, Hill came that much closer to figuring out where he was. After the fourth shot, he had him in the rifle's sight.

"I got him," Hill said.

"Where?" Francis asked. Hill let him look through the rifle sight. The sniper stood up from behind a boulder and started shooting again.

"Okay," Hill said, "I'm gonna shoot at him."

Hill pulled the trigger, but he'd aimed too high, and the sniper dropped down.

"You shot too high," noted Francis, stating the obvious.

"Yeah, yeah, yeah," said Hill.

The sniper moved to the left, and Hill fired a second shot. A burst of dirt in front of the boulder indicated that he was off his mark again.

"You shot too low," Francis said.

"Yeah, yeah, yeah."

"Sergeant Hill!" Francis said, mimicking the way Hill himself gave orders as a drill sergeant. "Practice your fucking fundamentals!"

Hill looked at Francis, then returned his attention to the scope. The sniper once again started to stand, preparing to fire at the camp.

"Got him, got him, got him," Hill muttered, and he pulled the trigger.

He blew off the lower left side of the sniper's face.

"Holy fuck!" Francis said. "You got him!"

The fundamentals.

CHAPTER 36

Blood and Embers

Because aid stations at combat outposts such as Keating can't depend on refrigeration, they don't store blood. It seemed to Cordova, however, that fresh blood might be the only thing that could save Stephan Mace, by providing him with red blood cells that would offer greater oxygen-carrying capacity and more clotting factors than the artificial stuff. So Cordova decided that he and his staff would attempt a "buddy transfusion."

Cordova had never done this procedure before, and he was scared of trying it now. Transfusions are almost always performed in a hospital or clinic, a controlled and sterile environment where a donor's blood can also be tested for disease before being given to the patient. Nevertheless, fresh whole blood has been successfully transfused under battlefield conditions since World War I, and Cordova, as a physician assistant, had been trained in the technique. A blood transfusion kit that had been left behind at the aid station by a previous unit would allow Black Knight Troop's medical team to take blood from someone else's arm and give it directly to Mace. The kit included five bags. It was risky, yes, but they had to do something, and there seemed to be no better options.

As the medics were starting to prepare for the procedure, Burton came to the aid station and announced, "If the fire keeps going, we're going to have to evacuate." To stay ahead of the blaze, Faulkner, Dannelley, Thomas, and Stone went outside to the Café, while most of the wounded ANA soldiers relocated to the Afghan Security Guard commanders' building. Mace was too badly injured to be moved, as were two ANA troops, the one with the mutilated abdomen, and another with a tourniquet on his leg. Courville went outside to assess the situation. How bad was this fire? And then he saw that the tall pine tree that stood between the operations center and the aid station was starting to burn.

Cordova continued to focus on Mace; to him, nothing outside that room mattered.

First they needed to know Mace's blood type. Cordova looked for his dog tag, but it wasn't around his neck. This wasn't unusual; because their Kevlar chest plates tended to press their dog tags into their breastbones, soldiers — especially the skinny ones — often tied them around their belt loops and stored them in their pants pockets. Indeed, that was where Mace's dog tag was. He was A-positive — good news, because so were Cordova, Hobbs, and Floyd. Out of these three matches, Floyd was elected to be the donor because, as the lowest-ranked and least experienced among them, he was deemed the least "essential." "Okay, Doc," Floyd said. "Stick me."

He rolled up his sleeve, and soon his dark-red blood began filling the collection bag, which contained an anticoagulant to keep it from clotting. After a struggle, Hobbs succeeded in plunging the receiving end of the system into Mace's neck.

A nervous Cordova kept a close eye on his patient. Studies have shown that dog tags carry unreliable information about blood type up to 11 percent of the time, so the physician assistant was on guard against any adverse reactions. There were none. Mace's pulse improved and could now be found not only in his neck but also on the inside of his thigh.

Even more important, Mace himself went from dazed to conscious. He started to complain about the pain in his leg. He asked for a cigarette, a request that was denied with a smile. They all started to joke around. Floyd was tall but very skinny, and the other medics often teased him about his manhood. Now Mace would be less of a man, the medics suggested, because he'd received Floyd's weak-ass blood. Others, too — most notably Rasmussen, one of Mace's best friends and partners in crime — came in and chatted with him. But fifteen minutes after the bag of Floyd's blood had been depleted, Mace's eyes started to wander off again. They would need to give him a second bag. Hobbs rolled up his sleeve.

*   *   *

Bundermann had some good news for the Apache pilots as they arrived on station: the Americans had taken back some land inside the camp. But the troops at Combat Outpost Keating still weren't sure where many of their guys were, so the pilots decided they would continue to avoid firing within the outpost.

For the next thirty minutes, Rasmussen fired smoke rounds at targets that Black Knight Troop wanted the Apaches to destroy in the hills and their environs. Bundermann would radio the pilots to tell them how close Rasmussen had come to the mark, and the pilots would saturate the relevant area with rockets and 30-millimeter rounds. Others joined Rasmussen in firing smoke rounds, another soldier marking where he thought an enemy Dushka team was hiding.

Bundermann had made it clear to the pilots that their top priority should be to kill the insurgents in the Afghan National Police station and the Urmul mosque, a source of clear and accurate machine-gun fire. Specifically, he requested that they drop as many Hellfire missiles on the mosque as they could.

It wouldn't be easy. In this narrow valley, with one smaller hill blocking access to the mosque from the north, the only way for either Lewallen's or Huff's Apache to get a clean shot was to head to the east and then make a westbound pass. They would come through the valley in one long, straight run that they hoped would not be interrupted by a Dushka or a lucky shot. If they made it safely, Lewallen could put a Hellfire into the mosque, then Huff could follow up with a second missile, pulverizing the enemy sanctuary.

They flew two and a half miles away from the camp then turned around, zooming east-to-west toward Combat Outpost Keating. As they approached, two Dushka shots found their mark in Lewallen's Apache.

"Shit," said Lewallen. Luckily, the shot hadn't seriously harmed the helicopter, but it had damaged its hydraulics and thus stopped it from firing its missiles. "I got a Hellfire malfunction," he told Huff. "I can't get my missile off the rail."

From the second Apache, Huff radioed that he would go ahead and try to make the shot, so as Lewallen flew over Observation Post Fritsche and took a left-hand turn, Huff turned right, leveled the bird, and let Wright, his copilot, take his shot. The Hellfire missile hit the mosque from the eastern side. At the same time, Huff and Wright's bird came under heavy machine-gun fire and lost the backup control system for its tail rotor. Lewallen had by now resolved the issue with his own Hellfire operating system, and he and Bardwell fired their missile, which hit the mosque from the south. Target successfully destroyed.

The two Apaches turned around and prepared to head back to Forward Operating Base Bostick for repairs. Other aircraft were now flying in and above the valley, dropping bombs. The walls of the shura building began to cave in. And something bigger was on its way: a B-1 bomber.

The B-1's pilot, Captain Justin Kulish, called in to Romesha. "What do you need?" he asked.

"Get rid of Urmul," Romesha replied. "Just level it." There was slim chance that any civilians were left in the small community, and they had to destroy the village in older to save themselves.

"All right," the pilot said, "get down, we're bombs away."

The first bomb hit the top of the Putting Green, straight above Urmul, and was then followed by a rapid succession of deep booms as the village was obliterated. Romesha could feel the bombs in his chest as their shock waves compressed his body and everything else in their path.

BOOM BOOM BOOM BOOM BOOM BOOM.

The shock waves hurt Romesha, but it was a good kind of hurt, a good pain. We have the upper hand now, he thought. Finally.

While bombs pummeled Urmul, Eric Harder passed the dining hall on his way to throw down more concertina wire on the southern side of the camp. On the radio, he heard someone—the B-1 pilot, he assumed— warn, "Hey, this one's gonna be close," and as he turned down to face the camp, he saw the impact of the shock wave shatter the glass windows on a bulldozer, and then he thought, Oh, shit, this is going to rip me to shreds. Harder ran to the side of the barracks to take cover from the succession of bombs. He sat there and listened to Urmul get destroyed.

A flock of U.S. aircraft now swarmed the valley, nineteen of them in all, each at a different altitude— A-10 Warthogs, Apaches, F-15Es, and a B-1 bomber. The sky was dark with rainclouds, and the air thick with a smell of explosives and chemicals that burned Harder's nostrils.

Every once in a while, the insurgents remaining in the mountains would take potshots at the camp, prompting the U.S. troops to shoot back a wall of bullets. Davidson was providing cover fire for Harder as he stretched the concertina wire.

"Do you think we're going to make it out of here?" Davidson asked him.

"I don't know what's going to happen," said Harder.

They had to stop the fire from spreading to the aid station via the burning pine tree. Someone had found a chainsaw, but not one of them had the first idea of how to use it.

When the Bastards were up at Observation Post Fritsche, the enlisted guys had a game they played: Name an occupation that Carter has never tried. It was remarkable: during his wandering years—after his stint with the Marines but before he enlisted in the Army—Carter had done just about everything. He'd scrubbed the bottoms of yachts in the San Francisco Bay Area, been a projectionist at a movie theater in Antioch, California, and served as an armed security guard in Oakland, a seasonal sales associate at Home Depot, and a hot-tub transporter. He'd worked at a sawmill and a motorcycle shop; he'd driven a flatbed tow truck.

And yes, he'd learned how to be a lumberjack for an excavating company.

"Carter can do it," said Private Second Class Kellen Kahn, a radio operator.

Hill tracked down Carter, who had recovered from rescuing Mace.

"With this chainsaw, can you cut down that tree?" Hill asked.

"I don't know," Carter replied. "Let me check." He grabbed the chainsaw and looked to see if it had fuel. He revved it, Leatherface-style, to find out if it worked. "Yeah," he said.

Smoke was now starting to emanate from the operations center. Carter knew he had to get this tree down, had to keep the aid station from going up in flames. The pine tree was tall, and he would have to angle the different cuts carefully to make sure it fell parallel to the Bastards' barracks and not on top of the aid station. Carter had earlier lost his protective eyewear, and the blaze was throwing embers onto the back of his neck. That didn't help his concentration.

But he made contact, he made his cuts, and the pine tree started slowly to topple. Cool, Carter thought, taking a few steps back.

Then the tree began spinning.

Waitaminute, he thought. This never happens....

The tree fell in the wrong direction, landing on the tactical operations center.

"Oh, shit!" Carter yelled. "Oh shit, oh shit!"

The roof of the operations center fell in, and the tree went with it, stopping the fire's path to the aid station but redirecting the flames downward. Carter wondered whether the fire in the operations center might not have caused an updraft, but regardless, troops started cheering: a disaster had been avoided because the tree was no longer a threat to the aid station. Carter himself felt a little sheepish. I can't believe they're cheering, he thought. But... I guess that did the job.

Carter climbed onto the tree with the chainsaw to clear some limbs that were blocking the walkway between the operations center and the Red Platoon barracks — potentially impeding a soldier's path to the aid station. "You're doing a good job, Carter," Hill told him. "But you're the most exposed person. You need to get down."

"I'm almost done," Carter said. "Just a sec."

"Get the fuck down!" Hill said. The incoming wasn't as bad as it had been, but it was still bad. This was no time for them to lower their guard.

The two Apaches had made it back to Forward Operating Base Bostick, but they were seriously damaged. Two other Apaches sent to Camp Keating returned soon afterward with similar battle scars. One of the birds had to execute an emergency landing. None of this boded well for further missions.

While the helicopters were being fixed up, Lieutenant Colonel Brown worked on a plan to air-assault a 150-man quick reaction force to Observation Post Fritsche, from which they would move down the mountain to help the men at Camp Keating. Here, too, there were complications. On September 10, First Lieutenant Tyler Parten, leader of the unit at Bostick that Brown would normally have been able to use as a QRF, had been killed in an ambush. Two other squad leaders had been badly wounded. As a result, it was decided that soldiers from the 1-32 Infantry Battalion would instead serve as the QRF. Two Black Hawks were launched to pick up those troops from bases in Kunar Province.

Three years before, Combat Outpost Keating had been established in part to help out the 1-32 Infantry, by stemming the flow of weapons from Pakistan to insurgents fighting 1-32 troops in the Pech Valley and other locations. Now the 1-32 Infantry was being called to return the favor, to save their brothers in arms at the same outpost.

As the troops prepared for this air assault, the sky filled with dark clouds bringing heavy rain, thunder, and lightning. The thunderstorm traveled through the Landay-Sin Valley, clinging to mountaintops and dumping water below. An MQ-1 Predator, an unmanned aerial vehicle used for reconnaissance by the U.S. Air Force and the CIA, was dispatched to Kamdesh to conduct surveillance of the battles at Keating and Fritsche, but the wind and weather iced its wings and caused it to veer and crash into the side of a mountain. It quickly became obvious that the bad weather was going to severely inhibit the QRF's ability to fly into the valley.

Back at the aid station, Cordova kept transfusing Mace with A-positive blood. After Floyd's came Hobbs's. Cordova's, Bundermann's, and Stone's were also used. As he was in the process of draining the fifth and final bag from the kit, Cordova was informed that a medevac was en route. He put a blanket and an oxygen mask on Mace and strapped him down. The young specialist was going to pull through. He was talking, breathing. Amid the horror of the day, at least they could be confident of one small victory.

At the operations center, Hill was focused on the stories that hadn't ended well. "We have fallen heroes," he said. "I need volunteers." It didn't matter that they were still encircled by what seemed to be hundreds of attackers intent on adding to the body count; this was what American soldiers did for one another: they left no one behind.

Hill and Bundermann made a plan involving two teams that would bound toward LRAS-2 and then up to the mortar pit. They'd escort Breeding, Rodriguez, and Barroga back to the operations center, carrying Thomson with them, and then the unit would be consolidated. Hill knew that some of the troops huddling at the Café were probably comparatively well rested, having worked solely on communications since early in the morning; they might even be eager to help in the field. And so they were: among the volunteers were Specialist Damien Grissette, who was usually in charge of water purification, and radioman Kellen Kahn.

Romesha looked up to see Hill and his men running toward him in the shura building; he didn't think this was part of the retrieval plan, but there was no time to argue about it. Romesha and his team bounded to the general area where Gallegos, Hardt, and Martin had last been seen, near LRAS-2. Sergeant Armando Avalos and Hill provided cover fire.

Rasmussen went around the laundry trailer. Underneath it was Martin, dead. It looked as if he'd tried to patch up some of his leg wounds and then low-crawl away from the enemy. He must have been spotted, because he'd been shot twice in the back of his head, at extremely close range.

Avalos and Kahn grabbed Martin, hauled him out, and dragged his body about seventy yards toward the shura building. Grissette met them on the way. "I got him," he said. He couldn't believe it. Just a few hours before, he and Martin had been running ammo around the camp. Then Martin was missing. And now, the ugly reality. Grissette began dragging his friend's corpse to the shura building. He felt it was the least he could do. He needed to do it. Once he'd made it there, Grissette broke down. "Man," he said, crying, *"not my boy!"*

"Stay with me, now," Hill told him.

"I'm good," Grissette said, composing himself. "I'm good."

Rasmussen was standing near the latrines when suddenly a Nuristani came out of one of the stalls; he was on the verge of shooting the man when he realized it was Ron Jeremy, the interpreter who hours before had warned the Americans of the attack. Given all the adrenaline and rage he was feeling, Rasmussen was surprised he hadn't just shot him on sight.

"Is anyone else in there with you?" he yelled.

"No," said the Afghan. Rasmussen didn't believe him, so he went in to check as Ron Jeremy ran off awkwardly, his legs stiff from hours of hiding from the enemy in the latrines, his knees pulled up to his chest.

Romesha spotted Gallegos's body from a distance as he ran to the LRAS-2 Humvee. Nearby, an insurgent lay on the ground; Rasmussen and James Stanley put more bullets into him, just to be safe. Then Romesha radioed to the others to take Gallegos to the aid station—he might still be alive, he thought. A few men would be needed for the task, since Gallegos was a big guy.

Armando Avalos was the first one on the scene. Gallegos was facedown on a rock with his hand under his head, as if he were taking a nap and using his forearm as a pillow. His body was wedged into a ditch that was covered by rocks and weeds. At first, Avalos thought his friend was still alive, but when he shook him, his body was limp and vacant. Gallegos's head fell to the side; his eyes were still open. Avalos was so shocked by the sight that he was all but oblivious to the RPGs exploding near him and the machine-gun fire that had picked up ever since he put himself out in the open.

After a second, he snapped to and hunkered down under the rocks in the ditch, in which he now realized Gallegos's leg was stuck. He used the sergeant's body as a roof, a shield. Two minutes later, he picked his way out of the ditch and ran to the latrines.

"Gallegos is stuck," Avalos explained to Romesha. "We'll need to lift him up to get him out."

With Hill and Avalos providing cover, Kahn, Dulaney, Romesha, and Grissette ran to Gallegos and under fire lifted him toward the sky to release his leg from the ditch. Then they dragged him toward the shura building. Hill had a gear cutter—a small, sage-colored tool containing a razor blade—that he and Romesha used to slice off Gallegos's gear and make him lighter to carry. Hill, Avalos, Grissette, and Kahn then placed their friend on a stretcher, and Hill and Avalos bore him to the aid station. There, they put him in a body bag.

"Don't seal that body bag," Courville told Hill. "We need Cordova to pronounce him dead."

"Why the fuck do we need a captain to pronounce him dead?" Hill asked. "He's fucking dead."

He stormed off to go get Martin's body and bring it to the aid station as well.

It was 6:40 p.m. The situation report was grim: eleven Americans wounded, six killed.

Kevin Thomson.
Joshua Kirk.
Michael Scusa.
Chris Griffin.
Vernon Martin.
Justin Gallegos.

All gone.

And Joshua Hardt was missing. As was Larson, too, now.

Where *had* Larson gone? Romesha wondered. He was supposed to link up with them in their bounding mission to LRAS-2, but after that plan fell apart, he vanished. A mystery.

Larson had been mentoring Hardt, and in something of a manic sprint, he was now frantically running around the camp looking for his protégé. Larson's body armor was weighing him down, so he took all his gear off. It wasn't necessarily the wisest move, but he didn't care—he thought speed was more important at this point than the added protection.

In talking with Romesha, he'd learned that Hardt's last transmission had been from one of the stand-to trucks. Larson tried to see the world as Hardt had seen it at that moment: If I were trying to get back to the shura building from that truck, what route would I take? he asked himself.

Larson figured that he and Hardt, thinking a lot alike, would've sought the same escape. He explored a number of paths, running and running, from the shura building to the showers to the giant rock and back around to the shura building. He knew he was being reckless, but he didn't care; he didn't want the Taliban to get his friend. But it was as if Josh Hardt had vanished, as if he had never been.

CHAPTER 37

The Long Walk Down

By now, Romesha and his squad had secured both the entrance to the outpost and the northwest of the camp, while Hill and his group controlled the north, northeast, east, and south. They were spread thin, but they felt confident that they could hold down those pieces of land. The one sector they did not yet have control of was the southwestern corner of the camp, near the mortar pit. The space was too open, and the incoming enemy fire too much of a confirmed threat, for Romesha and Red Platoon to make it there. "You've done enough," Breeding told Romesha on the radio. "We'll see you later."

"What do you think the odds are that Hardt was taken off the COP by the enemy?" Bundermann asked Romesha, also on the radio.

"I'm eighty percent sure his body is not on the COP," Romesha said.

Bundermann told others in the operations center to start distributing night-vision goggles and thermal sights. They needed to prepare for nightfall.

The members of the quick reaction force had only the sketchiest idea of where they were headed and what they would be facing when they got there. The operations officer at Forward Operating Base Bostick, Major Jack Kilbride, had pulled together a very detailed report to be passed on to the QRF, but because the ad hoc force was assembled so hastily, the information didn't filter down to them before they were picked up. They'd flown in from Kunar Province that morning, two rifle platoons from the

1-32 Infantry, led by Lieutenants Jake Miraldi and Jake Kerr. The commander of the rescue effort for Combat Outpost Keating was Captain Justin Sax, whose troops had been in nearby Barg-e-Matal for most of the previous two months. Miraldi's platoon had been the initial force to retake Barg-e-Matal after it was overrun; once they'd cleared the area, they were counterattacked and very nearly pushed out of the village by the enemy.

That morning, at Combat Outpost Joyce in Kunar Province, Sax and the other officers had received what they considered to be a rather "skimpy" situational update—skimpy in the sense that it was apparent that no one in charge had any real idea of what was going on. Sax and Miraldi agreed that they could not even begin to plan a rescue based on the little information they had received.

By 9:30 a.m., Sax and Miraldi were at Forward Operating Base Bostick, meeting with Brown, Portis, and other members of the leadership of 3-61 Cav. They were told that the men at Camp Keating had been forced into three concrete buildings in the center of the outpost, much of the rest of which was on fire. Enemy positions were constantly being identified and reported, and as they were plotted on the map in the Bostick operations center, Miraldi was taken aback: they were everywhere. Miraldi knew this would be a tough mission—and for some, very likely a final one: from what he now knew, he was sure he and Sax would lose men.

The original plan had been to drop Portis, Salentine, Birchfield, and the QRF at the "link-up point" midway between Observation Post Fritsche and Combat Outpost Keating, nearest to the southern side of the camp, which would've been their fastest approach; but once it was confirmed that the proposed LZ had an active enemy presence, that seemed foolhardy. An alternative would be to land the bird north of the outpost, near the Putting Green. They could clear that area, establish it as a firebase, move on to capture the Afghan National Police building, parts of Urmul, and the entry control point, and then, finally, retake the camp.

But when the Apache pilots came in, they poured cold water over that plan. The insurgents at the Putting Green and on the northern side of the river in general were just too strong, their forces too deadly; the Black Hawks taking the QRF troops to the area would be at significant risk of being shot down. Portis suggested that the Black Hawks instead fly as many of the QRF troops as possible to Observation Post Fritsche. Bad weather was coming in; soon their options might be limited to none. Sax told everyone that he was "going to fly in, get on the ground, assess the situation, talk to the guys on the ground, and we'll do a deliberate clearing on the way down to Keating, since we'll probably have contact." Portis, Salentine, and Birchfield would join him.

Because the Black Hawks had to fly there in a roundabout way to avoid the insurgents' powerful antiaircraft weapons, it took them forty-five minutes to get to the landing zone at Observation Post Fritsche. They flew so high they hit storm clouds and were drenched by a combination of snow and freezing rain—an ominous sign with terrible ramifications, as Sax well knew. Shit, this weather's coming in, he thought. We're not going to be able to get the next lift in. That would mean the QRF might have only thirty-five troops. They'd been told they'd need at least one more platoon's worth of guys, up to an additional forty soldiers, to go down the mountain. There went that idea.

They landed safely. The enemy fired a couple of mortar rounds at them, but they missed, and for the most part, the fighting at Observation Post Fritsche had died down.

The troops at the observation post all looked terrified.

The word from Forward Operating Base Bostick was, indeed, that the next flight wouldn't be coming in for some time, given the rough weather. Sax preferred to wait until all the men from 1-32 Infantry arrived, but Portis didn't want to hesitate another second before heading down the hill. They were receiving reports that some soldiers from Black Knight Troop were still getting hit, and others were looking for bodies. "We have enough guys," Portis insisted. "We need to get down there."

"Come on, come on, come on," Birchfield echoed, "let's go, let's go, let's go."

Portis and Sax finally agreed that if the rest of Sax's men didn't get there by 2:00 p.m., they would move out without them. It was just before noon.

"I need the best scout to lead us down," Sax told Portis. "Who's conducted this mission before?" Portis recommended Salentine and Birchfield. Portis also made sure that Stickney, the head mortarman at Observation Post Fritsche, had enough ammo to support the QRF, and Bellamy worked on grid coordinates with the team as well, just in case they ended up needing mortars during their hike down.

"We're not going to take any trails down," Birchfield said. "They've been watching us." He was certain that every known path was either booby-trapped or ready for an ambush. "We'll be breaking bush," he said, meaning they would be blazing their own trail.

At 2:00 p.m., with no additional troops having arrived, they set off. The hike would take at least four hours, and the decline was so steep that Sax told his men to empty their packs of everything other than ammo and water.

Miraldi briefed the platoon. Birchfield would guide them down from Observation Post Fritsche to an outcropping of rocks, from which they would follow some defunct power lines to the top of the Switchbacks. They would clear the Switchbacks, establish fire support and overwatch, and move into Camp Keating. They would almost surely be ambushed along the way, Miraldi acknowledged; what the QRF lacked in numbers, it would have to make up for with its speed and ability to mass and coalesce as a single, brute force.

The instant they left the wire of Observation Post Fritsche, enemy machine-gun fire began blasting them. Miraldi's troops returned fire while air support was called in. An A-10 Warthog zoomed in on the enemy in a strafing run, and then the QRF continued down the hill. The men slowly made their way through the mountain's rough profile. Above them, they could see nearly every kind of aircraft that they knew existed. Sometimes the A-10 Warthogs and F-15 fighter jets flew so close that they knocked the soldiers off their feet.

By 4:00 p.m., the QRF had reached the rocky outcropping, which afforded a good strategic view of the valley. While the men rested, Portis and Salentine relayed grids to the Air Force radio operators,[89] who coordinated with the pilots to drop bombs at targets on the mountains below them and across the valley. The QRF troops would spot groups of anywhere from twenty-five to fifty fighters trying to regroup to attack the camp again, and they'd radio the guys in the sky.

"Two above the Switchbacks, one above the Diving Board."

BOOM, dead.

After half an hour, they moved on. In places, the ground was slick and

---

[89] Technically called JTACs, for "joint tactical air controllers," these radiomen communicate with the pilots and tell them where to target their munitions.

challenging to negotiate. At one point, Specialist Kyle Barnes, a twenty-year-old soldier from 1-32 Infantry, slipped. Barnes hated this journey. The footing was slick, the descent was steep, and the M240B machine gun slung around his neck didn't make it any easier. As Barnes picked himself up, he pivoted on his right foot and — from the bizarre angle he'd fallen into — saw, right off the trail, a dead insurgent. Five feet to the corpse's left was another enemy fighter crouched down with a walkie talkie in his hand, wearing a white hat and looking away from the trail. His head was moving.

He was alive.

Barnes whispered to the person behind him. He thought it was Miraldi, but it turned out to be Specialist Paul Labrake, the radio operator for Miraldi's platoon.

"Sir, there's a dude in the woods," Barnes said. Worried that his machine gun would cause a dangerous ricochet that could hurt his fellow troops, Barnes drew his 9-millimeter Beretta pistol from his thigh holster.

"What?" asked Labrake.

"There's a fucking dude in the woods," Barnes said.

"Shoot him!"

Barnes unloaded a magazine into the insurgent's chest. The expression on the enemy's face seemed to indicate to Barnes that he was taking his death almost in stride, like a warrior.

Eight troops had already passed the two insurgents without seeing them, and they were shocked when they heard the sudden drilling sound of Barnes's automatic pistol firing. Miraldi, a few yards behind them, was confused. As the platoon took cover behind him, Miraldi shouted, "Barnes, what are you doing?"

"There's guys in the woods!" Barnes screamed in his thick South Boston accent.

"No shit, Barnes!" said Miraldi. "Where? How many?"

Barnes started shooting again as Miraldi ran down to him. The two insurgents were both now definitely dead. Miraldi sent two of his men to inspect the area the insurgents had been huddling in, where they found an RPG launcher with about five rounds, two AK-47 assault rifles, chest racks with magazines, some pineapple grenades, a radio, and a bag of flatbread. Barnes had killed one of the insurgents with his Beretta. The other had been mortally wounded long before that moment, much of his right leg having been stripped of flesh. The QRF troops took all of the insurgents' gear and returned to their hike. To Salentine, the dead insurgents didn't look Afghan or even Pakistani.

Labrake noted that enemy radio traffic suggested the insurgents were retreating. He'd also made contact with 3-61 Cav troops in the operations center below. They'd recovered six of their dead but were still missing one man.

Portis heard Cordova announce over the radio, "Anybody else got A-positive blood, I need to know! Come to the aid station if you do." It was uplifting just to hear his voice, Portis thought, though the message itself was depressing. Out there, there was only one thing you needed extra blood for.

An unsettling calm descended over the valley as the QRF trudged through debris left by the 120-millimeter mortars, trees shattered by bombs and shrapnel, and fields reduced by the Willie Pete to smoldering ash. Soon they arrived above the Switchbacks.

"We need to skirt the outside of this field," Birchfield said. "We get ambushed here a lot."

It was a strange, otherworldly experience. As they arrived at the midpoint of the Switchbacks at around 6:30 p.m., Portis started noticing many more dead Taliban bodies. He realized he'd been counting enemy dead on his way down the hill. There were more to count now. He told himself that when he got to a hundred, he would stop.

They proceeded down the remainder of the mountain, the smoke and fire from Camp Keating's burning buildings so heavy now that they couldn't see much of the land in front of them. Miraldi and Salentine took one of the rifle squads down the hill to the outpost while Sax, Portis, and the remainder of the 1-32 Infantry company conducted overwatch from the Switchbacks.

The rest of the QRF—the late arrivals to Observation Post Fritsche, delivered at long last—were on their way down and had been able to proceed more quickly because the initial QRF force had already secured the way. They were being guided by Specialist Victor De La Cruz, who had fought valiantly at Observation Post Fritsche earlier that day using TOW[90]

---

[90] TOW stands for tube-launched, optically-tracked, wireless-guided.

missiles, repeatedly exposing himself, and had a left leg full of shrapnel to show for it.

Salentine and Miraldi entered the wire. The insurgents in Urmul were still firing at the outpost, which was also engulfed in flames. Salentine and Miraldi and their men cleared every building on the western side of the COP, from the mortar pit to the center of the camp. The QRF members were greeted by wounded troops whose arms and legs were covered with gashes and blood. The battered men looked at once haunted and relieved.

Miraldi called back to Sax on the radio. "Looks like we're okay here," he said.

Portis had hit his one-hundred mark and stopped counting insurgent corpses; he and Sax led the other troops from the Switchbacks down to Keating. Men from 1-32 Infantry joined with the two Latvian trainers to secure the eastern side of the camp. It looked as though only two buildings were not on fire; in one of them, the aid station, Miraldi saw a soldier transfusing his blood into Mace. In the other—what had been the Red Platoon barracks but was now the new operations center—Miraldi introduced himself to First Sergeant Burton.

Lieutenant Shrode was sitting at the door on the north side of the barracks with Bundermann, coordinating air support on the radio, when he spotted Miraldi—which was a bit weird, since the two of them had been pals in college, playing football together at West Point. Miraldi had been a fullback and Shrode a middle linebacker, so with one on offense and the other on defense, they'd had some epic battles in practices on the gridiron, a number of which had ended with both of their heads ringing. They hadn't seen each other since graduation. Shrode stood, and they shook hands.

"How're you doing, Cason?" Miraldi asked.

"Way better now that you guys are here," Shrode said.

Sax, in charge of security for the camp, had his men fill sandbags and establish fighting positions. Birchfield checked the maintenance shed, the stand-to trucks, and other areas; Taliban bodies riddled with bullet holes were scattered throughout the camp. He met up with Romesha at the shura building and assigned troops to guard specific positions, clear various buildings, and inspect the outer perimeter.

Birchfield and some of the men from 1-32 Infantry were on their way down the hill when they saw something of note—or someone, rather. They radioed Bundermann: amid the strewn corpses of enemy fighters littering the southern side of the camp, they could see the body of a U.S. soldier. Hill and Francis went to the spot as directed—near the maintenance shed, close to Stand-To Truck 1, at the edge of the camp.

It was Hardt.

Rigor mortis had begun to set in. He had three entrance gunshot wounds on the left side of his head; his skull had suffered multiple fractures. Gunpowder residue indicated that he had been shot in the head at close range. He also had gunshot wounds to the left side of his chest, his left leg, and his left arm. Hill got a stretcher, and he and Francis carried Hardt's body to the aid station.

Hill found Bundermann.

"We're all accounted for now," he said. It was just after 8:00 p.m.

Hill and Francis sat down with Birchfield and told him who had been killed. There were seven: Kevin Thomson, Joshua Kirk, Michael Scusa, Chris Griffin, Vernon Martin, Justin Gallegos, and Joshua Hardt. Stephan Mace was banged up pretty good, but Doc Cordova had expressed optimism about his chances so long as they got him on a bird as soon as possible.

Birchfield thought about Scusa. The last time he'd seen him, the specialist was talking about his son. Indeed, it was always the same thing with Scusa: Connor did this, Connor did that, Connor is walking, Connor is eating solid food. He was a very proud father, as well as a hardworking soldier. And now he would never see his boy again. Birchfield started crying. Then he stopped, realizing this was not the time for it. Those men were gone, and that was tragic—and he would mourn them, later—but right then he had a job to do.

Romesha and Larson were sitting in the shura building smoking Camel Lights and drinking Dr. Peppers that Larson had grabbed from the Red Platoon barracks. The spicy fizz was like mother's milk to the two men, who were in awe that they had lived to see the end of the day.

Everything had started to slow down. The aircraft were in the midst of releasing the last of the sixteen tons' worth of bombs they would drop on the enemy that day. Troops weren't yet standing out in the open, but the enemy fire wasn't nearly as intense as it had been.

Soldiers from the 1-32 had volunteered to clear the landing zone so the medevac could—finally—land, but 3-61 Cav wouldn't have it. Soon Salentine, Romesha, Larson, Damien Grissette, Ryan Schulz, and Stephen Cady were heading across the bridge to the landing zone.

Larson threw a frag grenade into the Afghan National Police shack there, but he missed the door by four inches and hit the doorjamb instead; the grenade bounced right back to his feet. The men quickly jumped behind the rocks as it exploded. No one had the inclination to laugh.

The men got back up, and Larson and Cady cleared the shack as they were supposed to—with their M4 rifles. No one was in there. The men then pulled security on the landing zone until the medevac came in for Mace—a helicopter that also was bringing in Lieutenant Colonel Brown.

Before the medevac arrived, Koppes had gathered Mace's stuff—his iPod, camera, laptop, and a couple of books—so he'd have it all when he got to his hospital bed in Germany. Rasmussen and Adams kept asking Koppes if he wanted to visit with his best friend before the bird left, but Koppes resisted. The memory of seeing his sister on her deathbed in Ohio was still fresh in his mind, even as he stood in that smoldering deathtrap in Kamdesh. Everyone was telling him that Mace was going to make it, but Koppes was convinced that if he went to see Mace in that state, it was going to be Eva all over again.

It was dark now. In addition to the rest of Sax's group from 1-32 Infantry, Special Forces troops had also arrived and were clearing Kamdesh Village and reinforcing Observation Post Fritsche. Portis went to the Red Platoon barracks, outside which he saw Bundermann's lanky silhouette. "You've done an incredible job," Portis told him. "I'm the commander again, you're Red-One."

As Bundermann was relieved of his command, he exhaled and rolled his shoulders.

"You've done an incredible job," Portis repeated.

There weren't many places to sleep at Camp Keating that night—just the Red Platoon barracks and the aid station, and the ground around them. Few slept, and none slept well. October in Afghanistan: it was chilly. Some of the troops were wearing only T-shirts and shorts, having been woken up suddenly that morning and then later having lost all their clothing to the day's fires. Bodies—living ones—were scattered throughout the small section of the camp that was still standing. Red Platoon troops crashed in their barracks while the Bastards slept on the deck of the Café, huddled together. They slept on body armor, which wasn't at all soft. They curled up in the fetal position, redolent with this day's worth of sweat and smoke.

Portis walked outside the Red Platoon barracks. The dying fires crackled in nearby buildings. A glowstick flickered a blue light. Then Portis heard a sound. Someone was singing.

...I ain't seen the sunshine
Since, I don't know when...

Portis walked into the barracks. Chris Jones and his guitar had both survived the attack, and Jones was playing Johnny Cash's classic "Folsom Prison Blues," sitting in the middle of the barracks and moaning in his Tennessee twang with Zach Koppes.

When I was just a baby
My Mama told me, "Son,
Always be a good boy,
Don't ever play with guns."
But I shot a man in Reno,
Just to watch him die.
When I hear that whistle blowin',
I hang my head and cry.

Portis shook his head at the moment. The white noise emanating from the radio was interrupted by a squawk. He thought about the soldiers who had been killed. His men. Just one night before, they'd all gone to bed thinking they would soon get out of this cursed valley surrounded by these ominous mountains. But the mountains had gotten them first.

CHAPTER 38

Saint Christopher

Y ou're going to make it," Cordova told Mace as he finished prepping him for travel. "You have a quick flight to Bostick; you're going to be fine. Just hang in there for another fifteen minutes." The entire medical team was filled with optimism about Stephan Mace. He'd been wounded before 7:00 a.m., and though he'd had five transfusions of blood, he was alert and speaking in complete sentences.

After supplies were flown in, other wounded men from 3-61 Cav would be flown out that night, including Cookie Thomas, Ed Faulkner, Josh Dannelley, and Andrew Stone. First Sergeant Burton insisted that anyone with any kind of an injury needed to leave that night, but many of the wounded—including Eric Harder and John Francis—refused. They would leave when everyone else did. They would leave when Combat Outpost Keating was shut down.

When Stephan Mace was fifteen, his mother had let him spend the summer in South Africa with his best friend, whose family was originally from there and who returned seasonally to help run hunting safaris. Mace's mother worried about him, especially about his pending five-hour layover in England. She fretted that he would miss his connecting flight, that he would lose his passport, that something would go dreadfully wrong. And once he arrived in South Africa, she was equally concerned about her precious Stephan and what might happen there. Surely something horrific would befall him on safari, some terrible incident with a lion or a rhinoceros.

So Stephan Mace's mother bought him a Saint Christopher's medal, which she attached to a dog-tag chain, knowing of his desire to enlist someday. It would keep him safe, she told him, since Saint Christopher was the patron saint of travelers. Fifteen-year-old Stephan rolled his eyes, but he put it around his neck and from that moment only rarely took it off.

When Mace landed at Forward Operating Base Bostick that night, he was met by Command Sergeant Major Rob Wilson, who noticed the medal and commented on it. Mace asked him to hold on to it for him.

"You're in good hands," Wilson told him. "Trust the doc."

"Okay," Mace said, looking up at Wilson.

Major Brad Zagol, a surgeon trained at West Point and Walter Reed, examined Mace, who had tourniquets on both legs and multiple penetrating wounds to his abdomen.

"I don't want to die," Mace told Zagol.

He didn't sound panicked, but he was clearly scared. Mace looked Zagol in the eye. They were in the aid station, fifty feet off the tarmac.

"I just don't want to die," he said again.

Zagol looked at Mace. "I'm going to get you home," he promised him.

The nurse administered a sedative to calm the soldier down, and the surgical team began giving him blood. Zagol was worried; even though parts of Mace's body that his heart had deprived of blood—his bowel, for example—were now receiving red blood cells, the legacy of his physiological shutdown was grim. Too many of his blood-starved organs, too much of his tissue, had already died. Medics in war zones talk about that first "golden hour": if they can start treating a patient within the first sixty minutes after he's wounded, the odds of his survival will be greater than 90 percent. It had been more than twelve hours now since Mace was wounded. His blood pressure was weak. And Zagol wasn't sure what to do with the tourniquets; he figured for now he'd leave them on until Mace got to Bagram, where he could get even finer medical care.

The surgeon opened up his patient's abdomen. The bowel looked dead. There were holes through the left side of the colon and most of the small bowel. Mace was bleeding near his left kidney. Zagol inserted cotton packs to stem the blood flow. As he did so, roughly thirty minutes into the operation, Mace's heart stopped.

Zagol began performing CPR. Mace's heart started beating again. But the beat wasn't sustained; it would come back for fifteen or thirty seconds at a time and then vanish. The surgeon inserted a tube into each side of Mace's chest to release any air or blood that had gathered in the chest cavity and might be interfering with his heart. Air began to flow out of the tubes.

An hour had passed. Mace's heartbeat had not returned in any real way. Zagol opened the left side of Mace's chest and cut open his ribs to make sure he hadn't missed a wound to the heart. Reaching inside Mace's body, he massaged his heart, clapping his hands together. He had used this technique once before, during his residency. Such massaging was a last-ditch measure, one that rarely worked. But Zagol would not give up on this soldier. He had told him he would get him home.

Ninety minutes into the operation, Zagol knew that Stephan Lee Mace, twenty-one years old, wasn't going to make it. He had been without a steadily beating heart for almost an hour. Zagol stepped away from the table and pronounced him dead. A second group of wounded soldiers had now come in from Keating, and twenty to thirty more would soon be on their way.

Zagol walked outside. For three minutes, he threw trash and cursed. It was the first time he'd ever been responsible for losing a patient. Several years later, he would still be questioning himself, wondering whether, if he had been a better doctor, he might have been able to save that young patient who had clung to life for so long and against such great odds, only to slip away once he'd finally been delivered to a safe place.

Mace's Saint Christopher's medal had ended up in the care of Robert Hull, who had been promoted to captain and was presently stationed at Forward Operating Base Bostick. The medal now needed to be returned to Mace.

When the announcement came over the FOB Bostick loudspeaker summoning Hull to the operating room, he was tending to some of the other wounded Black Knight troops who had been medevacked in. Hull was crushed to hear that Mace hadn't survived the operation. The captain took a step toward the O.R., intending to put the chain around Mace's neck, but Wilson stopped him. He wanted to protect Hull from the tragic scene.

"Sir," Wilson said, "I'll give it back to him."

Hull handed Wilson the medal, and the command sergeant major walked through the swinging doors of the operating room to return the medallion honoring Christopher the martyr to its place around the neck of Stephan Mace.

Cordova wanted to find out about Mace, so he tracked down First Sergeant Burton at the Red Platoon barracks. He knew Mace had gotten to Forward Operating Base Bostick alive. Had he made it through surgery?

Burton didn't say a word, nor did he need to. He looked at Cordova with pain in his eyes.

Cordova walked away, shattered. He couldn't bring himself to tell Courville, Floyd, and Hobbs — maybe later, but not now, not now. He went into a small side room to be by himself.

Miraldi's platoon was assigned the eastern half of the outpost, and the troops took up residence in the one ANA barracks that was still standing. Afghan soldiers began trickling in after Lakis and Dabolins found them in their hiding places; they had not fought, nor defended the outpost. The 1-32 Infantry troops had them stay in a separate room. Not only had the Americans seen Afghan security forces run away from battle before, but for all they knew, these particular guys could all be Taliban in stolen ANA uniforms. Eventually, Sax's men forcibly took the weapons from the Afghans and posted a guard outside their room.

Having heard about the ANA troops' weak, cowardly, and in some cases treasonous performance the day before, as well as the rising tensions that had followed, Brown decided that they would be first to be shipped out the next day. Before their flight left, Lakis informed the assembled Afghans that due to weight constraints on the helicopter, they could bring along only one bag each. He looked at the congregated ANA troops and noticed one with an especially large satchel. He tried to grab it to see how much it weighed, but the ANA soldier pulled it away from him, and his fellow troops responded in a hostile manner. Lakis talked outside with the ANA commander about the incident. The ANA commander walked up to the soldier with the large bag, snatched it away from him, and dumped out its contents. Out spilled all sorts of objects pillaged from the U.S. troops, from digital cameras to protein-drink mixes.

*　　*　　*

The Bastards' barracks at Combat Outpost Keating during the October 3, 2009, attack. *(Taken from U.S. Army investigation)*

Stand-To Truck 1, in which Hardt, Griffin, and Faulkner attempted a rescue effort. *(Taken from U.S. Army investigation)*

*   *   *

On Sunday, October 4, Brown and Portis walked the grounds of the outpost with Romesha, Hill, and Larson to get a grasp on what had happened. They assessed the damage, trying to figure out which entrances
the insurgents had used to enter the camp, which buildings and trucks
had been damaged and how. Dead Taliban remained inside the wire,
gruesome and gray. The Americans were also trying to figure out what
could be salvaged and what they would need to destroy before the camp
was abandoned.

Salentine led a team into Urmul to make sure all the enemy fighters
had cleared out. When he came back, he told Portis, "If you think Keating looks bad, go check out Urmul. It's Armageddon."

Enemy radio traffic indicated that the insurgents would try again to overrun the outpost, so Miraldi's platoon was on full guard duty late into the
night. Luckily, there was no new attack, just small firefights as Black
Knight Troop shipped out men and equipment over the next two days.
Harder was assigned the task of securing the video camera that had been
placed atop the maintenance shack for surveillance; an insurgent in the
mountains fired at him, and he slid down the roof, nearly breaking his
leg. But compared to what had transpired but a few days ago, this was
almost the stuff of comedy.

The day after the battle brought ten local leaders from Kamdesh, Mandigal, and Urmul to the gates of Combat Outpost Keating. They asked for
Portis, who came out to meet them. Were they there to apologize? To offer
their condolences? To offer to help? No, they wanted to know if they could
collect the bodies of the insurgents in and around the camp.

Portis seethed. He told them they could send elders and women to collect the dead, but the appearance of any fighting-age males would be
considered a threat.

The elders from Urmul said they had been hiding in Agro since the
Taliban told them to flee. Could they return to their homes now?

No, Portis said. The outpost was still being fired upon, and the United
States Army would continue to bomb the Switchbacks and Urmul in
response. Those spots and the surrounding mountains would not be safe
for the next forty-eight hours. Portis wrote in his journal that night:
"They walked away upset. I walked away pissed off."

Portis wasn't the only one seething. The night before, he'd sent troops into the original, burning operations center to retrieve classified equipment and documents. Cady was tasked with securing any Afghan currency that was still intact from the two safes — Portis wanted him to finish his task of paying the contractors. Cady could barely contain his contempt as he handed over a small fortune to the head Afghan Security Guard, just a day after he and his men had proved worse than useless.

George and Brown had long discussed the best way to close Combat Outpost Keating. They had debated whether it was better to leave it intact or destroy it. This had been an ongoing discussion, and they again went over the options. Leaving it standing for Afghan forces or local authorities to use could be problematic; they recalled how 6-4 Cav left Combat Outpost Lybert, only to have insurgents falsely claim to have taken it by force.

George and Brown decided that they would remove everything they could and then they would bomb the hell out of the outpost, leaving nothing behind. Even if they had wanted to undertake a major salvage job, there weren't going to be enough helicopters to haul all of the equipment, and they weren't going to spend the money and effort to remove the Humvees that had been shot up or the tons of stockpiled ammunition. The brigade brought in a team of engineers. Crater charges were placed in each of the Humvees, and detonation cord wrapped around all the damaged ammunition. Explosives were attached to anything that an enemy fighter could possibly use for either fighting or shelter. U.S. Air Force observers were given just under a dozen grid points on which to drop their bombs.

Night finally came upon them, bringing to a close October 6, 2009. Members of the QRF flew out first, followed by the Bastards. The last to fly out were the members of Red Platoon. Burton pushed every group to conduct head counts, over and over. He was terrified that they were going to inadvertently leave someone behind at the camp, in the dark of night, as the United States abandoned the outpost forever.

Bundermann stood on the landing zone waiting. He couldn't leave Combat Outpost Keating soon enough. Hurry up, let's get out of here, let's get out of here, he said to himself.

Brown waited until the last helicopter was on the ground before he pulled the trigger and ignited the thermite grenades per the engineers' instructions. They would have fifteen minutes before the explosion destroyed the outpost—more than enough time to clear the area. The men linked up by the shura building, then exited out the gate of Combat Outpost Keating for the last time. Everyone boarded the helicopter. Burton and Brown paused at the back deck of the bird. Each wanted to be the last soldier to leave the camp. Portis watched them, shaking his head.

"Get on the damn bird," Burton told Brown. Brown stepped into the helicopter, and the first sergeant followed, convinced he was the last man out of Combat Outpost Keating.

But Romesha and Larson had rear security for the helicopter and had been standing next to the edge of the ramp. They waited and watched Burton enter the helicopter, then they looked at each other and stepped up on the bird at the same time—the very last to leave, just as they had wanted.

The helicopter rose and made its way down the valley. Bundermann looked out the back hatch of the bird and took in the tranquility of the mountains, and beyond them the stars. The men waited for the explosion. And waited.

It never came. Something was wrong with the timer or with the explosives.

After Brown got back to the operations center at Forward Operating Base Bostick, a B-1 bomber flew over Camp Keating and dropped several tons' worth of bombs on it. The next day, another B-1 dropped even more. Surveillance from a Predator drone on October 8, however, indicated that structures at the outpost were still standing. Worse, the Predator captured images of fourteen insurgents trolling around the camp and removing ammunition from the ammo supply point. Another B-1 bomber was cleared to target the insurgents, but its equipment malfunctioned. Instead, the two Predator drones over the site each fired two Hellfire missiles at the fleeing Taliban. "Bad" Abdul Rahman Mustaghni and the thirteen other insurgents were obliterated, and at long last, Combat Outpost Keating was gone forever.

CHAPTER 39

Two Purple Hearts and
Just One Scar

Combat Outpost Keating, after the United States bombed the camp. *(Taken from U.S. Army investigation)*

As was standard procedure, on October 10, General McChrystal ordered an official "15-6" investigation into what had gone wrong at Camp Keating. Major General Guy Swan III was appointed as investigating officer. He gave a progress report to McChrystal on November 3 in Kabul and handed in his full findings on November 9. Swan noted that Camp Keating had had a number of serious vulnerabilities, including "insufficient overhead cover for battle positions," an "oversized compound relative to troop strength," and a mortar position that should have been more defensible. He faulted four officers—George, Brown, Porter, and Portis—for their "failure to improve COP Keating's base defense and AT/FP" (that is, "antiterrorism/force protection") "plans at the troop and squadron level."

Porter, who had since been promoted to major, "bears the greatest responsibility," Swan concluded. The captain had rejected recommendations for additional protection, including lumber and sandbags that were already available at the outpost. He hadn't even let his lieutenants inspect the Claymore mines to make sure they were working, Swan noted.

Lieutenant Colonel Brad Brown "also bears significant responsibility," Swan's report stated. Brown was criticized for having known that the outpost was in a "precarious" position, given that he had visited it several times, beginning with his attendance at the memorial service for Captain Yllescas. Moreover, Brown knew that Porter "was not a strong leader," so he should have been more sensitive and paid more attention to security plans at Combat Outpost Keating.

In addition, Swan faulted Captain Stoney Portis, who had assumed command of the outpost less than two weeks before the attack, for the fact that "he made no significant improvements in force protection." Portis had increased the amount of time that troops were on "stand-to" guard duty, but he hadn't added patrols, checked the Claymore mines, assigned extra personnel to "stand-to" battle positions, or switched up response patterns or battle drills.

Finally, Swan faulted Colonel George, because as brigade commander, he bore overall responsibility, and having visited the outpost twice, he also knew firsthand of the outpost's vulnerabilities.

Swan volunteered a recommendation that the "obviously indefensible or high risk COPs and OPs" should be closed. Brown had briefed McChrystal on brigade plans to shut down Combat Outposts Keating and Lowell as well as Observation Post Fritsche, the report acknowledged, but a number of other pressing matters had interrupted those plans, including the Afghan elections, the siege at Barg-e-Matal, and the search for MIA soldier Bowe Bergdahl. Moreover, according to Swan, the plan to abandon Combat Outpost Keating had itself "inadvertently undermined the focus on current base defense and preparedness." Troops "were unclear, even confused, about their mission for anything beyond 'defending the COP.'" Furthermore, Swan declared, the base was undermanned.

Brown was furious when he read the report. *Every* base in his area of operations was undermanned. Between them, Combat Outpost Keating and Observation Post Fritsche had had three out of the ten platoons total in the squadron—and those ten had been fashioned out of an original eight, so that their troops were already stretched thin. Combat Outpost Lowell had two platoons. Observation Post Mace and Observation Post Bari Alai had only one each. Swan had asked Brown why he hadn't repositioned more forces to Combat Outpost Keating, and Brown had explained that as it was, the rest of the squadron had barely enough troops to defend itself and keep the road open. Swan told him he should have asked Colonel George for more men, but George knew how thin they were, he was aware that every unit had the same problem—that was precisely *why* they had worked so hard to close the small outposts. But Swan hadn't been tasked with looking at the larger problems of Regional Command East, or of Afghanistan as a whole. He was focused solely on Combat Outpost Keating that deployment. That had been his order.

On December 27, 2009, McChrystal determined that there was a need for him to issue a "memorandum for the record" stating the obvious: many of the decisive factors identified in the investigation as having contributed to the attack on COP Keating were the fault of people far above the colonel, lieutenant colonel, and two captains—namely, himself and other generals. The Army assessed the value of the loss of Combat Outpost Keating at $6.2 million, including LRASs, radios, machine guns, Humvees, and night-vision goggles.

In a letter acknowledging his formal reprimand, Brown, on January 2, 2010, wrote that while he felt "a sense of personal accountability for every soldier killed or wounded in this unit, and most acutely those who died on 3 October," there were other factors that the Army needed to consider.

He had long tried to close Combat Outpost Keating, he noted, believing that it "and the other isolated outposts in Kamdesh District served little functional purpose in the counterinsurgency effort, exacerbated ethnic and tribal tensions to the advantage of the insurgency, and placed a majority of the squadron's resources in tactically untenable positions."

As to Porter's failures as commander, Brown admitted that he had been "aware of the leadership issues at COP Keating, and had asked and received approval" from Colonel George "to change command of that troop ninety days after their arrival in theater." After October 3, Brown had learned that instead of complaining to him about problems at the outpost, including serious concerns about force protection, the troops had decided instead to wait for their new commander, Stoney Portis, to arrive and resolve the issues.

"Leadership issues" notwithstanding, Brown didn't think the heaps of criticism being flung at Porter were fair. Could Combat Outpost Keating have been better fortified? Sure, Brown concluded, but it wasn't as if any of them could have done anything to change the fact that the outpost was located at the bottom of a valley surrounded by three steep mountains teeming with enemy fighters. Soldiers under Porter—and generals above him— were looking to blame someone, and while Porter might not have been a strong commander, at the end of the day, his failures paled in comparison with the challenges posed by the camp's geography and the command's decision to scatter small and remote bases throughout one of the most dangerous corners of the world. Brown called the October 3 battle "not only a tactical victory for the coalition, but a resounding operational defeat for the Taliban and the enemies of Afghanistan. The Taliban's loss of key leaders and fighters severely weakened their sway with the population in both Nuristan and eastern Kunar." Brown was talking about the overall picture in the region—"Bad" Abdul Rahman and hundreds of his fighters dead, the former HIG commander Mullah Sadiq in Afghanistan and beginning to play a positive role—but this remark later prompted a U.S. State Department official to ask, "If that's a victory, what does defeat look like?"

After reading letters from Brown, Major General Scaparrotti, and Colonel George, McChrystal decided to assign the "memorandum of reprimand" against Brown to be a local filing—meaning that it would not follow him to his next assignment. It was a black mark, but McChrystal's move downgraded the punishment.

On April 9, 2010, McChrystal went to Forward Operating Base Fenty to present the Silver Star—the third-highest award for valor bestowed by the United States—to Andrew Bundermann, Chris Cordova, Jonathan

Hill, and Thomas Rasmussen. Silver Stars would also be awarded to Eric Harder, Brad Larson, Keith Stickney, Victor De La Cruz and, posthumously, Justin Gallegos. Portis and Brown also recommended that a number of troops receive other recognitions, including a Medal of Honor for Ty Carter and a Distinguished Service Cross for Clint Romesha.[91]

A Taliban spokesman, calling from an undisclosed location on October 9, proclaimed to reporters that the U.S. bombing of Combat Outpost Keating and Observation Post Fritsche "means they are not coming back. This is another victory for the Taliban. We have control of another district in eastern Afghanistan. Right now Kamdesh is under our control, and the white flag of the Taliban is raised above Kamdesh."

The first propaganda video posted by the Taliban, on November 18, was a complete sham. Purported to be footage of the assault on Combat Outpost Keating, the film in fact showed an attack on Combat Outpost Lowell—which closed down a few weeks after Camp Keating did— along with some old clips of Combat Outpost Lybert, which had been shut down in 2008. Nonetheless, inexplicably, on November 30, 2009, the director of national intelligence's "Open Source Center" released the video to the public, accepting the Taliban's claim that it depicted the attack on Camp Keating. Members of the U.S. media in turn took the U.S. government's word for it. To those who had served at the actual outpost attacked on October 3—and whose fellow troops had been killed there—this was another slap in the face. One outpost, another outpost, they were all the same to those who were safe at home.

In 2010, the Taliban released a legitimate video of the October 3 attack. The footage showed insurgents preparing for the assault in the mountains, chanting "Allahu Akbar," and firing upon Camp Keating. "The prophet Mohammed, peace be upon him, says if you throw an arrow toward the enemy, it is as good as freeing a slave for the sake of Allah," one insurgent yells.

"God is great!" and "The Christianity center is under attack!" shout others. "If you fight for God, then you will definitely be going to Heaven!" Once the insurgents breach the wire, one cautions, "Mujahideen have entered the base—don't fire at the base anymore." Another screams triumphantly,

---

[91] Both Jared Monti and Robby Miller received posthumous Medals of Honor.

"These are the American tanks!…This is their advanced technology! Our technology is our faith and belief in one God!"

Black Knight Troop remained in Afghanistan, working out of Forward Operating Base Bostick. After a memorial service on October 11 featuring a twenty-one-gun salute, Taps, and "Amazing Grace," as well as remarks eulogizing each fallen hero, the surviving soldiers came together around a bonfire. Stoney Portis tried to give them an inspirational pep talk. John Francis, Jonathan Adams, and Jeffrey Hobbs reenlisted.

Four days later, Black Knight Troop was back in action. Taliban insurgents attacked members of the Afghan Border Police and attempted to overrun Checkpoint Delta. Portis ordered White Platoon to take four Humvees out to the area, where they had never been before. Before they left, Portis bought the platoon a case of Red Bull energy drink for forty dollars.

Back to work.

Ed Faulkner, Jr., was sent to recuperate at Fort Carson, in Colorado, where his wounds were treated and he was promoted to private second class. He was initially encouraged to rejoin the Bastards at Forward Operating Base Bostick. "Don't you want to be a real man and return to Afghanistan with your unit?" an officer asked him.

Faulkner admitted that he didn't think he was capable of going back there. He had too much going on in his head, he said—too many voices, too many nightmares. An Army physician told him he had posttraumatic stress disorder. Already in a precarious and unstable place emotionally, he had been tipped into a chasm by the battle for Combat Outpost Keating. The loss of his friends Michael Scusa and Chris Griffin had left him racked with guilt. He, Griffin, and Hardt had been in that stand-to truck trying to save Gallegos, Mace, Martin, Larson, and Carter. Five out of the eight of them were now dead.

Faulkner's commander at Fort Carson suspected he'd gone back to using meth, which he believed was contributing to his paranoia and manic behavior. He decided it would be better to discharge the private before he got into so much legal trouble that the Army had to court-martial him.

At Forward Operating Base Bostick, Jonathan Hill heard about what the officers at Fort Carson were pushing on Faulkner. It didn't surprise him. Before 3-61 Cav deployed to Afghanistan, Faulkner had come to him and told him he wanted to admit himself for treatment of a drug problem. Hill respected him for it, but others thought he was playing games and just trying to avoid heading into combat. After being wounded on October 3, Hill thought, Faulkner had needed someone in his chain of command to look after him. While the injury itself might have been new, it had hit the old scar, both physically and psychologically, and reconjured old pains and ghosts. He had shown that when given attention and cared for by Salentine, Birchfield, and Hill, he was able to straighten up and become a decent soldier. "Please look after Faulkner," Hill told a member of their Family Readiness Group back at Fort Carson. "He's going to really struggle." But to his commanders, including Lieutenant Colonel Brown, what mattered was the seemingly inescapable fact that Faulkner would not abide by the Army's rules. Hill saw the young man as a falling leaf that the Army wanted to rake up and dispose of.

Faulkner was told he would need to put in for a discharge. From the perspective of the commanders of 3-61 Cav, the Army was giving him the opportunity to end his service under honorable conditions. A date was picked: April 1, 2010.

The decision incensed Faulkner's father, Ed senior, who reached out to his congressman. Sure, his son had messed up by possessing hashish at the observation post in Afghanistan, but he had paid for his mistake, having been busted down from specialist to the lowest level of private, and forfeiting four months' pay in the process. He needed psychological therapy, not humiliation, said his father. The congressman reached out in turn, and Lieutenant Colonel Dan Chandler responded that Private Faulkner's "abuse of illegal drugs placed the lives of his comrades in serious danger." Ed senior pointed out that his son had never actually been accused of being under the influence of the hashish and had performed honorably until he was injured during the attack on Combat Outpost Keating. Back at Fort Carson, he'd even been promoted. But as far as the Army was concerned, this was the end of the line for Ed Faulkner, Jr. So Ed Faulkner, Sr., boarded a plane for Colorado and accompanied his son home on the date agreed.

As soon as Faulkner got back to Burlington, North Carolina, he retreated into his own head, keeping in touch with friends mainly through his Facebook page. Faulkner was haunted. He dreamt about Iraqis coming to his family's door, ringing the doorbell, and bringing him their dead babies. He lamented to his father that he could have done something to save Chris Griffin's life as they ran from the truck. When the sun was in the sky, he would have flashbacks; when the moon was out, he was constantly being scared awake by nightmares. Michael Scusa had once comforted Faulkner by saying, "It's all good, man. It's all good." But Scusa wasn't able to say that anymore.

Later in April, Faulkner started in a carpet-cleaning job, for which he had to get up at 6:00 a.m. every day. His boss was showing him how to use the cleaning system on his van when Faulkner stepped into a bucket of scalding hot water. The blistering that resulted hurt worse than his bullet wound, he said.

The outpost never left him. Faulkner would stay up late at night watching insurgents' videos on YouTube. He told a friend from 3-61 Cav, Brian Casey, that he heard gunfire and saw Taliban on a daily basis. His father took him to a Greensboro Grasshoppers minor league baseball game. As they left the game, the stadium's management started shooting off fireworks. Faulkner hit the ground as if he were under attack.

Once, in the middle of the night, Faulkner's mother, Sharon, couldn't find her son. He wasn't in his bed, but his truck was still in the driveway. He didn't answer his cell phone. She got in her car and drove around the neighborhood looking for him. He wasn't anywhere. When she returned, as she pulled into the driveway, she saw a shadow in the bushes in front of the house. She walked over and found her son crouched down, acting as if he had a rifle and were looking through its scope at an enemy across the street. He picked up an invisible radio and started talking into it, as if in combat.

Faulkner's mother guided him to his bed. The next morning, he remembered none of it.

At the end of July, Ed Faulkner, Jr., ran naked into the street, yelling that the end of the world was coming. He stopped cars and asked drivers if they'd been saved and accepted Jesus Christ as their Lord and Savior. He was picked up by local police, who called his sister, Sarah Faulkner Minor. She told them that her brother had recently been discharged from the Army and had two Purple Hearts, one earned in Iraq and the other in Afghanistan. He had shrapnel injuries and was suffering from PTSD, she said.

"I knew it," said the police officer on the other end of the phone. "When we detained him, he was talking on the radio to fellow soldiers who weren't there." Both were imaginary, of course—the soldiers *and* the radio.

The officer said that the police didn't want to arrest Faulkner, but they would commit him. Sarah agreed; she didn't want him to hurt himself or anyone else. When she visited him in the psychiatric wing of Alamance Medical Center, she at first walked right past his room—with its mattress thrown to the floor and its occupant covered from head to toe by a sheet, the room clearly belonged to someone else, someone unhinged, she thought. Whoever that is, bless his heart, she said to herself before realizing it was Ed. She walked in and tried to make conversation, but it didn't sound like his voice when he spoke. Something had taken him over. He scared her.

"I can't sit in this nuthouse," he told her.

The realization took the wind out of her: My brother is very mentally ill right now.

"This is the end for me," he said. "You have no idea how I feel, I'm so stressed out, I don't know why I did what I did, I don't know why it happened."

She tried to tell him to give his life over to God, that only He, not drugs, could save him, but her brother seemed beyond saving.

"There's all this noise in my mind," he told her. "It won't stop. It won't quiet down."

Faulkner was transferred to a local veterans hospital for a couple of days, assigned a social worker, and then discharged. His parents were not impressed by the quality of care their son received, which seemed casual and oblivious, when clearly he needed serious help. "If you're out in a storm, you seek shelter," Ed senior would say. "He has a storm going on in his brain." But his government, his country, provided his son with no such cover.

Faulkner met a woman named[92] Charline in August. She told him she was bipolar and suffered from manic depression. For the first time in a long while, Faulkner didn't feel alone: Charline knew how he felt. She had a young daughter, whom he helped with her homework—a normal life, or almost. He moved into Charline's two-bedroom apartment within weeks of meeting her.

Charline was on government assistance and lived in subsidized housing provided through the Burlington Housing Authority. Prescribed assorted medications, including methadone and Xanax, she'd been investigated a few times by the local police for selling her narcotics. To his family, all of this seemed cause for alarm, but Faulkner was unyielding. "I don't have to

---

[92] Not her real name.

live in the biggest house," he said to his sister. "I don't need life's finest. So what if she's on welfare? So what if she's in government housing? Those people are closest to God."

Charline got on the phone. "I love your brother," she told Sarah, in a spaced-out and rambling fashion.

"I can tell you're on drugs," Sarah replied. "Lock them up. My brother was addicted to pain pills—keep them out of his reach." Charline promised she would. After all, she had a little girl and had to keep her medications out of her hands as well.

On the night of September 15, Charline found Faulkner drifting off to sleep in his parked truck. When she asked him what was wrong, he didn't answer. She helped him stumble out of the vehicle and into her bed.

The next morning, Charline woke up and got her daughter ready for school. She took her to the bus stop. When she came back, she was surprised to see that Faulkner hadn't moved an inch. She realized he wasn't breathing. She called 911 and tried to revive him. The fire department arrived and took over the CPR.

The first responders noticed that there were several buckets of murky water in the hallway. It wasn't clear whether the apartment had functioning electricity or plumbing. The mattress on which Faulkner was lying was riddled with cigarette burns. The apartment was packed with piles of clothes and trash. The bathroom was coated in filth.

The police and an ambulance got there at the same time. The emergency medical technicians ran in and confirmed what the firefighters had already ascertained: Faulkner was dead. They put him on a stretcher and wheeled him out, placed him in the back of the ambulance, and sped off to the emergency room. An autopsy indicated that his cause of death was acute methadone toxicity.

A few days later, a Veterans Administration office worker called Ed Faulkner, Sr. "Would you please let your son know that he's late for his appointment?" he asked.

As word of Faulkner's death spread, Hill—who by then had transferred out of 3-61 Cav—called Carter at Fort Carson to discuss how thoroughly the Army had turned its back on their friend.

"I kinda think he was the ninth victim of Keating," Carter said. "And I honestly don't think he'll be the last."

Epilogue

The mountains of northeastern Afghanistan are more foreboding than words can express—magisterial, with breathtaking peaks and narrow valleys. During helicopter rides, I see little villages, hamlets, single homes nestled in obscure nooks. Anyone might be living there.

I arrive at Forward Operating Base Bostick in October 2011. The officers of the 2-27 Infantry, the "Wolfhounds," have lost nine troops by this point in their deployment. Captains Tim Blair and Matthew Schachman take me to the entrance of the lieutenant colonel's office, where seven photos hang from the wall, troops killed mainly by IEDs on the treacherous roads. Four of them[93] were in a Humvee targeted because the enemy mistakenly thought Blair was in it, he tells me.

The eighth photo, of Staff Sergeant Houston Taylor, isn't up yet; he was killed just a few days before my visit, at a cell-phone tower several hundred meters below a brand-new observation post. They won't be hanging a photograph of the ninth soldier who died here, Private First Class Jinsu Lee, who took his own life at Forward Operating Base Bostick on August 5, 2011.

It boggles the mind that just five years ago, Captain Aaron Swain and his team can have left this base on ATVs to scout the location for what

---

[93] Specialist William S. Blevins, of Sardinia, Ohio; Staff Sergeant Kristofferson B. Lorenzo, of Chula Vista, California; Private First Class Andrew M. Krippner, of Garland, Texas; and Private First Class Thomas C. Allers, of Plainwell, Michigan.

would become Combat Outpost Keating. The Wolfhounds don't leave the wire or walk down the road without intense preparation and full body armor; most often, they are also ensconced in enormous mine-resistant trucks. Northern Kunar Province is no less dangerous.

Kabul doesn't seem any safer: just after my arrival on this trip, my second to Afghanistan, insurgents staged their deadliest attack yet on Americans in that city, using a car bomb to target a military convoy. I also spend a few nights in the confines of Forward Operating Base Fenty; whereas Ben Keating once wandered freely through the markets of Jalalabad, troops must now fly in helicopters to travel just a few miles down the road, to Forward Operating Bases Hughie or Finley-Shields. The roads are too dangerous.

I've come here to get as close to Camp Keating as I can, but the U.S. military has all but ceded Nuristan, deciding that, as then-Colonel Donahue suggested back in 2005, there isn't any reason for U.S. forces to be there. "Nuristan has no strategic value," says one public-affairs officer at Forward Operating Base Fenty. "The Afghan forces run it now." There is one remaining base in the province, at Kala Gush.

So I can't get into Nuristan at this time — not to Urmul or Kamdesh Village or the former location of Combat Outpost Keating — because no one will take me. Schachman jokes that in the Wolfhounds' area of operations, you can do anything once. So theoretically, we *could* make our way to Kamdesh to see the former site of Combat Outpost Keating. The problem would be getting back.

"I could put on my PT's[94] and jog down to Asadabad," Schachman says with a smile. "Once."

The hard work here in northeastern Afghanistan continues. The Wolfhounds devote much of their time and energy to maintaining the security of a section of the road from Asadabad to Naray, the same road that Lieutenant Colonel Brown and some of his men worked on securing two years ago. They try to get the village elders to assume responsibility for parts of the road. They offer assurances to villagers that they will benefit from contracts to pour the asphaltlike substance on the still-unpaved swath. They, like the other soldiers whose stories I have attempted to tell in these pages, are trying to do their very best in an impossible part of

---

[94] "Physical Training" clothes — shorts and a T-shirt.

the world, both to help the Afghan people and to eliminate the bad guys. They are paid modestly and have endured years away from those whom they love most. They are generally ignored by the American people and the American media.

Days before I get to Forward Operating Base Bostick, a B-10 recoilless rifle round hit the center of the camp, not far from Schachman's hooch. When I share this information on Facebook—where I've accumulated a fair number of friends and acquaintances from 3-71, 1-91, 6-4, and 3-61 Cavs—troops and former troops speculate that it must have been the same B-10 that haunted Camp Keating in 2009, the one that badly wounded Sergeant Shane Scherer[95] and, to a lesser extent, First Sergeant Ronald Burton.

Some of the Wolfhounds tell me that in Kamdesh District, Mullah Sadiq and HIG are fighting it out with the Taliban. Other interesting developments: before 3-61 Cav left Afghanistan in 2010, Kamdesh elder Abdul Rahman had become the district administrator for Kamdesh, and "Big" Gul Mohammed has since been assigned to serve as the local chief of the Afghan National Police.

Major Dominick Edwards is, when I land at Forward Operating Base Bostick, in charge of the entire area of operations while his commander is on leave. A North Carolina native, Edwards is forty-one and has a devoted wife and three children back home in Hawaii. He's reasonably confident that the Afghan National Army and National Police will be able to assume control of the area within the next couple of years.

There has been little public discussion of what happened at Combat Outpost Keating. The scope of the 15-6 investigation was limited largely to the matter of whether there was adequate force protection at the outpost, not addressing tougher questions such as whether those troops should have been in that valley at all, or whether the military had even larger issues to resolve. When I mention the Wolfhounds' nine fallen soldiers to Edwards and ask him if their lives were worth the infrastructure constructed, or even the enemy killed, he quite candidly admits he doesn't know. That will be for history to judge, he says.

---

[95] In an email to me, Lieutenant Colonel Brown called this "maudlin romanticism," noting that there were B-10s all over Afghanistan, and differentiating between the Taliban at Combat Outpost Keating and those at Forward Operating Base Bostick.

*   *   *

Specialist Brian Casey of 3-61 Cav was on his way back to Camp Keating from R&R when his friends were attacked on October 3, 2009. His three best friends at the outpost were Michael Scusa, Chris Griffin, and Ed Faulkner.

Casey wasn't there for that one battle, but he, too, carries the scars from being in Afghanistan. There have been times when he has scared his family. One morning after a bender, he woke up to find the whole downstairs of his house trashed. He thought his dogs had gotten into a fight. They hadn't—*he'd* done it.

Casey has since pursued help. But still, some nights, if he hears an odd noise, he will go load his shotgun and patrol his house for a few minutes before he realizes how frightening and strange his actions are.

Of all the troops who served at Combat Outpost Keating, Faulkner suffered the most immediately consequential case of PTSD. Some of his friends think his overdose was purposeful, though there's no evidence of that. "He took the easy way out," says Casey.

A 2008 study by the RAND Corporation concluded that almost 20 percent of service members who served in Iraq and Afghanistan reported some signs of either PTSD or major depression. By now, more than two and a half million Americans have served in those two wars, meaning that the number of Iraq and Afghanistan veterans suffering from those particular long-term effects is somewhere around five hundred thousand. The RAND study indicated that only about half sought treatment. How effective that treatment may prove to be is obviously an open question; Faulkner, for example, was in treatment.

Alex Newsom returned to Afghanistan. Based at Forward Operating Base Fenty in Jalalabad, Newsom—formerly of 1-91 Cav, now with Special Forces—worked with Afghan National Army commandos to fight the Taliban. As I was working on this book, I heard from him periodically via email and on the phone. He was always cryptic about what exactly he was doing, but he wanted me to know—he wanted me to tell you—that all was not lost in Nuristan, that troops had not died in vain.

In April 2012, the U.S. military posted pictures from a Special Forces mission to Kamdesh Village. The Taliban were on the verge of overrunning Upper Kamdesh, threatening to slaughter the inhabitants if they didn't side with them. For two weeks, the Taliban had been deliberately and methodically attacking locals in the middle of the night. Then, in early April, ISAF special operations troops and 120 ANA commandos entered the area under cover of darkness. They were there for five days, fighting and beating back up to three hundred insurgents.

"The people that we supported kept up the fight long after we left," Newsom reported to me, referring to his time with 1-91 Cav. He had a joyful reunion with Mawlawi Abdul Rahman—"I heard you guys needed some help," Newsom told the new district administrator. Then, at a district center in Upper Kamdesh, he saw former HIG leader Mullah Sadiq. "He looked pretty ill, but he's on our side," he confided.

"Our relationships that we established years ago were paramount in the success of the liberation of that particular village," Newsom insisted. "Without any American presence for two and a half years, these people we supported, they kept the fight up. All they needed was equipment. These are good people. There is hope." For Captain America, still running through the mountains of Nuristan, the fight goes on.

Captain Alex Newsom of U.S. Special Forces with Mawlawi Abdul Rahman (*to his right*) and others as U.S. forces and Afghan commandos fought back against Taliban insurgents in Kamdesh Village in April 2012. *(Photo courtesy of U.S. Department of Defense)*

*   *   *

On May 21, 2012, President Obama and the NATO allies announced that in the summer of 2013, Afghan government forces—ready or not—would take the lead on providing security throughout the country, and that U.S. combat forces would see their mission end come midnight, December 31, 2014. (It seems likely, nevertheless, that Special Forces units such as Newsom's will remain in the country beyond that date, conducting counterterrorism missions.)

At the NATO summit, in Chicago, the president took questions from reporters. I had solicited suggestions from the troops you've met in these pages as well as from their families, and I'd selected two, both from members of 3-61 Cav.

Asked now-Captain Stephen Cady: "If this handoff and withdrawal prove premature, what plans are in place for dealing with an Afghanistan that's fallen apart or is, possibly, again, under Taliban rule?"

"I don't think that there's ever going to be an optimal point where we say, 'This is all done, this is perfect, this is just the way we wanted it, and now we can...wrap up all our equipment and go home,'" the president said, speaking more from the heart than usual—probably because he felt he was conveying something directly to the fighting men, instead of just to a White House reporter. "There's a process, and it's sometimes a messy process, just as it was in Iraq. But think about it. We've been there now ten years...the Afghan security forces themselves will not ever be prepared if they don't start taking that responsibility" for their own security.

The president continued, "The large footprint that we have in Afghanistan, over time, can be counterproductive.... No matter how much good we're doing and how outstanding our troops and our civilians and diplomats are doing on the ground, ten years, in a country that's very different, that's a strain, not only on our folks but also on that country, which at a point is going to be very sensitive about its own sovereignty. So I think that the timetable that we've established is a sound one, it is a responsible one. Are there risks involved in it? Absolutely. Can I anticipate that over the next two years there are going to be some bad moments along with some good ones? Absolutely."

But, he said, "I think it is the appropriate strategy whereby we can achieve a stable Afghanistan that won't be perfect, we can pull back our troops in a responsible way, and we can start rebuilding America."

I then relayed a question from Eric Harder: "Do you feel that the reporting you receive from the Pentagon fully represents what the on-ground commanders assess? Is there any disconnect between what leaders feel the public and the president want to hear versus what is actually occurring on the ground?"

"I can't afford a whitewash," the president said. "I can't afford not getting the very best information in order to make good decisions....The danger a lot of times is not that anybody's purposely trying to downplay challenges in Afghanistan. A lot of times it's just the military culture is, 'We can get it done.' And so their thinking is, How are we going to solve this problem? not Boy, why is this such a disaster? That's part of the reason why we admire our military so much and we love our troops, because they've got that can-do spirit."

The president said that he thought he had "set up a structure that really tries to guard against that, because even in my White House, for example, I've got former officers who have been in Afghanistan, who I will send out there as part of the national security team of the White House, not simply the Pentagon, to interact and to listen and to go in and talk to the captains and the majors and the corporals and the privates, to try to get a sense of what's going on. And I think the reports we get are relatively accurate in the sense that there is real improvement in those areas where we've had a significant presence."

Harder was at that moment in Afghanistan, unsure that the president was really getting the full story.

When Harder returned from his second tour in Afghanistan in 2012, he kept a low profile. Memories of the outpost stayed with him, as did some of its artifacts, including a fifty-pound marble slab that had once been mounted right next to the front door on the wall outside the operations center. It read:

In honor of
1LT Benjamin D. Keating
3rd Squadron, 71st Cavalry
Regiment
Killed 26 November 2006 while
conducting mounted
reconnaissance near Kamdesh

Not much had survived the attack or the accompanying fire that ravaged the camp; the men of 3-61 Cav had been told to pack up only essential equipment. But to Harder, the plaque that bore Ben Keating's name fit that definition. He and some others ripped the slab from the wall of the devastated compound and carefully put it into a helicopter's sling load to the nearby forward operating base, FOB Bostick. There it ended up in a Conex storage container, shipped back to Fort Carson in Colorado. For a bit, the slab lived in a Fort Carson broom closet, until Harder brought it to his mother's garage in Minnesota. It wasn't as if he wanted to remember his time at the Outpost; he didn't, not really. But he knew that he had one last mission related to the place: he called Ken and Beth Keating to see if they wanted it. They did.

Harder was not the first soldier from the outpost to make such an effort. When they were up at Observation Post Fritsche, the Bastards of Black Knight Troop kept stumbling upon memorials to Staff Sergeant Ryan Fritsche — first a slab that had been made to stand at the OP but was still wrapped in butcher paper, then a memorial bracelet with Fritsche's name on it, which Jon Hill gingerly placed on a shelf in his hooch beside his family photos.

After the October 3, 2009, attack, Hill went into what was left of the Bastards' barracks, where there was little remaining but a four-inch-thick carpet of ash. The light caught an object buried in the soot, and Hill squatted to retrieve it. It was the Fritsche bracelet. Hill headed to the operations center and asked Burton to make sure the marble memorial still up on the OP wouldn't be left in Kamdesh; he wanted to get it home to the Fritsche family. Sergeant John Francis was tasked with that assignment. Back in Colorado in 2010, an altruistic postal worker promised Francis he'd get the slab to Indiana.

In July 2012, the town of Martinsville, Indiana, unveiled the stone from Observation Post Fritsche in its War Memorial park. Volitta Fritsche invited both Hill and Francis to speak at the dedication ceremony, though Francis by then was back in Afghanistan.

"I am extremely proud to know that the stone is home," Hill said. "You know, I never met Staff Sergeant Fritsche in person, but he is my brother in arms. And just like all my brothers and sisters in the ranks, this is what we do: we take care of each other."

*　　*　　*

On December 14, 2012, Harder boarded a flight to Boston, bearing the fifty-pound marble slab, tightly wrapped in cardboard. After landing at Logan Airport, he rented a car and drove to Portland, Maine, where he and Ken Keating had coordinated by email to meet at a Pizzeria Uno. Neither knew what the other looked like, but the soldier sent Keating a text and watched an older man check his cell phone, and it flowed from there.

They spent the day together. Harder learned all about Ben's life and the lives of those who missed him, about Ben's Christian faith and the apple orchard where he worked for two years before deciding to get his act together and go to college.

Harder had never known his own father; Ken Keating was now without a son.

Before Harder left, he asked Keating to tell him what he planned to do with the marble slab. Ken took a couple days with his response. Then he called Harder and told him: he had spoken with the funeral director who handled his son's funeral. Ben lay at the family burial plot all alone, his grave marked by the standard granite issued by the Veterans Administration, but his father and mother planned to erect a family monument that would incorporate the marble slab from Combat Outpost Keating as a tribute not only to their beloved son, but to all the soldiers who put their lives on the line at the outpost that bore his name.

It would be as close to permanence as one can get.

One freezing January 2013 afternoon in Tioga, North Dakota, Clint Romesha's cell phone rang.

Romesha had left the Army and now worked as a safety specialist for a company that did construction around oil sites. He was sitting in his truck in a spot that had decent cell phone service; he'd been told that a senior military official would be calling him around a certain time and to be by his phone.

He reached into his pocket, grabbed his cell phone, and looked to see who was calling: the phone number was blocked. This had to be the call, Romesha thought.

"Hello?" he answered, and a secretary on the other end of the line asked if she was speaking with Clint Romesha.

She was.

"President Obama would like to speak with you," she said.

Romesha was stunned. Nervous. *Don't say something stupid,* he told himself.

The president told Romesha that he would soon be awarding him the Congressional Medal of Honor. He offered his congratulations and told Romesha his actions honored the country.

"For me, this isn't about me," Romesha said. "It was everyone that day up at COP Keating."

For all the glory bestowed on Romesha, he had remained torn apart because of those he couldn't save that night, those no one could have saved.

"My granddaddy used to teach me, you know, 'When you tell someone you're going to do something, you do it. Your actions are what make you.' And I know I'm hard on myself, but it still hurts," Romesha told me.

When President Obama had called, there were seventy-nine living Medal of Honor recipients. On February 11, 2013, Romesha became the eightieth—to go along with the thirty-seven Army Commendation Medals, twenty-seven Purple Hearts, eighteen Bronze Stars, and nine Silver Stars awarded to the men of Black Knight Troop, 3-61 CAV, who served at Combat Outpost Keating.

Black Knight troops filed into the East Room of the White House along with the children of Gallegos and Kirk; the widows of Scusa and Hardt; the grieving parents of Mace, Thomson, Griffin, and Martin. Before the ceremony, Romesha's almost-two-year-old son, Colin, punctured some of the somber tension in the room, climbing and inspecting the lectern, briefly playing hide-and-seek with the bemused onlookers. A military escort returned Colin to his mother's arms in the first row.

"Colin is not as shy as Clint," President Obama noted. "He was in the Oval Office and he was racing around pretty good and sampled a number of apples before he found the one that was just right.

"Every day at the White House we receive thousands of letters from folks all across America," the president continued. "And at night, upstairs in my study, I read a few."

The president noted that roughly three years before, he'd received a letter from Vanessa Adelson, the grieving mother of Stephan Mace.

"She had received the condolence letter that I'd sent to her family, as I send to every family of the fallen. And she wrote me back," he said. "'Mr. President,' she said, 'you wrote me a letter telling me that my son was a hero. I just wanted you to know what kind of hero he was.

"'My son was a great soldier,' she wrote. 'As far back as I can remember, Stephan wanted to serve his country.' She spoke of how he 'loved his brothers in B Troop.' How he 'would do anything for them.' And of the brave actions that would cost Stephan his life, she wrote, 'His sacrifice was driven by pure love.'"

After turning to Romesha to note that the award he was about to bestow upon him, the nation's highest military decoration, "reflects the gratitude of our entire country," the president began to tell the story of the fight for Combat Outpost Keating. He noted that General Swan's investigation had concluded that the outpost was "tactically indefensible," but "that's what these soldiers were asked to do — defend the indefensible," the president said. And he continued:

> There were many lessons from COP Keating. One of them is that our troops should never, ever, be put in a position where they have to defend the indefensible. But that's what these soldiers did — for each other, in sacrifice driven by pure love. And because they did, eight grieving families were at least able to welcome their soldiers home one last time. And more than forty American soldiers are alive today to carry on, to keep alive the memory of their fallen brothers, to help make sure that this country that we love so much remains strong and free.
>
> What was it that turned the tide that day? How was it that so few Americans prevailed against so many? As we prepare for the reading of the citation, I leave you with the words of Clint himself, because they say something about our Army and they say something about America; they say something about our spirit, which will never be broken: "We weren't going to be beat that day," Clint said. "You're not going to back down in the face of adversity like that. We were just going to win, plain and simple."

Handling the attention wasn't that plain and simple for Romesha, who would agree to and then back out of attending the State of the Union address as a guest of First Lady Michelle Obama. The focus on his valor, with the weight of the guilt for the men who were lost that day, was almost too much to bear. He wanted to spend time with his battle buddies and their families.

"I stand here with mixed emotions of both joy and sadness for me today," a very emotional Romesha told reporters outside the Oval Office, noting that he was "feeling conflicted with this medal I now wear." The joy that came with the medal was "countered by the constant reminder of the loss of our battle buddies, my battle buddies, my soldiers, my friends. I accept this tremendous honor on behalf of all soldiers who served with me that day. This award is for the eight soldiers that didn't make it and for the rest of the team that fought valiantly and magnificently that day. I will forever be humbled by their bravery, their commitment to service, and their loyalty to one another."

The overcast skies shielded the crowd from what otherwise might have been a brutal summer sun on Saturday, June 22, 2013, at the Riverside Cemetery in Springvale, Maine. The slab that Eric Harder had delivered six months prior was now mounted within the Keating family headstone, along with these words:

THE MARBLE PLAQUE WAS REMOVED FROM A BUILDING AT COM-BAT OUTPOST KEATING, NURISTAN PROVINCE, AFGHANISTAN, BY SOLDIERS WHO SUCCESSFULLY DEFENDED THE OUTPOST AGAINST A DEADLY ASSAULT BY AN OVERWHELMING FORCE OF ENEMY FIGHTERS ON OCTOBER 3, 2009. ONE OF THOSE SOLDIERS PRE-SENTED THE PLAQUE TO THE KEATING FAMILY. THE PLAQUE IS INCORPORATED IN THIS MONUMENT TO HONOR BEN, FOR WHOM THE OUTPOST WAS NAMED IN 2006, AND ALL AMERICAN PERSON-NEL WHO SPENT TIME INSIDE THE WIRE AT COP KEATING DURING ITS THREE-YEAR EXISTENCE. OUR NATION IS INDEBTED TO THEM FOR THEIR INDIVIDUAL AND COLLECTIVE SACRIFICES.

Surrounded by almost ninety friends and family, including Harder, Ken and Beth Keating began a simple ceremony. Ken Keating recalled Ben, "a young man in the prime of his life who combined a sharp mind, great physical strength, and a tender heart. Loved both by older women and young children, Ben filled a room with his presence. However, he was also stubborn as a mule and a master of sarcasm; he could drive any-body nuts, and he often did. Although he freely admitted that he usually entered a room with the conviction that he was the smartest one there, I know he would be the first to acknowledge that he is not the main story today."

That was because, Ken Keating continued, the "most important pur-pose of this ceremony" was "to dedicate the upper half of the monument in honor of all the men and women who have raised their right hands and sworn an oath to defend the Constitution of the United States of America against its enemies in the global war on terror during the last twelve years, with a particular focus on FBI and CIA agents, special forces, reg-ular army and national guard troops who spent time behind the wire at Combat Outpost Keating, Kamdesh District, Nuristan Province, Afghan-istan, during its three-year existence."

Gallegos, Griffin, Thomson—Ken Keating listed all eight of the troops killed on October 3, 2009, while also paying homage to all the units that had deployed to the outpost named after his son.

"With scheduled troop drawdowns, the newspaper headlines and talk-ing heads on television will turn their attention to other stories, and the limited notice American citizens have taken of events in Iraq and Afghanistan will fade altogether, but there will still be soldiers, Marines, sailors, and airmen standing watch around the world to safeguard our way of life," Ken Keating said. "It is my hope that this monument, despite its restrictive focus on the history of COP Keating and the sacrifices made there by a small group of men on a single day in 2009, will bear constant witness to all who pass by this place of the unshakable courage and determined faithfulness of the men and women who in fulfillment of the oaths they have sworn confront danger on land, at sea, and in the air."

Harder spoke next, from prepared remarks clutched in his hand. But after reading a couple points from the papers, he crumpled them up and said what he needed to, explaining how he came to be there, one of the last men to set foot at Combat Outpost Keating in 2009, honoring the memory of the first to die there in 2006.

Beth Keating then turned to prayer, thanking Jesus "for the men and women represented by the words on this monument. The marble quar-ried from the mountains of Afghanistan and the granite quarried here in New England speak to the strong, steadfast courage of those who served at Combat Outpost Keating. We pray that all who pass by this place days, weeks, and years ahead, will take a moment to reflect, to give thanks, and to appreciate anew the freedoms we enjoy."

That same month, Ty Carter—now a staff sergeant based at Joint Base Lewis-McChord in Washington state—pulled over at a gas station near White Branch Falls, Oregon. He picked the area because it was a rare spot where his cell phone still had something of a signal. He was expecting a phone call from the president.

It was the same basic drill as had happened with Romesha, mixed with Carter's classic attitude. A week before, a White House official had phoned and wanted to know if Carter would be available for a phone call from "a high-ranking military official" at a set time. "No," Carter said. He and his family would be nearly impossible to reach, vacationing in Redwood National Park.

"You really need to be," the official suggested. So Carter rearranged the dates of his family vacation, and at the set day and just before the designated time, Carter pulled over the family's camper and waited for the president to ring.

"You can't park that here," the gas station attendant told him, so they moved to an adjacent space.

Roughly twenty minutes late, the call came to Carter's cell phone from a blocked number; a woman on the other end of the line wanted to know if he was prepared to accept a phone call from the president. Carter said he was. President Obama's voice came on the line next. He thanked the soldier for his service, asked about his family, and explained how he came to approve him for a Medal of Honor.

Two Medals of Honor for the same battle is very rare. In fact, the award for Carter marked the first time in almost a half century that one battle resulted in two living service members being awarded that highest of honors. Specialist Fourth Class Raymond Wright and Sergeant Leonard Keller received the Medal of Honor for actions during a battle in the Ap Bac zone in Vietnam on May 2, 1967. President Johnson awarded their medals in 1968.

There was a more recent battle that resulted in two Medals of Honor, but Sergeant First Class Randall Shughart and Master Sergeant Gary Gordon both received that honor posthumously, having been killed in the

"Black Hawk Down" fight in Somalia on October 3, 1993 — exactly sixteen years before the attack on COP Keating.

The rarity of the event, the history-making nature of his award, may have been a bit too conceptual for Carter at that moment, however. He was primarily focused on not seeming too nervous or saying anything too stupid.

Unlike Romesha's, Carter's was a crooked path to this rare honor, and there were some concerns among some of the higher-ups that his past — being kicked out of the Marines for fighting, a broken first marriage, and an arrogance that rubbed some of his comrades the wrong way — might prevent him from being awarded the medal. Ultimately, however, the sworn statements from his fellow troops and the backing of Portis and Brown resulted in the paperwork proceeding through the complicated Pentagon bureaucracy to then Secretary of Defense Panetta to President Obama.

During the August 26 ceremony at the White House, President Obama not only described Carter's "courage on the battlefield," he also took considerable time "to recognize his courage in the other battle he has fought. Ty has spoken openly — with honesty and extraordinary eloquence — about his struggle with posttraumatic stress — the flashbacks, the nightmares, the anxiety, the heartache that makes it sometimes almost impossible to get through a day. And he's urged us to remember another soldier from COP Keating who suffered, too, who eventually lost his own life back home, and who we remember today for his service in Afghanistan that day — Private Ed Faulkner, Jr."

Carter had once thought those troops claiming PTSD were just trying to get out of work. Only when the symptoms hit him did he realize how wrong — and ignorant — he'd been, and he vowed to use the attention on him from the Medal of Honor to try and destigmatize the condition. "Let me say it as clearly as I can to any of our troops or veterans who are watching and struggling," President Obama said during the ceremony. "Look at this man. Look at this soldier. Look at this warrior. He's as tough as they come. And if he can find the courage and the strength, to not only seek help, but also to speak out about it, to take care of himself and to stay strong, then so can you. So can you."

In the course of my conversations and interviews for this project, I was told by one recently retired general with experience in Afghanistan that he hoped this book might have an impact on the nation in wars going forward.

How so? I asked.

"The wars of the twenty-first century have been outsourced by the American people to our government in D.C. and to our military," he said. "With an all-volunteer force, the American people are no more connected to our armed forces than the Roman citizens were to the legionnaires. And now we even pay for wars with tax cuts. So, whose war and whose Army is it?"

The general hoped that at least some members of the public would, through reading this book, come to a greater understanding of just what war entails, just what the sacrifices mean. "I worry it is becoming too easy for the United States to use force," he added. "There are not enough domestic constraints."

Colonel Shamsur Rahman, of the Afghan Border Police, tells me that most of the fighters who attacked COP Keating were local, from the surrounding area.

Did the Americans do any good while they were there? I ask him.

"There was progress there," he says, "but when the progress was about to be completed, the bad guys would come and burn it down. The intentions were good, but the insurgents wouldn't allow it." And the locals were terrified. "If they participated, the bad guys would target them, kill them. Many people died that way."

Colonel Rahman also points a finger at the power player present throughout this book, the enemy that neither the American troops nor the ANA can go after: he says that Pakistan's intelligence services played a role in the attack. "The ISI told the fighters, 'The Americans are leaving, make a statement,'" he tells me. "'Make sure damage is done.'"

Many U.S. troops have found the way their government is waging war in Afghanistan simply farcical, given the immense role played by that country to the east, and the official policy of denying that reality. Sure, myriad American drones are buzzing about in Pakistan killing bad guys (and, inevitably, some innocents), remotely piloted by Americans thousands of miles away, in places such as New Mexico. And yes, when the time came to do away with Osama bin Laden, President Obama gave the go order, and American Special Forces went to Abottabad and killed the leader of Al Qaeda. But it's worth noting that in this book—about the bad guys who killed Americans, ANA soldiers, Nuristanis, and other Afghans who fought for their country—Pakistan is mentioned far more often than are bin Laden and Al Qaeda. That fact, however, is so inconvenient for policy makers as to be, within the larger scheme of war planning, almost ignored.

Soldiers die in war. Sometimes troops are lost in battle, and sometimes they're killed by the terrain. Sometimes they die because of carelessness or accidents, and sometimes because of wind and trees, random twists of fate, the nature of life. Aircraft carriers that haven't seen any action at all may nevertheless return to port with fewer sailors on board: some fell overboard, some contracted illnesses.

The ephemeral desires of generals for control of specific territories—the drive to claim particular plots of land that will soon enough lose their importance, if indeed they ever had any to begin with—inform a mindset that is long established. Its existence doesn't make casualties any less tragic, of course; it simply makes them unsurprising to any soldier.

And yet, there is no sugar-coating the tragedy of Combat Outpost Keating. In 2006, the U.S. Army went into this particularly dangerous part of Afghanistan and set up, throughout the region, small combat outposts, observation posts, and provincial reconstruction teams that quickly became ripe targets for a strengthening insurgency. The bases were frequently small, generally difficult to defend, and sometimes quite far from any available air support. The troops who fought there often felt as if they were on their own. And in some ways, they were.

Once Colonel Nicholson committed to sending troops into Nuristan, the Army had an obligation to make sure they received enough support to accomplish their mission. I do not see evidence that the men of Camp Keating, throughout the lifespan of the outpost, ever got that level of support. From the outset, President Bush and Defense Secretary Rumsfeld did not send enough troops or resources—not even close—to succeed at the counterinsurgency, the "nation building," that was becoming the goal in the Afghanistan war. (President Bush has since admitted as much, however little attention that part of his legacy—his reluctance to listen to the generals who suggested that the war would cost more money, and require more manpower, than predicted in initial projections—may get in his presidential library and in the history books.) Then, when President Obama and Defense Secretary Gates finally did surge troops and increase resources in Afghanistan, General McChrystal was still forced to ration critical assets. The closure of Combat Outpost Keating was delayed because most of the available helicopters in the country were devoted to Barg-e-Matal. Squadrons and battalions were chronically undermanned; while the Pentagon investigation pronounced Melvin Porter of 3-61 Cav "weak" as a leader, we might do well to recall that his commanders were themselves so understaffed when it came to captains that they kept him in place for three extra months because they had no one to replace him with.

By October 3, 2009, President Obama had been commander in chief for eight months, during which period top officials in his White House had been consumed by the politics of their squabbles with the Pentagon, with both the politicians and the Pentagon brass feeding a beast of dysfunction that did not serve U.S. troops with the professionalism and urgency they deserved. The generals, for their part, were confused as to precisely what the president wanted them to do in Afghanistan and how he saw this war upon which he'd pledged to place a renewed focus. President Obama's first national security adviser, Jim Jones, would ultimately leave his post in 2010 amid grumblings from senior officials over his lack of success in improving relations between the White House and the Pentagon.

That said, no president—neither President Obama nor President Bush before him—could be expected to focus on battle maps of Kunar and Nuristan in order to discern what might be best for the troops in a specific area of operations. The Ranch House, Wanat, Bari Alai—all of these disasters preceded the assault on Combat Outpost Keating, and all followed the same pattern, in which an overwhelming Taliban force attacked a small, remote U.S. base. It has been said that the United States did not fight a ten-year war in Vietnam; rather, it fought a one-year war ten times in a row. Perhaps the same will one day be said of Afghanistan.

It is not only with the benefit of hindsight that McChrystal's lack of urgency about closing Combat Outpost Keating might seem tragic. George and Brown had been planning for the withdrawal for nearly a year, but McChrystal refused to take the request as seriously as he should have. And while the lack of air assets would become an obstacle by July, McChrystal's initial considerations were political: he was worried about getting ahead of President Obama, and then about upsetting President Karzai. Realpolitik is not an ideal; it is, instead, the absence of one.

I did not write this book to convey lessons to be learned. I wrote it so that you as a reader (and I as a reporter) might better understand what it is that our troops go through, why they go through it, and what their experience has been like in Afghanistan. There are far superior military minds that can judge what went wrong and what policies might be formulated to guard against future disasters, future Combat Outpost Keatings. But one conclusion I cannot escape is that the saga of Combat Outpost Keating illustrates, above all else, the deep-rooted inertia of military thinking. Instead of seriously reconsidering the camp's location, the Army defaulted to its usual mindset: We're already there, let's just fortify the camp a little more. That might be a fine way to go about establishing, say, a new Starbucks in a sketchy neighborhood, but it's beyond glib in this context.

It was easier for me to get *to* Forward Operating Base Bostick than it was to get back. The military system is more interested in moving men to the enemy quickly, less interested in pulling them out. Such thinking—easy to advance, difficult to retreat—is burned into the military brain. Hence, the outpost was originally put in its precarious location so it would be near the road to facilitate resupply, but it stayed there even after the troops all but stopped using the road, within months of Lieutenant Ben Keating's death. This was a symptom of what President Obama, in May 2012, would refer to as the "How are we going to solve this problem?" mindset, the one that avoids asking instead, "Boy, why is this such a disaster?"

Unfortunately, the military doesn't have much concept of irony, since the actual definition is so often the opposite of the literal definition of so many actions (a dynamic perfectly captured by Joseph Heller). But naming an outpost after a soldier whose very death exemplified why the outpost should not have been there in the first place? That would seem to qualify.

Why, then, did the camp remain where it was? One reason was that the commander who stopped using the roads for resupply, Lieutenant Colonel Chris Kolenda, led an effective force in the region. Although he and his lieutenants discussed moving the outpost up the mountain to a more secure location—as Observation Post Fritsche was; no one was killed there either on October 3, 2009, or before—Kolenda ultimately ruled that the relocation would have rendered his men more vulnerable than they already were. Perhaps that was a fair judgment at that juncture, given the command with which 1-91 Cav controlled its area of operations, but for a different unit, at a different time, under different leadership, the ruling could be second-guessed.

So why did the successful efforts of the 1-91 Cav ultimately prove so ephemeral? In part because, as is true of politics anywhere in the world, the tides of history in Nuristan were turned by individual leaders—men such as Fazal Ahad, who was killed in 2007; Lieutenant Colonel Kolenda and Captain Joey Hutto, who left Afghanistan in 2008; and Captain Rob Yllescas, who was killed later that same year. The vacuum Ahad left behind took time to be filled. Yllescas was never truly replaced; however hard Pecha may have worked, his predecessor's assassination had an impact on the way he led. It also, and perhaps even more significantly, drove a larger wedge between the troops of 6-4 Cav and the citizens of the surrounding area. As one Kamdesh resident told me in November 2011, Kamdeshis always felt stuck between the Americans and the insurgents; the one thing they knew for sure was that the latter would be there long after the former were gone.

And here, Lieutenant Colonel Brown's question becomes salient: Where was the Afghan government in all of this? Why didn't it at least try to fill the shoes of Ahad, the Hundred-Man Shura, Kolenda, Hutto, or Yllescas? And if there really was no Afghan capable of assuming a leadership role in Nuristan, then was America always destined to fail there, no matter how many Rob Yllescases were sacrificed at the altar of counterinsurgency? The innocent people of Nuristan and Kunar Province surely deserved better from their leaders.

All that I can tell you with certitude is that the men and women of 3-71 Cav, the 1-91 Cav, 6-4 Cav, and especially 3-61 Cav deserved better. They are heroes, and they have my appreciation and eternal gratitude. I wish they had a command structure and a civilian leadership that were always worthy of their efforts.

Glossary and Military Terms

Operational Units of the U.S. Army:

- Field Army (comprising three to five corps)
- Corps (two to five divisions)
- Division (four brigades, or approximately ten thousand to eighteen thousand soldiers)
- Battalion or Squadron (three to five companies, or five hundred to six hundred soldiers)
- Company or (for Cavalry) Troop (three to four platoons, or one hundred to two hundred soldiers)
- Platoon (three to four squads, or sixteen to forty soldiers)
- Squad (four to ten soldiers)

OFFICERS:

- General (four or five stars)
- Lieutenant General (three stars)
- Major General (two stars)
- Brigadier General (one star)
- Colonel
- Lieutenant Colonel
- Major
- Captain
- First Lieutenant
- Second Lieutenant

NONCOMMISSIONED:

- Sergeant Major of the Army
- Command Sergeant Major or Sergeant Major
- First Sergeant or Master Sergeant
- Sergeant First Class
- Staff Sergeant

- Sergeant
- Corporal or Specialist
- Private First Class
- Private E-2
- Private

1-32 Infantry — The 1st Battalion, 32nd Infantry Regiment, is part of the 3rd Brigade Combat Team of the 10th Mountain Division. The unit served in Regional Command East in 2006–2007 and again in 2009–2010.

1-91 Cav — The 1st Squadron, 91st Cavalry Regiment (Airborne), is a light airborne reconnaissance squadron based out of Schweinfurt, Germany, and part of the 173rd Airborne Brigade, based out of Italy. Bulldog Troop was assigned to Combat Outpost Keating from 2007 to 2008.

3-61 Cav — The 3rd Squadron, 61st Cavalry Regiment, is part of the 4th Brigade Combat Team, 4th Infantry Division, based out of Fort Carson, Colorado. Black Knight Troop was assigned to Combat Outpost Keating in 2009.

3-71 Cav — The 3rd Squadron, 71st Cavalry Regiment, is part of the 10th Mountain Division, based out of Fort Drum, New York. Able Troop was assigned to Combat Outpost Keating (then known as PRT Kamdesh or Combat Outpost Kamdesh) in 2006, after Barbarian and Cherokee Troops had helped establish the outpost.

6-4 Cav — The 6th Squadron, 4th Cavalry Regiment, is part of the 3rd Brigade, 1st Infantry Division, and was at the time based out of Fort Hood, Texas. Blackfoot Troop was assigned to Combat Outpost Keating in 2008.

10th Mountain Division — a light infantry division of the U.S. Army designed for quick deployment and harsh conditions, based out of Fort Drum, New York, and assigned to Regional Command East in 2006–2007.

A-10 Warthog — a single-seat straight-wing jet aircraft with superior maneuverability at low speeds and low altitudes, designed specifically to provide close air support for troops on the ground. The Army says Warthogs are primarily used for the cannon on the front, but the aircraft has the ability to be outfitted with precision munitions.

Afghan Border Police (ABP) — a division of the Afghan National Police that is responsible for securing the country's more than thirty-four hundred miles of borders as well as its airports, and also for overseeing immigration. As of 2009, the ABP boasted some twelve thousand troops.

Afghan National Army (ANA) — the primary military branch of the Afghan government, supervised by the Ministry of Defense in Kabul. Training ANA soldiers has been one of the greatest challenges of the war for the coalition, and statistics regarding precise troop strength and ability have proved to be extremely unreliable. As of 2009, there were roughly ninety thousand ANA soldiers.

Afghan National Police (ANP) — the national police force of the Afghan government, supervised by the Ministry of Interior in Kabul. As of 2009, there were approximately ninety-three thousand Afghan police.

Al Qaeda—a global network of Muslim extremists that uses terrorist tactics to try to defeat countries and governments that its leaders consider to be evil. Al Qaeda leaders, in particular Osama bin Laden, planned the 9/11 attacks on the United States while living in Afghanistan.

Apache—The four-blade, two-rotor, two-engine Boeing AF-64 Apache helicopter is the U.S. Army's primary attack helicopter and has been compared to a "flying tank." It is typically armed with a 30-millimeter M230 chain gun, Hellfire missiles, and Hydra rockets and manned by a two-person crew consisting of a pilot and a copilot/gunner.

AT4—a recoilless antitank weapon that fires 84-millimeter rockets.

B-1—The Boeing B-1 long-range heavy bomber airplane has a wingspan of 137 feet extended forward, is 146 feet long and 34 feet high, and can fly at speeds of more than nine hundred miles per hour. A B-1 can carry dozens of five-hundred- and two-thousand-pound bombs, Quick Strike naval mines, cluster munitions, joint air-to-surface standoff missiles, and other weapons. The B-1 requires a four-person crew consisting of an aircraft commander, a copilot, and two weapon systems officers.

B-2—The Northrop Grumman B-2 Spirit, aka the Stealth Bomber, has a wingspan of 172 feet and is 69 feet long and 17 feet high. The B-2 can travel at high subsonic speeds while carrying either conventional or nuclear weapons. It requires a two-pilot crew.

bandah—a small shack, typically used by sheep- and goat-herders and consisting of a crude stone shelter for the herder and a separate pen for his animal.

Black Hawk—The Sikorsky UH-60 Black Hawk is a utility transport helicopter designed to move a fully equipped eleven-person infantry squad under most weather conditions. It requires a crew of four—two pilots and two crew chiefs—and carries two 7.62-millimeter machine guns.

CAS—"close air support," describing helicopter or plane support for ground troops in contact with hostile forces.

Chinook—The Boeing CH-47 Chinook helicopter is a big twin-engine chopper with two rotors. Generally used to transport ground forces, supplies, ammunition, and other cargo, it is large enough to carry two Humvees. Two pilots and an observer can sit in the cockpit—flying a Chinook requires a pilot, copilot, and another crew member—while the main cabin can hold thirty-three troops in full gear. A Chinook can accommodate three machine guns and has a triple hook system under its belly to carry large external loads. Its normal cruising speed is 149 miles per hour, but it can travel as fast as 184 miles per hour.

Claymore—An M18 Claymore antipersonnel mine measures roughly 8.5 inches wide by 3.25 inches high by 1.5 inches thick and weighs 3.5 pounds. When triggered, the C-4 explosive will propel seven hundred steel balls in the direction clearly indicated on the casing by the words "FRONT TOWARD ENEMY."

Combat Outpost Kamu—the name of Combat Outpost Lowell until 2007.

Combat Outpost Lowell—the outpost established in 2007 near the hamlet of Kamu, east of Combat Outpost Keating, before it was renamed in honor of Private First Class Jacob Lowell.

counterinsurgency—An effort to quell a rebellion or insurgency, the tactic of counterinsurgency (or "COIN") as applied in Afghanistan is based on separating the insurgency from the general population through a two-pronged approach: defeating the enemy militarily while at the same time winning over the rest of the population with a taste of some of the tangible results—schools, government, infrastructure—to be reaped from an alliance with the United States and the Afghan government.

Dushka—a Russian-made heavy antiaircraft machine gun, belt fed and mounted on a tripod. The name is elaborated from the acronym DShK, for "Degtyarev Shpagina Krupnokaliberny." Vasily Alekseyevich Degtyaryov and Georgi Shpagin designed the weapon; *Krupnokaliberny* means "large-caliber." In Russian, the word *dushka* means "sweetie."

embedded tactical trainer (ETT)—a trainer of Afghan troops who lives and works alongside his trainees.

F-15—a highly maneuverable tactical jet fighter armed with a 20-millimeter, six-barrel cannon with 940 rounds of ammunition, heat-seeking, short-range air-to-air missiles, and advanced medium-range air-to-air missiles. With a wingspan of 42.8 feet, the F-15 is 63.8 feet long and 18.5 feet high and can fly at speeds up to 1,875 miles per hour. The F-15A and F-15C require just one pilot; the F-15B, F-15D, and F-15E require two.

Forward Operating Base Bostick—the name of Forward Operating Base Naray from 2008 on. The base, located near Naray in northern Kunar Province, has served as squadron headquarters for troops in the area since 2006. Before that, it was used primarily by Army Special Forces.

Forward Operating Base Fenty—the name of Jalalabad Airfield from 2007 on, named in honor of Lieutenant Colonel Joseph Fenty.

Forward Operating Base Naray—the name of Forward Operating Base Bostick before it was renamed in honor of Captain Tom Bostick, who was killed in 2007.

HESCO—a wire mesh container with a thick fabric liner that can be filled with dirt and joined with others to form a portable, easily constructed barrier.

HIG—Hezb-e-Islami Gulbuddin, an Afghan political party/insurgency founded in the 1970s by Gulbuddin Hekmatyar. Many of the insurgents in Kamdesh District were affiliated with HIG.

Humvee—a "high-mobility multipurpose wheeled vehicle" (HMMWV), a four-wheel-drive vehicle used by the military.

IED—an "improvised explosive device," or homemade bomb, often used by insurgents to target U.S. vehicles.

Jalalabad Airfield—a U.S. base in the city of Jalalabad, Nangarhar Province, adjacent to the Pakistan border. It was renamed Forward Operating Base Fenty in honor of Lieutenant Colonel Joseph Fenty, who was killed in 2006.

Jingle truck—an ornately decorated truck, covered with chimes and paintings, usually belonging to a local private contractor; so named because of the sound made by the decorations.

Kom—the preeminent ethnic group in Kamdesh District.

Kushtozis—an ethnic group in Kamdesh District that has had a longstanding history of feuding with its rival community, the Kom.

LMTV—a "light medium tactical vehicle," a large military truck that can carry more than two tons of cargo.

LRAS—a "long-range advance scout" surveillance system, an expensive device that allows thermal-optical surveillance at a range of up to fifteen miles.

M16—a gas-operated, magazine-fed assault rifle that weighs slightly more than 7.0 pounds and measures 39.5 inches long.

M203—a single-shot, pump-action (sliding-barrel) grenade launcher, measuring 39.0 inches long and weighing 3.5 pounds when loaded with 40-millimeter grenades.

M240—a belt-fed, air-cooled, gas-operated, fully automatic machine gun measuring 49.0 inches long and weighing 27.6 pounds, capable of firing as many as two hundred rounds per minute in ten- to thirteen-round bursts.

M249—A lightweight, gas-operated, one-man portable automatic weapon measuring just over 40.0 inches long and weighing 16.5 pounds, the M249 is also called a SAW—short for "squad automatic weapon"—and can fire up to 750 rounds per minute. Two M249s are issued to each infantry squad.

M4—A gas-operated, magazine-fed, shoulder-fired rifle weighing more than 6.0 pounds and measuring almost 30.0 inches long, the M4 can fire up to 950 rounds per minute and is semiautomatic, firing in three-round bursts. A variant model, the M4A1, is fully automatic.

Mark 19, or MK19—A belt-fed automatic grenade launcher that shoots 40-millimeter grenade cartridges and is designed not to overheat even after prolonged firing, the Mark 19 is over 43.0 inches long and weighs 78.0 pounds without its tripod. Because of its size, the Mark 19 is often mounted on a Humvee.

Mawlawi—an honorific title bestowed upon high-ranking Islamic scholars.

medevac—short for "medical evacuation," the term used to denote the helicopter ambulance that rescues wounded soldiers in the field.

MICH ranger headset—the modular integrated communication helmet (MICH) ranger communication system is a microphone/sound-transmission setup that enables communication even amid extremely noisy conditions such as intense combat.

mIRC—an Internet relay chat (IRC) client for Microsoft Windows, much like Instant Messenger, used by the military (and others) for instant communications.

mortar—an explosive projectile fired indirectly from a cannon, or tube. Mortars can be used to fire at targets that are both out of sight and far away—for example, over mountains.

MRE—a "meal ready to eat," a single unit of basic rations provided to troops by the U.S. military.

mullah—an Islamic clergyman or leader of a mosque.

mujahideen—Literally meaning "Muslims who strive in the path of God," the Arabic term has come to mean "holy warriors," a catchall for Islamist insurgents or fighters. In Afghanistan in the 1980s, the mujahideen comprised a number of loosely affiliated insurgent groups fighting the Communist Afghan government and the occupying USSR troops. In modern-day Afghanistan, many insurgent groups refer to themselves by this word, and some U.S. troops use it, or its short form *muj,* to refer to them as well.

Observation Post Fritsche—the observation post established to watch over Combat Outpost Keating, sitting on the mountain to the south of the outpost, near Upper Kamdesh.

Observation Post Warheit—the name of Observation Post Fritsche until the name was changed in the winter of 2007–2008 in honor of Staff Sergeant Ryan Fritsche.

PRT—a "Provincial Reconstruction Team," typically made up of representatives of the U.S. military, foreign service officers, and experts on construction, who work together on development in those areas of a country where stability is most urgently needed. PRTs have played a key role in counterinsurgency programs.

QRF—a "quick reaction force," an armed team prepared, on short notice, to support another unit on a mission and in need of assistance.

Regional Command East—one of the territories of Afghanistan as divided up by the United States and coalition forces. RC-East was formed in 2006 and comprised fourteen provinces—Bamyan, Ghazni, Kapisa, Khowst, Kunar, Laghman, Logar, Nangarhar, Nuristan, Paktika, Paktiya, Panjshayr, Parwan, and Wardak—covering 43,000 square miles (about the size of Virginia) and sharing 450 miles of border with Pakistan. Initially, Kapisa, Parwan, and Panjshayr provinces had no combat brigades assigned, only PRTs, hence when Nicholson took over the region in early 2006, he only thought of himself as being in charge of eleven provinces. All fourteen provinces were considered part of RC-East when NATO/ISAF assumed responsibility for the entire region later that year.

RPG—a "rocket-propelled grenade," an explosive warhead affixed to a rocket shot from a shoulder-fired weapon.

SAW—See M249.

shura—a consultation with village elders, or leaders, that is an important element of governance in majority Muslim countries.

Sked—a hard plastic stretcher used for carrying dead or wounded troops. Troops commonly refer to the stretcher by the name of the company that makes it, "Skedco."

TacSat—a tactical microsatellite system enabling sophisticated communications on the battlefield.

Taliban—an extremist militant Muslim political and religious group that ruled over much of Afghanistan from 1996 until the U.S. invasion in October 2001, imposing strict interpretations of Muslim law.

TIC—"troops in contact," meaning a firefight.

Notes and Sourcing

For this book, I interviewed more than 225 individuals over the course of nearly two years, many of them multiple times. Some of those interviews were conducted in person, some by phone, some via Skype, and some by email. I have made use of primary documents, where noted; throughout, I have employed the term "memo" to mean any military document, though technically, different kinds have their own complicated names.

Many of those with firsthand experiences of the events related here were invited to read sections of the manuscript to double- and triple-check passages for accuracy. I have chosen not to list sources in the military by their rank because such titles are ephemeral.

Although most of the information presented in this book comes from firsthand interviews and Army documents, I have drawn from some other sources as well. Specific citations are listed in the endnotes for individual chapters, but additional books not listed below on which I relied for general information and inspiration included the following:

- Adamec, Ludwig, and Frank Clements. *Conflict in Afghanistan: An Encyclopedia.* Santa Barbara, California: ABC-CLIO, Inc., 2003.
- Barrington, Nicholas, Joseph Kendrick, and Reinhard Schlagintweit. *A Passage to Nuristan.* London: I. B. Tauris, 2006.
- Bowden, Mark. *Black Hawk Down: A Story of Modern War.* New York: Grove, 1999.
- Cloud, David, and Greg Jaffe. *The Fourth Star: Four Generals and the Epic Struggle for the Future of the United States Army.* New York: Crown, 2009.
- Grau, Lester, ed. *The Bear Went over the Mountain: Soviet Combat Tactics in Afghanistan.* Fort Leavenworth, Kansas: National Defense University Press Publications, 2005.
- Hankin, Erin, and Steven Jeffrey. "Challenges of Treating Modern Military Trauma Wounds." *Wounds International,* May 2011.
- Harnden, Toby. *Dead Men Risen: The Welsh Guards and the Real Story of Britain's War in Afghanistan.* London: Quercus, 2011.
- Herr, Michael. *Dispatches.* New York: Vintage, 1991.
- Jalali, Ali Ahmad, and Lester Grau. *The Other Side of the Mountain: Mujahideen Tactics in the Soviet-Afghan War.* Fort Leavenworth, Kansas: Books Express, 2010.
- Junger, Sebastian. *WAR.* New York: Twelve, 2010.
- Krakauer, Jon. *Where Men Win Glory: The Odyssey of Pat Tillman.* New York: Doubleday, 2009.

- Marlantes, Karl. *Matterhorn: A Novel of the Vietnam War.* New York: Atlantic Monthly Press, 2010.
- Marlantes, Karl. *What It Is Like to Go to War.* New York: Atlantic Monthly Press, 2011.
- Moore, Lieutenant General Harold (Retired), and Joseph Galloway. *We Were Soldiers Once...and Young: Ia Drang—The Battle That Changed the War in Vietnam.* New York: Random House, 1992.
- Naylor, Sean. *Not a Good Day to Die: The Untold Story of Operation Anaconda.* New York: Berkley, 2005.
- O'Brien, Tim. *The Things They Carried.* New York: Broadway, 1998.
- Raddatz, Martha. *The Long Road Home: A Story of War and Family.* New York: Penguin, 2007.
- Stewart, Rory. *The Places in Between.* New York: Harcourt, 2004.
- Strand, Richard. Nuristan website: http//:www.nuristan.info.
- Tanner, Stephen. *Afghanistan: A Military History from Alexander the Great to the War Against the Taliban.* Philadelphia: Da Capo, 2009.
- Woodward, Bob. *Obama's Wars.* New York: Simon & Schuster, 2010.

Sources for Book One

For book 1, the following individuals were interviewed:

Nick Anderson
Kevin Jonathan "Johnny" Aruajo
Ross Berkoff
Terry Best
Adam Boulio
Rhonda Bradbury, mother of Brian Bradbury
Frank Brooks
Michael Callegan, father-in-law of Buddy Hughie
Chris Cavoli
Moises Cerezo
Matt Chambers
Jenny Claiborn, sister of Buddy Hughie
Dennis Cline
Matthew Cole, then of Salon.com, who was generous enough to share with me some of his recordings as well as his thoughts about his time embedded with 3-71 Cav
Ryan Coulter
Judy Craig, widow of Heathe Craig
Chris Cunningham
Darian Decker
Pat Donahue
Karl Eikenberry
Tony Feagin
Kristen Fenty, widow of Joe Fenty
David Fisher
Adones Flores
Benjamin Freakley
Matt Gooding

Chris Grzecki
Jason Guthrie
Matt Hall
John Hawes
Scott Heintzelman, brigade operations officer for Colonel Mick Nicholson
Michael Hendy
Mike Howard
Erik Jorgensen
David Katz, U.S. State Department
Beth Keating, mother of Ben Keating
Ken Keating, father of Ben Keating, who like his wife, Beth, was incredibly generous in sharing with me their son's emails and letters home, which helped me explain his point of view. Thoughts attributed to Ben were either expressed in letters or stated to individuals who relayed those thoughts to me.
Dustin Kittle
Jessica Lewis, sister of Ben Keating
Daniel Linnihan
Heather McDougal, girlfriend of Ben Keating
Tim Martin
William Metheny
Matt Meyer
Dr. Gerald Meyerle, a research analyst in CNA's Stability and Development Program. Meyerle is one of three authors of *Counterinsurgency on the Ground in Afghanistan: How Different Units Adapted to Local Conditions*, published by CNA in November 2010.
Charlee Miller, mother of Joe Fenty
Brian Molby
Paul Monti, father of Jared Monti
Matt Netzel
John "Mick" Nicholson, Jr.
Javid Nuristani
Tamim Nuristani
Cheryl Lee Nussberger, mother of Pat Lybert (now Cheryl Lee Patrick)
Shawn Passman
Aaron Pearsall
Nick Pilozzi
Terry Raynor
Josh Renken
Jeremiah Ridgeway
Kevin Roland, who knew Buddy Hughie from the Oklahoma National Guard
Donald Rozman, who investigated the helicopter crash that caused the death of Lieutenant Colonel Fenty and nine others
Jessica Saenz
Michael Schmidt
Adam Sears
Steve Snyder (not his real name)
James Avant Smith
Sean Smith

Pete Stambersky
Jesse Steele
Richard Strand, Nuristan expert
Dennis Sugrue
Thom Sutton
Aaron Swain
Richard Timmons
Gretchen Timmons, wife of Richard Timmons
Unnamed Special Forces officers
Tracy Vaillancourt, mother of Brian Moquin, Jr.
Jason Westbrook
Jeffrey Williams
Dave Young

Everyone I interviewed informed the book in some way, even if he or she is not specifically cited in the chapter-by-chapter endnotes that follow.

Prologue: Focus

Information about the conversation between Whittaker and Lockner came from interviews with both men. For more on Whittaker, please see his own book at www.lulu.com/spotlight/jacobwhittaker.

Donahue's thoughts about Nuristan were expressed in an interview with him.

David Katz and Richard Strand were both incredibly helpful sources not only for the prologue but for the entire book. Their expertise about Nuristan may be unparalleled in the Western world.

Interviews with Nicholson and Warheit also informed this chapter.

"The Man Who Would Be King," by Rudyard Kipling, first appeared in *The Phantom Rickshaw and Other Eerie Tales* (part of the *Indian Railway Library*), published in 1888 by A. H. Wheeler & Co of Allahabad. The ebook version was posted in 2003 and may be downloaded through Project Gutenberg.

Information about the attack on Combat Outpost Keating was taken from the Army's investigation into the attack and the author's myriad interviews (see notes on book 3).

Note on "Allahu Akbar" from survey of religion scholars.

The quotes from insurgents came from videos of the attack posted on the Internet by enemy forces. They were translated by Javid Nuristani.

Chapter 1: Every Man an Alexander

Memories of Mefloquine nightmares were recounted by many interviewees. In 2009, the Army issued a policy directive listing the drug as the third choice to combat malaria. See Patricia Kime, "New Concerns Rising over Antimalaria Drug," *Army Times,* April 11, 2012.

Information about the convoys came from interviews with Berkoff, Decker, Gooding, Johnson, and Pilozzi. Ken Keating and Heather McDougal shared emails and photographs from Ben.

Information about the attacks in March 2006 came from the Pentagon's public-affairs office and news accounts.

Information about Ben Keating's thoughts and past came from his family and his emails home.

The quote "...allies and enemies were often indistinguishable until it was too late" is from Frank Holt, *Into the Land of Bones: Alexander the Great in Afghanistan* (Berkeley: University of California Press, 2005).

The Spartan mother's admonition to her son to return "with your shield or on it" originated in an essay by Plutarch, "Sayings of Spartan Women," which was included in his miscellany *Moralia:* "Another, as she handed her son his shield, exhorted him, saying, 'Either this or upon this.'" In 2003, a fact-checker for "The Straight Dope" column and website investigated how likely it was that the anecdote was historically accurate, given that Plutarch was not writing contemporaneously with the Spartans' era of military glory. He ultimately concluded that the quote was "anecdotal, uncorroborated, and far removed from the source" but nevertheless "plausible" ("The Straight Dope," September 23, 2003).

Information about Nicholson's views and background came from multiple interviews with him.

The fact that briefings often relied on Wikipedia references was taken from 3-71 Cav background materials obtained by author.

The statement "I changed my mind" can be found in George W. Bush, *Decision Points* (New York: Random House, 2010). President Bush spoke at the Virginia Military Institute on April 17, 2002. The quote "had a strategic interest in helping the Afghan people build a free society" is also taken from *Decision Points.*

The strategy for 3-71 was related in interviews with Donahue, Nicholson, Berkoff, Timmons, and Eikenberry.

The stories about Keating at a U.S. base and then in a marketplace were related in emails written by Keating in May 2006. The base was then a PRT in Jalalabad and is now a U.S. base called Forward Operating Base Finley-Shields, mentioned on p. 485.

The map, drawn by the author, is based on information from the "Afghanistan Facilities 2006" map by the Defense Logistics Agency.

Chapter 2: "Major Joe Fenty, Hard Worker"

Information about Fenty's convoy came from an interview with Berkoff.

Biographical information about Fenty was taken from interviews with Kristen Fenty, Miller, and Cavoli.

Biographical information about and emails from Berkoff were provided by Berkoff.

Information about HIG was provided by Berkoff, Strand, and Katz.

George Crile's *Charlie Wilson's War: The Extraordinary Story of the Largest Covert Operation in History* was published in 2003 by the Atlantic Monthly Press, New York.

Michael Crowley, "Our Man in Kabul? The Sadistic Afghan Warlord Who Wants to Be Our Friend," *New Republic,* March 9, 2010.

"U.S. Bombing Raid in North Afghanistan 'Targeted Fugative Hekmatyr,'" Agence France Presse, December 13, 2003.

Information about and emails to and from Fenty were provided by Kristen Fenty; further information came from interviews with Byers and Cavoli.

The map, drawn by the author, is based on information from the United Nations' Development Programme and Afghanistan Information Management Services.

Chapter 3: Like Just Another Day on the Range

Information about 3-71 Cav's arrival at Forward Operation Base Naray came primarily from interviews with Snyder, Stambersky, and Berkoff.

As mentioned, one useful book on Operation Redwing is Marcus Luttrell and Patrick Robinson, *Lone Survivor: The Eyewitness Account of Operation Redwing and the Lost Heroes of SEAL Team 10* (New York: Little, Brown, 2007).

Information about Nuristan and Kunar Provinces, and Afghanistan in general, came from many sources, including Katz and Strand as well as Richard Strand, *Nuristan Provincial Handbook: A Guide to the People and the Province,* ed. Nick Dowling and Tom Praster (Arlington, Virginia: IDS International, 2009). Additional information came from Jerry Meyerle, Megan Katt, and Jim Gavrilis, *Counterinsurgency on the Ground in Afghanistan: How Different Units Adapted to Local Conditions* (CNA Stability and Development Program, November 2010).

Information on the problematic borders was provided by Berkoff and Strand as well as by Joshua Foust, "Sub-National Administrative Boundary Discrepancies in Eastern Afghanistan," *Cultural Knowledge Report*, August 7, 2008, Human Terrain System–Research Reachback Center.

Information about the insurgent attack on the three Marines came from an interview with the one survivor, Brian Molby.

Accounts of the mission in the Kotya Valley were provided by myriad interviewees, including Berkoff, Swain, Byers, Hawes, Cunningham, and Fisher.

George Scott Robertson's book *The Kafirs of the Hindu Kush* was first published in 1896, in London, by Lawrence & Bullen.

Information about the Dawlat was taken from Daan Van Der Schriek, "Nuristan: Insurgent Hideout in Afghanistan," *Terrorism Monitor* 3:10 (May 2006), published by the Jamestown Foundation of Washington, D.C., as well as from Barnett Rubin, *The Fragmentation of Afghanistan,* 2nd ed. (New Haven, Connecticut: Yale University Press, 2002).

Information about ethnic groups, as well as other details about the people of Nuristan, came from the aforementioned *Nuristan Provincial Handbook: A Guide to the People and the Province,* plus Strand and Katz.

Information on the presentation by the Foreign Military Studies Office at Fort Leavenworth was provided by 3-71 Cav officers.

Chapter 4: War, Fate, and Wind

Descriptions of the mountaintop landing were provided by Pilozzi, Netzel, and Gooding.

Information about the Korangal Valley came from Nicholson, Katz, Strand, and Berkoff.

Information about Moquin and Netzel came from Netzel and from Vaillancourt, Moquin's mother, who also shared the letter he wrote her.

Details about the hike were gathered from interviews with Hendy, Larson, Netzel, and Passman.

Details about the flora and fauna of the region came from interviews with troops from all four years covered in this book, as well as from *Wildlife Surveys and Wildlife Conservation in Nuristan, Afghanistan, Including Scat and Small Rodent Collection from Other Sites,* published in August 2008 by the Wildlife Conservation Society/United States Agency for International Development, Afghanistan Biodiversity Conservation Program.

Kristen Fenty provided the auther with her late husband's notebook.

Information about the operation at Chalas was provided by Brooks and Jorgensen.

Accounts of Fenty's conversations were provided by Kristen Fenty and Nicholson. Information about Kristen's delivery came from her and Miller.

The story of the LRAS incident that Keating investigated is drawn from Keating's "Memorandum for the Record: AR 15-6 Investigation Concerning the Destruction of LRAS, Serial Number: 0582, on Abbas Ghar Ridge," obtained by the author, and from letters Keating wrote to his father describing his feelings about the matter.

With a script by Iva Hoth and illustrations by Andre Le Blanc, *The Picture Bible* was published by David C. Cook in 1978.

Keating's conversations were drawn from his emails home as well as from interviews with Beth Keating and Timmons.

Chapter 5: "This Whole Thing Is a Bad Idea"

Accounts of the Chalas operation were provided by Brooks, Jorgensen, Netzel, and Berkoff.

Details about the helicopter crash were drawn from the Army's investigation into the incident, as well as from interviews with Nicholson, Metheny, Rozman, Berkoff, Timmons, Brooks, Pilozzi, Cavoli, and Sears. The comments that Task Force Centaur's commanders had done the troops "an injustice by sending them to war before they were ready," that the "proficiency of crew members is not up to standards," and that the Task Force was "at best marginally prepared to conduct air operations" in Afghanistan were taken from the report on the Army's investigation into the helicopter crash.

Descriptions of the conversation between Joe and Kristen Fenty were provided in interviews with Kristen Fenty and Miller.

Chapter 6: Maybe That's Just the Wind Blowing the Door

The aftermath of the accident was described by Brooks, Pilozzi, Timmons, and Nicholson. Information about thermal imaging and other details came from the report on the Army's investigation into the crash, obtained by the author.

The account of Kristen Fenty's hearing the news came from interviews with her, Richard and Gretchen Timmons, Nicholson, and Howard.

The emails from Ben Keating were provided by his father.

Chapter 7: Monuments to an Empire's Hubris

Information about the plans to go to Kamdesh District and the meeting with the Kamdesh elders was taken from interviews with Swain, Snyder, Howard, Fisher, Byers, Timmons, and Berkoff.

The differences between Donahue's and Nicholson's views were extrapolated from interviews with both men.

Biographical information about Tamim Nuristani came from an interview with him.

Information about Snyder's mission and subsequent ambush was provided in interviews with Snyder, Swain, Howard, Fisher, and Nicholson.

Information on the village-hopping plan was furnished by Howard and Berkoff. Details about the specific mission to Hill 2610 came from interviews with Howard, Flores, Schmidt, Brooks, Cunningham, and Grzecki.

Information on the illegal timber industry came from Yaroslav Trofimov, "Taliban Capitalize On Afghan Logging Ban," *Wall Street Journal,* April 10, 2010, in addition to interviews with Lieutenant Colonel Chris Kolenda (source for book 2) and Lieutenant Colonel Brad Brown (source for books 2 and 3).

Information about Jared Monti was shared by his father, Paul Monti.

Chapter 8: Hill 2610

Information about the mission to Hill 2610 came from the Army investigation into the incident, as well as from interviews with Howard, Flores, Cunningham, Paul Monti, Hawes, Garner, Grzecki, Chambers, Smith, Linnihan, and Berkoff.

Information about Pat Lybert was provided by his mother, Cheryl Lee Nussberger (now Cheryl Lee Patrick).

Paul Monti expressed his thoughts during an interview.

Information about Brian Bradbury came from an interview with his mother, Rhonda Bradbury, and from a conversation he had with Garner.

Information about Heathe Craig was gleaned from an interview with his widow, Judy.

Details about the aftermath of the operation at Hill 2610 were taken from interviews with Nicholson, Howard, Berkoff, and Schmidt.

The map, drawn by the author, is based on information from Cunningham, Garner, Grzecki, and Hawes, as well as after-action reports.

Chapter 9: "This Will Happen to You"

Information about the issues with the road came from an interview with Sugrue.

Whittaker recalled his concerns during an interview.

Information about the air assault onto Landing Zone Warheit was provided in interviews with Schmidt, Johnson, and Howard.

Information about projects in the area was gathered from interviews with Schmidt, Howard, Sugrue, Snyder, and Lang. Other information was taken from *The National Risk and Vulnerability Assessment 2005,* published by the Afghan Ministry of Rural Rehabilitation and Development and the Central Statistics Office.

Information about medical aid for locals came from Schmidt, Johnson, and Araujo, as well as from ISAF cables about the incidents.

Information about Yunus and his murder was derived from interviews with Nicholson and Sugrue, Keating's letters, intelligence sources, and ISAF cables.

Some information about the development projects was taken from Scott Peterson, "In Afghanistan, U.S. Troops Tackle Aid Projects–and Skepticism," *Christian Science Monitor,* October 2, 2006; and idem, "Spinning Pop Tunes to Beat the Taliban," *Christian Science Monitor,* October 4, 2006.

Chapter 10: The Abstract Threat of Terror

Brooks's view of the outpost was conveyed in an interview with him.

The patrol up the hill to Kamdesh was described in interviews with Howard, Feagin, Johnson, Larson, Araujo, Howe, and Raynor.

Netzel described the patrol with Keating in an interview, and Keating wrote home about his experiences in letters shared by his father.

Chapter 11: The Enemy Gets a Vote

Information about the September 11, 2006, ambush came from interviews with Cline, Passman, Saenz, Boulio, Cerezo, and Netzel.

Information about the meeting between Gooding and Howard was taken from interviews with them.

Information on adrenaline was taken from Dave Grossman and Bruce K. Siddle, "Psychological Effects of Combat," Academic Press, 2000, and David Swink, "Adrenaline Rushes: Can They Help Us Deal with a Real Crisis?" *Psychology Today's* "Threat Management" blog, January 31, 2010.

Keating's thoughts and remarks were excerpted from letters and emails to his father and to Gooding.

Information about the visit to Mandigal was provided in interviews with Saenz and Boulio.

Information about tensions between Keating and Gooding was taken from letters from Keating to his parents and interviews with Gooding.

Matthew Cole, "Watching Afghanistan Fall," Salon.com, February 27, 2007.

Information about the shura came from interviews with Gooding, Feagin, Boulio, and Cole.

Collateral-damage information was provided by Sears, Anderson, Hendy, Bozman, and Gooding.

Stambersky provided information about the ambush on his convoy, as did Berkoff and Gooding.

The account of the shift from PRT to outpost is based on interviews with Nicholson, Howard, Feagin, Berkoff, and Gooding.

Chapter 12: Matthias the Macedonian and the LMTV

Information about Howard's order to drive the LMTV to the Kamdesh outpost came from Stambersky, Brooks, Berkoff, Sutton, and Gooding. When asked about it, Howard himself said he had no recollection of giving the order.

Information about the LMTV convoy to the outpost was provided by Stambersky, Williams, Brooks, Martin, Steele, and Coulter.

Information about the situation at the outpost upon Keating's return came from interviews with Mathis, Gooding, Westbrook, and Ridgeway.

Keating's "you do the math" quote appeared in Cole's *Salon* story.

Steven Pressfield, *The Afghan Campaign* (New York: Broadway, 2006).

Keating's feelings about being a liar were expressed in a letter home.

Information about the LMTV's being parked at the Kamdesh outpost and about Keating's decision to drive it to Forward Operating Base Naray came from interviews with Stambersky, Williams, Netzel, Cerezo, Johnson, and Gooding, and also from a copy of the report of the Army's investigation into the LMTV rollover, obtained by the author.

Information about the LMTV's rollover came from interviews with Cunningham, Gooding, Cerezo, Netzel, Mathis, and Garner, and also from the report of the Army's investigation into the incident.

The instant messages between Keating and McDougal were shared by McDougal.

The description of Ken and Beth Keating's hearing about their son's death came from interviews with them.

Chapter 13: The 7-31

Information about winter at the outpost came from interviews with Gooding, Hendy, Cerezo, Sears, and Anderson.

Information about the ANA and its trainers was drawn from interviews with Best and Gooding.

Information about Buddy Hughie came from Best and from Hughie's sister, Claiborn.

Information about the meeting with Governor Nuristani was provided by Nuristani and Nicholson, as well as by a memo about it obtained by the author.

The saga of Fazal Ahad was related in interviews with Nicholson, Gooding, and Berkoff, and also in ISAF memos obtained by the author.

Information about the tour's being extended was taken from interviews with Howard, Brooks, Berkoff, Jorgensen, and Eikenberry.

Eikenberry's comments on the "violent spring" appeared in Robert Burns, "U.S. Commander Wants to Extend Some Combat Tours in Afghanistan as Violence Intensifies," Associated Press, January 17, 2007.

Information about the memorial service was gleaned from a video of the service provided to the author.

Ken and Beth Keating expressed their reservations in interviews.

Chapter 14: Buddy

Information about the mission to save this young Afghan man came from interviews with Gooding, Boulio, Johnson, Best, Claiborn, Roland, and Hall.

The text of the night letter was taken from an ISAF memo obtained by the author.

Information about the murder of Fazal Ahad came from Nuristani, Nicholson, Howard, and Gooding, as well as Army memos obtained by the auther.

Remarks from the dedication of FOB Fenty were included in a staff report published in *Army Times,* May 7, 2007.

Chapter 15: "Don't Go Down That Way"

Information about the commando mission at Kamdesh Village came from interviews with Nuristani, Nicholson, Paparo, Howard, Gooding, Hall, and Schmidt.

Information about the ambush on the ANA troops came from Best, Pearsall, Steele, Sears, Anderson, McHugh, Kittle, and Guthrie.

The comments made by Abdul Raouf were reported by Kim Barker of the *Chicago Tribune* on May 13, 2007.

Information about Gooding's and Berkoff's departures was drawn from interviews with them.

Sources for Book Two

For the section of book 2 dealing with 1-91 Cav, the following individuals were interviewed:

Wayne Baird
Bert Baker
Nic Barnes

Bobby Bostick, brother of Tom Bostick
Carrie Bostick, aunt of Tom Bostick
Robert Cusick
Chris Doneski
Nicholas Dubaz
John Faulkenberry
Sarah Faulkenberry, wife of John Faulkenberry
Rob Fortner
Frank Helmick
Hank Hughes
Joey Hutto
Scott Ingbretsen
Kenneth Johnson
Brandon Kennedy
Chris Kolenda
Jennifer Lowell-Hetfleisch, sister of Jacob Lowell
Kyle Marcum
Nick McGarry
John McHugh
Bryan Morrow
Alex Newsom
Matthew O'Neill, then with HBO, who was embedded with 6-4 Cav and was generous
    enough to show me some of his footage
William Ostlund
Sam Paparo
Chip Preysler
Jesse Queck
Shamsur Rahman
Brenda Keeler Bostick Richardson, mother of Tom Bostick
Jim Richardson, Tom Bostick's stepfather since 1983
Dave Roller
Nate Springer
Jonathan Sultan
Stan Trapyline
Unnamed Special Forces soldiers
John Wilson

For the section of book 2 concerned with 6-4 Cav, the following individuals were interviewed:

Ryan Bodmer
Steven Brewer
Chris Briley
Brad Brown
Andrew Bundermann
Ronald Burton
Chris Cordova
Amanda Cuda
Randy George

Adam Laman
Tom Nelson
Jim Markert
Joe Mazzocchi
Kaine Meshkin
Donald Parsons
Dan Pecha
Karen Pfeifer, widow of Chris Pfeifer
Chris Safulko
Shane Scherer
John Spiszer
Kyle Tucker
Rick Victorino (not his real name)
Red Walker (not his real name)
Jim Witherington
Dena Yllescas, widow of Rob Yllescas

Chapter 16: "There's Not Going to Be Any Ice Cream"

Information about the battle of Saret Koleh came from Roller, Newsom, Faulkenberry, Fortner, Wilson, Barnes, Baker, Morrow, Hutto, Kolenda, Sultan, Johnson, and Springer.

Information about Bostick's genealogy was provided by his family. Sion Record Bostick's recollections of the capture of Santa Anna were recorded in the *Quarterly of the Texas Historical Association,* October 1901. Accessed on the Texas A&M University website.

Information about Lowell came from his sister, Lowell-Hetfleisch, and Kolenda.

Information about the water-pipe project came from Kolenda and Springer. The phrase *"Zar, zan, zamin"* is said to have been popularized in the West by Louis Dupree's *Afghanistan* (Princeton, New Jersey: Princeton University Press, 1980). The 2011 study referred to in the footnote is, again, Paul Fishstein and Andrew Wilder's *Winning Hearts and Minds? Examining the Relationship between Aid and Security in Afghanistan* (Medford, Massachusetts: Feinstein International Center at Tufts University, 2011).

Chris Kolenda, *Leadership: The Warrior's Art* (Carlisle, Pennsylvania: Army War College Foundation Press, 2001).

The activities at Camp Kamu were described in interviews with Newsom, Faulkenberry, and Baird.

The discussion of what insurgents were called was informed by numerous interviews with troops who didn't want to be quoted using terms that their commanders would deem inappropriate.

Information about Ryan Fritsche came from interviews with his mother, Volitta Fritsche, as well as with Hutto. Another resource was Volitta's book, *Why Ryan?,* self-published in 2009.

Information about the interactions between Fritsche and Wilson was taken from interviews with Wilson and Barnes.

Chapter 17: "Bulldog-Six, Where Are You?"

Accounts of the battle of Saret Koleh were provided by Roller, Newsom, Faulkenberry, Fortner, Wilson, Barnes, Baker, Morrow, Hutto, Kolenda, Sultan, Johnson, and Springer.

The account of events at FOB Naray was drawn from interviews with Hutto and Doneski.

The story of Fritsche's family hearing the news of his death came from Volitta Fritsche and her book.

Information about the recovery operation came from interviews with Preysler, Ostlund, Hutto, Wilson, Morrow, Newsom, and Roller.

Chapter 18: Balloons

Information about Hutto came from an interview with him.

Information about Faulkenberry's recovery was provided in interviews with him and his wife, Sarah Faulkenberry.

Kolenda's decision to reduce the number of road missions was recounted in an interview with him.

Information about operations at the outpost during this period was gleaned from interviews with Hutto, Newsom, and Roller.

Information about Chris Pfeifer's wound and treatment came from interviews with his wife, Karen, Baker, and Newsom.

Information about training to become a medic was shared by Donald Parsons of the Department of Combat Medic Training at Fort Sam Houston.

Information about life at OP Warheit was taken from an interview with Roller.

Information about the meeting at Parun came from interviews with Paparo and Katz.

Kutto and Colenda's reaching the conclusion that the Americans were in the midst of an insurrection was related in interviews with both men.

Information about the August 2007 Ranch House attack was taken from interviews with Preysler and Ostlund. Additional information came from two investigations into the later Wanat incident that referenced the Ranch House: the Army's official "AR 15-6 Investigation Findings and Recommendations into the Incident at Wanat, August 13, 2008," and a second study by the staff of the U.S. Army Combat Studies Institute, entitled *Wanat: Combat Action in Afghanistan, 2008* (Fort Leavenworth, Kansas: Combat Studies Institute Press, 2010). Other details were taken from the Army public-affairs story "Sky Soldier Awarded Distinguished Service Cross," written by Staff Sergeant Brandon Aird, September 17, 2008, and from Keith Rogers, "Soldier's Courage Reigns Despite Being Outnumbered and Enemy within Meters," *Las Vegas Review-Journal*, July 4, 2010.

Dealings with locals were described in interviews with Roller, Hutto, Ingbretsen, Briley, and others.

Events at the September 6, 2007, shura were recounted in an ISAF memo obtained by the author.

A description of ghee was provided by Strand.

Marcum expressed his thoughts during an interview.

Information about Chris Pfeifer's final days was taken from interviews with his wife, Karen, Sarah and John Faulkenberry, and Baird.

Chapter 19: If You're the Enemy, Please Stand Up

Dealings with locals were described in interviews with Newsom, Roller, Hutto, and Kolenda, as well as in ISAF memos obtained by the author.

Information about the Mandigal shura was gleaned from interviews with Ingbretsen and Hutto.

Disagreements among brigade officers were recounted in interviews with Preysler, Kolenda, Ostlund, and other, anonymous individuals.

Disagreements between Hughes and Roller were described by the two men (who are now friends) as well as by Newsom and Johnson.

Information about the shots fired at the outpost, and Hutto's investigation into their source, was shared by Hutto in an interview.

Winter at Observation Post Fritsche was described by Marcum in an interview.

Information about the ambush at Gawardesh was provided by Cusick and Kolenda, as well as in the U.S. Army's narrative for the posthumous Medal of Honor awarded to Miller.

Information about Shabbaz was taken from ISAF memos obtained by the author and from an interview with Hutto.

Cusick and other Special Forces soldiers who preferred to remain anonymous described in interviews their conflict with Kolenda, and Kolenda offered his take on it, too. The plans for an "Operation Commando Justice" were detailed in an ISAF memo obtained by the author and also discussed on background by military officers and troops. Preysler and Kolenda weighed in on the mission's being scrubbed. Votel's comment when I recounted the events as they'd been related to me was, "This could have happened, but frankly I do not recall. I do know I would not have done something deliberate like that to the CJSOTF"—Combined Joint Special Operations Task Force—"since we had a very good relationship and had supported a number of their operations in Kunar and Nuristan with helicopters and other resources. This was probably a function of priorities if anything."

Hutto, Roller, and Kolenda provided information about the PowerPoint presentation.

Hutto and Kolenda shared information about the shuras. Memos obtained by the author also contained details about the Hundred-Man Shura.

Karzai's statement "The Taliban are not strong" was taken from C. J. Chivers, "Karzai Cites Taliban Shift to Terror Attacks," *New York Times,* June 20, 2007.

The attacks on the outpost were described by Kolenda, Hutto, Newsom, Roller, Hughes, Marcum, Briley, and others who were there, as well as in memos obtained by the author.

Chapter 20: "We Will Go to Kamdesh Next"

The attacks on the outpost were described by Kolenda, Hutto, Newsom, Roller, Hughes, Marcum, Briley, and others who were there, as well as in memos obtained by the author.

The incident involving Laman was recalled in interviews with Laman, Briley, and Roller.

The incident involving Marcum was described by him in an interview.

Hutto and Roller provided information about Cali.

Kolenda's comments about Bostick on the occasion of the renaming ceremony were included in Staff Sergeant Brandon Aird's Army public-affairs story "Afghanistan Base Renamed in Honor of Commander Who Died in Combat," July 11, 2008.

Information about the attack on Wanat came from interviews with Ostlund, Kennedy, and Queck, as well as several other sources: the Army's official "AR 15-6 Investigation Findings and Recommendations into the Incident at Wanat, August 13, 2008"; a study by the staff of the U.S. Army Combat Studies Institute, *Wanat: Combat Action in Afghanistan, 2008* (Fort Leavenworth, Kansas: Combat Studies Institute Press, 2010); and the first draft of the latter, U.S. Army Combat Studies Institute document. Other resources included Greg Jaffe, "The Battle of Wanat," *Washington Post,* October 4, 2009, and Mark Bowden, "Echoes from a Distant Battlefield," *Vanity Fair*, December 2011.

Information about 6-4 Cav's coming into Afghanistan was taken from interviews with Spiszer, Markert, and Nelson.

In interviews, Kolenda and Hutto described their farewell.

David Roller's email home was provided by him.

Chapter 21: Chess with No Rules

Biographical information about Rob Yllescas came from interviews with his widow, Dena, who also shared many of his emails and pictures home.

Details about Yllescas at the outpost were provided by Mazzocchi, Meshkin, Safulko, Tucker, Briley, Victorino, and others.

Details about various attacks on the outpost were offered by Mazzocchi, Meshkin, Safulko, Tucker, Briley, Victorino, and others.

Biographical information about Meshkin was taken from interviews with him.

Biographical information about Mazzocchi came from interviews with him.

The meeting with Abdul Rahman was described by Meshkin and also covered in a memo obtained by the author.

Victorino shared his thoughts in an interview. Information about the lowering Army standards from Eric Schmitt, "Army Recruiting More High School Dropouts to Meet Goals," *New York Times,* June 11, 2005; and Eric Rosenberg, "Criminal Past Less a Barrier for Army Enlistees," Hearst News Service, October 14, 2007. Jingle air crash information from memo obtained by author.

Briley related his thoughts in an interview.

Casualty information came from an ISAF memo obtained by the author.

Biographical information about Safulko was provided in interviews with him.

The incident involving Franklin was described by Meshkin.

Chapter 22: After He Finished Washing the Blood Off

Information about the October 13, 2008, shura was taken from an ISAF memo obtained by the author.

Information about the October 25, 2008, attack was provided in interviews with Mazzocchi, Tucker, Safulko, Meshkin, and Briley.

Information about the attack on Yllescas came from interviews with Tucker, Briley, Safulko, Mazzocchi, Walker, and Victorino.

Information about Yllescas's early medical treatment was furnished by Brewer and Cuda.

Information about the medevac that was sent to get Yllescas came from Spiszer, Markert, and Nelson.

Mazzocchi's interaction with the local man whose wife was wounded was described by Mazzocchi in an interview.

Information about Amin Shir came from an interview with Walker. Information regarding his current location was provided by Victorino.

Dena Yllescas described in several interviews how she learned of her husband's injury. She also contemporaneously expressed many of her thoughts and feelings in her blog at http://yllescasfamily.blogspot.com.

Mazzocchi's conversation with Commander Jawed was recalled by Mazzocchi in an interview.

The shura meeting was described in interviews with Meshkin, Mazzocchi, and Tucker.

Information about Pecha's assignment to the outpost was provided by Pecha in interviews.

Markert's feelings were expressed in interviews with the author and also relayed in a contemporaneous email to a fellow officer.

President Bush's bedside visit was described by Dena Yllescas; information was shared with his office. Bush's jog with Christian Bagge was reported in Richard Benedetto, "Amputee Iraq Vet Fulfills Wish, Jogs with Bush," *USA Today,* June 27, 2006.

Chapter 23: What Was Wrong with Kaine Meshkin

The November 2008 attacks on the outpost were described by Pecha, Meshkin, Mazzocchi, Safulko, and Tucker in interviews.

Information about Rob Yllescas's medical treatment was provided by his widow, Dena, in interviews and in her blog at http://yllescasfamily.blogspot.com.

The excerpt from "You Save Me" by Kenny Chesney, written by Brett James and Troy Verges, from Chesney's 2005 album *The Road and the Radio,* is used by permission.

The description of the craniotomy procedure was based on information from the website for the Mayfield Clinic for the Brain & Spine, http://www.mayfieldclinic.com/PE-Craniotomy.htm, and was reviewed by Ron Warnick, M.D., and Mary Haverbusch, R.N.

In interviews, Mazzocchi, Safulko, and Pecha shared information about the plans for the outpost after Yllescas's death.

Meshkin recalled his response to Yllescas's death in interviews. His interactions with Dena Yllescas were described by both of them.

Information about the plans made by George and Brown was offered by both men in interviews.

Brown's outreach to Kolenda and Pecha was recalled in interviews by all three men.

The attack statistics were provided in an ISAF memo obtained by the author.

Chapter 24: The Puppies

The January 2009 attacks on the outpost were described in interviews with Pecha, Meshkin, Mazzocchi, Safulko, and Tucker.

Information about the Kamdesh radio station was offered by Bodmer and Markert.

Details about President Obama's plans for Afghanistan were provided in official announcements by the President; in interviews with White House advisers Denis McDonough and Ben Rhodes, White House press secretary Robert Gibbs, and Pentagon spokesman Geoff Morrell; and by other, unnamed sources.

Mullen's and Gates's views of McKiernan were described by unnamed Pentagon sources.

Events at the February 15, 2009, shura were recounted in an ISAF memo obtained by the author.

Pecha and Tucker's meeting with the contractors was recalled by both men in interviews.

Information about the cost of various projects was furnished by an unnamed source.

Safulko told the story about the dogs turning and their subsequent end in an interview.

The unrealized plans for a new observation post, to be named after Yllescas, were described by Pecha, Markert, Spiszer, and Victorino.

Information about the attack on Bari Alai came from interviews with Spiszer and Markert. Pirtle's concerns, expressed to his parents, were first reported on HDNET's "Dan Rather

Reports: What Happened at Bari Alai," on September 12, 2011. Wade Zirkle of the Fox News Channel claimed on May 15, 2009, that the ISAF was investigating whether the ANA might have been involved.

The email from Brown was provided to the author by Brown.

The closure of COP Lybert was described in an interview with Spiszer and also in Michael Gisick, "Fateful Day Brings Post Back to War's Reality," *Stars and Stripes,* September 25, 2008. In an interview, Cheryl Lee Nussberger recalled her concern over the enemy's propaganda video about the closure of the base named after her son.

Chapter 25: Pericles in Kamdesh

Information about 3-71 Cav's arrival at the outpost was taken from interviews with Bundermann, Burton, and Cordova.

Safulko recalled his conversation with Kirk in an interview. Kirk's schedule was shared by his wife, Gavin-Kirk, in an interview. Information about Kirk during his time with 1-91 Cav came from interviews with Kolenda and Springer.

Thucydides, *The History of the Peloponnesian War,* translated by Richard Crawley (London: Dover, 2004).

Information about the attack that wounded Shane Scherer was gleaned from interviews with Scherer, Witherington, Cordova, and Safulko.

Sources for Book Three

A major source for the information presented in book 3 was the November 3, 2009, "AR 15-6 Investigation re: COP Keating Attack of 3 Oct 09 Department of the Army," by Major General Guy Swan III, along with its supporting documents, obtained by the author. These are collectively referred to as the "Swan report" below.

In addition, the following individuals were interviewed for book 3:

Jonathan Adams
Vanessa Adelson, mother of Stephan Mace
Armando Avalos
Kyle Barnes
Janpatrick Barroga
Jordan Bellamy
Kirk Birchfield
John Breeding
Brad Brown
Connie Brown, mother of Vernon Martin
Jory Brown
Shane Brown, a Burlington, North Carolina, police staff sergeant
Andrew Bundermann
Cashet Burks, girlfriend of Vernon Martin
Ronald Burton
Stephen Cady
Ty Carter
Dan Casey

Kerri Griffin Causley, mother of Chris Griffin
Christopher Chappell
Chris Cordova
Shane Courville
Martins Dabolins
Kevin Daise
Josh Dannelley
Nicholas Davidson
Noor Din
Seward Dinsmore, uncle of Josh Kirk
Mark Dulaney
Faruq (not his real name)
Ed Faulkner, Sr., father of Ed Faulkner, Jr.
Cody Floyd
John Francis
Jeremy Frunk
Megan Gavin-Kirk, widow of Josh Kirk
Randy George
Robert Gibbs
Robert Gilberto (not his real name)
Justin Gregory
Damien Grissette
Eric Harder
Olivia Hardt, widow of Josh Hardt
Mary Henry, mother of Eric Harder
Jon Hill
Robert Hull
Jeff Jacops
Greg Jaffe of the *Washington Post,* who was incredibly generous with his time, his impressions from the period when he was embedded with 3-61 Cav, and his reporting on the aftermath of the October 3, 2009, attack
Chris Jones
Kellen Kahn
Bernadette Kirk-Bonner, mother of Josh Kirk
Kyle Knight
Jeffrey Kology, a Burlington, North Carolina, police investigator
Zach Koppes
Janis Lakis
Brad Larson
Ross Lewallen
Amanda Marr, former wife of Justin Gallegos
Brittany Martin, widow of Vernon Martin
Stan McChrystal
Brendan McCriskin
Denis McDonough
Matthew McMurtrey
Aaron Miller

Sarah Faulkner Minor, sister of of Ed Faulkner, Jr.
Jake Miraldi
Geoff Morrell
Mark O'Donnell
Dante Paradiso
Melvin Porter
Stoney Portis
Ted Preister
Tom Rasmussen
Ben Rhodes
Daniel Rodriguez
Dan Rogers
Clint Romesha
Debbie Routson, mother of Kevin Thomson
Ben Salentine
Justin Sax
Mike Scaparrotti
Cason Shrode
Jayson Souter
James Stanley, Jr.
Keith Stickney
T. G. Taylor
Albert "Cookie" Thomas
Jessica Tingley, sister of Josh Kirk
Nick Paton Walsh
Stuart Webb
Rob Wilson
Jordan Wong
Cynthia Woodard, mother of Michael Scusa
Christopher Wright
Brad Zagol

Chapter 26: The General's Competing Considerations

Heraclitus' precise words, as quoted in G. T. W. Patrick's *Heraclitus of Ephesus: The Fragments of the Works of Heraclitus of Ephesus on Nature* (Chicago: Argonaut, 1969), were "Into the same river you could not step twice, for other <and still other> waters are flowing. To those entering the same river, other and still other waters flow." There have been various interpretations of this quote.

The description of Porter's command was drawn from interviews with Porter, Brown, and myriad troops and officers from 3-61 Cav, as well as from the Swan report.

Mullen's and Gates's views of McKiernan were passed along by unnamed Pentagon sources.

McKiernan's telling Gates, "You're going to have to fire me," was first reported in Rajiv Chandrasekaran, "Pentagon Worries Led to Command Change," *Washington Post,* August 17, 2009.

Gates's and Mullen's remarks were taken from a transcript of the May 11, 2009, press conference.

The assessments and views of McChrystal were taken from interviews with McChrystal and other, anonymous Pentagon officials and military officers.

The June 2, 2007, exchange between Senator Lindsey Graham and McChrystal was taken from a transcript of the hearings. This was first noted as a troubling moment for White House officials in Bob Woodward, *Obama's Wars* (New York: Simon & Schuster, 2010), a conclusion that was later confirmed by White House officials. McChrystal shared his views in an interview.

A certain wariness toward the White House in general and Vice President Biden's office in particular was reflected in interviews with anonymous Pentagon officials.

Greg Jaffe's interview with McChrystal ran in the *Washington Post* on June 16, 2009, and was entitled "Gen. McChrystal, New Afghanistan Commander, Will Review Troop Placements." Woodward's story appeared on July 1, 2009, also in the *Washington Post,* under the headline "U.S. Says Key to Success in Afghanistan Is Economy, Not Military."

Plans for the closure of COP Keating were related in interviews with George, Brown, Scaparrotti, McChrystal, and other, anonymous officers and NCOs.

Biographical information about Breeding was provided by him in interviews.

Information about the mortar pit came from interviews with Breeding, Rodriguez, and Barroga.

Information about Kevin Thomson was gleaned from interviews with his fellow troops and his mother, Debbie Routson.

Disagreements between Porter and his troops were reported in interviews with Porter and many other troops.

Biographical information about Romesha came from interviews with him.

McChrystal's July 6, 2009, tactical directive was issued by NATO/ISAF.

Information about the attack that wounded Jacops was taken from interviews with Jacops and Cordova.

Brown's presentations to McChrystal and others were described in interviews with Brown, McChrystal, George, Scaparrotti, and others. McCrystal's competing considerations were summarized in interviews with McCrystal, Scaparrotti, George, and Brown.

The account of Bodmer's time alongside 3-61 Cav was taken from interviews with Bodmer, Brown, and Shrode.

Information about Operation Mountain Fire in Barg-e-Matal came from interviews with McChrystal and George.

For book 3, I interviewed more than fifty of the troops stationed at COP Keating and OP Fritsche on the day of the attack, including Adams, Avalos, Barroga, Bellamy, Birchfield, Breeding, Jory Brown, Bundermann, Burton, Cady, Carter, Casey, Chappell, Cordova, Courville, Dabolins, Daise, Dannelley, Davidson, Dulaney, Floyd, Francis, Frunk, Gilberto, Gregory, Grissette, Harder, Hill, Hull, Jones, Kahn, Knight, Koppes, Lakis, Larson, McMurtrey, Portis, Rasmussen, Rodriguez, Rogers, Romesha, Salentine, Shrode, Souter, Stanley, Stickney, Thomas, and Wong. Descriptions of the camp itself and the general esprit de corps were elaborated from interviews with all of them. After-action reports written by all surviving troops informed this section of the book.

Biographical information about Kirk was gathered from interviews with his wife, Gavin-Kirk; sister, Tingley; and uncle Dinsmore. The email from Kirk was shared by Gavin-Kirk. The description of Kirk in battle came from 3-61 Cav troops.

Biographical information about Zach Koppes was provided by him in an interview. The "hang-fire" incident was described in interviews with Wilson, Romesha, and Koppes.

Chapter 27: The Deer Hunters

Biographical information about Ed Faulkner, Jr., was furnished by his father, Ed Faulkner, Sr., and sister Faulkner Minor. Law-enforcement incidents from Faulkner's youth were summarized by Shane Brown of the Burlington Police Department in an interview.

Events involving Nelson were recounted by anonymous members of 3-61 Cav.

The incident with Faulkner and the hashish was described by Hill, Francis, and other members of 3-61 Cav.

Biographical information about Salentine was provided by him in an interview.

Biographical information about Rogers came from an interview with him.

The conversations between Hill and Salentine were recalled by both men in interviews.

Information about Walsh and Webb was drawn from interviews with both men. Their report, which featured the exchange that began "Do you ever think to yourself, 'Why am I here?'" as well as other quotes in this section, aired on August 17, 2009, and was accessed on the http://www.channel4.com website.

Various family members of 3-61 Cav troops shared their concerns about their loved ones' wasting away. Joshua Hardt's statement, "We barely have food," was cited by his wife, Olivia Hardt, in an interview.

Biographical information about Joshua Hardt, details about his relationship with his wife, and emails to her were provided by Olivia Hardt.

Information about 3-61 Cav's activities outside COP Keating came from interviews with Brown and George.

Observations related to the voting at Urmul and elsewhere were provided by officers and ranking NCOs of 3-61 Cav, including Brown, Shrode, and Hill. Information about alleged voter fraud at Barg-e-Matal came from Pentagon and State Department sources.

Biographical information about Justin Gallegos was shared by his ex-wife, Amanda Marr.

Biographical information about Eric Harder was provided by him in an interview.

Information about Vernon Martin came from interviews with his mother, Connie Brown; wife, Brittany Martin; and girlfriend, Cashet Burks. Grissette and Thomas recounted conversations they had with Martin in interviews.

Differences between Porter and Hull were recalled by both men in interviews.

Tensions between the White House and the Pentagon were described in interviews with officials on both sides, as well as by McChrystal and Kolenda. Woodward's article, accompanied by the redacted version of McChrystal's report, was published in the *Washington Post* on September 21, 2009, under the headline "McChrystal: More Forces or 'Mission Failure.'" Nancy Youssef's story "Military Growing Impatient with Obama on Afghanistan" was published on September 18, 2009, by McClatchy Newspapers.

Brown's outreach to Sadiq was related by Brown and also by Greg Jaffe of the *Washington Post,* who generously shared a copy of Brown's letter.

Chapter 28: Send Me

Biographical information about Portis was provided by him in an interview.

Portis's first interactions with the men of 3-61 Cav were recalled by Portis, Shrode, Courville, Breeding, and others.

Information about Chris Griffin came from interviews with his mother, Kerri Griffin Causley, as well as Portis and Salentine.

The events at George and Brown's shura at Kamdesh were recounted by George, Brown, Portis, and other attendees, including one officer who wished to remain anonymous.

The report that Portis heard about the shura attended by HIG and Taliban leaders, as well as an account of his conversation with the Afghan National Police chief, were elaborated in an email he sent to Brown, which was in turn included in the Swan report. Portis's briefing of his officers was described in interviews with him and the officers.

Intelligence information came from the Swan report and was confirmed with various sources within 3-61 Cav.

The interview with Faruq was conducted via Skype. Faruq's remarks were translated by Javid Nuristani.

The interview with Ishranullah was conducted on paper, again through Javid Nuristani.

Information about McChrystal's trip to London was gathered from an interview with McChrystal and from media coverage, including John Burns, "McChrystal Rejects Scaling Down Afghan Military Aims," *New York Times,* October 1, 2009; and Alex Spillus, "White House Angry at General Stanley McChrystal Speech on Afghanistan," *Telegraph,* October 5, 2009.

Chapter 29: Elevator Ride

Portis, Salentine, and Birchfield described the chopper ride in interviews.

Information about Abdul Rahman's plans came from Faruq.

Information about Hill's and Harder's activities was shared by both men in interviews.

Scusa and Dulaney's conversation was reported in interviews with Dulaney.

The interview with Noor Din was conducted on the phone, with translation from Javid Nuristani.

Information about the insurgents' arrival in Urmul and surrounding areas was drawn from interviews with Faruq, Ishranullah, and Din, as well as from the Swan report. The quote "There were a lot of foot soldiers from all the surrounding villages" came from an interview with a former resident of Nuristan.

The story of the Afghan National Police chief's coming to the outpost and all following details were recounted in interviews with those on duty at the time: Davidson, Gregory, Wong, Souter, Stanley, and Daise.

Quotes from insurgents were taken from videos of the attack posted on the Internet by enemy forces. They were translated by Javid Nuristani.

Chapter 30: "Wish Me Luck"

Information about events at the aid station came from interviews with Rodriguez, Cordova, and Courville.

Events in the Bastards' barracks were described in interviews with Hill, Harder, Frunk, Dulaney, and Adams.

Events at the mortar pit were related in interviews with Rodriguez, Breeding, and Barroga. Thomson's autopsy results were included in the Swan report.

The content of Bundermann's radio call to the mortar pit and his initial actions in the operations center were recalled by him in interviews.

Events in the Red Platoon barracks were detailed in interviews with Romesha, Dannelley, Jones, Davidson, Gregory, and Knight.

The attack on OP Fritsche was described by Stickney and Bellamy in interviews.
"Black Knight_TOC" and "Keating2OPS" communications were included in the Swan report.

Chapter 31: GET SOMETHING UP!

Events at LRAS-2 were recounted in interviews with Larson.

The activities of ANA soldiers and ASGs were relayed by Lakis, Carter, Dabolins, Burton, and Cady and recorded in the Swan report.

Activities in the Bastards' barracks and the run to the ammo supply point were covered in interviews with Hill, Harder, Carter, and Francis.

Events in the shura building were described by Davidson, Knight, and Gregory in interviews. Kirk's autopsy results were included in the Swan report.

Activities in the aid station were summarized by Cordova, Courville, and Floyd in interviews, as well as in Stone's after-action report, incorporated in the Swan report.

Activities at the shura building were recalled by Courville, Davidson, Rasmussen, and Stanley. Activities at the aid station were reported by Cordova and Courville.

Activities at LRAS-1 were related by Koppes, Dannelley, and Jones in interviews.

The conversation between Francis and Dulaney was repeated in interviews with both men.

Breeding and Rodriguez described events at the mortar pit.

mIRC chat between <TF_DESTROYER_BTL_CPT> and <TF_PALEHORSE_BTL_CPT> was reproduced in the Swan report.

Accounts of the activities at the Bastards' barracks were provided by Hill, Carter, Frunk, Rogers, Francis, and Harder.

Activities at the aid station were described in interviews with Cordova, Courville, Floyd, Chappell, Harder, and Francis.

Events at FOB Bostick were covered in interviews with Brown, Portis, Salentine, and Birchfield.

Events outside the Red Platoon barracks were recalled by Romesha, Gregory, Rasmussen, and Jones.

Daise's activities were related by him in an interview; myriad troops heard his "Enemy in the wire" call throughout the camp.

Chapter 32: "They've Got an RPG Pointed Right at Me"

<Keating2OPS> and <Black Knight_TOC> mIRC chat was contained in the Swan report.

Bundermann, Burton, and others in the operations center shared details about activities there.

The F-15 bomb drops were described in the Swan report.

The conversation between Hill and Francis was recounted in interviews.

Activities in the aid station were recalled by Hill, Courville, Romesha, and Floyd in interviews.

In interviews, Koppes, Romesha, and Francis reviewed the events at LRAS-1.

The plan to rescue the men stuck at LRAS-2 was explained in interviews with Bundermann and Romesha as well as in Faulkner's after-action summary, which was included in the Swan report. Griffin's autopsy results were also part of the Swan report. Many troops heard Hardt's last words on the radio.

Larson and Carter recalled the events in LRAS-2 in interviews. Gallegos's and Mace's autopsy reports detailed their wounds.

Thomas described his activities in an interview.

Chapter 33: Taking This Bitch Back

Portis summarized events at FOB Bostick and in the medevac.

Carter and Larson's conversation was related in interviews with both men.

Romesha, Lakis, Dabolins, Gregory, Jones, and Dannelley described their efforts to fight back.

Activities in and around LRAS-2 were detailed by Larson and Carter in interviews.

Bundermann and Shrode recalled activities inside the operations center.

Diagram information came from interviews as well as the Swan report.

Bundermann, Romesha, Hill, and Burton recounted their conversations about consolidating the outpost and fighting to take it back.

Romesha, Gregory, Rasmussen, Dulaney, Dannelley, and Jones all talked about the moment when they decided to go out and take the outpost back.

Chapter 34: The Apaches

Interviews with Lewallen and Wright informed this chapter, as did an interview with Bundermann.

Information about Apache weapons systems was provided by Boeing.

Romesha, Rasmussen, Dulaney, Dannelley, and Jones all described in interviews their activities to take back the outpost.

In interviews, Hill, Davidson, Rogers, and Gregory reviewed their efforts in the middle of the outpost.

Thomas recalled the Latvians coming into the barracks.

Hill and Francis both recounted their conversation in interviews.

Romesha, Jones, Dannelley, Dulaney, and Rasmussen talked about their push to the shura building/entry control point.

In interviews, Carter and Larson detailed their escape from LRAS-2.

Chapter 35: The Fundamentals

In interviews, Harder and Francis described their push to the ANA side of the outpost.

Breeding, Rodriguez, and Barroga covered events at the mortar pit.

Events in the aid station were recounted by Harder, Cordova, Courville, and Bundermann.

Larson and Romesha's conversation was related by both men in interviews. Romesha, Larson, Rasmussen, and Chappell reviewed the activities in the shura building.

The conversation between Brown and Lewallen at FOB Bostick was recalled by both men.

In interviews, Hill and Francis told the story of Hill's shooting the sniper.

Chapter 36: Blood and Embers

Information about the transfusions given to Mace came from Cordova, Courville, and Floyd; a more general explanation was provided by a presentation by Captain James R. Rice, *Battlefield Blood Transfusion* (Tactical Combat Medical Care, Fort Sam Houston).

Lewallen, Wright, Bundermann, Harder, Davidson, and Romesha all described the air support.

Additional information came from Amy McCullough, "Saving Outpost Keating," Airforce-Magazine.com, October 2010.

Carter, Kahn, and Hill recalled Carter's efforts to chop down the tree.

Brown, Lewallen, and Wright furnished information about the helicopters during interviews.

Information about the QRF was taken from interviews with Brown, Sax, and Miraldi.

Information about the MQ-1 Predator was drawn from the Swan report.

Information about the recovery of fallen soldiers came from interviews with Hill, Bundermann, Romesha, Avalos, Kahn, Rasmussen, Grissette, Stanley, Dulaney, and Courville.

Larson and Romesha both recounted Larson's actions in interviews.

Chapter 37: The Long Walk Down

Romesha and Bundermann described their conversation over the radio in interviews.

Information about the QRF's arriving at FOB Bostick, flying into OP Fritsche, and proceeding down the mountain came from interviews with Brown, O'Donnell, Sax, Miraldi, Portis, Bellamy, Salentine, Birchfield, Barnes, and Shrode.

The account of the recovery of Hardt's body was provided by Hill and Francis in interviews. Hardt's autopsy results were included in the Swan report.

Salentine, Romesha, Larson, Grissette, Cady, Bundermann, Portis, Jones, and Koppes supplied details about the end of the day.

Chapter 38: Saint Christopher

Information about Mace's leaving COP Keating was drawn from an interview with Cordova.

Information about Mace's Saint Christopher medal came from his mother, Vanessa Adelson.

Information about Mace's arrival at FOB Bostick was provided by Wilson and Zagol. Mace's autopsy results were included in the Swan report. Hull provided the details about the Saint Christopher's medal.

Information about the ANA was derived from interviews with Sax, Miraldi, Brown, Lakis, and Dabolins as well as from the Swan report.

Brown, Portis, Salentine, Romesha, Hill, and Larson shared in interviews their recollections of their last days at COP Keating.

Portis's interactions with Kamdesh elders were recalled by him in an interview. Portis's journal excerpt was shared by him.

Details about troops leaving COP Keating were taken from interviews with Brown, Portis, Burton, Romesha, and Larson. Additional information and photographs came from the Swan report.

Anonymous sources supplied information about the drone strike on Abdul Rahman. Other information came from a memo obtained by the author. Local media reported on his death, including Abdul Moeed Hashmi, "Commander Mustaghni Killed in Kamdesh Air Raid: Badar," in *Pajhwok Afghan News,* October 10, 2009.

Chapter 39: Two Purple Hearts and Just One Scar

The Swan report; McChrystal's December 27, 2009, "Memorandum for the Record"; and Brown's January 2, 2010, letter acknowledging his formal reprimand are here quoted from directly.

Brown's personal response was described by him in an interview.

The quotes from insurgents were taken from videos of the attack posted on the Internet by enemy forces. Translations were furnished by Javid Nuristani.

The Taliban spokesman was quoted in Todd Pitman, "U.S. Forces Leave Isolated Afghan Base after Attack," Associated Press, October 9, 2009.

Details about the end of Ed Faulkner, Jr.'s, time in the Army, and the end of his life, came from interviews with his father (Faulkner, Sr.), sister (Faulkner Minor), Hill, Faulkner's own Facebook page updates, Brown, Casey, police reports, Kology, Shane Brown, and the North Carolina medical examiner's autopsy report.

Similar accounts of Hill and Carter's conversation were shared by both men in interviews.

Epilogue

The author's visit to FOB Bostick took place in October and November 2011.

Casey told his story and expressed his thoughts in an interview.

The RAND study referenced in the text is Rerri Ranielian and Lisa Jaycox, eds., *Invisible Wounds of War: Psychological and Cognitive Injuries, Their Consequences, and Services to Assist Recovery* (Santa Monica, California: RAND Corporation, 2008).

Information about Newsom and his Special Forces work came from interviews with him.

Obama's press conference was held in Chicago on May 21, 2012.

Information about the president's Medal of Honor phone calls with Romesha and Carter came from interviews with those two men. The White House ceremonies were on February 11, 2013, for Romesha and August 26, 2013, for Carter. Information about Fritsche's marble slab came from Hill. Information about Keating's came from Harder and Ken Keating.

Detailed Map

The map used at the beginning of the book is from the United States Geological Survey website, published in 2007 online only. It was taken from the Natural-Color-Image Map of Quadrangle 3570, Tagab-E-Munjan (505) and Asmar-Kamdesh (506) Quadrangles, Afghanistan, by Philip A. Davis (image processing) and Kenzie J. Turner (cartography) and prepared in cooperation with the Afghan Geological Survey and the Afghanistan Geodesy and Cartography Head Office under the auspices of the U.S. Agency for International Development, AGS Open-File Report (505/506) 2005-1102-C; USGS Afghanistan Project Product No. 087. The information about bases and locations came from numerous interviews with troops who served in the area conducted by the author and military maps obtained by author. The design is by the author in conjunction with graphic designer Steve S. Bottorff, responsible for the execution. Some information does not appear on the map, which is intended as a tool for readers and not as an authoritative and definitive source.

An Important Note
and Some Thanks

I asked the surviving commanders of the four main Cavalry troops profiled in this book—Matt Gooding of 3-71, Joey Hutto of 1-91, Dan Pecha of 6-4, and Stoney Portis of 3-61—to survey their soldiers (and former soldiers) from COP Keating, and the families of those who have been lost, to select a short list of military charities to whom I could give some of the proceeds from this book, and to whom you can give as well, if you are so moved.

They say the following organizations have been of help to their troops and their troops' families:

Army Emergency Relief
200 Stovall Street
Alexandria, VA 22332
www.aerhq.org

Snowball Express
1333 Corporate Dr., Suite 105
Irving, TX 75038
www.snowballexpress.org

Defenders of Freedom
706 Stratford Lane
Coppell, TX 75019
www.defendersoffreedom.us

Tragedy Assistance Program
    for Survivors, Inc.
1777 F Street NW, Suite 600
Washington, DC 20006
www.taps.org

Fisher House Foundation, Inc.
111 Rockville Pike, Suite 420
Rockville, Maryland 20850
www.fisherhouse.org

Wounded Warrior Project
899 Belfort Road, Suite 300
Jacksonville, Florida 32256
www.woundedwarriorproject.org

The more than 225 troops, family members, and others listed in the endnotes were above and beyond helpful. Thank you. Thank you not only for your help, but for what you do and how much you sacrifice. I hope this book is worthy of what you've been through. Ross Berkoff provided vital advice and assistance, as did former Army translator Javid Nuristani. Berkoff and David Roller, in their own inimitable ways, forced me to make this project more ambitious than my original conception. They wanted to make sure that the story of the Americans in Kamdesh was as comprehensive as possible, honoring the hard work and sacrifice of their brothers in arms, especially those who had been lost.

At Little, Brown and Company this book found strong support from my editor and friend Geoff Shandler and the former executive vice president and publisher of Little, Brown, Michael Pietsch. New Little, Brown publisher Reagan Arthur has been a strong supporter of the paperback edition. I was fortunate to have as my Little, Brown teammates a number of talented and dedicated individuals, including Liese Mayer; Ben Allen, Dorothy Straight, and the whole Boston team; Eric Rayman; Nicole Dewey, Michelle Aielli, and Amanda Brown; and Denise LaCongo and everyone else in New York who helped make the inside of the book look so great. Literary agent Christy Fletcher helped nurse the project from its infancy.

In writing and editing this book, I received incredible help and advice from three journalists: Jeffrey Goldberg, who offered valuable writing suggestions, and Matthew Cole and Greg Jaffe, both of whom spent time with the U.S. troops in Kamdesh and were generous with their time, observations, and reporting. The eminent Nuristan experts David Katz and Richard Strand helped keep me honest, accurate, and less ethnocentric. Military bloggers Mark Seavey and Bill Roggio and Joshua Foust of the American Security Project were encouraging and enthusiastic early readers. My mother and father were diligent proofreaders and, as they've been since birth, warm and aggressive cheerleaders for their son.

Many troops and officers reviewed passages as well, offering suggestions and corrections. I'm not listing them because I don't want any of them erroneously blamed for any mistakes in the book or conclusions with which the Pentagon disagrees. But I could not have done it without them.

In January 2013 I began an exciting new job as anchor of *The Lead* and chief Washington correspondent for CNN. I'd like to thank Phil Kent, Jeff Zucker, Ken Jautz, Amy Entelis, Sam Feist, Eric Sherling, and Virginia Moseley for their confidence in me. I am so excited about all the brilliant people on my staff: Federico Quadrani, Katie Hinman, Suzanne Nelson, Melanie Buck, Alexis Weiss, Elizabeth Chmurak, Dan Donahue, Rick Saleeby, Jess Metzger, Shaneika Dabney, Ed Meagher, Cassie Spodak, Dana Davidsen, Jason Seher, Tyler Sloan, Arielle Hawkins, Kim Berryman, Sherisse Pham, Rachel Giberman, Kathleen Skinski, Adia Jacobs, Michael Brevner, Michelle Poley, Reza Baktar, Jose Nunez, Christopher Walter, Gerard Sisnette, Dewana Williams, Ruby Gutierrez, Paul Miller, Clayton Green, Christopher Garrett, Gary Krakower, Joe Brownlee, Michael McMullan, Kara Day, Christie Corologos-Medina, David M Robinson, Brett Tyler, Sonya Dowhaluk, Rahmin Atarod, Marco Arreaga, Insley Fowler, Dave Bacheler, Chris Bortner, Brian Burch, Patricia Carroll, Warren Channell, Adilson Kiyasu, Edwin Lora, Douglas McKinley, Chris Parks, Brendan Polmer, Ashley Powell, David Ridgeway, Jean Renaud, Allison Gollust, Edie Emery, Megan Grant, Erin McPike, Steve Dolce, Sarah Baker, Nancy Baker, and Jennifer Scoggins. Almost immediately after starting at CNN, I went to North Dakota for what would quickly end up being a prime-time hour about Clint Romesha. Thank you to all who worked on that show, including Jennifer Rizzo, Adam Levine, Bud Bultman, Mike Mount, Jessica Metzger, Ken Shiffman, Jen Hyde, Courtney Yager, Tim Lister, Max Newfield, Dave Herrod, April Hock, Blake Luce, Mike Chedwick, Karen Nolan, Meg Pearlstein, Jeremy Moorhead, Jeremy Harlan, Jim Spellman, Josh Braun, Pallavi Reddy, Patrick Ford, Jonathan Kemp, John Cowan, Christina Roberts, John Cooke, Matt Scheibner, and Gary Wilkinson. In August, we did it again for Ty Carter; among those who worked so hard on the Carter documentary were many from the previous doc, as well as Eric Marrapodi, Andy Segal, James Evans, Brandi Harrison, Steve Keller, John Torigoe, Ken Tillis, Khalik Abdallah, David Catrett, John Bena, and Trino Escobedo. I'm proud to work for a news organization that would devote so much time and expense to honoring the troops by telling their stories at a time that so many elected officials and so many in the public have tuned the war out.

I owe a thank you to ABC News for the opportunities and adventures of the last nine years, with special appreciation to Bob Iger, Anne

Sweeney, Ben Sherwood, David Westin, Diane Sawyer, Ted Koppel, Peter Jennings (R.I.P.), Charlie Gibson, George Stephanopoulos, Robin Roberts, James Goldston, Shelley Ross, Jon Banner, Tom Cibrowski, Jim Murphy, Tom Bettag, Leroy Sievers (R.I.P.), Rick Kaplan, Michael Corn, Jeanmarie Condon, Robin Sproul, Virginia Moseley, and Amy Entelis, as well as all the hundreds of talented producers, correspondents, editors, camera people, soundmen and -women, and others with whom I've had the pleasure to work—all of whom I'm not listing here only because I don't want to forget anyone. Special thanks to my friends and colleagues with the ABC News White House team (Mary Bruce, Stephanie Smith, Sunlen Miller, Ann Compton, Devin Dwyer, Jon Garcia, and Barry Freeman) and those with whom I worked on the campaign trail, in Afghanistan (Ely Brown), in Iraq (Zoe Magee and Ray Homer), and in New Orleans after Hurricane Katrina and the ensuing failure of the levee system (Sarah Rosenberg).

R.I.P. to a crew I worked with in Iraq: cameraman Alaa Uldeen Aziz, 33, and soundman Saif Laith Yousuf, 26, killed in 2007.

I am generally not a war reporter, and I want to take a personal moment to praise and thank those who are, those who live in the muck and mire for months—if not years—on end, away from their loved ones. In particular, I want to single out those who have risked so much to report for ABC News, including Martha Raddatz, Bob Woodruff, Mike Boettcher, Carlos Boettcher, Matt McGarry, Nick Schifrin, Doug Vogt, and Miguel Marquez. At CNN I've already benefitted from the courage and excellence of Nick Paton Walsh, Nick Robertson, and Arwa Damon, to name a few. To all of you, and the many others who toil similarly for other media organizations, you and your work humble me.

To my family—Mom, Dad, Shelly, Stone, Aaron, Laurie, Isaiah, Delilah, Lisi, Becky, Hanan, Talia, Ellie, Debby, Andy, Sam, Nathan, Linda, Tom, and Bob—I love you. Thank you for being my family.

And lastly—but most importantly—this book could not have been written without the patience, support, and love of my amazing wife, Jennifer, and the hugs, kisses, and laughter of my beloved children.

Index

663

About the Author

Jake Tapper is anchor of the CNN daily news show *The Lead with Jake Tapper,* as well as being the network's chief Washington correspondent. In addition to other journalism awards he has received, Tapper is the only reporter to ever be honored three years in a row by the White House Correspondents' Association with the Merriman Smith Memorial Award for excellence in presidential news coverage under deadline pressure. He is the author of *Down and Dirty: The Plot to Steal the Presidency.* He lives in Washington, D.C., with his wife, daughter, son, dog, and two cats.